DR. CHARLES BURNEY

DR. CHARLES BURNEY

A LITERARY BIOGRAPHY

BY

ROGER LONSDALE

OXFORD

AT THE CLARENDON PRESS

Oxford University Press, Walton Street, Oxford OX2 6DP

Oxford New York Toronto
Delhi Bombay Calcutta Madras Karachi
Petaling Jaya Singapore Hong Kong Tokyo
Nairobi Dar es Salaam Cape Town
Melbourne Auckland
and associated companies in
Beirut Berlin Ibadan Nicosia

Oxford is a trade mark of Oxford University Press

Published in the United States
by Oxford University Press, New York

British Library Cataloguing in Publication Data
Lonsdale, Roger,
Dr. Charles Burney: a literary biography.
1. Burney, Charles, 1726–1814
I. Title
780'.92'4   ML423.B9
ISBN 0–19–812885–1

Set by Latimer Trend & Company Ltd, Plymouth
Printed in Great Britain by
The Alden Press, Oxford

TO MY FATHER
AND MOTHER

PREFACE AND ACKNOWLEDGEMENTS

SOME brief explanation of the relationship of this biography to the late Dr. P. A. Scholes's *The Great Doctor Burney* (1948) may be helpful. During the 1950's several large collections of unpublished Burney family papers came to light. My first purpose has been to investigate and describe such of this new material as directly concerns Dr. Burney himself. It includes a correspondence of approximately 1,500 letters between Burney and his relations and friends, notebooks which he used while working on his *History of Music* and other books, and some 150 fragments of the autobiography which he completed towards the end of his life and which was thought until recently to have been entirely destroyed by his daughter Madame d'Arblay.

A number of these letters, usually censored to some extent, were printed in Madame d'Arblay's *Memoirs* of her father and in her *Diary and Letters*. Otherwise, of this manuscript material only about 100 letters were known to Dr. Scholes. This fact perhaps sufficiently explains why, although I have inevitably often been indebted to Dr. Scholes's devoted research into particular aspects of Burney's life and times, I have nevertheless had to provide what amounts to a new biographical framework.

The new material does not merely contain fresh factual information about Burney's life: it makes possible, and indeed essential, a new approach to his personality and to the nature of his career as a whole. Inevitably, because of the sheer quantity of material available, I have not found it possible to deal at length with all of Burney's many activities and interests. In pursuing what have seemed to me to be the central elements in his career, I have not usually felt it necessary to describe in detail a number of interesting topics which previous biographers of the Burneys have fully documented already, although I have tried to indicate where such investigations can be found. Thus, Professor Joyce Hemlow, the first explorer of the new hoards of Burneyana, has already admirably described the many domestic excitements and upheavals in Burney's family during his lifetime in her *History of Fanny Burney* (1958). Similarly it has not seemed to me necessary to imitate or reproduce the informative and entertaining descriptions of eighteenth-century musical life in general which Dr. Scholes provided as the background to his biography nor have I attempted any radical reassessment of Burney's strictly musical achievement. I have described such of his musical activities as are biographically central: less important, if interesting, musical material in the unpublished papers will have to wait until Burney's correspondence is eventually published in its entirety.

It will be apparent from my title that I have approached Burney basically as an author; but as he remained a professional teacher of music until the age of seventy-eight and as most of his books concern music, my use of the word 'literary' may require explanation. My approach is not an arbitrary abstraction from Burney's musical career. What I hope I have demonstrated is that his chief ambition and achievement was to be accepted as a 'man of letters' rather than as a 'mere musician'. At the mid-point of his career he began consciously to labour to transcend his original profession. It is this transition, and the social as well as literary achievement which it represents, that I have tried to document: the unprecedented way in which Burney, a professional musician, succeeded in capturing a polite literary audience for his books, and was duly rewarded with an equally unprecedented welcome into the most distinguished intellectual and social circles of his time.

This basic approach to Burney's career was originally adopted by his daughter Madame d'Arblay, although it has since been ignored. In most other respects, however, my account of him differs from that of his first biographer, whose zealously adoring portrait of an invariably good-natured and almost saintly father has succeeded very largely in controlling subsequent descriptions of him. The charm which his daughter attributed to him will still I trust be apparent in this book: the fact that an intensely ambitious, almost at times ruthless, side to his character must also now emerge will perhaps make him more recognizably human and for that reason need not diminish the affection with which he is usually regarded. In any case, I have tried to use the new material which has been made available to me in such a way as to enable Burney for the first time to tell his own story as far as possible, with the assistance of his friends and with the minimum of interference from his daughter.

I am greatly indebted to the following owners of private collections of manuscripts, who have allowed me to examine and quote material in their possession and have often gone to much trouble to assist me: Mr. Gerald Coke of Bentley, Hampshire; John R. G. Comyn, Esquire, of Turnastone, Herefordshire; Professor F. W. Hilles of Yale University; Mr. and Mrs. Donald Hyde of Somerville, New Jersey; Mr. Brooks Shepard, Librarian of the School of Music at Yale University; and the Warden of All Souls College, Oxford.

I wish also to thank officials of the following libraries for permission to quote material in their custody: the Berg Collection of the New York Public Library; the Folger Library, Washington; the Houghton Library, Harvard; the John Rylands Library, Manchester; and the Pierpont Morgan Library, New York. It is a pleasure to acknowledge the skill and patience with which my requests have been treated in the other libraries where I have done much of my work: the Sterling Memorial Library, Yale University; the Bodleian Library, Oxford; and the British Museum. Mr. Vincent Quinn, the Librarian of Balliol College, Oxford, and his staff have also dealt cheerfully with what must often have been tiresome demands.

During the two years which I spent at Yale I benefited from the advice and assistance of Professor Frank T. Brady, Mr. Herman W. Liebert, Dr. Robert A. Metzdorf, Mr. Brooks Shepard, and Miss Marjorie Wynne. Mrs. C. Sladitz of the Berg Collection of the New York Public Library particularly facilitated my work there. Since my return to Oxford I have been indebted for corrections, suggestions, and information to Mr. John Barnard, Mr. John Bryson, Professor Bertram Davis, Professor Herbert Davis, Mr. Martin Dodsworth, Mr. H. D. Johnstone, Dr. C. B. Oldman, Signor Gian Carlo Roscioni, and Professor James Sutherland. I am particularly grateful to Professor Joyce Hemlow, who helped me in the early stages of my research, when I was able to benefit from her unrivalled knowledge of the Burneys and of the daunting collections of the family's papers; and to Dr. L. F. Powell, who patiently read through the manuscript as it neared completion and to whose encouragement and criticism I owe much. Finally I would like to thank those friends—they will recognize themselves all too easily—who good-naturedly listened to far too much about this book while it was being written.

My greatest debt is to Mr. James M. Osborn of Yale University. He first encouraged me to work on Dr. Burney and enabled me to do so by making his own great collection of Burneyana available to me. I learned a great deal from him during my two years at Yale, while working with him on other projects. Any pleasure he may take in this book will be a poor return for the unvarying generosity and encouragement which I received from him and from Mrs. Osborn at Yale and which have continued since my return to Oxford.

R. H. L.

Balliol College, Oxford
May 1964

CONTENTS

LIST OF PLATES

(between pages 254 and 255)

DR. CHARLES BURNEY
From the portrait by SIR JOSHUA REYNOLDS. *By permission of the Trustees of the National Portrait Gallery*

THOMAS ARNE
From an engraving by J. GILLRAY *after* F. BARTOLOZZI

THOMAS TWINING
From an engraving by C. TURNER *after* J. J. HALLS

SIR JOHN HAWKINS
From the portrait by JAMES ROBERTS *in the Faculty of Music, Oxford, by permission*

DR. CHARLES BURNEY
From the drawing by GEORGE DANCE. *By permission of the Trustees of the National Portrait Gallery*

A fragment of Burney's 'Memoirs', with Madame d'Arblay's deletions and alterations (*British Museum, Add. MS. 48345, f. 3v*)

ABBREVIATIONS AND CUE TITLES

MEMBERS OF THE BURNEY FAMILY

CB   Charles Burney, Mus.D. (1726–1814).

CB Jr.   Charles Burney, D.D. (1757–1817), schoolmaster and classical scholar.

FB   Frances Burney (1752–1840), novelist and diarist, who married General Alexandre d'Arblay in 1793.

MANUSCRIPT COLLECTIONS

Barrett   Barrett Collection in the British Museum (Egerton MSS. 3690–708).

Berg   Berg Collection of the New York Public Library.

B.M.   British Museum, excluding the Barrett Collection.

Bodleian   Bodleian Library, Oxford.

Comyn   Collection of John R. G. Comyn, Esquire, of Turnastone, Herefordshire.

Hyde   Collection of Mr. and Mrs. Donald F. Hyde of Somerville, New Jersey.

JRL   John Rylands Library, Manchester.

Osborn   Collection of Mr. James M. Osborn of New Haven, Connecticut. Now (1986) in the Beinecke Rare Book Library at Yale University.

PML   Pierpont Morgan Library, New York.

Details of smaller collections to which reference is made are given in section I of the Bibliography.

BURNEY'S WRITINGS

Frag. Mem.   Fragments of his 'Memoirs' and related materials (British Museum and Berg and Osborn Collections).

Handel Commem.   *An Account of the . . . Commemoration of Handel*, 1785.

Hist. Mus.   *A General History of Music*, 4 vols., 1776–89.

Mercer   The *History of Music*, ed. Frank Mercer, 2 vols., 1935.

Metastasio   *Memoirs of Metastasio*, 3 vols., 1796.

Rees   Articles contributed to *The Cyclopaedia; or, Universal Dictionary of Arts, Sciences, and Literature*, ed. Abraham Rees, 45 vols., 1802–20.

Tours   *Dr. Burney's Musical Tours in Europe*, ed. Percy A. Scholes, 2 vols., 1959.

OTHER WORKS

Country Clergyman   *Recreations and Studies of a Country Clergyman of the Eighteenth Century,* ed. Richard Twining, 1882.

DL   *Diary and Letters of Madame d'Arblay,* ed. Austin Dobson, 6 vols., 1904–5.

ED   *Early Diary of Frances Burney, 1768–1778,* ed. Annie Raine Ellis, revised edn., 2 vols., 1907.

GDB   Percy A. Scholes, *The Great Doctor Burney,* 2 vols., 1948.

Gent. Mag.   *The Gentleman's Magazine.*

Grove   *Grove's Dictionary of Music and Musicians,* 5th edn., ed. Eric Blom, 9 vols., 1954.

Hemlow   Joyce Hemlow, *History of Fanny Burney,* 1958.

Hill–Powell   *Boswell's Life of Johnson,* ed. G. B. Hill, revised L. F. Powell, 6 vols., 1934–50.

Johnson, Letters   *Letters of Samuel Johnson,* ed. R. W. Chapman, 3 vols., 1952.

Mem.   Madame d'Arblay, *Memoirs of Doctor Burney,* 3 vols., 1832.

RES   *Review of English Studies.*

Thraliana   *Thraliana: The Diary of Mrs. Hester Lynch Thrale (later Mrs. Piozzi) 1776–1809,* ed. Katharine C. Balderston, 2nd edn. corrected, 2 vols., 1951.

Walpole, Corresp.   *Correspondence of Horace Walpole,* ed. W. S. Lewis and others, vol. 1– , 1937–   (in progress).

'Worcester Memoranda'   'Memoranda of the Burney Family 1603–1845' (typescript in the Osborn Collection).

In quotations from manuscripts, letters or words inserted to complete the sense are indicated by square brackets [ ].

Lacunae in the text, where the manuscript has been torn or deleted, are indicated by angle brackets ⟨ ⟩. When the missing letters or words are obvious, they have been supplied.

I

CHILDHOOD AND FIRST YEARS
IN LONDON

1726–1751

I

ACCORDING to an account of the Burneys written by a member of the family in the nineteenth century,[1] a James Macburney came south from Scotland with James I in 1603. The family historian, however, could relate no more of him; nor, indeed, is it certain whether he was father or grandfather (though surely the latter) of a second James Macburney, born in about 1653 in the village of Great Hanwood in Shropshire, who became, as secretary or steward to the Earl of Ashburnham, 'a gentleman of a considerable patrimony'. His son, a third James Macburney and the father of the subject of this biography, was also born at Great Hanwood in 1678, but later attended Westminster School under the celebrated Dr. Busby, his father having acquired a house in Whitehall. Although 'originally intended . . . for a Physician', the younger James Macburney preferred to amuse himself with the acquisition of such polite accomplishments as dancing, playing on the violin, and painting. In 1697, at the age of eighteen, he eloped with Rebecca Ellis, a young actress. His outraged father revenged himself by marrying 'his female domestic', to whom and to their son Joseph he left his entire fortune at his death.

Restless, irresponsible, cheerful, and now impoverished, young Macburney was obliged to support his family—his wife presented him with fifteen children in twenty years, nine of whom survived—by the professional practice of his talents as a musician, dancer, and painter. His life, we are told, 'was a succession of gaieties and troubles, & the number of places he appears to have liv'd at, proves the unsteadiness of his conduct.

[1] 'Worcester Memoranda.' This typescript, presumably a copy of an untraced manuscript, formerly belonged to Dr. Scholes, who describes its provenance, *GDB*, i.1 n.

. . . the versatility of his disposition was such, that tho he tried various professions, he continued in none of them long; the consequences of which, were what might naturally be expected.'[1] Macburney's sporadic career as a dancer and musician explains his friendship with such men as Charles Fleetwood, later a manager of Drury Lane Theatre; Isaac, the celebrated dancing-master and his natural son, Matthew Dubourg, an eminent violinist; and John Weaver, an important pioneer of theatrical dancing early in the century.[2]

For a time, during the reign of Queen Anne, Macburney 'had the place under the governm^t of licencer of the Hawkers & Pedlars, wch he lost on the accession of George the first'.[3] By 1720 he had moved to Shrewsbury and, losing his wife in that year, married again promptly and rather more shrewdly than in 1697. This second wife, Ann Cooper of Shrewsbury, was 'daughter to a Herald painter', 'had a small fortune, & had received an offer of marriage from the celebrated Wycherley the Poet'. Macburney now settled comfortably in Shrewsbury, apparently as a portrait painter.[4]

The second Mrs. Macburney bore him five more children, of whom the last two, Charles and Susanna, were twins, born in Raven Street, Shrewsbury, on 7 April (Old Style) 1726.[5] The boy was named after Charles Fleetwood, his godfather.[6] As for his surname, although the twins were christened 'Mackburny', the prefix was apparently dropped at about this time. Their elder brother Richard had in fact been christened 'Berney' three years earlier. The reason for this change is no more certain than the precise date at which it occurred, although we may compare Burney's suggestion in 1799 that Charles Macklin the actor had altered his name from McLaughlin 'to get rid not only of its *Paddy* appearance but of its harshness'.[7]

Susanna died at the age of eight, but Charles and his elder brother Richard had already been sent to the village of Condover, some four miles from Shrewsbury, where they remained

---

[1] 'Worcester Memoranda'; *Frag. Mem.* (Osborn), printed with alterations by FB, *Mem.* I. x–xv.   [2] See *post*, pp. 6, 7.
[3] *Frag. Mem.* (Osborn) deleted by FB.   [4] 'Worcester Memoranda'.
[5] FB gives 12 April, *Mem.* i. 1; but CB gives the correct date on his eightieth birthday in a letter to Lady Crewe, 18 April (New Style) 1806 (B.M. Add. MS. 37916, f. 16) and elsewhere.   [6] CB to CB Jr., 19 Apr. 1806 (Comyn).
[7] *GDB*, ii. 315: *Monthly Review*, xxx. 306.

in the care of an old woman named Nurse Ball until 1739. Since Fanny d'Arblay carefully destroyed her father's account of these early years in his 'Memoirs', it is difficult to establish the reason for this semi-orphanage of the two boys. Fanny herself, however, revealingly defended her suppression of these pages in a letter to her sister in 1820:

What respected his family, mean while, was utterly unpleasant— & quite useless to be kept alive. The dissipated facility & negligence of his Witty & accomplished, but careless Father; the niggardly unfeelingness of his nearly unnatural Mother . . . furnish matter of detail, long, tedious, unnecessary,—and opening to the publick view a species of Family degradation to which the name of Burney now gives no similitude.[1]

Although Burney was always to speak affectionately of his rural childhood in Condover, to enjoy lapsing into the local dialect, and to pride himself on remembering the dances, games, customs and friends 'of more than 60 years ago, as well as if I had quitted my nurse and Shropshire Village but 6 months',[2] this desertion by his negligent father and 'nearly unnatural' mother inevitably had some effect on the sensitive boy. It is not difficult to trace in his later career an endless, if harmless, desire to compel affection and admiration which would compensate for the inevitable insecurity of his childhood.

By about 1737 Charles Burney was attending the Free School in Shrewsbury. No registers of its pupils at this period have been preserved, nor is Burney's name entered in the notebook in which Hotchkiss, the headmaster, recorded some of his scholars. There can be no doubt, however, that Burney did attend the school, for he mentioned the fact repeatedly.[3] He probably walked to school each day, for, as Hotchkiss noted, there were 'several country boys' who could not be expected to attend catechism on Sundays. Since the school was in a poor state at this time,[4] Burney would not receive a very valuable continuation of the humble education which had begun under

---

[1] FB to Esther Burney, 20 Nov. 1820 (Barrett).
[2] CB to Twining, 10 Mar. 1804, copy (Osborn); to Mrs. Fermor, draft [? July 1809] (Osborn); to Malone, 9 Nov. 1806 (Bodleian, MS. Malone 38, ff. 133–4).
[3] *Frag. Mem.* (B.M. Add. MS. 48345, ff. 18, 22); CB to Mrs. Thrale, 6 Nov. 1778 (JRL, Eng. MS. 545. 5): *European Mag.* vii (1785), 163.
[4] J. B. Oldham, *History of Shrewsbury School 1552–1952*, 1952, pp. 60, 64, 65.

Nurse Ball. As Fanny d'Arblay observed rather solemnly, her father was eventually to make a striking progress 'through disadvantages of so lowering a species' to his place as 'not only one of the best informed, but one of the most polished, members of society'.[1]

James Macburney had meanwhile remained in Shrewsbury until about 1737 and had then, after a year in Dorset, removed to Chester to enjoy the patronage of George, third Earl of Cholmondeley, 'who procured him the place of Surveyor of the Window-lights'. By 1739 Macburney seems at last to have felt some compunction about the two boys he had left at Condover, for, at about this time, Richard, aged fifteen or sixteen, was sent to London as apprentice to his half-brother Thomas, 'an eminent Dancing Master';[2] and late in 1739 Charles, aged thirteen, joined his family at Chester, leaving his 'uncultivated and utterly ignorant, but worthy and affectionate old nurse', Dame Ball, 'with agony of grief'.[3]

On 25 December 1739 Burney entered Chester Free School as a King's Scholar, on the nomination of Prebendary Prescott, a prominent citizen and music-lover.[4] Chester, indeed, was at this time 'a very musical place'[5] and it was not long before the direction that Burney's career was to take had become clear. Although at Condover his musical education had been very limited—a fragment of the index to his suppressed 'Memoirs' mentions only that he had been 'Fond of ringing' and 'Still more of Psalm singing'[6]—Chester offered plenty of scope to an ambitious choirboy who could seize his opportunities: 'The first Music he learned was of Mr Baker the Organist of the Cathedral, who being distressed for an assistant during a fit of the Gout, taught him to play a Chant on the Organ before he knew his Gammut or the names of the keys. And this single Chant . . . was all that he was able to play to the Choir during his master's first fit of the Gout.' The fourteen-year-old boy quickly learned the rudiments of musical theory, added a few

[1] *Mem.* i. 4–5.
[2] 'Worcester Memoranda'; *Frag. Mem.* (B.M. Add. MS. 48345, f. 22).
[3] *Mem.* i. 4–5.
[4] F. G. E[dwards], 'Dr. Charles Burney (1726–1814). A Biographical Sketch', *Musical Times*, xlv (1904), 436.
[5] *Handel Commem.*, p. 26 n.; CB to Mrs. Crewe, 27 Oct. 1800 (Berg).
[6] B.M. Add. MS. 48345, f. 18.

more pieces to his repertoire and, when Baker was next afflicted
by gout, was able to perform at another service to great applause
before an audience 'composed of the first people of Chester and
its neighbourhood'.[1]

The stimulation afforded by the musical life of the town was
reinforced by the sight of the famous composers and performers
who passed through Chester on their way to or from Ireland.
The most notable of these visitors was George Frideric Handel,
who stayed in Chester for a few days in 1741. It is not difficult to
imagine the effect on the schoolboy: 'I watched him narrowly',
Burney recalled in 1785, 'as long as he remained in Chester',
and he was rewarded by hearing a rehearsal of part of *The
Messiah* before its first public performance in Dublin.[2]

Early in 1742, however, Burney returned to Shrewsbury,
having officially left Chester Free School on 27 March 1742.[3]
He himself later explained that, as a result of his success as a
singer in Chester, his half-brother James, now the organist of
St. Mary's Church in Shrewsbury, had sent for him to sing in a
concert and had persuaded him to stay as his assistant.[4] The
index to a missing portion of Burney's 'Memoirs', however,
contains at this point the cryptic, if more frank, explanation,
'Run away to Shrewsbury', and there are confirmatory references in fragments of the narrative itself to his 'flight' and
'elopement'.[5] Presumably this sudden removal was caused
both by friction with his parents and by the ambition of pursuing his musical studies with his thirty-seven-year-old half-
brother in Shrewsbury.

Although James Burney made his new assistant work hard,
it was not long before Charles realized that his half-brother
could teach him very little, 'want of science as well as fancy'
preventing his voluntaries on the organ 'from rising above
poverty & common-place'. The sixteen-year-old student was
therefore obliged to pursue his musical education 'without
Instructions or example', until he heard recitals by two famous
organists who were visiting Shrewsbury: William Felton of
Hereford and William Hayes, a predecessor of James Burney
at St. Mary's and the newly appointed Professor of Music at

[1] B.M. Add. MS. 48345, f. 22; for Baker, see *GDB*, i. 12–13. Cf. *Hist. Mus.* ii.
95 n.   [2] *Handel Commem.*, p. 26 n.   [3] See *ante*, p. 4, n. 4.
[4] B.M. Add. MS. 48345, f. 22.   [5] Ibid., ff. 3, 18.

Oxford. Their technique and the personal encouragement which they gave the young musician stimulated him, as he later recalled, 'so forcibly . . . that I went to work with an ambition & fury that w^d hardly allow me to eat or sleep'. For the first time, the capacity for almost unremitting industry which was to characterize the whole of Burney's later career can be clearly recognized:

The Quantity of Music I copied at this Time, of all kinds, was prodigious, & my activity & diligence surprised every body. For besides writing, teaching, tuning and playing for my Brother, at my *momens perdus*, I was educating myself in every way I was able. With copy books I improved my writing so much, that my Father w^d not believe I wrote my Letters myself. I tried at least to keep up the little Latin I had learned. Practiced both the Spinet & Violin many hours a day, wch with reading, transcribing Music & poetry, attempts at Composition, and my brother's affairs filled up every hour of the longest day. Indeed I had a great passion for angling, & whenever I c^d get time to pursue that sport, I ran no risk of losing my time if the Fish did not bite, for I had always a book in my pocket, wch enabled me to wait with Patience their Pleasure.[1]

His earnest self-education did not, therefore, render Burney unbearable, although Fanny d'Arblay relates that he tied a piece of string to one of his toes at night in order that a neighbouring apprentice might wake him as he passed the house early in the morning. The purpose of this device was not, however, as Fanny piously states, to enable him to resume his studies with the dawn but, as the manuscript of his 'Memoirs' reveals, 'to meet some other boys at a Bowling-green'. Burney also enjoyed dancing lessons from his father's old friend John Weaver, now more than seventy years old. As so little is known about Weaver, who contributed essays on theatrical dancing to the *Spectator*, it is unfortunate that nothing remains of passages in Burney's 'Memoirs' described in the index as 'Weaver' and 'Pranks by him & my father'. Nevertheless, a later description of his old age in Shrewsbury has survived.[2] The relentless zeal with which Burney pursued his studies was, however, real

---

[1] *Frag. Mem.* (B.M. Add. MS. 48345, f. 1); *Mem.* i. 8.
[2] See the present writer's note, 'Dr. Burney, John Weaver and the *Spectator*', in *Famed for Dance: Essays on . . . Theatrical Dancing in England, 1660–1740*, New York, 1960, pp. 59–61.

enough. His love of poetry led him to defy poverty by borrowing and transcribing the whole of the works of Prior, his favourite poet, as well as extracts from Shakespeare; and his 'Memoirs' also describe French lessons and instruction on the violin from Niccolà Matteis, an Austrian musician who had settled in Shrewsbury.[1]

With his literary and musical education proceeding so rapidly, Burney was already building 'aerial Castles' in the future; but just when he was contemplating a plan of joining 'a strolling company of players . . . to teach and accompany the Actors in their songs', his father—'who I believe, loved me very affectionately'—urged him to return to Chester and early in 1743 he was reunited with his family. Undistracted by work for his half-brother and 'inflamed with a rage for composition', Burney was able to continue his studies more zealously than ever, even if the servants (and probably his family as well) were baffled by the 'lessons, sonatas, songs, & concertos' which 'Master Charley' tirelessly produced. Having repaired an old spinet belonging to his eldest sister, he 'was incessantly at it, either practicing or composing', except when playing with professional musicians in the town.[2]

The continual arrival of musical visitors in Chester only inspired Burney to greater efforts. In the summer of 1743 Matthew Dubourg, a celebrated violinist and Master of the King's Band in Ireland, called to see his old friend, James Macburney. When Burney, now aged seventeen, was presented to him as 'a young & humble musical student', who would be gratified by hearing the master perform, Dubourg suggested that they play a piece by Corelli together. Apart from his pride in being able to acquit himself tolerably well—'for I never had accompanied a great player before'—Burney found Dubourg's playing a revelation. There was, indeed, another striking fact about the great violinist: 'Dubourg was a man of wit, who had been admitted into good company without, as well as with, his fiddle.' This second revelation evidently surprised Burney at the time and may well have initiated his acute awareness of the social status of the musician in the eighteenth century, the

[1] *Frag. Mem.* (B.M. Add. MS. 48345, f. 2); *Hist. Mus.* iii. 516 and n.; *Mem.* i. 10.
[2] *Frag. Mem.* (B.M. Add. MS. 48345, ff. 1, 3, 4, 22).

escape from which was to lie at the heart of his own ambitions and achievement.[1]

Although Burney's 'Memoirs' describe other musical events in Chester at this time, the crucial moment came in August 1744[2] with the arrival of Thomas Augustine Arne, who had just spent two years with his company of musicians in Dublin and who was now returning to London to take up the post of composer to Drury Lane Theatre. At Shrewsbury Burney had already heard and admired Arne's music for *Comus*, *The Masque of Alfred*, *The Blind Beggar of Bethnal Green* and for Shakespeare's plays, but now, hearing Arne's compositions performed by his own company, directed and accompanied by the composer himself, his 'delight was inexpressible'. Arne was acquainted with Baker, Burney's first teacher,[3] and perhaps as a result eventually saw some of the young musician's compositions. Although he pointed out their weaknesses, Arne strongly recommended that 'so industrious a youth, with such a disposition for the art w^ch [he] was studying', should be placed under the guidance of some 'eminent Master in London'. Although this suggestion struck Burney and his father 'very forcibly', the great expense involved in such a scheme prevented their taking it seriously. The financial problem can be appreciated from a remark about James Macburney made by the family historian: 'as his health declined in his Old Age, his circumstances kept pace, and his family were left to lament, that his talent for pleasantry, & love of sociability, overcame his prudential care, either for himself or them.'[4]

Arne's suggestion was, however, by no means disinterested, for on a second visit he offered to take Burney to London as his own apprentice, 'for £100 premium, & exempt my father from all further expence'. Although this sum was much smaller than the cost of paying for 'a first-rate Master, and for board, lodging

---

[1] *Frag. Mem.* (B.M. Add. MS. 48345, f. 3); in *Hist. Mus.* iv. 651, CB dates Dubourg's visit 1744.

[2] There has been some disagreement over the date of Arne's arrival in Chester. Arne's last performance in Dublin was on 30 May 1744—W. H. Cummings, *Dr. Arne and Rule, Britannia*, 1912, p. 34; this apparently misled Scholes into the statement that Arne reached Chester in May—*GDB* i. 19. H. Langley, *Doctor Arne*, 1938, p. 38, suggests that Arne stayed in Dublin until the autumn. 'August' is written over 'Autumn' in the manuscript of CB's 'Memoirs'.

[3] H. Owen and J. B. Blakeway, *History of Shrewsbury*, 1825, ii. 226 n.

[4] 'Worcester Memoranda'.

& cloaths' normally involved in sending a student to London, it was still much more than Macburney could afford. At last resigned to the impossibility of extracting money from Macburney and realizing that an apprentice who could play on the violin, tenor, harpsichord, and organ would be 'a more profitable than expensive part of his Family', Arne eventually agreed to take Burney to London without insisting on any payment. Not surprisingly, the offer was eagerly accepted:

> My father & I, dazzled by the Idea of avoiding expence in going to the Capital; of being instructed by a Master of the first abilities and fame among the natives of our Island; and of hearing all the great performers and compositions of other countries, made no objection. . . . The bargain . . . was struck, the Articles drawn, and covenants exchanged in a legal & regular way.

Accordingly, the eighteen-year-old apprentice, legally bound to Arne for seven years, accompanied his new master to London, arriving there in time for the opening of the season at Drury Lane in September 1744. In the circumstances it is understandable that neither Burney nor his father had paused to consider what was involved in 'total dependance on a Master, who if avaricious, selfish, sordid, and tyrannical, might render the best part of my life slavish & miserable'.[1]

II

A young musician could hardly have hoped to make a more auspicious entry into London musical life than under the direction of Thomas Arne who, at the age of thirty-four, was already the leading English composer of his day. Arne had been engaged at Drury Lane Theatre 'as composer of Songs, Dances and Act tunes, at a Salary of £3 a week; & Mrs Arne as principal singer, at the same salary'. He was, however, apparently not content with this reward for their joint services and it was soon clear that he regarded Burney as another primary wage-earner for the household. The work by which Arne expected his apprentice to earn his board and lodging and to supplement his own income was, however, well within Burney's powers, for it consisted mainly of transcribing the music which his master wrote for Drury Lane, teaching it to the less important performers, giving lessons to Arne's scholars, and

[1] *Frag. Mem.* (B.M. Add. MS. 48345, ff. 5–6).

playing in various orchestras. As there was no vacancy in the band at Drury Lane in the autumn of 1744, Burney was at first employed there only occasionally,

as a supernumerary Violin or Tenor . . . in pantomimes or musical pieces, when some of the performers in the orchestra were wanted on the stage, as Chorus singers; or behind the scenes in serenades, processions and other musical purposes, for stage effect. And for this I was not in Salary, but p^d by the night; only s5 each time: To wch I had no claim, nor did I consider myself degraded by the meanness of the pay, as there were others, much my seniors, who performed on similar occasions on the same terms.[1]

Although Burney was evidently untroubled by the fact that all his earnings went straight into Arne's pocket, the sight of older musicians reduced to earning a living in the same humble way as himself can only have increased his ambition of making a rapid success of his own career.

A good example of Burney's work for Arne appears in his account of a concert performance of his master's *Masque of Alfred* in March 1745. This masque had been written, to a libretto by James Thomson and David Mallet, for a fête given by the Prince of Wales at Cliveden in August 1740.[2] It is now remembered mainly because it concludes with Arne's famous setting of 'Rule, Britannia!' Arne worked his apprentice hard during the preparations for its revival and in his 'Memoirs' Burney remembered having to make a 'fair score' of the work, transcribing the vocal parts separately and in some cases teaching them to the singers, attending rehearsals 'to correct the books', and taking advertisements to the newspapers. When he first arrived in London he enjoyed such work and would have done so even more on this occasion, 'had my master been prosperous'. Unfortunately, this performance of *Alfred* for the composer's benefit was a financial disaster.[3]

Fanny d'Arblay later caused some confusion by stating that her father 'had the advantage of setting to music a part of the mask of Alfred' and that this task brought him the friendship of one of the librettists, James Thomson the poet.[4] Burney composed music, however, only for a drastically revised version of

---

[1] *Frag. Mem.* (B.M. Add. MS. 48345, f. 7).
[2] W. H. Cummings, op. cit., pp. 111–15.
[3] *Frag. Mem.* (Berg).   [4] *Mem.* i. 16.

Alfred by David Mallet in 1751. Fanny's footnote—'Upon its revival; not upon its first coming out'—seems to point to this later production; but as Thomson had died in 1748 it was not Burney's music for *Alfred* which brought them together.[1]

In any case, it was far from Arne's intentions that his apprentice should already be producing original compositions: it was more important to take every opportunity of exploiting Burney's earning power. Accordingly, during Lent 1745, Arne sent him with a letter of introduction to Handel, who engaged him to play in the orchestra he had assembled for performances of his new oratorios, *Hercules* and *Belshazzar*. Handel, Burney wrote later, 'at this time "did bestride our musical world like a Colossus" ', and by attending rehearsals and playing in his orchestra Burney was able not only to earn money for his master but to gratify his own 'eager curiosity in seeing and examining the person and manners of so extraordinary a man, as well as in hearing him perform on the organ'.[2]

Burney's first year in London must have been exciting and stimulating for so ambitious a young man, previously confined to the musical resources of Shrewsbury and Chester. Before long he had obtained a regular place in the Drury Lane orchestra, probably because his master had soon been appointed its leader; and from the summer of 1745 he played in the band at the Vauxhall Gardens, to which Arne had also become composer.[3] At Drury Lane, Vauxhall, and Arne's house in Great Queen Street, Lincoln's Inn Fields, where he lived as one of the family, Burney met numerous professional musicians and he also visited some of the more celebrated composers of the day, including Dr. Pepusch, Roseingrave, and Geminiani.[4] At the home of Arne's sister, Mrs. Susannah Maria Cibber, the famous actress, he would even more acutely feel himself at the centre of the city's artistic life, for here 'he found himself in a constellation of wits, poets, actors, authors, and men of letters', including most notably David Garrick, whose rapid rise to fame would be an inspiration to any young provincial in search of celebrity in the metropolis.[5]

[1] See *post*, pp. 28–29, 34–35.
[2] *Frag. Mem.* (B.M. Add. MS. 48345, f. 8); *Hist. Mus.* iv. 666–7.
[3] W. H. Cummings, op. cit., pp. 35–37.
[4] *Hist. Mus.* iv. 636 and n., 644 n.; article 'Roseingrave', Rees, vol. xxx.
[5] *Mem.* i. 14.

After a year with Arne, Burney took a long holiday with
friends in Lincolnshire in the autumn of 1745, having no
doubt been willingly released by his master for the months in
which his earning power was smallest.[1] It was probably on his
return to London after what had been 'one continued series of
mirth, amusement & festivity' that Burney first felt restless in
his apprenticeship, which still had six more years to run. The
cause was certainly not disillusionment with life in the capital.
In the months after his return, after a period of trepidation,
London was full of patriotic 'joy and hilarity', when the Jacobite
invasion was crushed by the Duke of Cumberland at Culloden.
Burney later recalled that whenever the Duke entered a theatre
he was greeted with an ovation and that 'songs of triumph'
were sung each night at the thriving Vauxhall Gardens, where
members of the Royal Family were frequent visitors during the
summer.[2] Burney made his own contribution to the patriotic
fervour, as well as to the history of the National Anthem, for
when Arne wrote a setting of 'God Save the King!' for a trio of
Drury Lane singers, he himself 'was dezired by some of the
Covent Garden singers wth whom I was acquainted, to set parts
to the old tune for that Theatre'.[3]

At any time, moreover, London offered all kinds of amusement for a young man and Burney's charm and vivacity had
won him a large and varied acquaintance. From his father he
had inherited a 'ready wit, & great flow of spirits' and, like
Macburney, he was to be throughout his life 'always an acceptable guest'. There, however, the resemblance ends. For
whereas his father had been self-indulgent and irresponsible,
had failed to apply his undoubted talents, and had always
found it 'more to his taste & disposition, to shine at a con-
vivial meeting, than to study his real advantage',[4] Burney's
ambition and desire to prove himself to the world were never to
be distracted either by pleasure or by suffering.

Burney had soon found that, with stimulation and opportunity all around him, his talents were being hampered rather
than developed. 'When I was a young man', the learned Dr.
Pepusch told him at this period, 'I determined never to go to

---

[1] *Frag. Mem.* (B.M. Add. MS. 48345, ff. 9, 22).   [2] *Frag. Mem.* (Berg).
[3] CB to Sir Joseph Banks, 29 July 1806 (Coke).
[4] 'Worcester Memoranda'.

bed at night, till I knew something that I did not know in the morning.'[1] This advice, which made 'so deep an impression' on the young apprentice, must also have had for him a heavy irony. In one of the notebooks, in which he collected information for his *History of Music* some thirty years later, Burney drafted an article on Thomas Arne, most of which he understandably decided not to print.[2] This unpublished account of Arne contains a severe indictment and explains Burney's growing restlessness in 1745:

It grieves me that gratitude does not oblige me to speak with more reverence of him as my Master; but the truth is, he was so selfish & unprincipled, that finding me qualified to transcribe music, teach, & play in public, all wch I c^d do before I was connected with him, he never wished I sh^d advance further in the Art. And besides not teaching or allowing me time to study & practice, he locked up all the B^{ks} in his possession, by the perusal of wch I c^d improve myself. . . .

Arne went to almost incredible lengths to prevent his apprentice from making any rapid progress in the art which he himself practised with so much skill. When Burney joined the Arnes and their relations in singing Palestrina on Sunday evenings in Great Queen Street, Arne 'was at the trouble of drawing out a Tenor part for me to sing by, lest in doing it for myself, I sh^d improve by examining how the several parts were constructed. . . . Indeed rather than not turn my small abilities to some lucrative acc^t he w^d have me employed in teaching, or playing any Instrument, at any place or price'. Even if the financial benefit was entirely Arne's, Burney enjoyed playing in the band at Drury Lane or for Handel's oratorios; but 'these were only my Evenings amusem^{ts}—in the morning Winter & Summer, when he had no Scholars to send me to, I was constantly employed as a Copyist of his own Compositions, either for the Playhouse or Vaux-Hall; & this under pretence that Norton, Lowe & Simpson, the Copyists for these places were not to be trusted with his precious Scores'.

Burney was discontented not only because he was writing himself almost 'into a consumption as an amanuensis'.[3] He was

---

[1] *Hist. Mus.* iv. 636 n.
[2] Osborn; CB's published account of Arne appears in *Hist. Mus.* iv. 655-7, 673-5. [3] *Frag. Mem.* (B.M. Add. MS. 48345, f. 22).

never to forget Mrs. Arne's kindness to him and he later claimed to have learned more from accompanying her on the harpsichord than from her husband: 'She was indeed, not only desirous of my professional improvement, but had a parental attention to my morals and conduct.' In return, Burney did his best 'to contribute to domestic harmony . . . and I did flatter myself, if I had continued longer with them, the union would have been of longer duration'.[1] For obvious reasons, however, the eventual disintegration of the Arne household was inevitable, for Burney wrote of his master that 'He never c^d pass by a woman in the street, to the end of his Life without Concupiscence [or, in plain Engl. *picking her up*, if her look was not forbidding, & impracticable. It has frequently happened in walking home with my Wife of a Night, if we have by some accident been separated for a few minutes, that she has been accosted by the D^r with that design, ere I c^d overtake her or he knew to whom she belonged.]'

Burney's letters tell more about Arne's 'whoredom' and his mistresses[2] but these quotations from his notebook will suffice to suggest the blend of frustration and disgust with which he had soon come to view the remaining years of his apprenticeship to his 'avaricious, selfish, sordid, and tyrannical' master. Five years of this servitude still stretched ahead of him when, in the summer of 1746, Burney met Fulke Greville, son of the Hon. Algernon Greville and grandson of Fulke Greville, fifth Lord Brooke. By the time that, as Burney put it, 'he honoured me with his Notice', Greville's fortune had been 'materially injured' by various kinds of extravagance and, at the age of twenty-nine, he had passed his peak as a 'buck' and was beginning to lead a quieter life than had been his custom. Greville remained, nevertheless, a fascinating figure to an ambitious apprentice to whom 'high society' had previously been closed. Descended from the friend of Sir Philip Sidney, Greville possessed every advantage of 'birth, and fortune and figure'. He had travelled extensively on the Continent, had a most refined taste in all the arts, was a noted tennis-player and trainer of horses, invariably travelled with two French-horn players who performed whenever he stopped, and was

---

[1] CB to François and Mrs. Barthélemon, 21 Oct. 1789, W. H. Cummings, op. cit., pp. 104–5.   [2] CB to CB Jr., 16 and 19 April 1806 (Comyn).

accustomed to entertain 'large parties of persons of the highest rank & fashion'. The range of Greville's interests and accomplishments impressed not only the ingenuous young musician: 'All these were striking and dazling circumstances to young ladies; but he had such a passion for the Turf & for play, as alarmed the fathers. He had lost considerable sums at White's and at Bath. . . .'[1] Horace Walpole recorded that, as recently as 1741, Greville had lost £15,000 at cards.[2]

Probably as a result of his visits to Italy, Greville boasted a highly sophisticated musical taste. His low opinion of professional musicians, however, was by no means untypical of the fashionable music-lover at this period. During the summer of 1746 Greville defied Jacob Kirkman, a famous maker of harpsichords, to produce a musician 'who had mind and cultivation, as well as finger and ear', a combination which seemed inconceivable to the aristocrat. To defend the honour of his profession Kirkman arranged a meeting at his shop between Greville and twenty-year-old Charles Burney, who was summoned, as he thought, only to demonstrate the qualities of some of Kirkman's harpsichords. His musical skill, lively intelligence, and ingenuous charm easily vanquished Greville's cynicism. Indeed, so impressed was Greville both by Burney's conversation and by his playing, that he wished to engage him on the spot as a domestic musician and companion. Reluctantly Burney had to explain that he was apprenticed to Arne. According to Fanny d'Arblay, Greville at once persuaded Arne to sell the remaining years of Burney's indentures, but this transaction was not, in fact, to take place for another two years. Nevertheless, Arne willingly agreed to accept 'a stated sum' for the temporary loss of his apprentice, who accompanied Greville to his splendid country house at Wilbury near Andover in Wiltshire.[3]

After a month of hunting and of visiting and entertaining his neighbours, Greville moved on to Bath, where Burney's performances of Scarlatti impressed his new master's aristocratic acquaintance, particularly Lord Holdernesse. Music was hardly the main interest of these visitors to Bath, however, and Burney watched with astonishment Greville and his friends gambling

---

[1] *Frag. Mem.* (Berg).   [2] *Corresp.* xvii. 126.
[3] *Mem.* i. 26–34; *Frag. Mem.* (Berg).

for as much as a thousand guineas at a time or racing their
horses in the fields. He observed also 'the tyranny of the master
of ceremonies Beau Nash', and used to rise early to watch 'the
great Ld Bolingbroke carried in a chair to the Pump-room for
privacy, before the rest of the company was assembled'. His
introduction to aristocratic society had to end, however, as
abruptly as it had begun, and late in 1746 he returned to Drury
Lane and to Thomas Arne.[1]

Although these weeks at Wilbury and Bath were not calculated to reconcile Burney to his drudgery for Arne, they were
not without effect on his life in London. Lord Holdernesse,[2]
who had been especially kind to him at Bath, invited Burney to
call on him and the young musician soon became a frequent
and welcome visitor. Holdernesse's encouragement gratified
Burney so much that it was to this nobleman that he 'most
humbly' dedicated his first published compositions, *Six Sonatas
for two Violins, with a Bass for the Violoncello or Harpsichord*, in
1747.[3] According to Fanny d'Arblay, it was at the house of
Lord Holdernesse that Burney first met William Mason, the
young Cambridge poet, who was a year older than himself and
who won fame in 1747 with his *Musaeus*, a monody on the death
of Pope. Although Fanny was mistaken in thinking that Mason
was already Chaplain to Lord Holdernesse, an appointment he
did not receive until 1754, he was already in the habit of making
frequent visits to London at this time and may already have
known his distant relative and future patron. Certainly, Burney's
long acquaintance with Mason dates from these years.[4]

Fulke Greville also came to London for the fashionable
season, and amused himself by introducing Burney to 'Gaming
Clubs' and to 'every scene of high dissipation which, at that
period, made the round of the existence of a buckish fine
gentleman'. The tone of Burney's description of Greville
gambling at Bath, which is all that survives from his 'Memoirs'
of this aspect of his life, expresses only surprised amusement. It
can be safely assumed that Fanny's lurid and melodramatic
descriptions of gambling and racing excursions with Greville

[1] *Frag. Mem.* (Berg).
[2] Robert d'Arcy, fourth Earl (1718–78), ambassador to Venice 1744–6, had
been an important supporter of London opera earlier in the decade.
[3] *Frag. Mem.* (B.M. Add. MS. 48345, ff. 11–12); *GDB*, ii. 340.
[4] *Mem.* i. 24; J. W. Draper, *William Mason*, New York, 1924, pp. 25, 45.

were very largely her own invention and were intended primarily to edify her readers with a picture of virtuous youth un-
corrupted by the vices of fashionable London.[1]

In April 1747 David Garrick returned to Drury Lane as joint
manager. Although, because of Greville's demands on his
time, Burney eventually lost his regular place in the orchestra,
Garrick gave him permission to use the music-room and watch
from behind the scenes when he was not engaged as a performer. Burney naturally made every possible use of this
privilege, 'particularly when *he* [Garrick] acted'. From this
period date many anecdotes in his 'Memoirs' concerning
Garrick, Quin, Mrs. Cibber, Mrs. Clive, and Mrs. Woffington,
which vividly communicate the enjoyment with which Burney
occupied his place in the wings. For example, to illustrate his
belief that Garrick 'c^d put off tragedy and put on comedy, like a
garment, at his pleasure', Burney described the actor at the end
of 'the most affecting scenes of King Lear', peering with great
satisfaction through the curtain at his deeply moved audience,
who were wiping their eyes and blowing their noses: 'Yes! yes!
My dears! you have it', said Garrick cheerfully, '& mopping
his fingers, ran into the green-room.' This story reminded
Burney of Samuel Johnson's reply to Garrick's complaint that
his friend's noisy conversation and laughter in the wings
'destroyed his feelings' when he was acting in tragedy: 'No, no,
Davy . . . Punch never feels!'[2]

Other 'curious scenes & incidents wch were concealed from
the public' concerned Burney's master, Thomas Arne. One revealing passage in Burney's 'Memoirs' describes a literal battle
between Arne and Mrs. Kitty Clive, whom Burney considered
to be 'the best comic actress, perhaps, that ever trod our stage,
[and] perhaps the worst singer'. Mrs. Clive tended to attribute
her own musical lapses to the musicians who were accompanying her:

When one night Mrs Clive having undertaken a song in wch she
was imperfect: as she was given to be out of time as well as tune; at a
hitch, she calls out aloud to the band, 'why don't the fellows mind
what they are ab^t?' At the end of the act Arne went up stairs in the
name of the whole band to remonstrate against her insolence, when
the only satisfaction he obtained, was a slap on the face. In return, he

[1] *Mem.* i. 36–46.　　[2] *Frag. Mem.* (Berg); cf. *Thraliana*, i. 177.

literally turned her over his knee and gave her such a manual flagellation as she probably had not received since she quitted the nursery; but as a proof that she had made a good defence, he came back without his wig, all over blood from her scratches, & his long point ruffles torn & dangling over his nails.[1]

The return of Garrick had done nothing to increase Burney's respect for his master for, like the other managers, Garrick feared Arne's early legal training rather more than he admired his music:

Garrick, ignorant what his musical merit may have been, had such an utter contempt for his vanity, and general Character, that he hardly ever qualified him wth any other title in Private, than the Rabscalion. Indeed all the managers knowing him to be a more regular bred attorney than musician, took care to tie him neck & heels in all contracts otherwise he w[d] not have been kept honest by his own Principles & probity. But though he was selfish, mean & rapacious after money, he spent it when acquired like a Child in gratifying his Vanity and incontinence.[2]

Arne's permanent shortage of money, however, worked to Burney's advantage, for it made his master all the more willing to release him to Greville for suitable compensation. In the autumn of 1747 Burney once more visited Wilbury. Greville took him to see James Harris of Salisbury, 'the most amiable, learned, & worthy of men', who was to be celebrated as 'Hermes' Harris after his book of that name, published in 1752, and who was to be a steady friend of Burney for many years. There were numerous 'neighbourly & accidental Visitors' at Wilbury, but Burney was more struck by two of the 'inmates' of the house. Thomas Broughton, Vicar of Bedminster near Bristol and Prebendary of Salisbury, had, at an earlier period, 'associated with the principal literary men of his time', and had written the librettos for a number of Handel's works.[3] Obliged to play the music of Handel for the benefit of Broughton, Burney was also expected to cater for the different needs of another guest, Samuel Crisp, 'a man of infinite taste in all the fine arts' and 'an excellent Scholar', who shared with Greville an unbounded admiration for Italian music, and who had

---

[1] *Frag. Mem.* (Berg).   [2] Osborn.
[3] Article, 'Broughton, Thomas', Rees, vol. v.

brought back from Rome 'the first large Pianoforte that was ever constructed'. Burney usually rose before the rest of the household to practise the works of both Handel and the Italians, in order to be able to gratify the admirers of both schools in the evenings. Never before had he enjoyed so pleasant an alternation of 'tranquil study and practice' and stimulating 'conversation and encouragement' from cultivated and widely travelled music-lovers.[1]

Burney's visits to Wilbury inevitably had an effect on his taste and ambitions. The joint influence of Crisp and Greville won him from his 'ancient worship' of Handel, Geminiani, and Corelli ('the sole Divinities of my youth') to a taste for such composers as Scarlatti, Hasse, and Pergolesi, which was to orientate his musical thought for the next forty years.[2] No less important was the effect on Burney's social awareness, for his ambition of escaping from the limitation of being 'a mere musician' clearly dates from this same period. He himself later 'used to boast that he had his education' at Wilbury, for his manners and conversation were inevitably and decisively influenced by intimacy with 'company . . . of the first class for birth, breeding, and conversation'.[3] He was significantly alert to similar circumstances in the careers of other musicians, writing in 1800 of J. C. Smith, the pupil of Handel, that 'he became acquainted, at Geneva, with some English gentlemen of learning and talents; which circumstance seems to have given a turn to his manners and conduct during the rest of his life'.[4] A few years later Burney wrote again of the importance of this acquaintance in Smith's life, which 'gave him a taste for, and procured him admission into, good company; so that he formed his character on models of a higher class than that of a mere musician'.[5] Once more the terms could hardly be more relevant to his own case.

After this second visit to Wilbury Burney returned to Drury Lane and to work for Arne, which must have seemed all the more tedious by comparison. At about this time, however, Fulke Greville fell in love with Frances Macartney, the third

[1] *Frag. Mem.* (Berg).
[2] CB to Twining, 14 Dec. 1781, copy (Osborn).
[3] *Frag. Mem.* (B.M. Add. MS. 48345, f. 22).
[4] *Monthly Review*, xxxi (1800), 418.
[5] Article, 'Smith, John Christopher', Rees, vol. xxxiii.

daughter of a wealthy Irish landowner. She was to be celebrated for her privately circulated poem, 'A Prayer for Indifference',[1] and Horace Walpole had written of her in *The Beauties* (1746), in verses which Burney, however, considered 'unworthy of the grace & beauty she posessed'.[2] During his courtship of Fanny Macartney, Greville sent Burney 'to teach her accompanyment, & the compositions of his favourite composers', a task which he found very agreeable, for the charming company of Fanny and her sisters was something 'new' to a young man 'who had then been intimately acquainted wth so few ladies of family & fashion'.[3]

Early in 1748 Greville married Fanny Macartney in a somewhat melodramatic manner. As a last wild gesture before settling down to married life, he eloped with Fanny, assisted by Burney and the Misses Macartney. (On his return from the wedding to beg pardon of his father-in-law he was greeted with the crushing observation, 'Mr. Greville has chosen to take a wife out of the window, whom he might just as well have taken out of the door.')[4] The fact that Greville asked Burney to give the bride away at this clandestine marriage indicates the confidence and esteem which he reposed in the young man. Similarly Burney stood proxy for the Duke of Beaufort as godfather to Greville's daughter, Frances Anne, who was baptized on 28 November 1748.[5] As Mrs. (and later Lady) Crewe, this child was to become one of Burney's dearest friends in the last three decades of his life.

Marriage now restricted Fulke Greville's extravagant amusements to some extent and he soon felt that Burney should become a more permanent member of his household. The lively, charming, and intelligent young musician had become so much a feature of Wilbury that Greville decided to purchase the remaining years of Burney's indenture to Arne. Fortunately, when Greville made his offer, Arne was 'out of Cash' and he

---

[1] *Oxford Book of Eighteenth Century Verse*, ed. D. Nichol Smith, pp. 426–8.
[2] CB's objection to the description is probably due to the fact that he identified Fanny Macartney as 'Flora' in *The Beauties*. Walpole's notes to the manuscript of his poem identify her as 'Fanny', *Corresp.* xxx, 328 n. 21.
[3] *Frag. Mem.* (Berg; and B.M. Add. MS. 48345, f. 10).
[4] *Mem.* i. 59.
[5] Registers of Newton Tony Church (I am indebted for this information to Dr. L. F. Powell); *Mem.* i. 60.

willingly transferred Burney's three remaining years of apprenticeship to Greville at Michaelmas 1748, for the sum of £300 (all of which sum, it may be noted, was clear profit). Thereafter, Burney wrote, 'I was entirely domesticated with Mr Greville, and accountable to him for my time.'[1]

Burney's status in the Greville household was curious, for he was at once apprentice, music-master, and intellectual companion. As he recalled with considerable pride some sixty years later, the delicate situation was handled tactfully: 'though only a Musician, I was never sent to the 2nd table'[2] and Mrs. Greville was careful about the way in which she referred to him: 'I was called the *Youth*. . . . My *lady* gave me that appellation, to steer clear of the too high title of young Gentleman, or too degrading address of boy, or young man.'[3] Fanny Greville did more, however, than smooth over the social complexities of which Burney was becoming increasingly aware, for the 'counsel, conversation, & love of literature' of this 'beautiful, charming & accomplished' woman, according to his own account, 'formed young Burney's character, [and] rendered his abode in the family at once delightful & useful to him during the rest of his life'.[4] The contrast with his life with Arne could hardly have been more acute, for at Wilbury he found peace in which to study, instruction and encouragement from men cultivated in all the arts, and entertainment in the form of the amateur theatricals of which the Grevilles were so fond. With other friends made at this period, John Hawkesworth and Richard Cox of Quarley, Burney was also to have 'connections of lasting and honourable intimacy'.[5]

When Burney had been living permanently with the Grevilles for only a few months, new pleasures were proposed in the form of a long visit to the Continent. Naturally it was expected that Burney would accompany them and that this opportunity of foreign travel would greatly excite him. On the contrary, Burney was extremely depressed. Some time earlier he had fallen in love with Esther Sleepe, 'a young person of beauty, wit, captivating manners and prudent conduct', whom he had

[1] *Frag. Mem.* (Berg).
[2] CB to Lady Crewe [Oct. 1807], draft (Osborn).
[3] CB to Mrs. Crewe, 5 July 1794 (Osborn).
[4] *Frag. Mem.* (B.M. Add. MS. 48345, f. 22).
[5] *Mem.* i. 59–61.

been meeting regularly at private balls held by his elder brother Richard, now a dancing-master in London. Burney could not marry without Greville's consent and he had been reluctant to seek it so soon after being rescued from the obnoxious Arne. Matters came to a head, however, with the prospect of several years' absence from Esther. Eventually he plucked up courage to show his master a miniature of his beloved:

M[r] Greville was so struck with her beauty that without my hinting a wish to complete our union till the full time of my apprenticeship was expired, he cried out, 'why don't you marry her?'—when I eagerly said—'*may* I?'—We lost no time; (the Marriage Act was not then even in contemplation) but the next day had the Gordian knot tied at May-Fair, where a Hymenaeal priest had always, as in the Fleet, a parental witness ready to make a present of a bride.[1]

Burney did not explain the need for the drastic haste with which the lovers married after receiving permission. As Miss Hemlow has convincingly demonstrated, when Burney married Esther Sleepe at St. George's Chapel, Hyde Park Corner, on 25 June 1749, he was already the father of a daughter born in the previous month.[2] To Miss Hemlow's argument for the date of the child's birth may be added the testimony of 'an extract from the records of the College of Arms which puts the date of Esther's birth at 1749', seen by Dr. Scholes in the possession of Canon F. d'Arblay Burney.[3]

After receiving only some nine months of service from his 'apprentice', Greville generously and good-humouredly released him from any further obligations and set off for Italy soon after Burney's marriage.[4] Many years later when, according to Fanny d'Arblay, he was in financial difficulties as a result of his passion for gambling, Greville had second thoughts about the affair. In a passage which she intended for her *Memoirs* of her father but eventually omitted,[5] Fanny relates that in 1773 Greville asked Burney (whom he now considered 'a man of easy fortune') to repay the £300 with which he had been freed from Arne. This was still, however, a considerable sum to a music-teacher with a large family to support and, on

---

[1] *Frag. Mem.* (B.M. Add. MS. 48345, ff. 11, 22); cf. *Mem.* i. 76–78.
[2] Hemlow, p. 6, and n. 2.   [3] *GDB*, i. 57 n. 1.
[4] *Walpole Corresp.* xx. 58.
[5] Barrett. CB refers to the quarrel in a letter to Crisp, 21 Jan. 1774 (Berg).

the grounds that Greville had quite voluntarily cancelled his articles with Arne twenty-five years earlier, Burney refused to consider the request and was prepared to take legal action in self-defence. He was deeply disturbed by this quarrel with his former patron, but his firmness convinced Greville of the unreasonableness of his demands and amicable relations were resumed after a series of placatory letters and meetings.

III

In the summer of 1749, with a wife and child to support, the twenty-three-year-old Burney was at last on his own, committed inevitably, in spite of his brief interlude in the higher social spheres to which Greville had introduced him, to a career as a professional musician. On 3 July, a week after his marriage, he paid the necessary fees to become a Freeman of the Musicians' Company and in the same month applied for the vacant post of organist at St. Dionis's Backchurch, which carried an annual salary of £30. If he had saved little money during his years with Arne and Greville, Burney had at least acquired many loyal and helpful friends, whose value was now to be demonstrated. With the support of such ardent music-lovers and powerful members of the Vestry of St. Dionis's, who elected the organist, as Sir Joseph Hankey, his brother Sir Thomas, and the Rev. and Hon. Alexander Hume (who became the ninth Earl of Home in 1761), Burney won an overwhelming victory over several other candidates in October after 'a long & tiresome struggle', the more comic aspects of which he described in his 'Memoirs'. In order to be closer to the church and to his 'zealous, hospitable, & friendly' supporters, Burney and his family now moved from the Fan Shop in the Poultry, where he had evidently taken lodgings, to a house in Fenchurch Street.[1]

With further assistance from Sir Joseph Hankey, Burney obtained another post a few months later. In March 1748 a great fire in Cornhill[2] had consumed the Swan Tavern where John Stanley, the blind organist and composer, had directed a famous series of fashionable concerts. During the subsequent

---

[1] *Frag. Mem.* (B.M. Add. MS. 48345, ff. 11–13); Records of the Musicians' Company, Guildhall MSS. 3091, 3098; Vestry Minutes of St. Dionis's Backchurch, Guildhall MS. 4216. Further material about CB's election was collected by F. G. E[dwards], *Musical Times*, xlv (1904), 438.

[2] *Gent. Mag.* xviii (1748), 138.

removal of the series to the King's Arms Tavern, Stanley and Sir
Joseph Hankey, who had a controlling interest in the concerts,
quarrelled over some issue described in a missing portion of
Burney's 'Memoirs'. The inevitable result was that, in the
winter of 1749, Burney was appointed to Stanley's place at the
organ and harpsichord for the new series of concerts. In spite of
the 'fear and trembling' with which he made his first appearance
—'being always extremely timid in public playing' at the best of
times—before an audience of Stanley's 'cross & indignant'
admirers, Burney acquitted himself well, playing a concerto
which he had written especially for the occasion, and his
'courage was frequently refreshed and invigorated by loud
applause'. His important role in these concerts brought him not
only a valuable addition to his income but the opportunity of
playing with some of the most famous musicians in the country.[1]

Before long Burney was appearing as a soloist in other series
of public concerts[2] and, as a result of his 'diligence & a regular
conduct', his reputation and prosperity increased rapidly: 'I
now began to be in fashion in the City, as a Master, and had
my hands full of professional business of all kinds, scholars at
both ends of the town, Composition, & public playing.' Among
his scholars Burney could count two of Handel's leading
singers, Giulia Frasi and Gaetano Guadagni, who was to be one
of the most celebrated male contraltos of the century. Burney's
task was 'to accompany him in his studies, and assist him in the
pronunciation of the English words in the parts given him in the
Oratorios by Handel.' These pupils brought him into contact
with the great composer himself, 'who used to bring an Air, or
Duet, in his pocket, as soon as composed, hot from the brain, in
order to give me the time & style, that I might communicate
them to my scholar . . .'. Handel's explosive temper, however,
could make such visits 'very terrific to a young musician', as
Burney discovered.[3]

In spite of his comfortable income and growing reputation as
a teacher and performer, Burney retained his ambitions as a
composer. From this point of view his important connexion was

[1] *Frag. Mem.* (B.M. Add. MS. 48345, ff. 13–14).
[2] *GDB*, i. 53.
[3] *Frag. Mem.* (B.M. Add. MS. 48345, ff. 14, 22); *Handel Commem.*, p. 35; *Hist. Mus.* iv. 495.

to be with James Oswald, 'the Scotch Orpheus', who owned a music-shop 'on the pavement of St Martin's church-yard'. Oswald, a noted performer of old Scots tunes on the 'cello, also composed similar melodies and, whilst he was still at Drury Lane, Burney had started writing accompaniments to these tunes and to those of other song-writers such as Henry Carey: 'afterwards', Burney recorded, 'I had a pleasure in working for him, by the sheet, as it amused me more than teaching'.[1]

At Oswald's shop Burney seems to have met a number of well-known writers and music-lovers, one of whom may have been Christopher Smart. Burney later wrote of Oswald, 'The first two or three ballads I ever printed, issued from his shop' and one of these ballads was entitled 'Lovely Harriote. A Crambo Song, the words by Mr. Smart. Set to music by Charles Burny. Printed by J. Oswald.'[2] As so little is known about Christopher Smart's curious and unhappy life, it is unfortunate that Burney was not urged to follow up a statement which he made many years later: 'I c^d give you a long hist^y of my acquaintance, intimacy and correspondence wth . . . Kit Smart, wch began as early as the year 1744 on my first arrival in London and continued through all the vicissitudes of his fame, insanity, poverty & imprisonment.'[3] An early draft of a passage in Burney's 'Memoirs' bears a note reminding himself to make an insertion in it: 'here Canonbury house—Newbury & Smart'.[4] If he did give any account of the poet, however, it would seem not to have escaped Fanny's censorship.

Nevertheless, various scattered pieces of new information about Smart can be found in Burney's papers. His statement that he met Smart in London as early as 1744, for example, is of interest simply because nothing has been known of the poet's whereabouts between January 1744 and July 1745, when he became a Fellow of Pembroke College, Cambridge.[5] As Fanny d'Arblay is rather reticent about the 'set' in which her father met Smart, it is possible that she regarded it as unsavoury in some way.[6] Although Smart was teaching at Cambridge between 1745 and 1749, he was frequently absent from the

[1] *Frag. Mem.* (B.M. Add. MS. 48345, f. 12); CB to CB Jr., 8 Feb. 1799 (Coke).
[2] *GDB*, ii. 342.   [3] CB to [? Malone], 5 May [1806] (PML).
[4] *Frag. Mem.* (B.M. Add. MS. 48345, f. 17); see *post*, pp. 36–37.
[5] E. G. Ainsworth and C. E. Noyes, *Christopher Smart* (Univ. of Missouri Studies, xviii. 4), 1943, p. 20.   [6] *Mem.* i. 17.

University,[1] presumably on visits to London, and Burney came to know him extremely well. The degree of friendship between them can be judged from an unpublished letter from Smart to Burney written in the summer of 1749, which is, incidentally, the first extant item in Burney's correspondence:

> Markett Downham Norfolk
> y[e] 29th of July 1749.
>
> My dear Charles.
>   I have left your last unanswered so long that I am under some apprehension, lest it shoud be now too late. You must know I am situated within a mile of my Harriote & Love has robd Friendship of her just dues; but you know the force of the passion too well to be angry at its effects. I condole with you heartily for the loss of your Father, who (I hope) has left behind the cole, which is the most effectual means of consolation.[2] I am as much a stranger as you to what is going on at Vaux Hall, for we are so wrapt up in our own snugness at this part of the kingdom, that we know little what's doing in the rest of the world. There was a great musical crash at Cambridge, which was greatly admired,[3] but I was not there, being much better pleased with hearing my Harriote on her spinnet & organ at her ancient mansion.—If you are still in the Kingdom I beg the favour of an immediate line or two, but if you are not, I hope even the Ocean will not, nay, he shall not cut off our correspondence & friendship—Y[rs] most inseparably C. Smart.[4]

Accompanying this letter is a partial transcript of it made by Fanny d'Arblay, probably intended for the volume of her father's correspondence which was at one time to supplement her *Memoirs* of him. Fanny also made some notes on Burney's friendship with Smart, including some remarks on this letter which have inexplicably been separated from it.[5] Some of her information was erroneous. 'Harriote' was not, as Fanny asserts, the daughter of John Newbery the bookseller whom Smart eventually married, but the sister of Jermyn Pratt of Downham with whom he had been at Cambridge. For Harriote Pratt Smart 'entertained a long and unsuccessful passion' and he

---

[1] Ainsworth and Noyes, op. cit., p. 34, n. 80.
[2] James Macburney died in June 1749, 'Worcester Memoranda'.
[3] Almost certainly the Installation of the Duke of Newcastle as Chancellor of Cambridge University on 1 July 1749. William Boyce provided the setting of Mason's *Installation Ode.* See *post*, p. 77.
[4] Houghton Library, Harvard.   [5] B.M. Add. MS. 48345, ff. 46–47.

wrote a number of poems about her, at least one of which, as we have seen, Burney set to music.[1] Fanny's notes state that Smart had given her father a number of his poems in manuscript, including 'On the Fifth of December'[2] and 'A burlesque or Parody or imitation of the Ode of Horace which never to the knowledge of Dr Burney had been published', and which she intended to print from 'a MS Copy in the Author's own hand'. Like Burney and his daughter, Smart's editors have not realized that his translation of Horace's 'Audivere, Lyce' (*Odes*, IV. 13) had in fact been printed in the *London Magazine* in September 1750.[3] Although Smart's manuscript has not appeared among Burney's papers, another text of the poem can be found in *Thraliana*, which was probably communicated by Burney to Mrs. Thrale.[4]

Smart's letter of 29 July 1749 was clearly written in ignorance of Burney's hasty marriage and in the belief that he was about to go abroad with the Grevilles. Nevertheless, it shows that the friends were usually in the habit of frequent correspondence and explains Smart's movements at a period of which all that has been known was that he left Cambridge for London 'sometime after the spring of 1749'.[5] Presumably he reached London later in the year and resumed his friendship with Burney. The reference to Vauxhall suggests that Burney had introduced Smart to Arne at a much earlier period than has been assumed and that the poet's songs were being performed there well before the summer of 1750.[6]

Burney introduced an even more significant figure into Smart's life a little later. It has hitherto been accepted as little more than a 'tradition' that it was Burney who brought together Smart and John Newbery, the bookseller and publisher, who was to be 'the most important figure in Smart's London existence',[7] the only evidence being a statement to that effect by Christopher Hunter, Smart's nephew, in his edition of his uncle's poems in 1791. Hunter states, however, that he had

---

[1] Ainsworth and Noyes, op. cit., p. 26; N. Callan, *Collected Poems of Christopher Smart*, 1949, i. 187–91.   [2] Callan, op. cit., i. 203.

[3] See the present writer's article, 'Christopher Smart's First Publication in English', *RES*, xii (1961), 402–4.   [4] *Thraliana*, i. 516.

[5] Ainsworth and Noyes, op. cit., p. 34.

[6] Cf. R. Brittain, *Selected Poems of Christopher Smart*, Princeton, 1950, p. 20.

[7] Ainsworth and Noyes, op. cit., p. 37; Brittain, op. cit., p. 21.

consulted Burney (who had also 'enriched the present collection with some original compositions') about his uncle's life.[1] Burney himself, moreover, confirms the story:

I brought him & Newbury (the Dr James' Powder bookseller, & excellent writer of Goody two-shoes, & Giles Gingerbread &c &c), acquainted. He had an apartment in his house where he compiled the 'Old Woman's Magazine,' &c and married the beautiful Nancy Carnan, daughter-in-law to Newbury whom ⟨he⟩ celebrated under the title of 'the Lass with the Golden ⟨Locks'⟩ whose carrots were 'the taste of the ancients: twas Class⟨ical hair'⟩.[2]

In this passage Burney appears to confirm a suspicion that Smart lived with Newbery before, as well as after, his marriage to the bookseller's step-daughter in 1753, for Smart was working for him by June 1750 at the latest and *The Midwife; or, the Old Woman's Magazine* began to appear in the following October.[3] At about this time Smart opened a subscription list for his *Poems on Several Occasions* and although Newbery did not publish the volume until 1752, when Burney had left London, the list itself suggests that 'Mr. Charles Burney' had done what he could to help his friend, by obtaining the names of his brother Richard, Arne, Fulke Greville, Sir Joseph Hankey and perhaps those of Garrick and his wife. In any case, by introducing Smart to the publisher who, for better or worse, was to encourage his strange literary projects, and to his future wife, Burney had already played a considerable part in the poet's early career in London.

Burney had other literary friends at this period about whom even less information has survived. The index to a fragmentary portion of his 'Memoirs' contains the entry, 'Acquaintance with Oswald, Honble & Rev. Mr Hume Thompson & Smollet'.[4] Although there is no other evidence that Burney knew Smollett, some information about his acquaintance with James Thomson can be gleaned elsewhere. Fanny d'Arblay, as has been mentioned already, mistakenly believed that Burney was brought into 'close contact' with Thomson when he composed music for

---

[1] *Poems of the Late Christopher Smart A.M.*, Reading, 1791, i. xviii.
[2] CB to Twining, 10 Mar. 1804, copy (Osborn). Lacunae in the copy where the original was torn have been supplied from Callan, op. cit. i. 202. See *post*, p. 363.
[3] Ainsworth and Noyes, op. cit., pp. 40, 73 n. 7.
[4] *Frag. Mem.* (B.M. Add. MS. 48345, f. 18).

Alfred. Although he did not in fact contribute to this work until 1751, three years after Thomson's death, Burney could easily have met the poet through Arne and seems also to have had frequent opportunity of seeing him at a slightly later period in the shop of James Oswald, 'the Scotch Orpheus'. No definite date, however, can be attached to a story of which Burney's friends were fond: 'Thomson, the poet, was so extremely indolent, that half his mornings were spent in bed. Dr. Burney having called on him one day at two o'clock, expressed surprise at finding him still there, and asked how he came to lie so long?—"Ecod, mon, because I had no *mot-tive* to rise", was his sole answer.'[1]

In 1747 Burney set to music Thomson's 'Ode on the Aeolian Harp', which, as he states in his 'Memoirs', 'was performed one morning at Lady Townshend's to whom I had the honour of being introduced by . . . Mr Hume'.[2] Elsewhere he expanded this account in a manner which suggests that he was accustomed to meeting Thomson in Oswald's shop. After mentioning a description of the Aeolian Harp in Kircher's *Musurgia Universalis* (Rome, 1650), Burney proceeded:

it was thence that Thomson the poet took it, who wrote an ode on this aerial instrument, which was set to music, and performed at a morning concert at viscountess Townshend's, mother of the present marquis.[3] . . . Oswald, the celebrated player of old Scots tunes on the violoncello, and composer of many new, passed for the inventor of the Aeolian harp; but as he was unable to read the account of it in the Musurgia, written in Latin, Thomson gave him the description of it in English, and let it pass for his invention, in order to give him a better title to the sale of the instrument at his music-shop in St. Martin's Church-yard.[4]

Through Oswald Burney also met Dr. John Armstrong, whose poetry he greatly admired. Indeed, he always firmly believed that Armstrong was the author of the celebrated poem, 'The Tears of Scotland', in spite of the normal attribution to

---

[1] 'Maloniana', in Sir James Prior, *Life of Malone*, 1860, pp. 415–16; also in W. Seward, *Anecdotes*, 4th edn., 1798, ii. 375. Hazlitt, who was fond of stories about CB, told it twice, *Works*, ed. P. P. Howe, 1930–4, xii. 66, and xvii. 106.

[2] *Frag. Mem.* (B.M. Add. MS. 48345, f. 12).

[3] George Townshend, fourth Viscount and first Marquis (1724–1807).

[4] Article 'Voice', Rees, vol. xxxvii. Cf. A. D. McKillop, *The Castle of Indolence and Other Poems*, Lawrence, 1961, pp. 206–9.

Smollett: 'Oswald, who set this song to music, and published it, assured a friend of ours, still living, that he had it from Armstrong in his own handwriting.' The evidence for Smollett's authorship, however, hardly supports Burney's second-hand story.[1]

The fact that, through James Oswald, Burney undoubtedly came to know a number of Scottish writers and music-lovers (such as the Rev. and Hon. Mr. Hume), only complicates a matter which, although relatively unimportant, has given rise to some confusion in the minds of both musicologists and literary scholars. Not long after Burney first came to know Oswald, the music-publisher 'obtained a patent for the sole publication of all Music composed, or pretended to be composed, by the dilettanti members of *the Society of the Temple of Apollo*.'[2] This patent was presumably the copyright grant given to Oswald on 23 October 1747.[3] All that has hitherto been known about this 'Society' came from the title-pages of certain compositions published by Oswald, which were composed or 'Corrected and approv'd of' by it; and from Fanny d'Arblay, who stated firmly that all the music which appeared under this rubric was in fact composed by her father and by him alone.[4]

Scholars have been curiously reluctant to pay any attention to Fanny's confident assertion. Frank Kidson rejected it and took the 'Society of the Temple of Apollo' to be one of the many groups of amateur and professional musicians which flourished during the century. Kidson even went so far as to speculate as to the political significance of the 'Society', assuming that its active members would include Oswald, Burney, John Reid, the Earl of Kellie, Thomson, and David Mallett.[5] Kidson's speculations have since been accepted as fact and new members have accordingly been elected to the 'Society'. Thus, for example, 'Smollett could not have missed knowing this group, composed largely of Scots, who were so closely associated in that period.'[6] Even Dr. Scholes, after quoting without comment Fanny's statement that her father was the only 'member' of the 'Society',

---

[1] *Monthly Review*, xvi (1795), 71 (this article contains other reminiscences of Armstrong); L. M. Knapp, *Tobias Smollett*, Princeton, 1949, pp. 57–61.

[2] *Frag. Mem.* (B.M. Add. MS. 48345, f. 12).

[3] F. Kidson, 'James Oswald, Dr. Burney, and "The Temple of Apollo" ', *The Musical Antiquary*, ii (1910–11), 39.   [4] *Mem.* i. 22–23.

[5] Kidson, op. cit., pp. 35, 38, 40–41.   [6] Knapp, op. cit., p. 60.

evidently accepted Kidson's theory;[1] and a scholar, who has recently read the fragments of Burney's 'Memoirs' on which the following elucidation of the problem is based, qualified earlier accounts only by adding the Rev. and Hon. Mr. Hume as a 'very active member' to the 'Society'.[2]

Although Fanny had contrived as usual to garble some of the information she was transferring from her father's 'Memoirs', her statement is substantially true. Under the 'patent' for music 'composed, or pretended to be composed' by the 'Society', Burney tells us, Oswald 'published his own compositions, a Cantata & six songs of mine, as well as whatever I afterwards composed for the Playhouse'.[3] The 'Society of the Temple of Apollo' was not, therefore, a club of dilettante musicians and Scottish writers, but a name under which Oswald published his own and Burney's compositions and occasionally works by other composers, 'corrected' or 'approv'd of' by the 'Society', which probably means that they were edited by Burney. In 1793 Burney went so far as to say that he had been at this period 'the *whole Society of the Temple of Apollo*'.[4] In his 'Memoirs' he repeatedly refers to the 'Society' as 'pretended'.

The misunderstanding that has arisen about the 'Society of the Temple of Apollo' was carefully fostered by James Oswald from the beginning and for the following purpose:

He persuaded Mr Garrick that the members of this Society were gentlemen of taste and talents, who met to shew each other their compositions, & have them tried under the direction of two or three Masters to point out to them their mistakes in counter-point. That some of the members had much original genius; and wd compose for the stage any pantomime entertainment, musical farce, or even incidental songs in serious dramas. . . .[5]

It is not clear precisely when Oswald made this suggestion to Garrick, but the manager of Drury Lane listened 'very attentively' to it. By the late summer of 1750 he was probably taking it very seriously, for his ambition of concentrating on productions of Shakespeare at Drury Lane had recently been

[1] *GDB*, i. 55–57.
[2] M. Benkovitz, 'Dr. Burney's Memoirs', *RES*, x (1959), 265.
[3] *Frag. Mem.* (B.M. Add. MS. 48345, f. 12).
[4] CB to FB [? 30 Oct. 1793], (Berg); see *post*, p. 368.
[5] *Frag. Mem.* (B.M. Add. MS. 48345, f. 12).

sorely tested by the enormously popular, if rather more flimsy and ephemeral, entertainment offered by John Rich, manager of the rival theatre at Covent Garden. Rich's 'pantomimes' exerted most of their appeal through exotic scenery and costume, elaborate theatrical machinery, lighthearted music, and the performances of Rich himself, 'the unrivalled Harlequin of the century'.[1]

Garrick had been deserted not only by his audiences, who had made it clear that they preferred pantomime to Shakespeare, but by most of his leading actors and actresses, for during the summer Barry, Mrs. Cibber, and Mrs. Woffington had followed Quin to Covent Garden. Garrick's prologue to the new season at Drury Lane in September 1750 expressed a bitter recognition of the financial necessity of compromising with popular taste:

> Sacred to SHAKESPEARE, was this spot design'd
> To pierce the heart, and humanize the mind.
> But if an empty house, the actor's curse,
> Shews us our *Lears*, and *Hamlets*, lose their force;
> Unwilling, we must change the nobler scene,
> And, in our turn, present you *Harlequin*;
> Quit poets, and set carpenters to work,
> Shew gaudy scenes, or mount the vaulting *Turk*.
> For, tho' we actors, one and all, agree
> Boldly to struggle for our—vanity;
> If want comes on, importance must retreat;
> Our first, great, ruling passion, is—to eat.[2]

Later in the autumn Garrick told Oswald 'that he sh^d give the dilettanti members something on wch to exercise their fancy very soon'.[3] In his 'Memoirs' Burney stated that the first commission was for music for the pantomime *Queen Mab* but, consciously or unconsciously, he was forgetting the music which he composed for *Robin Hood*, a work which elsewhere he variously describes as a 'comic opera' and an 'English burletta' and which was first performed as an after-piece to *The Alchemist* on 13 December 1750. Although *Robin Hood*, with a libretto by Moses

---

[1] J. J. Lynch, *Box, Pit and Gallery: Stage and Society in Johnson's London*, California Univ., 1953, pp. 232–6.
[2] *Gent. Mag.* xx (1750), 422.
[3] *Frag. Mem.* (B.M. Add. MS. 48345, f. 14).

Mendez, 'went off pretty well' according to the prompter, its short run was brought to an end by the illness of Beard, the leading male singer in the cast.[1] It was later described as 'having little more than musical merit to recommend it'.[2]

This last consideration doubtless encouraged Garrick to ask Oswald's 'Society', almost immediately afterwards, to help him 'to attack Rich in his strongest hold' by providing the music for *Queen Mab*, a pantomime devised by and starring Henry Woodward, Drury Lane's answer to John Rich, 'who delivered to Oswald, in writing, subjects for the tunes that were to paint the several scenes & events of the piece; in which Puck the Fairy had several Songs that were written by Garrick, and sent to Oswald for the Society to set, who delivered them to me'.[3] *Queen Mab* was a much more elaborate piece than *Robin Hood* and Garrick timed the production perfectly, the first performance taking place on 26 December 1750: 'It was exhibited in the Christmas holidays, with splendid decorations, a great pomp of machinery, and everything that could *elevate and surprise*. Woodward was a most excellent *Harlequin*, and through the rest of the season the success was so great, that Rich began to tremble on his throne.'[4] Another of Garrick's biographers bore testimony to the importance of *Queen Mab* in winning back lost ground from Rich:

The people crowded for above forty nights to see this exhibition, which it seems had a kind of novelty to recommend it from the fable. This decided the victory in favour of Garrick; and a print, called the Steel Yards, was published, in which Mrs. Cibber and Mrs. Woffington, with Quin and Barry, were put into one scale; and Woodward, in the character of Harlequin, and Queen Mab, in the other. The first scale kicked the beam.[5]

Queen Mab was performed forty-six times before the end of the season and, various additions and revisions having taken place, it was still being produced at Drury Lane in 1775.[6] Christopher

[1] *The London Stage 1660–1800, Part 4*, ed. G. W. Stone, Jr., Carbondale, 1962, i. 226–8.
[2] *Biographia Dramatica*, 1782, ii. 311.
[3] *Frag. Mem.* (B.M. Add. MS. 48345, f. 14).
[4] A. Murphy, *Life of Garrick*, 1801, i. 119.
[5] T. Davies, *Memoirs of Garrick*, 1780, i. 929.
[6] D. MacMillan, op. cit., p. 309.

Smart, it may be noted, gave his friend's success some publicity with an account of *Queen Mab*, '*now acting with* astonishing *applause*', in his magazine *The Midwife*.[1]

The triumphant success of the pantomime, for which Burney could take at least some of the credit, doubtless encouraged Garrick to commission more music from the 'Society of the Temple of Apollo' before the end of the season, for an elaborate production of a greatly revised version of *The Masque of Alfred*. As James Thomson had died in 1748, David Mallet, the co-author of the original libretto, was free to make extensive alterations and he transformed the two-act masque into 'a regular Tragedy of five acts, with incidental songs, duets and Chorus'.[2] As Garrick himself wished to appear as Alfred drastic revision was involved, since in the original version the main character had been the Hermit, played by Quin. Mallet was obliged to rewrite much of his own earlier share of the libretto and, of Thomson's contribution, only 'three or four single speeches, and part of one song' were retained.[3] The trend towards elaborate production continued: 'In decorations of magnificent triumphal arches, dances of furies, various harmony of music and incantations, fine scenes and dresses, this masque exceeded every thing which had ever before made its appearance on the English stage.'[4]

As most of the original songs had been dispensed with and new ones had been added, Burney had a great deal of work to do. Mallet had rather dogmatic views on the nature of the settings he required, for he wanted 'all the songs to be adapted to old Scotch tunes', perhaps encouraged in patriotic nostalgia by James Oswald, but doubtless inspired also by a desire to provide *Alfred* with some authentically 'ancient' music. Burney, however, received the suggestion coldly:

I indulged him in 2 or 3; but as Alfred was not a Scotsman, I thought it w^d be ridiculous to confine all the songs to Scotish melody. I therefore new set all the rest except 'Rule Britannia', wch had been so happily set by my Master Arne, that I always very early in life

---

[1] i. 145–51.

[2] *Frag. Mem.* (B.M. Add. MS. 48345, f. 15).

[3] Mallet's 'Advertisement' to *Alfred: A Masque. Acted at the Theatre Royal In Drury-Lane*, 1751.

[4] T. Davies, op. cit. ii. 37–38.

thought it the most pleasing and the best song that ever was produced by a native of England in our language.[1]

After great preparations and with high expectations, *Alfred*
appeared at Drury Lane on 23 February 1751 with George Ann
Bellamy and David Garrick in the leading roles. Burney was
playing at a public concert on that evening although, as he
admitted, 'I fear my performance there was not meliorated by
my anxiety for the fate of my offspring at Drury Lane.' The
following extract from his 'Memoirs' not only illustrates the
vivid quality of the surviving fragments of this work but the
combination of excitement and anxiety with which, to the end
of his life, Burney saw his works presented to the world at large:

I hardly staid to play the final Chord of the last piece on the Organ,
ere I flew out of the concert-room into a Hackney coach, in hopes of
hearing some of my stuff performed (if suffered to go on) before it
was finished; but neither the coach-man nor his horse being in so
great a hurry as myself, before I reached Temple bar, I took my
leave of them, & 'ran like a Lamp-lighter', the rest of the way to
the Theatre; and in a most violent perspiration, clambered into the
Shilling Gallery, where scarcely I c^d obtain admission, the rest of the
House being extremely crowded, wch did not diminish the sudorific
state of my person. I entered luckily, at the close of an Air of Spirit,
sung by Beard, which was much applauded—This was such a cordial
to my anxiety & agitated spirits, as none but a diffident and timid
author, like myself, can have the least conception.[2]

In spite of the applause which gratified Burney's ears at that
moment and in spite of the unprecedented pains that had been
taken with the production, *Alfred* had only moderate success. It
was performed each night until 9 March (with the exception of
an amateur performance of *Othello*, for which Christopher
Smart wrote the Prologue and Epilogue, on one evening), but
on 21 March the theatres closed because of the death of the
Prince of Wales and, after the reopening in April, *Alfred* received only one more performance.[3]

Nevertheless, James Oswald duly published Burney's music
to *Robin Hood*, *Queen Mab*, and *Alfred*, which in each case was

[1] *Frag. Mem.* (B.M. Add. MS. 48345, f. 15).
[2] *Frag. Mem.* (B.M. Add. MS. 48345, f. 15). The reference to Beard and his 'Air
of Spirit' make it clear that this passage is about *Alfred*; cf. the libretto, 1751,
pp. 48–49.   [3] MacMillan, op. cit., pp. 21–22.

attributed to the 'Society of the Temple of Apollo'. Burney, indeed, never 'set his name' even to the extremely popular songs from *Queen Mab*, 'nor was he known to be the author of this music for 20 years after it was composed'.[1] It is unlikely, however, that a young composer with theatrical ambitions would withhold his name from Garrick after so exhilarating a triumph as *Queen Mab* and a later statement by Burney suggests that his identity was not long concealed: 'I earned the liberty of the Theatre in Drury Lane in the year 1751 by Music I composed for Queen Mab, Robin Hood, & Alfred.'[2] At the end of the 1750–1 season Burney must have been more than satisfied with the direction which his career was taking, even if, now that he had left Fulke Greville, his social aspirations must be limited once more to those of a 'mere musician'. At the age of twenty-five he had established himself as a prominent performer and teacher, and in his first season as a composer for the theatre had acquitted himself well. If his ambition at this period was to follow in the footsteps of his old master Arne, he had already sufficiently impressed David Garrick to be sure of future commissions.

Whatever lofty plans Burney was constructing, however, were rudely shattered in the spring of 1751 by a severe illness, which confined him to his bed for three months with an apparently incurable fever. Even Dr. John Armstrong, sent by the Rev. Alexander Hume, who also insisted on paying all the fees, could not diagnose it, but eventually insisted that Burney leave the smoky atmosphere of London. The situation could hardly have been more depressing for a young man on the edge of a successful career in the capital, even if, fifty years later, he could describe his journey by litter to Canonbury House in Islington ironically enough: 'In my passage thither, whenever the Chairmen stopt to rest me, & themselves, I had the exhilerating comfort of hearing passengers say—'Ha! poor soul! he's going to his long home!'[3]

In the cleaner air at Canonbury House—an old 'palace' of Queen Elizabeth which had become 'an humble lodging house, and a receptacle for convalescent citizens'—Burney's fever

---

[1] *Frag. Mem.* (B.M. Add. MS. 48345, f. 22).
[2] CB to CB Jr., 14 Feb. 1793 (Berg).
[3] *Frag. Mem.* (B.M. Add. MS. 48345, f. 16).

abated. No doubt his spirits were improved also by the company of John Newbery, who rented part of the house for himself and his family, and of Christopher Smart who, like Goldsmith in later years, was living with the bookseller while in his employment.[1] Yet, although Burney's condition improved, 'a consumptive cough, night sweats and . . . a manifestly tender state of health' persisted and Armstrong expressed the conviction that he would never recover his health in London. Conveniently, Sir John Turner, M.P. for King's Lynn in Norfolk and a powerful citizen of that town, on behalf of the Corporation offered Burney the post of organist at St. Margaret's Church. The normal salary of £20 a year had been increased by subscription to £100, 'as an encouragem^t ⟨to⟩ a regular bred musician of some character to come down from the capital to instruct the children of the principal families in the town & Neighbourhood in Music'.[2]

Although this special subscription enabled Burney to maintain his dignity in accepting an otherwise humble post in a provincial town, it was with understandable reluctance, and only at Armstrong's insistence, that he accepted Sir John Turner's proposal. In September 1751 he travelled alone into Norfolk, leaving behind him his wife and three children for five or six months and, for some nine years, all his unfulfilled ambitions.

[1] See *ante*, p. 28.   [2] *Frag. Mem.* (B.M. Add. MS. 48345, ff. 17, 22).

II

KING'S LYNN AND THE RETURN
TO LONDON

1751–69

I

CHARLES BURNEY travelled alone to King's Lynn in September 1751 'to feel his way, & know the humours of the place, & prices of Lodgings, provisions, &c.'.[1] Some ten years later, during a visit to Lynn to see his constituents, Horace Walpole admitted of its citizens that, 'to do the folks justice, they are sensible and reasonable, and civilized; their very language is polished since I lived among them. I attribute this to their more frequent intercourse with the world and the capital, by the help of good roads and post-chaises, which, if they have abridged the King's dominions, have at least tamed his subjects'.[2] Yet even if Walpole was to be favourably surprised by the growing sophistication of Lynn, the reaction of the young Burney to the provincial town was predictable. Seven years in London, in the course of which he had won the friendship of many leading musicians, actors, and writers, as well as members of the aristocracy, and a high reputation as a teacher and composer, had inevitably transformed the raw apprentice from Chester into a polished young man, who was deeply shocked at finding himself consigned to a cultural backwater. Also missing his wife acutely, Burney poured out his heart to her within a week of his arrival in Lynn:

it Shames me to think How little I knew my self, when I fancy'd I shou'd be Happy in this Place. O God, I find it impossible I shou'd ever be so. Wou'd you believe it! that I have more than an Hundred Times Wish'd I had Never Heard its Name. Nothing but the Hopes of acquiring an independant Fortune in a Short Space of Time will keep me Here, tho' I am too deeply enter'd to retreat without great loss. But Happiness Can't be too dearly Purchas'd. I greatly dislike

---

[1] CB to CB Jr., 20 Dec. 1799 (Berg).   [2] *Corresp.* ix. 350.

this Place, in short, & wou'd gladly Change it for London at any Rate.

Neither Sir John Turner nor the citizens of Lynn to whom he introduced Burney answered the expectations of a young man accustomed to metropolitan tastes and fashions. Worst of all, the musical facilities were dreadful: 'The Organ is Execrably bad ... & Add to that a Total Ignorance of the most known & Common Musicall Merits that runs thro' the Whole Body of People I have yet Convers'd With. Even S[r] J[ohn Turner] Who is the Oracle of Apollo in this Country is extreamly Shallow.' Blended with this youthful musical snobbery, however, was the genuine disappointment of an ambitious composer who had counted on finding at Lynn at least an informed and admiring audience to stimulate him to creativity:

the bad Organ & the Ignorance of My Auditors must totally extinguish the few Sparks of Genius for Composition I may have, & entirely Discourage Practice. for Wherin wou'd any pains I May take to Execute a Meritorious tho' Difficult Piece of Music be repaid if like Orpheus I am to perform to Stocks & Trees. In short, I wish I Cou'd Make a good retreat, that is Without Offending the Gentlemen Who have been at pains as they thought to Serve Me, & before 'tis too late to be reinstated in My London Business.

Fanny d'Arblay deleted several lines at the end of the letter, but, with considerable difficulty, enough words can be made out to indicate that Burney intended to remain in Lynn only until Christmas, when he would receive the first quarterly instalment of his salary, before returning to his scholars in London.[1]

By the time the three months he allowed himself had elapsed, however, Burney's attitude had changed, for on 19 December 1751 he wrote a long and cheerful poem, telling Esther to prepare to leave London, and promising her at least good wine at Lynn, good music, if only from his own hand, and quiet evenings which could be spent in reading their favourite authors.[2] After his first violent reaction to the provincialism of

[1] CB to Esther Burney [Sept. 1751] (Osborn). This is CB's first extant letter, printed by FB, *Mem.* i. 88–90 with alterations.

[2] *Mem.* i. 91–94. It is perhaps significant that, although Esther had requested the final half-yearly instalment of CB's salary from St. Dionis's Backchurch on 16 Oct. 1751, CB did not officially resign his London post until Easter 1752. His letter of

Lynn, Burney had, as usual, quickly made friends, and he had soon found that Lynn and the surrounding district contained more interesting and cultivated inhabitants than he had at first imagined. An entry in the index to his 'Memoirs' of this period reads 'Clergy & Physicians finding me fond of books civil & friendly'. These new friends included Dr. George Hepburn, who had been the intimate friend and physician of Sir Robert Walpole; the Rev. Thomas Pyle, the Vicar of St. Margaret's, once a noted religious controversialist; and the Rev. Charles Squire, the headmaster of Lynn school, whom Burney described as 'a man of learning, and a general purchaser of new books'.[1] Sir John Turner, Mayor of Lynn in 1737 and 1748 and its M.P. since 1738, and his brother, Alderman Charles Turner, the Collector of Customs, were less cultivated but more powerful friends, with whom Burney dined regularly, as he did at the homes also of Alderman Walter Robertson, Mayor in 1747 and 1761, and Mr. Stephen Allen, a wealthy merchant.[2]

If Lynn society was somewhat crude by comparison with the artistic and aristocratic company Burney had been accustomed to keep, the town was by no means complacent about its barbarism. As Horace Walpole realized, Lynn was becoming much less provincial at precisely this period, and the engagement of a noted young musician such as Burney clearly indicates the community's anxiety to improve itself. Burney could hardly avoid enjoying the status that his polished manners and taste conferred on him, for 'good society' welcomed him with open arms, not only in Lynn but for miles around. Mrs. Mackenzie, for example, at Narborough, engaged Burney to give her harpsichord lessons immediately on his arrival at Lynn, and, to his delight, treated him so much as a cultivated guest and so little as a 'mere musician' that he declared, 'had I been rich, I w^{d} have paid for admission, instead of receiving money for my journey & instructions'. Another lady, who sixteen years later was to become the second Mrs. Burney, made a small mistake which was significant in several ways: 'His air was so lively,

---

resignation came before the Church Vestry on 23 Jan. 1752, Vestry Minutes of St. Dionis's Backchurch, Guildhall MS. 4216.

[1] *Frag. Mem.* (B.M. Add. MS. 48345, f. 18); Hill–Powell, i. 208 n. 3, vi. 362.
[2] *Frag. Mem.* (Osborn).

and his figure was so youthful, that the most elegant as well as beautiful woman of the place, Mrs. Stephen Allen, took him for a Cambridge student, who, at that time, was expected at Lynn.'[1]

His future brother-in-law, Arthur Young, found that by 1758 Burney was 'held in the highest estimation for his powers of conversation and agreeable manners, which made his company much sought after by all the principal nobility and gentry of the neighbourhood.'[2] Notable among his Norfolk patrons were such men as Charles, third Viscount Townshend at Raynham; Sir Andrew Fountaine at Narford; John Hobart, Earl of Buckinghamshire at Blickling; Thomas Coke, Earl of Leicester at Holkham; William Windham at Felbrigg; and, perhaps most important of all, George Walpole, the eccentric third Earl of Orford at Houghton. Lord Orford, nephew to Horace Walpole, had at once shown interest in Burney's musical activities in Lynn and district,[3] and frequently invited him to Houghton, where his guests were free to wander through the elegant apartments looking at the magnificent collections of paintings they contained. To his acquaintance with Orford and the other noblemen of Norfolk mentioned above Burney later attributed his previously neglected education in painting and sculpture.[4]

At Houghton and the other great country houses Burney soon discovered that he had no reason to feel that his migration to Lynn had completely cut him off from sensitive and cultivated society. On the contrary, he found that his 'studies . . . were much invigorated & benefitted by the good taste and encouragem' he received at Houghton, where Orford was always anxious 'to call natural genius into notice and encourage its cultivation'.[5] Grateful for Orford's generous patronage, Burney made it his business to introduce to Houghton one of his new Norfolk friends, to whom he was to remain deeply attached for some thirty years. William Bewley, who was four months younger than Burney himself, was a surgeon in the

---

[1] *Frag. Mem.* (Berg): *Mem.* i. 88.

[2] *Autobiography*, ed. M. Betham-Edwards, 1898, p. 23.

[3] CB to Orford, 18 Sept. 1752 (untraced; transcript in Scholes Papers, Osborn). For Orford see R. W. Ketton-Cremer, *A Norfolk Gallery*, 1948, pp. 162–87.

[4] *Tours*, i. 148–9. CB deplored the dispersal of the Houghton paintings, *Monthly Review*, xxvii (1798), 66.   [5] CB to Orford [1791], draft (Berg).

village of Great Massingham, some ten miles east of Lynn. Perhaps because of his unattractive, almost uncouth, appearance, Bewley was an excessively shy man, who to the end of his life only rarely and with extreme reluctance ventured further from his home than to Lynn. His unprepossessing appearance, however, was quickly discounted by the wit, intelligence, and good nature which Burney soon perceived in Bewley, and which can be clearly seen in his later letters to the musician.

Burney shared—or soon came to share—all Bewley's many interests, ranging from literature and music to electrical experiments, and we may believe Fanny d'Arblay's assertion that this friendship did much to stimulate in her father,

that love and pursuit of knowledge, that urge its votaries to snatch from waste or dissipation those fragments of time, which, by the general herd of mankind, are made over to Lethe, for reading; learning languages; composing music; studying sciences; fathoming the theoretical and mathematical depths of his own art; and seeking at large every species of intelligence to which either chance or design afforded him any clew.[1]

Although the range of Burney's interests undoubtedly increased at Lynn and although, as he had feared, his new environment hardly stimulated him to throw all his energy into composition, he was not simply resigning himself to the musical apathy around him. Perhaps as a result of his grumbling, the 'execrable organ' in St. Margaret's was replaced in 1754 by a magnificent new instrument built by John Snetzler;[2] and, as an entry in the index to his 'Memoirs' suggests—'parson Davil's aversion to Voluntaries / Cram them down his throat'[3]— Burney enjoyed his unchallenged supremacy in the town's musical life. Nevertheless, neither his musical activities in the church and the town nor his busy social life was fully satisfying. If he and his charming wife received many more invitations than they felt able to accept, the explanation was not merely that their family was increasing rapidly in size, with the birth of Fanny in June 1752 and of Susan in January 1755. (Two

---

[1] *Mem.* i. 107.
[2] *Frag. Mem.* (Osborn; B.M. Add. MS. 48345, f. 17); *GDB*, i. 77–80.
[3] *Frag. Mem.* (B.M. Add. MS. 48345, f. 18).

sons, both named Charles, were buried in October 1752 and
January 1754.[1]) Burney's natural intellectual curiosity and his
ardent, if unfocused, ambition also help to account for the
fact that he and Esther increasingly came to enjoy 'an evening
at home', when they could pursue 'a course of reading together'
which covered 'history, voyages, poetry, and science, as far
as Chambers's Dict^y, the French Encyclopédie, & the Philosophical transactions could carry us'.[2]

Some idea of the extensive nature of the reading which
Burney now undertook can be obtained from a fragment of
a notebook, dating from his years at Lynn, which contains
quotations and references on a variety of subjects from poetry
to ancient history, in English, French, Italian, and Latin.[3]
Ever reluctant to waste time, he read the great Italian poets on
horseback as he travelled round Norfolk, with the aid of a dictionary which he compiled himself.[4] He was assisted and encouraged in his Italian studies by Vincenzo Martinelli (1702–
85), the author of *Istoria Critica della Vita Civile* (London, 1752),
whom he frequently met through Lord Orford at Houghton.
Although Burney later considered that he was not 'a deep
scholar even in his own language', Martinelli was an unusual
and valuable acquaintance to find in Norfolk and the music-
teacher had much to learn from 'a man of strong parts, with
much wit & Italian humour', who knew the works of the major
Italian poets by heart.

Significantly, however, Burney was becoming increasingly
curious about the history and theory of his own art and, having
missed an opportunity of visiting Italy in 1749, he satisfied his
curiosity to some extent by questioning Martinelli and 'picked
his brains as much as I c^d ab^t Musical hist^y, & anecdotes, as
well as literature in general'.[5] In addition to collecting such
information about the history of music, moreover, Burney was
also laying the foundation of his great library of books on the
subject;[6] and even if he was not fully aware at the time of the
direction in which his interests were turning, he himself was

---

[1] *GDB*, ii. 316; Hemlow, p. 7.   [2] *Frag. Mem.* (Osborn).
[3] B.M. Add. MS. 48345, ff. 23–36.
[4] *Mem.* i. 107–8. The dictionary is now in the Osborn Collection.
[5] CB to J. C. Walker, 2 Feb. 1801 (Osborn); Martinelli to CB, 27 Feb., no year
(Osborn).
[6] CB to W. Crotch, 17 Feb. 1805 (Coke); Mercer, ii. 1032–6.

later to date the beginning of his musicological activities as
early as 1753, when he spent some time 'in translating & illustrating wth Notes' d'Alembert's *Élémens de musique suivant les
principes de Rameau* (1752).[1] He was even more impressed by
Rousseau's controversial *Lettre sur la musique Française* (1753),
which he later described as 'the best piece of criticism on the art,
perhaps, that has ever been written' and which he also translated whilst he was at King's Lynn.[2] When the Grevilles sent
him the score of Rousseau's operetta *Le Devin du village* (1752)
from Paris, Burney, who was profoundly affected by the Frenchman's musical thought, paid tribute to his new hero by preparing an English version of the work, which was to be taken
down from the shelf and performed a decade later.[3]

As yet, however, Burney was working to no particular
purpose in collecting books and making notes on the history
of music and he lacked the courage to attempt the publication
of his translations. Indeed, although he had originally moved
to Lynn merely to recover his health, his comfortable existence
in the small town, his numerous friends on every social level,
his growing family and the excellent new organ, seem eventually
to have dampened some of his ardour to return to the strenuous
pursuit of his ambitions in London. Burney knew well enough
that there could be no substitute for the stimulation and opportunity which London offered, for he made a point of visiting
the capital for a month or six weeks every winter 'in order to
rub off rust and revive friendships'.[4] Yet when, after some
three years at Lynn, he seemed to be resigning himself contentedly to a career as an organist and teacher in the provincial
town, his friends began to feel it necessary to remind him of
his duty to himself.

Samuel Crisp, whom Burney had met through Fulke Greville
at Wilbury in 1747, was particularly disturbed by his young
friend's apparently complacent existence among the 'foggy
aldermen' of Lynn:

But really, among friends, is not settling at Lynn, planting your
youth, genius, hopes, fortunes, &c., against a north wall? Can you

[1] Notebook (Osborn).
[2] Bewley to CB, 18 Mar. 1763 (Osborn); article 'Accompaniment', Rees, vol. i.
[3] See *post*, pp. 70–73.
[4] *Frag. Mem.* (B.M. Add. MS. 48345, f. 22); *Hist. Mus.* iv. 452.

ever expect ripe, high-flavoured fruit, from such an aspect? You underrate prices in the town, and galloping about the country for higher, especially in the winter—are they worthy of your talents? In all professions, do you not see every thing that has the least pretence to genius, fly up to the capital—the centre of riches, luxury, taste, pride, extravagance,—all that ingenuity is to fatten upon? Take, then, your spare person, your pretty mate, and your brats, to that propitious mart, and,

'Seize the glorious, golden opportunity,'[1]

while yet you have youth, spirits, and vigour to give fair play to your abilities, for placing them and yourself in a proper point of view.[2]

Although Burney hardly needed to be reminded of his duty to himself, this letter may have been instrumental in inciting him to inform the Churchwardens of St. Margaret's on 1 February 1755 that he intended to resign his place as organist as soon as a replacement could be found and by Michaelmas at the latest: 'The subscription being expired which first induced me to reside in this Town, and my success in other respects falling short of my expectations; the organ salary is too inconsiderable to retain me in your service.' He added that he objected to being responsible for the mechanical care of the organ, but the real cause of his resignation was undoubtedly the lack of scope in Lynn for his talents and ambitions.[3]

It was perhaps purely coincidental that, a fortnight after handing in his resignation at St. Margaret's, Burney was writing a long letter to Samuel Johnson, a forty-five-year-old author and lexicographer in London. Burney had read with excitement Johnson's *Plan for a Dictionary of the English Language* while he was still an apprentice to Arne in 1747.[4] Two years later he had seen and admired Johnson's *Irene* at Drury Lane[5] and in 1750 had started to read *The Rambler*, which he may well have seen first in Christopher Smart's *The Midwife*, for he

---

[1] Crisp slightly misquotes Rowe's *The Fair Penitent*, I. i. 156.

[2] Crisp to CB, n.d., *Mem.* i. 128–9. According to FB Crisp went abroad soon after writing the letter, which she dated 'some years' before CB's return to London in 1760. A. R. Ellis, *ED*, I. xliv, suggests a date of 1756 or 1757; but Crisp left England soon after the failure of his play *Virginia* in 1754 and Garrick's refusal to perform a revised version in 1755. As CB was planning to return to London by 1755, the letter can be dated no later than 1754.

[3] Vestry Minutes, St. Margaret's, quoted *GDB*, i. 81.

[4] CB to Johnson, 14 Oct. 1765, draft (Hyde).   [5] Hill–Powell, i. 197 n. 5.

later stated that 'Smart, the poet, first mentioned them to me as excellent papers, before I had heard any one else speak of them.' On his arrival in Norfolk, Burney had been shocked to discover that Johnson's essays were virtually unknown and he made it his business to recommend them wherever he travelled, with the result that, 'Before I left Norfolk in the year 1760, the Ramblers were in high favour among persons of learning and good taste.'[1]

Late in 1754 news of the imminent publication of the long-awaited *Dictionary* reached Lynn, and Burney enthusiastically collected the names of six inhabitants of Lynn and district, including his own, who would require copies of the great work. This success seemed to justify the opening of a correspondence with the writer from whose works he had already derived so much instruction and entertainment, and on 16 February 1755 Burney wrote a long, carefully wrought, and very humble letter to Johnson, ostensibly to inquire where copies of the *Dictionary* might be obtained, but also expressing all his admiration and gratitude:

Though I have never had the happiness of a personal knowledge of you, I cannot think myself wholly a stranger to a man with whose sentiments I have so long been acquainted. . . .

It is with great self-denial that I refrain from giving way to panegyric in speaking of the pleasure and instruction I have received from your admirable writings; but knowing that transcendent merit shrinks more at praise, than either vice or dulness at censure, I shall compress my encomiums into a short compass, and only tell you that I revere your principles and integrity, in not prostituting your genius, learning, and knowledge of the human heart, in ornamenting vice or folly with those beautiful flowers of language due only to wisdom and virtue. I must add, that your periodical productions seem to me models of true genius, useful learning, and elegant diction, employed in the service of the purest precepts of religion, and the most inviting morality.

Burney concluded his letter with more elaborate compliment and more profession of his own humility on the occasion:

I ought to beg pardon of the public as well as yourself, Sir, for detaining you thus long from your useful labours; but it is the fate of

---

[1] Hill–Powell, i. 208 n. 3; *Mem.* i. 117–18.

men of eminence to be persecuted by insignificant friends as well as enemies; and the simple cur who barks through fondness and affection, is no less troublesome than if stimulated by anger and aversion.

I hope, however, that your philosophy will incline you to forgive the intemperance of my zeal and impatience in making these inquiries; as well as my ambition to subscribe myself, with very great regard,

Sir, your sincere admirer, and most humble servant,

Charles Burney.[1]

Seven weeks passed, and Burney was probably despairing of ever receiving any acknowledgement from Johnson, when the reply came, dated 8 April 1755, not only apologizing for the delay and informing him that copies of the *Dictionary* should be ordered from Dodsley, but giving every sign of sincere appreciation of Burney's flattering letter:

Your civilities were offered with too much elegance not to engage attention; and I have too much pleasure in pleasing men like you, not to feel very sensibly the distinction which you have bestowed upon me.

Few consequences of my endeavours to please or to benefit mankind have delighted me more than your friendship thus voluntarily offered, which now I have it I hope to keep, because I hope to continue to deserve it.

As if to prove this last statement, Johnson invited Burney to favour him 'with another letter; and another yet, when you have looked into my Dictionary'.[2]

Burney could hardly have hoped for so much. At Easter 1755 the Churchwardens of St. Margaret's decided to advertise for a new organist,[3] and Burney expected to leave for London within a few months. Nothing could be more gratifying than the prospect of intimate friendship with the man whom he considered the greatest English writer of his day. Burney took Johnson's invitation literally and replied, with almost indecent haste, on 14 April 1755. This second letter was even more complimentary than the first, although there was little Burney could add apart from expanding the account of his excitement

---

[1] CB to Johnson, 16 Feb. 1755, *Mem.* i. 119–20; a draft of this letter is at Texas Christian University.
[2] *Letters*, i. 68–69; also *Mem.* i. 121 and Hill–Powell, i. 286.
[3] Vestry Minutes, *GDB*, i. 81.

at the imminence of the great *Dictionary*. That, at least, is the
impression given by the text of the letter printed by Fanny
d'Arblay, who, however, carefully changed one paragraph,
which reveals the main purpose of the letter to be an attempt
by Burney to consolidate the friendship offered by Johnson.
After admitting that he had begun to despair of an answer
and expressing his pleasure in being invited to write again,
Burney continued:

having Determined at the Close of the Ensuing Summer to fix my
future abode in London, I cannot help rejoicing that I shall be an
Inhabitant, & exulting that I shall be a fellow Citizen wth Mr John-
son. & were it possible ever to be honoured with a Small Share of his
Esteem, I sh^d regard it as the Most grateful Circumstance of my Life.
& shall I add, that I have a female Companion whose Intellects are
sufficiently Masculine to enter Into the true Spirit of y^r Writings, &
Consequently to have an Enthusiastic Zeal for them & their Author?
How Happy w^d Y^r presence Make us over our Tea, so often
Meliorated by y^r productions.[1]

Perhaps with no other intention than to simplify her narrative,
Fanny altered the first words of this paragraph in her version to
read, 'If, which is probable, I should fix my future abode in
London . . .', thus removing the firmness of Burney's plan of
returning to London during the summer of 1755.

Although at a later date Burney inscribed on the draft of
this letter the remark that 'This neither had nor required an
immediate answer', he undoubtedly hoped that the correspondence would continue. Johnson, however, did not manage to
'bestow a line or two' on his devoted admirer in Norfolk, as he
had been politely invited to do. The publication of the *Dictionary* in April 1755 probably occupied him fully, and the letter
from the country organist lay forgotten in Gough Square. In
any case, during the summer of 1755 Burney's plan of returning
to London collapsed. As Fanny d'Arblay chose not to discuss
the matter, she throws no light on the reasons for its failure.
The only possible explanation derives from two letters written
by Burney in 1806 from Bristol, where he was trying to recover
his health, in which he recalled that, fifty years earlier, he had

---

[1] CB to Johnson, 14 April 1755, draft (Hyde). Scholes (*GDB*, i. 89–90) printed
FB's text, *Mem.* i. 122–4, but the text of the original had already been printed,
albeit carelessly, by Mercer in his edition of *Hist. Mus.* ii. 1027–8.

'recovered in a few weeks time from a more alarming cough than the present' by means of 'the Waters & Air of the Hot-Wells'.[1] If Burney's 'fifty' is taken as a round number, an 'obstinate cough' and the necessity of a journey to Bristol may well explain his failure to leave Lynn for London in 1755.

Although the first of his three attempts to return to London had failed, Burney was waiting only for a full recovery of his health before trying once more. Certainly Johnson's silence did not dampen Burney's admiration for his writings. With William Bewley, who used to venture occasionally from Great Massingham for 'a musical & literary debauch' at Lynn,[2] Burney read and discussed the works of Johnson, and other notable writings of the decade such as David Hume's *History of England*, the first volume of which appeared in 1754 and the second in 1756. Bewley, who, like Burney, was a fanatical admirer of Johnson,[3] found that the works of these two great men made him increasingly dissatisfied with those of lesser writers. Writing to ask Burney to lend him the second volume of Hume's *History* in March 1757, Bewley added, 'I almost dread to make the Request, when I reflect to what coarse dishes I must sit down when it is over.—Why did I ever read *Hume* or *Johnson*! Wretch that I am, my Acquaintance with those great Fellows has given me a Taste for high living not at all adapted to my Situation. Had I not known them, I might have injoy'd the *Rolts* &c of these times in Peace. . . .'[4]

If 'high living' was, for the retiring Bewley, only a metaphor for literary excellence, it had a much more literal meaning for Charles Burney. The works of Hume and Johnson made him dissatisfied not only with inferior writers but with the inferior society of Lynn and the mediocrity of the life he was leading at the age of thirty. Perhaps partly as a reflex action to the admiration for Johnson expressed in Bewley's letter, twelve days later, after a silence of two years, Burney wrote once more to the great lexicographer, on 26 March 1757. Johnson had, after all, invited Burney's opinion of the *Dictionary*

---

[1] CB to Mrs. Fermor and Miss Willis [Sept. 1806], draft; CB to CPB, 17 Sept. 1806 (Osborn).

[2] CB to Lord Orford [5 Sept. 1783], draft (Osborn).

[3] Hill–Powell, iv. 134.

[4] W. Bewley to CB, 14 Mar. 1757 (Osborn). Bewley refers to Richard Rolt (1725?–70), a prolific miscellaneous writer.

and it need not be too late to reopen the correspondence. In any case, a suitable occasion for resuming it had recently appeared with the publication in the previous June of proposals for Johnson's edition of Shakespeare. Once more Burney had assiduously collected the names of six subscribers.

His letter opened with fervent praise of Johnson's 'admirable Dictionary: a Work, I believe, not yet equaled in any Language. For not to Mention the Accuracy Precision & elegance of the Definitions, the Illustrations of Words are so judiciously & happily selected as to render it a Repository &, I had almost said, Universal Register of whatever is sublime & beautiful in english Literature.' Thus Burney's eloquent adulation, which there is no reason to think insincere, unrolled, supported by a quotation from a French notice of the *Dictionary* in the *Bibliothèque des Savants*. Nevertheless, Burney declared, he would not have presumed to write had he not learned of the proposed edition of Shakespeare. The news, however, had not given him unqualified pleasure, as he explained in an entirely complimentary manner:

But, shall I venture to tell you, not withstanding my Veneration for you & Shakespear, that I c^d not partake of the Joy wch the selfish Publick seemed to feel on this Occasion—no, far from it; I c^d not but be afflicted at reflecting that so exalted, so refined a Genius as the Author of the Rambler sh^d submit to a Task so unworthy of him as that of a mere Editor. for who w^d not grieve to see a Paladio or a Jones undergo the dull Drugery [*sic*] of carrying Rubbish from an old Building when he sh^d be tracing the Model of a New?[1]

Since Johnson had undertaken the edition, as he told Sir John Hawkins, for 'the want of money',[2] he probably did not fully appreciate Burney's views on his literary pursuits. The summer and autumn of 1757 brought Burney no reply, and in December he wrote once more.[3] This time Johnson answered at once, apologizing for his failure to acknowledge the earlier letter (he had written a reply, but had mislaid and forgotten it), which had gratified him extremely, 'not only because I believe it was sincere, but because praise has been very scarce'. Only two of his friends had been optimistic about the success

---

[1] CB to Johnson, 26 Mar. 1757, copy by CB (Berg); *Mem.* i. 124–6.
[2] Hill–Powell, i. 318 n. 5.   [3] Not extant.

of the *Dictionary*,[1] and, Johnson added, 'Yours is the only letter of good will that I have yet received, though indeed I am promised something of that sort from Sweden.'[2]

Scandalized that it should be left to the Swedes to appreciate Johnson's achievement, Burney evidently sent the subscriptions he had promised as soon as possible, and took advantage of a polite inquiry after Mrs. Burney, to request on her behalf a list of Johnson's contributions to the *London Magazine*.[3] Johnson replied, with relative promptness this time, in March 1758, apologizing for the fact that his edition of Shakespeare, promised for Christmas 1757, had been delayed until the summer. 'I did not promise them more than I promised myself', he remarked of his subscribers, in a useful phrase which Burney later had occasion to borrow.[4] For Mrs. Burney, Johnson promised a list of his writings in the *London Magazine*, but, if he ever managed to compile it, this valuable document does not appear to have survived.[5]

Not long after receiving this letter Burney at last called on Johnson in London. The actual date of this meeting is, however, uncertain and it has been all too easily confused with a later one in 1760.[6] Nevertheless, the details of these two visits which Burney himself gave to James Boswell make it clear that the first took place 'soon after' he received Johnson's letter of 8 March 1758 and was to Gough Square; and that the second was made in 1760 to Johnson's rooms in the Temple, to which he had moved in 1759.[7] In 1765 Burney recalled a visit to Johnson which had taken place 'about the year 1759', its purpose being the delivery of a subscription of five guineas from Fulke Greville to the edition of Shakespeare.[8] Although this could refer to the first of the two meetings mentioned above, it may have been a quite separate visit, for Burney later recorded that he 'frequently visited' Johnson 'before & after I left *Lynn*'.[9]

In any case, Burney was at last able to converse with the

---

[1] Chapman suggests Birch and Langton.
[2] Johnson to CB, 24 Dec. 1757, *Letters*, i. 104–5; Hill–Powell, i. 323–4.
[3] Not extant.   [4] See *post*, p. 159.
[5] Johnson to CB, 8 Mar. 1758, *Letters*, i. 105–6; Hill–Powell, i. 327–8.
[6] *Mem.* i. 126; *GDB*, i. 93–94 and n.
[7] Hill–Powell, i. 328–30 and iv. 134.
[8] CB to Johnson, 14 Oct. 1765, draft (Hyde).   [9] *Frag. Mem.* (Berg).

man whom he and Bewley so greatly revered. In Gough Square
Burney 'dined and drank tea with him, and was introduced to
the acquaintance of Mrs. Williams', and then followed Johnson
to his garret, where he 'found about five or six Greek folios,
a deal writing-desk, and a chair and a half. Johnson giving to
his guest the entire seat, tottered himself on one with only
three legs and one arm.' Thus precariously situated, they
earnestly discussed the edition of Shakespeare, Johnson showing the volumes which had already been printed to this representative of his provincial subscribers 'to prove that he was in
earnest', although the edition was not in fact to appear until 1765.
Johnson may well have been impressed by the literary knowledge which the country music-teacher displayed, for Burney
proved that his evenings of reading at Lynn had indeed been
purposeful by discussing such writers as Theobald, Warburton,
Mallet, and Bolingbroke.[1]

Although once more it may be no more than accidental,
contact with Johnson coincided, as in 1755, with an attempt
by Burney to leave Lynn for London. A letter from Mrs.
Greville reveals that he planned this return for the summer of
1758, but had again abandoned it by the autumn. Mrs. Greville
expressed once more the conviction of Burney's friends that
he was wasting his talents in the provinces, as well as depriving
them of his company. The reference in the first sentence of the
following paragraph is to Will Fribble, a character in Garrick's
Miss in her Teens, which Burney had played at Wilbury:[2]

Friend *Will*, What has been the matter with you? thou art but a
Fribble I see, & if any thing Comforts me for your not coming to
London, it is the fear I should be under of that smoaky Town's not
agreeing with your feeble Constitution. au reste, voyez vous, mon
Ami, I had no doubts of your Succeeding well if you would but have
had a little patience & certainly London is the place to make money
in; but, *Will*, you have no Soule—so God bless you, & make you
prosperous in the way you chuse for yourself.[3]

Fanny Greville's references to Burney's poor health may

[1] Hill–Powell, i. 328–30.   [2] *Mem.* i. 60, 113–14.
[3] Fanny Greville to CB and Esther Burney, 2 Oct. [1758], (Osborn). The dating
of this letter is made possible by an amusing account it contains of an amateur performance of *Julius Caesar*, in which Fulke Greville played Mark Antony. An equally,
if unintentionally, amusing review of the play, to which Mrs. Greville refers, appeared
in *The Salisbury Journal* for 2 Oct. 1758.

point to the reason for the failure of this second attempted departure. In any case, it would appear that Lynn was reluctant to part with him, for the Corporation Records for 29 August 1758 direct that 'a yearly Salary of twenty pounds be paid by the Mayor and Burgesses to Mr. Charles Burney, Organist, as an encouragement for him to remain and teach Musick in this Town'.[1] This unusual public supplementation of his normal salary officially acknowledged Burney's importance to Lynn, and could only make it more difficult for him to tear himself away from the town.

Of the remaining eighteen months which Burney spent in Norfolk, little is known; but in 1760, at the third attempt, he at last succeeded in bringing his family back to London. One reason for leaving his many friends at Lynn and for exchanging 'tranquillity & social Happiness' for 'the Tourbillon of London' was his desire to give his children a better education and start in life than was possible in Lynn.[2] In 1762, indeed, Burney was to say that, once the children were settled, he and his wife had intended to return to 'a peacable and quiet retirement from the bustling frivolousness of a capital'.[3] This statement was made, however, under peculiar circumstances and should not perhaps be taken too seriously, for there can be no doubt that in 1760 Burney was intent on giving himself a last chance of winning fame (though whether it would be musical or literary he himself probably could not have said) in the metropolis. This is clear from the longest of his accounts of the removal which has survived:

though he loved & respected the persons with whom he lived [at Lynn] and passed his time very agreeably, finding his family increasing, having 6 Children, he was ambitious of a larger field of action in order to provide for his children & rise in his profession above the rank of a country organist; he therefore in the year 1760 ventured on speculation, to quit his provincial establishment and try to bear the fatigues and air of London. But this was not done so rashly as many thought: when he quitted London it was for want of health, and in hopes of returning thither whenever his health w[d] allow it.[4]

[1] *GDB*, i. 82.
[2] *Frag. Mem.* (Osborn).
[3] CB to Dorothy Young [Oct. 1762], *Mem.* i. 141.
[4] *Frag. Mem.* (B.M. Add. MS. 48345, f. 22).

Accordingly Burney, his wife and six children came to live in Poland Street. For all his dread of life in the capital, he was not to live permanently elsewhere for the remaining fifty-four years of his life.

II

Although it is not certain precisely when he brought his family back to London, Burney and Esther, his eldest daughter, were certainly in the capital by April 1760, when the little girl performed at a concert which featured various infant prodigies.[1] It seems likely that Burney, now no more than a thirty-four-year-old provincial music-master, was doing his best to draw attention to his return to London. The device certainly succeeded, for Esther, who remained a notable harpsi-chordist for much of her life, caused a mild sensation by her performance at the age of ten (not nine, as advertised) and inevitably much of the credit for her precocious technique went to her father: 'This sample of his method of teaching procured him scholars and a great boarding-school in Queen Square Bloomsbury.'[2] Although his post as music-master to this school, which was run by a Mrs. Sheeles, brought Burney a sub-stantial income for a number of years, Fanny d'Arblay evi-dently thought it beneath his later dignity and she did her best to delete every reference to it in her father's 'Memoirs' and other papers.

Esther's precocious talents brought Burney not only offers of 'more scholars than he could undertake' but some important patrons: 'The late Duke of York, to whom he had the honour of being introduced by the late Earl of Eglinton, was so capti-vated by some of the most wild and difficult lessons of Scarlatti, which he had heard his little daughter play, that his Royal Highness desired him to put parts to them in the way of Con-certos. . . . They were frequently performed to his Royal Highness and his friends. . . .'[3] Alexander Montgomerie, Earl of Eglinton, who was a friend of the Duke of York as well as of the young James Boswell at precisely this period, was extremely

---

[1] *Public Advertiser*, 23 April 1760.

[2] *Frag. Mem.* (B.M. Add. MS. 48345, f. 22).

[3] *European Mag.* vii (1785), 163. The short biography of CB in which this story appears was undoubtedly authorized, if not written, by CB himself.

fond of music. Some three years later, indeed, Boswell was rather offended at being expected to travel in a coach with Eglinton and Hugh Barron, another precocious musician patronized by the nobleman, who had performed in the very same concert as Esther Burney in April 1760.[1] From Boswell we also know that James Macpherson, the 'author' of *Ossian*, was frequently at Eglinton's house at this time. On at least one occasion Burney met him there and heard him sing some old Erse songs which he claimed to have learned from his mother and which had never been written down. Burney, who was already alert to any opportunity of gathering unusual information about the history of music, promptly ruled some lines on a piece of plain paper and recorded the melodies as specimens of 'national music'.[2]

His influential friends and patrons ensured that Burney's return to London was a success: 'Pupils of rank, wealth, and talents, were continually proposed to him; and, in a very short time, he had hardly an hour unappropriated to some fair disciple.'[3] Although he had soon to face numerous other problems, it seems that to the end of his life Burney never had any difficulty in obtaining a full complement of musical scholars. Inevitably his daily round of teaching the daughters of the aristocracy and the wealthy middle classes brought him in contact with their parents, who helped him to establish his own children in useful careers. His eldest son James, for example, had been sent to a naval school in October 1760: two years later the Hon. Colonel Cary, brother of Lord Falkland and father of two of Burney's pupils, was instrumental in obtaining a good place for the boy on a frigate.[4] Later in the decade, Charles, his second son, was admitted to the Charterhouse 'at the nomination of his Grace the Duke of Marlborough' in February 1768.[5]

As important as his new prosperity was the fact that Burney's health showed no signs of deteriorating in the smoky air of London. On the contrary, it was his wife's health which began

---

[1] *London Journal*, ed. F. A. Pottle, 1950, p. 252.
[2] CB to E. Bunting, 24 Sept. 1808, draft (Osborn); article 'Ossian', Rees, vol. xxv.   [3] *Mem.* i. 135.   [4] *Frag. Mem.* (Berg).
[5] — to CB, 9 May 176[7] (Osborn); document concerning CB Jr.'s academic career (Osborn), quoted *GDB*, i. 344; cf. *Mem.* i. 152, where FB says that Lord Holdernesse nominated CB Jr.

to give cause for anxiety. Although she travelled to Bath and Bristol in 1761 in search of a cure, her husband joining her as soon as Mrs. Sheeles's school broke up, she did not improve. Professionally he had never been more successful but prosperity was now 'rendered comfortless' by the dread of losing Esther. On 27 September 1762 she died, leaving Burney almost deranged with grief. Her death, he wrote, 'almost broke my heart' and for a fortnight he 'did nothing but meditate on my misery'.[1] All his projects and ambitions seemed empty and meaningless: 'I have lost the spur, the stimulus to all exertions, all warrantable pursuits. . . . all is lost and gone in losing her— the whole world is a desert to me!'[2] Two months later he was still bewildered by Esther's death and he admitted that it was fortunate that his teaching forced him 'to plunge deeply & precipitately into Bustle' and to leave the house in Poland St.: 'Home is so little Home—& contains such Mementos of my once Happy State.' Yet he believed that no one would have engaged him as a teacher, if they had known how impossible he found it to concentrate on the lessons he was giving.[3]

Struggling through her father's papers sixty years later, Fanny d'Arblay came across 'a vast mass of elegaic laments' on Esther's death, including translations from Dante and Petrarch.[4] (An 'Argument of Dante's Inferno' drawn up by Burney has survived but it is inscribed 'for M^{rs} St. Allen ab^t the year 1765' which, as will become clear, is a very different matter.[5]) The cover of a tactful letter from his Norfolk friend William Bewley, which refers only indirectly to Burney's loss, is filled with drafts of lines of verse on Esther.[6] Even if hard work at his teaching and at the school, as he recalled, 'forced me to a temporary inattention to myself and the irreparable loss I had sustained',[7] a considerable domestic problem remained, for the thirty-six-year-old Burney had been left with a family of six children of whom the eldest was aged only thirteen.

Burney's friends were anxious for him to engage in some pursuit which would enable him to escape his morbid reflec-

---

[1] *Frag. Mem.* (B.M. Add. MS. 48345, f. 19; Osborn; Berg).
[2] CB to D. Young [Oct. 1762], *Mem.* i. 140–4.
[3] CB to Mrs. Allen, 1 Dec. 1762 (Berg); extract, *Mem.* i. 145–6.
[4] *Mem.* i. 147, 150–1.   [5] Osborn.
[6] Bewley to CB [?1763] (Barrett).   [7] *Frag. Mem.* (Osborn).

tions. William Bewley, for example, wrote in March 1763 to ask him to recommend a reliable treatise on the theory of music, adding, 'I expect nothing of this kind from my Country-men unless you, my dear friend, would undertake it, who are, I am satisfy'd, equally well qualifyd, both with regard to *le fond des choses*, & a clear, agreeable manner of presenting them.' Bewley also urged Burney to publish the translations of d'Alembert and Rousseau which he made some years earlier at King's Lynn.[1]

This was perhaps the first of the crucial periods during the 1760's when Burney might well have embarked on his 'literary' career several years earlier than was in fact to be the case. Apparently, however, he did not share Bewley's confidence in his powers as a writer on music and instead turned back to the theatre and to his old theatrical friends. In the summer of 1763 he spent two weeks with Mrs. Cibber in Berkshire and in the following winter accompanied her to the opera and the theatre.[2] David and Mrs. Garrick were also particularly kind to him 'in the midst of this affliction'[3] and it was from Garrick that a concrete suggestion about an outlet for his restless creative ambitions eventually came.

In the summer of 1763 Garrick was making plans for the conduct of Drury Lane Theatre during his imminent absence on a journey to France and Italy. One of the most important of the productions which were to appear while he was abroad was his new adaptation of Shakespeare's *A Midsummer Night's Dream*. Although a number of musical adaptations of the play had appeared earlier in the century under various titles, notably Garrick's own *The Fairies* in 1755, this production was to be the first under its original title since 1662, and, indeed, the only such performance between that date and 1816. With George Colman who, with George Garrick, was to be left in charge of Drury Lane, David Garrick discussed his adaptation during the summer of 1763. Their expectations of its success were considerable: 'I live in hopes of seeing it a favorite entertainment of next winter', Colman told Garrick in June 1763.[4]

[1] Bewley to CB, 18 Mar. 1763 (Osborn).
[2] *Frag. Mem.*; CB to FB, June 1763 (Berg).
[3] *Frag. Mem.* (Osborn).   [4] Colman to D. Garrick, 18 June 1763 (Folger).

More than any other play by Shakespeare, *A Midsummer Night's Dream* demands songs and incidental music, and Garrick, doubtless remembering the success of Burney's music for similar material in *Queen Mab* in 1750, as well as wishing to assist his unhappy friend to resume his theatrical career, engaged him as a musical director for the production. Burney's contribution to the production was, however, unknown until 1946, when a copy of the libretto was discovered, which contained 'A Table of the Songs, with the Names of the several Composers'.[1] Of the thirty-three settings listed, twelve were by Handel's pupil, J. C. Smith, perhaps carried over from his music for *The Fairies* in 1755, and fourteen by Burney. Thus, although a number of other composers provided an occasional song, by far the greater part of the new music was by Burney himself.

Although its musical aspect has only recently been clarified, the adaptation itself has long been the subject of some argument. Recent investigation has arrived at the conclusion that the original adaptation of Shakespeare's play was by Garrick and that, after his departure for the Continent in September 1763, Colman made further alterations.[2] Burney himself, in an account of the production in his 'Memoirs', was somewhat confused about the identity of the adaptor. At the time he had understood that 'this Cookery' had been the work of Garrick, who 'always spoke of it to me, with the anxious affection of a parent'. However, in March 1806 he read in Isaac Reed's edition of *Biographia Dramatica* (1782) that Colman had been responsible for the adaptation, and he added a note to his 'Memoirs', in which he concluded that Garrick must have 'suffered me to suppose the *alteration* & *additions* to be his own, in order to interest me the more in its Fate'.[3] Burney apparently never checked the 1812 edition of *Biographia Dramatica*, in which appears a statement by Colman to the effect that the original adaptation had definitely been by Garrick and that he, Colman, had only attended rehearsals and had been little more than a 'godfather' on the occasion.[4]

---

[1] A. Loewenberg, 'Midsummer Night's Dream Music in 1763', *Theatre Notebook*, i (1945–7), 23–26.
[2] G. W. Stone, '*A Midsummer Night's Dream* in the hands of Garrick and Colman', *PMLA*, liv (1939), 467–82.   [3] *Frag. Mem.* (Berg).   [4] iv. 43.

Although this is basically a true description of the situation, Colman played a rather larger part than he cared to admit, for, as the diary of William Hopkins, the prompter, tells us, the adaptation was 'got up with a vast deal of Trouble to all concerned, but particularly to Mr. Colman, who attended every Rehearsal, and had Alterations innumerable to make'.[1] The reason why neither Garrick nor Colman was anxious to admit responsibility for the adaptation, and, presumably, why Burney mentions the production only in his 'Memoirs' and Fanny d'Arblay not at all, is not difficult to discover. All the high hopes invested in the play were shattered on 23 November 1763, the first and only night on which it was presented. The expensive and elaborate production 'failed about as completely as any play ever did on the eighteenth-century stage'.[2] Only charming performances by the children in the cast persuaded the audience to let the play reach its conclusion. The scene in which Shakespeare's lovers fall asleep caused particular displeasure, for 'The next day it was reported, the Performers sung the Audience to Sleep, and then went to Sleep themselves.'[3] The review in the *St. James's Chronicle* for 24 November confirmed the disastrous nature of the production, and Burney himself admitted that 'scarce any body w^d come to hear' the play, 'and those who did come, could hardly be kept awake by the utmost efforts of the performers'.

Colman had no choice but to cancel the performance planned for the following day, but, reluctant to waste entirely 'so much Pains and Expence', he rapidly converted it into a two-act farce, which he presented on 26 November as *A Fairy Tale* and which, according to Hopkins, was 'as pleasing a Farce as most that are done'. Burney relates that Colman retained only the comic songs from the original production, but these unfortunately 'shared the same neglect, and were withdrawn after one performance'. Thus, although the farce continued to be presented until the end of the season, the composers involved, and particularly Burney, 'who had done their best, & severally expected to establish an interest in the Theatre and in the favour of the public', suffered 'great . . . humiliation'. Some forty years later Burney could add the wry observation that

---

[1] Quoted MacMillan, p. 100.   [2] Stone, op. cit., p. 473.
[3] MacMillan, loc. cit.

'we unfortunate champions being thus levelled by a general calamity, may be supposed to part better friends than we met'.[1] Nevertheless, at the time the disastrous failure of *A Midsummer Night's Dream* must have dealt a bitter blow to his theatrical ambitions, particularly as he had carried most of the responsibility for the musical side of the production.

The series of catastrophes and disappointments which had begun with the death of his wife continued two months after his unhappy return to the theatre. Late in January 1764 occurred what Burney described as 'an event of considerable importance in my affairs'. This event was the death of Fraser Honeywood, a wealthy and somewhat eccentric London banker and M.P. for Steyning in Sussex, who had paid Burney a yearly salary of £100 for instruction in music. At his death Honeywood could still hardly play the simplest lessons, for Burney's real function had been to dine and converse regularly with the lonely old man, the usual subject being politics, 'concerning w^ch', Burney observed, 'I was too indifferent, and indeed, too prudent, to dispute': £100 a year was not a sum to throw away in the heat of argument. This rather peculiar relationship—'We agreed very well, but did not amuse each other much'—ended with Honeywood's dying intestate, by which Burney lost not only a large and steady part of his income, but, as he always believed, a considerable legacy. To the end of his life Burney regarded this as one of his major misfortunes.[2]

After the failure of his theatrical ambitions, the loss of a substantial part of his income, and with the constant worry about his large family of young children on his mind, Burney next attempted a solution to some of his problems by means of a second marriage. Stephen Allen, the wealthy Lynn merchant who had been a close friend of the Burneys, had died in April 1763, leaving a fortune of £40,000.[3] The beautiful and intelligent Mrs. Allen, with whom Burney had corresponded since leaving Lynn, had been in London during the following winter. Not long afterwards, Burney found himself 'very seriously impassioned' and with her husband's funeral baked-meats

---

[1] *Frag. Mem.* (Berg). This remark seems to imply that there had been some rivalry between the different composers involved in the production.

[2] *Frag. Mem.* (Berg); *Gent. Mag.* xxxiv (1764), 47; CB to Lady Crewe, 18 Apr. 1806 (B.M. Add. MS. 37916, f. 16).

[3] Young, *Autobiography*, p. 101.

hardly cold, he precipitately made his feelings known in some verses to Mrs. Allen, who responded to his declaration of affection by forbidding him to see or write to her for twelve months.[1] This 'rebuff' was probably administered between April and June 1764, for a letter from Burney to Mrs. Allen survives which can be dated in April, since it contains an account of the marriage of Lady Susan Fox-Strangways to William O'Brien the actor, which astounded London in that month.[2] The fact that by June 1764 Burney was on his way to settle two of his daughters in Paris suggests that he had by then abandoned for the time being any hope of providing a second mother for them.

By taking the fifteen-year-old Esther and nine-year-old Susan to Paris, Burney not only reduced the size of the family in Poland Street but without extra cost provided the two girls with a very desirable female accomplishment, the French language. Knowing that he would never be able to leave fortunes to each of his numerous children, Burney was anxious at least to give them a good education, 'to enable them to shift for themselves, as *I* had done'.[3] At the same time, by taking the girls to France himself, Burney also fulfilled his long-frustrated desire to visit the Continent. When David Garrick had set off for Italy in the preceding September, Burney had given him a list of music to obtain for him, and asked him also to send a report on 'the present State of Music in Italy', a phrase which, significantly enough, was to appear in the title of Burney's first important publication. From the letter which Garrick eventually wrote in response to this request it appears that Burney had himself been contemplating such a journey, although Garrick was anxious to persuade him that he would find Italian music intolerable, 'all execution without Simplicity or Pathos'. In Italy, according to Garrick, music 'has lost its nature, and it is all dancing the slack rope, and tumbling through a hoop. . . . I fear good Musick is the needle in a bottle of hay.' Burney, however, knew Garrick's ignorance of music well enough not to take seriously such an attack on the Italian music he admired so much.[4]

---

[1] *Frag. Mem.* (Berg).
[2] CB to Mrs. Allen [April 1764] (Osborn); MacMillan, p. 106.
[3] *Frag. Mem.* (Berg).
[4] D. Garrick to George Garrick, 2 Jan. 1764 (misdated 1763), F. A. Hedgcock,

Nevertheless, since he could not yet manage a journey to Italy himself, Burney compromised with a visit to Paris, and, having settled his daughters with a 'prudent & worthy female' and engaged masters to instruct them, he was free to explore the 'Theatres, Public buildings, &c', before hastening back to London for the reopening of Mrs. Sheeles's school on 13 July 1764.[1] A highlight of his stay in Paris was a meeting with David Hume, at this period secretary to Lord Hertford, the British Ambassador. Through Lord Eglinton Burney had obtained a letter of introduction from Michael Ramsay, an old friend of Hume, which recommended him as 'one of the most ingenious & deserving of musicians'. Burney also delivered to Hume 'a brochure, which reflected upon some political and some poetical questions' written by Fulke Greville. Armed with these introductions, Burney made a suitable impression on the philosopher, whom he found 'very civil & Friendly'.[2]

Fanny d'Arblay considered that her father's visits to the libraries and bookshops of Paris marked

the real, though not yet the ostensible epoch, whence may be traced the opening of his passion for literary pursuits.

And from this period, to the very close of his long mortal career, this late, though newly chosen occupation, became all that was most consoling to his sorrows, most diversifying to his ideas, and most animating to his faculties.

All that Burney now lacked, according to his daughter, was some subject which would 'amalgamate his rising desire of fame in literature, with his original labours to be distinguished as a follower of Orpheus'.[3]

III

Burney's life was never as orderly as Fanny would have liked. Her desire to locate the birth of his literary career in Paris may perhaps be best explained as some kind of tribute on her part to the memory of her French husband. Burney himself claimed that

David Garrick and his French Friends [1912], p. 174; D. Garrick to CB, 5 Feb. 1764 (Comyn; quoted *Frag. Mem.*, Berg).   [1] *Frag. Mem.* (Berg).

[2] Ramsay to Hume, 5 June 1764 and Greville to Hume, 6 Sept. 1764, J. Y. T. Greig and Harold Beynon, 'Calendar of Hume MSS. in the Possession of the Royal Society of Edinburgh', *Proceedings of the Royal Society of Edinburgh*, lii (1931–2), 72, 105.   [3] *Mem.* i. 159–60.

he had conceived the first, albeit vague, idea of his *History of Music* as early as 1753; and whilst it is possible that, in the libraries and bookshops of Paris, he first realized how much material was available on the Continent for musicological research, he was to engage in no very obviously 'literary' activities for another five years. His first project on his return from Paris in the summer of 1764, indeed, was the compilation of a 'Ladies' Catchbook', which was to be suitably 'free from licence and indelicacy'. Yet again he was doomed to disappointment, for he soon discovered that other music publishers in London had anticipated his idea.[1]

Thus, in spite of Fanny's conviction that the seeds of literary ambition had been firmly planted during his visit to Paris, Burney in fact continued to waver, ready to respond to pressure from any friend with more decisive plans than himself. For most of the decade that friend was David Garrick, and although it is now clear that Burney's protracted flirtation with the theatre was very largely a waste of time and energy, it must have seemed to the lonely and middle-aged music-master the only remaining hope of fulfilling his ambitions. Only William Bewley in Norfolk appears to have had any faith in Burney's literary abilities and he was too removed from the scene of action for his views to carry much weight. In London during the 1760's Burney had no literary friend sufficiently persuasive or interested to give him the confidence to abandon his recurring theatrical ambitions.

When he returned to London in 1760 Burney had been acquainted with at least three men of letters of some reputation, although for various reasons none of these friendships was to develop into an important influence on his career during the decade. At least in the case of the most distinguished of these writers this must appear surprising, for there are no indications that his reverence for Johnson's writings diminished after his return to London. Nevertheless, apart from a celebrated interview at the Temple in 1760, during which Burney furtively deprived Johnson's hearthbroom of some bristles to send as a literary trophy to William Bewley,[2] the friendship of the two men seems to have made little progress during the next ten years.

[1] *Frag. Mem.* (Berg; B.M. Add. MS. 48345, f. 19).
[2] Hill–Powell, iv. 134.

If the relationship was hindered by any reserve at either end, it is more likely to have been found in Johnson than in Burney, to whom the prospect of conversing with the lexicographer had been one of the inducements which brought him back to London. Johnson, however, made little effort to conceal his scorn and suspicion of music and musicians. Hawkins recorded Johnson's remark that music 'excites in my mind no ideas, and hinders me from contemplating my own'; and he added his own suspicion that 'music was positive pain' to Johnson.[1] Similarly Boswell heard Johnson's opinion that music 'was a method of employing the mind, without the labour of thinking at all'.[2] Even harsher was the statement attributed to Johnson that 'no man of talent, or whose mind was capable of better things, ever would or could devote his time and attention to so idle and frivolous a pursuit'.[3]

Burney may well have been discouraged by such views and the only definite evidence of any contact between the two men in the 1760's is an exchange of letters in 1765 concerning Johnson's edition of Shakespeare, which had at last appeared in October of that year. Burney wrote in some embarrassment, for 'a certain Delicacy' had hitherto prevented him from pointing out that, when he had brought Fulke Greville's subscription money some years earlier, Johnson had omitted to give him any receipt. He had therefore been obliged to give Greville the receipts belonging to his Norfolk friends, who now wished to collect their copies of the edition.

Most of the letter, however, was concerned with his delight in Johnson's Preface to the edition, which 'has awakened in me all that Esteem & Veneration wch your other writings had inspired but wch had slumbered a little perhaps during your long Silences'. As for Shakespeare himself, Burney's attitude was in many ways typical of his age, although he seems to have been somewhat reactionary in his suspicion of the 'enthusiasm' for the plays which David Garrick had fostered so carefully. In 1757 Burney had politely doubted whether an edition of Shakespeare was a worthy task for Johnson and he now complained again that 'Criticism has already done so much for that Anomalous Author who is so Seldom a proper object for

---

[1] *Life of Johnson*, 1787, p. 319.   [2] Hill–Powell, v. 315.
[3] Boswell's *Life of Johnson*, ed. J. W. Croker, 2nd edn., 1835, x. 135.

its Labours.' Nevertheless, Johnson's Preface had afforded him 'more Pleasure, I had almost said Rapture, than any Production of equal length I have ever read—the Richness & Elegancy of the Language! the Elevation & Originality of of [*sic*] thoughts! together with that mildness of Dissent so charming in controversy & in all enquiries after Truth! have enchanted me.'

Burney, however, admired the Preface quite as much for its qualifications about Shakespeare's genius as for its defence of his irregularities. It is not always remembered that the Preface was valued by its first readers for its restrictive as well as for its apologetic character. As Boswell later observed, 'A blind indiscriminate admiration of Shakspeare had exposed the British nation to the ridicule of foreigners.'[1] Similarly Burney felt that national pride in Shakespeare had reached the point at which it would be useful for Johnson's strictures to be translated into French to prove to that nation that 'we are not so blinded by Prejudice & national Pride as to let his great & real Defects escape Censure. They call him a Goth & a Barbarian because his Faults are glaring & his Beauties for the most part are not to be understood but by those who possess greater knowledge in our Language than Foreigners can perhaps ever arrive at.'[2]

Johnson's reply to this letter was polite but brief, and its tone confirms that the two men were no more than acquaintances.[3] Although their relationship at this period can receive no further documentation, a letter from Burney to Fulke Greville contains an interesting addition to his views on Shakespeare, as well as a balanced and objective statement of his attitude at this period to the man who, some ten years later, was to be so intimate and revered a friend. Defending Johnson's style against a reviewer's strictures, Burney wrote:

Let his errors & false reasoning be pointed out,—let his too constant use of flowery & learned Language be censured, but allow him what he has—originality & depth of thought let the Vehicle of Conveyance be what it will. I never look on Johnson as a perfect Writer —or Man,—but he has *Giant* talents, & Virtues which are known only to few of those who see nothing but Inflation of style,—& awkward bulkiness in his Figure.

[1] Hill–Powell, i. 496–7.
[2] CB to Johnson, 14 Oct. 1765, draft (Hyde).
[3] Johnson to CB, 16 Oct. 1765, *Letters*, i. 178; Hill–Powell, i. 500.

This last sentence suggests that Burney was at least in the habit of meeting Johnson occasionally, and this impression receives some support from another remark in this letter to the effect that Greville was 'perhaps less biased either by Friendship or habit of Admiration, than myself', in evaluating Johnson's writings. It would be difficult to estimate the extent of what Burney here describes as 'Friendship'. His letter concludes:

At the Time Johnson's Edition & Notes came out, I admired his Courage for daring to censure the real vices & defects of this wonderful Author, & yet, as I thought, defend him where defensible. There certainly has long been a Shakespeare *Mania* in this Country.— Garrick has abetted it for his own sake. . . . I have neither seen nor read any of his plays for many Years; but there are strokes of *Mental anatomy* in him that I can never forget, & that seem to me like Gleams from some Superior Being.[1]

Although Burney's friendship with Johnson was obviously restricted, the two men had one conversation at this period which has since become celebrated. It concerned the mental health of Christopher Smart, another friend with whom Burney might have hoped in 1760 to establish a useful literary connexion. This conversation, notable quite as much for what it tells us about Johnson as about Smart, is too well known to need repetition here.[2] Although Boswell did not date it and separated it from Burney's accounts of his visits to Johnson in 1758 and 1760, it probably took place on one of these occasions and certainly during Smart's confinement between 1757 and 1763.

The fact that Burney asked Johnson for news of Smart indicates that he had not entirely lost sight of his old friend during his years in Norfolk and, indeed, it is reasonable to suppose that before 1757 they met during Burney's winter visits to London. It has been suggested that on at least two occasions Smart and Burney co-operated on literary and musical ventures, although both instances must be approached with great caution. In 1756, shortly before his confinement, Smart and Richard Rolt began producing *The Universal Visiter*, under an agreement with the bookseller, Thomas

---

[1] CB to Fulke Greville, n.d., copy (Berg). FB inscribed it '—68'.
[2] Hill–Powell, i. 397; CB also related the conversation to Mrs. Thrale in 1777, *Thraliana*, i. 176.

Gardner, which has itself been the subject of much discussion.[1] Ultimately it became necessary for Smart's friends, including Johnson and Garrick, to help him out with material for the periodical. Burney was not numbered among these friends until 1939 when R. B. Botting described a set of *The Universal Visiter* which had been annotated with the initials of the contributors by a certain 'Anne Gardner'.[2]

Although he was unable to identify Anne Gardner, Botting assumed reasonably enough that she was some relative of the publisher of the magazine and accordingly in a position to identify contributors. At the end of an essay entitled 'Some Thoughts on Beauty, with Historical Instances of its Fatality to several Illustrious Ladies in England,' in the last number of the magazine in December 1756,[3] appears the attribution, 'Dr. B. to please A. G.'. Botting's confident suggestion that this enlists Burney as one of Smart's kind friends at this difficult period in his life is neither unpleasing nor inconceivable. Although Burney did not receive his doctorate until 1769, it is possible that Anne Gardner made her annotations after that date. Similarly, although he was living in Norfolk at the time, he could, as has been suggested, have kept in touch with Smart through his annual visits to London. On the other hand, there is no evidence that Burney was ever acquainted with an Anne Gardner and it is difficult for anyone familiar with his lively prose to believe that he could have compiled this dreary list, drawn mainly from English history, of beautiful but unhappy women. 'Dr. B.' might just as well be identified as Johnson's friend, Dr. Richard Bathurst, who died in 1762.

Burney himself is the authority for the statement that in 1769 he provided Smart and Newbery with a humorous musical setting of Bonnell Thornton's burlesque 'Ode to St. Cecilia'. His date of 1769, however, which he gives in a note supplied to Malone for the third edition of Boswell's *Life of Johnson* in 1799, must be rejected on several grounds, but the evidence on which a true date can be based is so slender and the various solutions to this small but puzzling topic are so numerous that discussion of it has been confined to an appendix. It

---

[1] Ibid. ii. 344–5; Ainsworth and Noyes, *Christopher Smart*, pp. 78–80.
[2] 'Johnson, Smart, and the *Universal Visiter*', *Modern Philology*, xxxvi (1938–9), 293–300. [3] pp. 543–51.

seems likely, however, that Burney set Thornton's ode in 1760 or 1763.[1]

Smart was released from the madhouse in 1763 but, although Burney could write later that their 'early friendship continued through all the vicissitudes of our several careers, to the time of his death',[2] the poet had long since ceased to provide Burney with a link with London literary life. In 1792 Burney recalled sadly that 'fanaticism . . . distorted his ideas, and, as if stung by the gad-fly, . . . made him run wildly about, in pain and terror; not knowing that he carried the enemy with him wherever he went'.[3] Smart had not forgotten his old friend in the madhouse, for two lines towards the end of his *Jubilate Agno*, which can be dated December 1762, mention Burney. Rather pathetically, however, they associate him with Thomas Arne, as though Smart's memory insisted on clinging to those early, happier years when they had first met: 'Let Arne, house of Arne rejoice with The Jay of Bengal. God be gracious to Arne his wife to Michael & Charles Burney.'[4]

In 1765 Burney subscribed to Smart's *Translation of the Psalms* but the poet's dependence on the charity of his friends had soon to be recognized more explicitly. William Mason, who had known Smart at Cambridge, suggested in 1766 or 1767 that the poet's friends promise him an annual subscription of one or two guineas[5] and Burney, as a friend of both Smart and Mason, was one of the first to agree to the plan. An unpublished letter from Smart to Burney in January 1768 acknowledges the receipt of two guineas for 1768 and that of a similar sum from a friend of Burney: 'I bless God for your good nature which please to take for a Receipt.'[6] After his release from the madhouse Smart seems to have been a fairly frequent visitor in Poland Street[7] and Burney's kindness to him continued until his death in May 1771.

It has recently been stated that Burney 'was one of the very few—perhaps the only one—of [Smart's] old friends who

---

[1] See Appendix I, *post*, pp. 485–90.
[2] CB to Twining, 10 Mar. 1804, copy (Osborn).
[3] *Monthly Review*, vii (1792), 38.
[4] *Collected Poems of Christopher Smart*, ed. Callan, i. 344.
[5] C. Price, 'Six Letters by Christopher Smart', *RES*, viii (1957), 145–8.
[6] Smart to CB, 4 Jan. 1768 (Houghton Library, Harvard).
[7] *ED*, i. 28, 66.

continued to help him to the end'.[1] Burney himself modestly
said only that 'Mason & Stonhewer were his benefactors to the
last'[2] but he undoubtedly did what he could to assist the poet.
Smart himself could describe his predicament with humorous
detachment. In 1808 Burney told one of his granddaughters
to ask Mrs. Thrale-Piozzi if she remembered

the Letter Smart, the Poet, wrote to Somebody who wanted to know
where he was:
Sir.
    After being *six* times arrested: *nine* times in a spunging house: and
three times in the Fleet-Prison, I am at last happily arrived at the
King's Bench.
                                                            Kitt. Smart.[3]

It was from the King's Bench prison that Smart wrote his last
letter to Burney, a request for money for a fellow-prisoner,
'whom I myself . . . have already assisted according to my willing poverty'. Mason seems to have been quite as active as
Burney in trying to relieve the poet's sufferings, but Burney
had been the closer friend and Mason, at an earlier date, had
often expressed distaste for Smart's activities. It is therefore
possible to accept Fanny d'Arblay's statement that, at his
death, the poet 'left behind him none to whom he was more
attached than Dr. Burney, who had been one of his first
favourite companions, and who remained his last and most
generous friend'.[4] Burney's loyalty to Smart did not end with
his death in 1771, as will be demonstrated later.[5]
    The third of Burney's literary friends who might, under
different circumstances, have influenced his career after the
death of his wife, was William Mason, whom Burney had
probably first met when he was still apprenticed to Arne.[6]
Their acquaintance was evidently renewed after Burney's
return to London in 1760 and on at least one occasion Mason
called in Poland Street to hear the celebrated Esther play on
the harpsichord. Unlike Johnson, Mason was passionately

---

[1] Christopher Devlin, *Poor Kit Smart*, 1961, p. 182.
[2] See *ante*, p. 68, n. 2.
[3] Marianne Francis to Mrs. Piozzi, 13 Aug. 1808 (JRL, Eng. MS. 582).
[4] *Mem*. i. 279–81; cf. *ED*. i. 133.
[5] See *post*, p. 363; and R. Lonsdale, 'Dr. Burney and the *Monthly Review*',
RES, xv (1964), 28–29.   [6] See *ante*, p. 16.

interested in music and Burney considered him 'nearly as good a Musician & Painter as Poet'. Since this may appear to be small praise to the modern reader of Mason's verse, it should be stated that Burney entirely approved of Mason's reputation in his lifetime as one of the three or four great poets of the period. Burney also found Mason an attractive and pleasantly un-affected personality, and there seems to be an implicit contrast with Samuel Johnson in an account of Mason which he wrote in 1764:

what pleases me most of all is his *Manner of Man*—he is innocently chearful (remember he's a Divine) in all respects Natural & un-assuming—no grotesk or Caricature Marks of Genius about him, but comfortably communicative & conversible without overawing or reminding you of his superiority—for a superior Man he doubtless is to every one in his Way except his Friend Mr Grey—in short I like the Man as much as his Writings, wch is saying a great deal for him, & more than I can say for any great Genius I have been acquainted wth in the Literary World.[1]

Although Mason visited London periodically he had become a Canon of York in 1762 and was to spend most of his life at his living at Aston in Yorkshire. For thirty years the two men corresponded on literary and musical matters, but the relation-ship extended no further.

Geographically removed from Mason and distanced no less effectually from Johnson by awe and from Smart by pity, Burney found only one friend in 1765 who could make any definite proposals as to the way in which he might employ his frustrated creative energies. In April 1765 David Garrick returned from his foreign travels and soon called to see Burney. In his derisive letter about Italian music in February 1764, Garrick had not tried to conceal his preference for a work which he had heard in France: 'I have felt more at the *first air* of *Rousseau* (in the Devin du Village) than at all the operas I heard at Turin, Genoa, Leghorn, Rome, & Naples.' Garrick had not been alone in succumbing to the simplicity and past-oral charm of *Le Devin du Village*, an operetta composed by Jean-Jacques Rousseau who, it should perhaps be stressed, was better known as a composer and critic of music than as a philo-

---

[1] CB to Mrs. Allen [April 1764] (Osborn).

sopher early in his career. The Grevilles had heard the work in Paris soon after its first production in 1752 and had sent Burney a copy of it. Whilst he was still at King's Lynn he had amused himself by translating the libretto into English *totidem syllabis*, so that his verse translation could be sung to the original music. Garrick had lost none of his enthusiasm for *Le Devin du village* by the time he returned to London in April 1765 and on his first visit to Burney suggested that his friend adapt the operetta for a production in English at Drury Lane. Burney was able to take down his translation from the shelf immediately. Within a few days he had sung it over to the Garricks and plans were being made to produce it during the next season, the winter of 1765–6.[1] Once again Burney was investing all his hopes in the theatre.

The necessity of making another journey to Paris in the summer of 1765 to retrieve Esther, his eldest daughter, however, interrupted plans for the production of what, in Burney's version, was to be called *The Cunning Man*, which was eventually postponed until the following season.[2] Burney's 'Memoirs', however, break off at the point at which he must have explained why the appearance of *The Cunning Man* was delayed for so long. When it was at last presented at Drury Lane, however, as an afterpiece to Otway's *The Orphan* on 21 November 1766, the moment could hardly have been better chosen, for Rousseau himself was in England and his quarrel with David Hume, who had been responsible for his arrival in the country, was then at its height. In November 1766, indeed, appeared Hume's

---

[1] *Frag. Mem.* (Berg, folder 4).

[2] Esther's return has been variously dated 1766 and 1767, Hemlow, p. 15 and *GDB*, i. 106; but for the following reasons it is clear that CB's second journey to France took place in the summer of 1765: (1) A letter from a Frenchman with whom CB and Esther travelled, dated 27 Aug. 1766, refers to the *quatorze mois* which had passed since their journey together, De Grange Blanche to CB (Osborn). (2) In the manuscript journal of his tour of France and Italy in 1770, CB states once that he had been in France in 1765 and twice that he had been there five years earlier. He also states that his 1770 journey was his third visit to France, so that he could not have been there in both 1765 and 1766. In each case Scholes mistakenly 'corrects' CB's date to 1764, *Tours*, i. 1, 29, 35, 38. (3) In the fragmentary index to his 'Memoirs', the entry 'I set out for Fr. a 2ᵈ time' comes under the general heading of 1765, *Frag. Mem.* (B.M. Add. MS. 48345, f. 19). (4) Mrs. Cibber, whom CB mentions as having wished to perform in *The Cunning Man*, died on 18 Jan. 1766, *Gent. Mag.* xxxvi. 103. This confirms that, although the operetta was not produced until Nov. 1766, plans for its production had begun in 1765.

self-justificatory pamphlet, *A Concise and Genuine Account of the Dispute between Mr. Hume and Mr. Rousseau.*[1] It was accordingly impossible for the innocent pastoral entertainment to escape some degree of involvement in the quarrel and Garrick may even have timed the production precisely to gain publicity from it. Even Fulke Greville as far away as Munich, where he was now Envoy Extraordinary to the Elector of Bavaria,[2] could not miss the connexion; and while he assured Burney that 'certainly you have contrived y^r translation charmingly', he added, 'Has not our friend Rousseau out done his usual out doings in Contradictions & Absurdity with his usual rapid glorious writing, I mean to poor Hume you see.'[3]

Whatever the interest in Rousseau aroused by the controversy, *The Cunning Man* probably suffered rather than gained from it. The complete absence of any of Rousseau's 'usual rapid glorious writing' from the naïve pastoral entertainment inevitably made it a disappointment in the context of the quarrel. In any case, the piece, which had enjoyed such success in France, did not appeal to the more robust English taste. According to Fanny, 'the drama was too denuded of intricacy or variety for the amusement of John Bull; and the appearance of only three interlocutors caused a gaping expectation of some followers, that made every new scene begin by inflicting disappointment.'[4] The simple charm of Rousseau's melodies could not compensate for the paucity of the action, nothing of which is omitted in Genest's summary of the plot: 'Phoebe consults the Cunning Man—he tells her that Colin has been false to her, but that he still loves her—at the conclusion they are reconciled.'[5]

Yet if *The Cunning Man* was scarcely the success which Burney and Garrick had expected, it was by no means a disastrous production. It received fourteen performances during the season and two more in 1768.[6] The *Monthly Review* considered that it did not discredit 'the gentleman who has taken the pains to introduce it on the English theatre';[7] and although it

---

[1] E. C. Mossner, *Life of David Hume*, 1954, p. 530.
[2] *Gent. Mag.* xxxv (1765), 539.
[3] Greville to CB, 14 Dec. 1766 (Osborn).
[4] *Mem.* i. 165.
[5] *Some Account of the English Stage*, Bath, 1832, v. 118–19.
[6] MacMillan, p. 228.   [7] xxxv (1766), 406.

was derided in some verses in the *Gentleman's Magazine*,[1] the letter columns of *The Public Advertiser* show that a certain amount of interest had been aroused. Some of the letters were probably no more than 'puffs', but others appear to be genuine complaints against the taste and behaviour of those who condemned the piece. Many of the letters predictably discuss the pastoral in the context of the Rousseau–Hume quarrel.[2] Burney himself, it should be added, evidently regarded the production as a success. The music was published in various arrangements, and the libretto appeared in two editions before the end of November 1766, and had been reprinted four times by 1792. In the second edition, dated 29 November 1766, Burney significantly added his own name as the adaptor to the title-page, as well as a note thanking the managers of Drury Lane for their assistance, the performers for 'their excellent representation of it', and the public, 'for their favourable acceptance of his feeble endeavours to contribute his mite towards their innocent amusements'.

Burney's latest flirtation with the theatre ended thus inconclusively, leaving him still tantalizingly on the edge of success. His close friendship with Garrick helps to explain the difficulty he found in resisting the spell of the theatre. Garrick, who had no children of his own, delighted in amusing the young Burneys in Poland Street, and Burney often spent week ends with the Garricks at their beautiful villa on the Thames at Hampton, which his host's 'Wit, humour, and constant chearfulness' and his wife's 'good sense, taste and Propriety' rendered 'a terrestrial Paradise' for the overworked and rather lonely music-teacher.[3] In the spring or summer of 1767 Garrick offered Burney yet another commission, inviting him to 'set to music an English opera called Orpheus'.[4] Thus Fanny dignified the work, although it was in fact no more than a burletta inserted in Garrick's farce *A Peep behind the Curtain*, produced on 23 October 1767.[5] Garrick's generosity extended elsewhere, however, for while reading over the libretto, Burney learned that François Barthélemon, a young French composer, had also been invited to provide a setting of the piece.

Burney's pride was deeply hurt, and he returned his copy of

---

[1] *Gent. Mag.* xxxvii (1767), 42.   [2] *GDB*, i. 111–16.
[3] *Frag. Mem.* (Berg).   [4] *Mem.* i. 170.   [5] *Grove*, i. 462.

the libretto without comment to Mr. Johnston at Drury Lane, to whom Garrick at once wrote a hasty and apologetic note:

Pray tell Mr Burney that I will sooner give up Every line that I Ever wrote than he sh^d have the least reason to be suspicious of my regard & Friendship for him—the affair of *Orpheus* was done in a hurry & without thought, but as I have not a greater opinion of anybody than of him I will pay Mr Barthelemon immediately for what he has done & be happy that he (Mr Burney) will take it under his Care & protection—I will have no Uneasiness about such a Trifle—You may say thus much to Mr Burney, or shew him this Scrawl, I can't write I have hurt my thumb.[1]

Burney quickly forgave Garrick's carelessness, but the affront to his pride had larger implications. He refused to continue with the setting of 'Orpheus' and resolved never again to compose music for the theatre. Ironically enough, the music which Barthélemon (who was married to Mrs. Arne's niece) provided for the burletta was so successful as to ensure him for some years a prosperous career as a theatrical composer. By that time, however, Burney's ambitions had taken a different direction, and, if any one incident can be seen as responsible for this crucial diversion of his interests, the brief misunderstanding with Garrick must assume that important role.

As Burney's seventeen years of spasmodic theatrical endeavour came to an end, the wretched luck which had dogged him since his return from Lynn in 1760 began to change. Fanny d'Arblay describes at some length an attempt by her father to obtain the post of Master of the King's Band, which she dates in 1765.[2] Since William Boyce held the post without interruption from 1755 until his death in 1779, Fanny's dating, as Scholes pointed out, must be incorrect. The purpose of her account, however, may well have been only to give her an opportunity of introducing an undated letter written by David Hume to Lord Eglinton, requesting an unspecified post for Burney.[3] Scholes argued that Fanny's date of 1765 should be altered to 1779, when Burney did attempt to obtain the Master-

---

[1] Garrick to Johnston, n.d. (Osborn).

[2] *Mem.* i. 185–8.

[3] Hume to Lord Eglinton, n.d. (PML), dated 'Spring 1767' in *Letters of David Hume*, ed. J. Y. T. Greig, 1932, ii. 132, where it is described as 'hitherto unpublished'; but FB printed it, *Mem.* i. 186–7.

ship, and that Hume's letter should also be dated in that year. As Hume had died in 1776, however, this solution can be dismissed at once. The truth would appear to be that Fanny, ever eager to dignify her father's career, was anxious to quote a letter by Hume on his behalf, but unwilling—if, in fact, she knew it—to admit the real object of the request: to ask for Burney the relatively humble position of 'Extra Musician' in the King's Band, which he duly obtained in 1767, an appointment which Dr. Scholes did not connect with Hume's letter.[1]

More significant than the small supplementation of his income resulting from this post was Burney's second marriage later in 1767. Mrs. Allen's sense of propriety having been satisfied, communications had been re-established between them, and, in spite of giving 'between 50 & 60 lessons a week, besides school scholars', when the London season was at its height, Burney had found time during the winter of 1766–7 to accompany her to the opera. By 'constant importunity' Burney persuaded the already middle-aged widow to ignore the disapproval of her family; travelled to Bristol to win over her brother to the match; conducted a correspondence with Mrs. Allen, which had such an 'Air of mystery and intrigue', that they 'seemed young lovers under age trying to out-wit our parents and guardians'; and finally won her hand during a summer visit to Norfolk. On 2 October 1767 they were secretly married, and it was some weeks before the children of either partner learned of it.

We may agree with Burney that it was a sensible match: 'no two persons had a better right to dispose of themselves than we had', for they had long been good friends, both had children to look after, and both were over forty. Stephen Allen's will had provided his widow with a dowry of £5,000 and his three children with £100 a year for their education and maintenance, until they were of an age to assume their individual fortunes. Although Mrs. Allen's wealth can hardly have appeared a disadvantage to her suitor, Burney's pride, as well as his prosperity as a music-teacher, rendered him unwilling to draw upon it: 'With my professional diligence, and the patronage and esteem of so many great families, wch made me in fashion with the less, I was well able to support and educate my children without

[1] *GDB*, ii. 321.

encroaching on the income of my wife. . . .' It was just as well
that his heart 'was attached to the lady's person, not her
property', for, just before the marriage, the merchant in whose
Russian enterprises Mrs. Allen had invested a large part of her
fortune went bankrupt. Perhaps with a sad irony, Burney concluded the account of his second marriage in his 'Memoirs'
with a description of his hopes at the time for an affectionate
union of his family with Mrs. Allen and her three children.[1]
Miss Hemlow has recently revealed the extent to which Burney's
children disliked their stepmother; and although the point of
view of the inevitably lonely, unhappy, and, in later years,
often sick woman can be documented by no extant material,
there can be no doubt that Burney's second marriage was, from
many aspects, an unsatisfactory move.[2]

In the autumn of 1767, however, it promised to solve one
of Burney's largest problems, his responsibility for his numerous
children. Moreover, free now of theatrical ambitions, he could
at last pursue the literary enterprises which had for so long
remained vaguely in the back of his mind. He had not yet, however, clearly defined the nature of his project, and, in addition,
he was by no means confident of his own powers: in Fanny's
words, 'the timidity of his Muse, not the dearth of his fancy,
long kept back the force of mind for meeting the public eye'.
Her account of the various undertakings he now considered,
however, is confused. Anxious to date the start of Burney's
literary career in 1764 with his journey to France, Fanny
states that, on his return, he worked first on a translation of
d'Alembert's *Élémens de musique*, abandoned it for Rousseau's
Dictionnaire de musique, and finally gave up that task for the
translation of *Le Devin du village*.[3] As has been stated already,
however, Burney had begun his translation of d'Alembert in
1753; and Rousseau's *Dictionnaire* was not published until 1767,
a year after *The Cunning Man* was performed. It is quite possible,
nevertheless, that during 1768, Burney thought of publishing
translations of either or both of these works; and equally likely
that the musicological research in which they involved him
brought to his attention—if he had not fully realized it before—
the absence of any history of music in the English language.

---

[1] *Frag. Mem.* (Berg; Osborn); Fanny Greville to CB, 29 Oct. 1767 (Osborn).
[2] Hemlow, pp. 35–40.   [3] *Mem.* i. 164–5.

No significant aspect of Burney's literary career, however, is so sparsely documented as the genesis of the *idea* of the great *History of Music*; and, before the period when we know that he was definitely working on it, occurred a curious episode which could be taken either as a last attempt to win purely musical distinction, or as a signal of loftier ambitions. In July 1769 the Duke of Grafton was to be installed as Chancellor of Cambridge University. It was customary for an Installation Ode, set to music by a prominent composer, to be performed at this cere-mony and, late in 1768 or early in 1769, Burney proposed himself to the Duke for the task. His offer having been accepted, Burney decided to imitate the precedent of William Boyce, the Master of the King's Music, who had set the Installation Ode in 1749 and, on the following day, had obtained the degree of Doctor of Music, after directing the performance of an anthem which he had written as an exercise.[1]

Early in 1769 Burney sounded his friend William Mason about the Ode itself, which was to be written by no less a poet than Thomas Gray, the new Professor of History at Cambridge, who was conveniently a close friend of Mason. Mason could only report, however, that Gray had not yet begun the Ode and that, in any case, he wished the fact that he was to write it to be kept secret. Burney was obviously anxious to get to work on his setting but Mason could offer only the discon-certing information that he himself had written the Installa-tion Ode in four days in 1749 and that Boyce had then been given only ten days in which to compose and rehearse his setting: 'I much fear you will not have more time given you on the present occasion.' Burney had also expressed a desire to provide a setting which would gratify Gray's predilection for Italian music,[2] but Mason advised him to meet the taste of the Univer-sity rather than that of the poet: 'Out roar Old Handel if you can.'[3]

It is unlikely that Burney ever came into any closer negotia-tion with Thomas Gray. The composer of the setting of the Installation Ode was also responsible for assembling a suitable orchestra and choir for its performance and, since the candidate for a doctorate had likewise to provide performers of his exercise

---

[1] *Grove*, i. 861.   [2] See *post*, p. 265.
[3] Mason to CB, 6 Feb. 1769 (Comyn).

at his own expense, Burney decided to employ the same musicians on both occasions. More for the benefit of his own exercise than for that of the Ode, we may suspect, Burney engaged a large orchestra of excellent London musicians, led by the famous violinist Giardini, undoubtedly relying on the expectation that the Duke of Grafton would meet the cost of transporting these performers to Cambridge. On submitting an account of the expenses involved, however, Burney was informed to his indignation that it must be cut by a half. As had been the case in his misunderstanding with Garrick in 1767, Burney was too proud to sustain such a rebuke and he haughtily resigned from the task.[1]

The setting of Gray's Ode was eventually composed by John Randall, the Professor of Music at Cambridge. An account of Randall which Burney wrote some thirty-five years later reveals the extent to which the affront to his pride still rankled. Randall—in Burney's opinion no more than 'a slight organ-player' and an undistinguished composer—obtained the commission of setting the Installation Ode in 1769, 'to the astonishment of all the musical profession, by undertaking to have it performed by the musicians resident in the university, without putting his grace to the expence of additional hands and voices from London, as Drs. Greene and Boyce had thought necessary on former occasions at Cambridge, and Dr. William Hayes at Oxford'.[2] It may be added that this was the first of a series of disappointments in Burney's life which he was to blame on his own reliance on the 'offensive & impracticable' proposals of Giardini, who presumably encouraged him in assembling so excellent an orchestra.[3]

According to a 'Letter from Cambridge', dated 9 April 1769, in the *St. James's Chronicle* for 11–13 April, Burney was then still intending to take his doctorate, in spite of the fact that Randall was to set the Installation Ode. Other details in this letter are, however, demonstrably inaccurate and it is perhaps more

[1] *Mem.* i. 210–12.

[2] Article 'Randal, John', Rees, vol. xxix. Gray's derisive comment on Randall's music is worth recording. A week before the Installation he wrote, 'the musick is as good as the words: the former might be taken for mine, & the latter for Dr. Randal's', *Correspondence of Thomas Gray*, ed. P. Toynbee and L. Whibley, Oxford, 1935, iii. 1065.

[3] 'Sketch of a Character' in a notebook (Osborn). See *post*, pp. 152, 227–8.

likely that Burney had immediately decided on the gesture of
retreating to Oxford. He matriculated from University College
on 20 June 1769, directed a highly successful performance of
his exercise two days later and took the degrees of Mus.B. and
Mus.D. on 23 June.[1] Although William Bewley gently mocked
this arrival at 'the pinnacle of all earthly dignity', Burney was
in fact hesitant at first about using the academic title which is
now inseparably associated with him: 'I did not for some time
after the honour that was conferred upon me at Oxford display
my title on the plate of my door; when M[r] Steel, author of
"An Essay on the melody of Speech," says, "Burney, why don't
you tip us the Doctor?" When I replied in provincial dialect,
"I wants daeycity, I'm ashayum'd"—"Poh, poh, (says he) you
must *brazen* it." '[2]

Burney accordingly 'brazened' it. His self-conscious relapse
into 'provincial dialect', however, serves to remind us of the
twenty-five years of frustrated ambition which had followed
his arrival in London from the provinces as an apprentice in
1744. At the age of forty-three, he was still little more than a
successful music-teacher, who had published some not very
inspired music[3] and who had at last had the good sense to bring
to a close a rather chequered career as a composer for the theatre.
The Oxford doctorate, however, marks the turning-point in
his life, the moment at which he made his last bid for fame,
no longer as a 'mere musician', but as a scholar and a man of
letters. Seven years were to suffice to bring him a European
reputation.

---

[1] J. Foster, *Alumni Oxonienses, 1715–1886*, 1887–8, i. 195; *ED*, i. 56; *Mem.* i. 213–14.
The manuscript of CB's exercise is in the Bodleian (MS. Mus. Sch. Ex. c. 15).
See *post*, p. 345.

[2] *Frag. Mem.* (Osborn). The story is told also in *Mem.* i. 214 and *Thraliana*, i. 137.
Joshua Steele (1700–91) published *An Essay towards establishing the Melody and
Measure of Speech* in 1775.

[3] For CB's musical compositions, see *GDB*, ii. 340–52.

III

MUSICAL TRAVELS

1769–1773

I

ALTHOUGH Burney himself always liked to consider that his
interest in the history of music dated from his years at
King's Lynn, there is little evidence to document its
gradual transformation from a hobby to a major preoccupation. In 1788 he more than once described his *History of Music* as
having been '30 years in meditation, & 20 in writing & printing'; and in 1807 he stated that he 'began to meditate a General
Hist^y of Mus.' after taking his doctorate at Oxford in June 1769,
adding that Dr. William Warburton, Bishop of Gloucester, had
been one of those who had assured him 'that the want of such a
work was a chasm in our literature'.[1] Although these two statements use the word 'meditate' in different senses, their general
import seems clear enough. By the time Burney returned to
London in 1760, he must already have been contemplating the
publication of a musicological work of some sort; but it was not
until 1769 that he was persuaded into the specific and highly
ambitious commitment of writing a *General History of Music*.
Certainly, he was talking freely of the work by 1770, had
evidently been engaged in research for some months and had
been greatly encouraged in his labours by the approval of his
friends.[2]

Burney's 'literary career' had already begun, however, with
the publication of *An Essay towards a History of the Principal
Comets that have appeared since the Year 1742* in October 1769. As
Fanny d'Arblay later observed, 'This opening enterprize cannot but seem extraordinary, the profession, education, and
indispensable business of the Doctor considered';[3] but in view of
his lifelong interest in astronomy, this 93-page pamphlet was

---

[1] CB to H. Repton, Nov. 1788, draft; to J. Huttner, 15 Aug. 1807 (Osborn).
[2] CB to W. Mason, 27 May 1770, copy (Osborn).   [3] *Mem.* i. 217.

a less eccentric publication than may at first appear. Both Burney and his first wife had been 'very fond of Astronomy'[1] and prefixed to his *Essay* was Esther's translation of a *Letter upon Comets* by the French scientist, Maupertuis. Telescopes had been a frequent topic of Burney's correspondence with his Norfolk friend, William Bewley, and his interest in astronomy was later to be manifested during his foreign travels, in his friendship with Dr. Shepherd, Professor of Astronomy at Cambridge, and in his pride in the fact that from 1774 he inhabited the former home of Sir Isaac Newton. One of his very last literary labours, indeed, was to be the composition of a long poem on the history of the science, written with the encouragement of Sir William Herschel.

It may still appear strange, however, that Burney should busy himself with an *Essay on Comets* when he was already searching bookshops and libraries for materials for his *History of Music*. Fanny d'Arblay, who was always willing to emphasize her father's attachment to his first wife (her own mother) at the expense of the second Mrs. Burney, had her own explanation. This joint publication of Burney's *Essay* and Esther's translation (seven years after her death and two years after his second marriage) not only represented 'a fond, though unacknowledged indulgence of tender recollections', but also expressed his desire that they should unlock 'in concert, the gates through which Doctor Burney first passed to that literary career which, ere long, greeted his more courageous entrance into a publicity that conducted him to celebrity. . . .'[2]

The anonymous publication of the *Essay* may have helped in some way to remove Burney's inhibitions about embarking on his new career, but he had no intention of spending much time on the pamphlet. Its immediate *raison d'être* was the return, in the autumn of 1769, of the comet predicted by Halley, which doubtless seemed to Burney an appropriate occasion for collecting some of the information gleaned in the earlier pursuit of his hobby. William Bewley, who saw the manuscript of the *Essay* in September 1769, considered that his friend, who was 'posting to the press with as much rapidity as a Comet down to its *perihelion*', should not be in 'such a pestilent hurry', but should endeavour to make the pamphlet a more careful and

[1] Ibid. 66.   [2] Ibid. 216–17.

learned study.[1] Burney, however, was anxious not only to publish while the reappearance of the comet was still a topic of general interest,[2] but to avoid any protracted interruption of his historical researches. The 'Postscript' to the *Essay* is dated 25 October 1769. In the following year it was reprinted at Glasgow in a smaller format and without the Dedication.

The *Essay* is perhaps of interest now only because its publication was attended by what were to be characteristic efforts on Burney's part to ensure its success. A dedication to a member of the aristocracy could do no harm and, 'the Countess of Pembroke being reputed to have studied Astronomy, & accustomed to Telescopical observations', Burney dedicated it to her. Fanny d'Arblay later learned that the Countess did not identify its author until after his death.[3] Even more significant was the way in which Burney exploited his friendship with William Bewley, who had recently become the chief scientific writer for the *Monthly Review*.[4] It can hardly be coincidental that Burney praised in his *Essay* some remarks by an 'ingenious' writer in that periodical, who turns out to be Bewley himself. Bewley also jocularly complained that, just when the *Essay* was about to be reviewed, Burney had sent him a present as a 'bribe'. His humorous protest against such gifts from friends who wished him to review their books—'Spirit of Equity! direct my steps, & enable me to preserve my critical integrity inviolate'[5]— was to be reiterated rather more earnestly in the following decade. Nevertheless, Bewley's short review duly appeared in December 1769, assuring his readers that the 'very sensible Compiler has been exceedingly industrious' and paying the particular compliment that 'even the ladies may peruse this Essay with improvement and pleasure'.[6]

The publication of the *Essay on Comets* was accompanied by another and rather different characteristic of Burney's later

[1] Bewley to CB, 27 Sept. 1769 (Osborn).
[2] Cf. *Gent. Mag.* xxxix (1769), 420, 508.
[3] *Frag. Mem.* (Osborn); *Mem.* i. 217–18.
[4] According to B. C. Nangle, *The Monthly Review: First Series, 1749–1789,* 1934, p. 4, Bewley contributed to the periodical between 1749 and 1783. The present writer has demonstrated that Bewley did not contribute until 1766 in 'William Bewley and the *Monthly Review*: a Problem of Attribution', *Papers of the American Bibliographical Society,* lv (1961), 309–18.
[5] Bewley to CB, 27 Sept. 1769 (Osborn).
[6] *Monthly Review,* xli (1769), 484–5.

career. Never robust, liable all too easily to become harrassed and over-anxious during the publication of each of his books, and obliged, because of his professional duties as a music-teacher, to restrict his literary labours to the night-time for many months of the year, Burney was troubled throughout his career by periodic attacks of rheumatism and other ailments. It was perhaps more than coincidence that in the autumn of 1769 an attack of rheumatism 'confined him to his bed, or chamber, during twenty days'.[1]

Having, to some extent, worked astronomy out of his system, Burney spent the winter of 1769–70 in putting in order the historical materials which he had collected during the preceding twenty years, and in searching for new information. Although, by the spring of 1770, he was confident that he had examined most of the relevant and available material in England, these initial months of research depressed him, leaving him confused rather than enlightened. He had discovered, in the first place, that the history of music could not easily be disentangled from a great many other fields of inquiry; and a letter to William Mason in May 1770, which contains the first discussion of his great undertaking, expresses also his disillusion with the writers who had previously written on the origins of music, and from whom he had expected to extract a great deal of reliable information:

The prospect widens as I advance. 'Tis a chaos to which God knows whether I shall have life, leisure, or abilities to give order. I find it connected with Religion, Philosophy, History, Poetry, Painting, Sculpture, public exhibitions & private life. It is, like gold, to be found, though in but small portions, even in lead ore, & in the coal mine; which are equivalent to heavy Authors, & the rust & rubbish of antiquity.

Burney had done his best with the 'heavy Authors', for he had 'got together & consulted an incredible number of Books & Tracts on the subject with more disappointment & disgust than satisfaction'. Most of them, he had discovered, merely reproduced without re-examination the conclusions and confusions of earlier writers. He himself was determined that his *History of Music* should not be yet another summary of his predecessors.

[1] *Mem.* i. 218.

'It is far more easy to compile a dull Book of bits & scraps from these writers, than to get any one to read it after it is done.' Already visualizing his *History* as a work which would appeal to readers who were neither musicians nor antiquarians, Burney's eagerness to arrive at his own conclusions and to avoid dullness at all costs led him, as he informed Mason, to make a drastic and unprecedented decision: 'I have therefore determined to fly to Italy this summer, & to allay my thirst of knowledge at the pure source, which I am unable to do by such spare Draughts as are to be attained from the polluted works through which it is conducted to us here'.[1]

No Englishman had previously attempted to write a large-scale *History of Music*, let alone cross Europe in search of materials; but, in Burney's opinion, such a journey would fulfil two important purposes: 'the one was to get, from the libraries to the *viva voce* conversation of the learned, what information I could relative to the music of the ancients; and the other was to judge with my own eyes of the *present state* of modern music in the places through which I should pass, from the performance and conversation of the first musicians in Italy'.[2] The attraction of Italy lay not only in the musical collections of its great libraries, but in the fact that Burney believed it to be the home of the most important contemporary music; and since he believed that, unlike the other arts, the music of antiquity could in no sense be described as 'classical' and that music had only recently approached perfection, modern music was in many ways the most important subject of his historical survey. In addition, he was well aware of the potential publicity value that his personal investigations would confer on his history, for it was with the deliberate aim of 'stamping on my intended History some marks of originality, or at least of novelty' that he 'determined to hear with my *own* ears, and to see with my *own* eyes'. There could be no substitute for personal testimony when it came to contemporary music: 'Learned men and books may be more useful as to ancient music, but it is only *living* musicians that can explain what *living music* is.'[3]

Before setting out for Italy Burney made various preparations

---

[1] CB to Mason, 27 May 1770, copy (Osborn); *GDB*, i. 148–50.

[2] CB to D. Garrick, 17 Oct. 1770, *Private Corresp. of Garrick*, 1831–2, i. 403–5.

[3] *Tours*, I. xxvii, 7.

to facilitate his travels and researches. An important step was the drawing up of a 'plan' of his *History*, both to formulate to himself the main aims of what would inevitably be hurried investigations in foreign libraries, and also to enable the scholars, librarians, and *dilettanti* whom he would encounter to offer criticism of his ideas, as well as to direct him most readily to fruitful sources of information. Although no copy of the 'plan' survives, the basis of it can be seen in the letter to William Mason quoted above, which Fanny d'Arblay, indeed, described as 'the opening view of his plan and of his tour'.[1] In this letter Burney discussed the various aspects and periods of both ancient and modern music with which he proposed to deal in his *History*, and requested suggestions not only from Mason but from 'your friend Mr Gray'. Thomas Gray, the poet, was deeply interested in music, but if he had in fact ever contributed any 'notions' on ancient music, Burney would not have been able to resist mentioning the fact somewhere in his writings; and, even if Gray had been willing to assist Burney, he would hardly have had time before his death in 1771. The 'Musical Definitions' attributed to Mason in the first volume of the *History of Music* are presumably those which he supplied in answer to Burney's letter.[2] In any case, having drawn up his 'plan', Burney had it translated into French and Italian;[3] and the extensive use to which he put it during his travels fully justified the trouble which he had taken over it.

Burney's problem, however, was not simply a question of picking the brains of the experts whom he was going to meet to the best advantage, but also one of obtaining opportunities of meeting them in the first place. Accordingly, from his 'friends amongst persons in power', he obtained letters to 'ambassadors and ministers from our Court' in France and Italy, although Fanny does not identify these influential persons. The 'persons of influence in letters and in the arts', on the other hand, can be named more easily, although Fanny mentions only Garrick.[4] The actor's assistance lay almost entirely in recommending Burney to the group of distinguished Frenchmen with whom he had become friendly during his own visit to the Continent in

---

[1] *Mem.* i. 221.   [2] *Hist. Mus.* i. 499–500.
[3] *Tours*, i. 187, 314.
[4] *Mem.* i. 221.

1763–5.[1] Garrick asked Burney to execute various commissions for him in Paris, and in return procured for him 'not only a very flattering reception, but innumerable acts of kindness and hospitality'.[2] Of Garrick's letters, only that to Jean Baptiste Suard survives, recommending Burney as 'a most amiable, honest & ingenious Man'.[3]

Not surprisingly, Burney's Italian friends resident in England provided many of the most valuable letters that he carried with him, and the names of Vincenzo Martinelli, a friend of his years in Norfolk, of Felice Giardini, the violinist, and of Giuseppe Baretti,[4] the writer, occur frequently in the account of his journey in Italy. English friends also helped, however, including Robert Strange, the engraver, Dr. Thomas Bever, the jurist, and Robert Hudson, the composer. The process was, in fact, a cumulative one, for the men to whom he was thus introduced in turn supplied letters for the later stages of his journey.

Thus equipped, on 5 June 1770, when most of his pupils had left London for the country, Burney arrived at Dover to embark for France. As he had forgotten his sword ('at this time the necessary passport of a Gentleman on the Continent'),[5] his departure was delayed until 7 June, and he had time to write a short letter to his daughter Fanny, in which, at this critical moment in his career, the characteristically close family feeling of the Burneys receives intense expression: 'continue to Love me & to believe that I love you—& that my Family is never nearer my Heart than when I am obliged to be far from them. it has ever been *Necessity* not *Choice* that has separated us.—had I an Ark like that of Noah I w^d have taken you all in it. . . . I hope to live to make you ⟨*torn*⟩ porcupines by the Wonders I shall have seen ⟨when⟩ I come to relate them'.[6] Some of Burney's adventures on the Continent were, indeed, to be even more hair-raising than he can have anticipated. Since the daily journal which he kept during his travels is perhaps the liveliest and most entertaining of his works, the temptation to quote extensively from his vivid descriptions of every aspect of French and Italian

---

[1] F. A. Hedgcock, *David Garrick and his French Friends* [1912], *passim*.

[2] *Tours*, i. 17, 22, 25.

[3] *Mémoires et correspondances historiques et littéraires*, ed. Charles Nisard, Paris, 1858, pp. 163–4; *Letters of Garrick*, ed. D. M. Little and G. M. Karhl, 1963, ii. 693–4.

[4] Cf. L. Collison-Morley, *Giuseppe Baretti and his Friends*, 1909, p. 227.

[5] *Tours*, i. 1.   [6] CB to FB, 6 June 1770 (Barrett).

musical life is hard to resist. Even lengthy extracts would hardly do it justice, however, and since the journal is now easily accessible in Dr. Scholes's recent edition, little more than a cursory summary of Burney's itinerary will be offered here, with particular emphasis on events which bear on his literary pursuits.

Burney reached Paris on 11 June 1770 and stayed in the city for almost two weeks. There were a number of notable libraries to consult and he spent some particularly rewarding mornings in the Bibliothèque du Roi 'making extracts from scarce books'.[1] As he detested French music and musical taste, he was less concerned to inquire dispassionately into the present state of music in Paris than to collect fresh evidence at concerts and the opera to confirm his prejudice. Although the two men whom Burney was most anxious to meet, Rousseau and Diderot, had left Paris for the summer, Burney profited from the hospitality and conversation of a number of other distinguished men, including Suard, the Abbé Arnaud, Pierre Roussier, the musicologist, and Jean Monnet, former director of the Opéra Comique.

Italy remained, however, the real object of his journey and on 24 June he set off for Milan, spending on the way three days at Lyons and two at Geneva. While at Geneva he could not resist visiting Ferney and, after being shown over the house by a servant, he accidentally met the seventy-five-year-old Voltaire. Burney did full justice to this encounter in his journal:

He was going to his workmen. My heart leaped at the sight of so extraordinary a man. He had just then quitted his garden, and was crossing the court before his house. Seeing my chaise, and me on the point of mounting it, he made a sign to his servant, who had been my *Cicerone*, to go to him, in order, I suppose, to enquire who I was. After they had exchanged a few words together, he approached the place where I stood, motionless, in order to contemplate his person as much as I could when his eyes were turned from me; but on seeing him move towards me, I found myself drawn by some irresistible power towards him; and, without knowing what I did, I insensibly met him half way.

It is not easy to conceive it possible for life to subsist in a form so nearly composed of mere skin and bone, as that of M. de Voltaire. He complained of decrepitude, and said, he supposed I was curious

[1] *Tours*, i. 17, 27, 30.

to form an idea of the figure of one walking after death. However his eyes and whole countenance are still full of fire; and though so emaciated, a more lively expression cannot be imagined.

After some conversation about contemporary English writers, in the course of which Burney suggested that the harshness of the 'periodical journals' had 'often silenced modest men of genius' such as Gray and Mason (an opinion which was later to offend William Bewley[1]), Voltaire obligingly showed his visitor round his estate: 'after which I took my leave, for fear of breaking in upon his time, being unwilling to rob the public of things so precious as the few remaining moments of this great and universal genius'.[2]

Burney eventually reached Milan on 16 July and his hectic and unremitting investigation of every conceivable kind of musical activity, which had been increasing steadily as he approached Italy, now reached the pitch at which it was to remain for some five months. During his eight days in Milan, Burney heard music in all the most important churches, at the opera, and at both public and private concerts; interviewed the most notable performers, composers, and scholars in the city; persisted in the face of initial reluctance on the part of the officials of the Ambrosian Library to admit him, and eventually obtained full access to its treasures; found time to visit the eminent astronomer, Padre Boscovich; and concluded his stay with an inspection of Count Portusali's fine private library, and with a banquet given by Count Firmian, the Governor of Milan. On 25 July Burney left for Venice, his heart warm with gratitude for 'the kind and honourable treatment' that he had received in every quarter.[3]

After three days at Padua, where he inquired assiduously about the composer Tartini, who had died there less than six months earlier, Burney reached Venice on 3 August. Although the public libraries held little of interest, he benefited from conversation with the Abbate Martini, a learned musicologist; and found that the lack of important materials on ancient music was amply compensated for by the quantity and quality of the 'living' music, which he heard in all forms, in the streets as well as in the famous *Conservatorios*, where orphan girls received

---

[1] See *post*, p. 107.   [2] *Tours*, i. 42–45.   [3] Ibid. 85.

elaborate musical education. His visits to these institutions later inspired Burney with a disastrous ambition to provide London with a similar Music School.[1]

On 19 August Burney left Venice and arrived at Bologna two days later. Personalities rather than libraries were his main interest in this city, and he enjoyed interviewing the celebrated castrato, Carlo Broschi, known as Farinelli, and Signora Laura Bassi, a noted female scientist, with whom he was able to converse knowledgeably on electrical experiments. In addition, there was an unexpected meeting at a concert with an infant prodigy whom he had often heard perform in London some five years earlier:

among the rest, who should I meet but the celebrated little German, Mozart, who in 1766 astonished all hearers in London by his premature musical talent. I had a long conversation with his father. . . . The little man is grown considerably but is still a little man. He has been at Rome and Naples, where he was much admired . . . there is no musical excellence which I do not expect from his extraordinary quickness and talents, under the guidance of so able a musician and intelligent a man as his father, who, I was informed, had been ill five or six weeks at Bologna.[2]

Although Burney was fully aware of Mozart's genius, he could hardly have conceived the eventual fame of the fourteen-year-old boy and, in any case, he had more immediate concerns. His 'chief business' in Bologna was to meet Padre G. B. Martini, whom Dr. Scholes described as 'the oracle of Europe in all that concerned the theory and history of music',[3] who was himself engaged on a huge *History of Music* in five volumes, the first of which had appeared in 1757, the second being published later in 1770.[4] This was a crucial interview for Burney, for his own ambitious undertaking could have been upset either by Martini's learned criticism of his 'plan', or by the discovery that his own intentions coincided too closely with those of the older historian. Fortunately, the two men liked and respected each other immediately: as Burney wrote, 'Upon so short an acquaintance I

[1] See *post*, pp. 149–53.
[2] *Tours*, i. 162; cf. CB's article on Mozart, Rees, vol. xxiv. Mozart and his father had visited London in 1764–5.   [3] *Tours*, i. 145 n.
[4] Vol. iii was published in 1781, but Martini was still working on vol. iv at his death in 1784.

never liked any man more. . . . It was impossible for confidence
to be more cordial, especially between two persons whose
pursuits were the same', and he was delighted to find that they
would not be competing in their histories and that he need not
alter his 'plan' to accommodate Martini's theories. As he made
a point of assuring his readers when he published his journal,

I had advanced too far to retreat before I could procure his book,
and when I had found it, my plan was so much digested as to render
the adoption or imitation of any other very inconvenient. Besides, as
every object may be approached by a different route, it may also be
seen in a different point of view: two different persons therefore may
exhibit it with equal truth, and yet with great diversity: I shall avail
myself of P. Martini's learning and materials, as I would of his
spectacles, I shall apply them to my subject, as it appears to me,
without changing my situation; and shall neither implicitly adopt
his sentiments in doubtful points, nor transcribe them where we
agree.[1]

With a generosity and equanimity which Burney was unfortunately unable to imitate towards his own rivals, Martini
put all the printed and manuscript resources of his great library
at his visitor's disposal, and before leaving Bologna on 31
August, Burney had spent many hours there in reading, transcribing, and making notes. The two historians did not meet
again, but corresponded until Martini's death in 1784.[2]

In Florence, where Burney arrived for two weeks on 1 September, the pattern which had established itself in other cities
was repeated: he worked hard in three great libraries, the
Laurentian, the Magliabechian, and the Palazza Rinucini; consulted scholars, composers, and performers; made notes on the
great Florentine art collections; and heard an almost incredible
amount of music. His energy was astonishing: to give only one
example, he travelled thirty miles overnight to the town of
Figline, where a festival, involving a great deal of music, was to
be held on the following day. Unable to find lodging after the
celebrations, he spent the whole of the second night travelling
back to Florence, where he renewed his investigations without
respite.[3]

    [1] *Tours*, i. 146.
    [2] CB to Martini, 6 letters, 1770–80 (Biblioteca Communale, Bologna; Osborn);
Martini to CB, 10 letters, 1771–84 (Osborn).
    [3] *Tours*, i. 174–6.

The proximity of Rome, however, began to exert an irresistible attraction, and leaving Florence on 16 September, Burney arrived reverently, four days later, in 'the capital of the world, for such it *still is* with respect to the arts'.[1] During his three weeks in Rome he worked hard and profitably in the Vatican Library and in the private collections of a composer named Santarelli and of the Abbate Orsini. Once more he indulged his interest in painting and sculpture, satisfying himself that certain information about ancient and obscure musical instruments could only be obtained from a study of these arts. Through the numerous other Englishmen whom he met in Rome, Burney was introduced to John Sackville, the third Duke of Dorset, at whose residence he spent several evenings in listening to Rome's leading performers. On 14 October he at last reluctantly set off on the final stage of his outward journey, having, as he stated himself, 'heard the most eminent performers, conversed with the principal theorists and composers, found many of the books, manuscripts, and antiquities which I had sought, and explained my wants with regard to the rest, to several friends at Rome, who kindly promised me their assistance in supplying them during my absence. . . .'[2]

Two days later he reached Naples, approaching the home of so many great Italian musicians with the highest expectations: 'My visits to other places were in the way of *business*, for the performance of a *task* I had assigned myself; but I came hither animated by the hope of pleasure'.[3] On the whole, however, Neapolitan music-making disappointed him, although he met Piccinni and Jommelli, two celebrated composers; discovered material of great interest in the Royal Museum at Portici; was able to 'ransack' the Royal Library for 'materials relative to music';[4] and was entertained with flattering attention by Sir William Hamilton, the British plenipotentiary at Naples, who arranged, amongst other diversions, a visit to Vesuvius, which had the historian of music scrambling on all-fours over the lava. Burney's uneasiness in Naples was caused not only by disappointment with the music he heard there, however, for by the end of October he was beginning to worry about his return to England. An original plan of being back in

[1] Ibid. 200. [2] Ibid. 238. [3] Ibid. 241.
[4] Ibid. 271–6, 280, 282–3.

London by October may well have been abandoned before he reached Italy,[1] and his new intention was to return by Christmas. As he recorded in his journal, 'I keep the exact number of days in the week and month, lest I should overstay my time'; but his anxiety was caused not only by a wish to resume his professional practice by the beginning of the fashionable season in the New Year, for

besides my own family and business which require my attendance in London, there is constantly another weight on my spirits, arising from the apprehensions of a war, which would either oblige me to pass all the winter in Italy, or ruin my health, and indeed greatly affect my affairs by the fatigue, difficulty, and expense of travelling home through Germany, and in danger too of being taken prisoner in a long sea passage, at which, on the mere account of sickness, I very much shudder. Every body here talks of war. . . .[2]

To the general fear of war with Spain was soon added the anxiety caused by a rumour that plague had reached London. 'I wish I were at home', Burney confided to his journal, but bad weather delayed the completion of his investigations in Naples: 'How I shall get home, or when, it is not easy to tell; but this is only another piece of my ill-luck, that Demon who never quits me.'[3] Twinges of rheumatism did not help to rescue Burney from this not uncharacteristic collapse of morale, but at last on 8 November he was able to begin his return journey. He could not, however, hurry through Rome, for he had to re-examine some manuscripts in the Vatican, hold a 'levee' of the copyists who had been working for him in his absence, and do many small pieces of research to which the willing friends of his first sojourn in the city had somehow forgotten to apply themselves. Not until 22 November did he begin a rapid, extremely uncomfortable and occasionally hair-raising journey by sea and land to Paris.

Even a short summary of Burney's travels cannot afford to ignore the sheer physical suffering which he so often endured, for he could not, of course, travel in the relatively comfortable but expensive manner of a young nobleman making the Grand Tour. Indeed, the ambition and enthusiasm which drove the middle-aged music-master to undertake his journey to Italy

[1] S. Crisp to CB, 18 May 1770 (Osborn).   [2] *Tours*, i. 263.
[3] Ibid. 276.

receive a new dimension when the alarming difficulties which he had to encounter are appreciated. One example—Burney's description of his crossing the Apennines on the journey from Sarzana to Genoa late in November—will sufficiently illustrate the point, and also make it easier to understand the collapse of health which immediately followed his return to England:

the first two posts were not quite unpleasant, though through a very wild country; but we had still two more to go in the night, and these were terrible indeed! Such as I shall never forget. During the first we had a rapid river to ford twenty times, which grew larger and larger —such rocks to climb and descend! But all this was nothing compared with the last post, when the road was always on the edge of a precipice, hanging over the river above mentioned; now a torrent was roaring below with such noise and fury as turned my head, and almost stunned me; had it quite done so it would have been for the better, for I neither knew what I did nor what any one of the Muleteers or Guides said. At every moment, I could only hear them cry out 'Alla Montagna!' which meant to say that the road was so broken and dangerous that it was necessary I should alight, give the Mule to the Pedino, and cling to the rock or precipice. I got three or four terrible blows on the face and head by boughs of trees I could not see. In mounting my Mule, which was vicious, I was kicked by the two hind legs on my left knee and right thigh, which knocked me down, and I thought at first, and the Muleteers thought my thigh was broken, and began to pull at it and add to the pain most violently. It was a long while ere I would consent to mount again, though I walked in great misery. Such bridges! Such rivers! and such rocks! amidst all the noise just mentioned, to pass, as are above all power of description! However, at length, about eleven at night we arrived at a wretched Inn or pigstye, half stable, and half Cow-house, with a fire, but no chimney, surrounded by boors and Muleteers, all in appearance cut-throatly personages, with no kind of refreshment but the cold veal, and some stinking eggs, and water *a bere*; after which repast and dosing in the smoak about an hour, we set off again to pursue the same most tremendous road. It is in vain to attempt to describe what I could not see—but I could feel that we clambered and crawled up and down rocks and mountains on narrow roads at the edge of precipices a 1000 feet above the torrents which were always roaring below.[1]

Burney eventually reached Paris on 8 December. His main concern was now to meet as many as possible of the eminent

[1] Ibid. 306.

Frenchmen whom he had missed in June. Baron d'Holbach and
the Abbé Morellet, who had both been absent from Paris in the
summer, had now returned and Burney was able to discuss the
history of music with them at length. The triumph of this short
stay in Paris, however, was the contrivance of an interview with
Jean-Jacques Rousseau, which was arranged through the bookseller Guy, 'one of the few people Rousseau suffers to approach
him'. It was with some trepidation that Burney climbed to the
fifth-floor apartment on the Rue Grenelle of the man whose
writings on music had so decisively influenced him:

I ascended in great *sogezzione*, as I knew so much of his character,
and had heard of the rebuffs which many had met with, and as I was
prepared by Gui for a cold reception. However, we got to the summit
at last, and entered a small room with a bed in it—Mde. la Gouver-
nante was the first person we saw,[1] at her needle, almost bent
double—She took not the least notice of us, nor we of her, and in a
dark corner was the Man Mountain, in a woolen night cap, great
coat and slippers—for which he apologized, and very civilly gave me
the best place near the fire—the reception was far better than I
expected—I begun immediately to tell him of my journey and errand
into Italy—and the account seemed to catch his attention—

A long conversation followed about Italian music, the music
of the ancients and Burney's version of Rousseau's *Le Devin du
village*:

All this while, we hit it off very well—He is a little figure, with a
very intelligent and animated countenance, with black eye-brows
and small piercing black eyes. After this, I had the courage to offer
him a copy of my plan in French, which had the appearance of great
length, it having been copied wide by the Abbé Morellet's Secretary.
He said he never read, and seemed coy, and afraid of it—However,
he took it in his hand, and begun reading to himself, and ere he had
got half way down the 1st page, he read aloud, and seemed caught
by it.

Rousseau expressed his approval of many features of Burney's
scheme:

and then went on with seeming eagerness to the end, and said several
very civil things which I dare not repeat. Ere I went away, I got him

[1] Thérèse de Vasseur, by whom Rousseau himself claimed to have had five
children.

to consent to let me send him the music of Jomelli's *Passione*, with the London edition of his *Divin du Village*, my Cunning Man, and we parted exceeding good friends. He did not bite, nor knock me down, but said he was very glad to have had the opportunity of conversing with one who loved and cultivated music so much, and was obliged to me for my communication.[1]

The last of Burney's many memorable interviews on this journey was with Denis Diderot, another man of letters who was greatly interested in music. Diderot not only discussed and praised the 'plan' of Burney's *History*, but presented him with 'a great heap of MSS.', containing his own speculations on such topics as ancient music, instructing Burney to destroy them if they were useless. Burney, who had admired Diderot ever since he had begun reading the *Encyclopédie* in Norfolk, was greatly flattered by this gift, and, in his printed journal, assured his readers that 'notwithstanding such a legal transfer, I shall look upon myself as accountable for these papers, not only to M. Diderot, but to the public'.[2] In spite of the anxiety of Diderot scholars to trace these papers, it is no easier to discover what became of them than to see what use Burney ever found for them: in the four volumes of the *History of Music* there are only two references to Diderot's 'MS. Reflex'.[3] It has apparently escaped previous notice, however, that part of the article on Diderot in Rees's *Cyclopaedia* (vol. xi), clearly contributed by Burney, contains the following statement:

During the musical reform that was attempting in France, he made remarks and reflections on the subject, sufficient to fill a 4to. vol. which still remains in manuscript, and in the hands of the writer of this article, to whom he presented them more than thirty years ago, but little use has been made of these remarks hitherto; yet in the course of drawing up the musical articles for the present Cyclopaedia, they will not be forgotten.

In 1802, therefore, Burney still possessed Diderot's manuscript and, although he hardly seems to have made much use of its contents in his later articles in the *Cyclopaedia*, it would almost certainly remain in his papers at his death. In any case, although Burney was never to make great use of Diderot's flattering

[1] *Tours*, i. 313–15.   [2] Ibid. 316.
[3] *Hist. Mus.* iii. 277 n., iv. 242 n.

gift, the gesture was an enormous encouragement to him at the time and cheered him over the last uncomfortable stage of his journey back to England in December. A storm delayed his crossing to Dover for five days, but on Christmas Eve he re-joined his family in the new Burney home in Queen's Square (the removal having taken place during his travels), after an absence of more than six months, 'heartily glad to find myself in old England again'.[1]

II

The daily journal which Burney kept during his travels reveals that the heroic terms in which his daughter later described his return in December 1770 are almost justified:

With all the soaring feelings of the first sun-beams of hope that irradiate from a bright, though distant glimpse of renown; untamed by difficulties, superior to fatigue, and springing over the hydra-headed monsters of impediment that every where jutted forth their thwarting obstacles to his enterprize, Dr. Burney came back to his country, his friends, his business, and his pursuits, with the vigour of the first youth in spirits, expectations, and activity.[2]

The journal is valuable, however, not merely because it con-firms her opinion of his ardent ambition and indefatigability, but because it brings his personality into a sudden focus which is not available at any earlier point in his career and which Fanny herself, in her long, verbose, and idealized biography of her father, was never to achieve.

During his strenuous travels Burney had by no means con-fined his interests to music. As his friend Samuel Crisp knew well, he was eager 'to grasp at every thing',[3] and from the first day of his journey, when he speculated on the geological rela-tion of England to the Continent, he had contrived to fit in with his exhausting musical investigations the incidental indulgence of such diverse interests as painting, sculpture, linguistics, astronomy, electricity, volcanoes, agriculture, and natural history. This endless curiosity was matched by his astounding

---

[1] CB to Crisp, 19–24 Dec. 1770 (Osborn). The postscript to this letter (which was begun at Calais) is dated on the evening of CB's return to London, 'Monday Night', i.e. 24 December. This clarifies the confusion in dating in the journal noted by Scholes, *Tours*, i. 318 n.

[2] *Mem.* i. 222.   [3] Crisp to CB, 18 May 1770 (Osborn).

energy, of which enough, perhaps, has been said already. His journal itself, by its stylistic charm, its vivid observation, and its good-natured and self-derisive humour, fully communicates the personality of the music-teacher who had managed so quickly to win the respect and friendship of the numerous scholars, *dilettanti*, men of letters, officials, travellers, and noblemen whom he encountered, most of whom entertained and assisted him with what might otherwise appear remarkable willingness. Burney's pride in the social success of his travels almost equalled his satisfaction with the books and manuscripts which he had bought or transcribed. His journal, indeed, reveals both sides of this social sensitivity: on the one hand, his responsiveness to kindness and voluntary assistance and his almost childish delight in 'condescension' from the nobility; and, on the other, his immediate resentment of any suspected coldness. The slightly absurd alternation of these reactions can be seen clearly, for example, in his relations with Sir Horace Mann, the British envoy at Florence, who seemed at first to snub Burney, and later was particularly civil to him.[1]

If Burney returned to London in triumph, as Fanny assures us, he was also completely exhausted and in poor health. He permitted himself, however, no relaxation. Some of the musical materials which he had obtained on his journey were so valuable that he had refused to be parted from them: 'the Choicest of my MSS & drawings of ancient Instruments . . . I am determined shall sink or swim with me', he had told Crisp from Calais. Inevitably, however, many of the books, manuscripts, and drawings he had acquired had been dispatched periodically to England as they accumulated, and on his return he found that they were still 'very much dispersed'. There was no hope, there-fore, of settling immediately to the writing of the *History of Music*; and in any case, while stormbound in Calais, he had already been contemplating another publication, as he had told Crisp: 'I long very much to tell you my adventures, viva voce, as well as to communicate to you my discoveries & to shew you my Journal, in order to avail myself of your Counsel as to the best manner of making them turn to some account in an honourable as well as profitable way.'[2]

---

[1] *Tours*, i. 176, 186, 191.
[2] CB to Crisp, 19–24 Dec. 1770 (Osborn).

Although the idea of publishing his journal had not been mentioned before his departure for Italy, it had been fully conceived by the time he reached Naples in mid-October 1770, when he had described it in a letter to David Garrick: 'As my general history must be a work of time, I intend publishing, as soon as I get home, in a pamphlet, or small volume, an account of the present state of music in France and Italy, in which I shall describe, according to my judgement and feelings, the merits of the several compositions and performers I have heard in travelling through those countries.'[1]

Early in 1771 Burney began to consider this plan in earnest. Although he feared 'the imputation of puffing, a Vice of wch authors are so frequently Guilty', he found it hard to resist the urge to inform the musical world, in an interim report on his progress with the *History of Music*, of the great success of his continental researches and interviews. Moreover, in the sense that he had carefully kept his daily journal up to date, the book was already written: the only problem was how much of it to publish. Naturally he consulted the friends whose opinion on such a matter he most respected, including Garrick, Mason, who was in London for the winter, Lord Holdernesse, his early patron, and John Hawkesworth.[2]

These friends were unanimous in assuring Burney that 'France and Italy had been so often described, that there was nothing new to tell', with the possible exception of his observations on the musical life of these nations, to which previous travellers had paid little attention. This advice was by no means unreasonable, for travel books at this period were pouring from the press and the reviewers were already showing signs of impatience. A few months later, for example, a writer in the *Critical Review* declared: 'So many authors, of late years, have published their travels into France and Italy, that works of this kind are come to be regarded as a stale commodity among the booksellers.'[3] In 1778 Samuel Johnson told Boswell, who was thinking of publishing an account of his travels in Europe: 'I give you my opinion, that you would lessen yourself by it. What can you tell of countries so well known as those

---

[1] CB to Garrick, 17 Oct. 1770, *Private Corresp. of Garrick*, i. 403–5.
[2] *Tours*, i. xxix; *ED*, i. 116; J. W. Draper, *William Mason*, p. 78.
[3] *Critical Review*, xxxii (1771), 143.

upon the continent of Europe, which you have visited? . . .
most modern travellers in Europe who have published their
travels, have been laughed at: I would not have you added to
the number. The world is now not contented to be merely
entertained by a traveller's narrative; they want to learn something.'[1] Burney received similar advice from his friends, to the
effect that 'I had better adhere to my primitive motive for
travelling in search of *Music*, which would be a new subject, and
which, they were pleased to say, I had treated in such a way as
would manifest my abilities to write its History'.[2] He therefore
decided to publish only a version of his journal from which all
non-musical narrative and observations were omitted.

After work on the preparation of the text of his book had
begun, Burney retired to the country to stay with the friend of
his years with Fulke Greville, Samuel Crisp, with whom he had
re-established contact in 1764, and who now lived in somewhat
cynical retirement from the world in lodgings in an almost
inaccessible house at Chessington in Surrey. Here, until Crisp's
death in 1783, Burney was frequently to seek the peace and
solitude that his literary labours demanded.[3] In the letter he had
written to Crisp from Calais, Burney had expressed a desire to
have his friend's opinion of his journal, and Crisp now read it
through. To Burney's embarrassment, Crisp disagreed completely and strongly with his other advisers. As he recalled many
years later, he was 'chidden very severely by . . . Mr Crisp, a
very competent judge of Music and all the fine arts of Italy,
where he had resided 5 years, and who, fond as he was of the
Music of that country, condemned the abridgement of my
journal, and assured me that my miscellaneous observations
had entertained him far more than the musical'.[4] It was now
too late, however, for Burney to alter his plans, and we may
suspect that he valued the opinion of Garrick, Mason, and
Lord Holdernesse more than that of Crisp, who for some years
had been out of immediate contact with the literary world, and
who was obliged, for the time being at least, to swallow his
protests at Burney's amputation of his journal.[5]

[1] Hill–Powell, iii. 300–1.   [2] *Tours*, i. xxix.
[3] *Frag. Mem.* (Berg).   [4] *Tours*, i. xxx.
[5] It should be explained at this point that CB later transcribed the omitted portions of his journal as part of his 'Memoirs'; and that, in Dr. Scholes' recent edition
of the *Tours*, the published and unpublished journals are conflated. In the preceding

Having at last sent his book to press, Burney, who had hardly rested since his return to England, collapsed in February 1771, and was confined to bed for some weeks. They were not weeks, however, that a man of his temperament could waste. Recently, William Bewley had playfully referred to him as 'the Man who has leave to write to Rousseau', adding that, 'This last *trait* gives me such an idea of your powers, that I shall find my vanity gratifyed in corresponding with you'.[1] Although Bewley was basically teasing him, Burney was indeed anxious to maintain a correspondence with the eminent men whom he had met in Paris. Accordingly, in March 1771, he wrote to Guy, the book-seller who had engineered his interview with Rousseau, en-closing a copy of *The Cunning Man*, together with other music, for the author of the original version. He was obliged to dictate the letter to one of his daughters since 'Il y a quelque Tems que j'ai eté reduit a l'Etat de garder le Lit par une Maladie severe & obstiné.'[2]

An undated draft of a letter to Diderot can also be ascribed to March 1771, for Burney once more employed an amanuensis and again mentioned his 'severe & obstinate Indisposition'. Clearly eager to enter into a regular correspondence, Burney told Diderot of the forthcoming publication of his journal and began the polite apologies, which he was to make to all his French friends, for the severe and derisive remarks on French music and musical taste in his book, in spite of the fact that all these 'enlightened' men had themselves condemned it during the controversy over French and Italian music some twenty years earlier.[3] Burney also told Diderot that, his ridicule of French taste notwithstanding, he planned to translate his book into French and hoped 'to submit [it] to y^r Correction'.[4]

By the third week of April, *The Present State of Music in France*

---

summary of CB's journey both portions were drawn upon. Two manuscripts of the omitted material exist (Osborn and B.M. Add. MS. 35112). About half the Osborn MS. is in the hand of an amanuensis. Also in the Osborn Collection are four pages of the journal transcribed in FB's hand, the text of which differs at points from the other published and unpublished versions. It is presumably an early transcript of part of CB's original journal.

[1] Bewley to CB, 6 Feb. 1771 (Osborn).

[2] CB to Guy, March 1771, draft, R. A. Leigh, 'Les Amitiés françaises du Dr Burney', *Revue de littérature comparée*, xxv (1951), 172–3.

[3] For Scholes's account of this controversy, see *Tours*, i. 322–6.

[4] CB to Diderot [March 1771], draft (Osborn).

*and Italy: Or, The Journal of a Tour through those Countries, under-
taken to collect Materials for a General History of Music. By Charles
Burney, Mus.D.* was in proof and William Bewley had agreed to
look over the sheets.[1] On 8 May Fanny was able to record in her
diary that 'My father's book . . . made its appearance in the
world the 3rd of this month', adding that 'Last Sunday was the
first day for some time past, that my father has favoured us with
his company in a sociable stile, having been so exceedingly
occupied by writing in those few hours he spends at home, that
he really seemed lost to his family; and the comfort of his society
and conversation are [now] almost as new as grateful to us'.[2]

Many of the friends who, in one way or another, had helped
Burney with his journey or his book received complimentary
copies of the *Italian Tour* (his own short title) and its publication
provided an excuse for further correspondence with his French
friends. Guy had already replied in April to his first letter and
had enclosed a note from Rousseau himself, which thanked
Burney for *The Cunning Man* and made some polite, if slightly
reserved, remarks upon it: 'Je ne vous parlerai pas des change-
mens que vous avez jugé àpropos d'y faire. Vous avez consulté,
sans doute, le goût de votre nation; il n'y a rien à dire à cela.'
Rousseau had added, however, some compliments about
Burney's visit which explain his great pride in this letter to the
end of his life.[3]

Guy's covering letter was probably rather more disturbing,
for he had made a request to Burney which threatened to involve him in a matter which had been one of the causes of
bitter contention during the quarrel between Rousseau and
David Hume in 1766 and 1767. George III had granted
Rousseau a generous pension, which, after much equivocation,
he had eventually declined. By 1770, when Rousseau was
reduced to earning a living by copying music, his friends, of
whom Guy was obviously one, were attempting to persuade
him to retract his objections and to accept the pension once
more. Rousseau's published correspondence makes it clear that

[1] Bewley to CB, 24 Apr. 1771 (Osborn).
[2] *ED*, i. 115–16.
[3] *Mem.* i. 257–8; *Corresp. générale de J.-J. Rousseau*, ed. Th. Dufour, 1924–34,
xx. 111. Leigh, *loc. cit.*, dates this letter mid-March, but Guy's covering letter,
dated 8 Apr. 1771, mentions that he has just received it from Rousseau. See
post, pp. 436–7.

he greatly resented his friends' efforts on his behalf;[1] but, if
Guy's letter to Burney told the whole truth, which must seem
unlikely in the circumstances, Rousseau had eventually agreed
early in 1771 to ask for a renewal of the Royal Pension:

voicy le fait: Sa Majesté, le Roy d'angleterre, a Eu la bonté de faire
une pension de Cent Guinées à M. Rousseau. En consequence M.
Rousseau en a Ecrit au Ministre qui a le Departement de ces Sortes
d'affaires, aparamment ou pour lui en faire des remercimens Sur la
bonté du Prince, ou Sur toute autre chose, c'est ce que je ne sçai pas.
Mais ce que je sçai bien que M. Rousseau n'ayant pas Eu de réponse
à cette Lettre aprehende qu'il n'y ait quelque chose qui ait deplu au
Ministre, et c'est le Silence de ce Ministre qui empeche M. Rous⟨seau⟩
a accepter la pension.

Guy went on to ask Burney to find out whether the Minister
in question had ever received Rousseau's letter:

et S'il étoit possible l'on peut determiner ce Seigneur a lui Ecrire un
mot de réponse, je Suis bien persuadé que M. Rousseau accepteroit
alors la pension: d'autant qu'un homme est toujours très honoré de
recevoir les Biensfaits d'une teste couronée.

Voyez, Monsieur, Si vous pouviez lui rendre ce Service, il Seroit
d'autant plus Beau que je vous jure il ignore que je vous enprie, et
qu'il ignore mon dessein: Si la chose réussit je le lui aprendrai alors.[2]

The whole affair was cloaked in mystery, as Burney must
have realized. Guy did not know precisely what or to whom
Rousseau had written and was obviously acting behind his back
in just the way that had infuriated him in the previous autumn.
Burney replied to Guy in May 1771, enclosing a letter and a
copy of his *Italian Tour* for Rousseau himself. He had to explain
that his efforts to clarify the situation over Rousseau's pension
had been fruitless: 'c'est en vain que j'ai fait toute la perquisi-
tion possible, de trouver le nom du Ministre à qui la Lettre
dont il s'agit fut addressée. Mais il y a arrive tant de Change-
ment de Tems en Tems dans notre Ministree que sans le date de
la Lettre ou le nom de la personne, c'est impossible de tirer au
Claire cette affaire.' If Guy could obtain more precise information from Rousseau about the letter Burney would try again,
but he advised that a fresh approach should be made to Lord

---

[1] *Corresp. générale de J.-J. Rousseau*, xx. 13–14, 27–28; cf. *Walpole Corresp.* iv. 434.
[2] Guy to CB, 8 Apr. 1771 (Osborn).

North. In any case he would gladly do everything in his power to help Rousseau: 'il n'y a rien au monde qui me serois plus de plaisir que de rendre quelque Service a ce grand Homme. Mais il faut Menager sa delicatesse, et vous pouvez contre sur Moi que je tacherai avec soins d'agir en telle sorte que je ne la blesserai pas'.

The British Government eventually offered Rousseau the arrears of his pension, but he flatly refused to accept the money, a fact which makes Guy's account of the situation, however well-meaning, all the more dubious.[1] If Burney had played any further part in this plot by Rousseau's friends, there is no evidence to document it. Similarly although he tried to prolong his correspondence with Rousseau himself in the letter which accompanied his *Italian Tour*, by asking him to point out 'mes defauts et les Erreurs naturels d'un Voyageur dans un pais etranger qui ne dois pas se fier de ses propres sens', Burney apparently received no reply for several years.[2]

These letters to Guy and Rousseau were probably written late in May 1771, when Burney told Crisp, 'I have had upon my hands no less than 8 or 9 Letters for Paris', which were to accompany complimentary copies of his book.[3] Four other recipients were Monnet, d'Holbach, Suard, and Diderot, and in his letters to them Burney once more apologized for his condemnation of French music, whilst expressing his confidence of their agreement with him and requesting their further assistance when they should feel so inclined.[4] The letter to Diderot mentioned that he had not had the 'Health & Leisure to attend to a Translation of my Book into French', and the idea never reappeared. From Diderot Burney obtained rather more response than from Rousseau, and they corresponded on musical subjects at least until the end of the year. Burney in fact spent part of June 1771 in helping François Philidor, a celebrated composer and chess-player, who had brought him a letter of introduction from Diderot, with a new English translation of his book on chess, *Analyse du Jeu des Echecs*; and

---

[1] Louis J. Courtois, *Chronologie critique de la Vie et des Œuvres de J.-J. Rousseau*, (*Annals de la Société J.-J. Rousseau* xv), Geneva, 1923, pp. 191, 196, 213, 217.

[2] CB to Guy and Rousseau, May 1771, drafts (Osborn). See *post*, pp. 183–4.

[3] CB to Crisp, 31 May 1771 (Osborn).

[4] CB to d'Holbach, to Suard, and to Diderot, 23, 24, and 27 May 1771, copies (Berg); Monnet to CB, 28 July 1771 (Osborn).

later in the summer he helped to choose a new piano for Diderot.[1]

In England, meanwhile, Burney's _Italian Tour_ had met with a highly favourable reception. By 3 June 1771 Fanny could record in her diary that 'My dear father has gained more honour by his book, than I dared flatter myself would have attended it. We hear daily of new readers and approvers'.[2] As late as the following April she was noting that the book was still finding an enthusiastic audience, although Burney was not yet ready to enjoy his success:

His book flourishes with praise, and we hear almost daily of new readers and admirers, and if he had time and inclination for it he might daily increase his acquaintance among the learned and the great. But his time is terribly occupied, and his inclinations lead to retirement and quiet. If his business did not draw him into the world by necessity, I believe he would live almost wholly with his family [and books].[3]

Elsewhere Fanny stated that, after the publication of his book, Burney received many 'letters the most flattering, from the deepest theorists of the science, and the best judges of the practice of the art of music'.[4] William Mason wrote to congratulate him, feeling sure that the journal would 'please generally in the form you have now put it', and telling Burney that Sir James Gray, the diplomatist and antiquary, who had himself been British minister at Venice, was anxious to meet the Italian traveller.[5] The Rev. Montagu North, Prebendary of Windsor, wrote offering any assistance to Burney's historical labours in his power;[6] and Dr. Joseph Warton, headmaster of Winchester, who had never met him, wrote instead to Garrick, saying that he had found the _Italian Tour_ 'most entertaining' and sending for Burney the 'Title & Contents of an old Treatise of Music', which he had discovered in the School Library.[7]

Burney was particularly delighted that such signs of interest in his book should come from a distinguished poet and critic,

[1] Diderot to CB, 18 Aug. 1771; CB to Diderot, 10 Oct. 1771; Diderot to CB, 29 Oct. 1771 (Leigh, op. cit., pp. 178–88; CB inscribed the last, 'answered Nov[r] 17, 1771'); and Diderot to CB. 26 Sept. 1771 (Osborn); _ED_, i. 123.
[2] _ED_, i. 120–1.   [3] Ibid. 174.   [4] _Mem._ i. 226.
[5] Mason to CB, 9 May 1771 (Osborn).
[6] North to CB, 31 May 1771 (Osborn).
[7] Warton to Garrick, 30 July 1771 (Osborn).

for Warton's voluntary assistance encouraged him in his ambition of writing a *History of Music* which would interest not only musicians and antiquarians. In his reply to Warton he therefore requested further historical information if, 'in the course of your extensive reading & still more deep & refined Thinking anything sh^d occur relative to my Subject': 'the work I have dared to attempt is so intimately connected with an Art wch you have so long & so happily exercised, that it is impossible to give a Hist^y of Music wch will not necessarily include a Hist^y of Poetry'.[1]

Yet although Burney valued the approval of his friends and of other scholars, he was also anxious that his *Italian Tour* should reach the general reader, not merely to help to pay for some of the expenses of his journey and of the book's publication, but also to interest potential subscribers in the *History*. The *Italian Tour* was at once a report on his progress and a display of his credentials, both as a historian and as a writer. As Burney realized all too well, reviews of his book in the monthly periodicals could have a decisive effect on the public interest in his great undertaking. Some reviews were, of course, less important than others. The first to appear, in the *Gentleman's Magazine* for May 1771, consisted largely of direct extracts from the book. The reviewer, who evidently knew Burney, did, however, emphasize the author's claims to be a historian of music, assuring the public that his 'ability in his profession is universally acknowledged; and his proficiency in literature is well known to all who are acquainted with him, otherwise than as a teacher of music'. Readers could expect both 'knowledge and entertainment' from a man who had so assiduously collected materials and established correspondences with so many learned foreigners.[2] In the same month the *London Magazine* gave Burney similar approval.[3]

The influence exerted by such short notices was not, however, comparable to that of the *Monthly* and *Critical Reviews*, a fact which Burney had not failed to consider. In February 1771 William Bewley had written to Burney inquiring after the progress of the *Opus magnum* (the *History of Music*) and adding, 'I apprehend, & lament, that I can be of little service to you: but

[1] CB to Warton [12 Aug. 1771], draft (Osborn); printed by J. Wooll, *Biographical Memoirs of Joseph Warton*, 1806, pp. 382–5.   [2] xli. 222–4.   [3] xl. 272–4.

if you could put me to any use, I should be happy'.[1] Burney's
reply evidently hinted that Bewley could indeed be of considerable service by reviewing the *Italian Tour* in the *Monthly Review*.
By 1771 Bewley had been a regular scientific reviewer for this
magazine for some four years; and although he had not yet met
Ralph Griffiths, he was well aware of the principles which the
editor laid down and which have been summarized as an
attempt 'to maintain a high standard of honesty himself, and to
ensure impartiality in the review. . . . He insisted that members
of his staff should not use their opportunities to help their
friends or attack their enemies'.[2]

A man of considerable integrity, Bewley instinctively supported these principles. In spite of his original and ingenious
scientific experiments, he himself was never to publish a book;
and from his obscure village in Norfolk, he considered that his
position on Griffiths's staff, which had come to him in middle
age, was the most satisfying and responsible role he was ever
destined to play. The anxiety which his friendship with Burney
caused him during the 1770's can only be understood in the light
of his deep and sincere desire to respect the much maligned
profession in which he invested so much of his own intelligence
and, in turn, to merit that respect by his own practice.

Bewley was not, however, surprised by Burney's suggestion
that he review the *Italian Tour*, for, as he told his friend in
April 1771, 'I have . . . long been communing with myself on
some casuistical niceties, or scrupulosities, quite habitual to me
in the exercise of my new profession. . . .' But eventually he had
decided 'in favour of common sense', and knowing that Griffiths
would be surprised by a request for a book on music from his
chief scientific and medical reviewer, he wrote to his editor, as
he told Burney, 'owning frankly at the same time that I was a
friend of your's; but that I was prompted to undertake the
office of your Critic solely with a view "to keep you out of
negligent or still more incompetent hands than my own";—
adding however "that if—which I did not think very likely—I
should find that I could not honestly—nay warmly—commend
the work, I should give him early notice to look out for another
Critic".' Although a refusal from Griffiths would amount to an

---

[1] Bewley to CB, 6 Feb. 1771 (Osborn).
[2] B. C. Nangle, *Monthly Review: First Series*, p. ix.

insult to his integrity, Bewley admitted that, in his heart, he would 'be obliged to commend his caution'; and he warned Burney that, in the circumstances, his desire to remain impartial would, if anything, inhibit his praise of his friend's book: 'Were you anonymous, & I your Critic, & unacquainted with the Author, I should express my sentiments of any thing laudable in your work much more warmly, than I now shall, *loaded.* . . .'[1] Ralph Griffiths, who apparently did not enforce his editorial principles quite as rigidly as Nangle has suggested, and who was perhaps disarmed in any case by Bewley's openness, soon sent him what he described as 'Dr Burney's *very entertaining* book'; and after this 'broad hint of *Master's*', Bewley wrote his review in better spirits, although he continued to warn Burney that his 'critical microscope' would be searching for faults as if the *Italian Tour* were by anyone but his closest friend.[2]

Fortunately Bewley found that he could sincerely admire 'the spirit & intelligence' of the book and he began to write his review in May, although the first part of it did not appear until September, and the second was further delayed until November 1771.[3] Although he was generally more conscientious and entertaining than his colleagues, Bewley's technique as a reviewer is not untypical of the *Monthly Review*. He began with a full and careful statement of the purpose of Burney's journey and then accompanied the traveller in some detail along his route. The review is characterized by the judicious and restrained approval which Bewley had warned his friend to expect; and, as if anxious to find something to criticize in order to prove his impartiality, he devoted the conclusion of the first article to a typically earnest defence of the integrity and discrimination of reviewers, in spite of their occasional fallibility, as a protest against some disparaging remarks on the profession which Burney had made to Voltaire.[4] The second article in November concluded, however, with a warm recommendation of his friend to the public as a future historian of music, the *Italian Tour* having fully demonstrated that he possessed all the requisites 'to the proper execution of an undertaking, which undoubtedly demands the

---

[1] Bewley to CB, 24 Apr. 1771 (Osborn).
[2] Bewley to CB, 18 May 1771 (Osborn).
[3] Bewley to CB, 26 Oct. 1771 (Osborn); *Monthly Review*, xlv (1771), 161–70, 337–44.
[4] Cf. *Tours*, i. 44; and see *ante*, p. 88.

united talents and acquirements of the scholar, the man of science, and the practical musician'.

Thus, without sacrificing his integrity, Bewley fulfilled his promise to Burney in the preceding May that 'the journal of a certain late itinerant Doctor of Music will be very handsomely received in one, at least of the two courts of critical inquisition established in these kingdoms'. Unknown to Bewley, however, Burney had already done his best to take care of the other 'court of inquisition'. The *Critical Review*, in June and July 1771, gave the *Italian Tour* even more space than Bewley, although all but four of these twenty-seven pages consist of simple extracts from the book.[1] The first article began favourably enough by making what was, at the time, an important point for Burney, whose growing ambition was to bridge in an unprecedented manner the considerable gulf that separated the musician from the world of polite letters. Burney, the reviewer assured the public, was by no means 'confined within the limits of his own profession': 'A commerce with the refined and enlightened part of the world are no less visible in the course of the work; the stile and manner in which he has treated his subject sufficiently shew it.'

Elsewhere, however, the reviewer voiced disapproval. He complained that Burney's decision to discuss only musical matters 'has in general, perhaps, been rather too strictly adhered to', for he had enjoyed 'some few accounts and observations of a less dry, and a more entertaining nature', which had survived in the published journal, and which he found so interesting 'as to make us wish for more'. The review concluded in July with general commendation of the book and of Burney's fitness for his great undertaking, but added a lengthy and severe protest against his 'bitterness and invective against the French', which the reviewer had been disappointed to discover in a writer who was proposing 'to give us a fair and impartial account of the music of all nations' in his *History*.

The first of these two complaints has a familiar ring: only one of Burney's friends had vigorously urged him to publish the whole of his journal and to intersperse his musical remarks with miscellaneous observations. The suspicion that Samuel Crisp had some connexion with this review seemed to justify an at-

[1] xxxi. 421–32; xxxii. 1–15.

tempt to read a passage in a letter from Burney to Crisp, written
not long before the first article was published, which Fanny
d'Arblay had thought fit to delete very firmly. (Some of her
deletions in her father's letters, in black ink, are beyond recovery, having defied all attempts to read them with the aid of
modern photographic devices. Other passages, such as that
under consideration here, can be read at the rate of about three
lines an hour with the aid of a magnifying glass, although it
would take a lifetime to decipher all of them, and the majority
turn out to concern only trivial family matters or such topics as
Burney's laundry.) Burney's letter to Crisp of 31 May 1771,
however, reveals that he had indeed contrived to arrange that
his friend should write the articles on his book for the *Critical
Review*.

When he wrote to Crisp Burney had seen the review in
manuscript and was troubled by two aspects of it. The first was
'the Expediency of such long Extracts—I feared like you that
they may either be too long for the Review or too much satisfy
the reader to make him inclined to purchase the Work'. This
matter, however, Burney was prepared to leave to the judgement of Archibald Hamilton, the publisher of the *Critical
Review*. There was, however, and not surprisingly, 'another
thing I believe it will be prudent to soften—the attack upon *my*
attack on Fr. music is perhaps a little too strongly urged, in
accusing me of *Injustice* & *prejudice*, two terrible Qualities in a
Historian! which it may even be dangerous to hint at—again—
my *Enthusiasm* in favour of *Italian Music*, at wch the Critique ⟨?⟩
hits a little too hard & will certainly raise the alarm among the
English musicians.' One English musician, indeed, had already
objected to the *Italian Tour* on these grounds, this dissonant
voice in the general chorus of praise belonging curiously enough
to Thomas Arne, who, 'hurt at not being mentioned' in his
former apprentice's book, had written to complain about this
omission, although his letter was otherwise 'full of Flomery as to
Manner of Writing &c'. Burney claimed, with some justification, that Arne's music was hardly relevant to an account of the
art in France and Italy: 'a Russian or Hottentot Musician has
equal right to complain of being neglected'. Otherwise he could
say, 'I hear Nothing but praise—& all agree in finding my
nonsense *Entertaining*.—this will probably sell the Book & get

Subscribers'. Understandably, therefore, Burney was anxious
that the generous reception that his book was receiving should
not be marred by the frank and almost severe public criticism
of one of his oldest friends. Crisp may have softened his review
before it was printed, but the tone of disapproval remains quite
firm; and it is possible that, still harbouring resentment at the
rejection of his advice about the content of the book, he refused
to make any alteration.

A further long deletion by Fanny in the same letter conceals
another aspect of the excitability which tended to affect her
father during the publication of his books. In this case his indignation was directed at his printers, and it was presumably
only his language which at this point provoked her censorship:
'I have found 2 or 3 Cursed typographi⟨cal⟩ blunders in things
that I had marked & Correc⟨ted⟩ in the press, which were
overlooked by the Corrector, and be d— to him. . . . why the
devil does not the public make haste in buying up this cursed
first Edit. in order to get a 2ᵈ more Correct?' Burney had, however, no real cause for complaint. Bewley and Crisp, while
contriving to preserve their integrity, had not let him down in
their reviews, and the public had followed their advice by welcoming the potential historian of music. The first edition of the
Italian Tour was sold out by 1773.[1]

Meanwhile the books, manuscripts, and drawings which he
had acquired in France and Italy had arrived and Burney was
ready to face the colossal task he had undertaken. Briefly he
sketched out for Crisp the plan he intended to follow, which
would trace music from its earliest known history among the
Hebrews, Greeks, and Romans, through 'our Monkish Writers'
on medieval music, up to 1600, after which date he was confident that 'Materials will not be wanting'.[2] During the summer
he printed, as a supplement to his *Italian Tour*, a pamphlet
entitled *A Letter from Signor Tartini . . . published as an important
lesson to performers on the Violin*, an eight-page translation of the
Italian text, which was also given.[3] This short work was no
distraction, however, from his main purpose, and later in the

---

[1] See *post*, pp. 130–1.

[2] CB to Crisp, 31 May 1771 (Osborn).

[3] Another result of CB's Italian journey was the publication, also in 1771, of a
collection of music 'annually sung in the Pope's Chapel during Passion Week'. See
GDB, ii. 347.

summer he was at last at work on the mass of materials he had
collected, at his wife's house at King's Lynn.

Although he can hardly have conceived that he would not
complete his *History of Music* for eighteen years, Burney permitted himself no illusions about the magnitude of his undertaking; nor, as the final paragraph of his *Italian Tour* had made
clear, did he wish the public to underestimate the task that he
had set himself, in spite of the success of his researches on the
Continent:

. . . with all these requisites, respect for the public, for the art about
which I write, and even for myself, will prevent precipitate publication: a history of the kind I propose, must inevitably be a work of
time; for after consulting the most scarce and valuable books and
MSS. and conferring with the most eminent artists and theorists; to
select, digest, and consolidate materials so various and diffused, will
not only require leisure and labour, but such a patient perseverance,
as little less than the zeal of enthusiasm can inspire. It is not the
history of an art in its infant state, whose parents are still living, that
I have ventured to undertake; but one coeval with the world; one
whose high antiquity renders its origin as doubtful as the formation
of language, or the first articulations of the human voice.[1]

III

Burney's caution about the rate of progress he could be
expected to maintain was justified, for the *History* did not
advance rapidly. Whilst he was in Norfolk in the summer of
1771 he paid a visit to his old patron Lord Orford at Houghton,
and met there John Montagu, fourth Earl of Sandwich (1718–
92), the notorious First Lord of the Admiralty. As Captain
James Cook had returned from his celebrated voyage round the
world earlier in the year, Sandwich had all the relevant papers
in his possession and was looking for a man of letters to put them
into a readable form. Burney took the opportunity to recommend his friend John Hawkesworth for the task and Sandwich
accepted the suggestion. This act of recommendation is attributed in the *Dictionary of National Biography* to David Garrick
on the strength of a remark in Prior's *Life of Malone* (1860),[2] but
Fanny d'Arblay's account of her father's part in obtaining the
commission for Hawkesworth would seem to be decisive; and

[1] *Tours*, i. 321.   [2] p. 441.

to this evidence can now be added a statement in a letter from Bewley in October 1771, 'You give me sincere pleasure in informing me of Dʳ H.'s appointment, in conseqᵉ of your lucky visit & recommendation of him at Houghton'.[1] Burney must have met Sandwich, who was a prominent figure in London musical life, before 1771, but it was perhaps a sign of his growing reputation that, not long after their meeting at Houghton, Sandwich invited Burney to Hinchingbrook for a few days to meet Captain Cook and Joseph Banks. Work on the *History* had to give way to so flattering an invitation, one result of which was that Burney's eldest son James accompanied Cook on his second voyage of discovery in 1772.[2]

By October 1771 the seeds of another distraction had been sown, as Fanny recorded in her diary: 'My father is at present most diligently studying German. He has an unquenchable thirst of knowledge; and would, if he had time, I believe, be the first linguist in England.'[3] In the same month Bewley wrote to congratulate him 'on the specimens you give me of your Teutonic Literature'.[4] It was not merely 'thirst of knowledge', however, which led Burney to the study of German, for he had soon discovered that he could not proceed with his *History* until he could read various learned works by German writers. If he had ever thought of evading this task, a letter which he received in August 1771, from Christoph Daniel Ebeling (1741?–1817), Master and Supervisor of the Commercial Academy of Hamburg, had made it into a duty. Ebeling, who had read Burney's *Italian Tour* and was planning to translate it into German, was anxious for patriotic reasons that the music of his own nation should receive equal attention in the *History*, and he wrote to advise Burney on the easiest ways of obtaining examples of German music and musical scholarship.[5] Burney's reply thanked Ebeling for offering to send him certain books, and assured him that 'I shall not rest until I am able to Read many of the Books you Mention'.[6]

Burney had, in fact, already commissioned Baron d'Holbach,

[1] Bewley to CB, 23 Oct. 1771 (Osborn); *Mem.* i. 267–9, 274–9; *ED*, i. 139–40.
[2] *Frag. Mem.* (Osborn); *ED*, i. 138; *GDB*, i. 193.
[3] *ED*, i. 140.
[4] Bewley to CB, 26 Oct. 1771 (Osborn).
[5] Ebeling to CB, 20 Aug. 1771, *GDB*, i. 199–201.
[6] CB to Ebeling, Nov. 1771, *GDB*, i. 201–3.

one of his Parisian friends, to procure certain German books for
him; but, although some of them were on the way to London
by December 1771, others had proved to be unobtainable or
were available only in German libraries.[1] This was not a
situation to which a man of Burney's thoroughness could easily
resign himself, for the books which Ebeling and d'Holbach had
been able to provide were 'so far from repressing my Curiosity
after the Musical Productions of the Germans that they excite a
fresh desire to see & hear more'.[2] The first suggestion that
Burney might make a second musical journey came in May
1772, when Sir William Hamilton, who had been so hospitable
to him at Naples, mentioned during a visit to Queen's Square
that he would be returning to Italy through Germany, whereupon Burney impulsively declared that he also might visit that
country in the course of the summer. Fanny perceptively noted
in her diary that his 'insatiable rage of adding to the materials
for his History' made the journey almost a certainty.[3] Although
Burney could not accept Hamilton's suggestion that they travel
together, he had made up his mind to visit Germany and the
Netherlands by the end of the month, when Fanny dutifully
commented, 'If the most indefatigable pains and industry will
render his work worthy of approbation, it will meet with the
greatest.'[4]

Burney was only too conscious that his zealous pursuit of
musical materials would seem merely eccentric to many:
'rambling thus all over Europe after a single Art will perhaps be
thought a greater Madness than that of which the Chevalier
Quixote was guilty of in strolling only thro' the kingdoms of
Spain after a single imaginary Mistress'. However, as he
frequently assured his friends, he was not one of those scholars
who could complacently compile books from the labours of
their predecessors; and having decided on a second expedition
to the Continent, he once more did his best to facilitate his
researches in advance, asking d'Holbach for any assistance in
his power in the way of introductions at Antwerp, Vienna, and
Berlin, and proudly boasting that he had already obtained
valuable letters to 'our Ministers & Consuls in the several

---

[1] d'Holbach to CB, 15 Dec. 1771 (Osborn).
[2] CB to d'Holbach, 2 June 1772, copy (Osborn).
[3] *ED*, i. 179.   [4] Ibid. 185.

Northern Courts' from Lord Sandwich '& other Friends of my
Enterprize'.[1] The crucial call on his route, however, was to be
at Vienna, where he particularly wished to meet Johann Adolf
Hasse, the composer, and Pietro Metastasio, the poet and
librettist of innumerable operas, for 'in Writing about the
Italian opera, they will be the Heros of my General History'. A
rumour, incorrect as it transpired, that Lord Stormont, the
British Ambassador, would leave Vienna before Burney arrived
there, caused him to fear that 'admission into the Libraries, or
access to the Learned that I may wish to consult' would be
made more difficult. Accordingly he wrote a curiously fulsome
and verbose letter to Count Firmian, whom he had met at
Milan in 1770 and who, he believed, had influence in Vienna,
asking to 'be honoured by your Countenance & extensive
Influence, in facilitating my researches'.[2]

This letter, 'a formal & formidable kind of thing', as he himself called it, apparently brought no reply; and Burney was
heartened no more by the discovery that James Harris (1746–
1820), the British Minister at Berlin, another crucial city to his
purpose, was no lover of music, although he was the son of
Burney's old friend 'Hermes' Harris. In spite of Burney's protest
that 'I am no more displeased with a Man for not loving or
understanding Music, than with his not having black eyes or
being 6 Feet high', there were obviously times when music-
lovers in high positions could be of particular service.[3] Sir
James Gray, the diplomatist, to whom Burney expressed these
anxieties, managed, however, to provide him with letters to
Hasse and to the insensitive Harris; 'Hermes' Harris sent
Burney another letter of introduction to his son, as 'a testimony
of regard to a person of y^r merit'; Baretti sent from his sick-bed
a vital letter recommending Burney to the Abbate Taruffi, a
friend of both Hasse and Metastasio; and Giardini provided at
least one letter to a musician at Berlin.[4]

Equipped with these letters, the invaluable series to various
diplomats contributed by Lord Sandwich, and the inevitable
German translation of his 'plan', Burney had crossed the Chan-

---

[1] CB to d'Holbach, 2 June 1772, copy (Osborn); cf. *Tours*, II. xii.
[2] CB to Count Firmian, 22 June 1772, copy (Osborn); cf. *Tours*, i. 83–84.
[3] CB to Sir James Gray, 25 June 1772, copy (Osborn).
[4] Gray to CB, 28 June 1772; Harris to CB, 30 June 1772; Baretti to CB, 24 June
1772 (Osborn); *Tours*, ii. 85, 95, 105, 173.

nel for the fourth time by 6 July 1772. As his journal reveals, during the few days in which he remained in France he listened attentively to any examples of that nation's music, presumably to reassure himself—and Samuel Crisp—that his harsh judgements upon it in his book had been fully justified. He found little improvement, indeed, even after he crossed the border into the Netherlands. At Brussels, where he arrived on 15 July, and at Antwerp, he spent eleven days, using libraries in both cities, but passing much more of his time in churches and theatres. He soon realized that useful manuscript and printed materials were going to be much harder to find than in Italy, and the 'present state' of music offered little alternative consolation to his ears. Moreover, as he proceeded into Germany, he was outraged by the almost intolerable travelling conditions and the marked contrast between the general poverty of the common people and the luxurious establishments of the aristocracy. He was also depressed by the surprising lack of interest in his inquiries on the part of the natives and the consequent difficulty of obtaining information. Accordingly, with only brief halts at intervening cities, he travelled rapidly to Mannheim, where he arrived on 6 August. Although there was little of interest in the public library, Burney spent his time profitably at the theatre and in listening to the famous Mannheim orchestra. Similarly at Ludwigsburg, while the library was useless to his purpose, he enjoyed conversing in Latin and Italian with a learned organist and was able to indulge his scientific interests by inspecting 'a very extraordinary astronomical machine or orrery'.[1]

Nevertheless, it was not until he reached Munich on 16 August that Burney could begin to feel that his journey was being justified. In this city Louis Devisme (1720–76), the British plenipotentiary, was of the greatest assistance, notably in gaining him admittance to the Elector's library, which he found to be 'more rich in old musical authors, and in old compositions, than any one that I have yet seen in Europe'.[2] Burney also had valuable interviews with the singers Guadagni (whom he had himself once taught[3]) and Regina Mingotti. Guadagni and Devisme, moreover, arranged that Burney should be presented to the Elector and Electress Dowager of Saxony, and he was

[1] Ibid. 40.   [2] Ibid. 47.   [3] See *ante*, p. 24.

delighted by the flattering interest they displayed in his journey, and by hearing both members of the royal family perform for his benefit. His ludicrously tactful description of the Elector's unremarkable figure—'neither too fat, too lean, too tall, nor too short'—reflects his usual lenience to royalty who treated him with civility.[1]

Heartened by his reception and discoveries at Munich, Burney left for Vienna on 24 August, on a dangerous and extremely uncomfortable journey, which lasted a week, down the rivers Iser and Danube, on a great raft constructed of lashed logs, the only protection against the inclement weather available on this curious 'boat' being a small cabin. Fortunately, the two weeks which Burney passed in Vienna (30 August to 13 September) more than compensated for the discomforts and indignities of the journey, for he found interesting material in the public and Imperial libraries; was willingly assisted by Lord Stormont, who had not, after all, left Vienna; and had a series of most rewarding and heart-warming interviews with Metastasio the poet, and the composers Hasse and Gluck, as well as being able to investigate every kind of music-making the city could offer.

Since, some twenty years later, Burney was to be engaged on a biography of Metastasio, his first pious impressions of the Imperial Laureate are not without interest. Before leaving England he had been assured by 'a person of very high rank . . . that he had been five years in Vienna before he could get acquainted with Metastasio'; and from another source he had learned 'that it would be in vain for me to attempt even a sight of Metastasio, as he was totally worn out, incommunicative, and averse to society on all occasions'.[2] Fortunately Burney had gone to great lengths to equip himself with suitable introductions and was eventually taken to see the poet by Lord Stormont; and the ease with which his characteristic charm overcame Metastasio's usual reserve is significant:

The poet is lodged, as many other great poets have been before him, in a very exalted situation, up no less than four pair of stairs. Whether modern bards prefer the sublimity of this abode, on account of its being somewhat on a level with Mount Parnassus, nearer their

[1] *Tours,* ii. 50–51.
[2] Ibid. 80.

sire Apollo, or in the neighbourhood of gods in general, I shall not determine. . . .

He received us with the utmost chearfulness and good-breeding; and I was no less astonished than pleased at finding him look so well: he does not seem more than fifty years of age, though he is at least seventy-two; and for that time of life, he is the handsomest man I ever beheld. There are painted on his countenance all the genius, goodness, propriety, benevolence, and rectitude, which constantly characterise his writings. I could not keep my eyes off his face, it was so pleasing and worthy of contemplation. His conversation was of a piece with his appearance: polite, easy, and lively. We prevailed upon him to be much more communicative about music, than we expected; for, in general, he avoids entering deep into any particular subject. He set off, however, by saying, that he could furnish me with very few new lights relative to my enquiries, as he had never considered them with sufficient attention; however, in the course of our conversation he discovered himself to have a very good general knowledge both of the history and theory of music; and I was very much flattered to find his sentiments correspond with my own in many doubtful particulars.[1]

Burney would willingly and profitably have stayed longer in Vienna but, anxious to conclude his journey before winter made travelling any less bearable, he set off in mid-September for Berlin, by way of Prague, Dresden, and Leipzig. At Dresden, John Osborn, the British Envoy, was particularly helpful, gratifying Burney by introducing him to the Elector and his family. On 28 September he reached Berlin for a stay of ten days, continued his relentless notetaking on every conceivable kind of musical activity, in churches and theatres, at concerts, some of which were arranged especially for his benefit, and in the streets, and attempted to meet every singer and instrumentalist of any reputation in the city. Especially rewarding, however, were a meeting with Friedrich Marpurg, another historian of music, 'who had so long laboured in the same vineyard as myself, that he was a perfect judge of the difficulties I had to encounter';[2] and a visit to the Court of Frederick the Great at Potsdam, where he had the privilege of hearing the musical monarch himself perform three *concerti* for flute at an evening concert.

The only remaining German city of musical importance was

[1] Ibid. 101–2.   [2] Ibid. 166.

Hamburg, where Burney arrived on 9 October. Here he at last met C. D. Ebeling, with whom he had been corresponding for a year, and who now put 'all his musical curiosities' at his disposal, and ensured that the traveller did Hamburg's musical life justice. Here also Burney spent many happy hours with C. P. E. Bach, with whose compositions he was much more familiar than with those of his father, J. S. Bach, whom he considered to be merely the composer of some dry and pedantic music for the organ. The end of his journey was now near, and he hurried from Hamburg through the Low Countries, arriving at Amsterdam on 20 October. His journal concluded at Rotterdam, after brief remarks on other cities. So exhausted was he at the end of his travels, that when the ship reached Dover, Burney could not be roused, and he woke to find himself halfway back to Calais. In spite of this strange incident, he was back in London by early November 1772.[1]

IV

In November 1772, immediately after his return to England, Burney went to stay with William Bewley at Great Massingham, to consult his friend about the form in which the journal of his second musical tour should be published.[2] Partly no doubt because Germany and the Netherlands were less familiar to English travellers than France and Italy, and partly as a concession to the advice so forcefully urged by Samuel Crisp, Burney decided to include in his new book 'miscellaneous' observations on other subjects than music and a general linking narrative of his journey. For this reason, *The Present State of Music in Germany, the Netherlands, and the United Provinces*, in two volumes, was almost twice the length of the earlier book; and for the same reason, Burney did not later bother to assemble any material omitted from the printed journal.

Having suffered considerably from the primitive means of transport available to him in Germany, Burney felt it a duty to devote several pages of his new book to accounts of the various hardships he had endured, including his journey down the Danube by raft, a later journey by water which obliged him to

---

[1] *Mem.* i. 230–2. FB states that CB returned in December, but this and other details are mistaken; evidently she partly confused his return in 1770 with that in 1772.   [2] Bewley to CB, 20 Nov. 1772 (Osborn).

'nestle' in the straw for warmth, and a night spent stuck in a bog after his coach-driver had lost the way. There were other exasperated passages describing in detail 'the villainous and rascally behaviour of postmasters and postilions', such descriptions being offered to his readers 'as the account of them may put future travellers on their guard, or, at least, prevent surprize, under similar circumstances'.[1]

Other aspects of the *German Tour* similarly suggest that, encouraged by the success of his first book, Burney was now deliberately aiming at a wider audience, composed not merely of readers with musical interests. The style is generally more relaxed, more humorous and subtler in tone. Much more direct biographical information about the most interesting personalities whom he encountered is given, in the form of short lives of such literary and musical celebrities as Mingotti, Metastasio, Franz Benda, Quantz, and C. P. E. Bach, which were perhaps intended in part as an attractive foretaste of the sort of writing that could be expected from his forthcoming *History of Music*.[2] At the end of his book, Burney's expanding literary ambitions became explicit in his apology that time had not permitted him to make his journal an account of '*the present state of arts and sciences, in general*'. Nevertheless, he added, '*poetry is so nearly connected with music*, that I could not help making some enquiries after the most eminent poets now living in Germany, and I shall here present my readers with what I found to be the general opinion there of men of taste and learning, with respect to their abilities'.[3]

This summary of 'general opinion', as well as some earlier remarks on the poet Frederick Klopstock, turn out, however, to be merely an unacknowledged but almost *verbatim* extract from a long letter on the subject from Dr. Mumssen, a physician whom Burney had met in Hamburg and who had introduced him to the celebrated poet.[4] Mumssen had offered his account of 'our modern Authors in Poetry & works of wit' as they appeared to what he called his own 'mind's eyes', and must have been surprised—perhaps gratified—if he ever discovered that his letter had been published as if it were the result of Burney's

---

[1] *Tours*, ii. 28–29, 63–70, 136, 157–8.
[2] Ibid. 54–57, 78–82, 173–7, 182–95, 215–19.
[3] Ibid. 241.   [4] Ibid. 212–13.

own assiduous guaging of German literary opinion.¹ Similarly, the account of the 'Singschüler' of Dresden in the *German Tour* is taken without any acknowledgement from a letter to Burney from Osborn, the British Envoy in that city.²

During his second expedition to the Continent Burney had probably kept his journal with a much greater sense of the form in which he would eventually publish it than in 1770, and on his return there would be little to do, apart from working in such information as that contained in the letters from Mumssen and Osborn. In spite of the fact that his busiest season as a music-teacher had already begun, his new book was in the press by 19 February 1773, although, as Fanny noted, her father was 'hurried and fatigued beyond expression, for this is a time of year when his business is at its height'.³ The book, however, went slowly through the hands of the printers. In March Fanny expected imminent publication and observed Burney's characteristic agitation: 'he is extremely anxious and diffident beyond any author that ever, I believe, existed. He has shut himself up entirely from all who know him, but his own family.'⁴ Nevertheless, it was not until 3 May 1773 that she could at last write, 'My father's German tour has been published this week.'⁵

Burney's anxiety over the reception of his second book was, if anything, greater than ever, and once more he did not hesitate to take advantage of his friends who had connexions with the important journals. As early as November 1772, Bewley had promised to be 'the earliest of your Harbingers', to atone for the delays in the publication of his earlier critique in the *Monthly Review*.⁶ In May 1773, when he had seen the printed volumes, he was able to assure Burney, 'I am delighted with them, & can with a safe conscience heartily recommend them to those whom it may concern'; and although there were 'two or three writers in my critical limbo, who have been waiting "in fearful expectation of judgement", ever since 1771', Bewley put them aside in order that the first part of his review might appear in June. The second article appeared in September 1773.⁷

---

¹ J. Mumssen to CB, 16 Oct. 1772 (Osborn); cf. *Tours*, ii. 241–2.
² J. Osborn to CB, 20 Jan. 1773 (Osborn); cf. *Tours*, ii. 150–2.
³ *ED*, i. 199.   ⁴ Ibid. 204.   ⁵ Ibid. 214.
⁶ Bewley to CB, 20 Nov. 1772 (Osborn).
⁷ Bewley to CB. 15 May 1773 (Osborn); *Monthly Review*, xlviii. 457–69; xlix. 212–24.

Lest it be thought that Bewley had lost his scruples about reviewing his friend's books, it should be mentioned that, in spite of an unspecified 'bribe'—the gift which Burney usually sent him at such a moment—he once more warned his friend of the caution that his own sense of integrity and his concern for the reputation of the *Monthly Review* imposed upon him:

I have given you a *good word*, as I said before, but I have yet been far from expressing to my own liking either my feelings or the cooler dictates of my judgement, with regard to your last two charming Volumes, in which you have gone on *crescendo* at a most rapid rate. We live in such a wicked, suspicious world, that an *honest* Reviewer is afraid of using any *warm* colouring in his sketches.—We have not an *universal* good character, & the sagacious reader is always ready to take the alarm at the least, impassioned declaration he meets with in our productions, though extorted from us merely by conspicuous merit.—Besides, I wish—as Reviewer only, by the bye—I had not known you.[1]

Although his review was accordingly restrained, Bewley left no doubt in his readers' minds of the 'conspicuous and various merits' of the *German Tour*, approving the inclusion of miscellaneous and non-musical narrative and observation; praising the biographical studies, which he considered to be 'delivered in an accurate, masterly, and pleasing manner'; and accompanying the traveller with an approving commentary throughout his journey. The review concluded with the important assurance to the public that Burney had described his travels in so 'pleasing and familiar a manner' that his book would be both 'interesting and intelligible' even to 'those who do not profess or cultivate music'. Since Burney had inserted in the *German Tour* proposals for his *History of Music*, Bewley emphasized that this new undertaking was already in 'great forwardness' and urged his readers to subscribe to it.

The *Critical Review* devoted three articles, which appeared in July, August, and November 1773,[2] to Burney's new book. Although there is no conclusive evidence, the reviewer may be identified once more as Samuel Crisp. In his 'Memoirs' Burney justified his preservation of the unpublished portion of his Italian travel journal by describing the approval which greeted

---

[1] Bewley to CB, 23 June 1773 (Osborn).   [2] xxxvi. 34–44, 81–92, 321–35.

the expanded form of the *German Tour*. His chief example of
this approval was the *Annual Register for 1773*, which had
printed extensive extracts from the book and had especially
applauded its unique 'cast and character'.[1] Burney transcribed
part of the article, noting that the editor of the *Annual Register*
was 'supposed to be Mr. Burke', although of this he was uncertain.[2] Thomas W. Copeland, in his study of Burke's contributions to this journal, has argued that this review is an
example of Burke's partiality to his friends, stating that 'Dr.
Charles Burney, whose *History of Music* was reviewed in 1773,
was a fellow member of the Literary Club.'[3] The review in
question was actually of the *German Tour*, but in any case,
Burney did not become a member of The Club until 1784 and,
in quoting the review, stated himself that he 'had then no
acquaintance' with Burke.

The relevant point is, in fact, precisely the opposite of Copeland's. Burney obviously valued the praise of the *Annual Register*
simply because it was *not* the work of a friend. In demonstrating
the success of his *German Tour* he did not quote the other leading
reviews because one was by Bewley and the other, it may be
assumed, was also by a friend, presumably Crisp. As in 1771,
the articles in the *Critical Review* consisted largely of extracts and
significantly concluded with a hearty assurance that Burney
need not apologize for including the 'miscellaneous' narrative
and that even more of it would have been welcome, as would
have been fewer of the detailed descriptions of various organs,
which were 'not only dry, but seem even useless, to all but
organ-builders'. Similarly, Crisp—if it was he—pointed out, as
in his earlier review, Burney's astonishing social success during
his travels: 'he must be possessed of some talents not common to
musicians, which could so early recommend a mere stranger
to the favour, protection, and assistance of so many great and
eminent persons in the course of his enquiries'.

Equally unusual in a musician was the ability to write
eloquently, and Crisp accordingly praised Burney's concise
'familiar journal stile'. Most striking of all, he believed, was
'that ardour, that enthusiasm, that indefatigable spirit, that
seems to have carried him through all obstacles, in pursuit of

---

[1] xvi. 166–88, 274–8.   [2] *Tours*, I. xxx–xxxi.
[3] *Our Eminent Friend, Edmund Burke*, New Haven, 1949, pp. 128, 145.

his darling object, music', although he ironically added that 'This warmth of imagination, the busy, money-getting world most sagely call madness'. Like Bewley, Crisp concluded his review by pointing out the proposals for the *History of Music* and encouraging his readers to subscribe.

In the course of his review Crisp correctly prophesied that one aspect of the *German Tour* would almost certainly cause its author some trouble. He was referring to the boldness of some of the passages on Germans and Germany, which included such frank comments as that on the celebrated singer Gertrud Mara: 'Her teeth are irregular, and they project too much.' Crisp had commented: 'As to the several young ladies, who, he has told all Europe, *are not handsome*; we shall leave it to them to revenge their own charms, the next time he comes in their way.' Similarly Crisp had suggested that Burney 'may do well likewise to keep out of the Prussian monarch's dominions for some time', having detected 'a secret sarcasm' in Burney's account of Frederick the Great's old-fashioned musical taste.

Crisp referred however, to only the more amusing of Burney's uncomplimentary observations, for the book as a whole was full of complaints about German travelling conditions; shocked descriptions of the terrible poverty of the common people which led to the greed, dishonesty, inefficiency, and poor food that he had so frequently encountered; and comparisons of this post-war condition of the poor with the splendour and luxury of the numerous courts, where music flourished so ostentatiously. Reluctantly, he was obliged to admit that he had sometimes found it hard to enjoy even the most attractive music in such circumstances: the first volume of his *German Tour* had concluded with the remark, 'though I love music very well, yet I love humanity better', and earlier he had written of the court of the Duke of Wurtemburg with little restraint:

His passion for music and shews, seems as strong as that of the emperor Nero was formerly. It is, perhaps, upon such occasions as these, that music becomes a vice, and hurtful to society; for that nation, of which half the subjects are stage-players, fidlers, and soldiers, and the other half beggars, seems to be but ill-governed. Here nothing is talked of but the adventures of actors, dancers, and musicians.—In this article I have perhaps gone beyond my *last*.[1]

[1] *Tours*, ii. 38, 125.

It was not easy for Burney to make such reflections on the harmful effects of a passion for music. The uneasy social position of the professional musician usually incited him to attempt to prove that music was highly beneficial to society, and he had laboured this point in the opening pages of his *Italian Tour*.[1]

Of the many unfavourable observations on Germany in his book, none, however, was to cause Burney more subsequent embarrassment than a sentence that was not even his own. In December 1772 he had received a letter from Louis Devisme, the British plenipotentiary in Munich, who remarked while discussing German music, 'if innate Genius exists, Germany is certainly not the seat of it; but it is that of perseverance and application'. Burney unwisely found occasion to quote the remark with approval in his book, attributing it to 'an accurate observer of human nature'.[2] (Burney lifted another remark from Devisme's letter which he must also have come to regret, to the effect that the sixteen-year-old Mozart had turned out to be 'one further instance of early fruit, which is more extraordinary than excellent'.[3])

Burney's reflections on Germany at once aroused protest. In July 1773 he received a letter from 'Mr Hutton of Lindsey House Chelsea whom Dr Hawkesworth takes friendly notice of'. James Hutton (1715–95), a former bookseller, a friend of John Wesley and a prominent Moravian, had travelled widely in Germany earlier in his life and wrote to object to Burney's description of that country's travelling conditions, which he had read in the *Monthly Review*.[4] To Hutton's bold suggestion that he correct certain passages in a future edition of his book Burney replied with some severity: 'I know not what interest you may have in the honour of Germany, but it cannot be stronger than mine for my own honour, when my veracity is attached.' Hutton, he argued, was ignorant of conditions in Saxony and Bohemia after the Seven Years War and he firmly assured him, 'I must own that I did not so much think how my Narrative would please the Inhabitants of Germany as to relate Things simply, & as they were . . . in general my remarks are given

[1] *Tours*, i. xxv–xxvi.
[2] L. Devisme to CB, 30 Nov. 1772 (Osborn); cf. *Tours* ii. 138 n.
[3] Cf. *Tours*, ii. 238.
[4] Hutton to CB, 2 July 1773 (Osborn).

undisguised & plain, just as they were set down on the spot in my Journal Book.'¹ The pious, good-natured and eccentric Hutton quickly retracted his objections and was soon earnestly assuring him of his affection, in his own curious manner: 'continue to love me at a distance as I shall certainly do you & when we are so happy as to meet one another here on Earth we shall be as if we had been long acquainted, & when we meet together with the Benevolent in Heaven, I shall say there comes Burney suum additurus Hallelujah. Amen.'² A little later Hutton told Mrs. Burney that he had had an opportunity of recommending her husband to the King and, upon her assuring him that Burney 'was much pleased to have had so good a friend speak of him before the King, "Madam", cried he, "I will speak of him before *God*, and that is doing much more!"'³

Whereas Hutton could quickly be converted from hostility into one of the most affectionate and affectionately regarded friends of the Burneys, the *German Tour* put some of his other friendships under severe strain. C. D. Ebeling, whose German translation of the *Italian Tour* had been published at Hamburg in 1772,⁴ who had been largely responsible for persuading Burney to undertake his second journey, whose introductory letters had been invaluable to the traveller and who had been of particular service to him in Hamburg, wrote to Burney in June 1773 to protest, not against the book as a whole but 'the interspersed remarks against German Genius in general'. What especially infuriated Ebeling and 'all true German' [*sic*] was the judgement on German lack of genius quoted from Devisme's letter, 'which indeed is very provoking, and for which I shal [*sic*] make you repent'. Ebeling sternly demanded the name of the man who had reached so insulting a conclusion:

Who is that terrae filius that dares to judge a whole nation! By wich [*sic*] degree of knowledge and genius, and observation and experience was he intitled to utter such an offending sentence? Does he understand the German language? What is his name? In the name

---

¹ CB to Hutton, 17 July 1773, copy (Osborn).

² Hutton to CB, 24 Jan. 1774 (Osborn). They met on 1 Apr., Hutton to CB, 2 Apr. 1774 (Osborn); *ED*, i. 303-12.

³ *ED*, i. 309.

⁴ CB had a few sheets of this translation in his possession whilst he was in Germany, *Tours*, ii. 170 n.

of all Germanns [*sic*], I desire you must deliver him to our revenge. But I neither have time nor ill humour enough to day to quarrel with You, and shall prove my passion to the [*sic*] next time when I write to You. Mr. Klopstock would not reed [*sic*] your Book when he found the above mentioned sentence, and so every honest and true son of Germany will do and must do.

Ebeling's letter included other threats, protests against Burney's account of German poverty, assertions that Germany 'invented 100 times more than any in the world, but that did it without noise', and retaliation in the form of an attack on English genius as embodied in such writers as Shakespeare and Milton.[1]

Burney replied at great length in July, admitting that he 'never was more mortified at the receit of a Letter' in his life; declining to reveal Devisme's name ('We English have an utter abhorrence & detestation of the Character of an *Informer*'); but giving Ebeling full permission to omit or criticize the offending passage in his projected translation of the book. He himself would omit it from a second edition of the *German Tour*. At other parts of Ebeling's 'open Declaration of War', however, he felt he must protest. His accounts of German poverty and the barrenness of the fields were intended 'more to expose the Tyranny of the Government, & despotism of Princes, than to insult the people, whom I pitied with all my Soul'. As for Ebeling's remarks on English poetry, Burney discussed with restraint the difficulty of appreciating poetry in a foreign language, adding, 'you blaspheme against our Milton & Shakespeare without *Connoissance de Cause*'. What mattered most of all to Burney, however, was his right to full freedom of speech: 'I would throw away my Pen, break my Ink-Bottle, & burn every bit of Paper in my House, sooner than let others guide me in *all* my opinions about Men, Things & Countries. I never will ask any Nation, City or Individual what I shall say of them, as I am certain that their vanity & self love would lead me further from the truth, than my own ignorance or prejudice.' And while he respected Ebeling's patriotism, he possessed his own: 'I love England—am proud of Breathing the same air as Locke, Newton, Milton, Dryden—Shakespeare &c. I bless myself in the liberty of our Government, & the Happiness it puts in our

---

[1] Ebeling to CB, 10 June 1773, *GDB*, i. 248-9.

power. . . .' It did not lead him, however, into extravagant claims for his nation in spheres in which it had achieved little. Nevertheless, his letter ended with an uneasily genial attempt to disarm Ebeling's indignation: 'I most cordially shake you by the Thumb, & beg you to make my book so palatable to your Country Men & friends as you can.'[1]

Ebeling, however, through ill-health took a less important part in the translation than Bode, the publisher, whose method of making the book 'palatable' to German taste did not present Burney in a very attractive light. Most of his comments on travelling conditions and the irresponsibility of the aristocracy were omitted and a sarcastic editorial commentary steadily pointed out all factual errors and attacked his pejorative observations.[2] In the following year, 1774, the German offensive against Burney was resumed by the young musician J. F. Reichardt (1752–1814) in the third chapter of the first volume of his *Vertraute Briefe eines aufmerksamen Reisenden*, which contained a bitter attempt to demonstrate Burney's carelessness, ignorance, lack of taste, mediocrity as a composer, determination to insult Germany and deliberate rudeness during his travels.[3] Needless to say, Devisme's unfortunate reflection on German genius again received particular attention, and although Burney omitted it from the second edition of the *German Tour* in 1775, it continued to cause him embarrassment until the end of the following decade. Finally, in the last volume of his *History of Music* in 1789, he made a public confession of his folly in having printed it, admitting that it was 'unjust, and founded on prejudice and ignorance' and that he had been 'as angry with myself as the most patriotic German can be, for ever having given admission to such a reflection'. The precise context of this humble apology will, however, be supplied on a later page.[4]

Certainly, in the months following the publication of his second book, Burney faced criticism from several quarters. In June 1773 Garrick heard him read over 'an Answer . . . to some complaints made by French writers, concerning his censure of

---

[1] CB to Ebeling, 15 July 1773, copy (Osborn).
[2] See *GDB*, i. 244–8 and *Tours*, ii. 36 n., 39 n., 131 n.
[3] See *GDB*, i. 251–3. Scholes rejects as baseless Reichardt's accusation of rudeness; but he was referring to a specific instance, forgotten by Scholes, of CB's failure to attend a concert at Berlin arranged in his honour, *Tours*, ii. 196.
[4] *Hist. Mus.* iv. 606; see *post*, pp. 327–9.

their Music'.[1] Burney explained this attack in his letter to
Ebeling in July: 'There is no peace for me here. A M. Framery[2]
of Paris, who intends to translate my History into French, has
Criticised my account of French Music, & sent me a long,
feeble & dull defence of it. . . .' Including Ebeling himself in the
complaint no doubt, he added, 'Nothing but Panygeric [*sic*]
will be believed; but my own feelings cannot be sacrificed to
Politesse.'

The outcry in France and Germany was probably drowned,
however, by the flattering reception which his books had
earned at home. The men whose friendship and opinion he
valued most could not have been more complimentary. Garrick
had written to say of the *German Tour* that 'nothing can be more
pleasing to his friends or more agreeable to the public; and that
it is clear, interesting, instructive, and delightful'.[3] Through
Garrick, Oliver Goldsmith, who had evidently never met
Burney, arranged that he should contribute the article 'Musician' to the 'Universal Dictionary of Arts and Sciences' which
he was proposing to edit, but which had been abandoned
before his death in the following year. Goldsmith's letter to
Garrick, which was duly passed on to Burney, was, however,
extremely complimentary: 'I am very happy that Dr. Burney
thinks my plan of a Dictionary useful; still more, that he will be
so kind, as to adorn it with any thing of his own. I beg you will
also accept my gratitude for procuring me so valuable an
acquisition.'[4]

Undoubtedly, Burney's ambition to reach a wide and not
necessarily musical audience had succeeded for, as he later
recalled himself, the fact that his *German Tour* had included
non-musical material 'procured me many more readers than
mere students and lovers of music. My publication was honoured with the approbation of the blue-stocking families at
Mrs. Vezey's, and Mrs. Montagu's and Sir Joshua Reynolds's,
where I was constantly invited and regarded as a member. . . .'[5]
Nothing could signal more precisely the moment at which
Burney made the transition from being essentially a professional

[1] *ED*, i. 226–7.
[2] Nicolas Framery (1745–1810) never executed this translation.
[3] *ED*, i. 214–15.
[4] Ibid. 225–6; *Mem.* i. 271–3; Hill–Powell, ii. 204 n. 2.
[5] *Tours*, i. xxx.

musician to being accepted as a man of letters than this admission to the polite literary coteries directed by Mrs. Vesey and Mrs. Montagu, where he joined their brilliant assemblies of writers, artists, statesmen, travellers, wits, and cultivated noblemen. As for Sir Joshua Reynolds, Mrs. Thrale remarked a few years later that he seemed to have 'set up as a Sort of Patron to Literature; so that no Book goes rapidly thro' a first Edition now, but the Author is at Reynolds's Table in a Trice'.[1] It is not surprising, therefore, to find that Burney's long friendship with the celebrated painter dates from this period.

There was one man, however, whose approbation meant more to Burney than that of the whole of London and he obtained it not long after the publication of his *German Tour*, when Baretti called with the message 'that Dr. Johnson will be very glad to see him; that he has read both his Tours with great pleasure, and has pronounced him to be *one of the first writers of the age* for travels!' 'Such praise', as Fanny properly observed, 'from Dr. Johnson, whom my father reveres above all authors living or dead, has given him the highest delight.'[2] Without doubt it was the expanded form of the second book that had won over Johnson who in March 1772 had declared to Boswell, with reference to the *Italian Tour*, that 'Dr. Burney was a very pretty kind of man; but he could not read through the book. I asked him why. He said, "Because I could not read about fiddles and fiddlestrings."'[3] This remark, which Boswell understandably omitted from his version of this conversation in the *Life of Johnson* and which has only recently been printed, confirms the impression that until 1773 Johnson had simply not taken Burney very seriously, his epithet 'pretty' dismissing him as basically negligible. The *German Tour*, however, revealed Burney in a different light, for Johnson could there examine his style and intelligence applied to other subjects than 'fiddles and fiddlestrings'. He later claimed to have read the book right through—'except, perhaps, the description of the great pipes in the organs of Germany and the Netherlands'—and told both Burney and William Seward that he had taken it as the

---

[1] *Thraliana*, i. 80.
[2] *ED*, i. 222; Johnson had written to Mrs. Thrale, 19 Feb. 1773, asking her to lend Mrs. Williams the *Italian Tour*, *Letters*, i. 301.
[3] *Boswell For the Defence*, ed. W. K. Wimsatt and F. A. Pottle, 1960, p. 51.

model, for 'size and form', of his own *Journey to the Western Islands of Scotland*, published in 1775.[1]

Burney acquired, as a result of his two journeys on the Continent, not only a vast and unique store of sources and information for his historical account of both ancient and modern music, but also a considerable reputation as a writer, many distinguished and influential friends, and an assurance that the *History of Music* itself would be awaited with the greatest interest. Inevitably these journeys, and the materials he had obtained, had proved expensive for a music-teacher, however prosperous, who had a large family to support. It is not quite clear how Burney financed his travels, although it is obvious that he must have invested a large part of his own savings and of whatever remained of his wife's fortune in them. He himself spoke at this time of 'fourteen or fifteen hundred pounds kicked down in my rambles & Bibliomania'.[2] On the other hand, both his books, which he had published at his own expense, sold well and must in part have reimbursed him. By October 1773, when he was already preoccupied with the *History*, the question of second editions of both works was raised. Writing to ask Arthur Young, his brother-in-law, for advice, Burney stated; 'My Italian Tour is reprinted & ready to deliver, not one copy of the first Edit. being left. I have corrected & somewhat enlarged it, to the amount of 10 or 12 pages.[3]—The German Tour has gone off so well, that of 1000 copies, Robinson says he imagines not one will be left by Jany next.'

Various booksellers had already attempted to persuade him to sell the copyright of his *Tours* and, although he was 'sorry to throw away two B^ks that have made their way, without Bookselling, or other Craft', Burney decided that, since he now wished to devote himself entirely to his *History*, he would do well to rid himself of 'all Trouble ab^t former publications'. After all, what now mattered most was that the books should be reprinted, to 'awaken attention in some to the subject of my

---

[1] *Mem.* ii. 78–79; Hill–Powell, iv. 186; W. Seward, *Anecdotes of Distinguished Persons*, 4th edn. enlarged, 1798, ii. 463.

[2] CB to Twining, 30 Aug. 1773 (B.M. Add. MS. 39929, ff. 59–64; draft, Berg).

[3] The additions are listed in a brief notice, perhaps communicated through Crisp, in the *Critical Review*, xxxvii (1774), 77, which ends, 'The Reviewers are happy to find the public opinion of this very entertaining work corresponding with theirs; of which the quick succession of a second edition is an irrefragable proof.'

great undertaking, & keep it alive in others' and he decided
that he might as well pass on the trouble involved to the booksellers.[1] In December he received an instalment of £150 from
George Robinson for 'one Half of the sole Copy-Right' of both
Tours[2] and Bewley congratulated him on his newly acquired
£300 early in 1774.[3] A second edition of the *Italian Tour* was
published immediately and the *German Tour* also reached a new
edition in 1775.

In July 1773 Burney left London to spend the summer with
Bewley in the peace of Great Massingham, intent on settling
down at last to uninterrupted labour on the *History of Music*. In
spite of the welcome given to his books by Dr. Johnson, the
'Bluestockings', and by the world of polite letters as a whole, he
had no intention of relaxing after his strenuous travels or of
enjoying the new areas of society which were now open to him.
As he wrote in August, 'My Friends often upbraid me for not
more frequently partaking of the Diversions of the Times, and
the Pleasures of Society. . . . Upon this occasion I have but one
short & true answer to make, which is, that "I have no Time to
be happy".'[4] Not until the *History of Music* had set the seal on his
reputation would he accept the social success which he relished
so much. Yet, in spite of this protestation, Burney was undoubtedly a happy man in the early summer of 1773, for he
began to write his *History* confident in the knowledge that he
had established himself as a phenomenon: a professional
musician who had been welcomed by London society as a man
of letters.

This fundamental social distinction was emphasized by
Fanny d'Arblay in writing about precisely this moment in her
father's life: 'From this period, the profession of Dr. Burney,
however highly he was raised in it, seemed but of secondary
consideration for him in the world; where, now, the higher
rank was assigned him of a man of letters, from the general
admiration accorded to his Tours. . . .'[5] Burney had had to
overcome a double prejudice. The social limitations of the professional musician can be most emphatically illustrated by

[1] CB to Young, 11 Oct. 1773 (B.M. Add. MS. 35126, ff. 157-8).
[2] Receipt dated 9 Dec. 1773 (Hyde).
[3] Bewley to CB, 8 Jan.–5 Feb. 1774 (Osborn).
[4] CB to Twining, 30 Aug. 1773 (B.M. Add. MS. 39929, ff. 59-64).
[5] *Mem.* i. 255.

Lord Chesterfield's definition of 'bad company': 'such as fiddlers, pipers, and *id genus omne*; most unedifying and unbecoming company for a man of fashion!'[1] A letter by Thomas Gray in 1763 demonstrates the corresponding prejudice of the 'man of letters':

> Poetry (w^ch, as you allow, must lead the way, & direct the operations of the subordinate Arts) implies at least a liberal education, a degree of literature, & various knowledge, whereas the others (with a few exceptions) are in the hands of Slaves & Mercenaries, I mean, of People without education, who, tho neither destitute of Genius, nor insensible to fame, must yet make gain their principal end, & subject themselves to the prevailing taste of those, whose fortune only distinguishes them from the Multitude.[2]

There had, of course, been many previous writers on music but their works were usually impenetrable to a polite literary audience. Burney's achievement was to convince his general readers that music could be discussed both elegantly and intelligibly; to meet them on their own literary ground, while dictating firmly his own musical convictions and taste; and to demonstrate that there was at least one professional musician who could display the 'liberal education, a degree of literature, & various knowledge' which Gray expected to find only in the poet. As for the genuine surprise caused by Burney's two *Musical Tours*, it was not for some three years that his close friend Thomas Twining felt able to describe their original impact and so to define precisely the gulf that Burney had succeeded in bridging:

> Do you know that I have often been provoked by meeting people who have been unwilling to believe that you write your own books, or *know* your own *knowledge*? I have heard it *supposed* 'that you got somebody to *draw up* your journals for you'. Nay, I have been *told* that Dr *Hawkesworth* was the man; by *excellent* judges of style & manner you may be sure. All this (excepting the *last* mistake,) is certainly very much to your honour, au fond.

Twining explained this frequent incredulity by the fact that 'we have had *no* experience of such a phenomenon as a professor of

---

[1] *Lord Chesterfield's Letters to his Son*, ed. C. S. Carey, 1912, ii. 106–7.
[2] *Correspondence*, ii. 811.

Music, & an artist, that was a man of letters, & a good writer.—
it is contrary to the uniform course of nature &c &c.'¹

This escape from the confines of his profession and his
acquisition of a general literary audience was Burney's proudest
boast, although at first he expressed his satisfaction only in the
most modest and self-deprecating way. In August 1773, he confessed to Mrs. Frances Crewe (the beautiful daughter of Fulke
Greville, his old master), who in later years was to be the
closest of his friends in 'high society', that he had never dared to
ask if she had read his *Italian Tour*. He had assumed that the
fear of being confronted with 'the Jargon of hard words & the
unintelligible Giberish of affected Science', which characterized
most books on music, had prevented her from doing so. Yet he
could assure her that there was nothing more difficult in his
Tours than in such children's books as *Giles Gingerbread* and
Goody Two-Shoes. Indeed, the most flattering tribute to his
books had been that none of his friends had 'ever complained of
not understanding me'.

Mrs. Crewe had also been teasing him about his sudden
fame: 'You laugh at your poor old acquaintance, & he laughs
at himself (he was always a *gigler* you know) when you tell him
of his being in the list of *great men*—Well, this Life, as far as I
know of it, is a strange mixture of Sense & Nonsense—Joy &
Sorrow—Affliction & Farce—a meer Tragi-Comedy, at which
one is inclined to cry & to laugh, all in a Breath.'²

So wrote Dr. Burney—'*the* Dr. Burney', as Fanny discovered
he had become during her summer holidays³—properly cautious
of luxuriating in his new celebrity. His sense of the ambivalence
of human experience was to be fully exercised in the next three
years, for the tragi-comedy had hardly begun.

---

¹ Twining to CB, 7 Mar. 1776 (B.M. Add. MS. 39929, ff. 76–79).
² CB to [Mrs. Crewe], 8 Aug. 1773, draft (Berg).
³ *ED*, i. 253.

IV

THE FIRST VOLUME OF THE
HISTORY OF MUSIC

1773–1776

I

ALTHOUGH his two *Musical Tours* won for Burney right of entry into London's most fashionable literary society, one of the most important consequences of his growing fame was, on the surface, nothing more exciting than friendship with a modest and retiring clergyman in an Essex village. Thomas Twining[1] had originally entered his father's tea business but in 1755, at the age of twenty, had removed to Sidney Sussex College, Cambridge, becoming a Fellow of the college in 1760. Four years later he obtained the living of Fordham in Essex and in this village and in Colchester, where he later became Rector of St. Mary's, Twining spent the remaining forty years of his life. Later in his career his translation of Aristotle's *Poetics* (1789) was to bring him a considerable reputation, but one of the earliest results of his classical training had been an intense interest in ancient music, a subject on which he had started to collect material before leaving Cambridge. He was equally interested, however, in the theory and practice of the art in modern times and was an accomplished amateur musician.[2]

In February 1773, Twining, who rarely visited London and

---

[1] Since Twining's letters to CB, almost entirely unpublished, will be referred to frequently in the next three chapters, the complex state in which they have survived must be described: (1) Original letters, 1776–85 (B.M. Add MS. 39929, ff. 65–362, with letters to other correspondents interspersed); (2) Twining's notes on his letters, 1773–82 (B.M. Add. MS. 39936, ff. 45–71); (3) Extracts, 1773–6, 1791–1801, copied by his half-brother Richard (B.M. Add. MS. 39933, ff. 69–173, Add. MS. 39934, ff. 9–10, 19–22, Add. MS. 39935, f. 53); (4) Extracts, 1773–1804, copied by his nephew Daniel in 1833 for C. P. Burney (Osborn); (5) Extracts printed in *Recreations and Studies of a Country Clergyman*, ed. R. Twining, 1882. Except in the period 1776–85, letters have often to be assembled from extracts in the different categories. (4) and (5) also contain extracts from CB's letters to Twining, few of which have otherwise survived.

[2] *Country Clergyman*, pp. 1–4, 14–20.

who had met Burney only briefly on one earlier occasion, paid an unsuccessful call on the musician in Queen's Square. Two months later, with considerable misgivings about such 'pushing' behaviour, he wrote to Burney from Essex, inquiring after the progress of the *History of Music* and offering to send some musical anecdotes which he had once heard from the composer Geminiani. The conclusion of his letter explained Twining's desire to correspond with Burney, for he described himself as 'a man, exceedingly fond of music, buried in the country, reduced, for all his musical enjoyment, to a short-compassed harpsichord, & his own no voice, & absolutely cut off from all conversation upon the subject'.[1]

The tone of Twining's complimentary, modest but intelligent letter was perfectly calculated to appeal to Burney, who, busy as he was at the time with the publication of his *German Tour*, replied at length later in the month. Although they were not to meet again until the summer of 1774, their correspondence at once assumed an affectionate and intimate tone. Burney was now forty-seven and Twining thirty-eight: as the clergyman's half-brother commented, 'They were far from young when they met, and they could ill afford to lose time. They soon became intimate, they soon became friends.' Twining said of Burney, 'I like the man, and I like the subject upon which he is engaged.'[2] Similarly, Burney's immediate confidence in his correspondent is strikingly clear from his second letter to Twining:

> Let us slap down our Thoughts as they come, without the Trouble of seeking or arranging them. I lament the distance between us, & the want of your Conversation & Counsel. I question whether we should recognize each other if we were to meet; and yet I feel so entirely off my guard with you that like some of our Common People and Servants, who, when they like Folks, give them, in the first Hour's Acquaintance, a History of all their Misfortunes, ill-usages, bad Places, & bodily complaints.—So I seem *inside-out* with you, & inclined to tell you every secret of my Life.[3]

It is significant that Burney should be slightly self-conscious about the lack of well-bred reserve which he was displaying.[4]

---

[1] Twining to CB, 7 Apr. 1773, copy (Add. MS. 39933, ff. 69–71).
[2] *Country Clergyman*, pp. 7, 8.
[3] CB to Twining, 30 Aug. 1773 (Add. MS. 39929, ff. 59–64).
[4] Cf. *post*, p. 232.

In London his remarkable social climb had already begun and the charm and 'correctness' of his manners, unique in a professional musician, had long been unimpeachable. His most intimate friendships were not, however, to be made in the increasingly distinguished social and intellectual circles which he entered with such pride. Samuel Crisp, William Bewley, and Thomas Twining were all highly intelligent but retiring men, living in the obscurity of tiny villages, who found some kind of vicarious satisfaction for their own repressed or frustrated interests and ambitions in encouraging and assisting Burney's rise to fame; and it was only with them or in his letters to them that Burney could relax sufficiently to reveal all his fears, hopes, and problems without restraint.

The charm, intelligence, and wit of Twining's letters would suffice to explain why Burney was so immediately attracted to the clergyman. Samuel Parr, indeed, considered that Twining possessed 'a talent for epistolary writing not surpassed by any of his contemporaries'.[1] It was not long, however, before Burney realized that Twining had many other qualities, upon which he was to become increasingly dependent. Twining was deeply learned in Latin and Greek, whereas Burney, largely self-educated, was no classical scholar; Twining had infinite leisure in his quiet parsonage, whereas Burney spent twelve hours a day for several months of the year in teaching; and Twining was invariably patient and equable, whereas Burney was highly excitable and liable to periods of the blackest depression. Like Bewley, who had only recently discovered that he might win a reputation for himself in scientific fields independent of Burney's activities, Twining did not realize until his late middle age that he had his own claims on the world's attention.

For at least ten years Twining was to put himself entirely at Burney's disposal, quelling twinges of personal ambition by persuading himself that he was no more than a contentedly indolent dabbler in scholarship, for whom life held no prospect of fame. When Burney genially declared in 1774 that Twining deserved a bishopric as a reward for his literary services, he replied: 'I would not be a Bishop for the world!—I could not wear my own hair as I do now, nor command my own time, nor keep my own company, nor follow my own fancies; nor

[1] *Country Clergyman*, p. 11.

sing opera songs; nor fiddle; nor play half a day upon the
harpsichord: nay I don't know whether I might shave myself!
Wish me well, but in some other way. I was not made for
dignities; and further they are quite *out* of *my reach*.'¹ In 1776 he
resorted once more to this image of himself: 'I know myself,
my *goods*, & my *bads*, pretty well. No man wou'd like fame & the
eyes of yᵉ world better. But I am timid, & indolent, & moreover, have all possible reason to doubt very much whether I
cou'd acquire any fame, worth having, if I were to *try*.'² As
friends and relations became more insistent that he use his
learning on his own behalf, various projects formed in his
mind, but for many years they were to be laid aside or abandoned if Burney needed help. Thus he wrote to his half-brother
in 1778:

'Why *am* I always correcting the MSS of others?'—because, Sir, I
am a mighty good-natured, obliging sort of a fellow, & always ready
to lend my friends my spectacles, such as they are; & then I am not
so very good-humoured but that I have a very pretty gift of fault-
finding.—'Why do I write nothing myself?'—Why, I do intend, if I
live & do well (tho' I shall not do well in that case,) to write 50
things. . . . You'll see, you'll see one of these days.³

Although, when Burney replied to Twining's first letter in
April 1773, he had just finished battling with the 'Scribling
Demon' who 'had scarce allowed me to eat or sleep for some
weeks' (the publication of the *German Tour*), he was preparing
to settle down immediately to work on his *History of Music* with
good humour and optimism, as is clear from the manner in
which he informed Twining of his plans:

I have at length got rid of . . . two brats that I have sent into the
wide World to shift for themselves. But notwithstanding the pangs of
Child Birth it will appear by a label prefixed to the back of one of
them, that I, like other Breeders, forgetting or slighting former
sufferings, determine to fall to again, & am preparing for another
Pregnancy—& having now found the secret of producing Twins, a
double Foetus may perhaps ensue more enormous than the last.⁴

The 'label' to which Burney referred was the leaf containing
'Proposals for Printing by Subscription, A General History of

¹ Twining to CB, 3–6 July 1774, copy (Add. MS. 39933, ff. 106–9).
² Ibid., 17 Sept. 1776 (Add. MS. 39929, ff. 105–7).
³ Twining to Richard Twining, 6 Nov. 1778 (Add. MS. 39929, ff. 178–9).
⁴ CB to Twining, 28 Apr. 1773 (Add. MS. 39929, ff. 54–56).

Music', which he had inserted in his *German Tour* and which also appeared in the second edition of his *Italian Tour* later in 1773. These 'Proposals' contain various 'Conditions': the *History* was to be 'elegantly printed in Two Volumes Quarto', with illustrations; subscribers would pay a guinea for each volume; and, while the names of subscribers would be printed in the *History*, non-subscribers would have to pay three and a half guineas for the two volumes.

The most important of the 'Conditions', however, was the third, in which Burney made two promises to the public: 'It is the author's intention to publish the first volume in the course of the next year, 1774. But, as the printing of this work will be attended with too great an expence for him to risk it against the public opinion, though it is in great forwardness, he cannot venture to send it to the press before *five hundred copies* are subscribed for.' Since he did not wish to remain long in suspense he added that, 'in order to render security reciprocal between the public and the writer, if the number of copies specified be not ascertained by next Christmas, he will abandon the enterprize, and return the money to the subscribers'. In April 1773, therefore, Burney had committed himself to two undertakings: the first, to obtain five hundred subscribers in eight months, and the second, to publish the first volume of his *History* within, at the most, twenty months.

Burney can hardly have doubted his ability to perform both these promises and the task of obtaining five hundred subscribers probably seemed the lighter of the two, for he looked confidently for support from his aristocratic friends, from the wealthy parents of his pupils, from the wider audience which his *Tours* had entertained, from his professional colleagues, and from antiquarians. In May 1773 Twining expressed what Burney himself must confidently have felt: 'The very mention, in your proposals, of abandoning the enterprise, hurt me; but I hope there is not the least doubt of your securing, without difficulty, the number you have fixt upon. You have deserved everything of the musical public, by the uncommon pains & expence you have been at, in order to procure them authentic information. It is a respect that is seldom paid to the public, & they ought to be grateful for it.'[1]

[1] Twining to CB, 28 May 1773 (Add. MS. 39933, ff. 73-78).

To Burney's surprise, however, the public seemed neither grateful nor even very interested and the subscription grew only slowly during the summer of 1773. At the end of July, however, he had an opportunity of disposing of all anxiety, for he received a letter from Messrs. Chandler and Davidson, '2 great Merch^ts in the City', informing him that they had been directed by a friend of theirs to guarantee that, when the list was counted at Christmas, he would subscribe for as many copies as were needed to bring the number up to the prescribed five hundred.[1] It was not only pride which made Burney refuse this gratifying offer. The enthusiasm of one rich and anonymous well-wisher was not enough to sustain his great undertaking, for his morale depended on the confident knowledge that a large and eager audience was awaiting his *History*. According to Fanny d'Arblay, he 'declined all sort of tie upon the event' and, loyal as ever to her father's reputation, she added that 'the subscription filled so voluntarily, that this generous unknown was never called forth'.[2]

Unsupported by the mysterious and 'munificent protector of his project', however, the subscription did not flourish as healthily as Fanny later suggested. By the end of August 1773, when half the period which Burney had allowed himself had expired, he was genuinely dismayed by the feeble response, especially since those who had already subscribed were largely dutiful friends and relations:

I find my Fr^ds better disposed to forward my Subscription than the Public at large. between 2 & 300, chiefly among my acquaintance, have already given in their Names; but I believe I could have en-sured full that Number, If I had chosen to employ personal Interest that way, for a set of Lessons or Concertos, which w^d have cost me but little Money to Print, & less labour to compose. People lye by, and wait to be asked—& if I were to spend my Time in soliciting Subscriptions, how, or when w^d my work be executed? . . . I must confess that the Zeal of a few *private* Friends, though a grateful Cir-cumstance to my Heart, is not an Incence of so sweet smelling a Savour to my Vanity, as an Author, as the voluntary offerings of the public would be.

He tried to persuade himself that potential subscribers were

---

[1] Dated 30 July 1773 and transcribed in CB to Crisp, 21 Jan. 1774 (Berg).
[2] *Mem.* i. 247.

merely lazy or that, 'sore from former ill-usage in Subscriptions', they were 'fearful that I should become too fat and lazy to write, if the *great profits* of my Work poured in upon me too fast, *d'avance*'.[1] For once Burney had no desire to emulate Samuel Johnson, Churchill's couplet on whom he may well have had in mind:

> He for subscribers bates his hook,
> And takes their cash; but where's the book?[2]

Such an explanation, however, could hardly console an author who, since his travels in Germany, had published an account of them and, without respite, had at once settled to work on another book. With one eye on the subscription list, Burney visited Oxford during the summer and then began writing his *History* while staying with Bewley at Great Massingham. During the autumn of 1773 he worked unremittingly at his great task, Fanny noting in her diary his 'late hours at night' and the fact that he was 'always shut up in his study'.[3] Samuel Crisp, on being informed of his friend's incessant toil, was not amused, as he told Fanny: 'As to that rogue your father, if I did not know him to be incorrigible, I should say something of that regular course of irregularity he persists in—two, three, four, five o'clock in the morning, sups at twelve!—is it impossible for him to get the better of his constitution? has he forgot the condition he was in the winter after his first return to England? . . . Certain it is, that he uses his thin carcass most abominably. . . .' Crisp felt, moreover, that Burney should not forget to make 'worldly use' of the 'Great and the Eminent' whose acquaintance he had recently made, and warned him, through his daughter, that his *History* must not cause him to neglect 'business' which, now that he had won a fashionable reputation, must 'prove his surest, firmest, best, perhaps his *only* Friend'.[4]

By the end of the year Burney must have felt that Crisp's warnings contained a great deal of wisdom, for at Christmas 1773, the appointed time for counting his subscribers, he was obliged to face the fact that his list 'barely amounted to 400'. The financial implications mattered less than the apparent lack of public interest in his great undertaking, for he had long been

[1] CB to Twining, 30 Aug. 1773 (Add. MS. 39929, ff. 59–64).
[2] *The Ghost*, Bk. III, ll. 801–2.   [3] *ED*, i. 263, 266.   [4] Ibid. 269.

resigned to losing money on the *History*. During the summer, when he had first become anxious about the subscription list, he had told Twining, 'I am now too far waded in Ink to retreat; & therefore pursue the Undertaking with all the Vigour of a Man in sight of the two Temples of Fame & Fortune, with the Goddess at the Door of each, beckoning him to come in.'[1] There was, however, a limit to what his pride could bear and, in spite of the years of preparation and strenuous travel, he might even have abandoned the *History*, as he had threatened, at the end of 1773, had not one avenue of escape remained. If, as Fanny stated, he had previously declined to consider the offer of his anonymous admirer, who had guaranteed to bring the list up to five hundred regardless of expense, Burney's arrival at the offices of Chandler and Davidson late in December 1773 must have been a humiliating moment for so sensitive a man. He reminded Davidson that in his 'Proposals' he had 'promised the Public to advance or retreat at that Time, & might be called on', and revealed that he had obtained only four hundred names. Davidson promptly told him that 'we are impowered to beg you to go on' and, when Burney modestly expressed his unwillingness to burden his generous admirer, assured him that their 'friend' would have subscribed for all five hundred copies if necessary. He therefore urged him to advertise his intention of proceeding with the *History*.[2]

Burney duly did so, although he felt obliged to admit unobtrusively that he had not yet obtained the full number of names:

The Time being now elapsed when Dr. BURNEY promised either to send his History of Music to the Press, or return the Subscription Money that had been deposited, finding that he has ascertained nearly the stipulated Number of Subscribers, he has the Honour to acquaint those who have favoured him with their Names, and those who may be inclined to encourage the Work in future, that he has determined to print it with all possible Expedition, and to keep the Subscription open till the first Volume is published, which the Author still hopes will be in the Course of the ensuing Year, 1774.[3]

Apparently Burney never learned, or never revealed, the identity of the 'young Man of Family & large independent

---

[1] CB to Twining, 30 Aug. 1773 (Add. MS. 39929, ff. 59–64).
[2] CB to Crisp, 21 Jan. 1774 (Berg).
[3] *Public Advertiser*, 6 Jan. 1774.

Fortune', who was so deeply interested in the *History of Music*; nor, surprisingly, is there any clue to his identity, nor even any particularly obvious candidate for the role among Burney's aristocratic acquaintance. Fortunately, his somewhat uneasy dependence on this patron was short-lived, for the apparent lack of public interest in the *History* turned out in the end only to reflect lack of judgement on Burney's part. His 'Proposals' had appeared towards the end of the fashionable London season, when most of his potential subscribers were preparing to leave for the country; and the list had been counted just before their return after Christmas. With the beginning of the new season and as soon as his advertisement of his intention to continue his undertaking had appeared, the situation changed dramatically. By the third week of January 1774 he could tell Crisp cautiously that 'Fashion begins, I think now, to operate'. He was suddenly receiving letters from 'People of rank, & high in Literature'; and 'Johnson puffs my Books—Mrs Montagu has desired my acquaintance'. Fulke Greville had suddenly subscribed for five sets of the *History* and Lord Sandwich had sent a list of eighteen names which he had collected, and required another five sets for himself. Realizing his own earlier lack of judgement, Burney was able to tell Twining, 'Scrip goes on rather swimmingly, now folks are come to town.'[1] By May 1774 the number of subscribers had almost doubled since Christmas and he could count '7 or 800 Names already of the first Persons of the Country for Ranks & Talents', including the Queen.[2] The first of his problems had eventually solved itself with less damage to Burney's pride than had at first seemed possible.

II

Burney's second promise to the public was to produce the first volume of his *History* during 1774. Early in the year, when the subscription was suddenly expanding, Burney derived further encouragement from the assistance offered to him by several scholars and travellers. Lord Mornington,[3] in a letter

---

[1] CB to Twining, 21 Jan. 1774, copy (Osborn).
[2] CB to Regina Mingotti, 3 May 1774 (Osborn).
[3] Garrett Wellesley, first Visc. Wellesley of Dangan and first Earl of Mornington (1735–81), had been a musical prodigy: Trinity College, Dublin, conferred a Doctorate of Music on him in 1764. He was father of the Duke of Wellington.

which expressed the highest admiration for the *Musical Tours*, offered his services in the field of 'the Musical Antiquities of Ireland', and announced that he had already 'sett on foot an Enquiry into the remote parts of the Kingdom' about the history of the Irish harp.[1] Simultaneously Thomas Pennant (1726–98), the traveller and naturalist, offered Burney information about Welsh music;[2] and a little later, in March 1774, Richard Twiss (1747–1821), a younger traveller, who had just returned from Spain, brought him examples of Spanish, Portuguese, and Provençal music. Twiss, however, quickly scandalized the Burneys by an uninhibited account of his travels, vividly described in Fanny's diary ('the most extraordinary evening I ever passed'), which made Burney vow that the young traveller would 'never see a *table-cloth* in his house again'.[3]

It was not long, nevertheless, before Burney had sunk into a new depression. The material offered by Mornington, Pennant, and Twiss might well be useful for the section on 'National Music' which he planned to include in his second volume, but his immediate concern was to publish the first volume during 1774, according to his promise to his subscribers. His earliest intention had been to commence his *History* in the eleventh century, with the 'invention' of counterpoint by Guido of Arezzo.[4] Of the history of earlier music he then knew little and he had found it hard to believe that the scanty materials available for an account of ancient Egyptian, Greek, Hebrew, and Roman music, and the 'barbarous' music of the early Christian Church, could or should be of any interest to the polite eighteenth-century music-lover. By 1770, however, he had realized that 'something must of course be said about the ancient music', and it was at this point that he had sought the help of William Mason and Thomas Gray.[5] His journey to Italy had been an attempt to supplement, or even to replace, the tedious and unreliable treatises which had already been written on ancient music, by obtaining original and authentic information at first

[1] Lord Mornington to CB, 30 Dec. 1773 (Osborn).
[2] Pennant to CB [? Jan.] and 11 Jan. 1774; CB to Pennant, Jan. 1774, copy (Osborn).
[3] Twiss to CB, 14 Mar. and [Mar.] 1774 (Osborn); *ED*, i. 289–302.
[4] CB to Twining, 28 Apr. 1773 (Add. MS. 39929, ff. 54–56).
[5] See *ante*, p. 85.

hand. On his return to England he was more confident of his ability to deal with the earlier history of music. He expected to be greatly assisted by Padre Martini's *History of Music*, the second volume of which he soon received from the author.[1] Classical authors would provide material for the history of Greek and Roman music; and from the Bible and 'some hebrew priests' Burney expected to obtain most of the information he would need concerning Hebrew music. The section on ancient music could be filled out with 'the Old Treatises in my possession & my drawings of ancient Instruments & remarks upon them'.[2]

Much of the work on this part of the *History* was as straightforward as Burney anticipated. Two notebooks dating from this period are almost entirely filled with material for his first volume, much of it transcribed by his daughters, Fanny and Susan. One of them, entitled 'Biographical Dict[y] of Ancient Greek & Roman Musicians', contains a somewhat disorderly mass of miscellaneous information gathered from various cyclopaedias and histories and from previous writers on ancient music, with a careful and very necessary index. The notebooks also contain drafts of parts of the relevant chapters of the *History*.[3] Such accumulation and condensation of historical, mythological, and biographical information about ancient music and musicians and the numerous deities associated with the art demanded, on the whole, only hard work and a great deal of transcription, much of which could be passed on by the busy music-teacher to his daughters.

It was, however, a different matter to describe the precise nature of ancient music, for almost the only confident statement that could be made about it was that it bore no relation to the theory and practice of any music familiar to eighteenth-century ears. The problem was not as simple as the complete absence of any information on the subject, but rather that ancient discussions of music were hopelessly scattered, incoherent and ambiguous. It was, indeed, precisely the fragmentary nature of knowledge about ancient music that, by the scope it allowed for imaginative speculation, had attracted so many ingenious, eccentric, and often incomprehensible scholars to write about it,

[1] Martini to CB, 7 Apr. 1771 (Osborn).
[2] CB to Crisp, 31 May 1771 (Osborn).   [3] Osborn.

especially since the sixteenth century. The tantalizing comments to be found in such authors as Plato, Plutarch, and Aristoxenus had, for example, engaged for many years the curiosity of so sensible a scholar as Thomas Twining, although he admitted that his patient study of them had been rewarded with few insights into the true nature of ancient music: 'I ran violently at these little openings, as Harlequin does at Columbine's door; but generally returned disconsolate, with my nose broke, & my arms crossed.'[1]

By April 1773, when he was at last free to begin writing his first volume, Burney knew that he could hardly avoid plunging into the chaos of earlier speculation about the theory and practice of ancient music. It was, as Twining had observed in his first letter, 'a subject about which, as after all, there is so little to be *known*, it is rather unlucky that there should be so much to be said'.[2] Burney accordingly had been struggling gallantly through 'all the dark & unfathomable stuff concerning Greek Modes & Hebrew psalmody, ab^t which we know nearly as much, as of the Musical System used by the Inhabitants of the Planet Saturn'. If the distasteful subjects must be dealt with, he told Twining, 'my Say will be much more to laugh at what others have written, perhaps, than to offer anything of my own concerning them.—The History of *Counterpoint* is certainly all that concerns a History of music. . . .'

Derision of earlier writers was certainly the easiest course to follow, although his self-confessed 'total neglect of Erudition' contributed something to Burney's anxiety to dismiss ancient music as a subject only for absurd and fruitless speculation. Equally important, however, was his reluctance to lose the good-will of the polite 'literary' audience which his *Musical Tours* had so successfully captured. Several hundred pages of dull and inconclusive technical speculation about ancient music would amount to nothing less than boorish and inconsiderate behaviour towards the unscholarly general reader whom he aspired to please. 'I could wish', he told Twining, 'to have my Book so divested of Pedantry & Jargon that every Miss, who plays o' top o' the Spinet should make it her manual.'[3]

---

[1] Twining to CB, 11 Apr. 1774, copy (Add. MS. 39933, ff. 98–103).
[2] Ibid. 7 Apr. 1773, copy (Add. MS. 39933, ff. 69–71).
[3] CB to Twining, 28 Apr. 1773 (Add. MS. 39929, ff. 54–56).

Twining did not at first appear to disagree with this ambition. He believed that 'Pedantry & Jargon' had always discouraged the general reader from the study of musical history: 'It is with great reason, that the histories of music hitherto published, have given the World in general an unfavourable opinion of the subject.' He also encouraged Burney's conviction that the only hope of entertaining his readers in this section of his book lay in ridicule of earlier scholars:

Obscurity & nonsense itself, will cease to offend, or even become amusing, when they are in the hands of a writer who sees them with unprejudiced eyes, gives them for what they are, & helps the reader to laugh at them. You cannot have much hope of instructing your readers in this part; but you will have many fair opportunities of diverting them by *just* ridicule. What disgusts & provokes one is the gravity of the Writers on ancient music who *will* talk about the scale, the genera, the modes &c, as if they really knew what they meant, & were present at Greek concerts every evening of their lives.[1]

When he began writing the *History* in July 1773, Burney decided to adopt a suggestion made by Twining, and proceeded 'to throw into a Dissertation, or preliminary Discourse, what guess-work, & ancient Authorities, have furnished me concerning the Doctrine of Modes, Systems, & Genera'. This plan had the advantage of clearly separating the more tedious technical sections from the main 'meerly historical' narrative and of thereby permitting his less serious readers to avoid it completely if they wished. The 'Dissertation' itself was to be characterized not only by refreshing mockery of earlier speculators, but by 'Humility' and frequent '*Confession of Ignorance*' on Burney's part, for he hoped that, by comparison with 'the solemn and decisive assurance' of earlier and bolder writers, such modesty would impress his readers as an attractive and reassuring novelty in itself.[2]

By August 1773 some progress had been made with the 'Dissertation' and Burney continued working hard during the autumn, when John Hawkesworth, a month before his death, heard part of it read aloud.[3] It was probably not until his

---

[1] Twining to CB, 28 May 1773, copy (Add. MS. 39933, ff. 73–78).

[2] CB to Twining, 30 Aug. 1773 (Add. MS. 39929, ff. 59–64); cf. Johnson to CB, 8 March 1758, on his edition of Shakespeare: 'where I am quite at a loss, I confess my ignorance, which is seldom done by commentators', *Letters*, i. 106.

[3] *ED*, i. 273.

worries over the subscription list were removed, however, that
Burney fully appreciated what scope for new depression his
discussion of ancient music offered him. The subject was even
more complex than he had suspected and he was not comforted
by the knowledge that antiquarians such as Thomas Pennant,
in addition to the young 'Misses', would be examining his work.
The problems which he had already encountered, he confessed
to Pennant in January 1774, were 'so multiplied & magnified
by examination & reflection, that I despair of having either
leisure or abilities to accomplish it in the Manner such Readers
as yourself may expect, or indeed in such a way as will at all
satisfy my own idea of what is wanted'.[1] William Bewley loyally
promised to 'brush up' his acquaintance with ancient music in
order that they might 'commune upon these matters in the summer'; but Greek modes and genera were essentially beyond his
capacity or interests, and his scientific preoccupations did not
promise well for Burney, as is suggested by the fact that it took
Bewley a month to complete the letter in which he offered his
assistance.[2]

In any case, Burney, pledged to publish his first volume before the end of the year, could not afford to wait until the
summer; and since it had soon become clear to him that Thomas
Twining knew quite as much about ancient music as he did
himself, and was infinitely more conversant with Latin and
Greek, he not surprisingly grew more and more dependent on
his new friend. From the summer of 1773, Twining had been
discussing various aspects of ancient music in his letters at considerable length, and Burney had soon admitted that it was
Twining, rather than himself, who should be writing the
'Dissertation'. In October Twining had modestly dismissed the
suggestion: 'as to your notion of my being qualified for such a
work as you are engaged in, . . . there is a monstrous stride
between seeing what *should* be done, & doing it'. Unwittingly
Twining thus defined precisely the roles that he and Burney
were to play in the partnership which produced the first volume
of the *History*. In the same letter Twining had begun to disagree
openly with some of Burney's theories about the Greek scale, in
order, as he tactfully explained, 'that our conversation may not

---

[1] See *ante*, p. 143, n. 2.
[2] Bewley to CB, 8 Jan.–5 Feb. 1774 (Osborn).

grow insipid, like that between Mr. Shandy & his wife, for want of a little seasoning of contradiction'.[1]

In April 1774, as his exhausting season of teaching was coming to an end, Burney appealed desperately to Twining for direct assistance. Although Twining had consistently played down his own knowledge of ancient music, he possessed so much material on the subject that he hardly knew how to begin helping his friend: 'You desire me to pop down my ideas, relative any way to your work. But what?—how? Whence? Where?—I have a 1000 things more, scrawled down in my papers as I read, about the Greek music.' There were, however, a number of topics which had especially interested him, his notes on which he offered to send Burney.[2]

In London the historian of music was working frantically: as Fanny noted, he 'pursues his work at all the leisure hours he can snatch from business or sleep'.[3] By June 1774 he had compiled a list of his most important problems and had dispatched it to Fordham with a letter which seemed to Twining 'the very picture of a man worried to death'. A slow and painstakingly careful scholar himself, Twining was annoyed that Burney should be 'forced to gallop & scramble to the press in so uncomfortable a hurry', but suddenly realizing the extent of his friend's anxiety to keep his promise to his subscribers of publishing during 1774, he agreed to give every assistance in his power.[4] Within a week his usual leisurely existence had been drastically transformed: 'You have sucked me into your tourbillon, & *your* hurry is *mine*, malgré moi.' As best he could, he dealt with the 'parcel of unanswerable questions' which Burney had sent him, adding his own basic 'creed' about the nature of Greek music and discussing the most reliable earlier writers on the subject. Most important of all, he sent Burney 'the only thing *like* a discovery that I ever made in it', a short treatise on one of the most troublesome topics which Burney had to face, the Enharmonic Genus in Greek music. This essay, and other material, Twining was able to take directly from notes he had collected to illuminate and supplement Plutarch's

[1] Twining to CB, 16 Oct. 1773, copy (Add. MS. 39933, ff. 83–92). Cf. *Tristram Shandy*, vol. vi, ch. xviii. Twining's humour owes much to Sterne.
[2] Twining to CB, 11 Apr. 1774, copy (Add. MS. 39933, ff. 98–103).
[3] *ED*, i. 316.
[4] Twining to CB, 28 June 1774, copy (Add. MS. 39933, ff. 104–5).

Dialogue on Music. He claimed little for his speculations but, if Burney wished, he could send more similar material: 'vous aurez mes opinions, mes scrupules, mes croyances, mes semi-croyances, mes demi-semi-croyances — mes conjectures — mes tâtonnements — mes vues — mes *entrevues* — mes lumières — mes lueurs — mes crepuscules — mes brouillants — mes tenêbres!'[1]

In spite of Twining's self-deprecation, Burney was delighted with his letter: 'you are a jewel of a man, to drudge for me in these pitch-dark & coal-black mines'. Arriving just when he had been fruitlessly poring over the confused 'authorities' on ancient music for several days, Twining's letter clarified many of his problems and cheered him enormously. He had found little with which to disagree and he admitted that Twining's 'creed' or basic convictions about the nature of ancient music was more elaborate and 'better founded' than his own.[2] As for Twining's hypothesis about the Enharmonic Genus, it is probable that Burney had already sent the section containing his own views on the subject to press and that he was obliged to cancel several pages to accommodate Twining's more learned and coherent theory.[3]

Although by the summer of 1774 the possibility of publishing the first volume of the *History* before the end of the year was slowly receding, with the learned and incisive assistance of Twining Burney might well have kept his subscribers waiting for no more than a few months, had not the one matter close enough to his heart to distract him from his great undertaking appeared at precisely this critical moment. Although Burney was preoccupied by this project for little more than a month, its consequences were to demoralize him for a much longer period and to make the fulfilment of his promise quite impossible.

III

Ever since his journey to Italy in 1770 Burney had been 'haunted' by the ambition of establishing in England a 'Public Music School' along the lines of the Conservatorios he had seen in Venice and Naples, in which poor but talented children could receive an elaborate musical education. Burney felt that

---

[1] Ibid. 3–6 July 1774, copy (Add. MS. 39933, ff. 106–11) and notes (Add. MS. 39936, ff. 51–53).   [2] CB to Twining, 13 July 1774, copy (Osborn).
[3] See *post*, pp. 491–2.

the scheme was a national concern, for it provided a way not only of raising England's musical reputation but also of obviating the need to import foreign singers at great expense for the London opera-houses. After his return from Italy he had drawn up a prospectus for such an institution and had at once won the interest and support of Giardini, the famous violinist. During 1772 he had expanded this 'Plan' and intended to print it on his return from Germany, 'either in a small Pamphlet, or in some other Form'.[1] Various schemes, however, of establishing the school under the patronage of the Royal Family, of the Fund for Decayed Musicians or by public subscription had collapsed and, distracted by his literary projects, Burney did not print his pamphlet. In 1774, however, a new scheme occurred to Burney and Giardini of establishing the Music School in the Foundling Hospital in London, where orphan children were already conveniently assembled and housed, and where a chapel, suitable for the public performances by the children which would provide much of the School's income, was available.[2] Giardini, moreover, was a Governor of the Foundling Hospital and, since 1770, had been in charge of such musical activities as already took place there.[3]

A summary of the short but eventful history of Burney's project, which has been related in part several times,[4] is justified not only by relevant new material but because its consequences have not hitherto been fully explored. Burney's 'Plan' in itself has always provided a problem, for during the nineteenth century it was usually listed among his publications. Dr. Scholes, who could find no traces of it, correctly concluded that it had never been printed.[5] This opinion could have been confirmed by examination of the biography of Burney in the *European Magazine* in 1785, which was undoubtedly based on information supplied by him, in which the work is listed as 'Plan of a Public Music School, M.S.'.[6] The all-important 'M.S.' was carelessly omitted in the later biographies which took their information from this article.

Two manuscripts of Burney's 'Sketch of a Plan for a Public

---

[1] CB to Giardini, 21 June 1772, copy (Osborn).
[2] CB to Twining, 13 July 1774, copy (Osborn).
[3] R. H. Nichols and F. A. Wray, *The History of the Foundling Hospital*, 1935, p. 211.
[4] *Mem.* i. 233–44; Nichols and Wray, op. cit., pp. 247–8; *GDB*, i. 261–3.
[5] *GDB*, i. 263, ii. 333.   [6] vii (1785), 164.

Music School After the manner of an Italian Conservatorio',
one of which is dated 'June 1774', have survived among his
papers.[1] This revised form of the 'Plan' contains various argu-
ments designed to persuade the Governors and Guardians of the
Foundling Hospital that the project was of the greatest national
importance and that the establishment in their care was the
only suitable basis for such a School. Although Burney was
undoubtedly sincere in his conviction of the importance of the
scheme, some of his enthusiasm can perhaps be explained by the
fact that his 'Plan' envisaged the appointment of Giardini and
himself as its two 'principal Masters' at a salary of £200 a year,
although the main burden of the teaching was to be carried by
four assistants at much smaller salaries.

Three of the fortnightly meetings of the Court of Governors
and Guardians of the Hospital discussed Burney's 'Plan'. The
Minutes of the first, held on 6 July 1774, record that Burney and
Giardini had intimated 'a Proposal for the Benefit of this
Hospital' to three of the Governors, and that the same three had
been empowered to receive and report on the proposal. Burney
read his 'Plan' to them on 12 July, and, not surprisingly, it was
'well received', for the three Governors whom he approached
had been carefully chosen. Sir Charles Whitworth, Treasurer
of the Hospital, seems to have been a friend of Burney, and
favourably predisposed to the scheme, and both Messrs.
Harrison and Scott had musical connexions with the Hospital,
which they doubtless hoped would become more profitable if
the School were established.[2]

The crucial meeting of the Court of Governors was held on
20 July 1774. Few of the numerous Governors attended these
meetings, especially during the summer, unless important
business was to be transacted and it is clear from the Minutes of
the following meeting that no announcement of the drastic
alteration to the basis of the Hospital proposed by Burney and
Giardini was made on this occasion. Of the nineteen Governors
who attended it is noticeable that many were friends of Burney.
Apart from Giardini, Whitworth, Harrison, and Scott, the other
Governors present included Lord Sandwich, the Rev. Martin
Madan, a keen music-lover, and John Stanley, the blind

[1] Osborn: both are in the hands of amanuenses, corrected by CB.
[2] Nichols and Wray, op. cit., pp. 211–12, 233, 238, 313.

organist, who already taught music at the Hospital. Since Daines Barrington, the lawyer and antiquarian, wrote especially to inform Burney that he had been urging his friends to attend this meeting,[1] it may be assumed that a number of the other Governors present (such as Benjamin Wilson, the painter, a friend of William Mason and, like Barrington and Burney, a Fellow of the Royal Society) were predisposed in favour of the 'Plan'.

Not surprisingly therefore the Minutes record that this small Court of Governors, packed with Burney's friends, decided that his proposal was 'likely to be of considerable advantage to this Corporation, and of National Utility', opened a subscription to bear the initial expenses, appointed a Special Committee to inaugurate the Music School on 28 July, and elected Burney a Governor of the Hospital. Carried away by the success of his 'Plan', Burney could concentrate on nothing else; an important visit to Fordham to confer with Twining about ancient music was postponed and, in Fanny's words, 'The hardly-fought battle over, victory, waving her gay banners, that wafted to the Doctor hopes of future renown with present benediction, determined him, for the moment, to relinquish even his history, that he might devote every voluntary thought to consolidating this scheme.'[2] By the end of July 1774 the Music School had been 'established in all its branches'. Sir Charles Whitworth— 'Allmost as eager as yourself for the Good Conduct of the Plan' —returned early from the country on 1 August to help Burney to ensure it.[3] Two days later, to Burney's 'indignant Consternation', Whitworth wrote again to inform him that the Court of Governors which met on 3 August had ordered the School to be closed.[4]

Burney later blamed the collapse of the School on the behaviour of his colleague Giardini,[5] but did not substantiate this charge. In any case, although the names of the Governors present at the Court of 3 August have not been preserved, it seems clear that this meeting was as packed with Burney's opponents as the previous meeting had been with his friends. Although the Music School was officially closed on the grounds that it was 'not warranted' by the Act of Parliament which had

---

[1] Barrington to CB, 19 July [1774] (Osborn).   [2] *Mem.* i. 241-2.
[3] Whitworth to CB, 25 July and 1 Aug. 1774 (Osborn).   [4] *Mem.* i. 242.
[5] 'Sketch of a Character' (Osborn). See *ante*, p. 78.

established the Foundling Hospital, at the time Burney bitterly attributed the 'illiberal, Gloomy and Tiranical principle' which had destroyed his ambitious scheme to 'a small Junto, a Cabal . . . collected together from 2 or 3 neighbouring streets'.[1] The memory of the disintegration of the School and, no doubt, of the loss of income involved in it, rankled for many years. Twice in the first volume of his *History* he deplored the absence of such a School in England[2] and, as late as 1785, described his unpublished 'Plan' (somewhat disingenuously, considering the nature of the Court of Governors which had approved it) as 'un-animously adopted in 1774, by the Guardians and Governors of the Foundling Hospital, and ordered to be carried into execution by Dr. Burney and Mr. Giardini, with professional assistants. This institution, so much wanted in our country, was soon suppressed by a small cabal, in the absence of the principal governors . . . .'[3]

Although his friends urged him to fight back or even to have the obstructive Act of Parliament altered, Burney abandoned the scheme 'without further struggle'.[4] His acutely sensitive pride could demean itself by argument no more on this oc-casion than during the misunderstanding with Garrick in 1767 or at Cambridge in 1769. During August he retreated at last to Essex to resume work on his *History* with Twining's help, carrying with him as much of his dignity as he could preserve.

Burney's dignity survived, however, for little more than two weeks. Between his visit to Twining and a short stay with Lord Sandwich later in the month,[5] the following advertisement appeared in the newspapers:

On Saturday next will be published,

Price One Shilling,

(Dedicated to the GOVERNORS of the
FOUNDLING HOSPITAL)

MUSICAL TRAVELS thro' ENGLAND,

By JOSEPH COLLIER, Organist.

☞ This work is printed on a proper Size to be bound up with the celebrated Musical Tours to France, Italy,

---

[1] CB's notes on a letter from A[ntony] S[hepherd], 4 Aug. 1774 (J. A. Sparrow).
[2] *Hist. Mus.* i. 387 n., 486.   [3] *European Magazine*, vii (1785), 164.
[4] *Mem.* i. 243.   [5] Sandwich to CB, 21 Aug. 1774 (PML); *ED*, i. 322.

Germany, Netherlands, and United Provinces, to which
it is intended as a Supplement.

Printed for G. Kearsley, in Fleet-street.[1]

The book was published on 20 August 1774 and three days
later the *London Chronicle* devoted more than a page to long
extracts from it. On seeing a copy of this newspaper, William
Bewley, who was staying at Houghton, 'raved & even foamed at
the mouth', although Lord Orford thought it no more than a
'harmless though extravagant parody'. Bewley, however,
assumed that the book was the work of 'a *personal* enemy' of
Burney and at once 'bespoke the Review of this production,
least it should fall into the hands possibly of a less competent
judge'.[2] His abusive notice of the parody, which appeared in
the *Monthly Review* in September, dismissed it as negligible and
tedious in so charged and violent a manner, however, that it was
more likely to attract than deter readers. Bewley significantly
felt it necessary to descend to the same level of humour as 'Joel
Collier' himself.[3] The ribald satire was not entirely without
merit, as the *London Magazine*[4] observed, and it sold well.

'Joel Collier's' *Musical Travels*, in fact, indulge in some coarse,
spirited, and not unamusing satire of Burney's *Tours*. The
direct parody, however, is only spasmodic, rarely personal and
usually confined to ludicrous parallels with Burney's journeys
and to quotations from his books made ridiculous by abstraction from their context. The parody had, nevertheless, been
explicitly instigated by Burney's attempt to use the Foundling
Hospital for his Music School and, in his more serious moments,
the satirist ridiculed that scheme as only the most recent and
extreme example of the contemporary triumph of luxury,
effeminacy, and corruption. The Dedication to the Governors
of the Hospital, written before the author had learned of the
failure of the School, congratulates them on the wisdom of their
new enterprise with heavy sarcasm:

---

[1] *Public Advertiser*, 18 Aug. 1774. 'Joseph Collier' was an error for 'Joel Collier'.
[2] Bewley to CB, 5 Sept. 1774 (Osborn).
[3] *Monthly Review*, li (1774), 242, quoted by Scholes, who was unaware that it was
by Bewley, *GDB*, i. 272. To avoid offending his readers Scholes silently omitted
part of the first sentence and inadvertently reversed Bewley's meaning in the ensuing grammatical patchwork.
[4] xliii (1774), 499–500.

men of narrow and contracted minds, who have neither *ear*, nor *voice*, nor *hand*, will still imagine, that it might prove of more national utility, to breed these adopted children of the public, to Husbandry, Navigation, &c. the objects of their original destination; than to convert one of the noblest of our public charities into a nursery for the supply of musical performers at our Theatres, gardens, and hops.— But this is a vulgar prejudice. . . . when we have rivalled the *Italians* in music, it will be time enough to think of our navy, and our agriculture. We have already (to our shame be it spoken) better sailors than fidlers, and more farmers than *contrapuntists*.[1]

Burney's reaction to 'Joel Collier' can be gauged only from remarks made by his friends. He was predictably distressed by the parody, especially as such friends as Lord Sandwich[2] and Twining were deceived by the advertisement and at first believed it to be a serious supplement to his own *Tours*. On realizing the true nature of the book, however, Twining was more concerned about its effect on his friend's morale than about any damage it might do to his reputation. The coarse parody, in fact, upset Burney so much that he even went so far as to contemplate abandoning his *History of Music*. Twining had to reprimand his friend severely for such folly: 'If there was the least *shade* of seriousness in your *shill-I-shall-I* about going on with your work, you deserve to be threshed. Shall the envy & ill nature of such a fellow be allowed to weigh a grain against the general approbation your introductory little works have met with?'[3]

Burney was not comforted by Twining's argument that the parody should be taken merely as a tribute to the celebrity of his *Tours*. Coming so soon after the infuriating collapse of the Music School and in the midst of his anxieties about the slow progress of his *History of Music*, 'Joel Collier' almost succeeded in breaking his spirit. In September 1774 he succumbed to a severe attack of rheumatism, which particularly crippled his right arm. Physical torment did not distract him from mental troubles, however, and in October Twining had to rebuke him once more: 'If you would give one farthing to annihilate the book, & all memory of it, you are a vain man.'[4] In his way, of

---

[1] 1st edn., p. vi. This passage was slightly revised in later editions.
[2] Joseph Cradock, *Literary and Miscellaneous Memoirs*, 1828, iv. 168.
[3] Twining to CB, 17 Sept. 1774, copy (Add. MS. 39933, ff. 114–15).
[4] Twining to CB, 13 Oct. 1774, copy (Add. MS. 39933, ff. 116–17).

course, Burney *was* an extremely vain man and the suggestion
that he attempted to suppress the parody by buying up all
copies of it was supported after his death by John Thomas
Smith, who doubtless received his information from Molesworth
Phillips, his close friend and Burney's son-in-law: 'The Doctor
was rendered uncomfortable beyond measure, by the publication of a small work, in which he was ridiculed under the
appellation of "Joel Collyer". Upon this squib, he, according to
calculations, expended full two hundred pounds in buying up
copies whereever they were offered for sale.'[1] F. J. Fétis later
explained the comparative rarity of the parody with a similar
story.[2]

Burney's acute concern for his own reputation makes the
story quite feasible, although the inevitable result would merely
be the appearance of new editions. By May 1775 Bewley had
read, at Burney's instigation, an expanded second edition,
which contained a reply to his own review, and had seen an
advertisement for a third, further expanded by an appendix.
Even Bewley, however, began to feel that his friend was taking
the parody too seriously: 'How could you be so serious about
that Joel Collier! Never surely was there any thing so execrable
as the *Additions*, in his second Edition, on which I threw away
two good shillings on your *recommendation*. Never surely was
there any thing so mortally stupid as the dull rogue's retort
upon his Reviewer.'[3] Fanny d'Arblay, either through ignorance
or through unwillingness to admit the popularity of an attack
on her father, stated that the parody misfired badly and was
never reprinted.[4] In fact, the second and third editions of 1775
were followed by a fourth in 1776, a fifth in 1785 and a sixth,
adapted to a new target, *Joel Collier Redivivus*, in 1818.

As for the authorship of the parody, although many attributions have been made, Dr. Scholes did not feel able to
reach a confident identification and Burney's papers have
provided no more positive information. If, however, the
Dictionary of National Biography had not garbled earlier statements into the wildest of all the attributions (to George Veal),
now accepted by most libraries, there would seem to be little

---

[1] J. T. Smith, *Nollekens and his Times*, 1828, i. 196.
[2] *Biographie Universelle des musiciens*, 2nd edn., Paris, 1860–5, ii. 336.
[3] Bewley to CB, 1 May 1775 (Osborn).   [4] *Mem.* i. 258–60.

reason for doubt about the authorship. The parody was attributed to John Bicknell (1746?–1787), a lawyer and miscellaneous writer, in his obituary notice in the *European Magazine*,[1] by James Boswell,[2] and by John Thomas Smith.[3] Internal evidence supports this identification, for Bicknell was a close friend of Thomas Day, the author of *Sandford and Merton*, and Day's hatred of foreign sophistication and the decadence of contemporary England can be paralleled constantly in 'Joel Collier's' *Musical Travels*. It is no surprise to find that the parody is attributed to both Day and Bicknell in an inscription in a copy of *Sandford and Merton* in the Bodleian Library,[4] or to learn that Day was a Governor of the Foundling Hospital.[5]

IV

The autumn of 1774 was one of the most depressing periods of Burney's life. His ambition of founding and directing the first Public Music School in England had collapsed; his books had been ridiculed in a ribald parody; rheumatic fever had crippled his right arm; and no hope remained of keeping his promise to his subscribers of publishing the first volume of his *History* during 1774. In September he worked irresolutely at Chessington, morbidly contemplating the abandonment of his great undertaking. Dissuaded by Twining from so foolish a decision, he returned in October to his new house in St. Martin's Street, Leicester Fields, the former home of Sir Isaac Newton. Although Fanny believed that her father was 'very much recovered',[6] he was still confined to his room, 'disabled' in both 'Body & Mind'. His illness meant that the publication of his book would be even longer delayed, but he tried to persuade himself that he would not be obliged to keep his subscribers waiting long, for the earlier chapters had already been printed.[7]

Thomas Twining, who continued to send Burney his learned theories about the nature of ancient music, began at this period to play an additional role, for his common sense, good humour, and encouragement were becoming as important to Burney as his knowledge of Latin and Greek. Twining perceived that

[1] xi (1787), 296.   [2] Hill–Powell, i. 315.
[3] See *ante*, p. 156, n. 1.   [4] *GDB*, i. 275.
[5] Nichols and Wray, op. cit., p. 382.   [6] *ED*, i. 328.
[7] CB to [Rev. Charles Davy], 3 Nov. 1774 (Osborn).

Burney's illness was largely psychosomatic and tried to persuade him that his anxiety about his book was unnecessary:

for heavens sake take care of yourself, & don't be hurried & plagued about your work;—I verily believe you have hurt yourself by your application, and continual worry about it. I wish I could persuade you not to care a farthing whether you publish within the time you had fixed or not. It is not possible now is it?—& have you not sufficient excuse? I wish you had not.—Be easy & cool; do nothing but just when you are in the humour, & even then let your mind make a bow to your body, first, & say, 'Pray Sir &c—?'[1]

To a man of Burney's temperament, however, such advice was futile, for, although he was still confined to his room at the end of November and was unable to write, he merely resorted to dictating the later chapters of his volume to his daughters:

Even illness took activity only from his body, for his mind refused all relaxation. He had constantly, when indisposed, one of his daughters by his side, as an amanuensis; and such was the vigour of his intellect, that even when keeping his bed from acute rheumatism, spasmodic pains, or lurking fever, he caught at every little interval of ease to dictate some illustrative reminiscence; to start some new ideas, or to generalize some old ones; which never failed to while away, partially at least, the pangs of disease, by lessening their greatest torment to a character of such energy, irreparable loss of time.[2]

During November he corresponded with Dr. James Lind (1736–1812), the physician, who was able to supply him with information about, and examples of, Chinese music, which he wished to mention in the *History*.[3]

By late November 1774, only the 'Dissertation upon the Music of the Ancients', barely a third of what was to be the first volume, had been printed, and early in 1775 Burney was obliged to take the step, which he had dreaded for so long, of making a public apology to his subscribers. Attributing the delay to his 'long and severe Indisposition', he begged them 'to indulge him with a few Months longer', adding that 'He can with the utmost Truth assure his Subscribers, that when he

[1] Twining to CB, 14 Nov. 1774, copy (Add. MS. 39933, ff. 118–25).
[2] *Mem.* i. 246.
[3] CB to Lind, Nov. 1774, draft, and 26 Nov. 1774; Lind to CB, 11 Nov. 1774 (Osborn). Cf. *Hist. Mus.* i. 38.

fixed upon the End of 1774, for Publication, he promised them
no more than he promised himself; however more than half the
First Volume is already printed; and the whole will be pursued
with all the Diligence and Expedition which his Health will
permit.'[1] If there was any comfort to be derived from the
situation, it was that Burney could adapt a phrase which Samuel
Johnson had used in a letter to him many years before, when
speaking of the subscribers to his edition of Shakespeare: 'I did
not promise them more than I promised myself.'[2]

In January 1775 Twining paid one of his rare visits to London, 'grinning like a dog, & running about the city' and calling
frequently on the Burneys. Fanny considered that he had 'not
only as much humour as learning, but also as much good
nature as either'.[3] Burney depended on all three of these
qualities in his friend, but conferences between them were
limited by the fact that, in spite of his crippled hand, Burney
could not afford to miss a music-teacher's most prosperous and
hurried season. Until the spring, therefore, he dragged himself
painfully from lesson to lesson, attending to the *History* whenever he could. Fanny told Samuel Crisp in April that 'He
teaches from nine to nine almost every day, and has scarce
time to write a page a week. Nobody besides himself could
write a word so circumstanced. His health and hand are, I hope,
rather better, however, very little, for never surely was an
attack more obstinate.'[4] With characteristic tenacity and
courage, however, Burney kept going: 'Every sick or failing
pupil bestowed an hour upon his pen. Every holiday for others
was a day of double labour to his composition.'[5] Many years
later, recalling his laborious life, Burney remembered being, at
this period, 'fully occupied by 2 trades at once, that of teaching
12 or 14 hours each day—and . . . on my return home at midnight finding a Printer's Devil waiting for the corrections of a
proof of my Hist^y at which, in winter all I was able to do, was
taken out of my Sleep'.[6]

In March 1775 he managed to write a letter to Crisp with his
own crippled 'paw', although, he added, 'not one straight

[1] *Public Advertiser*, 19 Jan. 1775.
[2] Johnson to CB, 8 Mar. 1758. See *ante*, pp. 51, 146, n. 2.
[3] Twining to CB, 26 Mar. 1775, copy (Add. MS. 39933, ff. 132–3); *ED*, ii. 10,
20, 24, 35–36.   [4] Ibid. 44–45.
[5] *Mem.* i. 246.   [6] CB to Lord Lonsdale, July 1804, draft (Osborn).

finger have I on my right hand. . . . such a hurried shattered worn-out post-horse as I am at present crawls not on the earth'. As for the *History*, it was 'at a dead stop now, page 352', the press having apparently caught up with author. About two-thirds of the first volume had therefore been printed, although he was already drafting the fourth chapter of 'The History of Greek Music' and the discussion of music at the Olympic and Pythian Games. In spite of the state of his health, Burney's spirits had improved surprisingly and he told Crisp the reason in his letter.[1]

In the previous October he had received a long letter from James Bruce (1730–94), the explorer who had recently returned from Africa and whose exploits were the subject of great interest and speculation, which were not diminished by the fact that he was extremely reluctant to give any authorized account of his explorations. It was therefore something of a triumph for Burney to obtain from Bruce a long account of the state of Abyssinian music.[2] His first intention was probably to reserve Bruce's information for the section on 'National Music' in his second volume; but his curiosity was aroused by a reference in the letter to an elaborate and very ancient drawing of a harp which Bruce claimed to have discovered in a cave near Thebes. The explorer had made a careful copy of it, which he now sent to Burney, who soon decided that a detailed depiction of so ancient an instrument was nothing less than a sensational discovery.

Throughout the winter of 1774–5 the gigantic Bruce was a frequent visitor in St. Martin's Street[3] and during these months Burney discussed the ancient harp with its discoverer. He had realized not only that Bruce's account of it was more relevant to the history of ancient than of 'national' music, but that its appearance in his first volume would anticipate any other publication by Bruce and greatly enhance the interest of his book to the general reader. Bruce eventually expanded his letter about the 'Theban Harp'[4] and also gave Burney permission to reproduce his drawing of the instrument. As Burney did not announce this 'scoop' to Crisp until March 1775, it is possible

[1] CB to Crisp, March 1775 (Barrett; *ED*, ii. 34–36).
[2] Bruce to CB, 20 Oct. 1774 (Osborn).
[3] *ED*, i. 321–2, ii. 7–8, 13–26, 31–33; *Mem.* i. 295–329.
[4] This addition runs from *Hist. Mus.* i. *222 (para. 3) to *224 (para. 1).

that he had only recently obtained Bruce's permission. As the chapter on Egyptian Music, in which Burney decided to insert Bruce's letter, had already been printed, he was forced to cancel a number of pages and to introduce a series of sixteen 'double pages', distinguished by asterisks.[1]

The inclusion of Bruce's letter made Burney only the more anxious to publish his volume. The troublesome 'Dissertation' was now printed and only the concluding chapters of the straightforward historical narrative remained. Counting on a peaceful summer of uninterrupted work at Chessington, Burney now expected his book to appear early in the autumn of 1775. Since he had come increasingly to rely on his friend's learned opinions, suggestions, and criticism, it is not surprising that as a final check he asked Twining to read over the sheets of the *History* which had already been printed. Earlier in the year he had sent some 200 pages to Bewley in Norfolk, but these had been returned by May at the latest[2] and during the summer the proofs were sent on to Twining, followed later by the manuscript of the remaining chapters.

During the summer of 1775 a number of minor tensions appear in Twining's letters to Burney, although the responsibility must be shared by both. The series of misunderstandings can be most simply explained by the fact that, although Twining had none of Burney's indefatigable energy and capacity for work to the point of utter exhaustion, he was a more scrupulous and learned scholar, and had studied the subject of ancient music much more thoroughly. Twining frequently commented on the unquestioning willingness with which Burney adopted his ideas, in some cases quoting his letters directly in the *History*. Moreover, stimulated at last to hard work for Burney's benefit, Twining inevitably began to consider the possibility of using his learning for his own fame, rather than simply handing over the fruits of his research to his friend.

These considerations lie behind Twining's letters in the summer of 1775. The most substantial of his contributions to the *History* was his hypothesis about the Enharmonic Genus, which Burney had taken over with only minor alterations. These

---

[1] See *post*, pp. 492–3.
[2] Bewley to CB, 2 Jan. 1775 (misdated 1774 by Bewley); and 1–6 May 1775 (Osborn).

changes affected only the style, which Burney seems to have tried to make more attractive for his general readers. In June 1775 he warned Twining of these changes in advance, before sending him the relevant sheets. Twining incorrectly assumed that his style had been too pompous and humbly begged frank criticism from Burney:

I had some fear when I sent you my scrawl, lest the genânte idea of writing something for the Great cyclops eye of the public to stare at, might have betrayed me into buckram & fancy, & given me a swing of the rump which I have not in my every day gait. If there is anything of this sort, for heaven's sake tell me so in plain prose; for I may one day be as foolish as my betters, & write a book about something or other; & if I do, 1000 to one but I write just as I have that paper.

As if to confirm that he was already contemplating a work of his own, Twining asked Burney if he thought that a translation and edition of Plutarch's *Dialogue on Music* would be worth undertaking.[1]

Burney's reply, which presumably accompanied the parcel of sheets containing Twining's 'Enharmonic Hypothesis', assured him that 'Our harmony of ideas will appear from the very few alterations I have made, either in the thoughts or words of your MS.'; and he expressed his delight that his friend was at last going to take 'an opportunity for a display of all your musical & other eruditions, as well as taste: so go to work'.[2] Twining discovered, however, that Burney's alterations to his essay were designed to dignify rather than to lower the style. He accepted most of them with genial derision:

And so your *diluting* & *lowering*, & all that, turns out to be *raising*, & it is *you* that have turned *my* coarse barragon[3] into broadcloth. . . . Almost all your alterations are amendments of my colloquial *bassesses*. I am glad I am not in your study—I might be provoked to throw the ink over your papers, or let a folio fall upon your toes, for your abominable good breeding. . . . I am very glad to find, however, that my errors in writing, are likely to lean to the *colloquial side*. . . . I had much rather write as the *vulgar* talk than as no body *ever talked*; I mean in the bloated bladderosity of the Johnsonian school.[4]

---

[1] Twining to CB, 9 June 1775, copy (Add. MS. 39933, ff. 136–7; Osborn).
[2] CB to Twining, June 1775, copy of memoranda (Osborn).
[3] Fustian.
[4] Twining to CB, 22 June 1775, copy (Add. MS. 39933, ff. 138–9).

Richard Twining's copy of this letter evidently omits a passage in which Twining must have explained that he did not seriously intend to undertake an edition of Plutarch's *Dialogue*, since he had already handed over most of his original discoveries about ancient music to Burney. Not surprisingly, Burney was aghast at the implication, intended or not, that he had deprived Twining of discoveries which his friend would otherwise have published himself: 'You work & mortify me by saying that my being in possession of your Enharm: System partly prevents your translating Plut.'s Dial.—If I acknowledge it in the Preface, which I will, & everything else most readily & gladly, if I have your leave, it will be yours *again* to do what you please with. . . . don't lay such a weight on my conscience.'[1] The copyist of Burney's letter in turn omitted a passage in which he protested about Twining's remarks on style, assuming that the reference to 'bloated bladderosity' was directed at his own prose. Twining now realized, however, that the exchange of ambiguous sentiments and complex disavowals was getting out of hand and, after a silence of almost four weeks, he replied late in July, firmly assuring Burney that he had intended no criticism of his style and that 'It was always about as probable that I should translate Plutarch, as that I should fly. When I give a man a thing, & wish it back again, it must be something of more value than my Enharmonic hypothesis.' In view of the amount of material Twining had collected about the *Dialogue*, it seems clear that he was simply being kind to Burney at this point. As for Burney's offer to acknowledge his help in his Preface, he mocked the idea with his usual modest good humour: 'Go to — you & your preface;—I desire none of your palaver. You had better have an engraving of my *joulter*, had not you? along with your own, in an oval frame, with Lyre & hautbois & trumpets & flying Music-books all round it; the motto—"caput inter nubila condit,"—to denote the sublimity, darkness & out-of-sightedness of my researches.'

Twining had, however, a particular motive for wishing to clear up these minor misunderstandings. For several weeks he had been reading the sheets of Burney's 'Dissertation' and the manuscript of later chapters, and, fully aware of his friend's desire to publish without delay, wished to put him into the right

[1] CB to Twining, 28 June 1775, copy (Osborn).

frame of mind for receiving the extensive criticisms he felt obliged to make. He brought his most affectionate tact to this delicate situation:

Don't think me a hypercritical caviller & a *faultmaker*: I am confident that no man ever discover'd faults or mistakes in the work of another, with a more unwilling eye, or with a feeling more similar to that *pure* displeasure which a man experiences in finding fault with himself. . . . I believe, indeed, that you & I, hardly, au fond, differ about anything.—Our souls, I believe, are of the same *temper*. But a *perfect* agreement in every opinion between two human creatures cannot be expected, till one soul is cut in halves, & put into two bodies. Nay, that would not do:—the two bodies would make a difference.[1]

Burney, however, was in no mood for welcoming such criticism, however necessary he knew it to be at heart. He had been detained in London until late in July and no sooner had he settled down to work at Chessington than the deterioration of his health resulted in his being ordered to Buxton.[2] He began to fear that, with about a quarter of the volume yet to be written, it would not be published even during 1775, especially as Twining's lists of suggested alterations and corrections were serious enough to necessitate the compilation of an appendix of 'Additional Notes'.

While Burney was at Buxton in August, Twining continued patiently with the painful task of criticizing and correcting the sheets and the manuscript of later chapters. He was glad that Burney had resigned himself to the necessity of adding 'supplements, & pentimenti' to the volume, for, considering the difficult circumstances in which the book had been written, this would reflect no disgrace on its author. He believed, moreover, that a frank confession to the public of those difficulties would not be harshly received.

You have not by the way, the least reason to be mortified at your mistakes &c: it is astonishing to me, that in the hurrying, uncomfortable, *filch-minute* way, in which you have been obliged to go on, with your ill health,—fatigue,—disabled hand, & no *choice* of *willing hours*—it is astonishing to me, how you can have done so much, & so

---

[1] Twining to CB, 24 July 1775, copy (Add. MS. 39933, ff. 140–1).
[2] CB to [Rev. C. Davy], 2 Aug. 1775 (Cambridge Univ. Library).

well as you have done. You must draw a sketch of all this in your pre-face, & then all your readers will be as much surprised as I am, at your perseverance, patience, *command* of *brain* &c.[1]

Twining's great affection for Burney did not, however, modify the frankness of his disagreements with his friend: if anything, it made him only more forthright and rigorous. Not without reason, Twining had come to care as much for the 'honour' of the *History* as if it had been his own work: 'I feel a tender interest in its welfare. Tender as fathers feel', he had told Burney in June. The unhappy author himself, tormented with rheumatism, appreciated that the unembarrassed honesty of Twining's criticism was only a sign of his loyalty, but his morale did not rise as he saw his defects and omissions laid bare.

Twining's criticism was not concerned only with facts, speculative theory, and classical references. Ever anxious not to alarm the 'Masters & Misses' and his polite literary audience, Burney had attempted to relieve the drier parts of his narrative with more attractive digressions comparing ancient and modern musical theory and practice, lengthy accounts of mythological characters connected with music, and translations—frequently his own—of Greek and Latin poetry, which in many cases had only remote relevance to his subject. Twining strongly disap-proved of Burney's attempts to satisfy simultaneously his scholarly and his social ambitions and insisted that he had his eye on the wrong audience. He agreed that Burney should try to avoid making his book impenetrable to all but learned musicologists; and, 'As to your *Masters & Misses*, if they will leave their novels & their plays for a history of music, let that history be as amusing as *possible*.' Burney's true audience, how-ever, lay between the two extremes:

to be amused with *any* sort of information, one must have a little stock of rational *curiosity* about the matter, & I have always found older folks than masters & misses unaccountably deficient in such curiosity. Do your utmost, therefore, the most you can reasonably expect of such readers, is that they will *read* the last half of the *last* volume, & look over the gays in both. But there are a sort of readers, between these, & the scientific folks you talk of, & whom you sup-pose to know everything before-hand; such as are capable of a little

[1] Twining to CB, 21 Aug. 1775, copy (Add. MS. 39933, ff. 142–3).

attention, & have previous knowledge upon the subject just sufficient
to set their curiosity in motion; & sense & taste enough to be pleased
when they see a subject that has hitherto been so treated as to produce nothing but disgust & ennui, made readable & entertaining.
Many such readers, I should hope you would have, & I think *they* are
the people one would fix one's eye upon *par preference*, if upon any.

For this reason, and also because he objected to them in
themselves, Twining disapproved of Burney's excursions into
mythology and his trite 'imitations' of classical verse. He had
begun to realize, in addition, that, if he was not careful, Burney
would have difficulty in cramming the whole history of music
into the proposed two volumes. Unless he omitted some of his
digressions, gave only thin treatment to Roman music, and had
dealt with the history of early Church music by the end of the
first volume, Burney would find himself in need of a third
volume, which Twining thought would be a great error.
Twining had no wish, however, to be dogmatic and he was still
embarrassed by the passivity with which Burney received his
criticism and suggestions, either altering his manuscript, expanding his 'Additional Notes', or apologizing abjectly for his
inability to include them: 'If I chance to tell you in the way of
conversation, that I have got a pimple upon my nose, I suppose
you'll be giving me reasons why you cannot mention it in your
history.'[1]

After three weeks at Buxton and a similar period sea-bathing
in Norfolk, Burney returned to London early in October 1775,
in better health but with his hand 'still *obstinately bent*'.[2] Finding
'the Press standing still just at the time when I can best attend
to it', he concealed himself from intruders in St. Martin's
Street, refused to see any visitors, and wrote urgently to Twining,
requesting the immediate return of such of the manuscript of
the later chapters as he had checked: 'If I don't get this vol. out
before X[mas] I shall break my heart—& there is so much to do to
it, & printers, if all was done on my part, are so little to be
depended on, that I expect to be harrassed to death by 'em, if I
do not first wear myself out.'[3] Twining returned part of the
manuscript on 16 October and the rest eleven days later,
apologizing for the length of time that he had spent on it,

[1] Twining to CB, Sept. 1775, copy (Add. MS. 39933, ff. 144–7).
[2] *ED*, ii. 85.   [3] CB to Twining, Oct. 1775, copy (Osborn).

although he knew well enough that his own painstaking scrutiny of the text was essential for a work written in such haste. Whereas Burney had almost reached the point of caring more about the publication of the book than its contents, Twining was anxious for it to be as perfect as possible, however long the subscribers had to wait: 'You & I draw together like a racer, & a carthorse; but then remember what it is we are drawing:— none of your light post chaises, or flimsy phaetons, but a great heavy-loaded, broad-wheeled waggon, swagging & creaking thro' terrible deep roads! Agree that my *pace* is better suited to the work. . . . I don't say it, God knows, to magnify obligation &c, but I have worked very hard: harder than I ever worked for myself, since I *finished my studies*.'[1]

Burney received the heavily corrected manuscript with due gratitude and humility, 'quite ashamed to see how much there was to *do* at my MS, & still more to see how much you *have done*'; but deeply grateful for the frankness of Twining's criticism: 'You have treated me with all the sincerity of a true friend.' In 'matters of opinion' Burney was 'now & then a patriot, & for Wilks & Liberty', but he accepted without question all Twining's corrections in 'matters of blunder & ignorance'.[2] He was reluctant, however, to exclude his verse translations, although, like Twining, he was beginning to worry about shortage of space. Twining's notes on his letter of 16 October show that he was still pressing for excisions: 'Other amputations possible. Putting up in case of Necessity, a new rail to keep off Poetry.'[3] Rather than omit any of his entertaining digressions, Burney decided to transfer the final chapter, on the music of the early Church, on which he had been working in October, to the beginning of his second volume. This decision made it inevitable that the second volume would be larger than the first, which was itself by now 500 pages long, but Burney regarded this problem as one that could be faced at some more convenient period. At the end of October, Fanny, 'the Doctor's principal amanuensis', was at last able to tell Samuel Crisp, 'The History has been this very day, for the first time since its long cessation, put into the press. It is now *rough* written to the end of the first

---

[1] Twining to CB, 16 Oct. 1775, copy (Add. MS. 39933, ff. 148–51).
[2] CB to Twining, 18 Oct. 1775, copy (Osborn).
[3] Twining to CB, 16 Oct. 1775, notes (Add. MS. 39936, f. 59).

volume, Preface and Dedication inclusive. When it is actually *published* we intend to keep the carnival.'[1]

Burney's Dedication to the Queen, mentioned by Fanny, was the work of Samuel Johnson. No account survives of the negotiations by which he had persuaded Johnson to write it and, like several other recipients of Johnson's generosity, he did not care to have it known that it was not his own work. In mid-October 1775, however, he made a veiled reference to it in a letter to Twining, who had been reading his chapter on Egyptian music. Twining thought that Burney should have 'stuck in some little bit of a *blushing* Note' about a compliment which James Bruce had paid him in his long letter. Bruce had stated that he would not himself expatiate on the implications of the ancient harp he had discovered, adding, 'I shall with impatience expect this detail from you, better qualified than any one I know now in Europe for this disquisition.'[2] The modest Twining felt that 'One should not *seem* to consent to a man's saying that in one's own book.'[3]

Burney, however, was characteristically unwilling to interfere with so flattering a compliment. His only response was the facetious suggestion that Bruce's 'flummery' would be less noticeable if he printed at the beginning of his volume '*Letters from the learned* on the Continent', '*Testimonials* from foreign & domestic Journals', and '*Verses*' to the author in different languages. While the inclusion of 'Joel' in the list of potential contributors of testimonials makes it clear that he was hardly serious, the passage communicates Burney's customary enjoyment in contemplating the compliments which such men as Rousseau, Diderot and Martini had paid him. As for verses 'To The Author', he told Twining: 'Pray get a good handsome copy ready, if you have a mind to be taken in tow to immortality. I am sorry Gray is dead—otherwise, perhaps, you'd have been so kind to have got a few lines from him in behalf of me & my work. Mason I am sure of—& Johnson—if he won't write, I have such fine things under his hand, already written!'[4]

This is Burney's only reference to the Dedication which Johnson had provided. He had received permission to dedicate his *History* to the Queen by May 1774.[5] (His *Musical Tours* were

---

[1] *ED*, ii. 85–86; *Mem*. ii. 127.   [2] *Hist. Mus.* i. *224.
[3] See p. 167, n. 1.   [4] See p. 167, n. 2.
[5] CB to R. Mingotti, 3 May 1774 (Osborn).

presented to her later in the month,[1] and it may not be coincidental that, in June 1774, he had been promoted from 'Extra
Musician' to 'Musician in Ordinary' in the King's Band.[2]) As
he was still hoping at this period to publish his first volume
during 1774, Burney may well have asked Johnson to write the
Dedication immediately. From 1772 onwards their friendship
had steadily improved, and in 1776 Burney noted that he had
been paying frequent visits to Johnson,[3] who had politely
looked over the early sheets of the *History*.[4] It is possible, however, that he received the Dedication from Johnson not long
before his reference to it in October 1775, for when, in that
month, as Fanny told Crisp, James Hutton had called in St.
Martin's Street, 'My father read to him his Dedication to the
Queen, which mightily pleased him, for he almost adores her
Majesty.'[5] Nevertheless, although Mrs. Thrale and others in
her circle eventually knew the true author of the Dedication,[6]
neither Burney nor his daughter ever admitted that it was not
his own work.

Burney was now irritated by any distraction from the completion of his volume, which involved only the revision of the
final chapters in the light of Twining's objections and suggestions, and the reading of proofs. Intensely gratified at every
other period of his life by attention from the aristocracy,
Burney for once begrudged the necessity of giving up two
evenings in November to entertain the 'great Volk', who were
crowding into the home of the 'little Volk' to hear his nephew
Charles Rousseau Burney and his daughter Esther perform
their celebrated duets on the harpsichord. One such evening
could be tolerated but, after the first, Lady Edgcumbe—as
Burney told Twining with unusual bitterness—went 'almost
down on her scraggy knees' to beg him to arrange another
concert to which she could bring her friends. Forced 'to sacrifice
another blessed day' to 'great Folk', Burney gave vent to a
surprising social resentment: 'If I wanted anything of them how
they'd hang on ere they'd let me enter *their* doors, much more
ere enter mine. Yet we must submit to the world's humours,

[1] L. Smelt to, CB 23 May 1774 (Comyn).
[2] Cf. *GDB*, ii. 321–2.
[3] *Frag. Mem.* (Berg).   [4] See *post*, p. 182.
[5] *ED*, ii. 88.   [6] *Thraliana*, i. 204.

when they produce nothing but Vanity—if one can keep off the *Vexation,*—of spirit.'[1]

In spite of Burney's impatience, Twining continued his frank and detailed criticism of the concluding chapters and proofs of the volume throughout November 1775. In addition to providing corrections and supplementary observations, he continued to express his disapproval of Burney's verse translations. Since Burney insisted on including them against his friend's advice, Twining felt that they should at least be accurate, and in several instances he pointed out the freedom of Burney's versions: 'there is scarce any resemblance. . . . No two things, that have two or three ideas in common, can be more different.' Burney evidently defended the 'poetical exaggeration' of his translations on the grounds that he wished to satisfy 'both those who want antient simplicity, & those who want modern poetical *concetti*'; but such little desire as Twining had ever possessed to gratify the 'Masters & Misses' was rapidly disappearing and he renewed his protests at Burney's ambition of catering simultaneously for different audiences with increased severity: 'Why *would* you translate that poor thing at all! you have put more specimens of these tame songs in, than I wish'd at last. . . . It reads horribly, I must needs say.'[2] Twining's mockery of particular examples obliged Burney in one case to cancel a page and substitute a new translation,[3] and in another to offer an alternative version of two lines in his 'Additional Notes'.[4]

In spite of the delays and inconvenience caused by Twining's objections, Burney could not fail to be deeply impressed by his friend's selfless zeal for the welfare of the volume; and even while they were arguing strenuously about the merit of his translations, Burney asked Twining if he might make some acknowledgement in his Preface of his friend's invaluable assistance: 'It will comfort my bowels,—ease my heart of a load, & flatter my vanity exceedingly if you will but just let me mention your name with only 3 words of acknowledgement for your intelligent & friendly zeal, & kind communications. . . .

---

[1] CB to Twining, 15 Nov. and Nov. 1775, copies (Osborn); cf. *ED*, ii. 93–127.
[2] Twining to CB, 27 Oct., 31 Oct., 13 Nov., 3 Dec. 1775, copies (Add. MS. 39933, ff. 152–72).   [3] See *post*, p. 492.
[4] Cf. *Hist. Mus.* i. 395 and 506 and *post*, p. 180.

would you have me groan under the weary load of ingratitude
to *you*? . . . Your delicacy shall be menagée: but my friendship &
gratitude must not be quite starved.'[1] Twining's reply discussed
the proposal at length. 'I shall be frighten'd out of my wits to
see my name in print', was his first reaction, but he eventually
confessed that 'it would be intolerable vanity, under a mask of
modesty, to be ashamed of the interest I have taken in your
work, or of appearing as *your* friend: if my *vanity* is at all interested
in the matter, believe me it is *there*. . . . One may *thank*, without
praising.—I shall see plainly, by what you say whether you set
me down as a puppy for giving my consent.' Characteristically,
Twining then proceeded to another devastating analysis of one
of Burney's translations.[2]

Considering the haste with which Burney wrote his first
volume and the technical nature of its contents, it is written in
remarkably composed and elegant prose. The Preface, the last
section to be written, is particularly assured and eloquent,
although its theme is in fact the diffidence with which the
author offered his work to the public and an account of the
many difficulties involved in its composition. After pointing
out that only England, of the major European countries, still
lacked a history of music, Burney informed his readers that, in
his attempt to fill this 'chasm in English literature', especially
by the use of manuscript materials, 'few modern writers have
expended more money and time, undergone greater fatigue, or
more impaired their health in the search of them, than myself'.
Then, as Twining had suggested, Burney begged the goodwill of
his readers:

If I might presume to hope, however, for any unusual indulgence
from the public with respect to this work, it must be from the
peculiarity of my circumstances during the time it was in hand. For
should the materials be found ill-digested, or the diction incorrect; it
is humbly hoped that part of these, and other defects, will be attributed to want of leisure and health, as well as want of abilities, to render it less unworthy the public patronage; for it may with the utmost
truth be said, that it was composed in moments stolen from sleep, from
reflection, and from an occupation which required all my attention,
during more than twelve hours a day, for a great part of the year.[3]

---

[1] CB to Twining, Nov. 1775, copy (Osborn).
[2] Twining to CB, 3 Dec. 1775, copy (Add. MS. 39933, ff. 170–2).
[3] *Hist. Mus.* i. xi.

After a long account of the tedious and often unrewarding nature of his researches—summarized at the opening of his 'Dissertation' by the sentence, 'I seemed to resemble a wretch in the street, raking the kennels for an old rusty nail'[1]—Burney attempted to mollify the various sections of his audience:

There are already more profound books on the subject of ancient, as well as modern Music, than have ever been read; it was time to try to treat it in such a manner as was likely to engage the attention of those that are unable, or unwilling, to read treatises written, for the most part, by persons who were more ambitious of appearing learned themselves, than of making others so. . . .

My subject has been so often deformed by unskilful writers, that many readers, even among those who love and understand music, are afraid of it. My wish, therefore, is not to be approached with awe and reverence for my depth and erudition, but to bring on a familiar acquaintance with them, by talking in common language of what has hitherto worn the face of gloom and mystery, and been too much 'sicklied o'er with the pale cast of thought;' and though the mixing biographical anecdotes, in order to engage attention, may by some be condemned, as below the dignity of science, yet I would rather be pronounced trivial than tiresome; for Music being, at best, but an amusement, its history merits not, in reading, the labour of intense application, which should be reserved for more grave and important concerns. . . .

If, therefore, a number of figures appear in the background, I hope they will give *relief*, and somewhat keep off the dryness and fatigue which a single subject in a long work, or a single figure if often repeated, though in different points of view, is apt to produce.[2]

Although the Preface was printed during December 1775, Burney could not fulfil his hope of publishing his book before Christmas. It was time, however, to call a halt to the stream of suggestions and additional notes which Twining was still communicating as he read over the last sheets. On Christmas Eve Burney wrote to him, 'If my book & self should live till a 2nd Edit. is wanted, not a tittle of your Criticisms & corrections shall be neglected; but at present more I could not do without ruin & destruction of the whole impression. 20 cancelled pages. 11 of addit. notes. 26 double & 2 of errata, will considerably inflame the reckoning with the printer & stationer, & make my

---

[1] *Hist. Mus.* i. 5.   [2] Ibid. i. xv, xviii, xx.

book, as I feared some time ago *600* instead of 500 pages.'[1]
Twining accepted Burney's decision, and the historian of music
must have echoed with some emotion the sentiment expressed
in the doggerel verses which his friend sent him at the New
Year:

> Let us pray
> That no more Antient Music
> May make me or you sick. . . .[2]

V

On 25 January 1776 Burney presented the first volume of his
History of Music to the Queen, to whom it was dedicated, 'at
St James's in full drawing room'.[3] According to Fanny d'Arblay,
the Queen received it 'with even peculiar graciousness': 'So delighted was Doctor Burney by the condescending manner of the
Queen's acceptance of his musical offering, that he never
thenceforward failed paying his homage to their Majesties,
upon the two birth-day anniversaries of those august and beloved Sovereigns.'[4] The volume was officially published on
31 January. Three days later the *Morning Post* printed Burney's
translation of 'Aristotle's Hymn to Hermias' and a long letter
from 'Crito', which praised every aspect of the *History*. Knowing
Burney's habitual precautions over the reception of his works,
we may suspect that this generous publicity was the result of
some private arrangement with the newspaper's editor, the
Rev. Henry Bate (later Sir Henry Bate Dudley), an intimate
friend of Garrick, if not of Burney himself.

Thomas Twining had already received his handsomely bound
copy of the book to which he had contributed so much. He
admitted that he had looked at once for Burney's acknowledgement of his assistance: 'I held up my fan, & looked thro' the
sticks as Fielding's squeamish lady did at the naked man.'[5]
Although he inevitably thought that Burney had been too generous, on the whole he approved the 'very pretty fat tight sleek

[1] CB to Twining, 24 Dec. 1775, copy (Osborn). For a discussion of the bibliographical information contained in this passage, see Appendix II, *post*, pp. 491–3.
[2] Attached to CB to Twining, 3 Jan. 1776 (Osborn).
[3] *Frag. Mem.* (Berg).
[4] *Mem.* ii. 71–72.
[5] Twining to CB, 27 Jan. 1776 (Add. MS. 39929, ff. 71–72); cf. *Joseph Andrews*,
chap. xii.

compact little eloge' in the Preface: 'And here, in order to satisfy the sentiments of friendship, as well as those of gratitude, I must publicly acknowledge my obligations to the zeal, intelligence, taste, and erudition of the reverend Mr. Twining; a gentleman whose least merit is being perfectly well acquainted with every branch of theoretical and practical music.'[1]

Burney's acknowledgement was hardly excessive, however, for he was indebted to Twining not only for such sections of his book as those on the Enharmonic Genus and on Rhythm in ancient music, but also for innumerable other ideas, suggestions, alterations, corrections, and refinements. Throughout this period of grappling with tedious and often intractable material, moreover, Burney had been sustained by the opportunity of frequent epistolary discussion with the enthusiastic Twining; and in addition to his dependence on Twining's classical learning, frank criticism, and painstaking scrutiny of both sheets and manuscript for such minor errors and omissions as appear in the 'Additional Notes' and 'Errata', Burney had come to rely on Twining's cheerful and tactful comfort and encouragement during the various tribulations which had afflicted him during the composition of the volume.

The extent of Twining's scholarly assistance can be fully appreciated only by examination of his letters to Burney; and it should be remembered that lengthy technical discussions of musical problems were often omitted from the copies of these letters which have survived, and that other detailed commentaries, which were sent separately with parcels of sheets or manuscript, are no longer extant. Even from the evidence that survives, however, it is noticeable how many ideas and phrases in Twining's letters were transferred directly to the *History*. J. T. Smith drew attention to one aspect of Burney's debt to his 'learned friend' when he wrote in 1828, 'The Greek with which his labours abound, was corrected, and indeed mostly provided, by the Rev. Mr. Twining; who held frequent intercourse with him as to his literary matters.'[2] It is a different matter, nevertheless, to say that Twining 'wrote the whole of the dissertation on the music of the ancients', as did the musician R. J. S. Stevens in the early nineteenth century, although he had the authority of Twining's nephew, Richard, who had

---

[1] *Hist. Mus.* i. xviii–xix.   [2] *Nollekens and His Times*, 1828, i. 196.

examined the correspondence.[1] An even more exaggerated assertion about Twining's contribution was made by Francis Douce on the fly-leaf of his copy of the *History*: 'The first volume of this work is said to have been written by the Revd Mr Twining.'[2]

Although these statements are far from the truth, the extent of Twining's contribution has been stressed in this study simply because the emphasis has recently moved so far in the opposite direction. Dr. Scholes, for example, did not take seriously the possibility that Burney had benefited from Twining's assistance to any great extent; and although he mentioned the invaluable and revealing Twining Correspondence in the British Museum in his Bibliography, he had clearly seen only the published material. It may be said in conclusion that, although the 'Dissertation' in Burney's first volume, to which Twining contributed most, is probably the least frequently consulted of his works, it would undoubtedly have been a very different and inferior study without Twining's assistance; and that if Burney had not been nursed out of his moods of depression by his friend's sensible, affectionate, and patient encouragement, the volume and, indeed, the whole *History*, might never have appeared at all.

Burney himself fully appreciated his debt. It was, after all, only with Twining that he could fully share his excitement at the volume's triumphant success. He could not, however, resist taunting his friend with the fact that the *Morning Post* had printed one of his derided translations:

That I should ever live to see the day when my ebullitions of Crambo nonsense should be so highly honoured!—why there now! —it never rains but it pours! If I am not in the *Poet's Corner* of that *judicious, candid,* & *decorous* paper the Morning Post to day I'm a rogue!—*You* pretend to taste, & judgement, & all that!—Why this sensible gentleman the Editor has selected the very thing which you rejected!

In more important ways, however, the publication of the book had been a success and the extra charge for non-subscribers had had a dynamic effect:

The house is a Fair, from morning to night; torn to pieces, Sir!

[1] J. B. Trend, 'R. J. S. Stevens and his Contemporaries', *Music and Letters*, xiv (1933), 136.   [2] Bodleian, Douce B. subt. 273.

The impatience of the public!! Would you believe it? people (so turned are the tables) with whose names I should, a month ago, have thought myself highly honoured, as well as gratified, are now begging as for our alms, during the frost, to be admitted as subscribers. The fame of the work, & the additional half guinea in its price, work prodigiously. All goes on smoothly as yet—but I dread what may come for all that.—I want to tell you the reception of our book most minutely, but it would fill a volume as big as itself to do it. 'Tis now the Town's talk, & none of the abuse reaches my Ears. I have had a great deal of flummery of people of high rank. . . .[1]

Twining, in the peace of Fordham, would not begrudge Burney his hour of triumph, although he would appreciate to the full his friend's generous reference to '*our* book'. Burney indeed, had already started to contrive a curiously complex way in which Twining's contributions to the *History* might receive detailed public praise, without his name being mentioned. On 30 January 1776 he sent a copy of the *History* to William Bewley at Great Massingham. As his letter to Twining reveals, Burney was still apprehensive about 'what may come for all that', in spite of the initial success of his book; and the manner in which he announced to Bewley the arrival of his volume was calculated to remind him of the importance of the notice it would receive in the *Monthly Review*:

I cannot find in my Heart to let this *Child* of my brain approach you without a word of recommendation. Pray receive him as the offering of your old Friend. If his language should be incorrect, or abound w^th *naughty words*; If he sh^d sometimes be *dull* & *stupid*; & at others *pert* & *trivial*; If he should discover a want of *knowledge* & *Reading*; or sh^d incline to *severity* & *calumny*; If you sh^d discover in him a propensity to *lying*, or hazardé assertions; a want of *diligence* in search of Information, or that he deals in old stories, & turns out a mere *Boar*; pray excuse his *errors* & *defects*, in consideration of the little Health & leisure I have had to render him more polished & fit for the world.

Burney was not averse to using pathos to engage his friend's interest:

It has always been my ambition to make him a welcome guest where ever he goes, & that neither Friends nor foes sh^d complain of his being useless or burthensome to them—Yet with all my anxiety & care his reception in the world may perhaps be such as will cover me with dishonour, &, instead of being a credit & comfort to me, corrode my heart wth chagrin, & bring my grey hairs wth sorrow to the Grave! In such a case you will, perhaps, heave a sigh for the fate of an Industrious & well intentioned Parent, whose Child was not *spoiled* for want of such wholesome correction as his affection & leisure w^d allow! But *You*, who will now *view*, & perhaps *re*view him without parental blindness or solicitude, will be more able than me to judge of his Vices, & Virtues, if he has any; & to recommend him to y^r Friends & to the world in general, if you sh^d find him worth y^r notice; &, Friendship to me apart, sh^d be able, without putting violence on y^r taste, Judgement, & sincerity, to say any good of him.[1]

This facetious self-pity was ill-timed, for Bewley had himself written to Burney on the same day in anything but a genial mood, explaining that he had just brought his son home with consumption, his daughter having died late in 1774. He had been trying to distract himself by writing a review of Joseph Priestley's *Experiments on Air* (1775), a work of particular interest to him, since it contained three of his own letters to the author. Anticipating Burney's request of the same day, however, Bewley wrote to say that he would defer this review to deal with the *History of Music*. Since his articles on the *Musical Tours*, Bewley had occasionally reviewed other books on music, although he had usually been obliged to ask Burney for help.[2] Now, quite apart from his usual uneasiness about reviewing a friend's book, Bewley knew that he was incompetent, by his own standards, to deal with so learned a work as the *History* and he was forced to request the author's assistance: 'With respect to [Priestley's] work—I feel myself perfectly at home; but with regard to yours, I am not so much Master of the subject as I ought to be.—My reading that way, in particular, has not been very extensive. Could not you point out to me the more original or *memorable* parts of your undertaking?—Perhaps your *preface*—I hope you have one—may enlighten me.'[3]

On learning of Bewley's situation, Burney apologized for the 'levities' of his previous letter but apparently repeated his

---

[1] CB to Bewley, 30 Jan. 1776, copy (Osborn).
[2] See R. Lonsdale, 'Dr. Burney and the *Monthly Review*', *RES*, xv (1963), 347.
[3] Bewley to CB, 30 Jan. 1776 (Osborn).

anxiety about the reception of his book. Bewley merely commented, 'You astonish me with your *repeated* croakings (in both
your letters) about *disgrace*.' He had fortunately made extensive notes on the 'Dissertation' when he had seen it in sheets
early in 1775, and by March 1776 had compiled an opening
article for the *Monthly Review*, 'which I should, in my present
frame of mind, be ill qualified to undertake *ab initio*'. Burney
had also sent him 'two well filled letters', which doubtless
pointed out the choicer sections of his volume.[1] Although
Bewley's review, as might be expected, was shorter and less
cheerful than usual, he managed to publish the first article in
March, and the second and concluding article in June.[2]

Since Bewley's loyalty had once more risen to the occasion in
such distressing circumstances, it is pleasant to observe that
Burney himself was simultaneously contriving to gratify Thomas
Twining. While most of Bewley's review consists of generalized
praise and exposition of the book, a conspicuous section of it is
devoted to particularly high praise of the pages on the Enharmonic Genus. In replying to Bewley's request for advice about
the review, Burney must have stressed this section, which was
almost entirely Twining's work. As Twining and Bewley never
met, and indeed barely knew of each other's existence, Twining
would take this praise as perfectly objective approval of his
contribution.

Twining confessed that he had blushed on reading the praise
of his Enharmonic hypothesis in the *Monthly Review*;[3] but in the
preceding month he had been gratified with similar praise in
the *Critical Review*, which published five articles on the *History*
between February and June 1776.[4] For this reason alone, it
could perhaps be assumed that some friend of Burney had
written this earlier review. Burney, moreover, had conversed in
January with Archibald Hamilton, the editor of the journal,
and had been horrified to learn that, although Hamilton
wished to begin reviewing the book in February, he felt that
none of his writers sufficiently 'understood the subject'.[5] Burney
was not a man who would willingly let the book on which his

[1] Bewley to CB, 3 Mar. 1776 (Osborn).
[2] liv (1776), 203–14, 438–46.
[3] Twining to CB, [14] Apr. 1776 (Add. MS. 39929, ff. 92–93).
[4] xli. 81–90, 185–93, 271–80, 337–44, 433–42.
[5] CB to Twining, 3 Feb. 1776, copy (Osborn).

reputation depended fall into incompetent hands and he may once more have arranged for Samuel Crisp to review it for Hamilton. Certainly, the praise of Twining's contribution does not seem accidental. The opening paragraphs of the first article contain the usual high general praise of Burney's 'accuracy, discernment . . . force of conjecture' and his 'perseverance and industry', and then proceeds to a superficial and almost entirely neutral exposition of the book's content. So neutral is it, in fact, as to give conspicuous emphasis to the praise of Burney's 'rhythmical enquiries', which were, like the Enharmonic hypothesis, almost entirely Twining's work, and which seemed to the reviewer 'in a particular manner happy, and to contain much classical knowledge and sagacity'.

Any suspicion that Twining himself wrote the review can be dismissed at once. Although he appreciated such unexpected and apparently detached praise ('a sensible man, the author of that article, I dare say!'), he was actually rather disgusted by the review as a whole: not only did he think the reviewer incompetent, but excessively fulsome in his praise. Not that it was undeserved: 'I assure you if I had reviewed your book myself (which I once really thought of doing—but in an unlucky hour of indolence, & mental flabbiness) I should have said that very thing, tho' I believe not quite in the same way; the substance wou'd have been exactly the same; but there is a little of the *Cant* of Panegyric—a certain swag & strut of words that can answer no end but to make people mistake truth for compliment.' Twining in fact upset Burney by preferring to such 'syrup' the articles on the *History* in the *London Review*.[1] They had both once suspected that its editor, William Kenrick, had written 'Joel Collier's' *Musical Travels* and had been prepared for more 'Collierism' on this occasion. Initially more detached, however, Twining was not unimpressed by the first article ('He seeks disagreements and faults, but keeps his temper'), although Burney, for whom anything short of the highest praise was an affront, tried to persuade him that the reviewer was offensively 'peevish & petulant'.[2]

Twining's objections to the fulsome tone of the *Critical Review*, in spite of the praise of his own contribution, would

[1] iii (1776), 102–10, 194–203.
[2] Twining to CB, 7 and 28 Mar. 1776 (Add. MS. 39929, ff. 76–79, 82–83).

seem meanwhile to have had some effect. The later articles of
the series become increasingly subdued and, compared with the
opening article, the last words of the review in June 1776 were
merely lukewarm: 'Upon the whole, we may venture to recommend this book to the perusal of the scholar and the gentleman,
as well as to the musician; and we sincerely wish the author
sufficient health and leisure, to enable him to complete his useful, extensive, and, if we may judge from such parts of it as are
already executed, well digested plan.' Almost certainly some
friend of Burney—perhaps Crisp, or even his own daughter
Susan, who contributed a review of a book on music to the
Critical Review three years later[1]—wrote these articles and, after
Twining's expressions of disgust, was advised by Burney to
reduce the quantity of vague panegyric. One small clue may
serve to confirm the suspicion that the review was written by
no casual hand. As a result of one of Twining's derisive attacks
on his verse translations in the *History*, Burney had supplied an
improved version of one of his worst couplets in his 'Additional Notes'.[2] In quoting this translation in the course of an
extensive extract from the book, the writer in the *Critical Review*
unobtrusively substituted the revised couplet. It is unlikely that
a casual reviewer would either have noticed the revision at the
end of the volume or, even if he had, would have taken the
trouble of substituting it in his extract.

In spite of the trouble which Burney took to ensure favourable
reviews, the success of his volume was assured long before they
had reached their final verdicts. By the middle of February
1776, some three weeks after its publication, very few copies
remained for sale and they were 'in the hands of the Publishers',
Becket and Robson, who had each subscribed for fifty copies,
and Robinson, who had taken six.[3] The 857 subscribers in
Burney's final list had taken between them 1,047 copies and it is
unlikely that many more had been printed. Published in a year
when such notable works as the first volume of Gibbon's
Decline and Fall of the Roman Empire, Adam Smith's *Wealth of
Nations*, and Priestley's *Experiments on Air* were also receiving
extensive treatment in the reviews, Burney's volume was never-

---

[1] xlvii (1776), 99–101; Bewley to CB, 29 May 1779 (Osborn).
[2] *Hist. Mus.* i. 506.
[3] CB to [Lord Mornington], 18 Feb. 1776, draft (Osborn).

theless one of the most fashionable books of the year. From scholars like Richard Hurd and Richard Gough, who considered that 'Dr. Burney has acquitted himself well',[1] to Mrs. Ord, from whom Burney received gratefully 'the Nectar & Ambrosia of Praise',[2] and his former master, Fulke Greville,[3] the verdict was unanimously favourable.

For all his efforts to cater for them, however, many of Burney's readers were incapable of judging the merits of his more learned chapters (although this did not in itself necessarily make them less eager to praise it). Horace Walpole, devouring quartos during an illness, admitted frankly that 'the first sections to be sure are to me absolute Hebrew', although he found considerable entertainment elsewhere in the volume. He was most diverted, however, by James Bruce's letter in the chapter on Egyptian music: 'Would you believe that the great Abyssinian, Mr Bruce, whom Dr B. made me laugh by seriously calling the *intrepid traveller*, has had the intrepidity to write a letter to the Doctor, which the latter has printed in his book, and in which he intrepidly tells lies of almost as large a magnitude as his story of the bramble. . . .'[4] To Burney's disappointment, Bruce's discovery, which later exploration has confirmed, was generally received with facetious incredulity. Jokes about the discovery of the 'Abyssinian lyre' by the 'Abyssinian liar' were commonplace until the end of the century.[5]

Otherwise there was nothing but praise for Burney. He was particularly gratified by applause from those of the 'great Volk' who were also proper judges of the more 'scientific' part of his volume. Lord Mornington paid him just such a tribute in May 1776: 'I never read any thing with more pleasure than your Elegant and judicious Dissertation, but I shall not think myself qualify'd to express my sense of its particular Beautys till I have allmost gotten it by heart. . . .' Mornington was already prepared, however, to assert that 'Your dedication to the Queen is the only Dedication I ever saw that was good and complimentary without Flattery.'[6] Two months earlier William Bewley

---

[1] Twining to CB, 7 Mar. 1776 (Add. MS. 39929, ff. 76–79); Gough to M. Tyson, 6 Mar. 1776, J. Nichols, *Literary Anecdotes of the Eighteenth Century*, 1812–15, viii. 619.
[2] CB to Mrs. Ord, [? Feb. 1776], draft (Osborn).
[3] [Greville] to CB, [Dec. 1776] (Osborn).
[4] *Corresp.*, xxviii. 248–9; for the 'story of the bramble', see ibid., p. 249 n.
[5] *GDB*, i. 268–9.   [6] Mornington to CB, 16 May 1776 (Osborn).

had expressed similar admiration: 'By the bye, the *Dedication*, in particular, appears to me to be one of the choicest *morceaus* we have, in that kind, in our language.'[1]

It is to be hoped that Burney, who must have been somewhat embarrassed by such compliments, accepted them with modest self-deprecation and passed them on to Dr. Johnson, who would derive little enough pleasure from the rest of the book whose Dedication he had written. In a collection of anecdotes about Johnson, Burney recorded that 'Upon D[r] J. reading at the author's request the first sheet of B——'s *Dissertation on the Music of the Anc[ts]* w[ch] is full of technical terms & particularly unintelligible to such as have never studied Music of any kind; he said, "the words are well arranged, Sir; but I do not understand one of them".'[2] In the same notebook Burney related that, on reading the second paragraph of his Preface, which asserts that 'The love of lengthened tones and modulated sounds . . . seems a passion implanted in human nature throughout the globe', Johnson had observed, 'The author . . . is I believe, right. All Animated Nature loves Music —Except myself.'[3] The only indication that Johnson ever voluntarily read either of the two volumes of the *History* published in his lifetime is a trivial marginal correction to a figure in his copy of the second volume (which he inscribed, 'Given by the Author to Sam: Johnson May. 16 1782').[4] In his Dedication for Burney's *Commemoration of Handel* (1785), however, Johnson borrowed his friend's sentiments in asserting that music 'seems to be one of the first attainments of rational nature; wherever there is humanity, there is modulated sound'.

Other distinguished and more musical subscribers were well satisfied, however. Through Suard, Burney sent a copy of his volume to Diderot, who assured him in April 1777 that he had read and re-read it 'avec grand plaisir'.[5] C. P. E. Bach, the

---

[1] Bewley to CB, 3 Mar. 1776 (Osborn).

[2] 'Johnsoniana', (Barrett); also in *Thraliana*, i. 176; cf. *post*, p. 383.

[3] Cf. *Mem*. ii. 77–78.

[4] Berg. The correction is on p. 246. Malone added a note: 'These figures were set down by D[r] Johnson; who never suffered any error in calculation to pass unnoticed.'

[5] CB to Suard, 25 May 1776 (Bibl. du Conservatoire de Musique, Paris; draft, Osborn); Diderot to CB, 12 Apr. 1777 (Osborn). Suard at first thought of translating the volume, with notes by Arnaud, *Private Corresp. of Garrick*, ii. 614.

celebrated composer, wrote an even more complimentary and affectionate letter, which ended with the hope that God would preserve Burney's life and health to the end of his great work.[1] Most pleasing of all, perhaps, was the reluctant acceptance of the volume by the already almost paranoiac Rousseau, who died two years later. The book was delivered to him by Andrew Lumisden, who duly described its reception in a letter to the author:

At first I found him a little peevish. He said that he had lost his memory, and could neither read, write or do anything: He therefore desired me to take back the book, because it was lost on him. However, I endeavoured to soothe him, and he accepted of your present. He expressed his high opinion of your abilities; and when I mentioned to him the so much disputed article of *counterpoint* he said he wished you were here, for he would communicate to you some ideas he had on that subject, but which he is unable to communicate in writing. He likewise told me that he had composed entire new music for his *Devin de village* and that he would prepare a specimen of it for you. I told him . . . I would call on him, and receive anything he had to send you. In short I left him in good humour, and much your friend. Pity that any weakness should mingle with such wonderful talents![2]

Rousseau did, however, begin to set down some of the ideas which the arrival of Burney's *History* had stimulated. It has always been assumed that his *Lettre à M. le Docteur Burney*, first printed posthumously in 1781, was no more than an 'open letter', which never reached, nor was intended to reach, the addressee.[3] This *Lettre* consists of observations on ancient music, an exposition of a new method of notation, and a rather fragmentary description of a dispute between Rousseau himself and the composer Gluck. It seems certain, however, that Burney did receive some communication from Rousseau before his death in 1778, which was at least related to the *Lettre* printed in 1781. In the autumn of 1777 Twining wrote in French (for a change) to congratulate Burney on various letters he had received from abroad: 'Je vous fais mes complimens sur tous les

[1] Bach to CB, 5 Sept. 1776 (Osborn).
[2] Lumisden to CB, 9 July 1776 (Osborn). The 'disputed article' was whether or not there was counterpoint in ancient music.
[3] *GDB*, i. 183–4. The *Lettre* appeared in Rousseau's *Traités sur la musique*, Geneva, 1781, pp. 375–427.

bonbons dont on vous regale d'Irlande, de France, et de la Chine; le tout pour l'embellissement de Monsieur le Tome second. Mais quel *poisson* que ce Jean Jacques? — *Desinit* in piscem. Il me semble qu'il y a là de la puerilité, de l'*humeur* — un certain depit enfantin, indigne d'un tel homme. Le titre de ce qu'il vous a envoyé, pique ma curiosité, mais me donne guere d'idee.'[1]

Twining himself, however, does little more than excite our curiosity and he does not mention Rousseau's communication again. In 1802 Burney made his only reference to the *Lettre* in telling a friend that 'Rousseau, a little before his death, wrote me a letter, making me the umpire between him and Gluck, in a friendly difference of opinion.'[2] Although from this evidence it seems possible that he actually received the *Lettre* which Rousseau addressed to him, it is remarkable that he never gave the fact more publicity, for he was not one to conceal friendly notice from great men. It can only be assumed that he considered Rousseau to be so eccentric in his old age that he decided to make no use of the *Lettre*. In the first volume of his *History* he had compared Rousseau to the Greek musician Archilocus, as if the Frenchman were already dead: 'A peevish, satirical, and irascible disposition, soured the public, and embittered their own existence.'[3] The letter from Twining quoted above, moreover, suggests that Burney thought Rousseau's communication childish and useless.

Since almost the whole first impression of the *History* had been claimed by subscribers or sold to the general public within a few weeks of publication, the indefatigable Burney had decided by April 1776 to prepare a second and extensively corrected edition. In that month he wrote asking Twining for any 'corrections, alterations, & contractions' he thought necessary. Although he was dismayed at the prospect of having to criticize Burney's book all over again, Twining began a careful re-reading and sent lists of detailed suggestions to be added to the many remarks which he had made before its publication and which Burney had been unable to include. Although he suffered another severe attack of rheumatism in his

---

[1] Twining to CB, 31 Oct. 1777 (Add. MS. 39929, ff. 147-8).
[2] CB to J. W. Callcott, 29 Jan. 1802 (Osborn).
[3] *Hist. Mus.* i. 363-4.

hand in May 1776, and had to visit Buxton once more during the summer, Burney worked hard on the revision of his book, incorporating new material, re-arranging and omitting sections, and working the 'Additional Notes' and 'Errata' into the text. From Chessington, where he spent September and October, Burney sent the copy containing all his revisions to Fordham for Twining's final comments.[1]

At first Burney seems to have spoken freely about his proposed second edition, the necessity for which was in itself a tribute to his book's success. As Andrew Lumisden remarked, 'I am not at all surprised that there should be so soon a demand for a second edition of this first volume. It is only a proof of its merit.'[2] In September 1776, however, it occurred to Twining that Burney's subscribers might 'grumble' at the immediate publication of so extensively revised and improved an edition: 'They will think their copies less valuable, when there *are* better; & every improvement in the new edit., will produce a correspondent defect in the old one, which they did not before discover.'[3] During October, however, having examined the revised copy, Twining changed his mind, for he thought it greatly improved (no doubt because most of the alterations had been suggested by himself): 'You will have made it a tight, sound, compact, spruce fellow.' Burney, meanwhile, had been uneasily pondering his duty to his subscribers, but had decided that he had no choice but to publish the improved edition. Twining now supported this decision whole-heartedly:

I don't see what is to be done, if they *will* grumble. The additions are not numerous enough to print separately. Very few of the possessors of the 1st Edit. perhaps, will ever *know* how much you have improved the 2d, if you don't trumpet it forth in the advertisement. . . . at least with respect to the *scrips*; keep *them* in ignorance, if you can, & *pen a whisper* in some corner of the 2d Edit. that may just say in the ear of the purchasers—aveta *una gioia!*—for I suppose, joking apart, that you mean to prefix some little *avis* to it, just to give an account, *what* you have done & why; & perhaps, to *menager* a little bit of apology to disarm grumbling scrips who *may* blunder upon your 2d Edit. & discover the secret.[4]

[1] Twining to CB, 9 Apr., [14] Apr., 18 May, 28 July, 22 Aug., 1776 (Add. MS. 39929, ff. 84–93, 96–104).   [2] Lumisden to CB, 9 July 1776 (Osborn).
[3] Twining to CB, 17 Sept. 1776 (Add. MS. 39929, ff. 105–7).
[4] Ibid., 7 and 21 Oct. 1776 (Add. MS. 39929, ff. 108–9, 112–13).

At this point, however, it becomes impossible to trace the fate of the revised edition with any certainty. Late in November 1776 Twining wrote, 'I rejoice that the regeneration or new birth of your book is in so fair a way.' Some additional corrections which he suggested make it clear that he was referring to the revised edition.[1] The only other possible reference to it occurs in June 1777, when Twining asked briefly, 'How goes regeneration?'[2] By this period, however, 'regeneration' might well refer to Burney's progress with his second volume.

All that can be stated with confidence is that no copy of the first volume, dated 1776, which contains any of the alterations, additions, and omissions agreed upon by Burney and Twining, has yet been discovered. On the other hand, all the revisions they discussed during the summer of 1776 are embodied in the official second edition of the first volume which was published in 1789 and which was undoubtedly printed from the revised copy prepared thirteen years earlier.[3] However Twining's two references to 'regeneration' are interpreted, it must be assumed that, late in 1776, Burney suddenly abandoned his plan of publishing a second edition, and that he merely reprinted the volume without any alterations. A passage (heavily deleted by Fanny d'Arblay) in a letter from Fulke Greville to Burney, which Fanny dated December 1776, appears to support this theory. Burney must have mentioned his new intention to his former patron, who replied 'I am glad to hear a 2^d Edit. of y^r 1st Book is going on, as I conclude there is a Demand for it, that makes it necessary—but is it ⟨? reset⟩ in the same ⟨ ? ⟩ with the 1st without Additions or Alterations, in hand—if so, 'tis pity more Copies had not been printed off at first—to have sav'd great Expence—how will the Plates hold out?'[4]

Only one explanation of this sudden change of mind can be offered. Towards the end of October 1776, when Burney seemed to have persuaded himself that a revised edition of his volume was both necessary and unlikely to offend his subscribers, Sir John Hawkins began to advertise the imminent publication of his rival *History of Music*. That Burney felt that

---

[1] Twining to CB, 29 Nov. 1776 (Add. MS. 39929, ff. 114–18).
[2] Ibid., 16 June 1777 (Add. MS. 39929, ff. 119–24).
[3] See *post*, pp. 342–3.
[4] [Greville] to CB [Dec. 1776] (Osborn).

his rivalry with Hawkins was the crucial moment in his career will be shown in the next chapter. It may merely be suggested here that the imminent appearance of Hawkins's *History* was sufficient to cause him to abandon his plan. It was no longer worth taking the slightest risk of offending his subscribers nor, in the new circumstances, was it wise voluntarily to reveal the defects of the first edition of his volume by so quickly publishing a second. Burney may also have feared that if the rival *History* appeared before his own second edition, the public would assume that his corrections and additions were the result of his reading Hawkins's treatment of the same subject. Whatever the reasons we attribute to Burney, he began once more to advertise his own first volume in mid-November 1776, a week before the rival *History* was published.[1] To enable him to do so, a new impression of his volume must have been printed.

The literary and musical worlds, in any case, were by no means as conscious of the shortcomings of his book as were Twining and the author himself. Burney had demonstrated the depth of his scholarship and the elegance of his literary powers so successfully that he had already fulfilled most of his long-frustrated ambitions. In less than seven years of strenuous and determined effort he had established himself as the leading authority on music in England and, perhaps, in Europe. He was accepted, moreover, as an eminent man of letters, who was welcomed into fashionable society and the most distinguished literary circles in a manner that no professional musician had ever previously enjoyed. Although her comments on this moment in her father's career are as usual somewhat exaggerated, Fanny d'Arblay understood the nature of his achievement and of his enjoyment of the applause that greeted it:

Greatly . . . to a mind like his, was every exertion repaid by the honour of its reception. The subscription, by which he had been enabled to sustain its numerous expences in books, travels, and en-gravings, had brilliantly been filled with the names of almost all that were most eminent in literature, high in rank, celebrated in the arts, or leading in the fashion of the day. And while the lovers of music received with eagerness every account of that art in which they de-lighted; scholars, and men of letters in general, who hitherto had thought of music but as they thought of a tune that might be played

[1] See *post*, pp. 198–9.

or sung from imitation, were astonished at the depth of research, and almost universality of observation, reading, and meditation, which were now shewn to be requisite for such an undertaking: while the manner in which, throughout the work, such varied matter was displayed, was so natural, so spirited, and so agreeable, that the History of Music not only awakened respect and admiration for its composition; it excited, also, an animated desire, in almost the whole body of its readers, to make acquaintance with its author.[1]

There was to be only one challenge in his lifetime to Burney's pre-eminence as an authority on music. It was delivered almost immediately and suppressed with equal rapidity.

[1] *Mem.* ii. 70–71.

V

BURNEY AND SIR JOHN HAWKINS

1770–1789

I

BURNEY wrote the first volume of his *History of Music* under great physical and mental strain. Throughout these years there was, however, one persistent cause of anxiety at the back of his mind which deserves to be treated as a separate topic. Although much of the material relevant to his rivalry with Sir John Hawkins was deliberately destroyed by his daughter, enough survives to document an episode in Burney's career which simultaneously reveals some of the least impressive aspects of his character and the determination with which he pursued his climb to fame.

While it may be surprising that no large-scale history of music had been attempted before the later eighteenth century in England, it is perhaps even more curious that two such ambitious works were undertaken and published in that period almost simultaneously. Not long after he had decided to commit himself to a *History of Music*, Burney learned that Sir John Hawkins (1719–89), author, magistrate, keen amateur musician, and friend of Samuel Johnson, had been engaged for many years on a similar task. Hawkins himself claimed to have started writing his *History* as early as 1759, and to have been collecting materials for an even longer period. The work had been suggested to him by Horace Walpole, who also helped him to obtain information and rare books from friends in England and on the Continent. Although his duties as a magistrate had limited his progress, the first volume of Hawkins's *History* was already in the press when Burney began writing his own work.[1]

Burney later admitted that his 'Courage was somewhat abated' when he first learned that he would be competing with

---

[1] Laetitia-Matilda Hawkins, *Anecdotes, Biographical Sketches and Memoirs*, 1822, pp. 101, 143; Walpole, *Letters*, ed. Mrs. Paget Toynbee, v. 14–15, and *Supplement*, ed. Paget Toynbee, i. 233–4; Hawkins, *History of Music*, 1776, Preface, vol. i.

so zealous an antiquarian as Hawkins, who had been assembling materials for so many years. While debating the wisdom of going ahead with his own *History*, however, he had come across a footnote in Hawkins's edition of *The Complete Angler* (1760), which had decisively 'revived [his] ardor for Action' and convinced him that he was competing with 'a Rival by no means formidable'. The passage which had so crucially put new heart into Burney occurred at the end of a long note by Hawkins on seventeenth-century music, in the course of which, in defiance of all contemporary opinion, he had boldly declared, 'And, now I am upon this Subject, I will tell the reader a secret; which is, that Music was in its greatest perfection in *Europe* from about the middle of the sixteenth to the beginning of the seventeenth Century; when, with a variety of treble-instruments, a vicious taste was introduced, and harmony received its mortal wound.' Hawkins had gone on to praise various Elizabethan composers, 'whose works shew deep skill, and fine invention'.[1]

To Burney such statements were not merely ridiculous: they amounted almost to blasphemy. By so gross an error of taste, Hawkins had condemned himself, Burney was confident, in the eyes of all music-lovers with any claims to sensibility. Hawkins's love of sixteenth- and seventeenth-century music deserved neither discussion nor refutation, for nothing was more central to Burney's musical beliefs than that the art had begun to escape 'barbarism' and to approach perfection only since the period so beloved by Hawkins. Burney himself was sustained in the earlier part of his *History* only by the prospect of eventually arriving at the promised land of the music of his own time. From the beginning of his work, indeed, he had felt it necessary to insert frequent asides and digressions to reassure 'persons of good taste and refined ears'[2] that his own taste was not being impaired by his immersion in the music of barbaric periods and that eventually he would arrive at the only era of musical history which was truly worthy of their attention. Unless this fundamental orientation of Burney's musical taste is fully appreciated, it is impossible to conceive the gravity of the accusations which he felt he could make against Hawkins and which by their mere recital revealed his rival to be both ludicrous and uncivilized:

[1] p. 238 n.   [2] *Hist. Mus.* i. 27.

Modern Music & Musicians are likely to have little Quarter from such a writer, who besides his little knowledge in the practice, delights so much in old musty Conundrums that he will not give a hearing to anything better. he confessed to me that he had not been at an Opera these 20 years—that he *never* was at the annual Concert for the Benefit of decayed Musicians—that he neither liked Tartini's Compositions nor his Book. (I'm sure he understands neither)—

In spite of this radical difference in taste, the two historians were at first openly curious about each other's progress, and even exchanged information, although Burney soon suspected that this was likely to benefit only his rival:

he made up to me two or three Times by way of acquaintance, & I naturally gave way to it & was as open & Frank as if he had been my Brother, till I heard several stories ab^t him well authenticated which made me shy—when I came back from Italy & Called upon him, he conversed with me pen in Hand, in the *Deposition* way.—This I did not much like—however I sent him my Book as soon as printed, & before publication—I did the same by my Edition of the Miserere of Allegri & the rest of the Music performed in the Pope's Chapel during Passion Week—& wished heartily to forget that we were in each other's way. however I have been advised by several who know him better than myself not to be too intimate with him nor too Communicative. my feelings are ever repugnant to reserve, Mystery & suspicion, however they must in the present Case, I believe, take place.[1]

Burney had soon learned to keep his discoveries to himself. At their first meeting he had blurted out praise of a certain obscure but important book, only to hear Hawkins, during their next encounter, repeat the information, as if it were his own discovery. Until they finally began avoiding each other, Burney merely cheered himself by detecting signs of weakness in his rival, rejoicing to observe Hawkins's difficulty with foreign languages or to hear him make a mistake about the contents of a manuscript, which he himself had already examined.[2]

In spite of his insistence that Hawkins deserved only derision from the serious music-lover, Burney's fear of his rival steadily increased and was soon causing him considerable inconvenience.

[1] CB to Twining, 28 Apr. 1773 (Add. MS. 39929, ff. 54–56).

[2] Ibid., 30 Aug. 1773 (Add. MS. 39929, ff. 59–64); this manuscript is described, *Hist. Mus.* ii. 413 n.

He had always intended, when he at last began writing his *History*, to publish the elaborate 'Plan' of his work, in order to stimulate interest among potential subscribers. The 'Advertisement' at the end of his *Italian Tour* in 1771 had stated, 'A General Plan of the author's intended History of Music, with Proposals for Printing it by Subscription, will be submitted to the public as soon as the work is sufficiently advanced to enable him to fix a time with any degree of certainty for its appearance.' Burney had made this promise on the assumption, however, that Hawkins would have published his *History* long before his own first volume was due. By April 1773, when he opened his subscription, there were still no signs of the rival work, and, reluctant to reveal any of his own intentions to Hawkins, he published only the bare 'Proposals': 'I heartily wished him to come out first, but finding how Voluminous he would be, & that there was little likelihood of his being out soon, I did not Chuse to let him know my Ideas & resources for the work I had undertaken. I have therefore only offered to the Public proposals in a Common form, without endeavouring to raise Expectation by magnificent Promises.'[1] Four months later Burney blamed the depressing state of the subscription list on this necessity for concealing his 'Plan' and stated, 'If I could know when the Knight's *last sheet* was in the press, I would perhaps retouch & publish my Plan.'[2]

Sir John Hawkins can have been no less aware of the developing competition, and some two months after the first appearance of Burney's 'Proposals' in his *German Tour* in April 1773, he replied with an announcement of the forthcoming publication of his own *History*, which was described as 'In the Press, And in great Forwardness', the third of his intended four volumes being already in the hands of the printers.[3] The literary world now began to observe the rivalry with interest: in August 1773, two months after the appearance of Hawkins's advertisement, Dr. Johnson, touring the Hebrides with Boswell, gave his views on the situation: 'Both Sir John Hawkins's and Dr. Burney's History of Musick had then been advertised. I asked if this was not unlucky: would they not hurt one another?

---

[1] See p. 191, n. 1.   [2] See p. 191, n. 2.

[3] *London Evening Post*, 17–19 June 1773; the same issue contains an advertisement for CB's *German Tour*, which draws attention to the proposals for his *History*.

—*Johnson.* "No, sir. They will do good to one another. Some will buy the one, some the other, and compare them; and so a talk is made about a thing, and the books are sold".'[1]

Burney himself, however, could not take so detached and sensible a view of the competition: or, at least, if there was to be 'talk', it must be entirely in his own favour, and, if books were to be sold, he was determined that they should be only his own. In the three tense and exhausting years preceding the publication of both works in 1776, however, it is almost impossible to describe with certainty Burney's attitude to Hawkins. The very fact that all mention of Hawkins was suppressed from his letters may, nevertheless, be taken as evidence that he felt an increasingly violent hatred of his rival. There can be no doubt that Fanny d'Arblay, while examining her father's correspondence after his death, deliberately and efficiently censored all references to Hawkins, with the result that, apart from the two letters to Twining already quoted, which never fell into Fanny's hands, only two references to Hawkins have survived in Burney's letters before 1791. (The exceptions are in two letters in 1784, which also escaped Fanny's attention.) Some kind of agreement must also have been reached with the Twining family, for the clergyman's half-brother and nephew similarly omitted all mention of Hawkins from their copies of the Burney–Twining correspondence. One copied passage referring to Hawkins has survived, but it does not name him and a second, probably copied by mistake, was later carefully deleted. That this censoring was deliberate and systematic becomes clear whenever it is possible to compare the copy with the original letter or with Twining's own notes on his letter. Between 1776 and 1785, the originals have survived and his relations did not interfere with their frequent discussion of Hawkins in this period. The Twinings followed similar principles in copying the letters by Burney in their possession. There is no mention of Hawkins, for example, in Daniel Twining's copy of Burney's letter of 28 April 1773,[2] the original of which, however, contains a long discussion of his attitude to his rival.

Although this situation is tantalizing, it is no more useful to speculate about the censored references to Hawkins than to try to guess what Christopher Welch was concealing when he

----

[1] Hill–Powell, v. 72.   [2] Osborn.

stated in 1911, 'I was intimately acquainted with Sir John
Hawkins's grandson, Colonel Hawkins, and . . . I have had
more than one conversation with him on the subject of the
relations of Dr. Burney with his grandfather, Sir John. I have
thus been favoured with a glimpse behind the scenes; but what
was then revealed it is neither necessary nor desirable that I
should disclose.'[1] It is clear, nevertheless, that one factor in
promoting Burney's instantaneous confidence in Twining in the
summer of 1773 was the fact that his new friend already disliked 'the Knight'. At an earlier period Hawkins and the
Twinings had been neighbours and had eventually quarrelled.
Burney later referred to this ill-feeling in 'The Trial of Midas
the 2^{d}', his verse satire on Hawkins;[2] and Fanny d'Arblay
confirmed that Hawkins was better known to Twining than
to her father, and 'yet more obnoxious, from having been at
variance with his family'.[3]

When Twining first wrote to Burney in April 1773 he was
able to supply some inside information about the progress of
Hawkins's *History*, the early sheets of which he had seen at the
bookshop of Thomas Payne, its publisher: 'Payne showed me
the first volume, beginning, as usual, from Mercury &c &c
with a crammed account of every thing that had been said,
disputed, & conjectured, over & over again, about the Music of
the Ancients. . . .'[4] Twining's notes on this letter make it clear
that he was referring here to Hawkins and reveal also that he
wrote again in July 1773 on 'Sr J. H. & his learning &c', although the copy of the letter omits this discussion.[5] There can be
no doubt that Hawkins was one of the many subjects upon
which Twining and Burney were in entire agreement and that
whatever information Twining could supply only confirmed
Burney's conviction that 'If Sr John had ever had any Taste, the
reading such a pack of old rubbish as he seems to delight in w^{d}
have spoilt it.'[6]

The only other reference to Hawkins in the copies of Twining's letters was later carefully deleted, but it suggests that

[1] *Six Lectures on the Recorder*, 1911, p. 116.
[2] See *post*, p. 206.
[3] *Mem.* i. 355; cf. *post*, p. 224.
[4] Twining to CB, 7 Apr. 1773, copy (Add. MS. 39933, ff. 69–71).
[5] Ibid., 7 Apr. and 22 July 1773, notes (Add. MS. 39936, f. 45).
[6] See p. 191, n. 1.

Burney was never quite as confident that his rival was merely a tasteless antiquarian dullard as he professed. By January 1774 he had begun to hope that he might publish his own first volume before Hawkins's *History* appeared, although Twining thought that the extra impetus this desire gave to Burney's already frantic hurry was quite unnecessary: 'I don't like the thought of your hurrying yourself on account of this *Knight of the freezing quarto*—if his whole Work came out tomorrow who would buy it?'[1]

Although no other discussion of Hawkins is to be found in the copies of the Burney–Twining correspondence, the rival historian is mentioned in two letters from Burney's friends, which suggest that they were supporting him solidly and that, in addition, he himself was by no means averse to the circulation of denigratory remarks about Hawkins, both as a man and as an author. As early as 1771, Bewley had replied to the news that Hawkins was also engaged on a *History of Music* with the comment, 'How came it into the head of this same Justice *Midas*—but that is not his name, I think, to write a history of Musick. It must be damnable.'[2] Burney had evidently already identified Hawkins as Midas, who preferred the rough pipes of Pan to the heavenly lyre of Apollo, a comparison he was to explore more fully six years later.[3] In January 1774 James Hutton, his Moravian friend, wrote, in reply to a letter from Burney, 'I cannot conceive a Man of a dark & rigorous turn fit to taste the fine amiable parts of Musick. I know not what Hawkin's plan is, but as I do not know him to be of a very benevolent Character I can not hope that he is able to taste or to make me taste any thing, but the summum Jus of a Session's Chairman. . . .'[4]

In so far as fashionable literary society interested itself in the competition, it shared James Hutton's feelings. The contrast between the rival historians was a marked one and was not confined merely to the opposition of antiquarianism and 'fashionable' taste. Burney was an elegant and charming writer, just as he was a highly agreeable member of society; Hawkins's

---

[1] Twining to CB, 31 Jan. 1774, copy (Add. MS. 39933, ff. 93–95).
[2] Bewley to CB, 18 May 1771 (Osborn).
[3] Cf. *Hist. Mus.* i. 272–3.
[4] J. Hutton to CB, 24 Jan. 1774 (Osborn).

prose was often pompous and awkward, just as he was an unattractive and unsociable personality. Even those who found
much to admire in Hawkins and were loyal in his defence, were
obliged to admit his limitations. Horace Walpole, who assisted him with his *History* and was anxious for its success,
described him as 'a very honest moral man, but of no brightness,
and very obstinate and contentious', adding that he was disliked by both 'the lower class' and 'the gentry'.[1] At his most
affectionate, Walpole thought Hawkins a 'harmless simpleton'.[2]
Samuel Johnson, who was usually angered by criticism of
Hawkins, was similarly prepared to admit and to exaggerate
humorously all his friend's defects: 'as to Sir John, why really I
believe him to be an honest man at the bottom: but to be sure
he is penurious, and he is mean, and it must be owned he has a
degree of brutality, and a tendency to savageness, that cannot
easily be defended'.[3]

It is not surprising, therefore, that the fashionable world was
on Burney's side from the beginning; and it is probably safe to
assume that David Garrick expressed the feelings of the
'Masters & Misses', as well as those of all persons of correct
literary and musical taste, one morning in 1775 during a visit to
St. Martin's Street: '"But pray, Doctor, when shall we have the
History out? Do let me know in time, that I may prepare to
blow the trumpet of Fame." He then put his stick to his mouth,
and in Raree-show-man's voice, cried, "Here is the only true
History, Gentlemen; please to buy, please to buy. Gad, Sir; I
shall blow it in the very ear of yon scurvy magistrate," [meaning
Sir John Hawkins, who is writing the same History].'[4]

By late 1775 expectation of both works was high. Burney's
volume, already a year overdue, was being hurried through the
press, but in spite of the delay there were still no signs of
Hawkins's work. Hawkins had his own supporters among the
antiquarians who followed the progress of his *History* with
interest and, in October 1775, it was confidently expected to
appear in the course of the winter.[5] Probably because his work
had overflowed into a fifth volume, Hawkins did not, however,

---

[1] *Last Journals of Horace Walpole*, ed. A. Francis Steuart, 1910, i. 398–9.

[2] *Corresp.* xxix. 193.

[3] *DL*, i. 58; and *Mem.* ii. 164, where FB ingenuously conceals the identity of the
subject of Johnson's remarks.

[4] *ED*, ii. 29.   [5] J. Nichols, *Literary Anecdotes*, viii. 581, 671.

publish for another year. The rivalry, nevertheless, was kept
before the public late in 1775 by a paragraph in the new edition
of Bishop Percy's *Reliques*, which stated, 'The reader will also
see many interesting particulars on the subject of these volumes,
as well as on most points of general literature, when Sir John
Hawkins shall publish his curious "HISTORY OF MUSIC in 5 Vol.
4to." a work, which the public has long expected with impatience, and from which, the known abilities of the author
lead us to expect much entertainment and instruction.'[1]

Twining read this 'glorious annunciation of the blessed
Knight' in January 1776, while waiting for the arrival of
Burney's first volume, and Percy's claims for Hawkins's com-
petence in 'general literature' and his assertion that the public
was eagerly awaiting the work struck him as ludicrous. He
suspected, however, that Hawkins was being supported by
some kind of antiquarian conspiracy:

> He c⟨om⟩es, he c⟨o⟩mes, the Hero comes!
> Blow yᵉ trumpet, beat the Drums!

We are to expect it, I see, with the primroses, & the violets; it will be
a pretty little bouquet for the spring:—light summer reading. He
does not write with the fear of young ladies before his eyes. He writes
to antiquarians & *old-English* grubbers. . . . there is not among any
set of people such a comfortable scratch-back confederacy, as among
these old ruin-diggers. Is it the consciousness of sneerers & scoffers all
round them—the *sound* feeling of ridiculability—that draws the knot
closer & forms the phalanx, back to back, for Mutual scrubbing, &
defence?—What a style of compliment & what continual *fadaises*
among the Steevenses, Farmers, Percys, Wartons &c. . . . I'll be
hanged if the Cavaliero did not give Dʳ P. a broad hint or so, that a
little notice of that sort wou'd be acceptable. . . .

In spite of his personal dislike of Hawkins, however, Twining,
unlike Burney, was essentially too fair-minded a man to deceive
himself about Hawkins's genuine qualities: 'Well, I shall read
his book, however: that he is a man of sense & parts I deny not;
and in 5 quartos, 'twill be hard if there is nothing worth reading.
I know likewise, that he is a patient, exact, painstaking man.'
He expected, on the other hand, that Hawkins's lack of classical
learning would mar the earlier part of his *History*, and he took it

---

[1] *Reliques of Ancient English Poetry*, 3rd edn., 1775, iii. xxxix.

for granted that 'in opinions & decisions of taste & judgement',
he would prove consistently erroneous.[1]

The first volume of Burney's *History* was published a few days
after Twining wrote these words. In anticipating Hawkins by
some ten months, Burney had the advantage of a considerable
amount of publicity, of having to stand comparison with no
earlier attempt at such an undertaking in English, and of
securing in his subscription list many readers who would not
wish to purchase both works. In his Preface he referred obliquely but politely to Hawkins—who was one of his subscribers—in assuring the public that he had written his *History*
without any 'view to rival others', but only 'to fill up . . . a
chasm in English literature', 'utterly ignorant that any one else
had undertaken to supply it'.[2] A less sensitive and ambitious
writer than Burney would have been content with the praise
his volume received, aware that Hawkins was aiming at a
basically different audience, and would have been prepared to
leave the literary and musical worlds to arrive at their own
verdict. He can hardly have doubted what that verdict would
be. Even his rival's most loyal supporters perceived that Hawkins must suffer from having allowed Burney to publish first:
Horace Walpole, for example, feared that the new volume would
'a little interfere with my friend Sir John Hawkins's on the
same subject'.[3] Burney was not, however, a man to be detached
about his own reputation.

II

After enjoying the initial excitement of the success of his
volume, Burney awaited the publication of the rival work,
which had been imminent for so long. Towards the end of
October 1776 Hawkins began to advertise his *History*, although
it did not appear until 23 November.[4] A week before its publication Burney inserted advertisements for his own volume in the
same newspaper, presumably as some kind of countermeasure.[5]
It has already been suggested that the publication of Hawkins's
History caused Burney to abandon his plan of a revised edition

[1] Twining to CB, 27 Jan. 1776 (Add. MS. 39929, ff. 71–72).
[2] *Hist. Mus.* i. xi.   [3] *Corresp.* xxviii. 248.
[4] *St. James's Chronicle*, between 24–26 Oct. and 21–23 Nov. 1776.
[5] Ibid., 14–16, 16–19 Nov. 1776; see *ante*, p. 187.

of his own first volume. Similarly, it is worth noting that in November 1776 Burney wrote his *Four Sonatas or Duets for two Performers upon one Piano Forte or Harpsichord*, which appeared shortly afterwards. Since he had published no original music since embarking on his literary career, it is possible that these compositions—very unusual at the time—were intended to remind the world of one of his chief claims to superiority over Hawkins: the simple fact that he was, after all, a professional musician. Twining forecast that the *Duets* would be extremely popular: ' 'twill be something *new*, as well as good, & run like wild fire'.[1]

Once Hawkins's five volumes were published Burney had little thought for anything else. Although most of his first volume had been printed several years earlier, Hawkins wrote his Preface (which is dated 20 August 1776) and his 'Preliminary Discourse' after the publication of Burney's book, and both sections refer directly or indirectly to it. In his 'Preliminary Discourse' Hawkins included Burney in a list of previous historians of music: 'At the beginning of this present year 1776, the musical world were favoured with the first volume of a work entitled "A General History of Music . . . by Charles Burney, Mus.D. F.R.S." The author in the proposals for his subscription has given assurances of the publication of a second, which we doubt not he will make good.'[2] Although Dr. Scholes described this paragraph as a 'not ungraceful brief reference',[3] the final words are either curiously awkward or else sarcastic; and while Hawkins was indeed often unfortunately pompous, he had also taken the risk of publishing his *History* without the safeguard of a subscription. It may, however, be over-subtle to detect in his remark a hint that Burney's subscribers would be lucky if they ever saw his second volume.

Parts of Hawkins's Preface were, nevertheless, quite unambiguously aimed at Burney. After justifying the publication of a *History of Music* by one who was not 'a professor of the science' on the strength of the many years he had devoted to collecting materials and to writing the work, Hawkins sneered at Burney's modest apology to his readers and description of the many

---

[1] Twining to CB, 29 Nov. 1776, 24 Jan. 1777 (Add. MS. 39929, ff. 114–18, 121–4); cf. *GDB*, ii. 348.

[2] i. xxi–xxii.   [3] *Life of Hawkins*, 1953, p. 127.

difficulties he had encountered in the composition of his book;[1] and followed these remarks with the implication that Burney had undertaken his *History* merely for financial profit:

Farther than the circumstances attending the peculiar situation of the author and the work may be allowed to entitle him to it, the favour of indulgence, or whatever else it is the practice of writers to crave of the public, is not here sued for, either on the ground of want of leisure, inadvertence, or other pretences; for this reason, that there can be no valid excuse for a publication wittingly imperfect: And it is but a sorry compliment that an author makes to his reader, when he tenders him a work less worthy regard than it was in his power to make it.

To be short, the ensuing volumes are the produce of sixteen years labour, and are compiled from materials which were not collected in double that time. The motives to the undertaking were genuine, and the prosecution of it has been as animated as the love of the art, and a total blindness to lucrative views, could render it.

Later, Hawkins seems once more to refer to Burney, who had travelled so assiduously across Europe in search of materials, in the course of defending the predominantly English sources of his own work: 'and to him that shall object that these sources are inadequate to the end of such an undertaking as this, it may be answered, that he knows not the riches of this country'.[2]

Hawkins's brusque rejection of mythological sources for the history of ancient music in his 'Preliminary Discourse'[3] may well have been provoked by Burney's extensive use of them. Similarly, while most of Hawkins's five volumes had been printed before the publication of Burney's *History*, there are a number of occasions when he seems to be glancing at his predecessor's *Musical Tours*. To give only one example, in describing the music of the German composer Hasse as 'effeminate' and 'greatly over-rated by some of our countrymen',[4] Hawkins undoubtedly had in mind the long and enthusiastic account of the composer in Burney's *German Tour*.[5] On a larger scale, moreover, Hawkins's *History*, and especially its closing pages, unrepentantly urging the thesis that music since Handel had become degenerate and corrupt and refusing to discuss any contemporary composers, represented, if only by implication, a

[1] See *ante*, p. 171.   [2] Preface, vol. i.   [3] i. xxiv-xxv.
[4] *History*, v. 324.   [5] *Tours*, ii. 94-95, 107-9.

deliberate and blunt rejection of Burney's celebration of the achievements of recent German and Italian composers in his two earlier books.

Since no material has survived to document Hawkins's attitude to Burney, it is difficult to estimate the bitterness with which he made these and similar remarks. For the purposes of this study it is perhaps sufficient to record that Burney was infuriated by them. What was worse was that fashionable London literary circles did not immediately make a laughing-stock of Hawkins. His five chaotically organized volumes were full of curious and recondite learning of every kind—detailed biographies and strange anecdotes, as well as dull explorations of medieval music—which appealed to the lover of obscure information quite as much as to the strict antiquarian and the student of musical history. Horace Walpole's verdict, delivered a few days after the publication of Hawkins's *History*, was not unfair:

My friend, Sir John, is a matter-of-fact man, and does now and then stoop very low in quest of game. Then he is so exceedingly religious and grave as to abhor mirth, except it is printed in the old black letter, and then he calls the most vulgar ballad pleasant and full of humour. He thinks nothing can be sublime but an anthem, and Handel's choruses heaven upon earth. However he writes with great moderation, temper, and good sense, and the book is a very valuable one.[1]

Immediately after the publication of Hawkins's *History*, *The St. James's Chronicle*, like other newspapers, began printing a series of extracts of amusing passages from the work;[2] and in December 1776 included a long letter designed to reassure 'common Readers' that Hawkins had written no mere scientific treatise, but 'a Magazine of interesting History and diverting Anecdotes', adding that 'the numberless Particularities respecting the Vocal and Instrumental Performers, and Musical Composers, will afford a perpetual Amusement to the Curious'.[3] In the following month a hostile letter was printed, deriding 'those barren, hackneyed, and uninteresting Anecdotes' which had been appearing; but this writer disclaimed any knowledge

[1] *Letters*, ed. Mrs. Paget Toynbee, ix. 445–6.
[2] 21–23 Nov., 23–26 Nov., 7–10 Dec., 1776; 11–14 Jan. 1777.
[3] 30 Nov.–3 Dec. 1776.

of music, and concerned himself only with Hawkins's remarks on John Gay.[1]

Burney began to fear that, in spite of his grotesque taste, his rival might yet capture a large audience. As he himself had so far published only the drier part of his *History*, which had given him little scope for favourable comparison with Hawkins, he began to contemplate some kind of retaliation against his rival's sneers and an exposure of his atrocious views, in spite of the fact that his friends assured him that the strange species of learning which occupied so much of Hawkins's volumes would never be taken seriously, and that its great price, six guineas for the five volumes, would deter many readers. Samuel Crisp, for example, who had been reading the extracts offered by the newspapers, wrote:

What stuff! Mice & Spiders coming out of their holes, to the Sound of the Lute![2] If I were not asham'd to name them together in the same Page, I should be apt to say, that this strange addle-headed fellow . . . puts one in Mind of some of the most ridiculous . . . extravagant unaccountable Tales of old Pliny—like him he crams into his Book all the Trash, all the Sweepings, that have been thrown into the Kennel a hundred years ago—at least if one may judge by the Extracts that every Newspaper is full of—His Book, on the same Subject with Yours, exhibits so vehement a Contrast, as cannot but do you more Service, than all the puffs of Reviews, Magazines, News papers &c put together—

Burney must, however, have already expressed to Crisp his intention of attacking Hawkins in print, for his old friend proceeded to offer some sensible advice, which Fanny d'Arblay later deleted: 'As matters stand, I think you would be wrong to excite a paper War by exposing him, as you may certainly risk your Reputation on a comparative view of the two performances, & leave it to the World to do you Justice.'[3]

Burney may have taken Greville's advice, but he still seems to have been connected with a series of attacks on Hawkins in *The Morning Post*, the newspaper edited by Garrick's friend Henry Bate. A cryptic and conspiratorial note from Garrick to Burney

[1] 17–19 Dec. 1776.
[2] Cf. the extract from Hawkins in *The St. James's Chronicle*, 7–10 Dec. 1776: 'The Wonderful Power of Musick in its Effects on Mice and Spiders'.
[3] [Crisp] to CB [Dec. 1776] (Osborn).

on 3 January 1777 refers to the 'exquisite' attack on Hawkins due to appear the next day, but the part played in the campaign by Burney himself is obscure, in spite of Garrick's warning, 'for Heavn's Sake take care', which suggests some degree of involvement.[1] Certainly Burney did not write these attacks, although he could have been the author of a poem abusing Hawkins in *The London Evening-Post* for 14–16 January 1777. In any case, it is clear that he at least began to collect ammunition, in case open warfare became necessary. His own copy of Hawkins's *History* contains many triumphant corrections and objections in his hand,[2] and he opened a new notebook especially to record some bitter 'Remarks on Sr J. Hawkins's General Hist^y of Music 1776'.[3] Burney began this onslaught with a detailed dissection of Hawkins's offensive Preface, which mocked its style, exposed its illogicalities, deflated its pomposity, and refuted with desperate earnestness every remark which Hawkins had directed, or seemed to have directed, at his predecessor. Since Hawkins claimed to have started writing his *History* in 1759, Burney felt it necessary to record triumphantly that he himself had begun to collect materials for his *History* six years earlier in 1753, ignoring the fact that Hawkins also claimed to have been gathering materials long before he started the actual writing of his book. Hawkins's sneer at writers who crave the indulgence of the public and his implication that Burney's only ambition was financial profit naturally outraged the musician, who defended himself at great length:

The author glories in his being in no Want of apologies or Indulgence, 'farther than for the Circumstances peculiar to his situation'. this is Manifestly a sneer at the humility of his predecessor, who Imagining his work may have suffered by the inevitable accidents of sickness & want of Time occasioned by that sickness as well as his Profession, wch tho' not that of a trading Justice, required at least as much of his Time as the K^t wanted for committing Vagrants & whipping poor prostitutes. The K^t was indeed tied down to no Time by a subscription having been rec^d—but he broke promises innumerable made in Advertisem^{ts} of speedy Publication. The inadvertence of fixing a Time for delivering the 1st Vol. of another Hist^y was the Cause of hurry, & hasty publication—If no such promise had been

[1] Incompletely dated in *Letters of Garrick*, ed. D. M. Little and G. M. Karhl, 1963, iii. 1271. Cf. *The Morning Post*, 31 Dec. 1776, 4 and 11 Jan., and 18 Feb. 1777.
[2] British Museum, c. 45, f. 4–8.
[3] Osborn. CB's attack on Hawkins appears on pp. 1–20, 148–57, 173–5.

made the subscription w^d not have filled: & when made to break it w^d have disturbed the author's Peace & perhaps have brought on him both private & Public Censure. There was no *necessity* for speedy publication on one side, but a manifest reason for it on the other.

Hawkins's 'Preliminary Discourse' received similar treatment; and selected chapters from all five volumes were subjected to equally stern analysis and refutation. When he resumed his critique later in his notebook, Burney arranged his angry comments on Hawkins under such headings as 'Passages & reflexions pointed at a late Writer on Music' (needless to say, Burney himself); 'Anachronisms & other blunders'; 'Inconsistencies'; 'Words coined—& obsolete'; and 'Omissions of Composers & Performers who died long before S^r J^{no} published his Hist^y & therefore had fair Claims to a Niche in it.'

Burney's frantic attempt to refute and deflate Hawkins hardly deserves longer consideration. His 'Remarks', however, contain a passage which points to another attack on his rival which he wrote almost simultaneously: 'The K^t being a mere *dillettante* of Gothic & oldfashioned Music, was not likely to embellish his Work with Reflexions suggested by good Taste or Science. & whenever he assumes the Character of Judge & Critic, he becomes a II^d Midas: constantly preferring bad to good; nor has he ever pointed out or praised any kind of excellence but what the Mob had previously approved.' Burney had compared Hawkins to Midas as early as 1771[1] and he now decided to complete the parallel with the myth, in which, for preferring the crude music of Pan to that of Apollo, Midas was crowned with the ears of an ass. During 1777 Burney wrote a long satiric poem in heroic couplets, entitled 'The Trial of Midas the Second or Congress of Musicians. A Poem in three Cantos'. One manuscript of the poem, in Burney's handwriting, was first described in 1933,[2] and a second copy, in the hand of an amanuensis with corrections by Burney, has appeared more recently among his papers.[3] Differences between the two manuscripts are slight, although the evidence indicates that the Osborn copy is the later version.

[1] See *ante*, p. 195.

[2] W. Wright Roberts, 'The Trial of Midas the Second', *Bulletin of the John Rylands Library*, xvii (1933), 322–32; reprinted in *Music and Letters*, xiv (1933), 303–12.   [3] Osborn.

Although he remained an assiduous and prolific versifier throughout his life, Burney had little talent as a poet. For all its shortcomings, however, 'The Trial of Midas the Second', a partial imitation of *The Dunciad*, at least succeeds in communicating some of the rage and indignation which Hawkins inspired in him. If nothing else impress the reader, the labour involved in the composition of so elaborate a poem (1,000 lines in length) must suggest that the busy music-master genuinely detested his rival.

In the first canto a crowd of music-lovers implores Apollo to punish 'a certain scribe malign' who has trespassed

> Within the magic circle of the Arts,
> Where Genius only draws and knows the Charts. . . .

The account of the new Midas which follows expresses all Burney's hatred of his rival, who is described as

> Unlicensed by the God or Muse divine;
> Unauthoris'd by Judgement, Talents, Taste,
> Unprincipled in present Lore or past;
> Without or Ear to hear, or Soul to feel,
> Without a Mask his malice to conceal;
> Who dared traduce his sons of high renown
> And try to blast each well-earn'd Laurel-crown:
> Denying all the feeling world allows. . . .

Midas, the crowd explains, accustomed as a magistrate to punishing thieves and whores, has now extended his activities to include the true sons of Apollo (contemporary composers) whom he lashes unmercifully. All that can be said in his defence is that, 'though the blood be black wch fills his heart', it is sheer 'ignorance' and 'False principles and prejudice' which prevent his recognizing the good even when he stumbles across it:

> Hence, ev'ry Rule he draws from Gothic works,
> From barb'rous Jargon, and unmeaning Quirks,
> Produc'd in impious and ill-fated Days
> When all thy sacred altars ceas'd to blaze,
> Thy Priests to sing, thy incence to expand,
> And not a Muse was worship'd thro' the Land!
> Black-Lettered Chains his cold Ideas bind
> Nor let Conviction beam upon his Mind;

> Eager with Fire and Faggot to pursue
> Whate'er is graceful, Elegant, or new—

Apollo, however, decides that he would confer too much honour upon the criminal by passing judgement himself, and consigns Midas to the decision of the crowd.

The trial itself occupies the second and third cantos of the poem. William Boyce, Master of the King's Music and a former friend of Hawkins, is appointed judge, Burney himself modestly declining to participate in the proceedings:

> Burney kept back; for him the cause must scare
> Lest the like Fate he sometime hence sh^d share—

The prosecution begins with a long indictment of Midas, describing his abuse of so many excellent composers and performers and his innumerable offences against Learning, Taste, and Wit. After Midas has pleaded 'Not Guilty', various witnesses for the prosecution claim to have been deliberately abused, ignored, or offended by him and expatiate at length on his crimes. After damning evidence from Science, Taste, Wit, Candor, and Fame, the Court declines to hear any more witnesses,

> Tho' Truth, Chronology, and many more
> To tell their Griefs, were waiting at the Door.

For the defence, an ancient 'Psalmodist' is produced, who offers an absurd tribute to Midas's love of strange and recondite information. This unhelpful witness is followed

> By one whose Nose a Cobweb close embrac'd;
> Whose fingers not with snuff were tinged but Rust,
> Corrosions far more precious than gold Dust.

Otherwise, no further witnesses appear on Midas's behalf, a fact which Burney explains with obvious satisfaction:

> For *Him* could Friendly Witnesses be found
> Who gain'd his neighbours hate for ten miles round?
> Him Twining, Stanley, Stevens, Hawkesworth, Burke,
> With many others Christian, Jew, and Turk,
> The Atrabilious humours in his Blood
> (To which an injured Friend is constant Food)

Had lost: His dang'rous Commerce all forsook,
Ere Coward Implications in his Book
Had multiplied his Foes, and want of skill,
Contempt had brought upon his name and quill.

Boyce, the judge, wishes to be lenient to Midas, if only
because of his praise of Purcell and Handel (although Burney
cynically explained this apparent evidence of good taste as no
more than an ignorant concession to popular fashion); but
eventually realizes that Midas has committed so great a crime
that acquittal is impossible. After the jury have found Midas
guilty, the defendant is allowed to speak for himself. His long
speech is very largely a versification of those parts of the Preface
to his *History* which had most offended Burney and which he
had already attacked in his 'Remarks'. Each assertion by Midas
is linked by footnotes to the relevant extract from the Preface,
although Burney transforms each statement so as to make it
self-evidently ridiculous or contradictory.

At the end of Midas's unrepentant, insolent, and pompous
speech, Boyce pronounces his sentence, to the applause of the
crowd:

> Learn hence, Ye Scribes! The world can never brook
> At once a hated man, and worthless Book.
> Uncommon as your deeds and fell Intent
> O Midas! now must be your punishment!
> To rid the World at once of such a name,
> And choke the Trumpet harsh of Evil Fame,
> To both I now consign a dirty Niche
> Deep in the darkest part of loath'd Fleet-Ditch.

The satire ends with a description, which owes something to
Pope, of the execution of the sentence on the appointed day. An
effigy of Midas and his 'Volumes five' are drawn upon a sledge
to the river:

> And when, as sentenced, in Fleet Ditch they're hurl'd,
> The Lake Oblivious of this upper World,
> Where all the Refuse of Terrestrial things,
> Hateful to sense, each neighb'ring Mortal flings,
> No Force Centrifugal creates a pause:
> With speed exceeding Gravitation's Laws,

> Through Water, Mud, and Dirt, they rapid pass,
> And penetrate the most obdurate Mass;
> Each diff'rent strata of the Globe they enter
> Nor stop one Instant till they reach the Centre.

Burney may at first have contemplated the publication of this elaborate satire on Hawkins, which must have taken up a considerable amount of his time. In any case, he certainly circulated it among his friends. Mrs. Thrale, for example, recorded in her journal late in 1777 that Burney had shown her

in Confidence a little Poem partly on the Plan & in the Spirit of the Dunciad in which are some exquisite Strokes of Satire well express'd, with great fertility of Allusion too & his personified Characters of Science, Wit, and Taste, are as happily finished as 'tis possible. . . .
The Portrait of Science is drawn with a masterly hand a Painter might paint from it—& as he read it me in the Post Chaise one Day I fancied it resembled Mrs Montagu. The Verses which close the Poem however, though they did not strike me more, I better remember, & will write down. They are full of Wit surely—or I know not what Wit is.[1]

Mrs. Thrale then quoted the conclusion of the poem. Later Burney must have presented her with the copy now in the John Rylands Library, which came from the collection of her adopted son, Sir John Piozzi Salusbury. Only once, however, did Burney himself refer to the poem in his surviving letters. Almost thirty years later, at the age of seventy-nine, he promised to read it to his friend, the Rev. C. I. Latrobe, adding, 'I think it w^d *divart* us sometime or other, over our old Port'.[2]

In 1777, however, Hawkins was not yet a subject about which to be genial. Burney published neither his 'Remarks' on his rival nor his long satiric poem, but he could not resist eventually taking active steps to ensure his downfall. Although George Steevens also seems to have been engaged on a private campaign against Hawkins,[3] the literary world as a whole was impressed by the scope and depth of the new *History of Music,* and merely amused by its disorderly method and its preference for sixteenth- and seventeenth-century music. In January 1777

---

[1] *Thraliana*, i. 217–18, where the poem is not identified.
[2] CB to Latrobe, 31 Oct. 1805 (Osborn).
[3] See Hawkins, *History*, new edn., 1853, i. x–xi.

both the *Gentleman's Magazine* and the *Critical Review* began a series of laudatory articles on Hawkins's five volumes and such favourable publicity for his rival undoubtedly shook Burney's confidence, especially as Hamilton, the editor of the second of these periodicals, had assured him that Hawkins would be treated in a very different manner: 'how do you, who live in the world, account for Hamilton's *private* declaration to *you*, & the *publick* proceedings of the *Crit. Reviewers*?', asked Bewley, adding that, 'Never surely was work of Mortal Man so fulsomely be-praised!'[1] To his horror, Burney discovered that Hawkins and his supporters in the *Critical Review* were beginning to exert their evil spell even upon the loyal Twining, who wrote in January 1777: 'I shall long to know what you think of Sr John. I have read some of his preliminary *Talk* in the Critical Review, & thought some of it better than I expected: but cannot get it out of my head, that he *must* have made many mistakes in the *antient* part of his work. I fancy you find it so.' Twining noted with his usual frankness that Hawkins had dealt more thoroughly with at least one aspect of Roman music than had Burney.[2]

Since Kenrick's *London Review* also began a not unfavourable account of Hawkins in the following month, Burney can have found little consolation in the suspicion that the 'Knight' himself was the author of the articles in Hamilton's review.[3] In self-defence, he was forced to call on the most trustworthy of all his supporters. In April 1776 Samuel Johnson had stated, in the course of a discussion about the *Monthly* and *Critical Reviews*, 'I think them very impartial: I do not know an instance of partiality.'[4] When Johnson uttered this opinion William Bewley was actually engaged in writing his review of Burney's *History*. Less than a year later, in February 1777, Bewley wrote for the *Monthly Review* a series of three articles on Hawkins's *History* which, almost single-handed, shattered its growing reputation.

The technique of Bewley's review was unusual. He had always been too conscientious to provide Griffiths with the collection of sparsely linked extracts which so often passed for reviewing at this period, but he had generally followed a set pattern which began with a summary of the author's past

---

[1] Bewley to CB, 19 May 1777 (Osborn).
[2] Twining to CB, 24 Jan. 1777 (Add. MS. 39929, ff. 121–4).
[3] CB to Twining, 31 July 1784 (Berg).   [4] Hill–Powell, iii. 32.

achievements, the intention of the present work and its general
merits or defects; and which then proceeded to a condensation
by summary and quotation of the book, with only intermittent
comment. Bewley's reviews of Burney's books had always
taken this basically expository form, which permitted the reader
to form his own judgement from the extensive extracts. For
Hawkins, however, Bewley adopted a different technique: his
intention was clearly to 'prosecute' the author, to argue a case
against him and to draw only upon material and extracts which
would support that argument. The reader of the review was
given little opportunity to arrive at his own conclusions.

The manner of his review was sufficiently unorthodox at this
time for Bewley to feel obliged to give his reader some explanation in his first article.[1] He immediately admitted that he
had been prejudiced against Hawkins before opening his
History of Music; and explained this bias by quoting the note in
praise of early English music in Hawkins's edition of *The
Complete Angler* (1760), which had given Burney new heart when
he read it and which he must have pointed out to Bewley as
triumphantly as he had to Twining.[2] Like Burney, Bewley now
quoted the passage as if, without further comment, Hawkins
had condemned himself in the eyes of all music-lovers with any
pretensions to taste. The thesis of the rest of the article was that,
in his new publication, Hawkins was as unrepentantly boorish
as ever: 'We were in hopes . . . that, in the course of sixteen
years, our Historian might have acquired a better taste, or at
least one somewhat more congenial with our own; . . . but had
soon the mortification of finding him maintaining the same
tramontane and Gothic opinions, and even speaking in the most
irreverent terms of the music "of the present day".'

It was not difficult to illustrate Hawkins's contempt for what
he had boldly and defiantly described as 'the *trash* daily obtruded on the world'. Bewley turned next to the chaotic structure of his *History*. Hitherto he had employed a tone of solemn
horror, as if in the presence of a blasphemer, in discussing
Hawkins's vicious taste. In the last pages of the article, however,
he suddenly became satiric and fanciful as he demonstrated
the characteristic irrelevance and disorder of the historian's
courageous and vigorous praise of the English madrigalists.

---

[1] *Monthly Review,* lvi (Feb. 1777), 137–44.   [2] See *ante,* p. 190.

Hawkins, however, had not merely described and praised the compositions of these and later musicians; he had assiduously collected a great deal of obscure and trivial information about them, having, as he had boasted in his Preface, even visited cemeteries in search of material. It was not difficult for Bewley to mock, for example, Hawkins's lengthy account of so humble an organization as 'the concert at the *Castle Tavern* in Pater-Noster-Row', which zealously informed his readers of the names and occupations of the carpenters, bakers and school-masters who had participated in it during the early eighteenth century. Such pages provoked Bewley to inspired derision, which greatly diverted his contemporaries and which, although it is obviously unfair, can still be amusing:

Honest souls!—we almost envy ye your temperate amusements and refreshments, closed by a sober and contemplative walk home by moon light;—but little surely did ye imagine, that your orderly and social meetings, and home-brewed potations would, like the *Memoirs of P. P. Clerk of this parish*, be thus minutely chronicled for the infor-mation of posterity. As little could Mr. *Samuel* Jeacocke, who 'mostly played the tenor' at these meetings, suspect that his name, his life and conversation, his proficiency in swimming and ringing, nay his very shop and habitation, should become the subjects of an history, from which Orpheus and Terpander—nay Apollo, and the Nine Muses—are excluded.

After two pages of such derision Bewley rather more gravely regretted the hostility of this first article and promised in his next 'to commend the Author's diligence, as an *Antiquary* and *Collector*; though we cannot speak well of his taste, or of his judgement in selection, as a *Conoscente* and an *Historian*'.

When Bewley resumed his review two months later, in April 1777,[1] his attitude and tone were, however, no more lenient than before. Ignoring his promise to give some account of Hawkins's antiquarian achievement, Bewley contrived to give the impression that the historian's mind was idiotically dis-ordered. The article concluded with a comparison of a paragraph from the *History* with a passage from Sterne's *Tristram Shandy* and an assurance that, if the review had been entrusted to 'our brother *Martinus Scriblerus*' (clearly Burney, from the account of his musical taste), Hawkins would not have escaped so lightly.

[1] *Monthly Review*, lvi. 270–8.

Although the third and final article of Bewley's review was delayed for four months, he had already succeeded in destroying Hawkins's reputation. Richard Porson, writing about Hawkins's *Life of Johnson* ten years later, must have had this review in mind when he sarcastically recalled that 'The witlings and critics of the day combined to run down that excellent book the "History of Music" in five volumes quarto; and their malice prevailed so effectually, for some time, that people who had any regard for their reputation were ashamed to have the book, or to know any thing about it.'[1] Bewley's review, like other attacks on Hawkins, was inevitably attributed to George Steevens. John Nichols thus wrote of his 'cruel and unwarrantable attacks on Sir John Hawkins's "History of Music": which for a long time much injured the sale of that valuable publication, to the very serious injury of "honest Tom Payne", one of the worthiest Booksellers that this country could ever boast.'[2] The review, still attributed to Steevens, was remembered as late as 1825 when Thomas Busby wrote, 'The elaborate and sarcastic character of the criticism, and its simultaneous appearance with a production from which much had been expected, led to a prodigious increase in the demand for the Review; but utterly prevented the success of Hawkins's History.'

According to Busby the 'laboured and severe commentary on the work' in the *Monthly Review* appeared only 'a few days after Payne's publication' and 'The public question was, how an article could have been prepared and printed with such apparent dispatch.' Although Busby's solution to the problem was that Steevens had seen Hawkins's *History* before publication, he must have been confusing other stories,[3] for Bewley's first article in fact appeared three months after the publication of the *History*. He may have been correct, however, in stating that for a time the review was attributed to Burney himself (although he was not yet writing for the *Monthly Review*, as Busby stated). Similarly, other sources agree with Busby that the unfortunate Tom Payne, the publisher of the *History*, who had 'sunk, in a dead stock, the whole of his precious capital', was ruined by the sudden collapse of Hawkins's reputation.[4]

Although Bewley's integrity and high conception of the

[1] *Gent. Mag.* lvii (1787), 652.   [2] *Literary Illustrations*, v. 428.
[3] See p. 208, n. 3.   [4] *Concert Room and Concert Anecdotes*, 1825, i. 133–4.

duties of a reviewer have already been emphasized, the assured and devastating mockery of his first two articles on Hawkins hardly prepare us for the conscience-stricken letters which he wrote to Burney between April and July 1777 and which bridge the gap between the second and concluding articles of his review. The situation suddenly becomes clear: Burney had persuaded his friend, evidently against his wishes, to undertake the review and had then dissociated himself from it. By April 1777 Bewley was 'quite *au desespoir*' at having had no reply from Burney, whom he had asked, with his characteristic desire to be scrupulously fair,

to assist me in pointing out what may *really* be meritorious in the Knight's publication;—divesting myself, *as a Reviewer*, of all prejudice against the Author, for running counter to all *my* notions of what a History of Music ought to be; but at the same time considering that due regard should be paid by *me, in that character*, to the gratification of the peculiar tastes of particular readers,—such as Antiquarians &c.—Had I not hoped for some little assistance from you, I really would not have undertaken the task—at least on so large a scale: though, in any case, I should have been provoked to have *given him a lick*, in consequence of the oblique strokes he seems to aim at his *predecessor*.

At the end of his first article Bewley had dutifully promised his readers a fair account of Hawkins's musical discoveries, for which he was relying on Burney's assistance since he himself was not competent to evaluate Hawkins's achievement. Burney had, however, remained silent and Bewley had been obliged in the second instalment of his review merely to continue 'mauling him for his extravagations'. Nevertheless, he was now determined that, in his final article, he would 'say all the *good* of him that I can', while at the same time justifying 'the general severity of the Critique by one or two select examples, out of several which occur to me'.

In spite of his anxiety to be fair to Hawkins, Bewley had inevitably been gratified by reports of the great amusement which his first article had caused:

Though I was not conscious that I had been more witty or humorous than becomes me, on this occasion; Griffiths wrote to me, about a month ago, that he had been accosted by Mr *Stephens* with many encomiums on Sr *John Hawkins'* Article;—& particularly this

flattering one;—that on visiting Johnson, he found him reading it, &
laughing so heartily, that he spilt his tea on his breeches. I really
don't know whether he did not scald himself; but I instantly wrote to
Griffiths, to keep a sharp eye on the breeches aforesaid, & secure
them for me, to be hung up among the other *Testimonia Clarorum
Virorum.*[1]

By the middle of May Burney had sent a supplementary account of Johnson's amusement to Bewley, who was delighted
by the knowledge that he had succeeded in entertaining the
great man whom he had admired from a distance for so long:
'I scarce knew whether I walk'd on my heels or my head,
when Griffiths told me of the two *Cynic's* high approbation
[Steevens & Johnson] of my first Article on the Knight; but
what sensations do I not feel on your topping the Climax!
Never was mortal Vanity so highly gratified as mine is, by the
"pleasant scoundrel" issuing from the *Os rotundum of Johnson.* I have
nothing further to wish for in this way.'

Bewley was not, however, to be distracted (if that was
Burney's intention) from his desire of ending his review with
some judicious praise of Hawkins, although Burney had so far
brought himself—with the greatest reluctance, we may suspect
—only to 'hint willingness' to assist with some discriminating
approval of his rival. Bewley's already complicated attitude to
Hawkins had not been clarified by the fact that he had been
involuntarily entertained by some of the material in the new
History, extracted 'from books which I never had seen, nor
could have an opportunity of seeing'. Once more Bewley sent
his plaintive request to London: 'I would fain soften the
deserved censure of the Knight by some honeyed words or other;
& would fain find out something praiseworthy in him, besides
mere *diligence.* The rule you hint at, as my guide, is by no means
sufficient.'[2]

Bewley should not perhaps have expected that, once his rival
had been decisively knocked down, Burney would voluntarily
hasten to the rescue. By the second week in June he had been
obliged to postpone his concluding article for yet another month
for Burney's only response to his requests for assistance had
been a letter containing further examples of Hawkins's defective

---

[1] Bewley to CB, 25 Apr. 1777 (Osborn).
[2] Ibid., 19 May 1777 (Osborn).

taste, contradictions, and omissions, probably transcribed from
the 'Remarks' in his notebook.[1] Since Hawkins had specifically
declined to deal with living composers, Bewley felt unable to
use most of this material and yet again he had to repeat his
plea, as 'a mere literary Reviewer' not 'a *professor*', for guidance
as to 'what may be reckoned curious or new, in a work of this
kind, & *in our language*'.

His conscience was, if anything, more troubled than ever. At
some gathering in Norfolk he had admitted to the authorship of
the two satirical articles on Hawkins, only to realize to his
'utter dismay' that he had been overheard by Horace Walpole.
Knowing that Walpole was 'the Knight's *friend*' and believing
also that 'he had written half the Knight's book', Bewley had
been greatly embarrassed and had anxiously 'begged him not to
peach'. Walpole had obligingly promised to keep the secret, but
this 'unlucky scrape' had only made it seem the more imperative that his final article should be responsible and balanced.
Without Burney's help this would be impossible:

> I wish too to favour poor *Payne*—a very honest man, as I am told—
> nay, & the poor devil of an Author too; though I do not mean to re-
> tract a syllable of what I have said.—Pray, assist me—I consider *you*
> as a perfectly *disinterested* man—for surely no two works, even on
> different subjects, can be so perfectly *aliene* as the two English
> Historys of Music! The Knight cannot possibly hurt *you*; but you
> have hurt *him* most confoundedly with your first Volume. You have
> given us a little *Tid bit* in *Quarto*—& after relishing . . . this dainty;
> the Knight's tough bull beef, & bollock's liver can never more go
> down.[2]

Another month passed without any response from Burney and,
in despair, Bewley at last wrote the article in July. Before he
sent it to Griffiths, however, the long-awaited letter from Burney
arrived and the article had to be postponed once more. In
reply, Bewley rehearsed his various anxieties for the last time.
While he was 'perfectly easy' about his *faux pas* with Walpole—
'He & I perfectly understand each other, & differ not much
about the matter'—he urged Burney to keep the story to himself, since Walpole '*professes* a great regard for the Culprit'. He
was grateful for Burney's assessment of Hawkins's researches

---

[1] See *ante*, pp. 203–4.   [2] Bewley to CB, 11 June 1777 (Osborn).

into Elizabethan music, but he could have wished for still more
information about the madrigalists to enable him 'to *flourish* a
little'. Although he assured Burney that he was 'fully sensible of
the Candour you shew in assisting me to laudify this tasteless
Goth', Bewley saw no reason why he should have been so
reluctant, since Hawkins could by no stretch of the imagination
be considered a serious rival. He also suspected that some of
Burney's apparent praise of Hawkins was really ironic ('Pray,
be *serious* as a *Judge* in what you write'). In conclusion, Bewley
tried to assure himself, as so often in the past, that Burney would
suffer rather than benefit from their friendship:

> Had I not known you—though it is very unlikely that, in that case,
> I should have undertaken this business—my principal or master
> stroke would have been to draw a *Parellele*—a Contrast, I mean, be-
> tween the two English Musical Historians. You have suffered by my
> acquaintance before this; & may rue the day you ever knew me. I
> am almost afraid to name you in the present article; though I have
> once plucked up heart to quote you. I know I am wrong in this; but,
> after all, there may be no great harm in it.[1]

Few eighteenth-century reviews can have been compiled
more conscientiously than Bewley's concluding article, which
finally appeared in August 1777.[2] After the four letters which
have been quoted—although some abuse of his earlier articles
by the reviewer of Hawkins's *History* in the *London Review*
probably helped[3]—it can be no surprise to find that Bewley
began his article with a solemn discussion of 'the leading
principles of our critical conduct', especially 'that first and
supreme duty which the critic owes to the Public' of detachment
and impartiality. Bewley's conscience set him a formidable
task, for he attempted simultaneously to justify the severity of
his earlier articles while bestowing some judicious praise on
certain aspects of Hawkins's *History*. Thus, while Bewley now
admitted that the sheer aggregation of obscure material in the
work was 'a striking monument of his patience and industry',
such praise is usually qualified almost as soon as uttered: 'He
has made the grave give up its dead. . . . he has not spared a
single cobweb of antiquity that lay *within his reach*: but then,

---

[1] Bewley to CB, 26 July 1777 (Osborn).
[2] *Monthly Review*, lvii (1777), 149–64.
[3] *London Review*, v (1777), 279; mentioned by Bewley, 19 May 1777.

such is the dust attending his operations, that his reader and pupil is generally left in the dark, blinded and suffocated by the clouds raised by his officious though well meaning *Cicerone*'. Bewley found it difficult to repress the comic manner of his earlier articles: 'Opening the fourth volume, for example, we there meet with old *John Mundy*, rubbing his eyes, on being most unnecessarily summoned, and dragged from his tomb in the cloyster at Windsor, where he had been deposited, and had quietly and deservedly been suffered to sleep ever since 1630. . . .' To Bewley, Hawkins's investigations of the Mundy family and of Dr. Blow's unmusical descendants seemed the 'results of a permanent and constitutional infirmity in our Historian. . . . a *love* of circumstance, and detail, be the subject or occasion what it may'. The scanty information offered about more recent musicians made a sharp contrast and Bewley quoted Burney's high opinion of Hasse to refute Hawkins's sneer at that composer. His long discussion of other omitted or abused names clearly leaned heavily on Burney's communications during the summer.

It was also from Burney, however, that Bewley had obtained advice about the praise which could properly be given to Hawkins's section on Elizabethan music and a page of rather grudging approval is bestowed on his courageously unfashionable claims for such composers as Tallis, Byrd, Wilbye, and Weelkes. Hawkins had, however, concluded his work with a defiant discussion of the degeneracy of music since the time of Handel and, supplied with ammunition by Burney, Bewley retaliated in his best style: 'Never surely did Mr. *John Immyns* himself, the founder and president of the Madrigalian Society, rave, with his "cracked counter tenor voice", from his chair at the *Twelve Bells ale-house* in Bride-Lane, with such *unenlightened* zeal against the corruptions and innovations of Handel and Bononcini!' Bewley's final verdict was that, although an occasional pearl or diamond might be found 'in the midst of various and heterogeneous substances of inferior quality', the valuable information in Hawkins's *History* was always 'blended and confounded with an inordinate mass of other matter, on which candour itself, in one of its most generous fits, cannot honestly bestow a more favourable appellation than that of *rubbish*'.

In effect, Bewley had not yielded an inch of ground and his display of impartiality probably only served to strengthen his condemnation. As Twining told Burney, 'O! the Review was excellent:—it *must* kill the man;—he can't live:—& yet 'tis all fair, & well deserved. I wish I cou'd know who wrote that article.'[1] Burney was not prepared, however, to entrust Twining with the truth. One of his most curious characteristics, indeed, was his determination to keep his closest friends in virtual ignorance of each other's existence, especially of his dependence on their different kinds of assistance. The reason for this behaviour is made clear by a troubled letter which Twining sent him in May 1781, asking him to deny a statement 'which I have heard positively asserted, but which I do not at all believe, because I must have known [it] from you. . . . that you were much en liaison with one Mr *Bewly* (so his name sounds) who is principally concerned in ye Monthy [*sic*] Review, & that he *assisted* you *in y^r History*: which I denied plumply.'[2]

Twining would obviously have been surprised and hurt to learn that Bewley, as well as himself, had always looked over the proofs of Burney's books and would also have been somewhat disillusioned by the realization that it was Bewley who had praised Burney and derided Hawkins in the *Monthly Review*. Another letter from Twining in October 1781 shows that, although Burney had been obliged to admit his acquaintance with Bewley, he must have stressed that his friend was merely a scientific reviewer and denied flatly that he had ever received any musical 'assistance' from him: 'Your account of y^r friend Bewley, likes me much: I had heard him spoken of as a very ingenious man, & a M^y Reviewer; but so much of him I did not know. I will set my informer right about his having assisted you.'[3]

But Twining was not yet quite satisfied and he renewed his inquiry in 1784, after learning that he himself had been identified as the malicious reviewer of Hawkins: 'Do you know that Payne thought, and had been told so, that I wrote the criticism upon Sr J.'s book in the M.R.?—I wish it were true, for it was an excellent thing. I have been told that your poor

---

[1] Twining to CB, 6 Oct. 1777 (Add. MS. 39929, ff. 143-6).
[2] Ibid., 4 May 1781 (Add. MS. 39929, ff. 254-7).
[3] Ibid., 10 Oct. 1781 (Add. MS. 39929, ff. 274-8).

friend Bewley wrote it; but I forget by whom. I think I never
heard *you* say.'[1] Burney had always been anxious to dissociate
himself from the review, but he could hardly refuse this second
request. In the course of his reply he casually and vaguely remarked, 'I believe it was poor Bewley who wrote the Monthly
Review of Sʳ Jnº.'[2] The dark deed of assassination had been
essential but he was not necessarily proud of it.

III

The ghost of Hawkins haunted Burney, however, as he continued working on the later volumes of his own *History*. In the
eyes of the literary world the victory was his, and he was confident that as a writer of elegant prose, in the construction and
exposition of his work and, above all, in 'taste', Hawkins could
not begin to compete with him. On the other hand, Burney
soon came to realize that his rival's five huge volumes had made
available a mass of material which he himself might never have
discovered and, as he proceeded with his own work, he found it
impossible to ignore his predecessor. The result was a perpetual
irritation with Hawkins. Sometimes he was obliged to alter his
own treatment of a subject simply to avoid the charge of
plagiarism. On other occasions it was no less aggravating to be
directly indebted to Hawkins, even if it was a debt he would not
think of admitting to the public. The very scope of Hawkins's
History presented Burney with a challenge; and in order to
compete he soon found that it would be impossible to complete
his own work in the two volumes he had envisaged. Psychologically, moreover, there was the general irritation of being
obliged to follow in another's footsteps instead of the excitement
of being a pioneer. This consideration in itself could serve to
explain the frequent discouragement and depression which
assailed Burney before he completed his last volume.

Even in the hour of his triumph over Hawkins in the autumn
of 1777, he communicated his annoyance to Twining, who
hastened to assure him that Hawkins had in no sense obviated
the need for another *History*: 'a *readable* History of Music is still
as much a desideratum as ever'. He admitted, however, that he
himself would not enjoy 'the necessity of squinting, & sideling,

[1] Ibid., 26 June 1784 (Add. MS. 39929, ff. 334–7).
[2] CB to Twining, 31 July 1784 (Berg).

& peeping all the way, to see what another man has done, where
he has built upon my ground, & where left it open, where he
has used my materials, & where his own &cᵃ'. As Burney had
already felt obliged to alter the first chapter of his second volume
simply to avoid Hawkins's path, however, Twining warned him
against making important omissions for this reason. The two
historians necessarily shared the same materials: Burney's
unassailable superiority would lie in his infinitely more attractive method of presentation; and as he approached contemporary music, the necessity of paying attention to Hawkins's
volumes would quickly disappear.

Burney had also asked Twining whether he should make any
reference to Hawkins in his later volumes, doubtless because he
would have relished every opportunity of mocking and criticizing
his rival. His friend, however, wisely discouraged such open
attacks:

I wou'd not *mention* him for the world: as to side flings, & back-
handed strokes, tho' 'tis tempting, & you will have perpetual openings,—I don't like them, & 'tis what *He* has done. I wou'd lose sight
of Sʳ J. Hawkins as entirely as possible. . . . You will work him
enough, without intending it. You have nothing to do but to go on:
is it worth while to lift up one's hand & level a blow at a man, whom
one is sure of knocking flat upon his back by fair accident?—Say I
right, bully Dʳ?[1]

Although the 'bully Dʳ' accepted the advice as far as direct
reference to Hawkins went,[2] he could not 'lose sight' of his rival
and his obsession did not diminish. In December 1778, when
Twining suspected that Hawkins's five great volumes were once
more depressing him, he loyally urged his friend to continue his
task, which, he argued, 'is, certainly, more a *desideratum* than
ever, since Sʳ J. H.'s publication: as teaching is *more* a desideratum to one of your scholars who has been ill taught, than to one
who is carte blanche: it is *wanted* both as doing and undoing'.
In the same letter Twining commented on the news that Hawkins had presented his collection of old books on music to the
British Museum: ' 'tis a stale trick; he thinks to save his fame,
as sinners save their souls, by an act of *Charity* at last'.[3] Twining's

---

[1] Twining to CB, 6 Oct. 1777 (Add. MS. 39929, ff. 143–6).
[2] But see *post*, pp. 265–6, 337.
[3] Twining to CB, 19 Dec. 1778 (Add. MS. 39929, ff. 185–8).

simile attracted Burney who cheered himself up by elaborating it in one of his more effective poems:

> In Ancient days of Superstition
> When Death approach'd the Sinner's door,
> He robb'd his kin, to shew contrition,
> And gave the Church his useless Store.

> E'en thus the Knight, in proud oblation,
> Bestows the Sweepings of each stall;
> And with them, to escape damnation,
> The dust, the cobwebs, worms & all.

> But pious protestants determine
> That Safety lies not in such querks;
> For whether clad in rags or Ermine,
> None 'scape the flames—but by *good Works*.[1]

Burney could not confine his resentment of Hawkins to his correspondence with the sympathetic Twining. Mrs. Thrale, at the height of her affection for him, noticed that he was 'envious' of Hawkins, a marked exception to his almost invariable good nature.[2] In 1784 his dislike of his rival found fresh nourishment, although it had seemed at first that some kind of reconciliation might be possible. Twining had recently purchased the blasphemous *History* at its considerably reduced price ('Think of *my* taking off Payne's hands, to his great joy, the *last* lingering copy'), and had diverted himself by placing it side by side on his shelf with the two volumes of Burney's *History* which had then been published: 'I congratulate you, & the Knight, upon your being such good friends.'[3] Burney was amused by this juxtaposition but he was able to describe an actual encounter with Hawkins, apparently the first since their uneasy acquaintance in the early 1770's: 'You mention the Cheek-by-jowlliad between me & the Knight—did I tell you of a real one lately between us twain?—I met him at Dr Johnson's & did not know him, he's grown so thin & old since I came from Italy. He came up to me—shook me by the paw—& more politely than I thought he cd truckle to, told me he ⟨was⟩ glad to see me &c—.'[4]

Any possibility of a precarious friendship between the two

---

[1] 'On Sir John Hawkins giving his Collection of old Musical books to the British Museum', in a notebook of poetry, p. 131 (Osborn).

[2] *Thraliana*, i. 458; see *post*, p. 231.

[3] See *ante*, p. 219, n. 1.   [4] See *ante*, p. 219, n. 2.

men rapidly disappeared. The scene of their meeting was significant, for a few months later, in December 1784, their common friend, Samuel Johnson, died, having appointed Hawkins
one of his executors. Both Sir John's fulfilment of his duties and
his decision to write a biography of Johnson displeased Burney:
'The knight, Sir John, and I met two or three times during his
sickness, and at his funeral. He steps forth as one of poor
Johnson's six or eight biographers, with as little taste or powers
of writing worthy of such an occupation as for musical history.'
Burney blamed Hawkins for the unworthy funeral service at
Westminster Abbey, which the executors decided should be as
cheap as possible, and he also suggested to Twining that Hawkins had been spreading baseless stories of Johnson's youthful
profligacy in London.[1] Although his own opinion of Hawkins's
biography has not survived, he must have enjoyed the harsh
treatment Sir John received from Boswell in 1791, especially
the latter's remarks on the 'dark uncharitable cast' of his
predecessor's *Life of Johnson*.[2] Burney himself contributed a note
rejecting Hawkins's account of the reception of *Irene* in 1749 to
the third edition of Boswell's *Life* in 1799.[3]

After 1784 occasional characteristic references to Hawkins
are to be found in Burney's letters—'There is no depending on
his information', 'That wooden block-head'[4]—but after 1789,
the year in which Burney completed his *History* and in which
Hawkins died, it is reasonable to suppose that the 'Knight'
obtruded very little. The only other references occur during
Burney's years with the *Monthly Review*, when his anxiety to
ensure that the new generation of musicologists respected the
earlier labours which had made their own work possible almost
forced him into a kind of truce with Hawkins, whose name he
often linked with his own, when pointing out what an easy task
musical history had become since the publication of the two
giant *Histories*.[5]

Burney could well afford such cautious generosity towards his
defeated rival; and it was only after the deaths of both historians that balanced comparison of their achievements became

[1] CB to Twining, 25 Dec. 1784, *Country Clergyman*, pp. 128–30.
[2] Hill–Powell, i. 27–28.   [3] Ibid. 197 n.
[4] CB to CB Jr., 14 [Jan.] 1805 (Coke); to Latrobe, 31 Oct. 1805 (Osborn).
[5] See R. Lonsdale, 'Dr. Burney and the *Monthly Review*', *RES*, xiv (1963), 352–3.

possible. Derision of Hawkins's five volumes had continued long after Bewley's review and had been revived in the year of his death by the publication of a catch on the rivalry by John Wall Callcott, which became extremely popular. The words 'Sir John Hawkins' and 'Burney's History' are carefully contrived to sound at certain points like 'Sir John Hawkins! Burn 'is History!' According to some sources, it was Callcott's catch which finally forced the bookseller to consign Hawkins's *History* to moulder 'in the profoundest depth of a damp cellar'.[1]

Although such stories may be exaggerated, there can be no doubt that for many years Hawkins's very real merits were greatly underrated. During the nineteenth century a reaction set in against the fashionable Burney, but the rivalry is not yet dead and the complementary qualities of the two histories are still being opposed to each other at the present day.[2] Most of the relevant considerations have already been stated or implied in this account of the competition. Burney's *History* is undoubtedly better written and more carefully organized, and his account of eighteenth-century music is important not merely for the first-hand information it contains, but because it embodies so completely and fundamentally the 'fashionable taste', such as it is, of the period. Hawkins, on the other hand, has often proved more valuable to later scholars as a repository of the obscure musical information which was the object of so much derision in his own lifetime. On the whole, justice has been done. Hawkins's book was republished in 1853, 1875, and 1963 and, although he had to wait much longer, Burney's *History* has been reprinted twice in recent years, in 1935 and 1957. The ultimate value of the two *Histories* is, however, less relevant to this study than the fact that Burney had established himself as the unchallenged arbiter of musical taste in England. The means by which he secured that position and defended it do not always reveal his character in a very attractive light, but the petty ruthlessness which his ambition made necessary can be understood, even if it is harder to condone it.

The preceding account of Burney's rivalry with Hawkins

[1] *Harmonicon*, ix (1831), 81.
[2] Cf. ibid., x (1832), 216; Hawkins, *History*, 2nd edn., 1853, i. viii–x; Scholes, *GDB*, i. 298–302 and *Life of Hawkins*, pp. 126–38: R. Stevenson, 'The Rivals'— Hawkins, Burney, and Boswell', *Musical Quarterly*, xxxvi (1950), 67–82; and C. Cudworth's introduction to a reprint of Hawkins's *History*, New York, 1963.

provides a suitable context for a story told by Fanny d'Arblay in her *Memoirs*, the full implications of which she deliberately concealed and which have never been understood, although the story itself has been retold more than once.[1] During one of Thomas Twining's visits to London (probably in 1777), Burney arranged to introduce him to David Garrick in St. Martin's Street. The two friends were awaiting Garrick, 'when a violent rapping at the street door, which prepared them for his welcome arrival, was followed by a demand, through the footman, whether the Doctor could receive Sir Jeremy Hillsborough; a baronet who was as peculiarly distasteful to both the gentlemen, as Mr. Garrick was the reverse'. Both Burney and Twining cried out in horror and were instructing the footman not to admit the unwelcome visitor, when,

strenuously flinging open the library door himself in a slouching hat, an old-fashioned blue rocolo, over a great-coat of which the collar was turned up above his ears, and a silk handkerchief, held, as if from the tooth-ache, to his mouth, the forbidden guest entered. . . .

The Doctor, whom Sir Jeremy had never before visited, and to whom he was hardly known, save by open dissimilarity upon some literary subjects; and Mr. Twining, to whom he was only less a stranger to be yet more obnoxious, from having been at variance with his family; equally concluded, from their knowledge of his irascible character, that the visit had no other view than that of demanding satisfaction for some offence supposed to have been offered to his high self-importance. And, in the awkwardness of such a surmise, they could not but feel disconcerted, nay abashed, at having proclaimed their averseness to his sight in such unqualified terms, and immediately within his hearing.

After a heavy pause the visitor seated himself 'with an air of domineering authority' in a chair near the fire and a further embarrassing silence ensued. At last, 'the intruder, after an extraordinary nod or two, of a palpably threatening nature, suddenly started up, threw off his slouched hat and old rocolo, flung his red silk handkerchief into the ashes, and displayed to view, lustrous with vivacity, the gay features, the sparkling eyes, and laughing countenance of Garrick,—the inimitable imitator, David Garrick.'[2] The anecdote is more, of course, than just

---

[1] Most recently by Carola Oman, *David Garrick*, 1958, p. 334.
[2] *Mem.* i. 354–7.

another example of Garrick's fondness for impersonation. Fanny could not resist using (and probably exaggerating) it in her *Memoirs*; but, unwilling both to offend Laetitia-Matilda Hawkins, who was still alive, and to resurrect the somewhat discreditable story of her father's rivalry, she altered certain details, retaining, however, the correct initials. Garrick's sense of humour, as well as the horror expressed by Burney and Twining, both receive an extra dimension when the obvious identification of Sir Jeremy Hillsborough is made. If any more evidence for that identification than the whole of this chapter is required, it can be found on a tiny scrap of paper, only an inch by an inch and a half in size, doubtless a memorandum made by Burney for his 'Memoirs', which is entirely filled by the words, 'Garrick sending in the Name of Sr Jno Hawkins—when Twin^g & I were making remarks on his hist^y'.[1]

[1] *Frag. Mem.* (Berg).

VI

BURNEY IN THE JOHNSONIAN
CIRCLE

1776–1784

I

FRANTIC and unremitting work in every spare moment had become so habitual to him that Burney found it difficult to relax after the publication of the first volume of his *History of Music* in January 1776, and he was eager to begin writing his second and concluding volume without delay. Thomas Twining was delighted, although he hoped that Burney ('poor perturbed spirit') would give himself plenty of time for a calm and comfortable completion of the work: 'Why, you are a hero of a man, to stare your 2^d Vol. in the face so soon! for my part, I am not at all afraid of it. But I desire to know, how long a time you allow for your 2^d Volume?—I hope to see no such hurry skurry work, such as squeezing & scrounging, & *deviltry* as there has been.' From his village parsonage Twining was prepared to continue advising, criticizing, and encouraging his busy friend in London but, perhaps realizing that he would be able to contribute less to the *History* as it moved away from ancient music, he felt it necessary to assure Burney of the importance of their correspondence to him: 'Let me just say, once for all, that your correspondence is, on ne peut pas plus, valuable to me: one of the pleasantest ingredients in the happiness of my life. . . . the same tastes—the same pursuits—the same hobby horses—in short there is no subject that is interesting to me, or that I wish to talk about with any man, but I *can* talk about it with you.'[1]

Inevitably, Burney's impetus of energy gradually failed. He could not resist basking temporarily in the warm approbation of the distinguished men and women who praised his book, and enjoying the new literary reputation which he had so painfully acquired. 'I hope ye Empress of Russia was well when you heard

[1] Twining to CB, 19 Feb. 1776 (Add. MS. 39929, ff. 73–75).

from her last', commented Twining derisively in March 1776.[1] Then, from April to the end of the year, Burney was preoccupied with the preparation of the extensively revised second edition of his first volume. In July and August he accompanied his wife to Bristol and himself travelled on to Buxton to nurse his rheumatism.[2] Twining could only approve such 'frisking & capering all over England', for he knew that Burney, more than anyone, deserved such a vacation. Nevertheless, he could not help worrying about the second volume: 'And so you have done nothing yet?—I see you will be in a bother at last, if you don't take care; I believe you *like* to be hurried.'[3]

By the end of 1776 there were new distractions. It was necessary, for example, for Burney to ensure the abrupt suppression of the challenge offered by Hawkins's *History of Music*, as well as to vent private rage and scorn at his rival in verse and prose. Simultaneously, it would appear, Burney was trying to turn his newly acquired musical eminence to some financial account, although the dating of this episode rests entirely on heavily deleted passages, which can be read only with the greatest difficulty, in a letter from Samuel Crisp in December 1776. It seems clear from this letter, however, that Burney already had some official connexion with the musical activities at the Pantheon, the magnificent new assembly rooms where concerts had been held since 1773, which he was now hoping to make more profitable and permanent. His ambitions apparently included becoming a Proprietor of the Pantheon and obtaining 'the management of the whole Band' there. On the strength of these expectations Burney had evidently given up, or was about to give up, his post at the boarding school for girls in Queen's Square where he had taught since 1760.[4]

The cryptic remarks, which are all that can be salvaged from the deletions, in Crisp's letter can be clarified by a passage in Burney's account of his relations with Giardini, the violinist, on whom he blamed so many of the disappointments of his life: 'by abetting his insolence & tyrannical Governm^t at the Pantheon I not only lost the Weight I had acquired with the Proprietors,

[1] Ibid., 28 Mar. 1776 (Add. MS. 39929, ff. 82–83).
[2] *ED*, ii. 141–2.
[3] Twining to CB, 22 Aug. 1776 (Add. MS. 39929, ff. 103–4).
[4] [Crisp] to CB [Dec. 1776] (Osborn).

but their Friendship, & a Sal^y of £100 p^r ann. wch had been voted me for carrying on their foreign Correspondence for 3 years, & wch w^d have been readily renewed had I chosen to relinquish him & his Principles'.[1] Although the evidence is scanty, it seems likely that Burney had acted as Foreign Correspondent to the Pantheon since about 1773 and that in 1776, at the instigation of Giardini, he tried to obtain greater control over the important musical activities at the assembly rooms, the only result of his ambitions being that his original connexion was severed.

This episode was probably of greater significance than may at first appear. The failure of Burney's ambitions at the Pantheon, which would have involved him irretrievably in the London musical world, probably gave greater compensatory importance to another connexion which he made at the same time and which soon brought him to the heart of the city's literary society. Early in January 1776 Burney had been invited to dinner by Sir Joshua Reynolds. Among the other guests were 'Dr Johnson whom I had frequently visited before & after I left *Lynn*—& Mr Thrale 1st Time.'[2] Burney's acquaintance with Johnson was increasing at this time, for on the same page of his pocket-book he noted that Drs. Johnson and Percy had called on him on 2 February, a few days after the publication of his *History*. It was with good reason, however, that Burney made a special note of his first meeting with Henry Thrale, the wealthy brewer, for it was through the Thrales that he was at last to enter into intimate friendship with Johnson and, indeed, into a social and intellectual circle which, for some eight years, was to influence his life decisively.

According to Mrs. Thrale, Burney was introduced to Streatham later in 1776 by William Seward, the young hypochondriac littérateur, whose father, like Thrale, was a brewer. During December, Mrs. Thrale stayed in London for a week and engaged Burney—now one of the most fashionable musicteachers in the city—to instruct her daughter Queeney. He gave the first lesson on 12 December 1776.[3] Although the rhap-

[1] 'Sketch of a Character' (Osborn). See *ante*, pp. 78, 152.

[2] Frag. of pocket-book, 8 Jan. 1776 (Berg).

[3] Mrs. Thrale's 'Children's Book', quoted by J. L. Clifford, *Hester Lynch Piozzi*, 1941, p. 149. CB mistakenly told Boswell that his acquaintance with the Thrales began in 1775, Hill–Powell, ii. 406.

sodic and impetuous Mrs. Thrale is not the first witness one would choose for a detached and balanced estimate of any of her contemporaries, her scattered remarks on Burney in *Thraliana* surprisingly enough constitute the most extensive objective account of his character which is available. The seemingly inexhaustible supply of material about the Burneys comes almost entirely from the family itself, especially from Fanny, and the fact that we are usually obliged to accept their own valuation of themselves is generally ignored. It is important therefore, that Mrs. Thrale's testimony be added to that of Burney's zealously adoring daughters, and her first protracted description of Queeney's music-master, dating from the late summer of 1777, deserves full quotation:

Doctor Burney was first introduced to our Society by M[r] Seward in the Year 1776—he was to teach our eldest Daughter Musick, & attended once a Week at Streatham for that purpose: but such was the fertility of his Mind, and the extent of his Knowledge; such the Goodness of his Heart and Suavity of his Manners that we began in good earnest to sollicit his Company, and gain his Friendship. few People possess such Talents for general Conversation, and fewer still for select Society, where no Restraint is laid upon one's Expressions & where Humour and good humour charm more than Wit and Philosophy—tho' Burney is never found deficient in either; and would be called a deep Scholar was he not without Pedantry, as he would be reckon'd a Wit was he not without Malice.—if ever the— Suaviter in Modo, fortiter in Rê—resided in mortal Man, tis surely in Doctor Burney—[1]

Burney had been introduced to Streatham at precisely the right moment. Henry Thrale was at his most affluent, the handsome house and grounds at Streatham were being improved and extended, and Mrs. Thrale's social and intellectual ambitions as a 'Blue-Stocking' were increasing.[2] Burney was not, however, welcomed as just one more literary adornment of the Thrale circle, for he came to fill a recently vacated position in the household. In July 1776 Giuseppe Baretti, Queeney's Italian master, who had been regularly resident at Streatham, finally quarrelled with Mrs. Thrale and walked out of the house. Burney, who arrived on the scene some five months later, soon developed into a replacement for Baretti

[1] *Thraliana*, i. 136–7.   [2] Clifford, op. cit., pp. 145, 153, 165.

and rapidly transcended his original function. As far as Mrs. Thrale was concerned, moreover, he provided a very welcome change, for none of her acquaintance could have contrasted more strikingly with 'the ferocious Italian', 'Haughty & Insolent and breathing defiance against all Mankind', who was 'so vile a Lyar' and characterized by a 'ferocious Temper' and by 'Violence' in conversation.[1]

Other members of her circle, as well as Mrs. Thrale herself, were aware of the contrast between Baretti and her affable and mild-mannered new favourite. 'You have got a *new* Friend now says Murphy—Doctor Burney; how can you like People of such different Dispositions? just says I as you can like *old Hock* & *Frontiniac*.'[2] In 1781, when she wrote verse characters of all the friends whose portraits by Reynolds adorned her house, Mrs. Thrale repeated the simile and once more contrasted Burney with 'his perfect Opposite Baretti'.[3] Burney, indeed, began his acquaintance with the Thrales with everything in his favour and *Thraliana* contains many affectionate and admiring tributes to his various qualities. Mrs. Thrale thought him 'the most modest of all human Creatures' and that his 'Parts almost rival his Virtues'. In 1779 she wrote, 'my Heart . . . runs forward a Mile to meet my dear Doctor Burney'.[4]

Not surprisingly Burney, in return, adored Streatham and its mistress. He felt at ease with, and was unawed by, Mrs. Thrale, who in that respect, as in many others, differed markedly from the other 'Blue-Stocking' ladies to whose *conversazioni* he was now being invited. Indeed, his daughter Fanny, when she had won her own way into the Streatham circle, was struck by the similarity between her father and Mrs. Thrale. Both, she thought, possessed 'a heart which . . . seems already fitted for another world'; and a little later she observed rather more specifically, 'I find the likeness perpetually; she has the same natural liveliness, the same general benevolence, the same rare union of gaiety and of feeling in her disposition.'[5]

In the end, however, Mrs. Thrale came to realize that there were limitations to Burney's character. She always found him intelligent, cheerful, and modest, and in a circle of brilliant wits

---

[1] *Thraliana*, i. 43–46.   [2] Ibid. 154.
[3] Ibid. 475; see *post*, p. 233.   [4] Ibid. 131, 343, 378.
[5] *DL*, i. 68, 85.

and egotists, his kindliness and self-deprecating charm could
not fail to afford a pleasant relief. The fault she eventually
detected, however, lay precisely in that modesty. In 1780
Fanny wrote that her father 'never thinks of his authorship and
fame at all, but . . . is respected for both by everybody for
claiming no respect from anybody'.[1] Burney's correspondence
with Twining, and other evidence, could be used to contradict
this statement. On the other hand, it is true enough of Burney's
social demeanour. It was, indeed, his very lack of self-assertive-
ness, his intense desire to please and to be liked, which seemed
to Mrs. Thrale to come close at times to servility: 'The Doctor
is a Man quite after my own Heart, if he has any Fault it is too
much Obsequiousness, though *I* should not object to a Quality
my Friends are so little troubled with.—his following close
upon the heels of Johnson or Baretti makes me feel him softer
though; like turning the Toothpick after you have rubbed your
Gums with the *Brush* & immediately applying the *Spunge* to
them.'[2] In 1788, when the happy Streatham circle had broken
up, she referred more bitterly to the same failing in a poem,
disposing of her former friend in the single line, 'And pliant
Burney bows from Side to Side.'[3]

In the period of their close friendship, however, Burney's
perpetual agreeableness, particularly to those more distinguished
socially or intellectually than himself, did not seem an important
flaw; and the only other weakness that Mrs. Thrale could
detect has already been amply illustrated. In September 1780,
after Burney had shown her a verse translation which he had
recently made, she wrote in her journal:

how happy, how skilful, how elegant is that dear Creature's Pen! but
his Mind is so elegant, every thing that comes from it, partakes of the
Flavour: yet there is no Perfection to be found in Character: Burney
is narrow enough about his own Art: envious of Hawkins, jealous of
Piozzi; till I listened a little after Musick, I thought he had not a
fault but Obsequiousness: *that* however is a *Vice de Profession*—so God
a Mercy Burney! I do love the Man; he is so much to my natural
Taste.[4]

There is nothing in Mrs. Thrale's account of Burney to contradict his daughter's descriptions of his charm, vivacity, and

[1] Ibid. i. 384.   [2] *Thraliana*, i. 368.
[3] Quoted by Clifford, op. cit., p. 330.   [4] *Thraliana*, i. 458.

humour. No well-known personality of the period seems to have been capable of inspiring affection so immediately and un-reservedly, nor to have aroused less hostility. Mrs. Thrale nevertheless supplements Fanny's image of her father. Fanny cannot have been unaware of her father's intense, if only spasmodic, bouts of professional jealousy. It is unlikely, on the other hand, that she saw his desire to be accepted by the 'great Volk' quite as clearly as did Mrs. Thrale, if only because, in a somewhat different form, she shared it. Certainly Burney him-self admitted that his position in society made it almost im-perative for him to court the favours of the great and he was prepared to make a distinction between genuine friendships and useful aristocratic acquaintances. In 1781, at a critical moment in the young man's career, Burney wrote to his son Charles: 'It has been said that *equality* of *Condition*, as well as similarity of disposition is necessary to firm & lasting Friendship—but call the Partiality of the Great by the name of patronage or what you will, it must still be a desirable thing in your Present Circumstances.' This distinction clarifies the nature of Burney's intimate friendships with such men as Twining and Bewley, his equals; and explains similarly his belief, expressed in the same letter to Charles, that a certain nobleman's 'Notice & Coun-tenance, were flattering & desirable favours', even if he felt obliged to add the somewhat disillusioned reflection that, 'Many such in the course of my Life have made me a Castle-builder. But I still remain a drudge amid the smiles of Wealth & Power.'[1]

In his old age Burney admitted that his anxiety to 'please' had been a conscious policy and its success had become one of his proudest boasts. In 1807 he told Lady Crewe, the daughter of Fulke Greville, 'my principles have always been to act with prudence & probity towards my friends—I have to boast that in my long life I have never lost one by a *quarrel*, except M[r] G[reville].—There must have been something very inoffensive at least, in my conduct & manners among my betters abroad & at home, to be so countenanced.'[2] In the context of Streatham, however, although Burney lacked what Mrs. Thrale called 'that Independent Spirit & lofty manner without which no Man

---

[1] CB to CB Jr., 25 Feb. 1781 (Comyn).
[2] CB to Lady Crewe [Oct. 1807], draft (Osborn).

can much please *me*', she could add that 'In Burney I *pardon* the
want on't'.[1] Yet, if her affection for Burney did not waver until
the final collapse of her circle in 1784, by 1780 she had found it
necessary to make the distinction between the 'Men I *love* best in
the World' and those 'I *like* best in the World', Burney being
one of the three in the second list.[2]

Twice in *Thraliana* she attempted to summarize Burney's
character in very different ways. In 1778 she 'rated' her
friends' qualities by marking them out of a total of twenty under
various headings. Burney scored high in 'Religion', 'Morality',
'Gen¹ Knowledge', and 'Manner'. His 'Person & Voice' were
moderately good (Johnson scored nothing in this category) and
his 'Scholarship' (purely classical, no doubt) won him only
eight marks. In 'Wit' and 'Humour' he was surprisingly deficient, but he received almost the maximum mark for 'Good
Humour', the fact that Johnson once more scored nothing under
this heading helping to explain much of Mrs. Thrale's gratitude
for Burney's presence at Streatham. Her three favourites,
Johnson, Murphy, and Burney, all received the same aggregate
of 110 marks in the nine categories, only David Garrick sur-
passing them with a total of 117.[3]

Three years later Mrs. Thrale wrote verse characters of all
the friends whose portraits by Reynolds were to be hung at
Streatham. Her lines on Burney, expressing in full her views on
his power of inspiring affection, his modesty, his openness of
manner as well as his social sensitivity, may suitably conclude
this account of her attitude to him. The 'portrait' followed that
of Baretti:

> See here happy Contrast! in Burney combine,
> Every Power to please, every Talent to shine;
> In professional Science a second to none,
> In social—if second—thro' Shyness alone;
> So sits the sweet Violet close to the Ground,
> While Holyoaks and Sunflowers flant it around:
> This Character form'd free, confiding, & kind,
> Grown cautious by Habit, by Station confin'd,
> Tho' born to improve and enlighten our days,
> In a supple Facility fixes its Praise:
> And contented to sooth, unambitious to strike,
> Is the favrite of all Men,—of all Men alike.

---

[1] *Thraliana*, i. 372.   [2] Ibid. 444 n. 4.   [3] Ibid. 329–30.

'Tis thus while the Wines of Frontiniac impart,
Their sweets to our Palate, their Warmth to our heart;
All in Praise of a Liquor so luscious agree,
From the Monarch of France to the wild Cherokee.[1]

Although this summary of Mrs. Thrale's affection for Burney
has drawn upon entries made in *Thraliana* over a period of some
five years, he had won her heart very soon after beginning his
duties at Streatham. The Thrales' plan 'to sollicit his Company'
in a non-professional capacity was, however, an eminently
practical one. After Burney had been teaching Queeney for
only a short time, Henry Thrale proposed that, instead of being
paid by the lesson, he should receive an annual stipend of £100.
In return for this, he was to visit Streatham once a week and,
after giving Queeney her lesson, dine and stay the night there,
travelling back to London as soon as he wished on the following
day. This arrangement continued until Thrale's death.[2] Since
Burney charged his scholars at this period an entrance fee of
four guineas, and half a guinea for each lesson thereafter,[3] he
was receiving from Thrale almost three times the normal fee.
He was being paid handsomely, moreover, in that he could now
enjoy the company and conversation not only of Mrs. Thrale,
but of a circle which included Garrick, Reynolds, Murphy,
Seward, Boswell, James Harris, and many of the 'Blue-Stocking'
ladies, who frequently adorned Streatham. There was, above
all, one aspect of weekly residence with the Thrales which
represented the fulfilment of an ambition of thirty years and to
which he gave the most important place in his doggerel autobiography for 1776:

This year I acquaintance began with the Thrales,
Where I met with great talents 'mongst females and males:
But the best thing that happen'd from that time to this,
Was the freedom it gave me to sound the abyss,
At my ease and my leisure, of Johnson's great mind,
Where new treasures unnumber'd I constantly find.

Huge Briareus's heads, if old bards have not blunder'd,
Amounted in all to the sum of one hundred;
And Johnson,—so wide his intelligence spreads,
Has the brains of—at least—the same number of heads.[4]

---

[1] *Thraliana*, i. 475.   [2] *Frag. Mem.* (Berg).
[3] Receipt for Miss Hoare's fees, 30 Sept. 1779 (Osborn); cf. *post*, p. 272. Scholes's
figures, *GDB*, ii. 56 and n., are incorrect.   [4] *Mem.* ii. 100–1.

Whenever Johnson was also staying at Streatham, Burney could talk to his heart's content to the man whom he had idolized for so many years. As he himself told Boswell, 'they had many long conversations, often sitting up as long as the fire and candles lasted, and much longer than the patience of the servants subsisted.'[1] For Mrs. Thrale, Burney's eagerness to sit up late in conversation with Johnson came as a great relief, for she had herself long since tired of such exhausting vigils.[2] She fully appreciated Burney's idolatry, for she later went so far as to say of Johnson that, 'Of all his intimates & Friends, I think I never could find any who much loved him Boswell & Burney excepted.' Typically, perhaps even jealously, anxious, however, to assert her own importance in this happy relationship, she went on to qualify her statement: 'as to Burney had they been more together, they would have liked each other less; but I who delighted greatly in them both, used to keep those Parts of their Characters out of Sight wch would have offended the other'.[3]

Johnson and Burney probably had few illusions about each other, however, and it would perhaps be more true to say that each managed to bring out the best qualities in his friend. Certainly, although Burney was devoted to Johnson to the end of his life and defended his personal virtues as loyally as any of his contemporaries, he remained fully aware of his failings and prejudices. His own soothing personality, however, clearly softened Johnson and he never seems to have suffered from the well-known roughness. As Burney wrote in 1781 of Johnson,

He is surely a great, a *very* great man, with all his prejudices, & imperfections. . . . I want his prejudices to be always attacked, & yet I wish his Genius & Virtues to be spared. He has many that the world knows nothing of, nor perhaps ever will believe. He is in private often pleasant, candid, charitable, to a degree of weakness, & as good-natured as a family mastiff, whom you may safely pat & stroke at the fire-side without the least fear of his biting you. The utmost he will do if you are a little rough with him is to growl.[4]

---

[1] Hill–Powell, ii. 407, introducing a collection of sayings by Johnson which CB remembered from this period.
[2] Clifford, op. cit., p. 149; cf. Hill–Powell, iii. 1 n. 2.
[3] *Thraliana*, i. 182; cf. Hill–Powell, ii. 427.
[4] CB to Twining [Oct. 1781], copy (Osborn).

As for Johnson, his affection for Burney from this period is all the more convincing because, as recently as 1772, he had been prepared to dismiss him as 'a very pretty kind of man'[1] and because he had to overcome his prejudice against musicians. By 1779, Johnson could have the following conversation with Fanny at Streatham:

'I love Burney: my heart goes out to meet him!'
'He is not ungrateful, sir,' cried I; 'for most heartily does he love you.'
'Does he, madam? I am surprised at that.'
'Why, sir? why should you have doubted it?'
'Because, madam, Dr. Burney is a man for all the world to love: it is but natural to love him.'

I could almost have cried with delight at this cordial, unlaboured *éloge*. Another time, he said,

'I much question if there is, in the world, such another man as Dr. Burney.'[2]

The other visitors to Streatham liked and respected Burney almost as much as did Johnson and Mrs. Thrale. Arthur Murphy the playwright, for example, declared: 'Dr. Burney is, indeed, a most extraordinary man; I think I don't know such another: he is at home upon all subjects, and upon all so agreeable! he is a wonderful man!' It cannot therefore be surprising that Burney's life became increasingly orientated towards Streatham, where he could so comfortably escape the tiring routine of a busy music-teacher's life, where wit and wealth abounded, and where he was always assured of the warmest welcome. By March 1777, only four months after his engagement at Streatham, he was invited to stay for several days[3] and later in the month the Thrales and Johnson accepted an invitation to St. Martin's Street for the first time, to the wide-eyed excitement of that household.[4] Mrs. Thrale's affection and generosity knew no bounds and their correspondence reveals the intimate geniality which their friendship had quickly attained. The temptation to slip away to Streatham became increasingly potent and Burney soon found it understandably

---

[1] See *ante*, p. 129.   [2] *DL*, i. 203; cf. *Mem.* ii. 175–6.
[3] Mrs. Thrale to CB, 5 Mar. 1777 (Osborn).
[4] Johnson to Mrs. Thrale, 19 Mar. 1777, *Letters*, ii. 166–7; *ED*, ii. 152–8; *Mem.* ii. 86–100; Hill–Powell, ii. 364 n. 3.

impossible to resist invitations for week-ends and longer visits which could conclude with such sentiments as 'remember that though you are more beloved than any Man I know in the World, you could give no more Pleasure to any one, nor does any one now want it more than Your H.L.T.'[1] or could describe the virtues which gave that pleasure so flatteringly:

What a Heart must yours be for Friendship and Liberality of Sentiment, that one should admire and prefer it to the Talents you possess!—but so it is: for they; numerous, elegant, and pleasing as they are, may be possessed by some other people perhaps in some *future* Time, but one does not expect *in this World*, (for you have drawn the Portrait but too like;) so much Heartfelt Kindness and Sympathy through the many turns of it, as you treat one with.[2]

Burney was fifty when he was introduced to Streatham: after twenty-five years of disappointments and frustrations which might have broken a less tenacious aspirant for fame, he had won, by the most strenuous labour, a considerable reputation as a man of letters. Streatham, and the cultivated, elegant life it contained, represented the most gratifying reward he could have envisaged, and it was crowned by the presence of Samuel Johnson. Burney had attained quite as much as he could have hoped for. As Fanny later wrote, 'Fair was this period in the life of Dr. Burney. It opened to him a new region of enjoyment, supported by honours, and exhilarated by pleasures supremely to his taste: honours that were literary, pleasures that were intellectual.'[3]

The only drawback was, of course, that Burney was not free to enjoy Streatham and the life it symbolized. A thousand sub-scribers were awaiting the second volume of his *History of Music* and while many of the most interesting of his contemporaries beckoned to him from Streatham, the drudgery of grappling with the 'Gothic' and 'barbarous' music of the Middle Ages summoned him to his desk. It was not as if any ambitions re-mained unfulfilled, nor as if his second volume could increase his reputation, for at best it could only confirm it. In the follow-ing account of Burney's work on the second volume of his *History* it must be remembered that Streatham was always

---

[1] Mrs. Thrale to CB [Dec. 1778] (Osborn).
[2] Ibid. [? 1778] (Osborn).   [3] *Mem.* ii. 73.

acting as a magnet, which persistently distracted him from the
kind of single-minded industry which had produced his first
volume. The 'new region of enjoyment' lay all before him and
he could make only brief and guilty excursions into it.

II

Burney had written the first volume of his *History* in two and a
half years. Eighteen months had passed since its publication
when a somewhat alarmed Twining wrote to 'scold' him for a
recent letter:

Why, you really talk about your opus magnum in a very cavalier
way; as if you did not care a farthing whether you finished it or not.
I tell you plainly I shall not suffer this. Why, pray, now what is the
matter? what are you afraid of? [—The lamb giving the lion a
lecture upon courage—smoke him.] Is not the worst half of your
labour over?—& have you not got with great credit thro' the most
unpopular, unpromising & dry part of it? What the deuce then
shou'd make you shrink now, when almost all drudgery, & gropery,
& poking is over; when you have plenty of materials to produce, &
every step will bring you into a more pleasurable country, where
neither *Moth* (the type of old books) doth *corrupt*, nor thieves break
thro' & steal—i.e. (for I am forced to *expound*) where you may have
recourse to your own ideas & taste which no man can have filched
from you, & where you can be *original* &c^a—Pray, good Mr Laziness,
think of all this; & jump up, & rub your hands, & give your breeches
a hitch up, & shew a little life & spirit. . . .

Yet if Burney found it difficult in the summer of 1777 to
resume the hard work which had produced his first volume, the
same letter from Twining reveals that he was also reluctant,
with Hawkins so recently vanquished, to permit any new
trespasser to stray into fields which he had marked out as his
own. For some years Twining had been turning over in his mind
various scholarly projects to which he might apply himself and
in April 1777 he had written to ask Burney whether the compilation of a 'Dictionary of Music' would be 'a feasible plan'.[1]
Although he had published only one volume of his *History* and
could make no progress with the second, Burney discouraged
his friend from this task, claiming so earnestly that he himself
had already planned such a dictionary that Twining had to

[1] Twining to CB, April 1777, notes (Add. MS. 39936, f. 63).

apologize for having presumed to contemplate such an under-taking. He could not resist, however, mocking Burney's anxiety to dominate English musicology: 'What a great, greedy, mono-polizing fellow you are—with half an enormous custard *in* your mouth, & half *out*, & running down your jaws, that you don't know what to do, nor when you shall ever be able to get your mouth clear again,—& yet crying "let that alone! that's mine!"—to a poor dog that wou'd have gather'd up a few crumbs that he did not think you wou'd stoop to pick up.'[1]

The realization that, while a friend as good-natured as Twining would not pretend to get in his way, other writers might well start taking up projects which he envisaged for him-self, probably helped to rouse Burney from his lethargy. In any case, Twining now embarked on an intensive campaign of goading his friend into activity, warning him that subscribers were already impatient for his second volume and offering any assistance in his power. He suspected that they were both suffering from 'a temporary *nausea*' after a surfeit of musical research, but he assured Burney that, before long, 'We shall be Aldermen again, with napkins under our chins, & greasing our chops as bad as ever.'[2]

During the summer of 1777 Burney at last resumed work on the *History* and, as Twining had hoped, was soon 'cover'd with the dust of old church-music'. By October 1777 Twining was delighted to hear that his friend had written thirty pages of the opening chapter, 'Of the Introduction of Music into the Church, and of its Progress there, previous to the Time of Guido'. Twining expressed his willingness to read the manu-script and promised his customary frank criticism: 'You shall have my mind, as usual, fairly turned inside out, as bare & raw as the wrong side of a rabbit-skin. It is not my common way of wearing it: I'd have you know it is in general, as soft & furry & strokeable a thing as a gentleman can carry about with him.' Burney was, however, already depressed by the fact that Haw-kins seemed to loom before him at every turn. He had been obliged to rewrite part of his opening chapter merely to avoid what might have seemed plagiarism; and, at the same time, the sheer scope of Hawkins's treatment forced him to compete on a

[1] Ibid., 16 June 1777 (Add. MS. 39929, ff. 135–8).
[2] Ibid., 30 Aug. 1777 (Add. MS. 39929, ff. 139–42).

comparable scale, which made progress much slower than he had anticipated. Twining discussed this problem at great length in October, especially warning his friend 'not to let the desire of being *different* from him, lead you to omit anything that *sh^d* be in your book', and assuring him that, 'As to the great historical high road, you must be content to be seen jogging on, sometimes behind him: you are both going to the same place, & nobody will suppose he leads you.'[1]

Ironically enough, while Twining was composing this cheerful and encouraging letter, Burney had already deserted his post. Only too glad to give way to temptation, when his wife went to visit her daughter Bessy Allen, who was at school in Paris, at the end of August 1777, Burney stayed with the Thrales at Streatham and at the end of September accompanied them for a fortnight to Brighton.[2] No work was possible in such distracting company, nor was it any easier when he returned to London in mid-October, for his wife joined him almost immediately with the distressing news that Bessy had eloped with an undesirable young man named Meeke.[3] So upset was Mrs. Burney that her husband had to take her into the country to recover. The tensions in the household at this period seem to have been well known to such friends as Mrs. Thrale and Dr. Johnson, who reflected that the insincere sympathy of her stepdaughters would be quite as hard for Mrs. Burney to bear as the loss of her own favourite child. As Johnson observed, 'it is impossible for her husband's daughters not to triumph, and the husband will feel . . . *something that does not displease him*'.[4]

Burney was, however, upset for his wife's sake and he wrote her a poem deploring the 'black ingratitude' of the event and the 'fruitless sorrow' expended upon it.[5] The effort of comforting his wife, moreover, prevented any progress with the *History*, as he told Mrs. Thrale (significantly expressing the hope that she would soon be back at Streatham):

that there are certain *Diavolini degl' Impedimenti*, or mischievous Sylphs & Gnomes that successfully forge Fetters for Resolution, even

---

[1] Twining to CB, 6 Oct. 1777 (Add. MS. 39929, ff. 143–6). See *ante*, pp. 219–20.
[2] *ED*, ii. 284; Clifford, op. cit., pp. 154–5.
[3] Hemlow, pp. 70–72.
[4] Johnson to Mrs. Thrale, 29 Oct. 1777, *Letters*, ii. 229–30.
[5] 'On My Wife's Birthday', 20 Oct. 1777 (Osborn).

wise Folks will deny; & yet, I seem surrounded with an Army of them, that prevent me from doing every thing I wish & intend.

'This erring Mortals levity may call,
    O blind to Truth! the Sylphs contrive it all.'[1]

At worst, however, Bessy Allen's elopement induced in Burney only 'Silence and Sulkiness' and an inability to apply himself to his work. If, nevertheless, as Johnson suspected, Burney was ever tempted to feel complacent about the behaviour of his own children, his self-satisfaction was cruelly shattered some two or three weeks later by the catastrophic news that Charles, his second son, newly entered at Caius College, Cambridge, had been sent down for stealing books from the University Library and selling them in London. Burney suffered the disgrace acutely, for he had struggled to provide Charles with an education infinitely better than his own and had high hopes that his son would have a successful career in the Church. The wretched Charles was forbidden to return to St. Martin's Street and retreated to the country, where he stayed until he obtained admission to King's College, Aberdeen, in the following year.[2]

Twining, who had received the manuscript of the first chapter of Burney's second volume at the end of October 1777,[3] returned it three weeks later with '7 sheets of remarks' and the assurance that he had 'fagged pretty hard' on his friend's behalf. Quite unaware of the disaster which had just blighted all Burney's hopes, Twining assumed his most jocular tone of encouragement: 'I *augure* all sorts of good things of y^r 2^d Vol. from this begin^g. . . . Get home early from your Misses; on with y^r gown; *enfonce* y^r self in y^r study; read, write, hunt, & spill y^r tea upon y^r papers.'[4] The tone of Twining's next letter, written a month later in mid-December, was completely different, for Burney had poured out to his friend all his anger and anguish at Charles's crime. Twining's new role was that of adviser and

---

[1] CB to Mrs. Thrale, 1 Nov. 1777 (JRL, Eng. MS. 545. 1). CB quotes *The Rape of the Lock*, i. 103–4.

[2] For a full discussion see Ralph S. Walker, 'Charles Burney's Theft of Books at Cambridge', *Transactions of the Cambridge Bibliographical Society*, iii (1962), 313–26. The earliest printed reference to CB Jr.'s 'crime', hitherto unnoticed, occurs in *Recollections of the Table-Talk of Samuel Rogers, to which is added Porsoniana*, ed. [A. Dyce], 1856, p. 315.

[3] Twining to CB, 31 Oct. 1777, notes (Add. MS. 39936, f. 64).

[4] Ibid., 18 Nov. 1777 (Add. MS. 39929, ff. 153–4).

comforter, pleading with the outraged father to show his banished son 'all the tenderness, affection & encouragement that *can* be shewn him', and deploring Burney's conviction that Charles was 'lost *for ever!*' Twining's many qualities are variously revealed throughout his correspondence with Burney, but nowhere more admirably than in this letter and in later letters on Charles's disgrace and the many problems which followed his 'crime'.[1]

Burney's children continued to distract him, although there could be pleasanter aspects to the problems they raised. No sooner had he managed to take a slightly more sensible attitude to Charles, as suggested by Twining, than he began to worry about the education of Richard, his youngest son by his second wife, who was a great favourite of Mrs. Thrale. This problem at least served to demonstrate the kindness of Mrs. Thrale and Johnson to the Burneys, for they both made great efforts to help to find a suitable school for the boy, Johnson writing to recommend Richard to Dr. Warton, the headmaster of Winchester. Although Warton could not offer a place immediately, he agreed to take Richard into his own house as a boarder until a vacancy occurred, and Johnson accompanied Burney and his son to the school early in 1778 to ensure that they were well received.[2]

These various catastrophes and anxieties, followed by the busiest season in Burney's professional year, prevented him once more from settling into the steady routine which his work required. More than two years had passed since the publication of his first volume when he wrote gloomily to Mrs. Thrale in March 1778, describing a visit to friends at Turnham Green and mocking his own low spirits with a feeble pun: 'I brought Books with me without curiosity to look in them—I brought writing Work, but was too *lache* to meddle with it. The few paltry Sprigs of Laurel I sometimes fancied I saw trembling before me in some degree of Verdure, have seemed shrivelled & withered so much of late, that I came hither to *Turn'em Green—* but alas! in vain. . . .'[3]

---

[1] Twining to CB, 17 Dec. 1777, 28 July 1778, 3 June 1779, 9 Nov. and 28 Dec. 1781, 18 Sept. and 28 Nov. 1782, 27 Jan. 1783 (Add. MS. 39929, ff. 155–7, 172–5, 203–5, 281–2, 291–2, 299–303, 306–7, 310–11).

[2] CB to Mrs. Thrale, 11 Jan. 1778 (Yale); Warton to Johnson, 27 Jan. 1778 (Winchester College); *ED*, ii. 286; *Mem*. ii. 81–84; Hill–Powell, iii. 367.

[3] CB to Mrs. Thrale, 8 Mar. 1778 (JRL, Eng. MS. 545. 4).

It was beginning to look as though there had been some justice in Hawkins's double-edged remark about the certainty of Burney's publishing the second volume which he had promised his subscribers. By May 1778 only the first chapter had been written and although William Bewley had heard that a sheet or two of it had already been printed,[1] little more can have gone to press, for as recently as April Twining had sent Burney a translation of a Greek epigram which was to appear at the end of the chapter.[2] To make matters worse, Burney was attacked at this time by 'an acute fever', which once more prevented his making any progress with the *History*, even if he had felt inclined to apply himself to it, which was unlikely in itself.[3]

Burney's spirits, energy, and pride were about to be dramatically restored, however, for London was already reading an anonymous novel entitled *Evelina*, which had been published in January 1778. The full story of the writing and publication of this novel, the result of a secret conspiracy between his daughter Fanny, the authoress, and her brothers and sisters, is too well known and too complex to bear repetition here.[4] Although she had once cautiously mentioned to her father her intention of publishing an anonymous book, Burney had not taken the idea seriously[5] and it was not until June 1778, six months after its publication, that he learned from his daughter Susan the identity of the author of the novel which was the subject of so much discussion. After Susan had rather nervously admitted that 'the book was written by her sister Fanny, with a determination never to own the sin she had committed', Burney opened the first volume with 'fear & trembling'. Fanny's dedicatory poem to himself, however, brought tears to his eyes and before long he had read enough of the novel to be delighted with its 'good sense & good writing'.

His excitement and enthusiasm, as reported by Susan to Fanny, who was at Chessington, grew rapidly. His first opinion that 'it has real merit' had become, a fortnight later, 'I wish I

[1] Bewley to CB, 4 May 1778 (Osborn).
[2] Twining to CB, 15 Apr. 1778 (Add. MS. 39929, ff. 163–5); cf. *Hist. Mus.* ii. 65–66.   [3] *Mem.* ii. 133.
[4] *ED*, ii. 222–54; *DL*, i. 21–64; *Mem.* ii. 121–71; Hemlow, pp. 53–104.
[5] *Mem.* ii. 169.

may die if I do not believe it to be the best novel in the language
Fielding's excepted—for Smollet's are so d—d gross that they
are not fit reading for women with all their wit.'[1] For a time,
however, Burney obeyed Fanny's wish for complete secrecy and
he enjoyed listening quietly to the excited praise of the novel
which he heard everywhere, especially at Streatham. Mrs.
Thrale was talking of nothing else and was forcing all her
visitors—Johnson, Burke, Lyttleton, Reynolds, Murphy, and
Seward among them—to read it. As Burney felt that he himself
could scarcely join in 'the concert of its praise', Mrs. Thrale
found it hard to believe that he had obeyed her instructions to
read the book, but she urged him to try to identify the author.
Eventually, when he was convinced that *Evelina* had met with
unanimous approval, he confidentially told Mrs. Thrale the
story of its secret publication by his second daughter, 'as a coup
d'essay, without my knowledge'. Mrs. Thrale's reaction was
characteristic: 'Lord! Dᵣ Burney! we must be acquainted —do
pray bring her with you the next time you come to Streatham'.[2]

Even to his own wife, to whom he read the novel every
morning in bed, Burney had not at first revealed the secret
which he shared with his children. Once he was convinced,
however, that *Evelina* could bring only credit to the family, he
could not resist telling the world that it was his retiring, embarrassed second daughter who had caused the literary sensation of
the year. By 22 July 1778 *Evelina* had passed the supreme test,
for Mrs. Thrale wrote to tell him on that day that Johnson was
'full of praises' of the novel, that he considered 'there were
passages in it which might do honour to Richardson', and that
he was still devouring it voraciously.[3] The fact that both Mrs.
Thrale and Johnson knew about Charles's disgrace at Cambridge[4] made Burney only the more eager to produce one of
his children who deserved only the praise and admiration of his
friends. On 27 July, in the highest spirits, he brought his reluctant daughter from her retreat at Chessington to Streatham
to face the literary fame which she had so unexpectedly and
dramatically acquired.

[1] *ED*, ii. 223, 230.
[2] *Frag. Mem.* (Berg); *Mem.* ii. 168–71.
[3] Mrs. Thrale to CB, 22 [July 1778] (Comyn); *ED*, ii. 249–50; *DL*, i. 48–49.
[4] *Thraliana*, i. 360 and n.; Twining to CB, 28 July 1778 (Add. MS. 39929, ff.
172–5).

III

Although after 1778 Fanny somewhat overshadowed her father, it can be stated without hesitation that Burney never suffered the slightest twinge of envy of her sudden rise to celebrity, of her intimacy with Mrs. Thrale, or of the way in which she involuntarily fascinated Johnson, Reynolds, Burke, the 'Blue-Stocking' ladies and in fact English literary society as a whole. It was, on the contrary, Burney himself who forced his daughter into society against her own wishes, and he never tired of hearing her novel praised: if anything, his pride in her achievement increased steadily rather than waned. Mrs. Thrale observed his and her own eclipse with wry amusement in November 1778:

> I heard of you at Reynolds's the other day, Mr Holroyd[1] of our Sussex Militia here told me how he had dined with you there, & how he had heard you were *Father* to the *Lady* whose Novel had been so much admired!—'Are you acquainted at all with that Lady Madam.' —'Yes Sir pretty well, *Dieu Merci*.'—'That is charming indeed!—but Mrs Thrale is acquainted with all the *great writers*.' This is a Fact.
>
> So *you* are only Father to the Fannikin now! and *I* am her Acquaintance.[2]

Burney certainly did not resent such a relegation to the status of proud parenthood and the excitement over *Evelina* in July 1778 seems in fact to have been instrumental in lifting him temporarily out of his lethargy as far as his own work was concerned. To Twining's sarcastic applause he made plans for beginning his second chapter:

> And so, you have actually roused yourself, & are going seriously to work? And full 6 weeks allowed for it!—to be sure you will get through ½ your 2d vol. in that time!—& the winter will come, when you will have your time charmingly to yourself:—Without joking, I wish you wou'd go on steadily, & keep your traces tight like a good draught-horse. Conceive me spitting, patting, stroaking;—anything, to get you on.

Changing his equestrian metaphor slightly, Twining attempted as patiently as ever to whip Burney into some degree of enthusiasm for his 'hobby-horse': 'Ay, Ay, right;—hoist your

---

[1] FB notes '*afterwards Earl of Sheffield*': John Baker Holroyd (1735–1821), first Earl.   [2] Mrs. Thrale to CB, 21 Nov. [1778] (Comyn).

elbows up to guard your precious eye-sight, & *crash* your way with a holla! through the hedge of these two first thorny chapters, & you'll find yourself upon the turf, in your own park, & canter at your ease to y^r very stable door.'[1]

As yet neither Twining nor Bewley had been informed about Fanny's authorship of *Evelina* and to the end of the year Burney amused himself by recommending the novel to his friends and awaiting their unguarded comments.[2] He could not, therefore, explain to Twining the difficulty he encountered, on returning to London in September 1778, in settling to the drudgery of writing a chapter on 'The Invention of Counterpoint, and State of Music, from the Time of Guido, to the Formation of the Time-Table', while Fanny was being detained at Streatham and enjoying the admiration of Johnson and Mrs. Thrale and other members of the circle. The proud father himself found it impossible to keep away from the scene of Fanny's triumph, and although he planned to take work with him to Streatham, he knew, as he told Mrs. Thrale, that it would be futile. His own ambition had almost disappeared once more:

I shall take the Liberty of bringing work with me, but with no great expectation of consequences—for who can patiently dig among the dead for Information or amusement when living sources are running to waste in one's reach? I have not set pen to paper for the press since I came home; but have idled my Time away in hunting old B^{ks} for intelligence, wch I have but seldom found, & still more seldom secured. The Eel of Science to me becomes more slippery every Day—my hooks are broken & decayed; and, from want of success, my former eagerness after this kind of fishing is greatly diminished.[3]

No result of Fanny's new celebrity gratified Burney more than Johnson's admiration and affection for the nervous authoress. He had heard that Johnson had formerly befriended such literary ladies as Charlotte Lennox, Elizabeth Carter, Hester Chapone, and Sarah Fielding, but, as he proudly re-

---

[1] Twining to CB, 28 July 1778 (Add. MS. 39929, ff. 172–5).

[2] CB to Twining, 1 Dec. 1778, copy (Osborn); Twining to CB, 19 Dec. 1778, 8 Jan. and 12 Mar. 1779 (Add. MS. 39929, ff. 185–90, 193–6); Bewley to CB [Nov. 1778] (Osborn).

[3] CB to Mrs. Thrale, 25 [Sept. 1778] (JRL, Eng. MS. 545. 6).

called in his 'Memoirs', he himself never knew Johnson to be as 'indulgent and kind' to a 'female author' as he was to Fanny. Indeed, Johnson had told him that no writer so young and inexperienced had ever analysed character so penetratingly or observed contemporary manners so accurately.[1] To Burney's delight, not long after Fanny had been startled out of anonymity, Johnson began calling at St. Martin's Street of his own accord. In October 1778 Mrs. Thrale told Johnson that 'the D^r writes me word how happy you make them in sitting to chat some times'.[2] It became accordingly easier to return such visits. On 31 October Burney 'took Fan in my hand & went to Bolt Court—where the good soul rec^d us with open arms, & was so pleasant & comical!'[3] This visit seems to have had a particular purpose, for three days later Johnson sent Burney two letters of introduction to friends in Oxford, who would be able to assist his researches in the Bodleian and in Christ Church Library, where Burney particularly wished to examine the great musical collection assembled by Dr. Henry Aldrich (1647–1710).[4]

On 3 November Burney set off for Oxford, 'to run my Nose into Cobwebs, & consult the Learned'. Later in the month, however, Johnson told Mrs. Thrale, 'Dr. Burney had the luck to go to Oxford, the only week in the year when the library is shut up. He was however very kindly treated, as one Man is translating Arabick, and another Welsh for his service.'[5] The disappointment over the Bodleian was easily outweighed by the kind reception Burney obtained as a result of Johnson's letter to Dr. Benjamin Wheeler, Canon of Christ Church, 'wch so perfectly answered the purpose, that a Vote or order was passed by the present Dean, that I sh^d not only have leave to examine Dr Aldrich's Collection of Music, but be permitted to take home any part of it to transcribe or consult at my leisure'. This auspicious start encouraged him to work in various Oxford libraries in each of the three following summers, particularly in Christ Church, and he compiled a catalogue of the Aldrich Collection which he duly presented to the College. As late as

[1] *Frag. Mem.* (Berg). [2] Johnson, *Letters*, ii. 260, 262.
[3] CB to Mrs. Thrale, 6 Nov. 1778 (JRL, Eng. MS. 545. 5).
[4] Johnson to CB, 2 Nov. 1778, *Letters*, ii. 266; and to Drs. Wheeler and Edwards, 2 Nov. 1778, copies by CB (Comyn); *Letters*, ii. 264–6.
[5] Ibid. 269.

1783 he still had some manuscripts from this collection in his possession.[1]

Johnson had provided not merely practical assistance but also greatly needed encouragement, for his interest, such as it was, in the progress of the *History* was becoming one of the most considerable factors which kept Burney at work. Slow as that progress was, from this period it was at least steady, after three years in which next to nothing had been achieved. By December 1778 Thomas Twining, who had at last settled on his own scholarly project, a translation of Aristotle's *Poetics*, and who had not written since July, was rejoicing '*exceedingly*' to find that his friend was once more 'going on in earnest & . . . up to the chin in materials.'[2] Later in the month he confessed that he 'had really almost despaired of your going on', and he urged Burney to 'Go on, with accelerated velocity, & knock everything down that is in your way'. Once more he assured his friend that Hawkins's five volumes had in no way obviated the need for another *History of Music* and he was delighted to learn that Burney had discovered materials in Oxford which had eluded his rival: 'I rejoice to find you have discover'd some things that have escaped the *nose* of a man who has scarce any other merit than that of being a good literary *pointer*:—i.e. of *finding* game for *others* to make the proper *use* of.' In spite of his new commitment to Aristotle, Twining asked to see such sheets of the *History* as had already been printed, as well as the manuscript of the second chapter, probably feeling that Burney would only continue writing if someone were pressing him, although the explanation he gave was different: 'you can *write*, it is true,—& think, & judge, perhaps, tolerably;—but for correcting the press,—& the sublime employment of examining syllables, & detecting the little frailties of commas, & figures &cᵃ you are nothing to me'.[3]

By early January 1779 Twining had read and was returning with comments the first eighteen pages of the manuscript of the second chapter. Most of Burney's material, Twining admitted, was now 'quite out the reach of my examination', and con-

[1] CB to —— [1781] (Ashmolean); to Twining, 10 Nov. 1783 (Add. MS. 39929, ff. 324–6). CB's catalogue is still in Christ Church Library, but until recently was attributed to William Crotch.

[2] Twining to CB, 7 Dec. 1778 (Add. MS. 39929, ff. 180–1).

[3] Ibid., 19 Dec. 1778 (Add. MS. 39929, ff. 185–8).

cerned 'a parcel of people that I never so much as heard of'. He rejoiced, nevertheless, that Burney had obtained admittance into the King's Library and added, 'I shall be glad to hear you are committed to the *Tower*—but take care of your *head*: old MSS have brought many a one to a *block*.'[1] Twining was referring both to the fate of Sir John Hawkins and to 'a Welch MS. in the possession of Richard Morris, Esq. of the Tower', which presented Burney with many problems. Although he believed that it was of great importance, he found it almost incomprehensible and it continued to trouble him until the summer of 1779, for in May Twining wrote, 'I can't help being diverted to see you sticking your quill into the brains of every *Welch Man* you come near, & sucking them 'till your cheeks meet, squeezing their poor heads with your two thumbs as a school-boy serves an orange, to make more come out than is in —& all to no purpose!'[2] Nevertheless, progress was being made. In February 1779, three years after the publication of the first volume, Twining returned the manuscript of the remainder of the second chapter, with a list of 'Errata' for the earlier sheets.[3] In spite of his professions of incompetence as far as medieval music went, Twining was able to help Burney by translating Latin treatises on music by Franco and Jean de Muris for the third chapter.[4]

Burney, busy as he was in the early months of the year as a teacher and with Twining zealously spurring him on with the *History*, could not resist distractions. In November 1778 William Bewley had sent him a long account of 'the musical exploits of the *gifted* babe at Norwich', a child named William Crotch, who, when barely two years of age, 'was first unexpectedly heard playing a part of *God Save the King*, or some other popular tune on his father's organ', and whom Bewley himself had heard at the age of 'about 3 years & 6 weeks old . . . play on the

---

[1] Ibid., 8 Jan. 1779 (Add. MS. 39929, ff. 189–90).

[2] Ibid., 12 May 1779 (Add. MS. 39929, ff. 199–202). CB dealt with the manuscript (now B.M. Add. MS. 14905) in *Hist. Mus.* ii. 110–14, 352. Richard Morris (d. 1779), a well-known Welsh scholar, had been chief clerk of foreign accounts at the Navy Office and was 'a leading figure among London Welshmen' (*Dictionary of National Biography*).

[3] Twining to CB, 1 Feb. 1779 (Add. MS. 39929, ff. 191–2); and notes (Add. MS. 39936, f. 65).

[4] Ibid., 12 Mar., 12 May, 3 June 1779 (Add. MS. 39929, ff. 193–6, 199–205); cf. *Hist. Mus.* ii. 176–208.

organ in Lynn Church several tunes, in a pleasing manner,
accompanying them with a *bass of his own invention*.[1] Before long,
Mrs. Crotch brought her precocious son to St. Martin's Street
to enable the historian of music to judge his talents for himself;
and, after some discussion with his friend Dr. William Hunter,
Burney decided to present his observations on the boy to the
Royal Society, of which he had been a Fellow since 1773.

On 18 February 1779 Burney read his *Account of the Infant
Musician Crotch* to the Society, and later sent the manuscript to
various friends for their comments. The response was flattering:
'Hermes' Harris wished that 'those, who write philosophically,
would write in the same Classical Stile with y^r Self, that is, with
purity and perspicuity'. Bewley thought it 'meritoriously
temperate, & philosophical' and Twining, 'satisfactory, well
drawn up, & very entertaining'. Later in the year the *Account*
was printed in the *Philosophical Transactions of the Royal Society*[2]
and Burney had a few copies printed for his own use. Further
compliments arrived on its publication from James Harris,
Andrew Lumisden, and, strangely enough, from Lord Monboddo.[3] Burney continued to take an interest in the precocious
and temperamental Crotch, who was appointed organist of
Christ Church, Oxford, in 1790 at the age of fifteen, and became Professor of Music in 1797.[4]

Not until the summer of 1779 was Burney able to resume
hard work on the *History*. Once again it was Samuel Johnson
who accidentally provided some of the inspiration. On 1 August,
on his way to stay at Chessington, Burney called at Streatham
and found that Johnson had been amusing himself by writing
parodies of the stilted verse of the Rev. Robert Potter, who had
recently published a translation of Aeschylus. The lines he had
chosen were taken from the *Medea* (ll. 193–203), but Mrs.
Thrale recorded in her journal that Johnson had 'translated
them seriously besides, & given them Burney for his History of

---

[1] Bewley to CB [Nov. 1778] (Osborn).

[2] Vol. lxix. Pt. 1, pp. 183–206.

[3] Harris to CB, 15 Mar. and 14 Oct. 1779; Bewley to CB, 29 May and 3 Sept.
1779 (Osborn); Twining to CB, 3 June and 17 Nov. 1779 (Add. MS. 39929, ff.
203–5, 218–19); Lumisden to CB, 10 July 1780 (Osborn); Monboddo to CB [1779]
(F. W. Hilles); CB to —— [Sept. 1779], draft (Osborn).

[4] Dr. Hayes to CB, 7 July 1779; CB to Sir James Lake, 23 May 1783 (Osborn).
See *post*, p. 387.

Musick'.[1] The passage was appropriate since it concerned the powers of music, although Burney could hardly claim that it was particularly relevant in the context in which he eventually placed it.

Nevertheless, the knowledge that his volume would once more contain so distinguished a contribution helped to fire him into activity, and after working hard on his third chapter at Chessington during August, he went in search of more material that might have eluded Hawkins in the following month. As he wrote in his doggerel autobiography:

> In September, to Cambridge I fly for a week
> Fresh materials for Volume the Second to seek
> In the manuscripts wch have been ages interr'd
> In Sepulchres whence they can ne'er be transferr'd.[2]

From Cambridge Burney went 'whisking to Oxford' and in college libraries in both universities made discoveries which he considered highly important.

Although some of his old enthusiasm seemed to have returned, the autumn of 1779 was marred by a letter from a somewhat aggrieved Twining, to whom Burney often neglected to write for long periods, except when sending parcels of manuscript for correction and criticism. Twining complained of Burney's habit of 'ceasing to write to me when your musical clue is dropped, & beginning again when it is resumed. I have sometimes been a little *afraid* that you lay me aside with your papers—& when you unclasp your memorandum books, out I come.—But enough, & too much of this. The very distant *idea*— the shadowy, hypothetical existence of such a thing is most unpleasant to me.'[3]

Although Burney was horrified by the suggestion, and although Twining was obliged to continue apologizing for having made it for several months, there was some truth in the accusation. Burney was busier than ever during his teaching season; Fanny's fame had brought an ever-increasing social life for both father and daughter; and Burney's thoughts were now much more decisively orientated towards Streatham than towards Fordham. The *History* did not dominate his life in the

---

[1] *ED*, ii. 256–7; *Thraliana*, i. 397–8; *Hist. Mus.* ii. 340 and n., where CB attributes the translation to 'a learned friend'.   [2] *Frag. Mem.* (Berg).

[3] Twining to CB, 29 Sept. 1779 (Add. MS. 39929, ff. 208–11); cf. *ante*, p. 226.

way it had before 1776; Twining knew much less about medieval music than he did about ancient music; and his contributions and opinions were inevitably less important to Burney. The correspondence between the two friends, particularly from the London end, accordingly suffered. Yet while Burney led a busy professional and social life in the metropolis or ransacked libraries in Oxford and Cambridge, Twining, in his quiet village parsonage, depended on their correspondence as a source of pride and entertainment. Certainly it meant much more at this period to the country clergyman than to the London man of letters, and Twining was accordingly more sensitive to Burney's long silences. He would probably have been even more sensitive if he had known that as many sheets of the *History* as were printed had been sent to William Bewley during the previous summer, for Burney still contrived to keep his most intimate friends almost completely unaware of each other's existence.[1]

During the autumn of 1779, however, Burney was at pains to convince Twining that he had been mistaken, and his friend rather more cheerfully resumed his scrupulously careful reading of the manuscript. Burney meanwhile worked away on the discoveries which he had made at Cambridge. In October Johnson told Mrs. Thrale, 'Dr Burney has passed one Evening with me. He has made great discoveries in a library at Cambridge, and he finds so many precious materials, that his Book must be a Porters load. He has sent me another sheet.'[2] Although it is not clear what useful criticism, other than stylistic, Johnson could offer, Burney obviously treasured the faintest signs of interest from his idol and continued showing him the proofs of his book, perhaps as some kind of return of confidence, since Burney saw the *Lives of the Poets* in both manuscript and proof at this period.[3] Stimulated by such interest, Burney made steady progress. Twining returned his third chapter—'Of the formation of the Time-table, and state of Music from that discovery till about the middle of the fourteenth century'—and some printed sheets with his list of 'Errata', late in November;[4]

[1] Bewley to CB, 3 Sept. 1779 (Osborn).
[2] Johnson to Mrs. Thrale, 21 Oct. 1779, *Letters*, ii. 310–11.
[3] Johnson to Mrs. Thrale, 2 Nov. 1779, *Letters* ii, 317–18; *Mem.* ii. 177–8; Hill–Powell, i. 71 n. 3.
[4] Twining to CB, 17 Nov. 1779 (Add. MS. 39929, ff. 218–19); and 26 Nov. 1779, notes (Add. MS. 39936, f. 67).

and in the following month sent his remarks on two sheets
which Burney had been obliged to cancel in his first chapter.[1]
By Christmas 1779 Twining could tell those of his friends who
were subscribers to the *History* and who had now been waiting
nearly four years for the second volume, that 'the 3^d chap. was
in the press, & the 4th getting forward in *paw*-script'.[2] A little
more than a third of the book had therefore been printed by
the end of the year.

The New Year, however, brought ill-health for Burney and
then the usual turmoil of the fashionable season, so that the
History had to be laid aside for the 'Masters & Misses': 'out
every day before 9, & hardly ever at home before 11. What a
Tourbillon is London to me at this time of the year!', he told
Twining in February 1780. Prevented as he was from making
any progress with his book, he learned with horror that a new
encroachment on territory he had claimed as his own was about
to be made. The discovery that Dr. Samuel Arnold was
planning to compile a 'Dictionary of Music' was made even
more distressing by the fact that he had managed to stifle
Twining's desire to undertake a similar task in 1777.[3] Burney
heard the news at a benefit concert for the Italian singer
Piozzi:

In a conversation with Giardini concerning some comical mistakes that were made in the night's bill of fare, he said he would send
it to Dr Arnold to be explained in his dictionary. 'Dict^y? what dict^y?'
quoth I.—'Why he is going to publish an explanation of Musical
Terms, & has been with me, to consult about several.'—*is* not this
vexatious? It seems as if somebody or other were to spit in every mess
of porridge I intended to taste.—And now the injury to you and the
Public, of which I was guilty in making *you* give up the design you
had formed of compiling a Musical Dictionary stares me in the face,
& smites my very heart.[4]

Twining consoled him, however, by agreeing that a complete dictionary would 'still remain to be done, after Arnold's is
out'[5] but reminded him that he would not be ready to undertake

---

[1] Ibid., 11 Dec. [1779], notes (Add. MS. 39936, f. 67); the pages affected were
Hist. Mus. ii. 33–50.   [2] Twining to CB, 6 Jan. 1780 (Add. MS. 39929,
ff. 222–3).   [3] See *ante*, pp. 238–9.
[4] CB to Twining, 28 Feb. [1780], copy (Osborn). This copy is incorrectly dated
1775.   [5] Arnold apparently never completed his 'Dictionary'.

such a work himself, 'till you have hawked & *grous'd* up all your *great* gob, which will stick in your throat for some time yet'.[1] There was nothing that Burney could do, however, until the summer. In March 1780 he lamented, 'Here's another week gone, & it is in vain I find now to wait any longer for leisure to write more. Every day increases my hurry, & narrows my meals & repose by new & unexpected engagements.'[2] His frenzied activity continued into April and staggered even that experienced student of human behaviour, Samuel Johnson, who commented to Mrs. Thrale, 'There has just been with me Dr Burney, who has given. What has he given? Nothing, I believe, gratis. He has given fifty seven lessons this week. Surely this is business.' The fact that he repeated this information to Mrs. Thrale five days later suggests that he was genuinely amazed by Burney's industry.[3]

By the time the London season came to an end, Burney had thus made little progress with his fourth chapter, 'Of the Origin of Modern Languages, to which written Melody and Harmony were first applied; and general State of Music till the Invention of Printing, about the year 1450.' Twining had read part of this chapter in manuscript by March 1780,[4] but no sooner was Burney ready to continue work on it than his long-awaited peace was shattered by the Gordon Riots in June 1780. The burning and plundering caused him great anxiety for his books and papers and, fearing that a Catholic neighbour was a likely victim of the mob, he hurriedly moved his most valuable possessions:

The first things I removed to the house of a friend were the valuable books and MSS. which had been lent to me; the next some writings to another; and thirdly, a coach-full of the MSS. I had collected for my 'History' in France, Italy, Germany, and elsewhere during my travels, and the greatest part of my life, I sent to Mr. Burney,[5] supposing him in a quiet part of the town, and intending to send more; but the second load was brought back, as likely to be more safe in my own house, there being a riot in his street, and a banditti levying money at pleasure of the inhabitants!

---

[1] Twining to CB, 22 Mar. 1780 (Add. MS. 39929, ff. 224–6).
[2] CB to Twining, 10 Mar. [1780] copy (Osborn).
[3] Johnson to Mrs. Thrale, 15 and 20 Apr. 1780, *Letters*, ii. 341–2, 345–6.
[4] See n. 1 above.   [5] CB's nephew, C. R. Burney.

PLATES

DR. CHARLES BURNEY (1781)

From the portrait by Sir Joshua Reynolds in the National Portrait Gallery, London

THOMAS ARNE

From an engraving by J. Gillray after F. Bartolozzi

THOMAS TWINING

From an engraving by C. Turner after J. J. Halls

SIR JOHN HAWKINS
From the portrait by James Roberts in the Faculty of Music, Oxford

DR. CHARLES BURNEY (1794)
*From the drawing by George Dance in the
National Portrait Gallery, London*

A fragment of Burney's 'Memoirs', with Madame d'Arblay's deletions and alterations British Museum, Add. MS. 48345, f. 3v

Disturbed as he was by these outrages, Burney's mind was full of another matter which seemed even more important. The opening of his fourth chapter was now in the press and he felt that his discussion 'Of the Origin of Modern Languages' ought, for once, genuinely to interest Johnson. It is curious, however, that in his letter to Twining Burney implied that he had shown no earlier sheets to Johnson.

I ventured in my great hurry to send a proof of nearly the beginning of the present Chapter to Johnson, begging him to correct it for me, & point out anything he disliked. However, he altered not a tittle, & wrote at the bottom—'this is an Excellent sheet indeed'. This I have put up in lavender & shall bequeath it to the Museum or Bodleian library. I never would consult him about anything where Music is concerned, as he is wholly deaf & insensible to it. But this Chap on the origin of modern languages is certainly within his ken, & he has convinced me that he has an *excellent Taste*, which I hope you will not dispute in the sentence he has so *justly* passed on my Sh[eet].[1]

At about the same time, however, Johnson forced Burney to face a problem which he had been evading for some time, although he must have already been aware that he could hardly hope to complete his *History* in the two volumes which he had originally envisaged. Twining had foreseen trouble as early as 1775, when he had urged Burney to 'amputate' parts of his first volume.[2] He had accepted Burney's decision to transfer his chapter on early Church music to the beginning of the second volume, with the comment that it would inevitably be 'cramped' and much larger than the first: ' 'Twill be, at worst, only giving us a second volume like a quarto bible;—a handsome squatty cube, that may be letter'd either upon back, or side, & stuck into its place any way, conveniently.'[3]

Until about 1780 Burney seems to have proceeded on this assumption that his second volume would merely be much longer than the first. As early as 1777, however, Twining had once more started to urge him to be as economical as possible: 'Adopt as many of my proposals for compression & omission

---

[1] CB to Twining, 11 June 1780, copy (Osborn); and *Country Clergyman*, pp. 80–84, where it is misdated 11 May 1780 and the passage concerning Johnson omitted.

[2] See *ante*, pp. 166–7.

[3] Twining to CB, 13 Nov. 1775, copy (Add. MS. 39933, ff. 166–9).

as you can find in y^r heart to do; for here is no dryness to make digressions & *ecarts* necessary as a relief, & y^r materials will gather upon you like a snowball. 'Twill be a cubic volume, I foresee.'[1] By the autumn of 1778 William Bewley believed that even a 'cubic volume' would not be enough: 'I . . . cannot conceive how you can possibly condense & pack all you have, & ought, to say, into one Volume.'[2] A year later Johnson observed that 'his Book must be a Porters load'[3] and early in 1780 made some remarks which greatly disturbed Burney:

Everyone I talk to on the subject frights me about the impossibility of getting all my necessary matter into one Vol. more. Johnson says it would be like a writer of the Hist. of Eng^d giving one Vol. to the Heptarchy, & *only* one to all the rest of all our annals. What shall I do? I dread having another Vol. on my hands, as well as the clamour of subscribers, who expected the work would be completed in 2 Vols. *Well, j'irai mon train*—I shall neither squeeze violently, nor amplify more than seems necessary for explaining, confirming, & illustrating in such a manner as to make my book intelligible & amusing—if I can.[4]

By May 1780, however, Burney had resigned himself to the necessity of a third volume[5] and was cautiously trying the idea out on such subscribers as Andrew Lumisden, who fortunately assured him that an additional volume was indispensable and that the public would willingly pay extra for it.[6] Burney himself seems to have been less confident that his subscribers, having already waited so long for his second volume, would welcome the fact that, even when it appeared, the *History* would be incomplete. To pacify them on the first count, he published an optimistic statement in *The Public Advertiser* for 17 May 1780 to the effect that 'The Second Volume . . . a great Part of which is already printed, will be published in the course of next Winter.' His new plan was to reach the end of the sixteenth century in this volume and to devote the third to the final two centuries, which constituted, after all, the period of musical history which really mattered.

[1] Twining to CB, 18 Nov. 1777 (Add. MS. 39929, ff. 153–4) and 26 Nov. 1779, notes (Add. MS. 39936, f. 67).   [2] Bewley to CB [Nov. 1778] (Osborn).
[3] See *ante*, p. 252.   [4] CB to Twining [1780], copy (Osborn).
[5] Bewley to CB, 24 May 1780 (Osborn).
[6] Lumisden to CB, 10 July 1780 (Osborn).

During the summer of 1780 Burney followed what had become a set pattern in recent years, retiring to the peace of Chessington in August[1] after visiting Oxford to rummage in the Bodleian Library like 'a hound in a rabbit-warren'.[2] In spite of his promise to the public, however, the knowledge that, because of his additional volume, he now had much more room in which to work, led Burney to relax his standards of relevance, and before long he was fighting a familiar battle with Twining. Not satisfied with competing with Hawkins in sheer scope and with triumphant descriptions of important manuscripts unknown to his rival, Burney still wished, as in his first volume, to cater wherever possible for the non-specialist reader. His first three chapters had been largely concerned with the theory of medieval music: thereafter, however, he deviated into literary history at every opportunity. In January 1779 Twining had warned him not to preoccupy himself with Provençal poetry,[3] but it was not until the autumn of 1780, when he was reading the manuscript of Burney's ever-expanding fourth chapter, that the argument began in earnest. Twining protested frankly that 'too large a part of the pages you sent me was occupied by *language*, & *Poets;* & to [sic] small a portion by *Music*'. Burney's long account of his favourite Italian writers, Dante, Petrarch, and Boccaccio,[4] was very interesting, but Twining thought 'their connexion with *Music* very slender, amounting to little more than the *general* connexion of *all* Poetry, & Music'.

Although Twining felt strongly that this section should be 'retrenched, or shortened', he admitted that it contained one piece of verse, the anonymous translation from the *Medea*, which was admirable.[5] In reply to his inquiry, Burney was able proudly to name the 'learned author' who had provided him with the translation: 'The passage from Euripides was first pointed out to me by Dr Johnson; and it struck me as so beautiful that I begged him to give me a Translation of it. There is a word in it that I want to change: '*o'erful* the saturated soul',—I like not—the rest I think charming—there's the true Smack of

---

[1] Mrs. Thrale to CB, 27 Aug. 1780 (Osborn); *DL*, i. 443.
[2] Johnson to CB, 31 July 1780, *Letters*, ii. 384; Twining to CB, 12 Oct. 1780 (Add. MS. 39929, ff. 238–41).
[3] Ibid., 8 Jan. 1779 (Add. MS. 39929, ff. 189–90); cf. *Hist. Mus.* ii. 221–50.
[4] Cf. *Hist. Mus.* ii. 319–46.
[5] Twining to CB, 4 Nov. 1780 (Add. MS. 39929, ff. 242–3).

la belle antiquité in it, according to my feelings—'.[1] In a part of
this letter which the copyist omitted, Burney evidently proceeded to defend his literary digressions and to accuse Twining
of enjoying only the 'gothic notes, & yᵉ accounts of MSS' in his
History. In reply, Twining reminded him that, 'The objection
which I have always heard to yʳ 1ˢᵗ Vol., when *any* has been
made, has been always that there was too much in it that had
nothing to do with Music. I feared that the same obj. might be
made here: however, it will *certainly not* be made by the readers
whose amusement you consult. I never objected, nor meant to
hint objection, to yʳ translations; I think as you do about the
necessity, or at least, the amusement of them.'

At the same time, Twining refused to retract his honest
opinion that Burney's literary topics and his own frequent
translations of medieval verse were irrelevant.[2] Burney nevertheless declined to accept these objections and in December
1780 Twining expounded his views for the last time. His
protests arose basically 'from an apprehension that you may
possibly find yourself pent up into a corner by these amusing
episodes, when you get to times of *real* Music, where your
materials must, I suppose, be abundant, & such as will be
intelligible & interesting to *all* musical people. If you are easy
about such consequences, I am easy. You best know your room,
& your resources.'[3] At heart, Burney's problem was once more
the nature of the audience which he hoped to address in his
History. Three years as a member of the Streatham circle, as
well as of the most fashionable literary society in London, had
done nothing to diminish his desire to appeal to readers who
were neither professional musicians nor antiquarians. Certainly,
it had not been his musical learning which had endeared him to
Mrs. Thrale; and Johnson, Burke, and Reynolds 'had neither
taste nor care for his art, and not the smallest knowledge upon
its subject'. It had been up to Burney to come to meet these
friends: 'Dr. Burney had too general a love of literature, as well
as of the arts, to limit his admiration, any more than his
acquirements, to his own particular cast; while the friends just

---

[1] CB to Twining, 7 Nov. 1780, copy (Osborn). In his reply (see n. 2) Twining
suggested that Johnson intended 'o'erfill', which was printed.

[2] Twining to CB, 21 Nov. 1780 (Add. MS. 39929, ff. 244–5).

[3] Ibid., 4 Dec. 1780 (Add. MS. 39929, ff. 246–7).

mentioned regarded his musical science but as a matter apart; and esteemed and loved him solely for the qualities that he possessed in common with themselves.'[1]

To Mrs. Thrale, whose lack of interest in music was such that Burney sometimes found it difficult to get through a lesson with Queeney without frequent interruption,[2] his *History* was no more than a 'heavy Book upon the Subject'; and the only aspect of his labours which appealed to her was his fondness for translating 'Monkish Rhymes', which, she believed, would 'contribute to egayer les Choses'.[3] Even if she confided these opinions only to *Thraliana*, Burney could not be unaware of Mrs. Thrale's attitude to his *History* nor could he help being anxious to afford her at least a little entertainment in his 'heavy Book'. The numerous verse translations which so irritated Twining in Burney's second volume not only represent part of his contribution to the literary life of Streatham but had in many cases actually received the approval of Mrs. Thrale and Johnson, sufficient justification, to Burney's mind, for their inclusion. *Thraliana* contains a number of poems by Burney, some of which duly appeared in the *History*, for which they were ostensibly translated. In addition to expressing her own conviction that Burney was an extremely elegant and skilful poet, Mrs. Thrale occasionally recorded similar praise from Johnson, who observed of one poem that 'These . . . are some of the few Verses which have as much Truth as Wit, and as much Wit as Truth'; and if that comment appear ambiguous, Mrs. Thrale noted later that 'Johnson says the following 8 Lines of Burney are actually sublime'.[4]

Burney had thus been led to believe both that he was a talented poet and that his translations provided one certain way in which he could entertain his dearest friends in what would otherwise seem to them an unreadable book. From the beginning of his second volume he had been rather pathetically apologizing to his readers for the necessity of discussing in detail many 'dry' aspects of medieval music. 'The history of barbarians can furnish but small pleasure or profit to an enlightened and polished people', he had written in his first chapter.[5] In his second he had apologized again, while hoping

[1] *Mem.* ii. 325.   [2] CB to Mrs. Thrale, 11 Jan. 1778 (Yale).
[3] *Thraliana*, i. 371.   [4] Ibid. 215, 341.   [5] *Hist. Mus.* ii. 41.

that a few of his readers 'will at least have curiosity and perseverance sufficient to travel with me to the dusty shelves of
Gothic lore, and to the gloomy cells of Monks and Friars,
where I am forced with great toil, and small expectation, to
seek my materials'.[1] Thus Burney proceeded with his account of
medieval music, anxiously assuring his readers that his own
taste was unaffected by the materials he was obliged to handle;
hastening to conclude a 'long article, to which very few
readers will, perhaps, wish me to return'; and avoiding another
learned exposition which, he felt, 'would be swelling my volume
with that, which if any one had patience to peruse, could afford
neither profit nor pleasure; and for which the highest reward I
could hope, would be the pity of my readers, for not having
found in all my researches any thing better to give them'.[2]

What sustained Burney—and, he hoped, his fickle general
reader—in this volume of his *History* was the fact that, in spite of
the recent explorations of 'the formation of our language' by
Dr. Johnson and of 'the early state of our poetry' by Warton,
Percy, and Tyrwhitt, he felt that he himself could properly
enter upon '*that* ground . . . in pursuit of my own game'. He
defended his literary excursions on the grounds that 'though I
may sometimes have hunted on the same manor as these
excellent literary sportsmen, and during the chace have
accidentally *run into them*; yet the chief objects of our pursuits
have been extremely different'. Accordingly, until music
acquired sufficient independent interest and dignity to be
worthy of his polite readers, Burney clung to his conviction that
music and poetry 'are so closely connected, that it is impossible
to speak of one without the other'; and in spite of Twining's
reiterated protests, his enormous fourth chapter, with its digressions concerning Provençal, Italian, and English poetry, as well
as his own verse translations, expanded rapidly.[3]

When his teaching season began early in 1781, the end of his
volume was still not in sight and, as Twining knew, he was now,
'as usual, torn limb from limb by business'.[4] For a time he
retained some hope of fulfilling his promise of publishing during
the winter, for 'the murmurs of the subscribers', as well as his
own longing to rid himself of his great burden, 'became such as

[1] *Hist. Mus.* ii. 85.   [2] Ibid. 98, 389–90.   [3] Ibid. 354.
[4] Twining to CB, 12 Feb. 1781 (Add. MS. 39929, ff. 252–3).

to sicken him of almost every occupation that turned him from its pursuit'. Fanny later described how he desperately tried to use every available moment, even on his busiest days:

uninterrupted attention grew more than ever difficult; for as his leisure, through the double claims of his profession and his work, diminished, his celebrity increased; and the calls upon it, as usual, from the wayward taste of public fashion for what is hard to obtain, were perpetual, were even clamorous; and he had constantly a long list of petitioning parents, awaiting a vacant hour, upon any terms that he could name, and at any part of the day.

He had always some early pupil who accepted his attendance at eight o'clock in the morning; and a strong instance has been given of its being seized upon even at seven; and, during the height of the season for fashionable London residence, his tour from house to house was scarcely ever finished sooner than eleven o'clock at night.

But so urgent grew now the spirit of his diligence for the progress of his work, that he not only declined all invitations to the hospitable boards of his friends, he even resisted the social hour of repast at his own table; and took his solitary meal in his coach, while passing from scholar to scholar; for which purpose he had sandwiches prepared in a flat tin box; and wine and water ready mixed, in a wickered pint bottle, put constantly into the pockets of his carriage.[1]

Such efforts were in vain and it was not long before he had abandoned his hope of publication before the end of the 1781 season.

IV

Burney was not, however, the only member of his family who was struggling to complete a book at this time. Many of Fanny's admirers, convinced that her talents lay in dialogue and were essentially dramatic, had insisted that she follow her successful novel with a play. Accordingly she had worked during 1779 on a comedy entitled 'The Witlings', encouraged by Johnson, Murphy, Sheridan, and Burney himself. Eventually, however, Burney and Samuel Crisp felt that Fanny's satiric comedy about the 'Blue-Stockings' might give offence and by the summer of 1779 the plan of having it performed during the following winter had been abandoned. Until the end of 1780, however, Fanny seems to have carried the play rather hopefully about with her, contemplating revision and alterations.[2]

---

[1] *Mem.* ii. 211–12.
[2] CB to FB, 2 letters [1779] (Barrett); *DL*, i. 315, 344, 449; Hemlow, pp. 129–38.

Burney nevertheless insisted that his daughter should continue a literary career which had opened so auspiciously and eventually persuaded her to begin a new novel, *Cecilia*, whose heroine was taken from the abandoned play. On the whole Fanny did not share her father's ambitions for her further fame; and the knowledge that she could no longer shelter in anonymity, that expectation would be higher and criticism more rigorous, only made the writing of the novel a more painful task. During the winter of 1780–1 Burney and Crisp made her retire to Chessington to work without distraction and when she eventually fell ill with a fever, Mrs. Thrale was convinced that Fanny's 'anxious earnestness' to please her father 'had caused much of the illness we lamented'.[1] Fanny herself was never happy about *Cecilia*. 'I think I shall always hate this book', she told Mrs. Thrale;[2] and from her letters to Susan Burney it is clear that she proceeded with it mainly to gratify her father: 'He will expect me to have just *done*, when I am so behind hand as not even to see land!—yet I have written a great deal, but the work will be a long one, & I cannot without ruining it make it otherwise. . . . I am *afraid* of seeing my father. . . . I cannot sleep half the night for planning what to write next Day, & then next day am half dead for want of rest.'[3]

No connexion between the literary activities of Burney and his daughter at this period seems hitherto to have been perceived, perhaps partly because Fanny herself later gave the impression that there was a considerable interval between the publication of the second volume of her father's *History* and *Cecilia*.[4] The evidence suggests, however, that Burney was greatly attracted by the prospect of the simultaneous appearance of the two works by father and daughter and, expecting at first that his own second volume would be ready early in 1781, he applied tremendous pressure in an attempt to make Fanny complete her novel at the same time. Only when it became clear that he could not complete his own volume before the following winter did Fanny return to St. Martin's Street and Streatham.

During the summer of 1781 Burney worked feverishly to

[1] Mrs. Thrale to FB, 20 Feb. [1781] (Barrett).   [2] *DL*, i. 463.
[3] FB to Susan Burney, 19 Feb. [1781] and n.d. (Barrett).
[4] See *post*, p. 446.

break the back of the remaining chapter of his book, having, as
he had told Twining, 'not above 150 pages . . . wanting' to
complete it, and several peaceful months ahead in which to
work '*under ground* in retirement—like a mole'.[1] As he began
work on this final stretch, he was anxious for Fanny likewise to
return to *Cecilia*, and, having 'long with regret, though with
pride, perceived that, at Streatham, she had no time that was
her own, earnestly called her thence'.[2] Mrs. Thrale was greatly
irritated by the loss of her companion, especially since she had
always been baffled by the intense family loyalty of the Burneys.
In August 1779 she had written in her journal:

> The Family of the Burneys are a very surprizing Set of People;
> their Esteem & fondness for the D^r seems to inspire them all with a
> Desire not to disgrace him; & so every individual of it must write and
> read & be literary: He is the only Man I ever knew, who being not
> rich, was beloved by his Wife & Children: tis very seldom that a per-
> son's own Family will give him Credit for Talents which bring in no
> Money to make them fine or considerable. Burney's Talents do in-
> deed bring in something, but still I sh^d expect a rich Linen-draper to
> be better beloved in his own house—and nobody is so much beloved.—[3]

Fanny's own fear of being patronized at Streatham also
occasionally offended her generous friend, and her departure
from Streatham in July 1781 at her father's insistence led to
one of Mrs. Thrale's most outraged protests:

> What a Blockhead Dr Burney is, to be always sending for his
> Daughter home so! what a Monkey! is not She better and happier
> with me than She can be any where else? Johnson is enraged at the
> silliness of their Family Conduct, and Mrs Byron disgusted: I confess
> myself provoked excessively, but I love the girl *so* dearly—& the D^r
> too for that matter, only that he has such odd Notions of superiority
> in his own house, & will have his Children under his Feet forsooth
> rather than let 'em live in Peace, Plenty & Comfort any where from
> home. If I did not provide Fanny with every *Weare*able, every *Wish*-
> able indeed, it would not vex me to be served so; but to see the
> Impossibility of compensating for the Pleasures of St *Martins Street*,
> makes me at once merry & mortified.[4]

---

[1] Twining to CB, 10 Oct. 1781 (Add. MS. 39929, ff. 274–8).
[2] *Mem.* ii. 217.
[3] *Thraliana*, i. 399.
[4] Ibid. 502; and cf. 400, 443 and Clifford, *Hester Lynch Piozzi*, p. 178, n. 1.

Fanny returned to St. Martin's Street, however, not simply because she disliked being the constant object of Mrs. Thrale's well-intentioned generosity nor because the social sensitivity from which all the Burneys suffered made 'home' and the company of the other members of the family especially agreeable. Burney was almost certainly now aiming at the simultaneous publication of his second volume and of *Cecilia* during the following winter. He himself worked hard at Chessington during the summer of 1781[1] and Fanny also retired there to try and complete her novel later in the year, ill-health having hindered progress earlier.[2]

Twining was also seriously ill during the summer and autumn of 1781, but he loyally told Burney that he would be prepared as usual to check and criticize 'anything that you wou'd give a farthing to have me read'.[3] Burney still relied so heavily on Twining's careful scrutiny of his manuscript and sheets, that, in spite of some misgivings about his friend's health, he accepted the offer: 'When I read your account of yourself I felt very uncomfortable at your having written so *long* a letter in spite of prudence & injunctions. But you still have courage to ask after opus Mag: & friendship to encourage the author to the old practice of employing you. I believe I ought not to abuse your kindness so far as to accept it,—& yet every sheet would terrify me that had not gone thro' your hands previous to printing.'[4] Accordingly, the 'Gobs'—as Twining called them—of the manuscript of the fifth chapter ('Of the State of Music, from the Invention of Printing till the Middle of the XVIth Century') were regularly dispatched to Fordham during the autumn of 1781. Materials for this period of musical history were abundant and, in his anxiety to finish his volume, Burney had at last decided to change his policy and to exclude anything but strictly musical matter.

Twining was understandably amused, early in November 1781, by the ultimate victory of his own convictions: 'What you say about writing for *Musical* readers &c^a is what I have *preached* to you often. I am glad that, at last, you confirm my ideas by your own; for we agree exactly. You will have enough

[1] *DL*, ii. 52.   [2] Hemlow, pp. 144–5.
[3] See *ante*, p. 263, n. 1.
[4] CB to Twining [Oct. 1781], copy (Osborn).

to do now without squinting at the Masters & Misses.'[1] In spite of
these measures it was already clear that Burney would be unable to cover even the whole of the sixteenth century in his
second volume and Twining noticed that his haste was resulting
in a lack of 'method' and of 'chronological arrangement'
which might confuse his readers.

This shortage of space, to which Burney was obliged to refer
several times in the volume itself,[2] had a somewhat ironic cause.
For all their mockery of Hawkins, both Burney and Twining
had lately discovered in themselves a growing admiration for
sixteenth-century music. Burney had spent a great deal of time
in scoring the works of the composers of the period, such as
Josquin des Prés, Okeghem, and Taverner,[3] and he found
himself discussing them at much greater length, and defending them much more warmly, than he had ever intended.[4]
Twining simultaneously confessed that he had been very fond
of early church music and madrigals at Cambridge and that he
had only been converted from this taste by Thomas Gray the
poet, 'who made me first turn my back upon all this, by his
enthusiastic love of *expressive* & *passionate* Music, which it was
hardly possible for me to *hear* & *see* him *feel*, without catching
something even of his *prejudices*. For Pergolesi was his darling.
. . . This was the *bridge* over which . . . I passed from *Antient* to
Modern Music.'[5]

Burney was inevitably self-conscious about even a partial
concession to Hawkins's taste and it is amusing to find that he
could now no longer resist directing barbed remarks at his rival.
As he brought his volume to its conclusion he attacked the note
in Hawkins's edition of *The Complete Angler* which had offended
him for so many years, sneered at a badly chosen musical
illustration quoted by his predecessor and took pleasure in
pointing out another example of Hawkins's technical ignorance.[6]
These and similar remarks were mere pin-pricks and Burney
still avoided mentioning Hawkins by name. Nevertheless, they

[1] Twining to CB, 9 Nov. 1781 (Add. MS. 39929, ff. 281-2).
[2] *Hist. Mus.* ii. 360, 380, 433, 512.
[3] B.M. Add. MSS. 11581-91 contain CB's copies and scores of these and later
compositions used in the last three vols. of *Hist. Mus.*
[4] *Hist. Mus.* ii. 485, 490, 507-11, 554.
[5] Twining to CB, 8 Dec. 1781 (Add. MS. 39929, ff. 287-90).
[6] *Hist. Mus.* ii. 553 and n., 565-6 and n., 573 n.

served to relieve a little of the resentment which he felt after six years of following gloomily in Hawkins's footsteps.

Until February 1782 Burney continued sending the manuscript of his fifth chapter to Twining, who dutifully read and criticized it.[1] By the middle of that month the chapter was complete and Twining was hoping that 'the Devils will work hard, & deliver you handsomely of this burning brat e'er long'. He had also heard for the first time of the impending publication of *Cecilia*, which had hitherto been kept as secret as possible.[2] Fanny had been shut up at Chessington with Crisp from November until January 1782, when she returned for the marriage of her sister Susan, 'after which, the Doctor kept her stationary in St. Martin's-street, till she had written the word Finis'.[3] She was as depressed as ever about *Cecilia* and only her father's insistence kept her at work upon it. His own volume, the last chapter of which was in the press by February 1782, could probably have been published during March. It can hardly be coincidental that, at the end of February, Fanny was horrified to learn that he confidently expected *Cecilia* to be printing within a month.[4] By March, however, the novel was in fact in the press,[5] although it was hardly Fanny's eagerness which had brought it to completion. 'But for my Father', she told Mrs. Thrale, 'I am sure I should throw it behind the Fire';[6] and in mid-March she wrote to Samuel Crisp, 'I would it were in my power to defer the whole publication to another spring, but I am sure my father would run crazy if I made such a proposal.'[7]

While the five volumes of *Cecilia* were in the press, Burney decided that a little advance publicity could do no harm. On 12 March 1782 a poem, entitled 'Advice to the *Herald*', appeared in *The Morning Herald*, describing the accomplishments of the various 'Blue-Stocking' ladies and including a reference to 'Little Burney's quick discerning'. Fanny was characteristically shocked, embarrassed, and fascinated by such vulgar publicity and endured it only to please her father, suspecting that the author of the lines was William Weller Pepys: 'my

---

[1] CB to Twining, 14 Dec. 1781, Jan. 1782, copies (Osborn); Twining to CB, 28 Dec. 1781 (Add. MS. 39929, ff. 291–2).
[2] Twining to CB, 14 Feb. 1782 (Add. MS. 39929, ff. 293–4).
[3] *Mem.* ii. 218   [4] *DL*, ii. 58.   [5] Hemlow, p. 149.
[6] FB to Mrs. Thrale, n.d. (Barrett).   [7] *DL*, ii. 72.

father is so delighted, that, though he was half afraid of speaking to me at all about them at first, he carries them constantly in his pocket, and reads them to everybody!' Although the secret seems to have been preserved in his lifetime, a draft of the lines in Burney's hand was discovered among his papers after his death.[1]

As far as his own volume was concerned Burney's remaining problem was that of mollifying his subscribers, who were expecting the *History* to be complete in two volumes and who might resent having to buy a third; and he therefore wrote an 'apology' for the decision he had been forced to take. His characteristically humble manner before his subscribers must have produced a long and profuse self-exculpation, but he wisely took the precaution of showing the passage to Samuel Johnson, to whom, incidentally, he had referred and paid compliments more than once in the course of his volume.[2] Johnson returned the manuscript with a brief and incisive note: 'Dear Sir, I have taken great liberties by shortening your paper, but have, I hope, omitted nothing important. A long apology is a tedious thing. I am Dr Sir &c Sam: Johnson.'[3]

Although Dr. R. W. Chapman could find 'no such thing' as this apology in Burney's volume, it appears at the conclusion of the book,[4] and it is not difficult to detect in it signs of Johnson's hand. Indeed, Burney had actually worked into it the opinion which Johnson had expressed two years earlier on the necessity of a third volume: 'My original intention was, to comprise the whole work in two volumes; but I soon discovered, with some degree of shame and mortification, that to have bestowed no more pages on *modern* Music . . . than upon the *ancient* . . . would be like allowing one volume, in a History of England, to the Heptarchy, and only one to all subsequent times.'[5]

After describing the unexpected aggregation of materials in the course of writing his second volume and the necessity of working 'in detail at particular parts, without bestowing much attention on the *whole*', Burney concluded with two paragraphs which seem to owe something to Johnson's cheerless view of

[1] Ibid. 73–74, 76–77, 78 n. CB's draft is now in the Osborn Collection.
[2] *Hist. Mus.* ii. 41, 219, 343, 354.
[3] Johnson to CB, 18 Mar. 1782, *Letters*, ii. 468.
[4] *Hist. Mus.* ii. 585–6.
[5] See *ante*, p. 256.

literary endeavour, in sentences of his own characteristic dignity:

It has never been my wish, or intention, to be always in the *Press*; or to keep memory and reflection on the rack, at the expence of every moment of leisure for enjoyment or amusement. My industry, in this undertaking, has not been stimulated by profit, and the reputation of an author becomes daily less alluring, as reflection shows it to be more uncertain. Yet, a repugnance to abandoning, unaccomplished, an enterprize, for which such pains and expence have been bestowed in procuring materials, would be still an incitement to new efforts, though every other should fail.

This apology, for the amplification of my original plan, seems due to my first Subscribers. I have been obliged, extremely against my inclination, to depart from the letter of my Proposals; but as it has been done with no selfish or sinister views, my wish being only to render my work more worthy the honour of their patronage, I venture to hope, that no great moral turpitude will be found in the addition, at some future time, of a THIRD VOLUME.

As had been the case with the dedication in the first volume, at least one of Burney's friends innocently praised Johnson's contribution. Twining wrote on 5 May 1782, 'Your conclusion, & the unhackneyed & pleasant way in wch you apologise for a 3^d Volume, likes me much.'[1] That Twining had already received his own set of the printed sheets of the volume by that date supports the suspicion that it could have been published much earlier than it was, and that Burney delayed its publication to narrow the gap between its appearance and that of his daughter's novel. The second volume of the *History* was eventually published on 29 May and *Cecilia* on 12 June, just two weeks later.[2] (The novel was published by Tom Payne and it is conceivable that, after Payne's heavy losses over Hawkins's *History*, Burney's conscience prompted him to suggest that this unfortunate bookseller should enjoy some of the inevitable profits arising from Fanny's novel.)

After writing to ask the author if he had 'any thing to offer—explanatory, or exculpatory &c &c.', William Bewley did his usual duty in the *Monthly Review*. He feared, however, that Burney had 'spoken rather too aenigmatically' about his

---

[1] Twining to CB, 5 May 1782 (Add. MS. 39929, ff. 295–6).
[2] Hemlow, p. 151.

promised third volume and asked permission to hint that work on it was already in progress.[1] Although he praised the new volume in his two articles,[2] Bewley, who was in poor health, employed much more direct quotation than in earlier reviews and devoted in all only some sixteen pages to the book. One valuable aspect of his review, however, was the graceful manner in which he passed over the need for a third volume, describing it as 'an arithmetical mistake (at which, however, we apprehend, the most intelligent of his readers will rather rejoice). . . . A cool compiler could have made a much better estimate; but your men of genius, and original thinkers, write under impulses which set all figures and calculations at defiance.' Burney had evidently given Bewley permission to state that work on the third volume had started, for the second article concluded with the assurance to the public that 'We are happy to learn, that he has already made a pretty considerable progress in this truly desirable work; animated, we doubt not, by the increasing facility and agreeableness of the remaining part of his task.'

Although there is no evidence as to the identity of the writer in the *Critical Review*, its four articles on the *History*,[3] in both manner and content, seem once more to have been written by some friendly hand. This review, in fact, appears to contain a careful anticipation of every criticism of the volume which might be made by a hostile reader. Burney's literary digressions, to which Twining had objected so consistently, were defended in the second paragraph of the first article; and in the following paragraph, the technical 'dryness' of parts of the volume, which he had always feared might prove indigestible to many of his readers, was stated to have been made attractive by his 'clear and elegant' style. In January 1783 the subject of the third article was Burney's fourth chapter and the reviewer, having declared that the author 'deserves considerable praise for his *poetical* abilities', proceeded to quote many of Burney's 'agreeable' translations, including the 'very beautiful' lines from the *Medea* (without indicating that they were not Burney's). In the following month the review concluded by assuring

---

[1] Bewley to CB, 21 Oct. 1782 (Osborn).
[2] Oct. 1782 and Jan. 1783; lxvii. 177–82, lxviii. 30–41.
[3] liv. 325–33, 405–14; lv. 49–59, 109–18.

Burney, on behalf of the public, that 'whoever has read the volumes already published would be more sorry than the author himself' if he did not complete his *History*, even if it entailed a third volume. His imminent arrival at the subject of contemporary music, moreover, was greeted with the confident expectation that his great knowledge and experience would 'not only render [it] pleasant, but instructive to his musical readers, by regulating and correcting the public taste in music, as sir Joshua Reynolds has done in a sister art'.

Warmly welcomed in this manner in the monthly journals, the second volume of the *History*, according to Fanny, 'was received with the same favour and the same honours that had graced the entrance into public notice of its predecessor. The literary world seemed filled with its praise; the booksellers demanded ample impressions; and her Majesty Queen Charlotte, with even augmented graciousness, accepted its homage at court.'[1] Burney's book was, however, undoubtedly overshadowed by *Cecilia*. '*Who* will read our *Histories of Music*, & our *commentaries* upon *Aristotle*, at *this* rate?', asked Twining, on hearing of the novel's success.[2] Yet no hint of jealousy ever appeared in Burney's ecstatic pleasure at Fanny's new triumph, for she had brought honour not only to herself but to all the Burneys; and he genuinely cared less for his own fame than for that of the family, as a whole, of which he was the head. Such pride was understandable when *Cecilia* could earn the wholehearted admiration of so busy a politician as Edmund Burke, who congratulated Burney 'on the great honour acquired to his family' by the novel.[3]

The family's double achievement was recognized in the *Critical Review*, which juxtaposed articles on both works, several pages of praise of *Cecilia* following the second article on the *History* in December 1782, introduced, somewhat disingenuously we may suspect, with the information that *Cecilia* was 'supposed to be written by miss Burney, author of Evelina, and daughter of the ingenious Dr. Burney, so well known in the literary world by his excellent History of Music'.[4] Apart from the *Monthly*

[1] *Mem.* ii. 213.
[2] Twining to CB, 18 Sept. 1782 (Add. MS. 39929, ff. 299–303).
[3] Burke to FB, 29 July 1782 (Comyn); *DL*, ii. 92–94.
[4] liv. 414.

Review, which rather surprisingly made some apologetic strictures on the novel, only Twining dared to offer any criticism,[1] and Burney seemed to hear nothing but praise of *Cecilia* in the course of his teaching, at the opera-house and at parties, all of which he carefully recorded and sent to Fanny, who was spending the autumn at Brighton with Mrs. Thrale.[2] His excitement and pride did not diminish and, in January 1783, when Fanny described a literary party at which, to her usual embarrassment, she had received many open compliments, she added that 'I went with my dear father, who was quite enchanted at the affair. Dear soul, how he feeds upon all that brings fame to Cecilia! his eagerness upon this subject, and his pleasure in it, are truly enthusiastic, and, I think, rather increase by fulness, than grow satiated.'[3] 1782 was one of the happiest years of Burney's life and with the most tedious part of his labour on the *History of Music* concluded, he was now determined to reap his reward and to enjoy his own and his daughter's fame to the full.

v

'Now you breathe free a little,' Twining observed in June 1782[4] and, indeed, Burney was at last determined to relax. His life had always been one of relentless industry and a struggle against time. In recent years the temptations of Streatham and of the flattering invitations he received ever more frequently had grown stronger; but although since 1776 he had been a fashionable figure and could be found at many literary parties and dinners, often in the company of his famous daughter, the burden of his *History* had always lain heavy upon his shoulders. His real business, he had always felt, when not earning as much as possible in the London season, was writing in his study, or rummaging in libraries. In 1778 Arthur Murphy had complained at Streatham, 'what a sad man is Dr. Burney for running away so!'; and Mrs. Thrale had replied, 'I often say Dr. Burney is the most of a male coquet of any man I know; for he only gives one enough of his company to excite a desire for more.'[5]

---

[1] See *ante*, p. 270 n. 2.
[2] CB to FB and Susan [July 1782] (Hyde); to FB [Oct.] 1782, 6 and 8 Nov. 1782 (Barrett). [3] *DL*, ii. 186.
[4] Twining to CB, 26 June 1782 (Add. MS. 39929, ff. 297–8). [5] *DL*, i. 203.

Burney had been no happier about the necessity of endless hurry than his friends; and after the publication of the second volume of his *History* in 1782, when he was in his fifty-seventh year, he resolved at last to enjoy himself, to participate more fully in the exciting intellectual and social life around him, from which he had been obliged so often to absent himself. For too long all his pleasure had necessarily been invested in the future. Now he was ready to converse with the living, to enjoy the present, and to take advantage of his great popularity, which for some years had been making demands upon his time that he could permit only at the expense of sharp pangs of conscience. In June 1781 Samuel Crisp had testified to Burney's social success in explaining the brevity of one of his visits to Chessington:

the Dr. would have stay'd longer, but was oblig'd to return, in order to make his appearance at Court this day; he is now at the Top of the *Ton*. He is continually invited to all the great Tables, and parties, to meet the Wits and Grandees, without the least reference to Music; and among the People, that neither employ him, nor care a straw for his Skill in an Art, which they never think about, he has now half a guinea a Lesson from all his scholars, the old ones as well as the new, and 4 Guineas Entrance; and has this year more Scholars and business than ever he had in his Life—there's for you![1]

Arthur Young, the agriculturalist and traveller, who was Mrs. Burney's brother-in-law, helped to explain Burney's popularity at this same period:

I never met with any person who had more decided talents for conversation, eminently seasoned with wit and humour, and these talents were so at command that he could exert them at will. He was remarkable for some sprightly story or witty *bon mot* just when he quitted a company, which seemed as much as to say, 'There now, I have given you a dose which you may work upon in my absence.' His society was greatly sought after by all classes, from the first nobility to the mere *homme de lettres*.[2]

As if in recognition of the fact that he had successfully completed his climb to celebrity, Burney spent part of the summer writing his 'Memoirs' at Chessington with Crisp.[3] The alteration

---

[1] *Burford Papers*, ed. W. H. Hutton, 1905, p. 63.
[2] *Autobiography*, p. 101.   [3] See *post*, p. 433.

in his behaviour was striking, as Fanny noted: 'My father is all himself—gay, facile and sweet. He comes to all meals, writes without toiling, and gives us more of his society than he has done many years. His third volume he is not tied down to produce at any stated time, and he has most wisely resolved not to make any promises to the public about it, nor to take in any subscriptions, but to keep free from all engagement.'[1] Although, after his return to London in the autumn, he resumed work on the *History*, he deliberately 'restored himself, in a certain degree, to his family, his friends, and a general and genial enjoyment of his existence'.[2] To his own fame was added that of his daughter, 'and the pleasure of his parental feelings doubled those of his renown; for the new author was included, with the most flattering distinction, in almost every invitation that he received, or acquaintance that he made, where a female presided in the society'.[3] Burney enjoyed this social life enormously and if Fanny, to whom most literary parties were embarrassing and distasteful, continued to accept invitations to such gatherings, it was very largely only to please her father. Not until 1784 could she convince him that she disliked the strain of such constant entertainment, for in that year she wrote, 'I have now a little broke my father into permitting my sending excuses; and, indeed, I was most heartily tired of visiting, though the people visited have been among the first for talents in the kingdom.'[4]

His own engagement book in the winters of the early years of the decade was always full. A fragment of it for 1784 concludes with the proud comment that 'My dinners & Conversationi increased this year so much that to 21 houses of old acquaintance 16 new were added, where I dined & spent evenings for the 1st time'.[5] A letter to his daughter Susan in April of the same year, which describes his social life during the past week, may serve to illustrate its strenuous nature, especially when it is remembered that all these engagements followed several hours of teaching in the 'terrible hurrying time of the year'. On the Monday he dined with Dr. Richard Warren. After another dinner engagement on Tuesday he moved on to 'a grand Conversatione', attended by all the leading 'Blue-Stocking'

[1] *DL*, ii. 95.   [2] *Mem.* ii. 214.   [3] Ibid. 259.
[4] *DL*, ii. 253.   [5] Osborn.

ladies, Sir Joshua Reynolds, Horace Walpole, the Bishop of St. Asaph, and Soame Jenyns, '& all the conversation People and wits one had ever seen'. On Wednesday he dined with the eccentric Lady Mary Duncan and on Thursday went to the opera at the Pantheon. On Friday he was again out to dinner, the guests including the Duke of Dorset and his mother, Lady Sackville; after some music, he went on to Mrs. Vesey's to meet 'all the *blues*' once more, and, as if that were not enough, 'H. Walpole & I after all the rest were gone sate the Candles out in talking over old times & old operas.' On Saturday he dined at the Royal Academy, sitting next to 'dear good Johnson'; drove on to the Opera; and then picked up Fanny to take her to yet another 'blue party'. As Burney himself asked, 'was not this a good day's work after the usual dayly Labour was over?'[1]

Part of Burney's pleasure in such engagements lay, of course, in his intense enjoyment at meeting 'great men', whether they were distinguished for rank or for intellectual prowess. The young William Beckford of Fonthill had caught that pleasure in a single phrase two years earlier, in a description of a musical evening which he had organized: 'Here were to be seen at one and the same moment, nay, on one and the same bench— H.R.H. of Cumberland rattling away like a dice-box—the Archbishop of York sitting next to Dicky Cosway, the Chancellor listening superciliously to Dog Jennings, Dr. Burney worshipping Lord North, who laughed incessantly. . . .'[2] His growing fame at this time received somewhat strange recognition from his friend James Barry, who depicted Burney in his painting 'Commerce, or the Triumph of the Thames', in the company of such eminent mariners as Drake, Ralegh, Cabot, and Cook. Barry attempted to forestall the puzzled and amused comments which greeted Burney's appearance in this celebration of the Thames by insisting that music had a natural connexion 'with matters of joy and triumph' and that Burney's historical labours had restored English music to an honoured position in Europe.[3] Nevertheless, the appearance of the fully

---

[1] CB to Susan Phillips, 26 Apr. 1784 (Osborn).

[2] J. W. Oliver, *Life of William Beckford*, 1932, pp. 112–13. Beckford's description of this audience may be partly fictitious, cf. Boyd Alexander, *England's Wealthiest Son*, 1962, p. 296, n. 13, but the point of the comment on CB would not be affected.

[3] *Mem.* ii. 340–2. Barry defended his depiction of CB, deplored the fate of his plan for a Public Music School in 1774, and praised his *History*, especially his

clothed Dr. Burney, standing in the water and gazing rather apprehensively over the outstretched arm of a naked Nereid, inevitably excited many comments. Richard Owen Cambridge wrote some verses linking Burney's appearance and an accidental fall into some water by Edward Gibbon; Twining, who saw the painting during a visit to London in April 1783, could not refrain from referring in a letter to the 'Nymphs sporting in the water with Dᵣ B. in the midst of them, playing an accompaniment to them,—I hope, *à testo solo*'; and many years later William Hazlitt was still unable to recall the picture without intense amusement, for in three different essays he described the ludicrous portrayal of Burney, 'swimming in the *Thames* with his wig on, with the water-nymphs'.[1]

In spite of his active social life and his determination to reap the reward of so many years of drudgery, a terrible irony was already overtaking Burney. Some of his close friends had died before he completed the second volume of his *History* in 1782. David Garrick's death in January 1779 had 'crushed the Spirits' of Burney, whom Mrs. Thrale described as his 'Obligée'.[2] Before his commitment to a literary career Burney had certainly owed much to Garrick's support and encouragement in the theatre, but, although that dependence had disappeared, Garrick had remained one of the best loved friends of his family, and Burney felt the loss deeply.[3] In April 1781 Henry Thrale had also died and the arrangement by which Burney received £100 a year for the privilege of visiting Streatham weekly had apparently come to an end. As if he were anxious that as little as possible at Streatham should change, however, Burney had been almost alone among Mrs. Thrale's friends in believing that she should not sell the brewery.[4] It was not long, however, before the atmosphere of Streatham and the happiness of its mistress were drastically transformed.

The period of unqualified enjoyment of life which followed

'animated translations', in his *Account of a Series of Pictures, in the Great Room of the Society of Arts, Manufactures, and Commerce, at the Adelphi*, 1783, pp. 62–65.

[1] *DL*, ii. 224–5; Twining to CB, 26 Apr. 1783 (Add. MS. 39929, ff. 314–15); Hazlitt, *Works*, ed. P. P. Howe, iv. 35, xvii. 223, xviii. 132.

[2] *Thraliana*, i. 363–4.

[3] For CB's account of a visit to Garrick on his deathbed, see *Mem.* ii. 203; his verses on Garrick's death (Berg) are printed in *Mem.* ii. 204.

[4] *Thraliana*, i. 500.

the publication of the second volume of his *History* lasted, indeed, only a few months. In April 1783, in the midst of an 'incessant hurry' of business which was worse than ever before, Burney received the news that his oldest friend, Samuel Crisp, was seriously ill. Fanny, to whom Crisp had been almost a second father for many years, hurried to Chessington, but he died on 24 April at the age of seventy-eight. His death could scarcely come as a shock to Burney and, in any case, he had to repress his own sorrow in an effort to comfort Fanny, who was greatly upset. Nevertheless, Burney had spent part of almost every summer since 1764 at Chessington and although Fanny preserved very little of his correspondence with Crisp, it seems to have been as affectionate and intimate as those with Bewley and Twining. He had valued the older man's judgement and advice ever since 1747 when they had first met and, as he wrote to Fanny, 'His wit, learning, taste, penetration, and, when well, his conviviality, pleasantry, and kindness of heart to me and mine, will ever be thought of with the most profound and desponding regret.'[1]

Burney found it difficult, in the summer of 1783, to abandon his old practice of retiring to the country house where he had written so much of his *History* and, at the same time, it seemed almost intolerable without his friend: 'Chessington and Mr. Crisp had seemed so indissolubly one, that it was long ere the painful resolution could be gathered of trying how to support what remained, when they were sundered.'[2] Before going to Chessington in the summer of 1783, however, Burney learned that William Bewley, whom he had known for only four years fewer than Crisp, was at last about to make a visit to London in August. Although they had met rarely in recent years and although Bewley had become increasingly preoccupied by his scientific interests, their lively, affectionate, and amusing correspondence had not flagged. Bewley's last extant letter, written in October 1782, had indeed lamented the fact that they never met: 'I love your handwriting, were it only from long habit; but I suspect that there are some *associated ideas* that make it more desirable. It is hard, methinks, that you & I, & half a dozen more; (—for, even my catalogue—hermit as I am—

[1] CB to Crisp, 12 Apr. 1783 and 2 letters to FB, Apr. 1783, *DL*, ii. 210–13.
[2] *Mem*. ii. 324.

extends so far)—cannot pass our days together, & commune with each other, instead of holding this distant language; though, sinner as I am, I ought to thank God for this expedient.'[1]

In mid-August 1783 Bewley at last managed to leave Great Massingham, the village in Norfolk where he had spent most of his life. His journey was no carefree jaunt, however, but a conscious farewell to the friends whom he had so rarely seen. A surgeon himself, he was unable to diagnose or cure his own illness, but, as his friend Lord Orford later told Burney, 'He was Himself so much Persuaded of his approaching end, that He told us the very manner in which He apprehended he would suffer.'[2] Accompanied by his wife, Bewley first visited Dr. Joseph Priestley, with whom he had been corresponding for fifteen years on scientific matters, and, after a week at Birmingham, continued his journey to London.[3]

One reason for Bewley's visit to London was to obtain expert medical advice but, perhaps convinced of the futility of it and certainly cheered by Burney's company, he postponed the consultation. Shocked by Bewley's appearance, Burney delayed his retirement to Chessington and the two old friends spent three or four days 'in the same chearful & cordial manner as 30 years ago, when we used, now & then, to have a musical & literary debauch, at Lynn'. They read, played music and saw the sights together, visiting the British Museum, the Pantheon, and the exhibition of Barry's paintings, which featured Burney himself. Most important of all to Bewley, however, was the fact that Burney now took him to meet Samuel Johnson for the first time.

Bewley must be considered one of the earliest and most ardent of all Johnsonians. 'I suppose there are many numbers of the Rambler, Idler, &c. that I have read at least a hundred times,' he had told Burney in June 1779, in reply to the unexpected news that Johnson, who knew of him as the recipient of the bristles stolen from his hearthbroom in 1760, had sent him, at Burney's suggestion, a signed set of his *Lives of the Poets*, inscribed '*For the Broom Gentleman*'. The modest Bewley had been so overwhelmed by this present that he had found it quite impossible to express his 'heartfelt thanks' to his own satisfaction. 'In my distress on this account, I have sometimes been tempted to make so gross a return for his spiritual food, as a fat Norfolk turkey', he told Burney in May 1780, several months after receiving the *Lives*. By the following August, however, he had still not managed to bring himself to his overpowering task: 'not a single line, nor even a Norfolk turkey'. Fifteen months later he was 'quite miserable on the score of Dr. Johnson', especially as he had just heard that some of the later *Lives of the Poets* were now on their way to Norfolk.

In the end, after two years of trying to compose a suitable letter, Bewley was obliged to ask Burney to thank Johnson on his behalf:

I sat down & expressed my feelings on the occasion in *black & white*; but what I had written did not come up to my ideas, & so here the letter remains, & it is now too late to send it, or to write another. In fact, though it did not sufficiently express either my gratitude, or my very high opinion of this last excellent work, yet the language of true, & feigned, gratitude, & of panegyric, resemble each other so nearly, that I was induced to suppress it rather on the latter account than the former; & so I must rely on *your powers*, as my own pen fails me, to represent to the Doctor the true state of my conscience on this occasion.

Although no account of the meeting between Johnson and the 'Broom Gentleman' in August 1783 has survived, we may assume that Bewley at last managed to express something of his gratitude to the man whom he had revered for more than thirty years.[1]

After a few days Bewley went to visit Ralph Griffiths, the editor of the periodical to which he had contributed so many reviews, and Burney set off for Chessington, leaving his friend apparently enjoying himself 'as much as a young man of five and twenty'. Early in September, however, Bewley, who was staying in St. Martin's Street, was suddenly taken seriously ill and Burney hurriedly returned from the country to find that the doctors were suspecting an intestinal cancer. After excruciating pain, Bewley went into a coma on 4 September and died on the following day.[2]

Burney was so upset by the death of his friend that he was

---

[1] Bewley to CB, 5 letters, 26 June 1779–5 Nov. 1781 (Osborn); *Mem.* ii. 180.
[2] CB to Lord Orford [5 Sept. 1783], draft (Osborn).

unable to attend the funeral and, 'quite worn out with grief', had to write to ask his son Charles, now a schoolmaster at Chiswick, to represent him.[1] The fact that Bewley was precisely the same age as himself only intensified his sorrow and he poured out his heart to Twining, the sole survivor of his three most beloved friends: 'He was born the same year as myself:— loved every thing that you & I love—Music—Books—fun—& had an *extent* & *depth* of Science that I have never met with . . . and with all this a humanity, & goodness of heart; & a simplicity of character, enlivened by natural & original wit & humour, which delighted everybody who conversed with him.' Since Twining had never met Crisp and Bewley, it was now futile to praise them, but Burney could not help himself: 'You speak warmly of old friends: I know you will forgive me—But they knew us, & we knew them before a lock was put upon the heart, by experience & distrust; and they had ever since the *entrée*, as *amis de la maison*.'[2]

As soon as possible Burney returned with Fanny to Chessington. Yet that formerly cheerful house was equally haunted by memories and Fanny knew that her father was 'extremely hurt & depressed' by the loss, within five months, of 'his two dearest friends, both of whom had been known to him, with encreasing affection & esteem, for more than thirty years'.[3] Burney had not failed to pay what public tribute he could to the memory of his shy and self-deprecating friend. His son Charles had recently become editor of the new *London Magazine* and he printed a generous eulogy of Bewley in the form of a 'Character of the Philosopher of Massingham', which was written by Charles but with Burney's suggestions and corrections.[4]

At Chessington in the autumn of 1783 Burney worked furiously at the third volume of his *History* in an attempt to forget his grief, for a moment's reflection served to remind him of his lost friends and of his own increasing age: 'I used to laugh at low Spirits & thought it impossible I sh⁴ ever indulge them; but alas! if I did not keep off foul fiends by forcing myself & by

---

[1] CB to CB Jr., 6 Sept. 1783 (Osborn).
[2] CB to Twining, 6 Sept. 1783, copy (Osborn).
[3] FB to Rosette Burney, 12 Sept. [1783] (Osborn).
[4] CB to CB Jr., 12 Sept. [1783] (Berg); *London Magazine, Enlarged and Improved*, i (1783), 258–9.

being forced into employm^t I sh^d sink under them. To see how easily the thread of life is snapped! to feel infirmities dayly increasing—the time of Life—Constitution—& a thousand gloomy Ideas crowd incessantly into my mind and devour me!'[1] London, when Burney returned to St. Martin's Street, was no less depressing. 'You and I have lost our friends, but you have more friends at home', Johnson had written to Burney on 20 September, returning to a cheerless Bolt Court after the death of his 'domestick companion', Anna Williams.[2] One of the most important friendships in the lives of both men, however, was also disintegrating: Streatham had been let in September 1782 and all that it had meant to both of them was disappearing likewise.

Burney did not easily bring himself to realize what was happening to Mrs. Thrale, although, by the time Streatham had been let, Fanny already knew of her love for Gabriel Piozzi. That it should have been Queeney's singing-master who finally brought about the break-up of the old Streatham circle was ironic in itself, for Burney had first heard Piozzi sing on 18 November 1776, two weeks before he was himself engaged to teach Queeney, and he had thereafter done everything in his power to help the accomplished Italian who had arrived in London with 'few patrons & no scholars'. In the summer of 1777, for example, Burney had obtained for Piozzi an engagement to travel with the Duke of Ancaster into Lincolnshire to teach his daughter and to perform himself in the evenings. Piozzi thought himself poorly treated, however, for he had been 'sent first to the 2^d table and kept at a great distance from the Duke & Duchess', and had eventually been forced to barricade himself in his room to avoid constant summonses to appear 'like an animal to shew his tricks'. He had eventually left Lincolnshire protesting that 'if he had left an eye behind him, he w^d not go back to fetch it'.[3]

For a number of years Burney had continued to feel himself partly responsible for Piozzi's welfare and sometimes held small concerts in his home to ensure that the Italian 'sh^d be well heard

[1] CB to Twining, 10 Nov. 1783 (Add. MS. 39929, ff. 324-6; copy, Osborn).
[2] Johnson to CB, 20 Sept. 1783 (Comyn; *Letters*, iii. 70). Dr. Thomas Lawrence, Johnson's friend and physician, had also died in June 1783.
[3] *Frag. Mem.* (Berg).

by real lovers & patrons of Music'. Piozzi's audience on these occasions was not, however, always composed of 'real lovers' of his art, for the most memorable of the evening concerts in St. Martin's Street was that at which Mrs. Thrale wickedly mimicked Piozzi behind his back, while he was favouring the distinguished company with one of his most expressive songs.[1] The irony of this behaviour does not need re-emphasis. In July 1780 she had met Piozzi at Brighton and had belatedly discovered in herself a sudden passion for music, as a result of which he was engaged to teach Queeney singing, while Burney remained her instructor on the harpsichord.[2]

Mrs. Thrale had soon perceived that there were limits to Burney's desire for the success of his Italian friend. By September 1780 she was noting in *Thraliana* that he was 'a Monkey to be jealous of Piozzi, he particularly recommended him to our notice', and later in the month she referred to his jealousy once more.[3] At this stage his irritation was probably caused only by the discovery that Mrs. Thrale could show affection of any sort for a musician other than himself. Having escaped the confines of his own profession, Burney adopted an attitude towards it which was almost identical with that of fashionable society. (Fanny once mentioned as a merit of the singer Pacchierotti, who was a favourite of the Burneys, that he had 'a mind superior to his own profession, which he never names but with regret'.)[4] No one could be more enthusiastic over the talents of a great singer than Burney, but he retained a strong sense of the social status of a musician. His account of Piozzi's unhappy engagement with the Duke of Ancaster deliberately laid emphasis on the fact that Piozzi had been treated very much as a 'mere musician', and Burney himself had acted as something of a 'patron' to the singer.

Burney had not at first, however, understood the change that had begun to affect Streatham after Henry Thrale's death. As Mrs. Thrale's passion for Piozzi became more intense, he had perceived 'a species of general alienation which pervaded all around at Streatham',[5] but he respected Fanny's friendship

---

[1] *Mem.* ii. 101–14. Virginia Woolf described this embarrassing occasion in 'An Evening at Dr. Burney's', *The Second Common Reader*, 1932, pp. 108–25.
[2] Clifford, *Hester Lynch Piozzi*, pp. 187–9.
[3] *Thraliana*, i. 455, 458.   [4] *DL*, i. 435.   [5] *Mem.* ii. 245.

with Mrs. Thrale sufficiently to ask no questions. Once, however, as he was bringing Fanny back to St. Martin's Street for the day, 'he almost involuntarily, in driving from the paddock, turned back his head towards the house, and, in a tone the most impressive, sighed out: 'Adieu, Streatham!—Adieu!' His daughter perceived his eyes were glistening; though he presently dropt them, and bowed down his head, as if not to distress her by any look of examination; and said no more.'[1] The comfortable and cultivated life of Streatham was coming to an end just when Burney was at last prepared to enjoy it fully. The advice which Samuel Crisp had given Fanny in 1780, in answer to a letter describing life with the Thrales, applied no less pertinently to Burney himself: 'Where will you find such another set? Oh, Fanny, set this down as the happiest period of your life; and when you come to be old and sick, and health and spirits are fled (for the time may come), then live upon remembrance, and think that you have had your share of the good things of this world, and say,—For what I have received, the Lord make me truly thankful!'[2] The difference was that, whereas Fanny had indeed enjoyed the best of Streatham, Burney had never quite had the time.

In the autumn of 1783, with Mrs. Thrale defiantly settled in Bath and awaiting the return of Piozzi from Italy, the survivors from Streatham pathetically attempted to create something that might resemble it. Johnson, who missed Streatham more than anyone, now formed the Essex Head Club—or, as Burney called it, the 'Sixpenny Club'—which met at a public house opened by Sam Greaves, a former servant at Streatham, who had 'chiefly attended' Johnson when he was visiting the Thrales. The setting of the club was, as Burney admitted, 'humble', but the members were all 'intimate fr[ds] among the admirers and beloved of the great moralist'.[3] Among them were Daines Barrington, James Boswell, Arthur Murphy, John Nichols, and William Windham.[4] Although Nichols included him in a list of 'constant members',[5] Burney was later 'obliged to abandon poor D[r] Johnson's 6[d] Club in Essex Street mainly for want of

[1] *Mem.* i. 248.   [2] *DL*, i. 323.
[3] *Frag. Mem.* (Berg); *DL*, ii. 235; *Mem.* ii. 261–2.
[4] Hill–Powell, iv. 253–4.
[5] *Literary Anecdotes*, ii. 553.

time to attend'.[1] His resignation did not, of course, take place
before Johnson's death, and, in any case, early in 1784 it became
possible for him to meet his friend elsewhere. A fragment of
Burney's pocketbook for 1784 contains the proud entry; 'Feb[y]
17th elected Member of *The* Club of w[ch] I had notice in a letter
from Eliot the Chairman of the Night at the next meeting.—
Inaugurated by S[r] Jos. Reynolds, D[r] Johnson, & M[r] Burke.
This was at 1st called the *Literary Club* by S[r] Jos. R.'[2]

It may appear surprising that Burney had not received the
honour of election to '*The* Club' earlier, considering the number
of his friends who were already members. A partial explanation
may be the fact that both Johnson and Burke were opposed on
principle to increases in membership,[3] and that Johnson only
reluctantly abandoned the original aim of electing only 'the
1st Man of every profession, if we c[d], to refer to in discussions
concerning things of w[ch] the rest were ignorant'.[4] Sir John
Hawkins, ironically enough, was considered to represent
musical scholarship, and his presence may have been sufficient
to exclude Burney for some years.[5] Burney's election in 1784,
however, was the result of a general agreement 'in ranking
[him] as a distinguished Man of Letters'.[6] During the next
twenty years, until he was confined by ill-health to his rooms,
Burney's membership of The Club was one of his proudest
boasts and few other members can have been more regular in
attendance.

By the spring of 1784 this new honour, which ensured him
regular meetings with Johnson, was compensating to some extent for the loss of Crisp and Bewley and the absence of Mrs.
Thrale. He had also undertaken a new literary labour, having
laid aside his *History* to write an account of the great choral
celebrations in Westminster Abbey in May and June, in commemoration of Handel. The frenzied activity in which this
involved him may also have helped to insulate him to some
extent from the steady collapse of the world he had been so
eager to enjoy. Whatever he may have suspected about Mrs.
Thrale's relationship with Piozzi, it was not until May 1784
that he was 'told all'. That distraught lady herself wrote to

[1] *Frag. Mem.* (Berg).   [2] Osborn.   [3] *Thraliana*, i. 107.
[4] CB to FB, 27 May 1800 (Osborn).   [5] *Thraliana*, i. 188.
[6] *Mem.* ii. 377–8.

Fanny, 'I love Dr. Burney too well to fear him, and he loves me too well to say a word which should make me love him less.'[1] She was not surprised, therefore, that he had 'behaved with the utmost Propriety'.[2] Burney was upset, however, as his daughter told Queeney Thrale in June:

My Father was too much prepared by the universal voice of rumour to be *much* surprised;—yet surprised he still was,—& never speaks to me of the matter but with a sigh for the frailty of human nature!—As he was not called upon for advice, but only told the business in confidence, he treated it with all possible chearfulness & delicacy to *her*,—but he was not for that reason at all the less shocked that she should thus fling away her talents, situation in life, & character;—for thus to quit all her maternal duties is a blot upon it never to be erased.[3]

Saddened by what he considered to be a disastrous step by one of his dearest and kindest friends, Burney nevertheless resigned himself to the inevitable. Mrs. Thrale herself was less surprised than Fanny at his attitude: 'I always *thought* I could manage with Charles well enough, but dear Fanny Burney wonders he softened so soon.'[4] She married Piozzi late in July 1784 and by 4 August was able to tell Queeney that 'Dr Burney has written a most affectionate Letter indeed'.[5] This letter of congratulation was written when he was frantic with worry over his book on Handel and he excused his delay in sending good wishes by the fact that he had been 'shut up in the *Spidery* scribling in the utmost hurry'. His letter was neither cold nor formal, although it inevitably lacked the spontaneous and cheerful intimacy of his earlier letters to her. Sadness could not help entering the letter, even as he sent his wishes for 'every species of happiness wch this world can allow'.[6] Mrs. Thrale's marriage had brought the happiest period of his life almost to its end: Streatham had been at the heart of that happiness and nothing would ever replace it.

Only one beloved friend remained in whom the spirit of those days survived and, having suffered a stroke in the previous

---

[1] *DL*, ii. 257.   [2] *Thraliana*, i. 594.
[3] *The Queeney Letters*, ed. Marquis of Lansdowne, 1934, p. 99.
[4] Ibid., p. 171.   [5] Ibid., p. 176.
[6] CB to Mrs. Piozzi, 30 July 1784 (JRL, Eng. MS. 545. 12); she replied warmly on 2 Aug. 1784 (Osborn).

summer and now deeply shocked by Mrs. Thrale's marriage, Johnson was only a shadow of his former self. Yet he had never, perhaps, been closer to Burney and his family than in these last months. In November 1783 Burney could proudly tell Twining that Johnson had recently been very kind to his erring son Charles (now a schoolmaster and a promising classical scholar), 'speaks of him to everybody with uncommon warmth & energy, for him; invites him to call frequently on him to talk philology'.[1] A little later Johnson made a request to Burney in which, considering his lifelong dislike of music, it may not be over-subtle to discover a peculiar pathos and, at least, a desire to draw closer to the friends who remained to him: 'Not six months before his death, he wished me to teach him the Scale of Musick:—"Dr. Burney, teach me at least the alphabet of your language." '[2] During the summer of 1784 Johnson visited his friend Dr. Taylor at Ashbourne, but he remained in poor health and spirits. When Burney asked him to write the dedication to his *Commemoration of Handel*, however, Johnson readily agreed: 'You shall certainly have what my thoughts will supply, in recommendation of your new book.'[3] During August and September they exchanged letters about the dedication, one of the last, if not the very last, of Johnson's literary labours. By 4 September the final form had been agreed upon and Johnson told Burney that he was delighted 'by finding that You like so well what I have done'.[4]

During the autumn of 1784 Burney was fully occupied with the difficulties and delays of publishing his new book. On 17 November, however, he received a note from Johnson, which if it could hardly have been briefer, could hardly have been more affectionate: 'Mr Johnson who came home last night, sends his respects to dear Doctor Burney, and all the dear Burneys little and great.'[5] It was soon clear, however, that the disintegration of Burney's circle of friends was almost complete and that the death of the man whom he admired more than any other in the world was imminent. Johnson was now seriously ill and Burney called twice to see him early in December, once

[1] CB to Twining, 10 Nov. 1783, copy (Osborn).
[2] Hill–Powell ii. 263 n. 4.
[3] Johnson to CB, 2 Aug. 1784, *Letters*, iii. 191.
[4] Johnson to CB, 4 Sept. 1784 (Coke; *Letters*, iii. 215–16).
[5] Johnson to CB, 17 Nov. 1784 (Comyn; *Letters*, iii. 248).

with Edmund Burke, who remarked afterwards, 'His work is almost done; and well has he done it!'[1] To all Johnson's friends it was clear that the end could not be far distant and Burney 'resorted to Bolt Court every moment that he could tear from the imperious calls of his profession'.[2] On 10 December came the warning that Johnson could survive only a little longer and Burney hurried again to Bolt Court. He could not, however, be admitted to his friend, but on the following day he conversed with Johnson for the last time. Two accounts by Burney himself of this final parting have survived and since both are unpublished they will be quoted at length. The first was written shortly after Johnson's death on 13 December 1784:

We have at length lost poor Johnson! he died as he lived, *en odeur de saintité*—I saw & rec[d] his Benediction on Saturday, and he expired on Monday. He had been so bad for some days, as to be able to see none but medical people, & his constant attendants, the Hooles & Langton; however on my desiring M[r] Hoole to let him know, if there was an opportunity, as he was said to be dozing, that I was in the next room, he soon returned & said he wished to see me—when he, sitting propt up in a great Chair, took hold of my hand & asked after the whole Family, particularly Fanny, who, I told him had been to enquire after him 2 days ago, when he said 'I heard of it but hope she will excuse my not seeing her; for I was unable to talk with her'—& then said 'God bless you!'—after w[ch] still holding my hands he made one of the most fervent & Eloquent prayers that was ever uttered in the last moments of a saint. I w[d] give the world to remember it Verbatim, but it is impossible for memory to do it justice. No one, I think, was by, but his old friend D[r] Taylor, with whom he was in the summer at Ashburn in Derbyshire—whose intellects at present are not very powerful, how ever he may have acquired the favour of poor Johnson in his younger years. When I came away, he said '*come again*!'—though for several days he had taken a final leave of all with whom he was able to talk—& said 'tell Fanny I think I c[d] throw the Ball to her yet'—[& his last words were 'Remember me to Fanny—'] w[ch] encouraged poor Fanny to go to Bolt court next day, Sunday; but after staying more than 2 Hours in hopes of seeing him, Langton came out of his room to tell her it was impossible, as he was too bad to be able to speak to any one—this you may be sure over-set our poor Fan[ny] terribly. He went off on Monday in a sleep, without the knowledge of young Des Moulins, who only was in the room, and imagined him still asleep some time after he expired. Though very uneasy for many years at the thoughts of death, he at last faced it with great courage, & talked of that, his affairs, and Funeral with perfect composure.[1]

In 1807, when he was over eighty, Burney wrote another account of Johnson's death, in which he supplied more details of his last words to him:

When Dr Johnson, a firm believer in the X^{tian} dispensation, & terrified at the approach of death imagining himself unworthy of Salvation, though guilty of no atrocious crimes, & possessed of more virtues of integrity, charity, benevolence & friendship than the rest of mankind—after languishing long in bodily pain & mental despair, 3 or 4 days before his decease, he seemed more tranquil, & prepared to meet his inevitable dissolution with fortitude. Being informed that there were several of his most intimate & anxious friends in the house, wishing, if possible, to see him once more!—before the fatal dart was thrown. He desired to get up, though extremely feeble, was wrapt in a Night gown, & desired that his friends sh^d be called into the next room one at a time in the order they had entered the house, & conversed a few minutes with each—at length it came to my turn to be called and having been so long acquainted with his Wisdom, worth, learning, piety, & friendship—I approached him with reverential awe & heart-felt affliction—He rec^d me kindly and affectionate[ly], & seizing both my hands, uttered an exhortation, to philanthropy, & X^{tian} & social virtues wth the eloquence & energy of a St Cyprian, without fanatacism or impracticable doctrines—& finished by this impressive precept—'Do all the good you can.'—a precept wch I have never forgotten—even the beggars in the street, while I was able to go out either on foot or in a Carriage were never refused a mite if I had one ab^t me to bestow![2]

That Burney did not forget Johnson's last words to him is clear from the number of occasions on which he referred to them in his letters. In 1799 he quoted the phrase, 'Do all the good you can' and added, 'This precept has penetrated deeply into my heart, & I cannot help thinking that my conduct since, on the side of benevolence, has been affected by it in some small degree.'[3]

[1] CB to Susan Phillips [Dec. 1784] (Comyn); the words in brackets appear to have been inserted by FB, although she may only have written over an insertion by CB.

[2] CB to Lord Lonsdale [? March 1807], draft (Hyde). CB's somewhat erratic punctuation has been retained.

[3] CB to E. Miller, 17 Sept. 1799, draft (Comyn); also CB to Latrobe, 31 Oct. 1805 (Osborn); to Lady Crewe, Jan. 1808 (Osborn). William Seward quoted

On 20 December 1784, with the other members of The Club, Burney attended the funeral of his 'dear & revered' friend.[1] His grief was inevitably modified by his awareness of the loneliness and suffering of Johnson's last years, which had sometimes made him a trying companion. 'I am . . . grieved to hear that he is such a raw-head & bloody bones, to his acquaintance', he had written to Fanny in October 1782, on learning of Johnson's behaviour at Brighton, where he was staying with Mrs. Thrale and Fanny.[2] The fervour of Burney's admiration for Johnson is, indeed, all the more convincing in that he never attempted to deny the great man's shortcomings. As he wrote to Twining five days after the funeral, 'I truly reverenced his genius, learning, and piety, without being blind to his prejudices. I think I know and could name them all. We often differed in matters of taste, and in our judgements of individuals. My respect for what I thought excellent in him never operated on my reason sufficiently to incline me to subscribe to his decisions when I thought them erroneous.'[3]

Beset as he was by various literary commitments, Burney almost certainly considered writing a biography of Johnson. On entering the Streatham circle he must soon have discovered that at least Boswell, Baretti, and Mrs. Thrale were given to writing down 'Johnsoniana',[4] and he himself began to follow their example, although only a fragment of his collection of anecdotes has survived.[5] The knowledge that Sir John Hawkins was writing a biography of Johnson can only have increased his desire that a fully competent hand should undertake so important a work. The bitterness of his account, in the letter to Susan Phillips already quoted, of the numerous potential biographers of his friend, who had already appeared by December 1784, can probably be explained by the fact that he himself was contemplating a similar work. Realizing that Susan would have seen long accounts of Johnson's 'circumstances, Funeral, Biographers &c' in the newspapers, he continued:

I will only tell you the Names of these last who are already writing

---

Johnson's last words to CB in *European Magazine*, xxxiii (1798), 241 and in *Biographiana*, 1799, ii. 601.   [1] *Frag. Mem.* (Osborn).
  [2] CB to FB [Oct. 1782] (Barrett).
  [3] CB to Twining, 25 Dec. 1784, *Country Clergyman*, p. 128.
  [4] *Thraliana*, i. 177.   [5] Barrett.

his Life: Sir John *Hawkins*, one of his Executors wth D[r] Scott . . . &
Sir Jos. Reynolds—D[r] Kippis; *Croft* whose life of the poet D[r] Young
is inserted in Johnson's Lives; *Boswell*; Tommy Tyers; The Editor of
the Johnsoniana, a M[r] Cook, who does not set his name to it, but who
suffered Kearsley to advertise it as ready for publication the day after
the good soul's death, & it is to be published to morrow. Besides these
a life of him is publishing every day in one of the News papers. Not
one of these Biographers has to my thinking a single Qualification
necessary for the work he so flippantly undertakes; nor one who
sufficiently reverenced his learning, Genius, & Piety; or who is
possessed of a style & abilities capable of doing them justice. Hawkins
& Kippis are both equally dry & dull—Croft, a fop who imitates
Johnson's style without being possessed of one of his Ideas: ' 'twas
very impudent says Burke the other day at the Club, to take a man
off in his own book'—meaning in his life of Young. . . . Tommy
Tyers is such a quaint, feeble, fumble-fisted writer, as is only fit for
Mother Goose's tales—& Boswell with all his Anecdotes, will only
make a story book, a kind of Joe Miller the 2[d] without address or
dignity of introduction or application in relating his bons mots—and
Cook, if we may judge of his talents by the Johnsoniana, will continue to spoil the best stories he picked up, by want of powers to
relate them.[1]

Burney's obituary notice in the *Gentleman's Magazine* for April
1814 confirms that for a time he thought seriously of writing a
biography of Johnson. After stating that he had been 'in habits
of peculiar friendship with Dr. Johnson, of whom he used to
relate many interesting anecdotes', the article proceeded:
'Indeed, *it is known*, that soon after the death of that Colossus of
Learning, he had some thoughts of giving a memoir of him to
the world; but the subject was so overwhelmed by various
publications, that he relinquished his design.'[2] Burney must also
have known that, with his *Commemoration of Handel* still unpublished and his *History* unfinished, he could hardly hope to be
able to devote the necessary time to a work of such importance.
In addition, he must soon have realized that James Boswell was
capable of something more than 'a kind of Joe Miller the 2[d]',
probably after the publication of his *Journal of a Tour to the*

---

[1] See *ante*, p. 287, n. 1: in the original letter CB enumerated the biographers,
from 1 to 6, above their surnames. Kippis and Croft apparently abandoned their
biographies. The other four were published as follows: Tyers in *Gent. Mag.* liv
(1784), 899–911 and lv (1785), 85–87, and separately in 1785; Cook in 1785;
Hawkins in 1787; and Boswell in 1791.   [2] lxxxiv, Pt. I, 421.

Hebrides in 1785. Late in 1787 he handed over such letters from
Johnson and anecdotes as he wished to appear in Boswell's
biography. His behaviour on this occasion, though mildly dishonest, was not unusual: anxious to be commemorated as an
intimate friend of Johnson, he was reluctant at the same time to
reveal to the public that his friend had written the dedications
to two of his books. Accordingly he omitted or altered passages
in any letters which would give away the secret, most of which
concerned the *Commemoration of Handel* in 1784.[1] To the editions
of the *Life of Johnson* which were edited, after Boswell's death, by
Edmond Malone, Burney contributed additional notes.[2]

In the years immediately following Johnson's death, when his
life and character were discussed, attacked, and misrepresented
by various biographers and, indeed, by any writer who felt inclined to do so, Burney's loyalty remained firm and even
militant. In the pages of the *Monthly Review* between 1785 and
1802 he carried on a discriminating warfare on behalf of
Johnson, never ignoring an unfair remark in the book he was
reviewing or failing to take the opportunity of praising his
friend when relevant.[3] In his old age his intimacy with Johnson
was one of his proudest memories, and it is not surprising to
find that when he met a representative of the literary generation of Wordsworth and Coleridge in person, he should have
talked of Johnson. Already, to Henry Crabb Robinson, Johnson
and his literary ideals must have seemed somewhat remote, but
he was clearly touched by the loyalty of Burney, who was about
eighty at the time, to his lifelong idol:

> The Doctor spoke with great warmth of affection of Dr. Johnson;
> said he was the kindest creature in the world when he thought he was
> loved and respected by others. He would play the fool among friends,
> but he required deference. It was necessary to ask questions and
> make no assertion. If you said two and two make four, he would say,
> 'How will you prove that, sir?' Dr. Burney seemed amiably sensitive
> to every unfavourable remark on his old friend.[4]

---

[1] See R. Lonsdale, 'Dr. Burney and the Integrity of Boswell's Quotations',
Papers of the Bibliographical Society of America, liii (1959), 327–31. Cf. Boswell's re-
marks on the anonymous authors for whom Johnson had written dedications, Hill–
Powell, iii. 1–2.   [2] See *post*, p. 393, and n. 7.

[3] See R. Lonsdale, 'Dr. Burney and the *Monthly Review*', *RES*, xiv (1963), 357–
8 and xv (1964), 30–32.

[4] *Diary, Reminiscences, and Correspondence of Henry Crabb Robinson*, ed. T. Sadler,
1869, iii. 485.

When Johnson died in December 1784 Burney had lost, within twenty months, three of his dearest friends, to whom Mrs. Thrale-Piozzi must be added as a fourth, since she had now disappeared from his life. Of his close friends only Thomas Twining, who rarely visited London, remained; and although Burney's 'acquaintance' had never been so large or so impressive, he did not expect to find new friendships at the age of fifty-eight to replace those of which he had been deprived. Instead, with melancholy never far distant, to the end of his life he fought off the 'foul fiend' by incessant labour and by the pursuit of new ambitions.

VII

BURNEY AND THE COURT: THE COMMEMORATION OF HANDEL AND THE COMPLETION OF THE HISTORY OF MUSIC

1784–1789

I

'H E dressed expensively, always kept his carriage': with these words Arthur Young capped his account of Burney's prosperity and social success.[1] The fine clothes and the carriage which were essential if Burney was to keep his place as a member of fashionable society can give, however, a misleading impression of his wealth. Certainly, as long as his house in St. Martin's Street remained full of his children, before his daughters married and his sons could support themselves independently, his financial resources were always under considerable strain. His literary activities brought him little or no profit and, indeed, the necessity of buying the rare books which were essential sources for his *History* constituted yet another formidable item in his expenditure. Only occasional glimpses of his financial difficulties can be obtained, however, for Fanny d'Arblay would undoubtedly remove most of the evidence. Nevertheless, in the summer of 1779, Mrs. Thrale noted Burney's problems, although her dislike of music perhaps explains something of her pity: 'Poor dear Man! he is sadly pressed for Pelf too I fear, the Times go *so* hard with him; his Book will never pay its own Expence I am confident, & in two or three Winters more—nothing new happening neither—people will be pretty sick of spending their Money to tickle their Ears. . . .'[2]

Although the Burneys, particularly Fanny, were ultimately too proud to let themselves become over-dependent on the generosity of the mistress of Streatham,[3] Burney's letters to Mrs. Thrale frequently thank her for unspecified gifts to his family

[1] See *ante*, p. 272 and n. 2.   [2] *Thraliana*, i. 395.   [3] See *ante*, p. 263.

and it is clear that he owed much more to her, in this purely material sense, than has perhaps hitherto been realized or admitted. That he found it possible—perhaps even necessary—to resign himself to being the recipient of Mrs. Thrale's 'patronage' is clear from a poem which he sent her in March 1778:

> Humiliation ne'er corrodes
> The Mind of those your bounty loads
> But grateful Souls your Boons receive
> With Joy as pure as you can give. . . .
> While some, to whom Fate grants the Purse
> Contrive to make each gift a curse;
> And Conflicts raise in ev'ry breast
> Whether to love or to detest
> The Cold, ungraceful, clumsy hand
> Which Pride & Insolence expand.
> Insolvent, yet I ne'er repine
> At Favours heap'd on me & mine,
> And though both numerous & great
> They no remorse or shame create
> For, by the Manner you bestow
> The Hearts acquire so warm a glow
> Of all who benefits receive
> As makes them feel like those who give.[1]

Even Fanny felt obliged to comment on her father's financial difficulties at this period, explaining that he never invested his earnings, but 'lived chiefly upon the principal of the sums which he amassed' in the hectic months of the fashionable season between January and June. As a result, 'his current revenue [was] almost incredibly below what might have been expected from the remuneration of his labours; or what seemed due to his situation in the world'.[2]

The trouble lay precisely in that 'situation in the world', which Burney was so anxious to maintain. His carriage was more than a mere symbol, however, as he gloomily explained to his daughter Susan in December 1783, as the new season was beginning:

Engagem[ts] come on too, much faster than either my health or spirits can fulfil, without effort, & inconvenience. Every day is

---

[1] CB to Mrs. Thrale, 8 Mar. 1778 (JRL, Eng. MS. 545. 4).
[2] *Mem.* ii. 212–13.

broken into—the heavy coach Jobb begins on Tuesday, at 4 Guineas a week, & 7ˢ the driver! my back aches at the Idea of the number of hours I must fag for this—indeed for the 1ˢᵗ Month all my Profits will hardly suffice—but I am unable to trapes through dirt & wet—& I am more likely to get cold in damp hacks, (wᶜʰ cannot always be got at the moment I want 'em) than in the streets.[1]

While society did not grow tired of music as rapidly as Mrs. Thrale had predicted in 1779 and it remained as important as ever for any self-respecting family to have a music-master for the girls, Burney's profession was still somewhat precarious. In hard times, when an attempt to economize became essential, a family's music-teacher would be one of the first expensive items to be relinquished. Thus, in December 1784, reflecting on the poor state of the 'polite arts' in 'this ruined country', Burney wrote to Thomas Twining: 'It is the same with music; many masters, once in great business, are now wholly scholarless, without any other cause assigned but the general declension of the kingdom. . . . The poor masters are certain sufferers on these occasions. I have felt their bankruptcies a little; but Mr. Burney very heavily.'[2] It is perhaps more than coincidental that, a few months later, Burney began contributing to the *Monthly Review*, receiving a useful supplementary income from his articles.[3]

Although he remained one of the most successful teachers of his day, Burney's financial situation was still precarious enough to explain, quite apart from other considerations, his many unsuccessful attempts to obtain musical appointments at Court. Since 1774 he had been a 'Musician in Ordinary in the King's Band', a nominal position which brought him an income of some £40 a year.[4] After the publication of the first volume of his *History* in 1776, he felt that he deserved a more important appointment. In 1779, on the death of William Boyce, the Master of the King's Band, Burney confidently expected the post. In 1806 he mentioned his galling failure in a letter describing the numerous disappointments of his life: 'I lost the reversion of the place of Master of the King's Band of £300 a year twice. 1ˢᵗ by Lᵈ Hert-

[1] CB to Susan Phillips, 17 Dec. 1783 (Osborn).

[2] CB to Twining 25 Dec. 1784, *Country Clergyman*, p. 127; CB refers to his nephew, C. R. Burney.

[3] See R. Lonsdale, 'Dr. Burney and the *Monthly Review*', *RES*, xiv (1963), 346.

[4] See *ante*, p. 169.

ford the Chamberlain, 4 of whose daughters were my scholars, and who had promised me the place in case of a vacancy; but asking the K[ing] on the death of Dr Boyce, whether his Majesty wished him to appoint any particular person, without mentioning my name, Stanley was appointed.'[1]

Although such an experience left Burney understandably disillusioned about the value of apparent 'Notice & Countenance' from the great—'I still remain a drudge amid the smiles of Wealth & Power', he wrote in 1781[2]—he continued to make every effort to supplement his income. In the summer of 1782, on the death of Joseph Kelway, organist in the Queen's Band and also of St. Martin's-in-the-Fields, Burney attempted to obtain both positions. He lost the election in his own parish church, however, to Benjamin Cooke;[3] and although Mrs. Thrale, Mrs. Boscawen, and William Seward exerted all their influence on his behalf, he was no more successful as far as the Queen's Band was concerned.[4]

When at last recognition of Burney's claims was made, the post he obtained was much less rewarding financially than the royal appointments at which he had aspired; but, at least, the honour came unsolicited, and the circumstances could not have been more gratifying. In December 1783 at Sir Joshua Reynolds's, Edmund Burke, who was Paymaster in the Fox–North Coalition Administration, drew Burney aside and informed him that the post of organist at Chelsea College was vacant; and that, although it carried an annual salary of only £20, he would obtain it for Burney if he desired it. The administration of which Burke was a member was on the point of collapse and although he spoke of the post to Burney 'as a thing he was ashamed of', he knew that this would be his last opportunity of using his power to help his friend.

According to Fanny, her father accepted the post primarily to show that he appreciated Burke's thoughtfulness: 'Trifling as this was in a pecuniary light, and certainly far beneath the age or the rank in his profession of Dr. Burney, to possess anything

---

[1] CB to Lady Crewe, 18 Apr. 1806 (Add. MS. 37916, f. 16; draft, Osborn).

[2] See *ante*, p. 232.

[3] C. F. Abdy Williams, *A Short Historical Account of the Degrees in Music at Oxford and Cambridge*, 1894, p. 136.

[4] Mrs. Thrale to —, 14 June 1782; and to CB, [? June 1782] (Osborn); W. Seward to CB [? June 1782] (Barrett); cf. *GDB*, ii. 324–5.

through the influence, or rather the friendship of Mr. Burke, had a charm irresistible.'[1] Her obsession with her father's dignity, as so often, distorted the truth. Burney's own account reveals not only his appreciation of Burke's kindness, but his eagerness to accept even so small a supplement to his income: 'I thanked him most heartily for thinking of me, & said that I was arrived at a time of life (57) when as it was unlikely that I sh[d] long be able to continue the constant drudgery of a Musical ABCdarian from morning to Night, it was time to aspire at something permanent for old age; I sh[d] therefore gratefully accept of the appointment he so kindly proposed.'[2] Accustomed by now to disappointment, however, Burney 'expected little' from Burke's promise to try to obtain an 'augmentation' of the basic salary. To his surprise, on 18 December 1783, the day before he lost office, Burke managed to secure an increase in the salary of organist at Chelsea College to £50 a year, on the grounds that 'the Organist had no apartments or allowance of coals, candles, or any other perquisites whatever, and the Duty of his Office required his attendance at a distance from London'.[3] A week later the new organist was inducted. Much of the routine work was performed by a deputy, to whom Burney paid £10 a year, although he himself usually played in the Chapel on Sunday mornings.[4]

This appointment, with its small but steady income, served to console Burney a little for former disappointments and to assure him that his deserts were not being entirely overlooked. It could be regarded, however, only as an initial step towards the honours which a man of his eminence in the musical and literary world might properly expect, and within a few months prospects of further preferment were being tantalizingly held out to him. In March 1784 Burney noted in his pocket-book the beginning of what was to be one of the most harassing episodes in his life: 'Mar. 2[d] Dine with directors of the Com. of Handel during its arrangement.'[5]

Burney was referring to one of the most celebrated musical occasions in England during the eighteenth century, the series

[1] *Mem.* ii. 373–4.
[2] *Frag. Mem.* (Berg); CB to Twining, 3 Nov. 1786, copy (Osborn).
[3] Records of Chelsea Hospital, quoted by F. G. E[dwards], *Musical Times*, xlv (1904), 576.   [4] *Frag. Mem.* (Berg).   [5] Osborn.

of performances of Handel's music in 1784 to commemorate the centenary of his birth (although it was later discovered that he was born in 1685, not 1684) and the twenty-fifth anniversary of his death. The concerts were also intended to demonstrate the flourishing state of music in England by assembling a greater number of vocalists and instrumentalists from all parts of the country than had ever been known to participate in a single musical performance; and to raise money for charity, notably for the Fund for Decayed Musicians.

The Directors of the Commemoration of Handel included Lord Sandwich, an old friend of Burney, the Earl of Exeter, Sir Watkin Williams Wynn, and Sir Richard Jebb. The Assistant Directors were all professional musicians of some eminence. Burney's curious status in the musical world seems to have precluded him from the second group, but, as his pocket-book shows, his views were invited at the highest level. Fanny's account of his connexion with the Commemoration is, however, one of her most misleading and idealized versions of a particular episode in her father's career and deserves at least partial quotation in all its attractive simplicity:

Dr. Burney, justly proud of the honour paid to the chief of that art of which he was a professor, was soon, and instinctively wound up to his native spirits, by the exertions which were called forth in aid of this noble enterprize. He suggested fresh ideas to the Conductors; he was consulted by all the Directors; and his advice and experience enlightened every member of the business in whatever walk he moved.

Not content, however, to be merely a counsellor to a celebration of such eclât in his own career, he resolved upon becoming the Historian of the transaction; and upon devoting to it his best labours gratuitously, by presenting them to the fund for the benefit of decayed musicians and their families.

This offer, accordingly, he made to the honourable Directors; by whom it was accepted with pleasure and gratitude.[1]

That Fanny's account of this happy episode—Burney's wisdom and experience respectfully consulted, his generous donation of the profits of his *Account of the Commemoration* to charity —bears little resemblance to the truth is clear from the very beginning of his involvement with the Directors. Such advice as

[1] *Mem.* ii. 380.

he was allowed to offer was probably based on his fear that musical considerations would be forgotten in the desire to gather as many performers as possible for the concerts and that the result would be merely colossal and chaotic uproar. A letter from Twining in June 1784 reflected Burney's opinion that the Commemoration would be no more than a noisy farce as well as his complaints about the way in which his advice had been completely ignored by the Directors: 'I'll be hanged if I did not *wish* that your prophecy—"I foresee that it will be *manqué*"— might be fulfilled, merely for their abominable neglect of your opinions, & hints.'[1] Burney himself later bitterly described the extent of his contribution to the planning of the Commemoration: 'I was invited to meet them . . . to 5 or 6 Dinners; but so far from doing any good, I c^d not edge in a Word—all I had to do was to stuff—drink—& be a witness to their importance & blunders.'[2]

So much, therefore, for Fanny's image of her father as a venerable counsellor on this occasion. Nevertheless, in spite of his resentment of the scant respect paid by the Directors to his advice, Burney, like the rest of London, was overwhelmed by the Commemoration itself. The chaos which he feared was not realized, for the enormous choir and orchestra ('more than five hundred voices and instruments') sang and played magnificently and with the most unexpected precision. The grandeur of Handel's music performed on such an unprecedented scale, the solemnity of the setting in Westminster Abbey, and the presence of the Royal Family and the cream of London society, made the Commemoration an occasion of unparalleled musical splendour, and a source of intense national pride. Three performances (the second in the Pantheon) were given on 26, 27, and 29 May 1784, and so successful were they, and so great the demand for tickets, that the King commanded two further performances in Westminster Abbey on 3 and 5 June. To his amazement, Twining who, like Burney, had expected 'little more than noise & confusion', learned that his friend 'had been *worked* prodigiously' by the concerts.[3]

In one way and another, indeed, Burney was to continue to

[1] Twining to CB, 26 June 1784 (Add. MS. 39929, ff. 334–7).
[2] CB to Twining, 31 July 1784 (Berg).
[3] Twining to CB, 26 June 1784 (Add. MS. 39929, ff. 334–7).

be 'worked prodigiously' by the Commemoration for many months to come. At the end of July 1784 he sent Twining one of the strangest letters he ever wrote, which reveals so much of the complex and troublesome situation in which he had quickly become involved, that it must be quoted at some length. Mere extracts, however, hardly serve to convey the frantic character of the letter, which, in spite of every effort Burney could make to distract himself with other items of news and inquiries about Twining's health and activities, keeps returning in fresh outbursts of mingled rage and defiance to his own anxieties.

The trap in which Burney found himself at the end of July had not at first been at all obvious. So impressed had he been by the Commemoration concerts that, before the series of performances had ended, he had decided to put aside his *History* for a week or two and to write an account of this most memorable of all English musical occasions. Fearing that other writers might have the same intention, he had quickly sketched a 'plan' of his book for the newspapers, 'to prevent others from spitting i' th' Porridge'.[1] At one of the performances at Westminster Abbey early in June he showed it to Lord Sandwich, who was naturally delighted that the great enterprise which, under his direction, had been so overwhelming a triumph, should be described for posterity by the leading musical historian of the period. Borrowing Burney's plan, he took it at once to the Royal Box and when the King voluntarily remarked that some competent hand should write an account of the Commemoration, Sandwich was able to produce it as evidence that he had already arranged for the execution of such an account by Dr. Burney himself: whereupon 'the K[ing] was pleased to say he was glad it w^d be in such hands; & wished to see it, when written in MS.'. Two days after the last performance in the Abbey the newspapers welcomed Burney's intention: 'The Commemoration of Handel is a circumstance by no means below the dignity of the Historic Muse, and it is with anxious pleasure we look forward to Dr. Burney's intended history of a transaction so extraordinary in the harmonic world.'[2]

---

[1] Cf. Dryden's Prologue to *Albumazar*, ll. 38–40:
  'Much like the meals of politic Jack Pudding,
  Whose dish to challenge no man has the courage:
  'Tis all his own, when once he has spit i' th' porridge.'

[2] *Morning Chronicle*, 7 June 1784.

Burney's first intention was to publish only a short pamphlet, selling for two or three shillings, which would describe each of the five days of the Commemoration and would be handsomely illustrated, by permission of the Directors, with the elegant engravings which had served as tickets for the concerts. He soon decided, however, to preface this narrative with a 'Sketch' of Handel's life, many details of which he could describe at first hand as a result of his contact with the composer forty years earlier. Both Burney himself, since he was anxious to resume work on his *History*, and the Directors wanted the book to be published without delay and he accordingly abandoned 'between 20 & 30 scholars' who were still on his hands and retired to Chessington early in June, expecting to complete it within a week.

That expectation soon disappeared, however, as Burney came to understand the problems of writing a biography of Handel and as the scope of his book as a whole steadily increased. Before long he had decided that it should be a quarto volume, selling for about fifteen shillings, which would be embellished with seven engravings and would contain, in addition to the life of Handel, an extensive preface and introduction, and a commentary on every item that had been well performed at each of the five concerts. He had also received permission to dedicate the book to the King, which in itself posed an additional literary problem, although he soon decided to draw on the same assistance with this task as in 1776.

Nevertheless, Burney returned to London with part of his book in manuscript, which he showed as soon as possible to Lord Sandwich and the other Directors, as well as to Joah Bates, who had conducted the huge musical forces at the Commemoration. At this point he received the first of the unpleasant shocks which were in store for him. After the passage from her *Memoirs* already quoted, Fanny proceeded to enlarge on her father's generosity in handing over all the profits of his book to the Fund for Decayed Musicians. Burney did not, however, arrive voluntarily at this munificent decision. The Fund had already benefited by £6,000 from the Commemoration and it had not occurred to Burney that the profits of his *Account* of it would go anywhere else than into his own needy pocket. The following conversation with Lord Sandwich must be placed in the proper context of Burney's financial insecurity:

after I had read my Preface & fragments of the rest to Ld Sandwich, Sr W. W. Wynn, Bates &c—Ld S. said—'you intend giving the profits of this acc^t to the Fund, Dr B.—don't you?'—'No, my L^d—I had no such intension—It will be a drop in the Ocean, after the thousands it has gained by the Commemoration—& yet though little for them to receive, it will be a great deal for me to give—There is not a Bookseller in London who w^d not readily give me a £100 for a Pamphlet on the subject. By paying a Guinea for my admission at each performance, & the loss of 4 entire days business my Sacrifice to the Commemoration & Fund has already been considerable, & the giving up my Copy right to the Pamphlet will make my contribution much higher than my share, or that of any one else.'—'His Majesty expects it'—says my L^d—'you w^d not I dare say be the only one who benefitted by the Commemoration.'—This staggered me—& made me feel very uncomfortable—though it did not convince me that I ought to comply. I fretted afterwards, & grumbled in the gizzard— till tired of both—I made up my mind ab^t it—& perhaps more heroically than wisely determined to sacrifice my youngest babe to please his M——y & their Lord^ps & Baronetships.

Burney's donation of the profits of his book to the Fund, as Fanny stated, was a considerable sacrifice, although the manner in which he did so hardly supports her belief that it 'manifested, perhaps, as generous a spirit of charity, and as ardent a love of the lyre, as could well, by a person in so private a line of life, be exhibited'.[1] The loss of the copyright was, however, only the first of his vexations. The King's desire to see the *Account* in manuscript proved to have been no passing whim and during July 1784 it had to be conveyed to His Majesty through one of the royal pages as it was written. By the end of the month the King had already seen the Preface and had retired to Windsor with the Life of Handel and the account of the first performance of the Commemoration. Burney now hoped to be able to start sending his manuscript to press within a few days and was meanwhile trying rather frantically to keep ahead of the two 'copyists' he had hired.[2] As he told Twining: 'the chief part as [*sic*] been written on scraps of paper with a pencil, *chemin faisant*, in going from scholar to scholar—the instant a sheet is written it is given to be transcribed on gilt paper for the Royal Eye.'

Although the necessity of submitting his manuscript to the 'Royal Eye' was clearly going to delay the publication of his

---

[1] *Mem.* ii. 383.   [2] CB to FB and Susan Phillips, 24 July 1784 (Berg).

book, Burney soon discovered that the real problem lay rather with the 'Royal Ear'. He was well aware that he now possessed an unprecedented opportunity of ingratiating himself with the King, who was taking so intense an interest in the book and to whom it was to be dedicated. If all went well, Burney would be able to expect the next musical appointment at Court as a matter of course. The royal taste was, however, extremely narrow and, in fact, exclusively confined to the music of Handel himself. Burney now found himself in a painful dilemma. Much as he admired Handel and impressed as he had been by the Commemoration, he was not prepared to exaggerate Handel's genius to the detriment of the later German and Italian composers whom he so much admired. The King's enthusiasm for Handel, which Burney had at first hoped to exploit, soon became a source of intense irritation. The situation was not improved by the fact that Joah Bates, the conductor of the Commemoration and the 'mediator' between Burney and the 'Royal Eye', was just as '*intoleratingly* fond' of Handel as the King and, indeed, encouraged his prejudice. In addition, Bates was making it clear to Burney that he expected his own important part in the Commemoration to be properly celebrated in the book.

The unfortunate author began to feel that his integrity as a historian was being seriously threatened and although he could see clearly enough that, if he were to act '*politically & wisely*', he must submit to the taste of Handel's 'insatiable & exclusive admirers', his self-respect overcame his usual subservience before the 'great Folk' and he poured out his anger at both Bates and the King to Twining:

> I see that I am in great danger of doing myself more harm than good by this Business.—however circumspectly I may act. But I will not write like an Apostate—I will not deny my liberal principles. I will not abuse the lovers of the best Music of Italy & Germany, & say that they are only admired *through fashion*, & want of good taste & judgement. I will ransack the language for terms of praise in speaking of [Handel's] best works—& the Manner in which they have been lately performed; but cannot, will not say that there is no other Music fit to be heard, or as well performed.

Nevertheless, Burney was tortured by this conflict between his duty as a historian and his knowledge that all kinds of honours might come to him, if only he could please and flatter the King.

His letter to Twining returned constantly to the problem: 'This one business has put all other businesses out of my head—& if my brain were microscopically examed [*sic*] *Handel* & *Commemoration* w^d be seen clinging to every fibre.'

Most humiliating of all were the attempts by the King and Bates to censor his book at every point where he had felt obliged to make some qualification about Handel's genius. Nor did such 'Handelomaniacs' appreciate his characteristic sense of humour:

neither his M——y nor Mr B. has the notion of a *Joke*—not the most innocent or insipid smile must be put on a single period—, *one key* of Panegyric is all they want.—fine!—very fine!—charming! exquisite! grand! Sublime!!!. These are all the notes (a Hexachord) I must use —Some time or other I'll shew you a passage or two that I have been obliged to expunge, or render utterly insipid, because they smiled a little—Now B. can smile & smile & still be dissatisfied—But then the K— does not like it—Into what a scrape am I got?—I may do myself irreparable mischief—& *can* I fear derive no good—considering the hands I am in.

Burney felt his position to be almost intolerable. The fact that he was being kept in London during the summer, a season when he usually retreated to the reviving 'tranquility & wholesome Air' of the country and when he should have been working on the long-delayed third volume of the *History*, was unimportant compared to the dangers of offending the King or of quarrelling with Bates. Worst of all was the affront to his pride and integrity, the degradation of slavery to the 'opinions & prejudices' of others, or of 'the State of a hireling ministerial Scribler'—'without the Pay', as he added bitterly. Burney's long lamentation to Twining ended with a renewed flurry of rage against the King and Bates ('my God!—what contraction, & childish prejudices —how deaf, as well as how blind are both to real Genius!') and, for good measure, against the Directors as a whole ('Les grands Hommes! qu'ils sont!'). Such anger was, of course, highly untypical of Burney, who was normally devoutly reverent towards royalty and the aristocracy; and he thought it wise to add a cautious postscript to his letter: 'You will instantly perceive that all I have written ab^t his M——y & Bates is rigorously Sub sigillo.'[1]

---

[1] Burney to Twining, 31 July 1784 (Berg).

Considering his defiant and abusive attitude to the Directors, it was ironic that in July 1784 Burney was called upon to act as Chairman of a General Meeting of the Society for the Support of Decayed Musicians and their Families, which had benefited so handsomely from the Commemoration, and which agreed to express its thanks to the Directors and to Joah Bates. Burney himself ('I am not accustomed to public Speaking') had to prepare and deliver a speech urging the Society to be 'more liberal & Charitable' than in the past with its newly acquired wealth. He was depressed by the fact that the meeting was marked by 'folly, & illiberality', but at least he made sure that his own efforts received the publicity they deserved, for his son Charles printed his speech in the *London Magazine* in the same month.[1] To Burney also fell the tiresome task of delivering the Society's thanks to the Directors;[2] and, coming on top of all his other vexations, his inevitable involvement in the quarrels of the Society at this period did not improve his temper.

By August 1784 it had become clear that his book would be delayed even longer than he had expected and he was obliged to fall back on a device to maintain public interest. Late in July he had had 'a single Page composed by the printer—, in order to have it to say in advertising, that it is in the Press & will be speedily published'.[3] On 9 August the advertisement to this effect duly appeared in the newspapers.[4] Burney probably expected that his book would be delayed for no more than a month after this notice to the public. By the end of August he had obtained a noble Dedication to the King from the ailing Samuel Johnson;[5] he himself had completed his manuscript; and the King had 'read & approved' it. Even if the adulation of King George in Johnson's Dedication bore little resemblance to Burney's true feelings, royal interference in the composition of the book had virtually come to an end by mid-August, and thereafter his resentment was gradually replaced by pride in the King's collaboration. In her *Memoirs* Fanny printed two 'critical notes' which the King had sent Burney on passages in the *Account of the Commemoration*, adding that her father, 'unwilling to

---

[1] iii (1784), 73–74; cf. *Morning Chronicle*, 31 July 1784.
[2] The address to the Earl of Exeter is dated 12 Sept. 1784 and signed by CB (Osborn).   [3] See *ante*, p. 303, n. 1.
[4] *Morning Chronicle*, 9 Aug. 1784.   [5] See *ante*, p. 285.

lose their purport, yet not daring to presume to insert them with the King's name in any appendix, cancelled the two sheets to which they had reference, and embodied their meaning in his own text'.[1] Although bibliographers have accepted this statement that the two sheets in which the King's observations appear were cancelled,[2] it is doubtful if this is what actually happened. Burney himself dated the manuscripts of the two royal notes July and August 1784 respectively, explicitly stating that the latter was 'Written by the King and enclosed with some MS. sheets which his Majesty had perused of the Acc^t of Handel's Jubilee.'[3] The book was certainly not in the press in July and probably not until September. In any case, it is worth noting that Burney absorbed the King's observations into his own narrative with hardly any alteration.

In September, when he had hoped to be free at last to retire to Chessington to resume work on the *History*, Burney was still obliged to spend most of his time in London in seeing the book through the press: 'my whole time, thoughts, and summers retreat are gobbled up by it'. His only consolation was the thought of what he would say about Handel in his uncensored *History*. Further contact with the 'noble or gentle' Directors of the Commemoration had, however, largely distracted his rage from the King, who at least knew something about music, even if it was only about that of Handel. He could not say as much of the Directors.[4] September passed in revision of his manuscript and in proof-reading, an irritating way of spending what was usually the most peaceful and productive period of his year: 'considering it is the most vacant time of the year for the real scholaring business, 'tis hard to be so pestered'. The *History* would have to wait yet another year: 'alas! poor Hist^y if it reach posterity, there will be more books wanting than of Livy'.[5]

Outwardly as urbane and civil as ever, Burney seethed within. His temper was not improved during October 1784 when Lord Sandwich and the other Directors wanted to know why his *Account of the Commemoration*, advertised as in the press early in

[1] *Mem.* ii. 384–6; cf. *Commem.*, pp. 80, 105.

[2] A. T. Hazen, *Johnson's Prefaces and Dedications*, New Haven, 1937, p. 31.

[3] C. Hill, *Fanny Burney at the Court of Queen Charlotte*, 1912, p. 46 and facsimile opposite p. 48.

[4] CB to Twining, 1 Sept. 1784, copy (Osborn).

[5] CB to CB Jr., 24 Sept. 1784 (Osborn).

August, had not yet appeared. Burney was able to tell Sandwich that, by mid-October, 160 pages had already been printed
and that the whole book would be ready by the end of the
month. A new problem, however, was being caused by the
engravers, and after explaining it, Burney indicated rather
coldly that he was in no mood to take the blame for the delay:

> The plates I fear will not be ready so soon; it was extremely hard
> to find any artists of eminence who w^d undertake to engrave one of
> them in less than 4 or 5 Months. After preparing the acc^t for the
> press, the correction of the proofs & attention to engravers have
> wholly occupied my time & thoughts . . . nor have I been able to be
> absent from London a whole week at a time since the Commemora-
> tion. . . . I find the pursuit of my gen^l Hist^y of Music impossible,
> while this recent & particular event constantly draws off my atten-
> tion from remote periods of time.[1]

Nevertheless, to placate the Directors, Burney published an
advertisement on 26 October to the effect that the book would
appear 'In the Course of next Month'.[2] Two weeks later, he had
little hope that this new promise would be fulfilled. The large
impression of his book ordered by the Directors—2,000 copies—
was printing slowly, and the engravers were making no better
progress with the plates.[3]

Burney had already discovered, in any case, that he was not
even going to be free to sit through the delay in gloomy passivity.
The main sources for his biography of Handel had been Main-
waring's *Memoirs of the Life of Handel* (1760), 'very deficient and
inaccurate', in Burney's opinion; contemporary newspapers and
pamphlets; and his own reminiscences of the composer. While
waiting for the engravers to finish the plates for his book, however, Burney came across important additional information
about Handel's early life, which obliged him to revise his
biography extensively. He explained the necessity of such
alterations and additions in a footnote to the biography itself:

> When I first began this *Sketch*, several of Mattheson's Musical
> Tracts in my possession having been mislaid, I was unable to consult
> them; but being since found, respect for my readers, and for truth,

---

[1] CB to Sandwich, 14 Oct. 1784, draft (Coke).
[2] *Morning Chronicle*, 26 Oct. 1784.
[3] CB to Sir Robert Murray Keith, 9 Nov. 1784 (Add. MS. 35532, ff. 364-5).

have induced me to cancel several leaves that were already printed, and to new write this part of HANDEL's Life, in order not only to correct the mistakes into which I had been led by trusting to his former English Biographer, but to insert from German writers such other incidents as concern HANDEL's younger years, of which, as we know but little in England, the admirers of this venerable master will be more particularly curious.[1]

While he was undoubtedly pleased to be able to improve his biography, Burney did not view the necessity of such revisions and cancellations quite so philosophically as Samuel Johnson, who wrote to him early in November, 'That your book has been delayed I am glad, since you have gained an opportunity of being more exact. Of the caution necessary in adjusting narratives there is no end. . . . a writer should keep himself on his guard against the first temptations to negligence or supineness.'[2] Burney was never consciously guilty of either 'negligence or supineness', as he hastened to assure Lord Sandwich later in the month when it was quite obvious that he would be unable to keep his latest promise to the public: 'I have cancelled the 1st sheet, new written it, & added 18 or 20 pages of new matter to other parts, deterrés from Mattheson & different German musical writers.' Three of the plates, all by his nephew Edward Francesco Burney, were still at the engravers, but the printed sheets were now ready for the inspection of the Directors. He assured Sandwich that he had not 'been very communicative of my printed sheets or proceedings' to anyone but the King, whose views were still being politely consulted.[3]

One specific instance of the King's continued interest in the book as late as November 1784 can be described. Burney eventually decided to include in it a list of 'all the collectors of Handel's works that come within his knowledge' and he was particularly anxious to obtain details of the manuscripts in the collection of the late Barnard Granville, who had been a friend of the composer. Through his daughter Fanny he was able to approach Granville's sister, the aged Mrs. Delany, who was also an intimate friend of the King and Queen. Mrs. Delany duly obtained the list in November but thought it proper to send it

---

[1] *Commem.*, p. 7 n.; CB to J. C. Walker, 2 Feb. 1801 (Osborn).
[2] Johnson to CB, 1 Nov. 1784 (Comyn; *Letters*, iii. 243-4).
[3] CB to Sandwich, 27 Nov. 1784, draft (Coke).

first to the King, who returned it with his approval and the direction that it be forwarded to Burney.[1]

By mid-November 1784 Burney had completed the necessary alterations and additions to his book, the result being something of a bibliographical monstrosity.[2] His Preface, which follows Johnson's noble Dedication and which is hardly less dignified in tone, expressed all his anxiety to maintain his integrity and self-respect. Having awarded Joah Bates the praise he deserved (and had, in fact, demanded), Burney carefully dissociated himself from the undiscriminating and exclusive admiration of Handel's music from which he and his book had suffered during the summer:

> However my mind may be impressed with a reverence for HANDEL, by an early and long acquaintance with his person and works, yet, as it amounts not to bigotry, or the preclusion of all respect or admiration of excellence in others, wherever I can find it, my narrative will be less likely to excite suspicions of improbability, or hyperbole, in such readers as were not so fortunate as to participate of the surprize and rapture of all that were present at these magnificent performances, and are able to judge of the reality of the sensations described.

Burney added that he would 'reserve the critical examination of the entire works of HANDEL for the last volume of my History', a statement which not only reminded his readers of his major undertaking but hinted that, as he had already told Twining, he would be less tactful and confined in his remarks on Handel when he could escape the scrutiny of the 'Royal Eye'.

The somewhat bizarre appearance of the 'Sketch of the Life of Handel' which follows the Preface is explained by the cancellations and insertion of double pages which had been necessary. The 'Character of Handel as a Composer' and the 'Chronological List' of his works which conclude it must have been added during November 1784, when Burney obtained the information from Mrs. Delany which appears at this point. Such additions to the biographical section were made easier by the fact that the second part of the book, the account of the actual

---

[1] Mrs. Delany to CB, 7 Nov. [1784]; to FB, Dec. [1784], (Comyn); *Autobiography and Correspondence of Mrs. Delany*, ed. Lady Llanover, 2nd series, 1862, iii. 242; *Commemoration*, 'Life of Handel', p. 46.

[2] For detailed bibliographical discussions of the book, see A. T. Hazen, *Johnson's Prefaces and Dedications*, pp. 30–32; and R. A. Metzdorf, *The Tinker Library*, New Haven, 1959, p. 272.

performances of the Commemoration, has entirely new pagination. In this section Burney described in detail the development
of the plan to hold the celebration and then analysed every item
which had been performed on each of the five days of the
Commemoration.

Although Burney's book was once more ready for publication
by November 1784, he was unable to keep his latest promise
that it would appear during that month, for the plates, by now
the sole cause of delay, were not expected to be completed even
by Christmas. Powerless in this aggravating situation, Burney
was in any case distracted from his irritation during December
by the death of Johnson, which has already been described.[1]
Later in the month he was asked to help a young Austrian
harpsichordist, the blind Maria Theresia Paradis, to establish
herself in London, by translating into English verse a 'Cantata',
which had been written about her in German. Burney obliged,
'in the best manner my little leisure for the gingling of Rhyme,
amidst the noise of so many other gingling keys will allow'. His
translation, with a prefatory narrative of the lady's life, was first
published by Burney's son, Charles, in the *London Magazine*, and
thereafter in many other periodicals and newspapers, presumably as part of a deliberate publicity campaign for her first public concert in March 1785. The translation was also published
separately as a pamphlet and Fanny records that 'Dr. Burney
took measures for having this narratory effusion set before our
Queen Charlotte, both in its vernacular and its adopted tongue.'
In spite of Burney's generous efforts, Mademoiselle Paradis
failed to obtain any permanent patronage or post in London.[2]

Vexation over his long-delayed *Account of the Commemoration*
was never far from Burney's mind, however, and in December
1784 a new anxiety appeared: not only was he not going to
profit from the book, but it began to look as though he might
even find himself paying for the expenses of its publication. On
Christmas Day he wrote to Twining:

What bitter histories I could give you of unforeseen plagues in this
business, besides those which from the beginning stared me full in the

---

[1] See *ante*, pp. 285–7.

[2] CB to Latrobe, 5 letters, 29 Dec. 1784–9, Feb. 1785 (Osborn); *Mem.* iii. 21–27. For
more detailed information about Burney's assistance to Mlle. Paradis see Hermann
Ullrich, 'Maria Theresia Paradis in London', *Music and Letters*, xliii (1962), 16–24.

^face! I shall only say, in few, that besides the disappointments of engravers, the grateful Musical Society for whom I have been royally commanded to write have as yet taken no proper measures for defraying the expenses of printing, paper, and plates; so that unless I redeem the sheets and plates, when finished, with my own credit and purse, the book will remain some time unpublished for want of money to pay the artists that have been employed.[1]

This particular problem must, however, have been solved. On 8 January 1785 *The Morning Chronicle* was able to report that 'We hear that Dr. Burney's long-expected account of the Commemoration of Handel, which has been several months waiting for plates, will be ready for publication in a few days. The principal artists in London have been employed in designing and engraving the prints for this work.'

A week later the engraver, who had 'prolonged the Throes & agonies of Parturition long enough to kill both parent & child', completed the outstanding plates. All three were by his nephew, E. F. Burney: the frontispiece, dated 8 January 1785 and two other plates, both drawings of the scene in Westminster Abbey during the Commemoration, dated 14 January 1785. By now Burney feared that public interest in his book, disappointed by earlier advertisements and promises, would have greatly diminished, as he explained to a friend, exploring further his favourite metaphor for publication: 'after going so *long* beyond my time some began to suspect it to be only a *Tympany* . . . & others a *false conception*, wch at length is brought forth not only *out of time*, but when the public is *out of tune*, & every wish & expectation ab^t it faded away'.[2] However, on 17 January 1785, Burney took 'splendidly bound' copies of his book for presentation to the King and Queen. He was honoured with an almost informal interview in the private audience room at St. James's, which he later described in some detail in his 'Memoirs'. Nothing pleased him more than the royal admiration for the many different talents of his family. After inspecting Edward Burney's drawings, the King declared, 'All your Family are geniuses'; and the Queen added that Fanny was 'a very extraordinary genius, indeed!' After expressing surprise at the size of the book, the King discussed with Burney the various performances it

<hr/>

[1] CB to Twining, 25 Dec. 1784, copy (Osborn).
[2] CB to R. Bull [Jan. 1785], draft (Osborn).

described. Having been so infuriated by the royal interference in his book during its composition, Burney now forgot all his grievances and humbly thanked the King for his criticism of the manuscript.[1]

Two thousand copies of the *Account of the Commemoration*, with a few copies on large paper for the King and Queen and the Directors, were printed,[2] but the number of copies sold had, of course, no financial interest for Burney. He was still, however, exposing his hard-won reputation to the critics and, moreover, for the first time he was publishing a book without the comforting knowledge that William Bewley would be protecting his interests in the pages of the *Monthly Review*. It is not, therefore, surprising to find that when he sent Twining a copy of the *Account* he dropped a hint that his friend might like to review it. Twining agreed enthusiastically, assuming that the article should be sent to the *Monthly Review* ('The M[y] Rev[w] is the *thing* —n'est ce pas?'), and quickly got down to work, asking Burney for 'any particular wishes as to anything that I *shou'd*, or shou'd *not*, say'. Although he completely lacked Bewley's misgivings over the idea of reviewing a book by a close friend, Twining felt that it would be wise to include in the review '*some* little objection, or petty criticism, or minikin diff. of opinion . . . if only for a *blind*, that the reviewer may not seem troppo amico'.[3] Burney replied immediately, accepting Twining's 'offer' to review his book and evidently asking whether the article could be written 'by the time M[r] H. mentions'. He had either failed to interest Ralph Griffiths in Twining's review, or else, knowing that the editor of the *Monthly Review* disliked publishing anonymous reviews sent to the periodical, did not even bother to try. 'M[r] H.' must refer to Hamilton, the publisher of the *Critical Review*, and the fact that Burney knew that he could have a friendly review published in that journal supports the suspicion that all criticism of his earlier books in its pages had been the work of Samuel Crisp or of other friendly hands.[4]

Twining quickly wrote an extremely long review, which he sent to Burney on 15 February 1785, with full permission to

---

[1] *Frag. Mem.* (Berg).

[2] There is a copy on large paper in the Lowell Mason Collection at Yale.

[3] Twining to CB, 5 Feb. 1785 (Add. MS. 39929, ff. 346–7); endorsed by CB, 'Answered Feb[y] 8th 1785'.

[4] Ibid., 11 Feb. 1785 (Add. MS. 39929, f. 348).

'amputate' it as necessary: 'cut, lop, chop, hack, hew,—*as* you please, & *when* you please'. Since Burney apparently feared that his earlier grumblings about having to write the book under pressure from Handel enthusiasts might have leaked, Twining assured him, 'I have been so cautious that I wou'd not even drop the slightest hint than [*sic*] any body living had *doubted* your sincerity. I w^d not even *imply* the accusation, by *defending* you from it.' He had, however, abused in passing '*exclusionists*, & the *Handelomaniacs*' and had noted, as he had promised, one small error in the book ('else how sh^d I be a Critic?'). Otherwise the review was such a 'dish of praise', that Twining humorously thought Burney would suspect the flattery had some ulterior motive:

I have but one thing to say—if I have given you *one iota* of com-mendation that did not come from my heart—from my real feelings & opinions—I am the greatest rascal upon earth.—I know you may think that I have a view to the *back-stairs influence*—but I—I'm sure I —I—don't mean—I don't desire—a tight Prebend or so w^d be a comfortable thing to me,—I don't say but *what* it wou'd—but as to that there, or anything in that shape—I'm sure I never thought no more about it than the child unborn.

At the end of his article Twining 'c^d not help mentioning your liberality. . . . I saw no reason why you sh^d not have due honour done you on that score.'[1] Even if Burney's 'liberality' had been somewhat grudging, it had cost him quite as much in hard money as if the gesture had been voluntary.

Twining's article appeared in the *Critical Review* in February 1785, probably cut down considerably by Burney or Hamilton.[2] Elsewhere Burney's book was also noticed with approval. Henry Maty welcomed it with a jaunty and flattering article: 'And here comes Dr. Burney, to relieve, what some will have thought, a dull review, as I have sometimes seen him happily come into company to relieve a dull company.' Maty commended Bur-ney's 'usual industry, accuracy, good sense, and sentiment'.[3]

As for the *Monthly Review*, Burney was safe enough in the hands of his friend, the elder George Colman.[4] Colman, how-

---

[1] Twining to CB, 15 Feb. 1785 (Add. MS. 39929, ff. 350–1).
[2] lix. 130–8.
[3] *A New Review: With Literary Curiosities, and Literary Intelligence, by Henry Maty*, vii (1785), 56–62.   [4] lxxii (1785), 279–86.

ever, seems to have suspected or even known that the 'manly
Dedication to his Majesty' was not the work of Burney for, after
discussing it, he continued, 'Some Critics have traced, in our
Author's graver style, a frequent resemblance of JOHNSON; and
where would be the wonder if our historian's long and intimate
acquaintance with that eloquent author, together with a warm
and deserved admiration of his copiousness and powers, should
often have inspired him with parallel conceptions, and sometimes betrayed him into similar expressions.' Colman detected
the influence of Johnson particularly, however, in a paragraph
in Burney's Introduction to his account of the performances.[1]
Nevertheless, he left no doubt in his readers' minds that Burney's pen was 'the fittest organ to echo to the world their original
design, its progress, and execution' that the Directors of the
Commemoration could have chosen. Memory of the great
musical occasion would long be kept alive by 'so learned and
lively a chronicle'.

In spite of the praise that his latest book received, Burney's
trials and anxieties were by no means at an end. Soon after its
publication his health predictably gave way and Fanny wrote to
warn him to take greater care of himself: 'You were beginning
to be ill that *Court Sunday*, & I did not like your looks,—but
thought them better afterwards; however, to be *never* spared—to
have no respite—toil, hurry, business & visiting succeeding, or
rather *galloping over* one another—I begin to think too much, not
only for mortal man, but for Doctor Burney himself.'[2] Before
long his pride took a severe blow, with the publication of the
satirical *Probationary Odes For The Laureateship: With A Preliminary
Discourse, By Sir John Hawkins, Knt.* If Burney was at first tempted to enjoy the mockery and parody of Hawkins, he would
soon find that he himself was one of the targets of the satirists.
Each of the public figures who is supposed to have composed an
ode to establish his claim to the vacant laureateship is supported
by a prose testimonial from another well-known personality.
Burney, strangely enough, appears as a witness to the poetical
powers of Michael Angelo Taylor, M.P. ('Most impertinently
and unwarrantably', thought Fanny[3]), in an essay, which if not
unamusing, is hardly the parody of Burney's style which it is
evidently intended to be. The gibes which must have hurt

[1] *Commem.*, p. 15. [2] FB to CB, 22 Feb. 1785 (Barrett). [3] *DL*, iii. 493.

Burney followed a discussion of Taylor's supposed ancestor, John Taylor the Water-Poet: 'I shall publish both the Taylors works, with the score of Michael's Ode, some short time hence, in as thin a quarto as my Handel's commemoration, price one guinea in boards.' With even more of a sting, there was a footnote mocking Burney's eventual pride in the King's interest in his book: 'This anecdote was majestically inserted in my manuscript copy of Handel's Commemoration, by that Great Personage to whose judgement I submitted it. (I take every occasion of shewing the insertion as a good puff.—I wish, however, the same hand had subscribed for the book.)'[1]

Burney was not therefore permitted to enjoy the King's contribution to his book, even in retrospect. Lord Sandwich, however, may eventually have provided some compensation, for there is a story, published after Burney's death, that the nobleman presented him with £100, 'which he accepted rather than disoblige his friend'.[2] Since Burney had told Sandwich that he could have sold the copyright of his book for precisely that sum, there may be some truth in the story. Burney, however, was now confident that a larger and more honourable reward would eventually come to him. Twining had shared this hope since the previous August: 'if you are not remember'd for this, & made amends hereafter by some notice or mark of favour to you, or to *your's* &c[a]—I know what I shall *think*, & what I will *say*, any where, & to any body'.[3] Only some royal appointment would sufficiently compensate Burney for the numerous embarrassments and anxieties which he had suffered during the summer and autumn of 1784, as well as for the months of his valuable time which he had so unwillingly taken from his *History*. Nothing could be much further from the truth than Dr. Scholes's conclusion that, 'In every way, then, Burney had a congenial task in the compilation of his *Account of the Musical Performances in Westminster Abbey and the Pantheon in Commemoration of Handel*.'[4]

II

Instead of honours and rewards, however, the months following the publication of his *Account of the Commemoration* brought Burney only disappointment and exasperation. On 15 March

---

[1] pp. xxxi–xxxiii.   [2] *Harmonicon*, x (1832), 216.
[3] Twining to CB, 27 Aug. 1784 (Add. MS. 39929, ff. 338–9).   [4] *GDB*, ii. 71.

1785 the *Morning Chronicle* reported that, 'On Sunday night Dr. Burney's house in St. Martin's-street, Leicester-square, was broke open, and two bureaus plundered of cash and banknotes to the amount of near 300 l.' Twining tried to comfort his friend with the news that, a few days earlier, Sir John Hawkins's house had been burned down: 'the comparison, my dear friend, may comfort you for *your* loss'.[1] The comparison, however, consoled Burney no more than the fact that both the historians had been satirized in the *Probationary Odes*, and he showed little of what his friend Pacchierotti, the singer, described at this time as his 'well known philosophy, ever prepared at any chance of life'.[2] In spite of strong circumstantial evidence, litigation against a former footman did not result in a conviction or the recovery of any of the money. Burney was infuriated by the situation and he listed with great care the expenses of the prosecution and the fees he had lost from his scholars through attending the trial, estimating his losses as £57. 2s. 5d.[3] All ended happily, however, for his eccentric friend and admirer, Lady Mary Duncan, insisted on presenting him with a banknote for the stolen sum.[4]

In March 1785, however, Burney's hopes of prosperity suffered another and much more fundamental blow, which he recalled in 1806 for the benefit of Lady Crewe: 'When the Duke of Rutland was Lᵈ Lieut. of Ireland, Mʳ Secretary Ord had procured me a promise of the place of composer and Master of the King's band in Ireland of £200 a year in case of a vacancy during the D. of Rutland's regency: a vacancy *did* happen, when the Prince of Wales knowing nothing of my claim asked the place of the Duchess of Rutland for Crosdill, young enough to be my grandson.'[5] Dr. Scholes pointed out that, although, according to Grove's *Dictionary of Music*, Crosdill was appointed to this post in 1783, the Duke of Rutland did not become Viceroy of Ireland until 1784.[6] A letter from Twining to Burney in April 1785, however, makes it clear that the *Dictionary* is in error and that this disappointment had only just happened. After lamenting the burglary in St. Martin's Street, Twining added, 'And Crosdill!——Well—many good things are due to you for

[1] Twining to CB, 1 April 1785 (Add. MS. 39929, ff. 356–7).
[2] Pacchierotti to CB, 2 May 1785 (Osborn).
[3] CB to FB, n.d. (Osborn).   [4] *Mem.* iii. 32–37.
[5] See *ante*, p. 295, n. 1.   [6] *GDB*, ii. 325–6; cf. *Grove*, ii. 541.

all this, & I hope they will come. . . . I wish the P. of W. had
been—quiet.—I hope,—I *will* hope,—that *Squire Madge* will *not*
be quiet, 'till he makes you some amends.'¹ 'Squire Madge's '
first opportunity of honouring the writer who had so painfully
devoted his time to the glory of his favourite composer had been
wasted, and Burney must have begun to wonder if he was ever
to receive the reward that he had been convinced for so long
was his due. He had no alternative, when the season came to an
end, but to attempt to forget his latest disappointment in hard
work on his neglected *History*.

Since the publication of his second volume three years earlier,
in 1782, Burney had made some progress on what he expected to
be the concluding volume in spasmodic periods of hard work.
Twining had supported him as loyally as ever and by April 1783
was returning part of the manuscript of the new volume with
his comments and his usual spirited encouragement to unremitting labour:

> Pray go on—let go your bridle—stick in both your spurs—smack
> your whip like a French postillion—gare, gare—there he goes—Lord
> have mercy on us—there's Dʳ Beauvoir laying a great bundle of old
> music in his way to stop him—he'll be killed—he'll ride over him!
> &cᵃ—I told you before, that I want to have you write some ten or
> dozen books more, when your history is done: nice *little* things, that
> will be mere refreshment of badinage to you after the labor 'im-
> probus' of your long work.²

Burney had responded so well to such urgent encouragement
that by the summer of 1783 he was already making notes for the
chapter on the rise of musical drama in Italy in the seventeenth
century, which was in fact to appear at the beginning of his
fourth volume. At last he felt that he had arrived at a period of
musical history in which he could exercise his discriminating
taste to full advantage and in which his research was fully
justified because self-evidently important. It was a great relief
after 'rummaging old Engl. *Madrigals* by your Weelks's—
Kirbies—Wilbies—& Bennets. What a mob of them have I
been forced to score.'³

¹ See *ante*, p. 315, n. 1.
² Twining to CB, 26 April 1783 (Add. MS. 39929, ff. 314–15). This passage is an
imitation of *Tristram Shandy*, vol. iv, chap. xx.
³ CB to Twining [? Aug. 1783] (Add. MS. 39932, ff. 165–6, incomplete).

During the autumn of 1783, when he was working furiously at Chessington in an attempt to forget his grief at the deaths of Bewley and Crisp, he sent Twining four and a half chapters, revised the rest of his third volume himself, and pushed on into what was to become the fourth.[1] By the time he was obliged to surrender his time to the service of the Commemoration of Handel in the spring of 1784, he had probably drafted the first chapter. He was unable to resume serious work on it, however, until July 1785, when he retreated with his family to Chessington.[2] He had now, however, much more to put in order than mere papers and books. His frenzied preoccupation with Handel during 1784 had protected him to some extent from the full realization of the number of friends he had recently lost: Bewley, Crisp, Mrs. Thrale, and Johnson. New friendships had to be made and his affections orientated in new directions; or, if it was impossible to replace those he had lost, and Burney himself suspected that this was the case, the attempt had still to be made.

One acquaintance who, according to Fanny, showed at this period 'an increasing desire of intimacy' with Burney was Horace Walpole, who invited him and Fanny to Strawberry Hill in September 1785. Both host and guests enjoyed the visit of 'a day and a half' and Walpole found Burney 'lively and agreeable'.[3] Burney, however, was looking for younger and less formidable friends. In November 1784, in fact, he had already made such an acquaintance with Christian Ignatius Latrobe (1758–1836), a Moravian clergyman in his mid-twenties,[4] who is still remembered as a minor composer and musicologist. Latrobe had been educated in Upper Lusatia and his knowledge of German was to prove useful to Burney on many occasions, the first of which had been in assisting him to translate the *Cantata* on Mademoiselle Paradis early in 1785.[5] Another new friend to whom Burney was to be attached for the next twenty-five years was Edmond Malone, whom he began to meet regularly after his election to The Club in 1784. When Burney returned to London in October 1785 he was suffering from the

---

[1] Ibid., 10 Nov. 1783 (Add. MS. 39929, ff. 324–6).

[2] *Queeney Letters*, ed. Marquis of Lansdowne, p. 111.

[3] Walpole to CB, 6 Sept. 1785 (Comyn; *DL*, ii. 483); Walpole, *Letters*, ed. Mrs. Paget Toynbee, xiii. 320; *Mem.*, iii, 64–70 (where the visit is misdated 1786); *Queeney Letters*, ed. Lansdowne, p. 114.   [4] *DL*, ii. 267.   [5] See *ante*, p. 309.

rheumatism which so often accompanied or followed periods of intense literary activity and which on this occasion caused 'pain, soreness, want of appetite, & all but want of sleep—wch even Laudanum does not give one'.[1] Confined to his room, he was nevertheless happy to answer a query from Malone about a musical term in *Twelfth Night*, the text of which Malone was preparing for his edition of Shakespeare. As he had written the section on music in Shakespeare's plays for his *History* at least two years earlier, Burney was able to supply Malone with some learned observations on the subject.[2]

Burney recovered from his rheumatism late in 1785 only just in time to plunge into his busiest season, work on the *History* being hindered as usual by 'the early & late hours wch business & other engagem^ts oblige me to keep. Dinners I am now obliged to deny myself, except a snap at home or in the Coach; but blue-stocking parties, & Consorts of music were never more rife than at present.'[3] Another blow to his efficiency and will to work on his *History* was the marriage of his 'librarian', his daughter Charlotte, to Clement Francis in February 1786. Burney seems to have depended heavily on her knowledge of his books and manuscripts and on her willingness as an amanuensis. Her departure hampered him for several months, and some idea of her responsibilities and usefulness to her father can be gathered from a description which she had sent her sister Susan in 1783 of an attempt to clean out and rearrange his study:

> I have had the pleasing & *recreative* task of finding new places (& places at Court are not more difficult to be met with) for every Book & paper, the ponderous weight of which, altogether, has *well nigh* worn the wooden legs of the old table to the stumps—so that I have been in an *abyss of literature* & at the most grievous *non plus* for new plans for these Books & papers, than for time to do anything for myself!—I have been in a situation only to be enjoyed by some of the fogrum codgers of the Royal Society; surrounded by learned papers, & fusty Books, Folios, Quartos, & Duodecimos up to my chin, & not knowing which way to turn for the depth of my Father's literary property that I have had to dig into, & investigate.[4]

---

[1] CB to FB, 31 Oct. 1785 (Osborn).

[2] CB to Malone, 17 Oct. 1785 (transcript in Scholes Papers, Osborn); Malone to CB, 15 Oct. (Folger) and 17 Oct. 1785 (Comyn). See *Hist. Mus.* iii. 334–44.

[3] CB to Charlotte Francis, 25 Feb. 1786 (Barrett).

[4] Charlotte Burney to Susan Phillips, 25–26 Oct. 1783 (Barrett).

Charlotte's facetious reference to the difficulty of obtaining places at Court had acquired some bitter irony by 1786, when Burney's thoughts were once more directed towards Windsor. In July 1785 the Duchess of Portland, the close friend of Fanny's acquaintance, Mrs. Delany, had died, and the King and Queen had sympathetically provided Mrs. Delany with a pension and a furnished house at Windsor.[1] Later in the year Fanny went to stay with the old lady and inevitably met the King and Queen during their visits to inquire about their friend's health.[2] Fanny did not exaggerate her father's satisfaction at this situation when she later wrote that 'The pleasure with which Dr. Burney received the details now transmitted to him, of the favour with which his daughter was viewed at Windsor, made a marked period of parental satisfaction in his life'; and that he read her letters describing her three weeks at Windsor 'with the highest vivacity . . . to almost all his confidential friends'.[3] Part of his pleasure was caused by the fact that, in spite of all his disappointments, it seemed that the King and Queen had not entirely forgotten his merit and deserts. Fanny let him know, for example, that on 3 December the Queen had said of Burney to Mrs. Delany, 'I think him . . . a very agreeable and entertaining man.' The King asked Fanny about her father's literary activities and Fanny herself mentioned him whenever a good opportunity presented itself.[4] Once more Burney must have felt certain that the next musical appointment at the royal disposal would be his.

A few months later he was able to discover whether his hopes had been justified. On 21 May 1786 he learned of the death of John Stanley, the blind organist who had been Master of the King's Band since the death of Boyce in 1779. Disappointed on that occasion, Burney's expectations soared once more, and early on the following day, a Sunday, he hastened to obtain the advice of his friend Leonard Smelt, who had been deputy-governor to the royal princes until 1781 and who now, as deputy-ranger of Richmond Park, remained a favourite of the King: 'Mr. Smelt . . . counselled him to go instantly to Windsor, not to address the King, but to be seen by him. "Take your daughter," he said, "in your hand, and walk upon the terrace.

---

[1] FB to CB, 24 Aug. 1785, *DL*, ii. 289–92; Hemlow, pp. 194–5.
[2] *DL*, ii. 300–49.   [3] *Mem.* iii. 59, 61–62.   [4] *DL*, ii. 311, 323, 342–3.

The King's seeing you at this time he will understand, and he is more likely to be touched by a hint of that delicate sort than by any direct application." '

Burney followed this advice and went to Windsor immediately, accompanied by Fanny. In separate parties, they both attended the royal promenade that evening but, although the King and Queen spoke to Fanny, they merely bowed to Burney. Both he and his daughter found the situation extremely embarrassing, and almost humiliating:

my poor father occasionally joined me; but he looked so conscious and depressed, that it pained me to see him. There is nothing that I know so very dejecting as solicitation. I am sure I could never, I believe, go through a task of that sort. My dear father was not spoken to, though he had a bow every time the King passed him, and a curtesy from the Queen. But it hurt him, and he thought it a very bad prognostic; and all there was at all to build upon was the graciousness shown to me. . . .

The expedition to Windsor was, in fact, futile, for Burney learned on his return to London the same evening that Lord Salisbury, the Lord Chamberlain, had appointed William Parsons to the Mastership as soon as he heard of Stanley's death.[1]

Burney was probably not exaggerating when he later wrote that the hasty appointment of Parsons by Lord Salisbury was made 'for fear I sh^d be named to the place by the K[ing] who wished I sh^d have it, and I was expected by all of the musical profession to be Stanley's successor'.[2] Certainly Burney was not alone in expecting that he would obtain the post. Mrs. Boscawen wrote to Mrs. Delany, 'I long to know your opinion of Dr. Burney's success, which I am sure has your good wishes, for the love you bear to his amiable daughter. I heard they were both at Windsor last Sunday, and I have great hopes that His Majesty *will* think him worthy to succeed the late Mr. Stanley.' Having learned of Burney's failure, she wrote four days later, 'I am sure you regret with me that *Lord Salisbury* had *a favourite* amongst the musical people, so as not to prefer *the most worthy*, and Dr. Burney is thus esteemed by so many people that I do not wonder they have given him the name of "the hare with many friends" '.[3]

---

[1] *DL*, ii. 356–60; *Mem*. iii. 71–78.
[2] See *ante*, p. 295, n. 1; this quotation is from the draft (Osborn).
[3] *Correspondence of Mrs. Delany*, ed. Llanover, 2nd series, iii. 352, 355; the reference

The fact that John Wolcot, the prolific satirist who wrote under the name of 'Peter Pindar', described Burney's failure to obtain the post in his *Ode upon Ode* suggests that the competition for the Mastership had been a subject of public interest. After describing the gracious reception which continental royalty had given the 'musty music-hunter . . . Much travel'd BURNEY', Wolcot contrasted with it the cold treatment which he had received in his own country:

> For, ere to SALISBURY's house the Doctor came—
> To get, as ODE-SETTER, enroll'd his name—
>   Behold! behold the *wedding was gone by*.
>
> Ah! how unlucky that the prize was lost!
>   PARSONS, who, daring, dash'd thro' thick and thin—
>   ECLIPSE the second!—got like lightning *in*,
> When BURNEY just had reach'd the *distance post*.[1]

Wolcot added that the 'mortified' Burney still generously admired 'his rival's art', and Fanny later confirmed that her father felt no resentment against Parsons.[2]

Burney had not been deceiving himself, however, in believing that the King would have given him the Mastership of the Band, had not Salisbury acted so hastily. Three years later, during his madness, the King returned to the subject in the course of a long and strange conversation with Fanny:

> He now spoke of my father, with still more kindness, and told me he ought to have had the post of Master of the Band, and not that little poor musician Parsons, who was not fit for it. 'But Lord Salisbury,' he cried, 'used your father very ill in that business, and so he did me! However, I have dashed out his name, and I shall put your father's in,—as soon as I get loose again!' . . .
>
> 'And what,' cried he, 'has your father got, at last? nothing but that poor thing at Chelsea? Oh fie! fie! fie! But never mind! I will take care of him! I will do it myself!'[3]

There are other indications, however, that the King was displeased by Salisbury's precipitate action and that he thought

is to Gay's fable, 'The Hare and Many Friends', in which the hare—'Her care was never to offend; | And every creature was her friend'—is politely deserted by the other animals in her hour of need.

¹ *Ode upon Ode: or, A Peep at St. James's*, 7th edn., 1787, pp. 38–39.
² *Mem.* iii. 78–79.   ³ *DL*, iv. 249.

highly enough of Burney to wish to make him some immediate amends for his new disappointment. The latest in Burney's long series of failures to obtain a royal post was followed so quickly by Fanny's summons to Court that it is surprising that biographers of the family have seen no connexion whatsoever between the careers of father and daughter at this period. It seems never to have been suggested, likewise, that the offer of a place at Court to Fanny came as anything but a complete surprise to the Burneys. Certainly, little evidence remains to indicate that Burney had been expecting such an honour for his daughter, but Fanny's horror of 'solicitation' may serve to explain its absence. Twining, it will be remembered, had hoped in August 1784 that the compensation for Burney's painful efforts on behalf of the royal taste for Handel would be 'some notice or mark of favour to you, or to *your's*'.[1] In January 1785 the Queen had remarked, when Burney delivered the royal copies of his *Commemoration of Handel*, that she thought Fanny 'a very extraordinary genius, indeed!'[2] Burney must have described this royal audience to Twining who exclaimed, 'I grieve for Miss B.! I wish the Queen knew what she is, *besides* being a genius.'[3] Although too heavy a burden should not be placed on so cryptic a remark, it would appear that Burney had been hoping for a royal post, if not for himself, for his celebrated daughter, who was now approaching middle age and whose chances of marriage were diminishing. His delight at the notice she received from the King and Queen later in 1785, when she was staying with Mrs. Delany, could bear the same interpretation.

In any case, it was clear enough at the time that the honour bestowed on Fanny in June 1786 was intended as some consolation to her father. Three weeks after Burney's abortive expedition to Windsor with Fanny, Leonard Smelt told Fanny that 'his Majesty's own intentions had by no means been fulfilled' by the election of Parsons, and, later in the same evening, explained that he had been commissioned to offer her a place 'in the private establishment of the Queen'. Smelt left no doubt in Fanny's mind that this honour was 'an intended and benevolent mark of goodness to her father himself, that might publicly manifest how little their Majesties had been consulted, when

---

[1] See *ante*, p. 314.   [2] See *ante*, p. 310.
[3] Twining to CB, 11 Feb. 1785 (Add. MS. 39929, f. 348).

Dr. Burney had again so unfairly been set aside'.[1] In another account of her conversation with Smelt Fanny stated that he pointed out to her that there were 'thousands of offered candidates . . . who were waiting and supplicating for places in the new-forming establishment' and that in such a position 'you may have opportunities of serving your particular friends,— especially your father,—such as scarce any other could afford you'.[2] The connexion was obvious to Lady Llanover: 'King George III. and Queen Charlotte wished to make Dr. Burney some amends for the disappointment of Lord Salisbury's not having appointed him Master of the Queen's band, which they considered he had a claim to expect. Mr. Smelt suggested the possibility of benefiting Dr. Burney *through his daughter*.'[3]

It is worth stressing that Fanny's appointment was offered as some sort of consolation for Burney's previous disappointments, both because recent biographers have ignored the fact and because Burney's subsequent conduct is hard to understand unless it is seen in this context. Although Fanny was extremely depressed by the prospect of leaving her family and friends for permanent imprisonment in the Court, she left the final decision to her father, and tried to conceal her own distaste for the honour conferred upon her. There was no question, however, in Burney's mind about the right course of action. His delight knew no bounds. 'I cannot even to my father utter my reluctance,' Fanny wrote, '—I see him so much delighted at the prospect of an establishment he looks upon as so honourable.'[4] On 19 June 1786 she was interviewed by the Queen and offered the position of Second Keeper of the Robes to Her Majesty. That his daughter should refuse such an invitation was inconceivable to Burney, as Fanny complained to her brothers and sisters: 'To have declined such a proposal would . . . have been thought madness & folly,—nor, indeed, should I have been *permitted* to decline it, without exciting a displeasure that must have made me quite unhappy.'[5]

Her brother Charles shared his father's enthusiasm at the great opportunity for family advancement which now lay before

---

[1] *Mem.* iii. 80–81.   [2] *DL*, ii. 363–4.
[3] *Correspondence of Mrs. Delany*, ed. Llanover, 2nd series, iii. 360. The Mastership in question was of the King's, not the Queen's, Band.
[4] *DL*, ii. 365.   [5] FB to Esther Burney, June 1786 (Berg).

them; yet he also sympathized with Fanny, wishing that their
father had weighed the matter 'with coolness, and deliberation,
and that your feelings had been more effectually considered'.[1]
Burney, however, had no intention either of cooling down or of
sympathizing with any misgivings on the part of his daughter.
Macaulay hardly exaggerated when he wrote,

> Dr Burney was transported out of himself with delight. Not such
> are the raptures of a Circassian father who has sold his pretty
> daughter well to a Turkish slave-merchant. Yet Dr Burney was an
> amiable man, a man of good abilities, a man who had seen much of
> the world. But he seems to have thought that going to court was like
> going to heaven; that to see Princes and Princesses was a kind of
> beatific vision; that the exquisite felicity enjoyed by royal persons
> was not confined to themselves, but was communicated by some
> mysterious efflux of reflection to all who were suffered to stand at
> their toilettes, or to bear their trains.[2]

Burney undoubtedly felt an almost religious reverence for
royalty; but he also knew that his whole family might expect to
benefit from Fanny's appointment. Above all, the King and
Queen had at last recognized his achievements and merits, and
after so many humiliating failures to obtain royal posts he was
not prepared to let anything stand in the way of his accepting
the present honour on behalf of his daughter. He was not a cruel
man and normally he was acutely sensitive to the feelings of
others, particularly of his children. Nor, indeed, was he consciously cruel on this occasion, for his excitement rendered him
temporarily insensitive to all other considerations. His inability
to communicate with his pathetically obedient daughter is clear
from his own description of their arrival at Windsor on 17 July
1786, the day on which Fanny entered royal service. Grimly
determined that nothing should prevent him from delivering
Fanny to the Royal Lodge, he still feared to the very last moment that it was all too good to be true: 'a long series of dis-
appointm[ts] rendered me sceptical & indeed incredulous ab[t]
every thing that concerns the favours of fortune & the patronage
of the great. . . . I durst not venture to regard the whole but as a
flattering dream from w[ch] misfortune, as usual, w[d] soon wake
me to lament its want of reality.'

---

[1] CB Jr. to FB [1786] (Osborn).   [2] *Edinburgh Review*, lxxvi (1843), 545.

Mere human frailty, at any rate, was not going to prevent Fanny from reaching her destination. Although she found their short walk from Mrs. Delany's house to the Royal Lodge, in Burney's own words, 'so formidable that I feared she would not be able to get thither'; although she 'turned pale, her lips trembled, & she found herself so ill that it was with the utmost difficulty she reached the lodge', there could be no question of turning back or of reflecting on the reasons for these signs of distress. The kindness of the Queen and the members of her household helped to calm Fanny and she did her best to conceal her wretchedness from her father, who eventually left in the highest spirits, rejoicing in the congratulations of all he met. As he wrote afterwards to Smelt, 'tho' I have been so fortunate as to marry 3 of my daughters to worthy & good Husbands, I never gave one of them *away* with the pride or pleasure I felt on Monday'.[1]

A marital simile occurred also to the dejected Fanny at the same time: 'I am *married*, my dearest Susan—I look upon it in that light—I was averse to forming the union, and I endeavoured to escape it; but my friends interfered—they prevailed—and the knot is tied. What then now remains but to make the best wife in my power? I am bound to it in duty, and I will strain every nerve to succeed.'[2] Only her father's exuberant pleasure at her new career helped to make her unhappiness bearable. Re-reading the letters which he wrote to her at this period many years later, she seems, however, to have been somewhat embarrassed by the material aspects of his delight. Two days after her immurement at Windsor, he wrote to her:

I see—& what is still more important to you & me—*you* see, a very comfortable, ⟨*deletion*⟩ magnificent prospect before you. Enjoy it in its full extent, and do all that your most warm & upright heart can dictate to make yourself useful & acceptable to your most excellent Royal Mistress, & I trust your life will be as happy, as well as splendid, as the most flattering dreams c^d suggest. I came away much comforted with these Ideas. . . .[3]

Fanny thought it necessary to delete various phrases in this passage, but 'magnificent' and 'as well as splendid', expressing

[1] CB to Smelt [21 July 1786], draft (Osborn; and, altered by FB, *Mem*. iii. 93–96).
[2] *DL*, ii. 382. [3] CB to FB, 19 July 1786 (Osborn).

Burney's material expectations for Fanny and her family, can still be read.

Although he spent the summer of 1786 working on the *History* at Chessington and visiting his brother-in-law Arthur Young in Suffolk,[1] Burney's thoughts were never far from Windsor. An event like the attempted assassination of the King early in August 1786 brought him rapidly back to London to make a loyal appearance at the next royal drawing-room.[2] As the summer passed, he began to reflect in a more characteristically paternal way about Fanny's new appointment. She dutifully tried to conceal her distress from him and he eagerly accepted her every effort at cheerfulness at its face value. Only when she bravely, if rather ambiguously, wrote to assure him that 'officially all goes on quite well & comfortably', did he admit to himself the misgivings which he had suppressed earlier and he replied with unintended irony: 'I sh^d have been broken hearted, had it been otherwise. . . . Honour, & distinction are something, in union with comfort, but without it, of little value in the estimation of humble & tranquil minds.'[3] When she received this letter Fanny was already so distressed by her first experiences of the cruelty of her superior, Mrs. Schwellenberg, 'that nothing but my horror of disappointing, perhaps displeasing, my dearest father, has deterred me, from the moment that I made this mortifying discovery, from soliciting his leave to resign'.[4]

With Fanny so honourably and, as he thought, happily settled, he turned his attention once more to his *History*, anxious 'lest I sh^d never be able to terminate a Work that has employed so much of my time & thoughts'. As Twining had always encouragingly predicted, once Burney reached the seventeenth century, materials were abundant, the music under discussion was at last almost fit for the attention of men of taste and he found it possible to write rapidly and enthusiastically. It must already have been clear, however, that he would need more than one volume to complete his great undertaking, for by September 1786 he was half-way through what was to become the second chapter of the fourth volume. Sometimes he felt that his colossal labour would never come to an end and he shared

---

[1] CB to FB, 31 July 1786 (Osborn).   [2] Ibid., 5 Aug. 1786 (Osborn).
[3] Ibid., 4 Sept. 1786 (Osborn).   [4] *DL*, iii. 10.

with Twining a dread of 'procrastination and age stealing on, and the feeling of being busied about what one may never finish, and of sacrificing "good days that might be better spent" to—I know not what. . . .'[1] He was cheered, however, by the fact that he was now writing a chapter on the development of oratorio, which was 'His M[ajesty]'s favourite Music',[2] and he worked with loyal zeal during the autumn of 1786, waiting only until he reached Handel before attempting to exploit the royal enthusiasm for that composer which had irritated him so much two years earlier.

Unsolicited royal interest in his writings caught him by surprise, however, providing him with several days of anguish in October 1786 and Fanny's *Diary* with one of the most acute of the anxieties recorded in that anthology of embarrassment. Late in September Fanny wrote to ask her father to lend her a copy of his *German Tour* for a 'loud lecture': presumably to be read aloud to the Queen or the Princesses if the opportunity arose. Burney complied with this request with some misgivings, for the book contained many adverse comments on travelling conditions in Germany and, worst of all, Louis Devisme's disastrous remark on German lack of genius.[3] He had found 'a copy of the pages reprinted'—evidently the second edition from which Devisme's comment was omitted—but, considering the origins of the British Royal Family, Burney still feared that the revised version 'w^d not go down well': 'I was betrayed by the late Mr Devisme to make a *national* reflection on the dulness of the Germans, wch they can never forgive. & indeed it was unjust & inconsistent. . . . It was flippant & offensive, & I long to make a public recantation of my Errors [&] rash declaration.' His admiration for so much German music and the kind treatment he had received in many German cities made this 'uncharitable & unjust conclusion very indefensible'. This avowal of his error, however, would avail nothing, he feared, if any member of the Royal Family should ever read similarly offensive passages in his book. He could not reject an opportunity of bringing his works to royal attention, but the book must 'be guardedly read, & previously prepared', and he himself carefully marked in pencil

[1] Twining to CB, 19 Oct. 1786, *Country Clergyman*, p. 139.
[2] See *ante*, p. 326, n. 3.
[3] See *ante*, pp. 124–7.

the sections of the two volumes which should be particularly avoided.[1]

Two weeks later his worst fears were fulfilled when the Queen suddenly asked Fanny to lend her copy of the *German Tour* to Princess Elizabeth. Although this request was intended as a compliment, Fanny was thrown into utter confusion—' 'tis all over with us for ever!'—but after appearing, as she realized, almost rudely hesitant, she brought the volumes to the Queen, 'out of breath, both with fear and consciousness'. Nervously she tried to explain that her father regretted many of the observations in his book, and that he was actually revising the very copy she had in her possession. By this time the King had appeared, and both he and the Queen good-naturedly began to inquire about the pencil marks in the book and to ask why Burney had sent his daughter his own marked copy. As soon as she had recovered from this hair-raising interview, Fanny sent a long account of her 'panic' to her father.[2]

Burney, who was now working 'incessantly' on the *History of Music* in London, read Fanny's report with horror: 'I trembled all the time I read your letter, at the tremendous situation in wch a strange concurrence of circumstances had thrown you.' He thought Fanny's attempted explanation of his pencil marks 'truly magnanimous & Heroic' and after discussing various other explanations which could be offered, apprehensively asked for further news of the situation.[3] Fortunately Burney's *German Tour* was not quite as important in the lives of the King and Queen as he and Fanny feared. A further ludicrous misunderstanding occurred, nevertheless, when the books reached their original destination: 'a most ridiculous mistake followed, from the marks made by my dear father: the Princess Elizabeth told Miss P[ort] she was going to read Dr. Burney's *German Tour*. "And I am quite delighted," she added, "that I have Miss Burney's set, with all the marks of her favourite passages!" '[4] This harrowing experience presumably induced Burney to make the long and abject apology which appears towards the end of the fourth volume of his *History* and which concludes with the assurance that he was 'as angry with myself as the most

[1] CB to FB, 2 Oct. 1786 (Osborn).
[2] FB to CB, 16 Oct. 1786, *DL*, iii. 72–76.
[3] CB to FB, 17 Oct. 1786 (Osborn).   [4] *DL*, iii. 76–77.

patriotic German can be, for ever having given admission to such a reflection' as Devisme's opinion.[1]

By November 1786 the turmoil caused by this narrow escape in Burney's loyal heart had subsided, and he felt that the time had come for him to attempt to obtain 'notice' from their Majesties. He was able to see Fanny whenever the Royal Family came to town, but he realized that he was more likely to enjoy an informal and protracted encounter with the King by visiting Fanny at Windsor. He was not insensitive to the possible embarrassments of such plans: 'there is something formidable in the throwing one's self in the way. It is like forcing the cabinet. And then if one goes in expectation of *Notice* which is not taken, there is a kind of let down of Pride so many pegs, that one is out of humour wth one's self.' In addition, frequent attendance at Windsor ostensibly to see Fanny was impossible without accommodation in the neighbourhood, as he had already realized on one occasion when the Queen suggested to Fanny that he stay to dinner at Windsor with her. Two acquaintances, Horace Walpole and Mrs. Garrick, lived close at hand, but his pride prevented him from using them: 'They are choice & select in the subjects of their hospitality, & I never loved to receive proofs of anybody's hospitality, but as a sort of favour done to *them.*' The happiest solution would be a spare bed, when possible, with the Smelts, who lived at Kew in a house recently given to them by the King, whose partiality for Smelt was such that Burney knew that 'as *his* guest, I sh^d have been almost sure of Notice'. Fanny later significantly deleted 'Notice' and substituted 'doing right'.[2]

If only he could meet the King, Burney was convinced that he now had a way to his heart. For some months he had been working furiously at his *History*, although he was still hampered by the loss of his 'librarian Charlotte'. By early November 1786 Twining had already 'over-hauled the whole of the 16th Cent^y, and what concerns the 17th Cent^y *in England*', that is, almost the whole of what became the third volume; and Burney had sent him another 'large pacquet', which would have been even larger if he had not been so recently deprived of all his amanuenses.[3]

[1] *Hist. Mus.* iv. 606.
[2] CB to FB, 3 Nov. 1786 (Osborn).
[3] CB to Twining, 3 Nov. 1786, copy (Osborn).

By now he was well advanced into the sixth chapter of the fourth volume, which concerned the history of Italian opera in England, and, as he told Fanny, 'had got as far as Handel's *Rinaldo* 1711, when I am come to a dead stop. For his 3 next Operas were never printed, & are only to be had in his Majesties Collect. or Mr Granvilles. The Operas are *Theseus*, *Amadige*, & the first *Pastor fido*.' Fanny deleted the rest of this paragraph, presumably because Burney went on to hint quite clearly that she should use her position near the King to obtain permission for him to use the manuscripts in the Royal Collection. The passage can, however, be read with some difficulty: 'It will be pity merely to name or talk of them unsight unseen, while copies are extant in the kingdom. I must leave room in my MS. for a detailed account if I sh^d ever be able to give one, & go on to something else. The first time I see Mr Malone, I shall mention to him my difficulty, perhaps he can help me.'[1]

The hint was taken and not only was permission obtained for him to borrow the royal manuscripts of Handel's operas but the King was thereby conveniently informed that Burney was now working on his favourite composer. Early in December 1786 Burney wrote to Fanny to inform her of his progress on these operas. The strangely formal tone of this letter, its detailed account of his work on the royal manuscripts, and its frequent exclamations at the King's graciousness in permitting him to use them, all suggest that it was primarily intended to be seen by, or read to, the King himself. (In the previous month Mrs. Delany had received a letter from Mrs. Montagu which was similarly intended for the 'royal eye'.[2]) In the course of his letter Burney hinted that he would appreciate an opportunity of seeing the score of another opera, *Radamisto*, and he eventually obtained his wish.[3]

Burney and his daughter now considered that the time had come for the contrivance of an interview with the King. In December 1786 he was invited to stay at Windsor for three days with Mrs. Delany, who conveniently thought it necessary to

---

[1] CB to FB, 3 Nov. 1786 (Osborn).   [2] *DL*, iii. 105.
[3] CB to FB, 4 Dec. 1786 (Osborn). CB seems eventually to have seen all the Royal Handel MSS., to which reference is made throughout his section on Handel's operas, *Hist. Mus.* iv. 222–436. For notes which he left with the manuscripts, see W. B. Squire, *Catalogue of the King's Music Library, Part I: The Handel Manuscripts*, 1927, pp. 31, 76, 80, 97.

obtain permission from their Majesties. As Fanny also felt it proper to inform the Queen that her father was arriving on 29 December, the King had no excuse for being unaware of his presence. On the first evening of Burney's visit the King duly called to inquire after Mrs. Delany's health but, as Fanny knew, 'not for that solely, though ostensibly, for his behaviour to my father proved his desire to see and converse with him'. The King at once began to talk about music and, in his excitement and ignorance of the correct ritual, Burney replied in a very informal manner, taking it upon himself to direct much of the conversation—'that was always thought high treason', according to Horace Walpole[1]—and eagerly following the King around the room instead of keeping his distance and speaking only when addressed. The King, however, accepted this conduct good-humouredly and their conversation lasted for almost an hour.

On the following day Burney went to Slough to visit the great astronomer William Herschel, whom he had met regularly at the Royal Society. In the evening the King again visited Mrs. Delany and Burney enjoyed a second conversation with him. On Sunday, 31 December, the last day of his visit to Windsor, Burney hoped to have an opportunity of presenting his respects to the Queen but, although he missed her at church ('I got in the wrong side the porch'), he met the King instead, who was so gracious as to urge him to stay longer.[2]

Delighted almost to ecstasy by such condescension, Burney was back at Windsor a week later. For this visit he had rehearsed, according to Fanny's instructions, a short 'speech' in which he was to thank the Queen for her kind treatment of his daughter. After dinner, his opportunity of delivering it arrived when both the King and Queen came to Fanny's apartment.

Nevertheless, no sooner did the King touch upon that dangerous string, the history of music, than all else was forgotten! Away flew the speech,—the Queen herself was present in vain,—eagerly and warmly he began an account of his progress, and an enumeration of his materials,—and out from his pockets came a couple of dirty books, which he had lately picked up, at an immense price, at a sale, and which, in showing to the King, he said were equally scarce and valuable, and added, with energy, 'I would not take fifty pounds for

[1] *Corresp.* xvii. 210; cf. *DL*, ii. 314, 440.
[2] CB to FB, 31 Dec. 1786 (Osborn); *DL*, iii. 144–50; *Mem.* iii. 97–102.

that!' Just as if he had said—little as he meant such meaning—'Don't hope for it to your own collection!'[1]

Later, as Burney noted in a pocket-book, the King took him to his evening concert, conversed with him freely, and also lent him 'some very scarce & curious MS. Compositions of Handel for my amusement' from the royal collection, which were brought to Fanny's apartment for his examination.[2]

On his return to London Burney wrote an exultant letter to Fanny, listing in detail the many musical topics upon which he and the King had found they were in striking agreement and accordingly praising the royal knowledge and taste. The narrow and exclusive enthusiasm for the music of Handel, which had so aroused Burney's scorn in 1784, no longer troubled him. He had returned to London with the manuscript scores of *Rodelinda* and *Scipio* and he resumed his historical labours with renewed zeal: 'This kind of work gives me more & more pleasure in proportion as imagination paints it to me as likely to be grateful in some small degree to our most beneficent & royal Master.' As this letter expresses Burney's adoration of the Royal Family so fervently and as his later contact with the King is only scantily documented, a quotation from it will serve to summarize his delight in Fanny's new position and the 'notice' it had obtained for him: 'It is impossible to be deeper penetrated with gratitude & sensibility at what happened. I know that it c[d] not be purchased by money, or by much longer & meritorious services than I can ever boast; & that some of the first people in the kingdom w[d] envy me, & be ready to cut my throat, if they knew in how very gracious, & condescending a manner I had been treated.' He did not intend to boast generally of the honour he had received, 'As I am certain if others were told, & *believed* it, that nothing but envy, spleen & abuse w[d] be excited by the narrative.' He had nothing left to wish for, since the prospect of material benefit from Fanny's position at court seemed to matter little by comparison. His hopes of 'notice' from the Royal Family hereafter, he felt, would be excited 'not now half so

---

[1] *DL*, iii. 158–9.

[2] *Frag. Mem.* (Berg); during this visit CB also obtained from Mrs. Delany the promise of an account of the singer Anastasia Robinson (d. 1755), who had been greatly celebrated some sixty years earlier. This narrative, with appropriate acknowledgement, appears in *Hist. Mus.* iv. 246–9. Cf. *Mem.* ii. 367–8.

much from vanity or ambition as—shall I venture to say, affection?'.[1]

III

Little information remains, however, about Burney's attentions to the Royal Family during the next two years, which are more sparsely documented than any similar period of his life after 1770. Various explanations can be offered for this lack of material, one of the most important being that the Twining Correspondence in the British Museum virtually comes to an end in September 1785. Although Twining was at last working hard on his translation of Aristotle's *Poetics*, there seems to have been no diminution of the intimate friendship between the two men: nevertheless, the most important source of information about Burney's literary endeavours after 1773 ends abruptly, soon after the publication of his *Commemoration of Handel*.

It is perhaps more than coincidental that there is a similar paucity of material from other sources. In about 1785 Burney's youngest son Richard committed some mysterious crime—or was involved in some kind of scandal—and, although there are dark references to his disappearance to India, his name is very largely dropped or censored from surviving family correspondence. In July 1787 Susan Phillips told Fanny that her father had received 'a letter f^m India—which he told us he dreaded to unseal'.[2] Clearly, Fanny very effectively suppressed all her father's letters in which any mention of Richard's crime occurred and her zealous censorship must provide one explanation for the absence of material at this period, and perhaps even for the suppression of the Twining Correspondence for the same years.

There can be no doubt, however, that, in spite of his flattering reception at Windsor during his two visits just after Christmas 1786, Burney very wisely did not expect continued attention from the King of the same sort. So overwhelmed was he by the royal condescension during his visit early in January 1787 that he seems to have been satisfied with the 'notice' he had already received; and after giving Fanny 'a poem on the Queen's birthday, to present', which, with some embarrassment, she delivered

---

[1] CB to FB, 8 Jan. 1787 (Osborn).
[2] Susan Phillips to FB, journal-letter, 19 July–9 Sept. 1787 (Osborn).

to her Royal Mistress,[1] Burney turned all his attention once more to his *History*. He continued to see Fanny at regular intervals, usually in London, but it is significant that in August 1787, when he visited her at St. James's, she found him 'full of spirits, full of Handel, full of manuscripts, and full of proof-sheets'.[2]

In his anxiety to rid himself of the burden which he had now been carrying for almost twenty years, Burney gradually sequestered himself as much as possible and during 1788, at least, ceased writing to almost all but family correspondents, another reason for the lack of material at this period. A man of his position had inevitably to maintain some sort of social life and in the early months of 1787 'dinners & Evening parties were so frequent that I hardly ever dined or passed an evening at home'. He regularly attended The Club and meetings of the Council of the Royal Society and it was professionally important for him to be seen at the opera and at the Concerts of Ancient Music. He declined, however, an offer of election to the Society of Antiquaries, stopped attending the Essex Head Club, and as the *History* neared completion was obliged to cut down on other engagements: 'I had generally a printer's d[evi]l waiting for me and often the Engraver of the plates to dismiss however late I went home.' Returning to a favourite image, Burney knew that 'the agony of bringing forth Twins was not very distant'.[3]

Some minor distractions, however, were flattering enough to demand some of his valuable time. Thomas Jefferson, the American Ambassador in Paris, asked Burney, whom he greatly admired, to supervise for him the construction of a harpsichord, and during 1786 and 1787 Burney gladly attended to this commission.[4] By June 1787, nevertheless, he had completed a draft of the fourth volume of the *History* and had started to revise the third, which was about to go to press immediately. Returning to chapters which had been written almost five years earlier, Burney found that there were many alterations and additions to be made, and he called frequently on the assistance of his young friend Latrobe, whenever he had to fall back on German sources of information. By 18 July 1787 he had received proofs of the

---

[1] See *ante*, p. 333, n. 1.   [2] *DL*, iii. 301.   [3] *Frag. Mem.* (Berg).
[4] *Papers of Thomas Jefferson*, ed. J. P. Boyd, Princeton, 1950– , ix. 579; x. 75–76, 117–18, 175, 393, 516; xi. 58–60, 140–1.

first sixteen pages of the third volume and he wrote hurriedly to Latrobe, who had been helping him with his account of the influence of Luther on metrical psalmody,[1] the section which was due to go next to press: 'I am plunged into the Press with my III[d] Vol. over head & Ears. . . . Hasten then, dear Soul! as I am called upon for more Copy; (the *Devil* is now at my elbow, help me to exorcise him, I entreat you). . . .'[2]

During the summer of 1787 Burney moved to the organist's apartment at Chelsea College, which had at last fallen vacant and which was much more suitable than the large house in St. Martin's Street, now that almost all his children had left home. Until the lease on the house expired, however, he kept most of his books and papers in St. Martin's Street, and seems also to have found it more convenient to live there during the winter, in his busiest teaching season.[3] In effect, nevertheless, Burney had now moved to what he facetiously described as the 'wooden-leg Hospital' where he was to spend the rest of his life. In July 1787 his daughter Susan visited him in his new home and sent Fanny a long account of the apartment. She found him wrestling with proof-sheets and later accompanied him to 'rummage' in the 'Poor old St. Martin's Street house', which 'looked very dark & dismal', in search of music and books.[4]

The pressure from the printers was now unremitting and took its usual toll. In September Burney visited his daughter Charlotte Francis at Aylsham, but in spite of handsome entertainment from aristocratic friends along the route, he was in 'very great & almost constant Rheumatic suffering'.[5] With his usual tenacity, however, Burney kept up with the press. The clearest picture of his frantic haste in these poorly documented years appears whenever the revision of his manuscript led him to consult Latrobe. Although a volley of letters was the usual result, a single quotation will sufficiently illustrate his reaction whenever confronted by the German language: 'I am so surrounded & bewildered with *Charman* books of all kinds, that I shall fret myself to Sauer-Kraut if you do not come & disentangle me soon. . . . poking out their meaning with a Dict[y] in my hand is so slow

---

[1] *Hist. Mus.* iii. 31 ff.
[2] CB to Latrobe, 14 June and 18 July [1787] (Osborn).
[3] *DL*, iii. 399, 406.
[4] Susan to FB, 19 July–9 Sept. 1787 (Osborn).
[5] CB to FB, 8 Oct. 1787 (Osborn).

& unsure, that I can neither spare the time, nor venture to use
what I may make out this way, if I c^d.'[1]

Otherwise, until November 1788 there was almost complete
silence, broken only by an impressive exchange of letters with
Edmund Burke. In July 1788 Burney evidently wrote to apologize for the fact that, in spite of Burke's kindness in obtaining
him his post at Chelsea College, he felt unable, for political
reasons, to vote for his friend at an election. Burke's reply
assured Burney that he bore him no ill-will and, indeed, thought
the better of him for refusing to violate his conscience. Burney's
reply in turn expressed undisguised relief: 'Instead of shunning
or fearing your sight in Society, my heart will now, as usual, go
out to meet you.' The draft of this letter shows even more clearly
how troubled he had been at the possibility of alienating an old
friend. Omitted from the letter as sent to Burke were references
to the 'painful doubt & irresolution' he had suffered and the
'shame & disapprobation of my conduct' he had feared.[2] It is
worth observing that beneath his invariably genial manner and
in spite of his intense desire always to please, Burney possessed a
tough core of integrity. Mrs. Thrale, indeed, had once recorded
that she believed him to be the only man whose pardon Johnson
had ever begged, after Burney had taken offence at an apparent
aspersion against his veracity.[3]

From July 1787 to November 1788 Burney worked desperately hard, night and day, to see the last two volumes of his
History through the press. As he and his friends had confidently
anticipated, his labours had become much pleasanter and easier
as he approached the music of his own time. There was no need
for entertaining digressions and he could write with full confidence that readers of taste would not be offended by the discussion of 'Gothic' or 'barbarous' music. He had not been able
to conceal his pleasure at this imminent prospect, even while he
was still concerned with music of the reign of James I: 'we are
now approaching better times, when productions of a superior
class will pour in upon us, and deserve insertion; of which, to
point out the peculiar beauties and excellence will be a much

---

[1] CB to Latrobe, 4 letters, 15 Dec.–22 Dec. 1787 and 1 letter, n.d., dated '1788'
by Latrobe (Osborn).

[2] Burke to CB, 1 Aug. 1788 (F. W. Hilles; partial extract, *Mem.* iii. 122); CB to
Burke, 8 Aug. 1788 (Fitzwilliam MSS., Sheffield; draft, Osborn; extract, *Mem.*
iii. 123).   [3] Hill–Powell, iv. 49, n. 3.

more pleasing employment, than to censure or ridicule the defects of such as were produced during this reign.'[1] From the beginning of his third volume, however, he had been able, a little to his own surprise perhaps, to take patriotic pride in the church music of such English composers as Tallis and Byrd and, at a later period, in the compositions of Henry Purcell. There was also frequent opportunity for striking satisfying blows at his old rival, Sir John Hawkins, sometimes only by implication in cases where their tastes differed completely, but on other occasions quite directly, although he still forbore to mention his old enemy by name. His use of the word 'trash', for example, could leave no doubt in the minds of interested readers as to the object of his scorn when he attacked 'the vulgar cant of such as are determined to blame whatever is modern, and who, equally devoid of knowledge and feeling, reprobate as _trash_ the most elegant, ingenious, and often sublime compositions, that have ever been produced since the laws of harmony were first established'.[2]

As has been suggested above, Burney must have known for some time that a fourth volume would be necessary, for after completing what was to be the third he had reached only the end of the seventeenth century. In spite of the extra volume, however, the problem of space remained with him until the end. When he came to write his chapter on the rise and progress of Italian opera in England during the eighteenth century, his gratitude for the King's generosity in permitting him to use the Handel Manuscripts in the Royal Collection obliged him to deal with that composer's theatrical works at enormous length. Earlier threats about the uncensored criticism of Handel which would appear in the _History_ were now forgotten and his lengthy and detailed discussion of the operas was obviously written primarily for the delectation of the King: for once Burney hardly cared about his general readers. He included, indeed, a direct compliment to the King's taste which, in July 1784, would have seemed inconceivable: 'happy for the art, when a sovereign's favour is founded on so firm a basis as the works of Handel! Indeed, our country would certainly now be less sensible of their worth, were it not for the royal countenance and

[1] _Hist. Mus._ iii. 325.
[2] Ibid. 112; see _ante_, p. 210.

patronage with which they have been long and steadily honoured.'[1] Burney himself, we may suspect, might have been 'less sensible of their worth' in other circumstances.

Although the fourth volume of Burney's *History* is the most valuable, there are many signs that it was written in haste and the organization of many chapters is often swamped beneath the mass of available material. Feeling it his duty to discuss the music of all the important European countries in turn at each period, he could often allow space for little more than lists, with brief comments, of composers and musicologists in chronological order. Haste was not the only explanation, for, in spite of the fact that his *History* in the end was more than twice as long as he had intended, shortage of space eventually became a problem once more. His four volumes in fact became progressively larger, containing respectively 522, 598, 622, and 688 pages. Towards the end of the fourth volume he frequently referred to his lack of space and in the end he was forced to omit the chapter on 'National Music' which he had promised from the beginning of his work. Many friends, such as Richard Twiss, Lord Mornington, Thomas Pennant, James Lind, and Joseph Cooper Walker had supplied him with examples of, and information concerning, the music of the various nations which they inhabited or had visited, and Burney himself had collected relevant materials from 'almost every quarter of the globe . . . with great difficulty and trouble'. The alternative to abandoning the chapter, however, was to publish a fifth volume and Burney was not prepared to strain the goodwill of his readers any further.[2]

Shortage of space, however, probably helped to solve a problem which had inevitably arisen towards the end of his work. Whereas Hawkins had declined to deal with any living composers or musicians, Burney aimed to bring his *History* absolutely up to date, the difference in attitude to contemporary music between the two historians sufficiently explaining their decisions. Burney knew that he faced the risk of offending his contemporaries, particularly those in England, either by what he said or did not say about them. He admitted eventually that 'living musicians are, in general, neither fair nor safe objects of history

[1] *Hist. Mus.* iii. 483–4.
[2] CB to J. C. Walker, 7 June 1789; and to E. Bunting, 24 Sept. 1808, draft (Osborn). See *ante*, pp. 142–3; and cf. *Hist. Mus.* ii. 114, 220, 352, 576 n.

or criticism',[1] but it was his lack of space which eventually
helped to excuse him from mentioning all but the most eminent
of his contemporaries. He did not, however, escape embarrassment on this account. The composer Barthélemon, for example,
wrote to remind him to do full justice to Dr. John Worgan
(1724–90), but Burney pointed out that it was impossible for
him to give a detailed discussion of one musician, while ignoring
others with equal claims. He gave Worgan, nevertheless, two-
thirds of a page of his valuable space, perhaps as a result of this
request.[2] Similarly, after the publication of the third and fourth
volumes, Robert Nares wrote to the *Gentleman's Magazine*, complaining that the *History* had not done justice to the later career
of the infant prodigy William Crotch, whom Burney himself had
brought to early fame in 1779.[3] Another instance of the same
problem will be discussed shortly.

Burney, however, was almost past caring about such objections. His fourth volume brought the history of music up to the
Handel Commemoration of 1787 (it had become an annual
event), dealt with opera in London to the end of the 1788 season,
and on the very last sheet mentioned the death of a musician
who died on 1 November 1788, 'while this sheet was printing!'[4]
His only thought, however, was to bring the work to an end:
'For several months I have worked from 12 to 18 hours a day.
. . . Indeed I began to fear, after all the time & expence bestowed on this perhaps romantic plan, that I sh^d leave it unfinished: as we are always *Tenants at the will* of Providence, and,
after 60, a clay cottage is a habitation doubly precarious.'[5] He
was much less disturbed than his friend Latrobe by the discovery in 1788 that the German writer Johann Forkel had
plagiarized extensively from his earlier volumes in the first part
of his *Allgemeine Geschichte der Musik* (Leipzig, 1788), and had at
the same time attacked him in other parts of his book: 'He &
others may censure & revile as much as they please, but I have
had too much trouble in writing my History, (in wch I have
most conscientiously endeavoured to speak with truth & candour both of Men & things to the best of my judgement) ever to

[1] *Hist. Mus.* iv. 521; cf. iv. 681–2.
[2] CB to Barthélemon [1788], draft (Coke); cf. *Hist. Mus.* iv. 665–6.
[3] *Gent. Mag.* lix (1789). 610.
[4] *Hist. Mus.* iv. 682.
[5] See n. 2 above.

think of bestowing more time & pains in defending it.'[1] Burney
nevertheless wittily exposed Forkel's debt to his own first
volume in a footnote.[2]

At last, on 4 November 1788, came the long-awaited moment
when Burney could write joyfully to his daughter Charlotte,
with a characteristic lapse into provincial dialect, '*de yaou knaou,*
that I yesterday gave the printer the *last* Chapter of my *tiresome*
History?—adad I did—hur——ra——h! Why ever since July I
have often worked at this Schtoff 17 & 18 hours out of the 24—
& now I shan't have occasion to fag above 12 mehap till all is
done.'[3] As he told his friend Humphry Repton, the landscape
designer, he had vowed either to complete the work 'or die with
the pen in my hand', and had used his friends, relations, and
correspondents 'like dogs', never being caught 'at home' and
'regarding all letters as totally unanswerable till one of those
events was come to pass'. With undisguised exuberance he
described the actual moment at which his great labour had
come, in effect, to an end:

Did you never dear Sir, see a child give an involuntary jump, from
the mere ebullition of animal Spirits, when musing o'er his playthings with seeming Sobriety?—A few nights ago, when I had just
sent the last copy, of the last Chapter, of the last Vol. of my work to
the compositor I caught myself in the fact. And if you were here, I'd
shew you how I jumped for joy at the thoughts of an entreprise being
so nearly terminated that had been 30 years in meditation, & 20 in
writing & printing; and for w[ch] I had so heavily taxed every amusement, & Social enjoyment, & in order to gain more time, drawn so
deeply from my sinking fund, Sleep.[4]

Work on the *History* had by no means finished, of course:
proofs had still to be read, plates prepared, indexes compiled,
and errata noted. Last of all, perhaps, Burney wrote his dignified and moving 'Conclusion'. If Samuel Johnson had been
alive, Burney would surely have consulted him about these
pages. Certainly Johnson's hand would have been detected in
them; and the fact that he had been dead for more than four
years does not make it impossible to identify in Burney's prose
signs of his undying reverence for his friend:

---

[1] CB to Latrobe [1788] (Osborn).   [2] *Hist. Mus.* iv. 603 n.
[3] CB to Charlotte Francis, 4 Nov. [1788] (Barrett).
[4] CB to Repton, Nov. 1788, draft (Osborn); extract, *Mem.* iii. 130.

I have at length arrived at the end of a work that has been thirty years in meditation, and more than twenty in writing and printing. Whether I have been too brief or too minute in my narrative must be left to the wants and intelligence of my readers. Ignorance and science are relative terms, and the same book, like a dictionary, may at once contain too much for one purchaser, and too little for another. My ambition has been to gratify reasonable curiosity concerning every part of my subject, without shrinking at difficulties; yet those who have previously had leisure and opportunity to draw knowledge from the same sources will think much might have been retrenched; while others, to whom the subject is wholly new, will be in want of many additions.

It is more than coincidental that Burney should mention a dictionary in this passage. It had been through Johnson's great lexicographic labour that Burney had first entered into correspondence with him; and in many ways he seems to have been encouraged into an equally monumental undertaking by the example which Johnson had given him. It would not be surprising to learn that when he wrote the last paragraphs of his *History of Music*, Burney had Johnson's Preface to his *Dictionary* open before him. Johnson had written: 'I have protracted my work till most of those whom I wished to please have sunk into the grave; and success and miscarriage are empty sounds. I therefore dismiss it with frigid tranquillity, having little to fear or hope from censure or from praise.' Burney wrote in 1789: 'The havock which death has made since this work was begun among my friends, and those I wished to please, who, of course, were the most willing to be pleased, is so great, that more than half my first subscribers have disappeared; and if any curiosity was excited, or interest awakened, towards the subject by the former volumes, it is not likely to be of much use to the present.'[1]

Fanny admitted that she knew little about the publication of the last two volumes of her father's *History*; and, indeed, proved it by stating in 1832 that the fourth was published some time after the third.[2] In fact, both volumes were published on 30 April 1789. Burney had not been idle since the last chapter had gone to press in the previous November. In January rheumatism, as so frequently, had accompanied his preparations for publication; but the fact that his great undertaking was at an end had kept him in good spirits, as Ralph Griffiths discovered: 'He, nevertheless, has still drollery enough to compare his present dolorous situation to that of the poor "Souls in Dante's Hell, stuck up to their chins in *Ice*—while the Devils are kicking their teeth down their throats". I do verily believe that this same pleasant friend of ours would still preserve his Comicality, even tho' he were writing, or acting, a Tragedy.'[1]

As soon as he recovered, Burney had set about preparing a second edition of the first volume of his *History*. Probably little remained to be added to the revised copy which he and Twining had prepared in 1776. The 1789 edition apparently contains all the alterations and omissions suggested by Twining thirteen years earlier, in addition to the correction of errata and the absorption of the 'Additional Notes' into the main body of the text. The most extensive alteration affected the Preface: the introduction to the 'Dissertation on the Music of the Ancients' was transferred to the Preface in the second edition, and what had originally been a (slightly absurd, according to Twining) series of catechistical questions and answers on the nature of music, was re-written and separated in the new edition from the Preface as 'Definitions'. As a result of Twining's persistent objections to Burney's fondness for mythological musicians, the first chapter of the historical narrative, 'Of Music in Greece during the Residence of Pagan Divinities, of the first Order, upon Earth', was extensively altered, many passages being omitted in 1789, others transferred and still others replaced.[2] A passage on 'reeds' in the Appendix entitled 'Reflections on the . . . Musical Instruments of Antiquity' was also extensively revised. All these and numerous smaller changes had been suggested by Twining in 1776, particularly in a letter of 17 September of that year.[3]

Almost the only alteration which had not been planned in 1776 was made to the illustrations of ancient musical instruments. Burney neatly inserted three small musical figures, which had been brought to his attention by Sir Joseph Banks and J. C. Walker, on gaps in the original plates. The new edition

---

[1] Griffiths to CB Jr., 8 Jan. [1789] (Osborn).
[2] Cf. *Hist. Mus.* i (1776), 257–99 and (1789), 262–99.
[3] See *ante*, pp. 184–7.

of the first volume went to press on 8 May 1789, nine days after the publication of the third and fourth volumes. Burney's haste can be explained by the fact that not a single copy of the first edition remained unsold and by his desire to publish the second while interest was being aroused by the two new volumes.[1]

Since there were no subscribers to the third and fourth volumes, it was more important than ever that Burney should receive favourable reviews. In spite of Professor Nangle's claim that Ralph Griffiths prevented his staff from praising the work of their friends or colleagues,[2] the editor of the *Monthly Review* evidently accepted Burney's suggestion that Twining should write the articles on his *History*. (Burney had himself been contributing to the *Review* since 1785.) Certainly, Griffiths considered this arrangement 'rather delicate', but he insisted on sending Burney the proofs of Twining's articles as if he were reviewing his own book. Griffiths, it should be added, was so impressed by Twining's abilities that he tried to enlist him as a permanent contributor. Twining did not, however, write again for the *Monthly Review*.[3]

Twining's review, which appeared in five instalments between October 1789 and March 1790,[4] consists for the most part of the usual extensive quotation. It is amusing, however, to find him solemnly pointing out to his readers some 'entertaining anecdotes' concerning Corelli in Burney's *History*, which, 'it seems, were communicated to him by a friend'. Twining himself had heard these stories from Geminiani and they had been the pretext for the letter which had opened his long correspondence with Burney in 1773.[5] It is also worth noting that, as in his review of Burney's *Account of the Commemoration of Handel*, Twining salved his critical conscience by noting a slight 'inaccuracy of construction' in the *History*.

The final article of the series concluded with the predictable celebration of Burney's arrival at the end of his great undertaking, an event with which Twining had additional sympathy since he himself had published his long-delayed translation of

[1] CB to Sir Joseph Banks, 10 May 1789 (transcript in Scholes papers, Osborn); to J. C. Walker, 7 June 1789 (Osborn). The inserted figures are marked with asterisks on Plate IV.   [2] See *ante*, p. 106.

[3] Griffiths to CB, 8 June [1789], [? Oct. 1789], and 20 Apr. [1790] (Osborn).

[4] *Monthly Review*, lxxxi. 289–302, 426–43, 537–53; i (N.S.), 121–33, 265–77.

[5] See *ante*, p. 135; *Hist. Mus.* iii. 552–4, 557–8.

Aristotle's *Poetics* in 1789. Although the fact that it was written by a close friend detracts from its value as a contemporary tribute to Burney, it is still impressive as a sincere testimony to that friendship itself. The work which Twining was praising owed much to his own wide learning, invariably frank and indefatigable criticism and spirited encouragement; yet no one knew so well as Twining how much the *History* had cost Burney in years of labour and in nervous strain. The conclusion of the review contains a reminder that one of his most important functions had been to provide Burney with moral support after the appearance of Hawkins's *History of Music*. This last blow at Burney's old rival was in a way, however, unnecessary, for Hawkins had died two weeks after the publication of Burney's last volumes:

To Dr. B. the praise is justly due, of having first begun to supply, in a masterly and able manner, a *vacuity* in our English literature. The *literal* vacancy, indeed, on the shelves of a library, was filled by another history of music before this was compiled: but the work before us, we hesitate not to pronounce, is the only one yet produced of the kind, in our own, and, we believe, in *any*, language, that can be read with satisfaction by *real* judges of the subject: the only one, in which they will find any thing approaching to an union of all the requisites of a good musical historian—a thorough knowlege [*sic*] of the subject; a sound and *unprejudiced judgement*; criticism equally supported by science and by *taste*, and much authentic and original information, rendered more interesting by a certain *amenity*, which is the general character of Dr. B.'s manner of writing, and which may best be defined, as the diametrical opposite to every thing that we call *dull* and *dry*. We do not recollect any literary undertaking, of equal labour both in research and execution, where that labour is more apparent to the reader when he *considers* the work, or less evident while he *reads* it.

Burney fell into less trustworthy hands in the *Critical Review*, whose first article on his volumes appeared in August 1789.[1] His critic can be identified as William Jackson, the organist of Exeter Cathedral and a composer of some pretensions. Although Burney knew him quite well and had mentioned him briefly in the *History*,[2] Jackson felt that less than justice had been done both to himself and to contemporary English music as a whole. Two

---

[1] lxviii. 94–103.   [2] *DL*, ii. 161–2, 175–7; *Hist. Mus.* iv. 675.

footnotes in the *History* particularly irritated Jackson. Burney had rather strangely printed in his third volume the anthem which he wrote for his Oxford degree exercise in 1769, hoping, in a long footnote, that 'the reader will pardon this *egotism*', which he justified on the grounds that it was commonly believed that he 'neither liked nor had studied Church Music'.[1] Rejecting the degree anthem as evidence of anything at all, Jackson declared that the real accusation that was made about Burney was that 'he has never given to the public an instance of his abilities as a composer, in *any* style'. He called on Burney to refute this if he could and suggested that he omit the whole passage from any future edition of the *History*. Jackson also belaboured another footnote in which Burney, without mentioning him by name, had disagreed with his *Thirty Letters on Various Subjects*, and had dismissed 'elegies'—Jackson's favourite species of composition—as the products of 'the more maudlin moments of artificial melancholy'.[2] This passage Jackson understandably considered to be 'in every view beneath the author to write'.[3]

Jackson's second and concluding article did not appear until December 1790, sixteen months later.[4] The passage of time had perhaps mellowed him to some extent. Noting Burney's abject apology to German musicians for his former remarks on that nation's lack of genius, he still considered, however, that the historian should make 'the same amende honorable to some of his countrymen, as he has done to those illustrious foreigners', in a new edition of the *History*, and he regretted the absence of any examples of English 'national melody' from the work. Jackson's review ended, however, with a generous tribute to Burney's achievement:

From the impartiality we profess, we have freely expressed our thoughts where we differed from Dr. Burney; but, when we dissent from an author who possesses such sources of information on a professional subject, it is with a due distrust of, and not a partiality to, our own judgement. We wish to be understood as recommending this work, as by far the most perfect that has yet appeared upon the subject in any country or language; and that it contains a greater mass of musical knowledge, as far as the history of the art is concerned, which is all that it professes, than seems possible to be collected by

[1] *Hist. Mus.* iii. 329 n., 351–3.   [2] Ibid., 92 n.
[3] *Critical Review*, lxviii. 99–100.   [4] Ibid., lxx. 618–32.

the labour of any one man; a labour, which nothing could support but a love of the subject, and conscious ability of being able to execute the task with success.

Burney breathed a sigh of relief on reading these words:

At length, after making my *trial* in the C.R. as long as Hastings's in West^r Hall, Judge *Jackson* has seemingly acquitted me of all *charges* except that greatest of all offences in his Eyes: the omission of *his* Praise. All his cavils, I am certain originated from that omission. . . .[1]

Nevertheless, Jackson's concluding remarks, 'regarded as the praise of an Enemy', were 'as favourable as I c^d possibly expect'. It had been the very first time in twenty years as an author, after all, that one of his publications had been exposed, in the *Monthly* or the *Critical Review*, to the mercies of a critic who was neither a friend nor a well-wisher and he had come lightly out of the encounter. Burney was not, however, accustomed to hostile criticism of any kind and he did not neglect later opportunities of taking his revenge on Jackson.[2]

Burney's *History* received other reviews, of course, including a long and respectful, if occasionally disapproving, survey of all four volumes in the *Analytical Review* by Mary Wollstonecraft in February 1790.[3] Before his various critics had reached their final verdicts, however, Burney was already brooding on conflicts which made such literary disagreements seem trivial. The 'feuds and contentions lately occasioned by Music in France', which he had described at length in his *History*,[4] were insignificant by comparison with the violence which erupted in that country a few weeks after the publication of his last two volumes. In May 1789 Burney must have felt that he had surely arrived at last at a period of well-deserved relaxation and peace of mind. Not, however, to the very end of his life did he manage to discover it.

---

[1] CB to CB Jr., 7 Jan. 1791 (Osborn).
[2] See R. Lonsdale, 'Dr. Burney and the *Monthly Review*', *RES*, xiv (1963), 355.
[3] vi (1790), 129–46; see R. M. Wardle, *Mary Wollstonecraft*, Lawrence, 1951, p. 107.   [4] *Hist. Mus.* iv. 630.

VIII

MEMOIRS OF METASTASIO

1789–1796

I

'How light y^r shoulders will feel when you have done with it!—You shall never do a stroke of hard work again—voyez vous?'[1] With these words of encouragement Thomas Twining in 1784 had looked forward to the completion of Burney's *History of Music*. When, in May 1789, he published the third and fourth volumes of his great work, Burney himself, now aged sixty-three, felt that he had earned some respite, after twenty years of indefatigable industry. During the summer he set out on a pleasantly nostalgic journey to King's Lynn and other parts of Norfolk. He was not, however, permitted to relax and to enjoy his freedom for long for, even if the full significance of the news which began to reach England from France in July 1789 was not immediately apparent, it was sufficient to alarm so unshakeable a conservative and monarchist as Burney. His own reaction to the French Revolution was stern and simple: '*Egalité* of condition in Society is impracticable nonsense. Nature has made our minds no more alike than our face & figure. There are tall minds, and tall bodies. Difference of intellect as well as of muscular strength will always occasion inequality.'[2]

Although his conviction of the essential evil of the upheaval in France was never to waver even momentarily, Burney could not dismiss the Revolution from his mind as easily as he could condemn it. Even in England it seemed that the old order, which he loved so intensely, might be in danger. Everywhere he went the talk was of France and to his horror he found that not all his friends and acquaintances shared the simple clarity of his own attitude. Old affections were suddenly

---

[1] Twining to CB, 12 Nov. 1784 (Add. MS. 39929, ff. 342–3).
[2] CB to CB Jr., 2 Sept. 1789 (Berg); to FB, 2 Oct. 1789 (F. W. Hilles).

strained and areas of society where Burney had formerly moved with ease and assurance were suddenly seen to be full of pitfalls and had to be re-explored cautiously. Such old friends as William Mason and Arthur Young, with whom Burney maintained an argumentative correspondence on the subject, at first inexplicably viewed the events in France with enthusiasm. Fulke Greville's daughter, the celebrated Mrs. Crewe, one of the most beautiful women of her day and a fashionable Whig hostess, had recently become a great favourite of Burney, but as her husband and friends were conspicuous 'democrats', he felt obliged to write her frequent, lengthy letters, discussing the latest news from France and deploring English sympathy with these events, with the desperate ardour of an evangelist struggling to save a soul from damnation. Even The Club was no safe refuge from the new pervasive spirit of disorder, when it contained such a member as Charles Fox.

Disturbed and almost bewildered by the French Revolution and its impact on England, Burney was unsettled and restless for other reasons. Although it had become an increasingly wearisome burden, his *History* had at least concentrated his mental powers for two decades. After its completion, his occupation was gone: unable to relax, he found that he was so accustomed to having some literary labour on his hands, even if he did not particularly enjoy it, that he immediately began looking for a new undertaking. The difficulty in 1789, however, lay less in finding fresh tasks than in persisting with them. During the summer he began a long poem on astronomy, a science which had always fascinated him,[1] but after writing 350 lines he laid it aside.[2] He doubtless felt that such a work was no more than self-indulgence and that, especially in such disturbing times, he should apply himself to some more serious project, befitting a musicologist of his European reputation.

The task on which Burney settled in the autumn of 1789 was the writing of a biography of Pietro Trapassi (1698–1782), known as Metastasio, an Italian who had settled in Vienna and who had been considered in his lifetime to be one of the greatest poets of the century. Both Voltaire and Rousseau had written of him in terms of the highest praise; his secular and sacred dramas had been set to music by such composers as

---

[1] See *ante*, pp. 80–81.   [2] See *post*, p. 384.

Jomelli, Hasse, Handel, Gluck, Haydn, and Mozart; and he had lived to see the publication of some forty editions of his works, as well as translations of them into French, English, German, and Spanish. Burney had revered him for many years. Preparing for his German tour in 1772, he had gone to great lengths to ensure a meeting with Metastasio in Vienna, where he was poet to the Imperial Court. Together with the composer Hasse, who had set many of his libretti, Metastasio was to be one of the 'Heros' of the *History*. During September 1772 Burney had visited the poet five times and, as he had related in his *German Tour*, had not been disappointed by the appearance and conversation of the great man.[1]

In spite of his interviews with Metastasio and his reverence for the poet's literary and moral virtues, Burney had not, in the end, discussed him at any length in the *History*. References to his collaboration with various composers inevitably abound in the long treatment given to Italian Opera, but lack of space presumably prevented Burney from giving a protracted study of the poet himself. In 1789 he undertook a biography of Metastasio explicitly to compensate for this omission. Five volumes of letters, which were included in an edition of Metastasio's works at Nice in 1785 and 1786, had arrived in England too late for Burney to quote them in his *History*; but, as he was to observe in the Preface to his biography, these letters 'seemed to furnish necessary materials to the completion of my musical annals'.[2]

In many ways, therefore, a biography of Metastasio was a logical and attractive undertaking for Burney. The poet had worked with many important composers and performers. Burney had met him in person and had obtained 'anecdotes & information concerning the principal incidents of his life' from Metastasio himself and from his friends in Vienna. He had also been personally acquainted with many of the poet's correspondents, such as Padre Martini, the composers Hasse and Jomelli, and the singer Farinelli.[3] Important as were Metastasio's musical connexions, however, and much as Burney respected his skill in writing libretti perfectly suited for musical settings, he also intensely admired him as a poet in his own right. For this admiration he had no less an authority than Samuel

---

[1] See *ante*, pp. 114, 116–17.   [2] *Metastasio*, I. iii; cf. iii. 325.
[3] CB to J. C. Walker, 1 July 1793 (Yale); *Metastasio*, I. xiii.

Johnson: Burney may have known that he had provided the enthusiastic Dedication to John Hoole's translation of *The Works of Metastasio* in 1767 and it is more than likely that he was familiar with Johnson's own translations from the poet, which Mrs. Thrale entered in her journal in 1777.[1]

Part of the attraction of writing a biography of Metastasio lay in the fact that it would demonstrate conclusively to the world that Burney was truly a 'man of letters', by no means confined to strictly musical subjects. If the 'literary' quality of his earlier books on music had already seemed remarkable to his contemporaries, Burney was now prepared to undertake a subject which was, if anything, more literary than musical. At the same time, he could hardly help being reassured by Metastasio's musical connexions and, in fact, it was the way in which the poet had succeeded in bridging the worlds of literature and music which he especially admired and even tried to imitate. He himself had no dearer ambition: and once, at least, he had admitted that he identified himself closely with Metastasio. On 8 April 1779, when a typical group had gathered at Streatham, Mrs. Thrale asked her friends to state who they would most like to have been if not themselves: 'Johnson said he would change with nobody but Hugo Grotius. Burney rather wished to be Metastasio.' As Mrs. Thrale explained, 'Burney desired to be still *more* a poet & Musician'.[2] The passage of time had not affected this desire. Sixteen years later Fanny reminded her father, 'you know, when we were all to choose who we would be if not our dear identical and always all-preferable selves, you fixed upon Metastasio; and indeed, in many, nay most respects, it would hardly be a change'.[3]

The biographical method which Burney decided to follow had first been employed by his friend William Mason in his *Memoirs* of Thomas Gray in 1775, 'the most agreeable species of biography that has ever been published' in Burney's opinion.[4] This technique, which was simultaneously being used by James Boswell in his *Life of Johnson*,[5] consisted basically of the interweaving of the subject's letters into the narrative. The Nice edition of Metastasio's letters had unfortunately aimed at no

---

[1] *Thraliana*, i. 211–12. Mrs. Thrale also translated Metastasio, ibid. 392, 435; ii. 771.   [2] *Thraliana*, i. 377.   [3] FB to CB, 13 May 1795, *DL*, v. 255–8.
[4] *Metastasio*, I. vi.   [5] Hill–Powell, i. 29.

particular chronology and Burney was obliged to spend some
time putting them in the correct order. He enjoyed, however,
the other employment of translating the letters from Italian and
significantly described himself as having been 'diverted' by the
task during the summer of 1790. It was not a word which he had
ever been able to use of his *History of Music*.[1]

His *Memoirs of Metastasio*, nevertheless, could not replace his
History and although he worked hard at translating the letters
during 1790, his enthusiasm gradually waned. By the autumn
he had turned to a new diversion and was rearranging and
cataloguing his enormous library, which had probably not been
completely transferred to Chelsea College until 1789, when
Burney finally left St. Martin's Street. Horrified at the number
of missing volumes and inexplicably incomplete sets, Burney
did his best to remedy these omissions: 'every time I have an
hour to spare in Town is spent at stalls & old book shops in
hopes of completing many valuable sets of books that have been
cruelly dismembered'. Miscellaneous poems, pamphlets, and
music were bound neatly together 'to the amount of 2 or 300
Vols' and so enormous was the collection—'Garrick, long since,
said I had script ev'ry stall in Moorfields'—that Burney had to
build a new bookcase, apparently grievously needed since, as he
wrote, 'I had hardly a table for my dinner or a chair to sit down
on, that was not loaded, without well knowing with what.' The
organization of his library seems to have begun in October 1790
and was still occupying him in December; and refinements to
his catalogue continued to be made during 1791. Burney was
looking ahead: as he told Fanny, his collection of books, 'now
I have room to find places for them, if completed, w^d be the
greatest comfort of my old age—Many of them excite my
curiosity now more than when first published.'[2]

During the following year work on Metastasio continued
sporadically, but it was to come to an end in the autumn of 1791
when Burney had reached the sixtieth year of the poet's life. He
was sustained in the work by none of the urgency which had
kept him tied to his *History* and he was easily distracted from it.
Although he was now in his mid-sixties he was still obliged to

[1] CB to R. Cox [Nov. 1791], draft (Osborn).
[2] CB to FB, 27 Oct. 1790 (Barrett); to Susan Phillips, 20 Nov. 1790 (Osborn);
to Charlotte Francis, 8 Dec. 1790 (Barrett).

make his living as a music-teacher in the fashionable season
between January and June, and his social life continued undiminished. During 1791 there were also a number of important
musical distractions, which inevitably took time and energy
from his literary activities. Burney was involved, for example, in
a plan to open the Pantheon as an opera-house in place of the
Haymarket, which had burned down in 1789, and he attended
conferences on the subject in the summer of 1790. The venture
began well in February 1791, Burney being appointed as 'foreign
secretary to engage singers from Italy and Germany' at 100
guineas a year. He had also invested a large amount of money
in the project, expecting considerable profit from it.[1]

In the early months of 1791, indeed, Burney was perhaps
more deeply and willingly involved in London's public musical
life than at any time since the completion of the first volume of
his *History* in 1776. To a man who had a great capacity for hero-
worship—a faculty which had had little exercise since the death
of Johnson—the arrival in England on New Year's Day 1791 of
the great composer Joseph Haydn was an event of the utmost
importance. Burney had long been an admirer of Haydn's
music and, according to Fanny d'Arblay, had already been in
correspondence with him for 'many years'.[2] As early as 1783
Burney had been scheming to obtain Haydn an engagement in
London and, as he had told Twining, at one time had some hope
of success: 'I have stimulated a wish to get Haydn over as opera
Composer—but mum mum—yet—a correspondence is opened,
& there is great likelihood of it, if these Cabals, & litigations
ruin not the Opera completely.'[3] This attempt, like similar
schemes by Haydn's English admirers in the 1780's, had failed,
but after the death of his great patron, Prince Esterházy, in
1790, the composer had at last been lured to England by the
impresario Salomon.

Some idea of Burney's rapture on this occasion can be
obtained from his opening remarks in his *History* on 'the admirable and matchless HAYDN! from whose productions I have
received more pleasure late in my life, when tired of most other
Music, than I ever received in the most ignorant and rapturous

[1] CB to CB Jr., 21 July 1790 (Osborn); to Lady Crewe, 18 April 1806 (Add.
MS. 37916, f. 16); *Gent. Mag.* lxi (1791), 174.   [2] *Mem.* ii. 327.
[3] CB to Twining [Aug. 1783], fragment (Add. MS. 39929, ff. 165–6).

part of my youth, when every thing was new, and the disposition to be pleased undiminished by criticism or satiety'.[1]
Salomon soon brought Haydn to visit the historian of music,
who was not disappointed: 'I have had the great Haydn here,
& think him as *good* a creature as *great Musician*.'[2] Burney
naturally wished to present Haydn with his *History* and sent
him the four volumes 'superbly bound' and accompanied by an
ecstatic poem welcoming him to England. To ensure that the
composer had no excuse for not reading his verses, Burney asked
Latrobe to translate them into German prose and early in
March sent his friend the following report:

Having met the $\begin{cases} \text{good} \\ \text{great} \end{cases}$ man, by accident, at the Professional Concert
soon after he had rec^d my present, he took the opportunity of making
fine speeches innumerable, *viva voce*, & by that means saved himself the
trouble of writing a letter, as he told me he intended to do. I afterwards met him at the Concert of Anc^t Music in Tottenham street,
whence I carried him home when it was over; & then he repeated &
added more *fine things* on my present, than he c^d have written on ten
sheets of Paper.

Burney had prophesied earlier in the year that 'It will be a
busy & memorable season in the Hist^y of Tweedle-dum and
Tweedle-dee Quarrels' and Haydn's first concert for Salomon
was duly delayed for some weeks by conflict between rival
theatrical and musical interests. Burney was already doing
everything in his power for Haydn, however; and having told
Latrobe that Haydn was to have a benefit concert in April
(later postponed until May), he added, 'I am now translating
for him, *totidem syllabis*, an Ital. Oratorio Chorus, which is to be
performed in English. Success attend him in all his enterprizes.'
His enthusiasm went even further for, encouraged by Haydn's
approval of his poem, he expanded it and allowed himself to be
'persuaded by 2 or 3 trusty friends to print it, upon a supposi-
tion that it may inform some of our musical folks how great a
Man we have at present the good fortune to possess'. In spite of
his ambitions as a poet, he explained to Latrobe that he would
publish his verses anonymously: 'I must entreat you to keep my

---

[1] *Hist. Mus.* iv. 599.
[2] CB to A. Young, 16 Feb. 1791 (Add. MS. 35127, ff. 84–88).

secret or I shall have all the envious brethren on my back, who
in the true *esprit du Metric*, imagine all praise bestowed on
others, a robery [*sic*] committed on their own little estate (if
they have any) in Parnassus. I shall not let even the printer, or
all my near relations into this secret—therefore Mum's the
Word.'[1] Thomas Twining, who was fascinated by Burney's
news of Haydn, saw the poem before publication and, with his
usual frankness, criticized part of it as 'dry, prosaic, and
cataloguish'.[2] Burney was not to be deterred, however, and in
May 1791 his *Verses on the Arrival in England of the Great Musician
Haydn* appeared in a shilling pamphlet of fourteen pages. His
anonymity enabled him to escape the envious criticism that he
anticipated, as well as to commend his own poem to the readers
of the *Monthly Review* in June.[3]

　　Burney's friendship with Haydn developed rapidly. In April
he described to Latrobe a visit by the composer to Chelsea
College:

I ⟨spent⟩ the day yesterday with the dear great & good Haydn,
whom I love more & more every time I see as well as hear him. In a
small party chiefly of my own family, we prevailed on him to play
the 1st Violin to his Instrumental Passione, for wch, though we cd
only perform it in 4 parts, though it consists of 16,[4] yet its effect was
admirable as executed by him, in a most chaste & feeling manner.
He played the 2d Violin only to several of his Quartets—while my
Nephews played the 1st & Tenor, & a Mr Gun of Cambridge the
Violoncello.[5]

Not surprisingly Burney's musical friends and acquaintances
pressed him to introduce them to the composer. The former
infant prodigy, William Crotch, now the organist of Christ
Church, Oxford, wrote to ask him to arrange a meeting; and it
was Burney who eventually brought Haydn and Latrobe together.[6] Twining was also greatly excited at the prospect of a

　[1] CB to Latrobe, 3 Mar. 1791 (Osborn).
　[2] Twining to CB, 4 May 1791, *Country Clergyman*, p. 148.
　[3] vi (1791), 223–4. There is a manuscript of the poem in the Berg Collection.
　[4] This work, better known as *The Seven Last Words of Christ*, was written for the
Cathedral of Cadiz in 1785 and published in its original orchestral form in 1787.
Arrangements for string quartet and chorus were published later.
　[5] CB to Latrobe, 24 Apr. 1791 (Osborn).
　[6] Crotch to CB, 8 Mar. 1791 (Osborn); Latrobe to V. Novello, 22 Nov. 1828
(B.M. Add. MS. 11730, f. 112).

musical evening in Haydn's company, which he promised to attend 'if it were even in the black hole of Calcutta (if it is a good hole for music)'.[1] Burney managed to arrange the small musical party at Chelsea College late in May, when Twining, Haydn, and a few other friends enjoyed 'an excellent Concert for real judges of good Music, unmixed and unannoyed by loquacity; in this Accademia Haydn himself condescended to play the Tenor'. Once again they played Haydn's *Seven Last Words of Christ*, which Burney now considered 'perhaps, the most sublime composition without words to point out its meaning that has ever been composed'.[2]

After this concert Twining could no doubt dispose of the fear which he had expressed in the previous February that Haydn, now in his sixties, had written himself out: 'If the resources of any human composer could be inexhaustible, I should suppose Haydn's would; but as, after all, he is but a mortal, I am afraid he must soon get to the bottom of his genius-box.'[3] The very reverse was, of course, to be the case, for his two visits to England in 1791–2 and 1794–5 were to stimulate Haydn to new imaginative heights. Burney's opinion of the great symphonies which he wrote for Salomon can best be summarized by the remarks he was to make after Haydn's benefit concert in May 1795. The new symphonies performed that evening seemed to him 'such as were never heard before, of any *mortal's* production; of what Apollo & the Muses compose or perform we can only judge by such productions as these'.[4]

Early in July 1791 Haydn received an honorary Mus.D. at Oxford. According to the composer's first biographers, Dies and Griesinger, Burney instigated this event and accompanied him to Oxford for the ceremony.[5] There is certainly nothing implausible in the story, but already Burney was becoming preoccupied by an anxiety quite acute enough to relegate even Haydn to secondary importance. After almost four wretched years at Court, Fanny had at last confessed to him, at the Handel Commemoration in May 1790, the distaste she felt for her royal post, the disastrous effect that her duties were having on her

---

[1] Twining to CB, 4 May 1791, *Country Clergyman*, pp. 147–9.
[2] *Frag. Mem.* (Berg); *DL*, iv. 459.
[3] Twining to CB, 15 Feb. 1791, *Country Clergyman*, pp. 143–4.
[4] CB to Susan Phillips, 8 May 1795 (Osborn).
[5] Vernon Gotwals, *Joseph Haydn*, Madison, 1963, pp. 35, 158.

health, and her anxiety to return from painful seclusion to her family and friends. As she had always feared, her father was greatly upset: 'how was I struck to see his honoured head bowed down almost into his bosom with dejection and discomfort!—We were both perfectly still a few moments; but when he raised his head I could hardly keep my seat, to see his eyes filled with tears!—"I have long", he cried, "been uneasy, though I have not spoken. . . . but . . . if you wish to resign—my house, my purse, my arms, shall be open to receive you back!" '¹ Burney was depressed not only by the prospect of losing a valuable and flattering connexion with the Royal Family. With the French monarchy in so precarious a situation, he was terrified lest Fanny's resignation should be interpreted as any kind of disloyalty.

In such troublesome times he desired no more than to take every opportunity of showing his devotion to the King and Queen, as he could in the following October when he was commissioned through Fanny to obtain two copies of Burke's _Reflections on the French Revolution_ for the Royal Family: 'What an honour to be en commerce de Livres wᵗʰ R[oyalt]y! Well, we shall grow rich in honour at least—however poor in Pocket.'² The rapid deterioration of Fanny's health soon made it clear, however, that she could not continue at Court and, after she had made futile attempts, a cause for depression in themselves, to obtain royal favours for her brothers,³ a letter of resignation was presented to the Queen. Although, by the end of 1790, Burney's anxiety over Fanny's health more than balanced his desire to retain the goodwill of the King and Queen, he was still relieved to learn in January 1791 that, while the Queen was unwilling to lose Fanny, there was 'no ill-will mixed with the reluctance', and that she had named him with 'much softness'.⁴

Although he anxiously assured all his friends of Fanny's loyalty—'She will risk the dying at her Majesty's feet to show her zeal before she can be spared'⁵—her situation was by now a matter of almost public interest. As William Windham told Burney, 'It was the common cause of every one interested in the concerns of genius & literature.'⁶ Boswell, Reynolds, and

¹ _DL_, iv. 392.   ² CB to FB, 27 Oct. 1790 (Barrett).
³ Hemlow, pp. 213–15.   ⁴ _DL_, iv. 449.
⁵ CB to A. Young, 16 Feb. 1791 (B.M. Add. MS. 35127, f. 84).
⁶ Windham to CB, 28 July 1791 (Osborn).

Walpole were all campaigning for her release and The Club even considered addressing 'a round-robin to the Doctor, to recall his daughter to the world'.[1] In so delicate a situation, when motives might easily be misinterpreted, it was reassuring to 'find that we shall not be blamed for the steps we have taken, when they come to be known'; but to the end Burney was filled with misgivings, as he told Fanny: 'God send this Catastrophe may be operatical!—any other w^d make you & all of us uncomfortable for the rest of our lives.'[2] By early July 1791, however, he had decided to bring her home regardless of the consequences, when he learned that her captivity was at an end and that the fear that 'like Agamemnon I had sacrificed you, my Iphigenia, to the state' had been unnecessary. On 7 July 1791, ailing but rejoicing, Fanny arrived at Chelsea, the Royal Family having parted with her in a reassuringly 'gracious & amicable manner'.[3]

Dining with Reynolds, Malone, and Burke in the following September, as he told Fanny, Burney heard Burke sum up her career at Court with the observation that 'if Johnson had been alive your hist^y w^d have furnished him with an additional & interesting article to his *Vanity of human wishes*'.[4] The disappointment was almost entirely Burney's own, however, and Fanny did not perhaps exaggerate in describing her break with the Royal Family as 'a blight to close, in sickly mists, the most brilliant avenues of his parental ambition'.[5] All this mental turmoil had its customary result and in August 1791 severe lumbago forced Burney to abandon a visit he had planned to make to Crewe Hall in Cheshire, at the invitation of Mrs. Crewe.[6] Reporting to her on his health in the following month, Burney admitted that he was suffering not merely from an old complaint: 'though I once thought I sh^d have died, I now only find that I am grown old'. Suddenly the indefatigable and cheerful Burney was disillusioned and purposeless, mocking the irrational tenacity with which he clung to life: 'We scramble &

[1] *DL*, iv. 424, 429–31; *Mem*. iii. 116.
[2] CB to FB, 14 June and [June 1791] (Osborn).
[3] FB to CB, 3 July 1791, *DL*, iv. 481–2; CB to FB, 6 July 1791 (Osborn); to Walpole, July 1791, draft (W. S. Lewis).
[4] CB to FB, 21 Sept. 1791 (Osborn); *DL*, v. 34.
[5] *Mem*. iii. 111.
[6] CB to FB, 17 Aug. 1791 (Osborn).

paddle ab^t to the last breath, to continue that existence with wch we pretend to be so *dissatisfied*.'[1] It is hard to recognize in Burney's dispirited complaints the man who, only a few months earlier, had been so flattered and excited by the friendship of Joseph Haydn. In September he confessed to Arthur Young that 'a listless & irresolute disposition has made my mind for some time past as flimsy as a dish-clout'. For the first time he recorded what was to be, to the end of his life, an annual sense of foreboding at the approach of winter, which would soon 'shew his d——d sour face, & chain me to my chimney corner, till after X^{mas}, when I shall be unfettered merely to be dragged into the hurry & din of London, wch are every year more & more insupportable. . . . Indeed Autumn wth all its golden gloss & variegated charms to Landscape Painters, is to me a constant memento mori, wth its withered leaves tumbling ab^t my ears.'[2]

Whatever work on Metastasio had been achieved in 1791 came to an end in September: 'Poor Metastasio lies stock still and has ever since I lost my amanuensis, Bessy Young, now Hoole.'[3] In any case, he had found the task less amusing than in the previous year: 'I was unable to divert myself by my own labour, so I applied to that of other people.' His reading had included the correspondence of Voltaire,[4] which had 'enlivened many a dull hour' and James Boswell's long-awaited *Life of Johnson*. In such revolutionary days Burney looked back more and more nostalgically to the great Johnsonian period and he was moved and gratified by the biography, in spite of the fact that, as he observed to Fanny, he had some reservations: 'I am glad Bozzy entertains & sometimes displeases you as he did me.'[5] If he had ever pursued his own plan of writing a biography of Johnson, there was some information, as he told Boswell himself, which he would have thought it prudent to omit:

Some indeed have thought that too many of the weaknesses, prejudices & infirmities of this truly great & virtuous Man have been

---

[1] CB to Mrs. Crewe, 9 Sept. 1791 (Osborn).
[2] CB to A. Young, 21 Sept. 1791 (B.M. Add. MS. 35127, ff. 125–6).
[3] CB to FB, 8 Oct. 1791, *DL*, v. 35–37. Eliza Young, daughter of CB's brother-in-law, married the Rev. Samuel Hoole on 15 Sept. 1791, *Gent. Mag.* lxi (1791), 873.   [4] Some notes by CB on Voltaire's letters have survived (Comyn).
[5] CB to FB, 4 Oct. 1791; and to R. Cox [Nov. 1791], draft (Osborn).

recorded; but what other Man c^d have had his private life so deeply & minutely probed without discovering vices or at least foibles, more hurtful to society than those wch you have disclosed? The most gratifying information wch I can give you concerning the effect of your narration is, that it has impressed y^r readers with a much more favourable opinion of the goodness of our Friend's heart than they had before conceived, though they were never insensible to his merits as a Writer. . . .

Indeed, if all his writings wch had been previously printed were lost, or had never appeared, your book w^d have conveyed to posterity as advantageous an Idea of his character, genius, & worth, as Xenophon has done of those of Socrates.

Burney was, in fact, so impressed that he recommended to Boswell 'the collecting & writing _Memoirs of the deceased Members of our Club_'. He could pay no higher compliment to Boswell's biographical talents than to say, '_you_ may make even Hawkins entertaining, for the first time'.[1] After Boswell's death, however, Burney spoke rather more severely of the biography to Edmond Malone:

It is too late now to soften or expunge the harsh and offensive opinion of living characters & their productions, uttered in private conversation by Johnson, without the least idea of their being made public. Among all the good qualities of our friend Boswell, wch were very numerous, _delicacy_ had no admission. He was equally careless what was said of himself, or what he said of others. But the memorabilia wch his diligence & enthusiastic admiration of the British Socrates have preserved are inestimable, & will merit the gratitude of posterity as long as the language of our country shall be intelligible.

With the return of Fanny from a recuperative holiday in the autumn, Burney's spirits revived and she found him 'all goodness, gaiety, and affection'.[3] He had now returned to the organization of his library and had set himself the task of making a '_Catalogue raisonné_' of all his books on music, 'describing the intention of the writer of each, & the success wth wch he has executed his design'. His musical library had been collected with great trouble and many of the volumes in it were extremely rare: accordingly he now decided to 'form them into a Corpus,

[1] CB to Boswell, 16 July 1791 (draft, Hyde; original, Boswell Papers, Yale).
[2] CB to Malone, 10 Oct. 1798 (Add. MS. 33965, f. 24; Mercer, ii. 1032).
[3] _DL_, v. 37–38.

or complete body of books & Manuscripts solely confined to the Practice & Science of Music. and if ever they are sold it shall be to some public Lib^y in the Lump. This is my present Hobby. . . .'[1]

He expected that in the New Year this work would be interrupted by the usual 'drudgery' of teaching, but the interruption which winter brought was, instead, his severest illness since 1751. In December 1791 he was confined to his room with rheumatism, but the attack seemed no more serious than on earlier occasions and Ralph Griffiths was encouraging him to amuse himself with extra work for the *Monthly Review*. By February 1792, however, he was in such pain that Griffiths wrote again urging him to abandon whatever reviews he had promised.[2] Fanny returned to Chelsea in the middle of the month to find him 'rather worse than better, and lower and more depressed about himself than ever. To see him dejected is, of all sights, to me the most melancholy, his native cheerfulness having a character of such temperate sweetness, that there is no dispensing with any of it, as its utmost vigour never a moment overpowers.'[3]

Burney's dejection was caused not merely by excruciating rheumatism, for between November 1791 and March 1792 he received a number of severe shocks, as if all that remained to link him to the happiest years of his past were being systematically destroyed. During 1791 he had corresponded with Lord Orford, the patron of his years in Norfolk, and had managed to obtain some financial support for their common friend John Hayes, who was in poor health. In November 1791 Orford himself died and Hayes, who bequeathed some handsome books to Burney, survived only some twelve months.[4] On 15 January 1792, a year after it had opened as an opera-house, the Pantheon was burned down and Burney lost both his post as Foreign Secretary and the £700 which he had invested in the project.[5] In the following month he lost one of the last of the intimate

[1] CB to R. Cox [Nov. 1791], draft (Osborn); see *post*, p. 476.
[2] Griffiths to CB [Dec. 1791], 31 Dec. [1791], and 21 Feb. [1792] (Osborn).
[3] *DL*, v. 57.
[4] CB to Orford, 17 Apr. 1791 and [1791], drafts (Berg); *Mem.* iii. 146–51; *Gent. Mag.* lxi (1791), 1164–5 and lxii (1792), 1059.
[5] *Frag. Mem.* (Berg); CB to Lady Crewe, 18 Apr. 1806 (B.M. Add. MS. 37 16, f. 16).

friends whom he had made in the 1770's. After a visit to Sir Joshua Reynolds, who had been in poor health for some time, he had reported in November 1791 that 'his spirits are depressed beyond revival by the Society of his acquaintance, or consolation of his friends'.[1] Reynolds died on 23 February 1792.

One of the fragments of Burney's 'Memoirs' contains a long and moving tribute to Reynold's genius and character, recalling their long friendship, their frequent meetings at Streatham, at The Club, and, especially when they were close neighbours in London, in their own homes. Both were amiable and good-natured men and their enjoyment of each other's company had been increased by the contrast with more strenuous friendships. Burney recalled that Reynolds had always kept his temper when Johnson and Burke, both of whom he admired intensely, had 'wounded his feelings' in the course of 'vehement debates', although he would afterwards complain confidentially to Burney of the 'rudeness and violence' with which they had treated him. Although his health prevented Burney from joining the other members of The Club at Reynolds's funeral, he wrote an 'Elegy' on his old friend.[2]

A few weeks after the death of Reynolds, Burney suffered another loss which depressed him even more. During a visit to London his elder brother Richard, the head of the Burney family in Worcester, was knocked down by a coach and left lying in the street with a serious brain injury.[3] The death of his brother ('the only one I had by the same mother'), with whom he had spent his early years of 'orphanage' at Condover and much of his time when he first arrived as a youth in London, only confirmed Burney's gloomy conviction that his own end was at hand. During April 1792 he prepared for death, writing 'farewell' letters to his daughters Fanny, Susan, and Charlotte, which were to be given to them on his decease, and in which as a 'last prayer' he praised their respective virtues and regretted that they could not be around him as he lay dying.[4]

In the spring, however, with the warmer weather, Burney revived a little. After a confinement of some six months he

---

[1] CB to R. Cox [Nov. 1791], draft (Osborn).
[2] *Frag. Mem.* (Berg); *DL*, v. 67; *Mem.* iii. 145–6.
[3] *Frag. Mem.* (Berg); *GDB*, ii. 124–6.
[4] CB to FB and to Susan Phillips (Berg); to Charlotte Francis (Barrett), Apr. 1792.

emerged from the sickroom in June 1792 and was able to accompany Fanny on visits to Mrs. Crewe's villa at Hampstead, and to attend a dinner given by Joseph Haydn, who was shortly to leave England, for the Musical Graduates, a club of Doctors and Bachelors of Music resident in London, who provided the dinner in rotation.[1] Later in the summer he confessed to Twining that 'last winter I had little expectation of extending existence to the present time'. His wife was ill and he himself was still crippled in his arm and hand.[2] By August, however, he had recovered his spirits sufficiently to enjoy helping Lord Macartney, a relation of Mrs. Crewe, to organize the 'musical establishment' he was taking with him on his famous embassy to the Emperor of China; and he took the opportunity to give Macartney a list of inquiries which might conveniently be made about the nature of Chinese music. Burney devoted a great deal of time to the problem of introducing European music to Chinese ears, and was agreeably surprised when Macartney expressed his gratitude by presenting him with an inscribed silver inkstand.[3]

Burney's arm was still crippled, however, and in September he was advised to try the waters at Bath. Towards the end of the month he was driven there, spending two nights with his old friend Richard Cox at Quarley in Hampshire. The past now seemed to haunt him and he 'fetched a sigh or two in passing' Fulke Greville's old country house at Wilbury, 'the happy residence of my youth & gigling days!'[4] At Bath he was delighted to meet Edmund Burke and his wife and although leeches and the pump had little effect on his useless arm, he stayed longer than he had planned. Late in October he set out on the return journey to London, spending a night at Reading on the

---

[1] *DL*, v. 89, 98; CB to A. Young, 17 July 1792 (Add. MS. 35127, ff. 161–2); *Frag. Mem.* (Berg).

[2] CB to Twining [? Aug. 1792], draft (Osborn).

[3] *Frag. Mem.* (Berg); CB to Mrs. Crewe, 27 Aug. 1792 (Osborn); CB to J. C. Walker, 1 July 1793 (Yale); *Mem.* iii. 217–18. J. L. Cranmer-Byng, *An Embassy to China*, 1962, p. 364, n. 22, suggests that an entry in Macartney's account-book for 22 Aug. 1792—'To Dr. Burney, balance for musical instruments—£76–1–4'— contradicts CB's statement in his Will that he 'positively refused all pecuniary reward' for his services, *GDB*, ii. 269. But CB clearly meant that he had refused the remuneration which Macartney thought that he had 'professionally' deserved for his assistance; whereas he would obviously accept repayment of any money he spent on equipping the small band which he organized for the embassy.

[4] CB to Mrs. Crewe, 8 Oct. 1792 (Osborn); to J. C. Walker, 1 Nov. 1792 (Hyde).

way. In the inn he remembered that the widow of Christopher
Smart, the unhappy friend of his earliest years in London, lived
in the town and he hired a waiter to guide him through the
unlit streets to her home. Time had robbed him in recent years
of so many of his old friends that he could not waste such an
opportunity, even if it were unlikely that Mrs. Smart, whom he
had not seen for forty years, would remember him:

She was alone in a back parlour; In to wch when I was introduced,
anonymously, we stared at each other for some moments, ere either
of us spoke—when I, breaking silence, asked her if she w^d permit a
friend of 40 years standing to claim and renew acquaintance with
her?—We then stared at each other with more prying curiosity. 'I
think, (says she, speaking first) I know who you are'—Do you? says I
—giving her still more time for recollection—I shall be much flattered if you do—'You are Doctor Burney'—says she. 'I knew you by
your voice.'—was not this an extraordinary reminiscence? I then
fancied I c^d trace through the ravages of time, remains of the features
of Nancy Carnan. Her figure is still good, & for her time of life, she is
still a fine woman. But a certain gravity, bordering on severity of
countenance, has obliterated almost all her juvenile sweetness & play
of features. Her life must have been rendered miserable by marriage,
& full of care & difficulties during her Widowhood. We talked over
old times near an hour; & though she well remembered my bringing
her Father-in-law Mr. Newbery & the Poet together, & by that
means, being the author of her unhappy Marriage, she seemed to forgive me, & we parted as good friends as if we had not met at such
a distant period.[1]

Reassured that the passage of time had not entirely destroyed
all the links with his past, Burney travelled on to London. His
pleasantly melancholy recollections of his youth could not protect him, however, from the insistent horror of the present.

II

Burney recovered his health and returned to the world just in
time to grasp the full horror of events across the Channel.
France was now at war with Prussia and Austria; the French
monarchy was on the point of collapse; and in August and
September 1792 the Revolutionary Commune ruthlessly
massacred its enemies. It would be hard to exaggerate the effect

[1] CB to FB, 2, 8, and 29 Oct. 1792 and to CB Jr., 18 Oct. 1792 (Berg); to
Charlotte Francis, 22 Oct. 1792 (Barrett); to Mrs. Crewe, 31 Oct. 1792 (Osborn).

which the daily news from Paris had on Burney. In September, just before setting out for Bath, he had written to Mrs. Crewe, 'I can neither think, talk, or write ab^t anything else than the abominations of France'. In one anguished cry he expressed all his regret for an era that seemed to have come so decisively to a conclusion: 'Is this the end of the 18th Cent^y, so enlightened & so philosophical?' His own firm conviction was that 'There is . . . no Tyrant so cruel, nor no Sovereign so worthless, as that of the Mob'.[1]

Repeatedly he insisted that his opinions were affected by no political commitments: as he told Mrs. Crewe, 'you may perhaps seldom converse with so mere a *by-stander* as myself'.[2] He was shocked not merely by the 'abominations' in France, however, for to his bewilderment he found that there were still English 'democrats' who were hoping that a similar social revolution would occur in their own country. In almost every letter he wrote in the autumn of 1792, Burney expressed his faith in the English constitution and his proud and defiant attachment to the existing structure of society:

To shake hands wth sweep-chimneys, Coal-heavers, churls, clod-polls, soldiers, & sailors, & assure them that they are our *true sovereigns*, have a right to our possessions without work or service, & that without education, cultivation of talents, or intellect, they are equal & even superior to those who have usually been thought men of learning, abilities, and genius. These are the reforms intended. . . . As to the *majesty of the people*, I own myself a determined rebel to all *tyrants*, but to none so much as to that monster. If we were really oppressed, old as I am, & crippled by Rheumatism, I w^d endeavour to pull a trigger against the oppressors, if fair means w^d not do.[3]

The execution of Louis XVI in January 1793 and England's declaration of war in the following month, however, helped to unify the country. Charles Fox's appearance at The Club could still upset the other members,[4] but patriotic hostility against France gradually replaced internal dissension.

The next event which, during the first half of 1793, greatly distressed Burney can only be understood in the context of his horror of everything French. In January his daughter Fanny

[1] CB to Mrs. Crewe, 19 Sept. 1792 (Osborn).
[2] Ibid., 31 Oct. 1792 (Osborn).
[3] Ibid., 2 Dec. 1792 (Osborn).
[4] CB to FB and Susan Phillips, 31 Jan. 1793, *DL*, v. 166–9.

met the handsome but penniless General d'Arblay amongst a group of French *émigrés* at Juniper Hall in Surrey. Before long they were intent on marriage, in spite of the fact that Burney had repeatedly warned Fanny to use the greatest caution in her relations with her new French friends, particularly Madame de Staël.[1] When he learned of Fanny's intention he was convinced that such a marriage could only be disastrous; and without forbidding it, he did everything in his power to persuade the middle-aged lovers to postpone the wedding until the impoverished General had some prospect of financial support to offer his wife. In his letters to Fanny, to her close friend Mrs. Locke, and to d'Arblay himself during the summer of 1793,[2] he insisted that his sole objection to the marriage was that they would have only Fanny's meagre royal pension to live on and that he himself could not afford to augment it.

Fanny believed that her father's 'dread of pecuniary embarrassment [was] secretly stimulated and heightened by a latent hope and belief in a far more advantageous connexion';[3] and certainly after the high promise of her summons to Court in 1786, Burney could not help feeling that she might have done more for the family than marry an impecunious French soldier. Yet behind these financial considerations undoubtedly lay instinctive dismay at the fact that his daughter should have chosen at such a moment to marry a Frenchman (even if d'Arblay had been driven from his native land), a Catholic and a Constitutionalist, who would probably never recover his confiscated property in France nor obtain any fitting employment in England. His disapproval of the match was somewhat softened after a tense first meeting with the polished and cultivated Frenchman,[4] but to the very end he refused to bless the marriage, even if he could do nothing to prevent it. Fanny was convinced that in time his attitude would change: certainly, she had no intention of surrendering her own preference for humble happiness with d'Arblay to the social life in London which she had never really enjoyed. Five days before her wedding she wrote to her brother Charles,

My dear Father—alas!—from prudential scruples—is coldly

---

[1] *DL*, v. 179–80, 183.
[2] CB to FB, May 1793, *DL*, v. 203–5; to Mrs. Locke, 11 July 1793 (Barrett); to d'Arblay, 11 July 1793 (Berg). [3] *Mem.* iii. 179–80. [4] Hemlow, pp. 232–4.

averse to this transaction—& my Heart is heavy from his evident ill will to it—yet he has not refused his consent—&circumstances are such that I feel myself bound in honour—& even in necessity—to here fix my fate—or to relinquish for ever a Person the most peculiarly to my taste, & whom I think the most peculiarly formed for my happiness, of any Mortal I ever saw or ever knew in my life.[1]

Burney declined to attend the wedding on 28 July 1793 and Fanny received merely 'a cold acquiescence, that left me to myself'.[2] By September, however, he had resigned himself to the situation and was writing, as Fanny had trusted he would, in his characteristically cheerful manner to his daughter and her husband.[3]

During the summer of 1793 Burney seems to have sought refuge once more in his biography of Metastasio, which had lain untouched for almost two years. In July he visited Edmund Burke at Beaconsfield and found not only pastoral escape from news from France and family problems, but positive encouragement of his literary enterprise: 'We read, we walked, we fed rabits, & made hay together. And having begun my Memoirs of Metastasio, I ventured to shew him some sheets of the MS. To wch he was so polite, that I am ashamed to record his flattering encouragement.'[4] Whilst at Beaconsfield Burney accepted an invitation from Mrs. Crewe's brother, who had recently married the eldest daughter of the Duke of Portland, to visit Bulstrode. This visit was a significant one, for although Portland's 'democratic' leanings ('I wish Cha. Fox had not infatuated this same D[uke]') somewhat disturbed Burney, the Duke cordially invited him to come again to Bulstrode.[5] In the following decade the friendship of the Duke of Portland and summer visits to Bulstrode were to provide some of the happiest weeks of Burney's last troubled years.

Although his attention had returned briefly to Metastasio, the biography was once more willingly laid aside late in the summer when the opportunity of practical assistance to the victims of the French Revolution presented itself. During the summer of 1793 Mrs. Crewe had seen at Eastbourne 'a great number

[1] FB to CB Jr., 23 July 1793 (Comyn).
[2] Ibid., 8 Aug. 1793 (Osborn).
[3] CB to FB, 12 Sept. 1793 (Barrett; DL, v. 218–20).
[4] Frag. Mem. (Berg).
[5] CB to CB Jr., 16 July 1793 (transcript in Scholes papers, Osborn).

of venerable and amiable Fr[ench] clergy, suffering all the evils of banishm^t & beggary with silent resignation', and had been moved to raise money among her female friends to supplement the tiny allowance made to these unfortunate priests by an official Committee established for the purpose.[1] The organization of her scheme began in the second half of August and she asked Burney to act as her London agent. As a gesture against French tyranny and as an exercise in 'benevolence', the work appealed to him; and he enjoyed corresponding about it with such important political figures as Burke and Windham.[2] By the autumn, however, he found himself acting as honorary secretary to a scheme which grew rapidly more complicated as advertisements, 'Plans', and subscription papers were published. His *'secretaryship'* had become a full-time occupation and his apartment in Chelsea College the 'general office' of Mrs. Crewe's generous project.[3]

As the official fund threatened to expire, the 'Ladies' Plan' assumed even greater importance: Fanny was persuaded to write a dignified pamphlet in support of it, especially valuable since male opinion of the scheme tended to dismiss it as 'Ladies' Nonsense',[4] and Burney applied himself to it with the indefatigable zeal which he had previously shown only in writing his *History*. Although Mrs. Crewe herself eventually grew alarmed at the demands he was making on himself, as well as at the size which her benevolent scheme had assumed, his responsibilities were clear enough in his own mind: 'You say, dear Mad^m, that *you* & I must lie by a little; we have done our share—But alas! if we do stop in our agency, who will relieve us?—I protest I see nobody likely to do it—& it will all tumble to Pieces, if left without such Props.'[5] Eventually it became clear that a fully paid secretary and clerical staff would have to be engaged, but nothing was done before Burney had spent much of the autumn carrying the organization on his own shoulders. He had found that the genteel benevolence of the enthusiastic ladies did not extend to the more practical aspects

[1] See p. 366, n. 3.
[2] CB to Mrs. Crewe, 26 and 27 Aug., 7 Sept. 1793 (Osborn); CB to Windham, 10 Sept. 1793 (Add. MS. 37914, f. 56); Burke to CB, 15 Sept. 1793 (Comyn).
[3] CB to FB, 25 Sept. 1793 (Osborn).
[4] Ibid., 4 and 23 Oct. 1793 (Berg); Hemlow, pp. 244–5.
[5] CB to Mrs. Crewe, 24 Oct. 1793 (Osborn.)

of the scheme: 'I have done nothing night & day since I wrote last, but read & write letters ab^t this *Plan* business. No Committee is as yet formed, no secretary or Clerks appointed; & as I was formerly the *whole Society of the Temple of Apollo*, I am now the whole Committee, Secretary, Clerks, & Porters, of the Ladies' Association for the Fr. Em. Clergy.'[1]

Burney must eventually have collapsed under the sheer weight of the work. Severe rheumatism and other 'maladies' confined him to his room in November and December 1793 and his illness alarmed even his family, who had grown rather accustomed to his frequent rheumatic attacks. By the end of January 1794, however, he was better, still crippled in hand and foot but glad that the 'very long & dispiriting confinement' was at an end.[2] At least he had the satisfaction of knowing that his 'indefatigable Measures & cares' on behalf of the French Clergy had resulted in a 'noble success' for the 'Ladies' Plan'; and although his interest in the well-being of the unfortunate priests continued, he was no longer called upon to run the scheme single-handed.[3]

III

Nothing, however, could prevent the steady flow of alarming news from France, for everywhere Burney read and heard about the terror of the guillotine and about French military successes. He came to understand that to the painful question he had asked in 1792—'Is this the end of the 18th Cent^y, so enlightened & philosophical?'—there could be only a tragic answer. When he was not shuddering at the latest news from France, he was thinking wistfully of the past, of the old order and values which were apparently fast disappearing. For one of the last survivors of the great Johnsonian circle, there could be no comfort in talk of reform and progress and when, in April 1794, he met Mrs. Thrale-Piozzi at a concert for the first time since her marriage in 1784, the memory of happier, calmer days quickly bridged the silent rift that had existed between them for ten years: 'Well, we talked, & laughed as usual, and I never saw her more lively, good humoured & pleasant in my

---

[1] CB to FB [? 30 Oct. 1793] (Berg); see *ante*, pp. 30–31.
[2] FB to CB Jr., 8 Jan. 1794 (Osborn); CB to FB, 25 Jan. 1794 (Berg).
[3] FB to CB, 17 Jan. 1794 (Barrett); Windham to CB, 30 Mar. 1794 (Osborn); CB to [Mrs. Crewe], 1 Nov. 1794 (Osborn).

life. My old affection for her all returned, & I w^d have done anything possible to have shewn it with the same empressement as in the best of Johnsonian, Thralian & Streatham times.'[1]

Yet if it was infinitely 'better to talk of our old acquaintance' than of the 'present monsters' in France, it was impossible to hide in pleasant memories from the 'revolution in the minds of men every where' which had occurred since 1789: 'Peace, tranquillity, content, benevolence, humility, politeness, and all religious & social Virtues, are not only neglected, but regarded as vices!! . . . Not to be content with anything, nor to agree wth any one in the change of what *has* been, & *is*, for what is *to be*—nor to be allarmed at the imminent danger of religion, morals, liberty, property, & life—constitutes modern freedom & heroism.'[2] Depressed by French victories and the disorder of the Allied resistance, Burney brooded repeatedly on this apparent collapse of traditional values during 1794:

all the powers & governments of Europe seem breaking up & in a state of rapid decay. Every thing is decompounding & disorganizing & seems likely *not* to leave a *wreck* behind! Principles are gone, at least those that were once thought wise & good—& in their place presumption, conceit, & experiments on Mankind as cruel as those lately made by Spalanzani & others on the meanest animals & reptiles. Every coxcomb is now become a legislator, and has a system of his own, wch if not adopted by others, he becomes a *Robespiere* to the utmost of his power.

But why plague you as well as myself with Politics?—Yet little as I have to lose of life or property, the events of the times haunt me day & night. The principles & horrors of France are making a terrific Progress on the Globe, & though a great part of it was *Mal gouvernée*, no region upon Earth w^d gain by such a Revolution as that now perpetrating.[3]

In March 1794 Burney told Fanny, 'There is no talking or thinking of anything else but the tremendous increase of discontent, danger, & unheard of profligacy & horrors.' This statement might seem to be contradicted by the fact that he was once more enthusiastically at work on his biography of Metastasio by the following spring. There is no inconsistency,

---

[1] CB to FB, 14 Apr. 1794 (Osborn).
[2] Ibid., 19 Mar. 1794 (Barrett).
[3] Ibid., 7 July 1794 (Barrett). Lazaro Spallanzani (1729–99) was famous for physiological experiments on small animals.

however, nor was he merely trying to escape from the horrors of reality. Late in 1792, in the course of one of the many refutations of 'democratic' ideas which he regularly sent Mrs. Crewe, he had written,

I sh^d think I did the world a signal piece of service, if, one night or other, when its inhabitants were all fast asleep, I could, by the wave of a magic wand, wipe away every idea of that kind, smack smooth, out of their brains, or send them down forever to the bottom of their *dimenticatos*; & in their room, pour into their precious noddles, with a large funnel, the love of Music, poetry, & the fine arts, or other good-humoured, amusing, & improving pursuits, ingenious or scientific, as they please. Let them study mathematics, optics, metaphysics, & all the *ics* & *tics* in the world, except *Politics*. How good-humoured & happy they w^d all come down to breakfast, the next morning![1]

Ill-health, family problems, and then the distressed French clergy had prevented him from seeing that his biography of Metastasio might serve as such a 'funnel'; but when he resumed work upon it in 1794, there can be no doubt that he realized that he possessed a wonderful opportunity for a defiant celebration of all that he feared was rapidly disappearing from the world. 'Peace, tranquillity, content, benevolence, humility, politeness, and all religious & social virtues': these were the qualities which Burney thought were being systematically destroyed, and they are the very qualities which are repeatedly emphasized in his account of Metastasio. Even if his eulogy of forgotten virtues could be only a futile gesture of protest, his work now had a purpose which it had hitherto lacked. As he wrote after the publication of his biography:

during these turbulent times, that the writings or virtue of a *Poet of the golden age* sh^d be properly appreciated or tasted, is hardly to be expected. Indeed the work was undertaken more to keep off the *foul fiend* Politics, than with any view to fame or profit. . . . during so total a revolution in the moral as well as political principles of mankind, when virtues are metamorphosed into vices, & è Contra, how can the mild effusions of so tranquil & benignant a heart as that of Metastasio, be thought worthy of display or admiration![2]

Not surprisingly, therefore, Burney's account of Metastasio is idealized and uninteresting. He was writing the kind of

---

[1] CB to Mrs. Crewe, 2 Dec. 1792 (Osborn).
[2] CB to J. C. Walker, 12 July 1796 (PML).

biography that he wished Boswell had written of Samuel Johnson, in which vices and failings were suppressed and only general virtues were celebrated. Although it has remained the most extensive treatment of the poet in English, it can rarely have been read in the course of the present century and it would not be easy to demonstrate that it deserved a better fate. Its dullness cannot be explained merely by the fact that Metastasio led an almost featureless life at the Imperial Court: for it is due equally to Burney's unqualified and nostalgic admiration for the poet and his correspondents, which prevented any appearance of his characteristic humour and irony.

The only interest of the *Memoirs of Metastasio* must now lie in its self-consciously reactionary nature. In this sense it hardly matters and is hardly surprising that Burney's idealized picture of the *'Poet of the golden age'* has since had to be replaced by a much sharper and more critical image of a man, 'always selfish, often servile, sometimes ungrateful, meanest in action when noblest in words', leading 'a life of idleness and indifference', 'not particularly happy, and perhaps [taking] a pleasure in being so as little as possible: to be wretched was at least some little excitement in this monotony'. Although Burney had several times conversed with Metastasio, the 'picture of rewarded philosophy and virtue' which he has left for posterity has had to be explained away as the result of his own self-deception and the carefully studied *persona* which the poet assumed for the benefit of visitors.[1]

In the spring and summer of 1794 Burney worked enthusiastically on this celebration of the Golden Age, probably spurred on in addition by the knowledge that Fanny was now working on a new novel and by the hope that, as in 1782, they would be able to publish their books simultaneously. He was also encouraged by a gesture of Joseph Haydn, who was making a second visit to England: 'The admirable composer & worthy man, Haydn, has brought me 2 or 3 of the best prints of Metastasio that have been engraved at Vienna.' Although Burney eventually decided to use only one of them as a frontispiece to the book, Haydn's flattering interest in his biography made him work all the harder. By July 1794 he was able to send the first part of the book to press. Before much progress had

---

[1] 'Vernon Lee', *Studies of the Eighteenth Century in Italy*, 1880, pp. 213–14, 218, 219.

been made, however, he was obliged to call a halt to the printing. Joseph Cooper Walker, the Irish antiquarian, had informed him that a new edition of Metastasio's letters had been published at Vienna, and Burney had desperately 'set all my engines to work' to obtain these volumes, in case they contained new biographical material. He had not forgotten the cancellations which he had been forced to make in similar circumstances in his *Commemoration of Handel* in 1784. In spite of Walker's confident statement, however, none of the librarians, collectors, booksellers, or recent visitors to Vienna whom Burney anxiously consulted throughout 1794 had heard of the new edition.[1]

No progress had therefore been made by the printers with the '2 thick 8vo Vols.' which he expected to publish when Burney returned from his summer travels in August and there was still no news of the mysterious Vienna edition of the letters. There was plenty of work to do, nevertheless, before the biography was complete and Burney applied himself to it during the autumn with the fierce energy of which, as he discovered almost to his own surprise, time had not deprived him: 'You know the rage with wch I stick to any business into wch I am heartily entered, & how I grudge my self every other enjoyment to pursue it. & but for that fury, I sh^d never have finished anything to the end of my life, wth the numerous engagem^{ts} & interruptions wth wch I have been tormented.' For almost the first time since the completion of his *History* in 1789, Burney was once more himself: enthusiastic, tireless, and cheerful. Not surprisingly his new and preoccupying employment put him in better spirits and in better health than he had enjoyed for years.[2]

The puzzling edition of Metastasio's letters still troubled him, however, and towards the end of the year he wrote to Marianne Martinez, with whose father Metastasio had lived for many years, in whose hands he suspected the poet's papers still lay, and whom he had himself met in Vienna in 1772.[3] Late in January 1795 Madame Martinez replied with the information that although no new edition of the letters had appeared, three volumes of *Opere Postume dell'Abate Pietro Metastasio* were in

---

[1] CB to J. C. Walker, 28 Nov. 1794 (F. W. Hilles).
[2] CB to FB, 17 Nov. 1794 (Berg); FB to CB, 21 Oct. 1794 (Barrett).
[3] *Tours*, ii. 106–7, 117, 119–20.

process of publication. To Metastasio's *Osservazioni da me fatte sulle Tragedie e Commedie Greche* would be added miscellaneous unpublished letters and poems.[1] Having ascertained the substance of Walker's rumour, Burney was now faced with the problem of obtaining these important volumes. Although friends, as well as his publishers, the Robinsons were already 'harrying the author' to finish his book,[2] three months of illness and confinement delayed his progress and gave the Vienna volumes an opportunity to arrive.[3] This, unfortunately, did not happen and when Burney eventually resumed his usual bustle of teaching and attendance at The Club, the opera, concerts, and literary *conversazioni* later in 1795, he was still laying 'traps' for the books. For once his busy social life helped him with his literary labours, for he was able to interest Lord Spencer, the First Lord of the Admiralty, in his problem. Spencer wrote to Vienna for the elusive volumes and even arranged that, when obtained, 'they shall be brought by a King's Messenger, against all rule'.[4]

Burney was extremely gratified by this aristocratic encouragement. Meanwhile, he took advantage of the delay in procuring the books by translating Metastasio's commentary on Aristotle's *Poetics*, which he intended to include in his biography. He now met with further encouragement, for some of his scholarly friends began for the first time to take an interest in his new work. By May 1795 he was bursting with pride on Metastasio's and his own behalf:

I am hallooed on prodigiously in my Metastasian Mania. All the Critics—Warton, Twining, Nares, & D[r] Charles,[5] say that his *Estratto dell'Arte poetica d'Aristotele*, w[ch] I am now translating is the best piece of dramatic Criticism that has ever been written—'God bless my Soul!' says Warton, 'I that have been all my life defending the 3 unities am overset'—Ay—quoth I—has not he made you all ashamed of 'em? You learned folks are only theorists in theatrical matters, but Metastasio had 60 years successful practice.—There!— Go to—

He had now recovered all his old passion for the 'idea' of Metastasio, in whom he found 'every thing that delights my

[1] *Metastasio*, i. xiii–xv.　　　　[2] W. Keate to CB, 1 Feb. 1795 (Osborn).
[3] CB to Mason, 10 May 1795 (Osborn).
[4] CB to Susan Phillips, 8 May 1795 (Osborn).　　　　[5] i.e. CB Jr.

heart & feelings—But basta—you know when I take up a favourite author, as a Johnson, a Haydn, or a Metastasio, I do not soon lay him down or let him be *run* down!'[1]

To reinforce the didactic character of his biography, which was already something of a saint's life, Burney decided to add to his chronological list of Metastasio's dramas 'a kind of analysis & indication of the moral view wch the bard had in writing each piece'. While working on this scheme he encountered and surrendered to the fatal temptation of 'translating a few songs & fragments of scenes in each drama to elucidate the doctrine wch he meant to inculcate'. It was a 'daring' plan and he was soon 'seized with a panic', but his ambitions as a poet could not be suppressed. Had not Mrs. Thrale and even Johnson praised his verses in happier days and had not the translations in the *History of Music* escaped criticism? He took the precaution, however, of hopefully explaining his idea to William Mason the poet, asking him to look over and correct his verse translations.[2]

Burney and Mason had been meeting and corresponding since about 1748. In their letters and published works they had disagreed on certain musical matters but the debate had been friendly and they had paid each other handsome compliments in print.[3] More recently their political views had conflicted, but the 'democratic' Mason had eventually seen the folly of his ways and had returned to the ranks—in Burney's opinion—of honest patriots.[4] Lately, however, he had grown somewhat testy and he expressed no great anxiety to see Burney's verse translations of Metastasio. As he also went so far as to disparage Metastasio as a dramatist, Burney tried to mollify him in his reply by requesting some notes on his views to be incorporated in the biography.[5]

Burney did eventually force Mason to look over some sample translations, perhaps encouraged in this persistence by a visit which he made in the same month to Horace Walpole, who, as he told Fanny, 'seemed main eager about my Metastasio, and, —would you think it?—charged me to give plenty of translations from his poetry'.[6] Mason, however, refused to be impressed.

---

[1] CB to FB, 7 May 1795 (Berg).
[2] CB to Mason, 10 May 1795, draft (Osborn).
[3] e.g. *Hist. Mus.* i. 499, iii. 146 and 480 n.   [4] *Mem.* iii. 191–2.
[5] Mason to CB, 23 May 1795 (Osborn); CB to Mason [8 June 1795], draft (Berg).   [6] CB to FB, 9 June 1795, *DL*, v. 258–61.

He clearly did not think very highly of the originals, considered that whatever force they once possessed had evaporated in translation, and frankly recommended 'literal prose Versions'.[1] Such authoritative advice must have dampened Burney's poetic ambitions considerably and he abandoned his plan of including extensive translations, although he retained a few of his versions in the main body of the biography. Those which had already been printed, however, now seem to have given him anxiety, for he cancelled the pages on which one of his longest attempts had appeared and presumably rewrote it.[2] Nevertheless, he included towards the end of his biography Mason's views on Metastasio, together with those of Gray, which the poet had also sent to Burney in June 1795.[3]

By the summer of 1795 two volumes of letters had already been printed and it was clear that a third would be necessary. Burney's translations of the letters, accompanied by a linking biographical narrative, eventually ran to page 280 of the third volume. After an account of Metastasio's death and a discussion of his literary achievement and reputation, he piously added a list of the poet's dramatic works with his discussion of 'the *moral object*' of each of these performances, 'in which he has not only administered cathartics to the irregular passions . . . but anodynes to virtue'; reflections on 'each class of Metastasio's poetical productions for music'; and similar remarks on his miscellaneous poetry. This section also includes a translation of the introduction to Metastasio's *Estratto* on Aristotle's *Poetics*, with a summary of the main body of the treatise. Lack of space had presumably forced Burney to abandon his original enthusiastic plan of printing the whole work. He did not miss the opportunity, however, of paying some compliments to Twining's translation of and commentary on the *Poetics*, which had been published in 1789.[4]

Little information about the completion of the *Memoirs* has survived, except in its own concluding pages. Burney seems eventually to have despaired of the arrival of the King's Messenger from Vienna with the volumes of Metastasio's posthumous

[1] Mason to CB, 28 June 1795 (Osborn).
[2] *Metastasio*, i. 129–32.   [3] Ibid. iii. 385–6.
[4] Ibid., 364–5, 367–8, 377–8. Manuscripts of CB's translation of chaps. i, ii, iii, and xii of the *Estratto* have survived (Berg and Osborn).

works; and although Mason's discouragement had been very largely effective, he could not resist concluding his work with forty lines of original verse addressed 'To the Shade of Metastasio'. A short quotation will conveniently serve to illustrate both Burney's poetic talents and the nature of his admiration for Metastasio:

> Thy lenient ethics mitigate each smart,
> And, while they flatter, purify the heart.
> The furious passions are at thy controul,
> And each emotion of the human soul.
> Lost must that mortal be, who hears in vain
> Thy moral lesson, or thy pious strain!

This poem was intended to conclude the work when Burney eventually sent the last third of his manuscript to press late in 1795. After the work had been printed and the press closed, however, Burney was obliged to add an appendix, which dramatically—and it is perhaps the only excitement in the whole work—describes the arrival in England of several copies of the long-sought _Opere Postume_ in the hands of 'an itinerant German _Colporteur_, or book pedlar', who had heard that the work was in demand in England.

Burney's problem had not, however, been solved, for since his arrival in England, a fortnight before the date at which Burney was writing, the pedlar 'had been hawking his _inestimable_ little bale of Metastasian goods, without success; owing to the price he set upon it being so enormous, that no importer of foreign books would venture to deal with him; nor would he part with a _single_ set, on any terms'.[1] Burney was understandably reluctant to buy the 'seven or eight copies of each impression of the work' which the German insisted on selling together, but eventually he had contrived, 'by the favour of a person in whose hands they were left for a day or two', to spend three hours looking over the volumes and hastily transcribing Metastasio's analysis of _Prometheus Unbound_ from the first volume, which he then printed 'as _addenda_ to the Memoirs of the Poet's Life and Writings'. At this point Burney's appendix assumes the form almost of a diary, for he next informs his readers that he has at last obtained a copy of the work, 'over which my power is unlimited'. Whether some dealer had at last been persuaded to

---

[1] _Metastasio_, iii. 393-4.

buy the whole stock from the pedlar or whether the King's Messenger had arrived dramatically from Vienna just in time with the copy ordered by Lord Spencer is not explained. Burney was now able to add at his leisure further extracts from Metastasio's remarks on Greek dramatists and some comments on the previously unpublished letters and on the poet's will.

Mention of Metastasio reappears in Burney's correspondence in February 1796. Just before the publication of his book he reported to Fanny with typical enthusiasm that he had arranged for a copy to be presented to the Queen,[1] who later told Fanny that she thought it 'a very pretty book' and that she was 'very much pleased with it'.[2] Burney had no financial interest in the sale of the *Memoirs of Metastasio* as he had sold the copyright to the Robinsons,[3] nor did he expect that it would cause a sensation. There were, however, readers who derived the same pleasure from the work that Burney had taken in writing it: that of celebrating forgotten virtues and the old order. There were complimentary letters from relations and friends; and Dorothy Young in Norfolk had a vision of Metastasio in heaven 'highly gratified' by Burney's tribute and

delighted with the delineation of a heart alive to every tender trick of sensibility—well might he exclaim with the Poet, 'He best can paint them who can feel them most.' Indeed he is worthy of such a Biographer, and towards the end of the next century may there arise another, with similar qualifications, to record with the same dignity of sentiment and elegance of language the merit of *him* now employed in the generous task of immortalizing his cotemporaries.[4]

If Fanny is to be believed, her father's 'imitations' of Metastasio were particularly approved by 'the best critics', especially by Horace Walpole, 'as so breathing the sentiments and the style of the author, that they read . . . like two originals'. Her summing-up of the reception of the book, however, is much more restrained than usual and, while it is necessary to read between her over-written lines, her account may be taken as substantially accurate: 'from the public at large, these Memoirs

---

[1] CB to FB, 6 Feb. 1796 (Berg).
[2] *DL*, v. 277.
[3] CB to Horace Walpole, Lord Orford [? Feb. 1796] (W. S. Lewis).
[4] D. Young to CB, 18 Feb. 1796; G. Steevens to CB, 19 Feb. 1796; A. Young to CB, 22 Feb. 1796 (Osborn).

obtained a fair and satisfactory approvance that kindly sheltered
the long-earned laurels of Dr. Burney from withering, if they
elicited not such productive fragrance as to make those laurels
bloom afresh.'[1]

The one tireless enthusiast for Burney's biography was his
Irish friend, Joseph Cooper Walker, who for many years urged
him to publish a further volume of Metastasio's miscellaneous
writings. Burney did not take this flattering suggestion seriously,
probably because he had learned to distrust the unremitting
panegyric with which Walker softened his frequent requests for
scholarly information and the loan of rare books. It is worth
noting that when Walker wrote to Burney in August 1796
praising the *Memoirs of Metastasio* at great length he had not yet
read them, as he admitted to a friend four days later.[2]

Although his admiration for Metastasio continued to the end
of his life, Burney rarely mentioned his biography of the poet in
later years and seems to have been uncharacteristically indifferent to its fate. It had been written as a gesture against the forces
of immorality and disorder and the fact that it evoked little
response was merely a triumphant demonstration of the growth
of these evils in recent years. Only once did he display any
anxiety about the work. Some three years after its publication
he learned that John Hoole, who had translated *The Works of
Metastasio* in 1767, was engaged on a translation of the poet's
Dramas and Other Poems. Suspecting that Hoole was planning to
prefix to it a new life of Metastasio, Burney wrote to point out
that this would inevitably imply that his own recent biography
of the poet was merely 'useless lumber'. He did not feel that it
was 'the part of an old friend' to foster such a suspicion and
suggested that a translation of one of the Italian lives of the
poet would be more appropriate.[3] Hoole evidently sympathized
with his point of view and, in the preface to his translation,
obligingly directed those of his readers who required information about the poet's life to 'the last publication of the ingenious
and indefatigable Dr. Burney'.[4]

---

[1] *Mem.* iii. 213-14.
[2] J. C. Walker to CB, 26 Aug. 1796 (Osborn); to Pinkerton, 30 Aug. 1796,
Literary Correspondence of John Pinkerton, ed. Dawson Turner, 1830, i. 420. Cf.
R. Lonsdale, 'Dr. Burney and the *Monthly Review*,' *RES*, xiv (1963), 355-7.
[3] CB to Hoole [Feb. 1799] (Berg).
[4] *Dramas and Other Poems; of the Abbé Pietro Metastasio*, 1800, i. ii.

Apart from this letter, there is nothing to suggest that Burney was insincere in his professions of indifference to the success of his *Memoirs*. Five months after the book's publication he wrote, 'As to the rapidity of its circulation, or even the Number of copies printed, I am as yet a stranger. All that I have hitherto discovered, & that, accidentally, is that among my fr^{ds} and acquaintance the book has had as many readers as I c^d have expected in more auspicious times.'[1] Yet if Burney's anxiety about his own success and reputation might appear to have diminished since 1789, his concern for that of his family had, if anything, only increased. The progress of Fanny's third novel, *Camilla*, for example, caused him much more alternate worry and pleasure than did his own work. It had been decided to publish *Camilla* by subscription and the problems which this raised preoccupied Burney, Fanny, and Charles from the summer of 1795 until the appearance of the novel in June 1796, some four months after his own *Memoirs*.[2] During the summer Burney tirelessly sent Fanny and other members of the family excited reports of his own ecstatic response to *Camilla* as well as every scrap of praise which he could pick up from his friends and acquaintances.

While his own enthusiasm for the novel knew no bounds, most admirers of Fanny's earlier novels considered that a steady deterioration had now set in. Burney could hardly be unaware of this general opinion, but it made him only the more determined that justice should be done: 'The work if it has fair play must do credit, not only to Fanny, but to us all—I never felt so jealous for the defence of any of her writings.'[3] Few of his friends, however, dared to state their true opinions, although Twining, as usual, frankly stated a preference for *Cecilia*, and Horace Walpole, whom Burney visited in mid-August 1796, was hard put to humour the proud father: 'Next arrived Dr. Burney, on his way to Mrs. Boscawen. He asked me about deplorable *Camilla*—alas! I had not recovered of it enough to be loud in its praise. I am glad however to hear that she has

[1] CB to J. C. Walker, 12 July 1796 (PML).

[2] FB to CB, 4 letters, 18 June–21 July 1795; CB to CB Jr., 3 letters, 11 Jan.–18 April 1796 (Berg; Bodleian, MS. Eng. letters, d. 74, f. 150).

[3] CB to FB, 12, 14, and 16 July 1796 (Berg); to CB Jr., 3 Aug. (Bodleian, MS. Don. c. 56, ff. 87–88) and 5 Sept. 1796 (Berg); to Susan Phillips, 8 Aug. 1796 (Berg).

realised about £2,000. . . .'[1] Burney, however, also reported this
encounter, managing to satisfy himself that the ailing Walpole
was in no fit state to judge so great a work of art competently:
'Ld Orford, to whom I made a short visit last week, is so feeble
and emaciated, that I am sure that he was not able to read
Camilla with the energy, zeal, & disposition to be pleased, w^{ch}
he possessed till very lately. He says "there are fine things in
it, as there must be in whatever Mad^e d'Arblay writes; but
he cannot say he likes it so well as Cecilia".' Burney, in fact,
suspected that Walpole was no longer quite sane. No one in his
right mind could fail to admire *Camilla*.[2]

The greatest source of pride and pleasure came from Fanny's
long accounts of the Queen's gracious condescension in accepting a set of *Camilla* from the hands of the authoress at Windsor.
This latest example of royal notice of his family inspired in
Burney the strongest emotions of loyalty and patriotism: 'How
glad I am to recollect that I have been all my life loyal to such
excellent sovereigns, & fighting & scolding with Wilkites—
Foxites—Democrats—revolutionists—Jacobins—& Anarchists,
without knowing that such gracious goodness to you & your
last born child Camilla were in the Womb of time!'[3] Satisfied
with his own contribution to literature, musical history and,
not least, morality, earlier in the year; deaf to any criticism, and
alert to any praise, of his daughter's new novel, Burney was
happier in the summer of 1796 than he had been for many
years. Even if his own dull biography and Fanny's verbose
novel were hardly the achievements he liked to believe, we
should not perhaps begrudge him a summer of triumphant
elation. As he grew older fate never tantalized him with such
happy interludes for long.

[1] *Corresp.* xii. 203–4.
[2] CB to FB, 23 Aug. 1796 (Berg).
[3] Ibid., 6 Aug. 1796 (Berg).

IX

'ASTRONOMY, AN HISTORICAL
AND DIDACTIC POEM'

1796–1801

I

FLUSHED with what he firmly believed to be the triumphant success of Fanny's *Camilla*, Burney made his usual visits in the summer of 1796 in a state of proud excitement. 'Bright again with smiling success and gay prosperity was this period to Dr. Burney', Fanny observed; but it was, as she added, 'not more bright than brittle!'[1] In spite of his apparent vivacity and high spirits, his severe illness in 1792 had had a lasting effect, 'namely, a slow, unfixed, and nervous feverishness, which had infested his whole system', and which, to the end of his life, could all too easily return, 'robbing his spirits, as well as his frame of elasticity; and casting him into a state the least natural to his vigorous character, of wasteful depression'.[2] Thus, in September 1796, he was thrown into sudden gloom by the departure of his favourite daughter Susan to join her husband, Major Phillips, in Ireland,[3] and worse followed almost immediately. During the summer Mrs. Burney had suffered again from the violent haemorrhages of the lungs which had frequently afflicted her in recent years. Yet since she had recovered on previous occasions, Burney obeyed her insistence that he leave her in the care of their old Lynn friend, Dorothy Young, and continue his country visits during September. On his return to Chelsea later in the month, he found her confined to bed, never to rise again. She lingered until 20 October, when she died after such suffering 'that she often wished an end to her pain'.

The voluminous family papers contain comparatively little about Burney's second wife, to whom he had been married for

---

[1] *Mem.* iii. 219.   [2] Ibid. 175
[3] CB to FB, Sept. 1796 (Berg); *Mem.* iii. 221–2; Hemlow, pp. 277–8.

twenty-nine years, partly because he himself was to destroy all his correspondence with her. Although Miss Hemlow's biography of Fanny has considerably restored the picture, Mrs. Burney inevitably appears in that account from the hostile viewpoint of her stepchildren. Some of the blame for the tension in the household, of which Burney himself can hardly have been unaware, must, however, rest with the children; and the bad temper which was Mrs. Burney's main failing can be partly explained by her loneliness and ill-health. Fanny admitted that 'Her Temper alone was in fault, not her heart or intentions'. Elsewhere, after repeating that this 'Temper the most unhappy' had marred Burney's second marriage, she added that 'whatever there might be to lament of flaw or defect, he was warmly attached to her, & owed to her his chief though not unbroken after-Happiness'.[1] On her deathbed, indeed, Mrs. Burney thanked her husband for his unfailing good humour and kindness during her 'long bodily suffering', when, she feared, she had inevitably shown 'impatience & . . . peevishness in pain'. This consideration should perhaps force us to give her rather more sympathy than her stepchildren were prepared to, but, in any case, there is no reason to doubt the sincerity of Burney's love for and dependence on her. He had admired her unusually wide reading and her conversational powers, but even more important was a 'coincidence of taste & principles' on all important matters which had resulted in a permanently 'sincere, cordial & chearing' relationship.[2]

Although the tribute to his wife's intellect and to her qualities as a companion in Burney's 'Memoirs' is convincing enough, its detachment hardly prepares one for the paralysing effect that her death had on him. In the preceding March Burney had written to Twining on the death of his friend's wife, assuring him that 'time, religion, & philosophical resignation to the orders of Providence' would eventually diminish 'the acuteness of your sorrows'.[3] He himself, however, showed little 'philosophical resignation' at his own loss in the following October. He returned to his apartment after the funeral 'disconsolate and stupified', acutely aware of the 'vacuum in my habitation and

---

[1] FB to Rev. S. Allen [1833], draft; FB's inscription on CB to Mrs. Allen, 1 Dec. 1762 (Berg).   [2] *Frag. Mem.* (Berg).
[3] CB to Twining, 21 Mar. 1796 (Osborn).

in my mind', and he remained in a state of comfortless despair for almost three months.[1] All his old pleasures and hobbies failed to distract him: 'time is heavy, & nights are sleepless. As yet only one subject occupies me—reminiscence of past times & present privations. Everything else is insipid.'[2] His children attempted to help him in vain: 'James and Charles dined here, and kept the monster at a little distance, but he was here again the moment they were gone. I try to read and pronounce the words "without understanding one of them", as Johnson said in reading my dissertation on the music of the ancients.'[3]

Fanny had feared that her father, who was now seventy, would 'require much watching and vigilance',[4] and Burney himself was desperate for some employment to 'make me forget myself and my sorrows'. He told his friends, 'I sit whole hours with my hands before me, without the least inclination or power to have recourse either to such business, or amusem^{ts} as I used to fly to with the greatest eagerness.' The composition of complex canons, which he had always recommended to others as a distraction from pain or sorrow, failed to amuse him; he was entertained by none of his thousands of books; the once infallible opiate of music, 'in my present state of mind . . . only promises disgust'; and 'For *conversation* I am unfit; as indeed I am for any employment of mind or body'. His ceaseless meditation on the past suggested only an occupation which inevitably aggravated his sorrow, 'the heartrending task of looking over & burning old letters and papers, that have been accumulating for many years'. At this period Burney destroyed at least 500 letters to his wife, which, if they had survived, would have provided a much needed perspective on the family. In early December 1796 'the melancholy business of seeking, perusing, sorting & burning, old family papers' was still his 'sole occupation since the sad Catastrophe, and . . . the only one to wch I can apply'. To Twining he now admitted that 'no expectation of such events is sufficient to fortify the mind against horror & affliction, whenever they arrive'.[5]

Fanny was extremely worried by her father's prolonged grief:

[1] *Mem.* iii. 225.   [2] CB to CB Jr. [Nov. 1796] (Berg).
[3] CB to FB, Nov. 1796, *DL*, v. 296–7; see *ante*, p. 182.
[4] *DL*, v. 300.
[5] CB to Latrobe, 14 Nov. 1796 (Osborn); to Twining, 6 Dec. 1796 (Berg).

'he wants some one to find out pursuits—to entice him into reading, by bringing books, or starting subjects; some one to lead him to talk of what he thinks, or to forget what he thinks of, by adroitly talking of what may catch other attention.'[1] Early in November 1796 she started to suggest what she hoped would be attractive projects for him, for she had soon realized that only by persuading him to immerse himself in some large undertaking could he be rescued from his gloomy meditation on the past: 'I want to say something of a *Dictionary of Music*—it would be an unrivalled work in your hands.' This suggestion evidently had no effect, for a week later she was offering two fresh ideas. The first was an attempt to convert his melancholy re-reading of the family papers into a more cheerful task: 'Sometimes I wish this search could be mixed with collecting for copying your numerous—and so many of them beautiful—manuscript poems.' The second suggestion was that Burney, Twining, and other friends should collaborate in a periodical.[2]

Both suggestions were to have repercussions. The first, however, cunningly appealing to Burney's poetic ambitions and affording an easy transition from his rummaging among his papers, took effect almost immediately. Although he was still brooding on the past and burning old letters at the beginning of December, he admitted that he had been astonished by the number of his poems he had discovered and, following Fanny's flattering suggestion, he 'reprieved' and transcribed many of those addressed to his two wives. In addition, he started to collect his 'miscellaneous' verse.[3] To direct this diversion of his energies the better and to help to amuse him during what should have been a festive season, Fanny and her baby son came to stay at Chelsea College just before Christmas 1796. Together they continued the investigation of his papers, but she perceived at once that hope lay in her father's old ambitions as a poet, for he had already filled two quarto notebooks with his verses and enough remained to fill a third. Burney had also come across 350 lines of the poem on astronomy which he had started, abandoned, and forgotten in the summer of 1789.[4] Listening to him read it aloud, Fanny had her moment of inspiration: in Burney's words, 'this Fanny was so partial to, as earnestly to press me to

[1] *DL*, v. 304.   [2] FB to CB, 8 and 14 Nov. 1796 (Berg; *DL*, v. 300–1).
[3] CB to FB, 2 Dec. 1796 (Berg).   [4] See *ante*, p. 348.

go on with it' and eventually he succumbed to her 'urgent entreating'.[1]

The poem which he had started more than seven years earlier had been inspired by the experiments with balloons which had fascinated the nation during the 1780's. As early as 1783 he had prophesied that his grandchildren would live to see 'a regular Balon stage established to all parts of the universe that have ever been heard of'. Fresh from an evening of conversation with the Duc de Chaulnes and Samuel Johnson (who had very little to say on the subject) about the Montgolfiers, Burney had declared, 'if I had wit enough, or energy of mind sufficient to be *mad* ab^t anything now, it w^d be ab^t *Balons*—I think them the most wild, Romantic, pretty playthings for grown Gentlemen that have ever been invented & that the subject, as well as the thing, lifts one to the Clouds, whenever one talks of it.' In September 1784 several members of The Club, including Burney, Burke, and Reynolds, had witnessed 'Lunardi's ascent in a balloon at the Tower'. When he began his poem in 1789 Burney had pursued the idea which had occurred to him six years earlier that, before long, 'parties might undertake voyages to the moon, perhaps to planets nearest the Earth such as Mars & Venus'.[2]

On rediscovering his poem in 1796, Burney was uncertain as to the best way of continuing it: 'My first idea was, in a sportive, but philosophical way, to have visited, & described the inhabitants of the Planets.' Fanny, however, judiciously urged him to make his poem a much more ambitious—and preoccupying—undertaking, and eventually he agreed to attempt what amounted to nothing less than a versification of the complete history of the science, to be entitled '*Astronomy, an historical & didactic Poem, in XII Books*'.[3] He began work on it in January 1797 rather half-heartedly, still reluctant to believe that he would ever enjoy life again: '*Time* only can blunt the edge of regret & sorrow for what we lose;—but quaere—does it not, likewise, diminish our appetite for what remains?'[4] Fanny, however, carefully tended his flickering interest, assuring him that such a

[1] CB to [Dorothy Young], 7 Feb. 1797 (Berg); FB to Esther Burney, 20 Nov. 1820 (Barrett).
[2] CB to Susan Phillips, 17 Dec. 1783; *Frag. Mem.*; CB to CB Jr., 24 Sept. 1784 (Osborn).
[3] CB to [D. Young], 7 Feb. 1797 (Berg).
[4] CB to J. W. Callcott, 24 Jan. 1797 (Osborn).

poem would 'add very considerably to the stock of literature, and in a walk perhaps the most unhackneyed. To conduct to any science by a path strewed over with flowers is giving beauty to labour, and making study a luxury.'[1]

By the end of January 1797 Burney had added 200 lines to his poem. He was still wavering, however, and was tempted by an alternative plan, suggested by Mrs. Crewe, that he and Fanny, with the help of Windham and Canning, edit a 'strictly anti-jacobinical, and professedly monarchical' periodical. The proposal was discussed for some weeks, but when Fanny declined to participate Burney returned to his poem.[2] Although by early February he had completed 600 lines, mainly by devoting sleepless nights to composition, he was uneasy about committing himself, at the age of seventy, to so large an undertaking. Since he had already dealt to his own satisfaction with 'Hesiod, Thales, Anaximander, Pythagoras, Plato, Eudoxus, Aristotle, &c., the heroes of astronomy, before the establishment of the Alexandrian school', it might appear that he had already conquered some daunting material. Nevertheless, Burney grew understandably 'more frightened' as he saw 'more of the plan of the building I have to construct, of which little more than a corner had caught my eye at first'. The necessity of manipulating 'technical Greek words' within his couplets presented a tiring problem in itself.

Reluctant to admit that his sorrow would not last for ever, Burney hesitated: 'I think, if I could a little get up my spirits and perseverance, this business would fasten on me. But, alas, 'tis too late in the day for amendment of any sort!' Fanny, however, was alert with brisk enthusiasm and excited admiration of the difficulties he faced and would conquer: 'I long to see the six hundred lines: pray work up Ptolemy, but don't ask me how! I can hardly imagine anything more difficult for poetry.'[3] On the astronomy poem she banked most of her hope not only for his recovery from present sorrow but for protection from future catastrophes. She judged her father's temperament accurately, for he was soon totally committed to his new task.

---

[1] FB to CB, 26 Jan. 1797, *DL*, v. 315–16.
[2] CB to FB, 6 Feb. 1797 and FB to CB, Feb. 1797, *DL*, v. 317–21; *Mem.* iii. 229–37.
[3] See *ante*, p. 385, n. 3 and n. 2 above.

II

Although Burney's didactic poem on the history of astronomy was never published and was, indeed, destroyed by the author himself, a compressed account of its curious career is justified on several grounds. It illustrates the extent of Burney's interests and the intensity of his ambitions as a poet; it came to the attention of several of his most notable contemporaries; and, however reluctantly it was undertaken, the poem gave him on the whole more unqualified pleasure during its composition than any other of his literary undertakings. His preoccupation with the poem, moreover, even if ultimately futile, at least helped to distract him from such family upheavals as the marriage, against his express wishes, of his widowed daughter Charlotte Francis to Ralph Broome, to whose republicanism he strongly objected, in 1798. Later in the same year Burney was able to escape his horror at the news that his eldest son James had eloped with his half-sister, Sarah Harriet, by losing himself once more in his poem.[1]

Burney was soon enthusiastically at work on his new pursuit, but his rising spirits were constantly threatened by new disappointments and occasions for sorrow. Although it has not hitherto been suspected that he ever possessed such an ambition, two statements by Fanny refer obliquely to the fact that he had hoped to be appointed Professor of Music at Oxford in March 1797. Ironically enough, the new Professor was the twenty-one-year-old William Crotch, whom Burney himself had helped to make famous in 1779.[2] In spite of this setback, Burney was fully recovered from his depression by the end of April 1797, engaging cheerfully 'in as much of my old fashioned hurry as I have been able to undertake', accepting invitations to dinners and literary parties, and attending concerts and the opera during the spring and early summer. His poem was not forgotten: 'after all this, instead of sleeping like a dull mortal, I take a flight upon Pegasus to the moon, or to some planet or fixt star'.[3] By July 1797 he had written eight of the twelve books which he planned.

The poem was, indeed, a necessary precaution. Since 1792, Reynolds, Gibbon, and Boswell had died; and the death of

[1] For an account of these disasters, see Hemlow, pp. 280–5.
[2] FB to CB, 4 Apr. 1797 (Berg); note by FB on CB's 'Johnsoniana' (Barrett).
[3] CB to FB, 4 June 1797 (King's Lynn Museum).

Horace Walpole in March 1797 was followed by that of Dr. Richard Warren, a close friend of Burney, in June[1] and, two weeks later, by that of Edmund Burke. Like Johnson, Burke had 'passions and prejudices' of which Burney had not been able to approve, yet he considered him 'certainly one of the greatest men of the present century' and had valued his friendship. He attended the funeral at Beaconsfield as one of the pall-bearers and found that Burke had left him a ring of remembrance.[2] The generous Mrs. Crewe now decided that Burney must be rescued from the dejection which was once more descending on him by means of a long summer excursion. On 29 July he set off for Crewe Hall in Cheshire, picking up Mrs. Crewe and her daughter at Beaconsfield, where they had been comforting Mrs. Burke. On the way they passed through Stratford, where Burney made a point of sitting in Shakespeare's chair, 'still remaining in his Chimney Corner', and wondered 'Whence c^d his sublime images spring? Not from what he c^d see, hear, or imbibe in such a mansion or habitation as this!'

Part of Mrs. Crewe's scheme was that Burney should revisit the scenes of his youth. At Shrewsbury, his birthplace, he found his way with 'as much local knowledge as I c^d have done near 60 years ago', although he was amazed to find the streets so 'narrow, dirty, irregular & ill built': 'How different were my ideas of this Town 60 years ago, on leaving Condover! I thought it then heaven upon *yearth*, and its buildings the most splendid on its surface.' Sadness, however, inevitably intruded and he did not visit the village of Condover, where he had spent his childhood:

there was no one with me to partake of the melancholy pleasure of visiting poor Nurse Balls habitation, and grave; & the graves of all my play-fellows, & rustic friends!—it was a melancholy part of my wandering through Shrewsbury, that there was not a single inhabitant living that I remember, or who remembered me, though when I left the Town more than 50 years ago, there was not a single housekeeper of any kind of consequence that I did not know and to whom I was not known! But such the term of our existence! and such in old age the melancholy events of the vital drama!

A visit from Crewe Hall to Chester, where he called at his old school and at the cathedral, which contained the first organ on

[1] *Gent. Mag.* lxvii (1797), 616–17.
[2] CB to FB, 20 July 1797, *DL*, v. 330–1; *Mem.* iii. 239–42.

which he had ever played, inspired similar emotions. Mrs. Crewe kept him so occupied with various excursions, however, that he was not allowed to grow dejected. On 26 August he set off for London, calling at Lichfield on the way to see the homes of three famous citizens of that town, Johnson, Garrick, and Dr. James (whose celebrated 'powders' had been sold by Burney's old friend, John Newbery). He was thus able to fulfil an ambition of carrying compliments 'from the Easy-Chair of Shakespeare' to that of Garrick.[1]

Burney was no longer haunted by the past as he had been a few months earlier. Although the letters which describe his summer travels contain sad reflections, the melancholy is rather self-indulgent, even wry at times. One reason for his reviving optimism was that William Herschel, the celebrated astronomer, had invited Burney to visit him during the summer. They had met frequently at the Royal Society and Burney was particularly anxious for Herschel—who 'after Newton will be my Achilles and Aeneas: c'est à dire, l'heros de la pièce'—to read and criticize his poem.[2] From Crewe Hall he had written to inform the astronomer of his progress:

I c^d not help frequently thinking of you by anticipation, & the great obligation [astronomy] has to your genius, diligence, & dexterity of observation. . . . & now, in approximating our own times I wish more than ever to communicate to you, not only my whole plan; but to consult you on some doubtful points of doctrine, & to be corrected in the theoretic part, wherever I may have misconceived the merit or demerits of anc^t Sages and fathers of the science.[3]

Before the science had become his devouring passion, resulting in his appointment as Court Astronomer in 1782, Herschel had himself been a professional musician, had published various compositions and had been an organist in churches in Halifax and Bath. He was therefore fully capable of appreciating Burney's eminence and he sent the historian of music 'a very polite and friendly letter', urging him to visit Slough and agreeing to discuss any aspect of astronomy he chose. He seems, however,

---

[1] CB to CB Jr., 19 Aug. 1797 (Comyn); to FB, 13 Sept. 1797, *DL*, v. 338–42; to Susan Phillips, 26 Oct. 1797 (Barrett). CB to FB, 2 Aug. 1797, *Mem.* iii. 243–9, is a garbling of the second and third of these letters.

[2] See *ante*, p. 387, n. 3.

[3] CB to Herschel [Aug. 1797], draft (Osborn).

hardly to have been prepared for the new role which Burney had assumed.

Burney made his visit late in September 1797. His original plan of staying with Lord Chesterfield near Slough having miscarried, he was eventually entertained to dinner and pressed to spend the night by the hospitable Herschel and his sister. After dinner, Herschel invited him to read as much of his poem as he had written, a request which even the poet himself considered excessively generous: 'Heaven help his head! my eight books, of from 400 to 800 lines, would require two or three days to read.' Eventually he read Book VIII, which dealt with Sir Isaac Newton and, to his intense pleasure, Herschel was surprised and suitably impressed: 'He gave me the greatest encouragement; said repeatedly that I perfectly understood what I was writing about; and only stopped me at two places. . . . The doctrine he allowed to be quite orthodox . . . .' Herschel made a confession, however, which would certainly have kept Burney far from Slough if it had been made before his visit: 'he told me—that he had never been fond of Poetry—He thought it to consist of the arrangem^t of fine words, without meaning—"but when it contained science and information, such as mine (hide my blushes!) he liked it very well".' Herschel's admission made his approval of Burney's didactic poem all the more gratifying and he was duly rewarded the next day with a reading of Book VII, which dealt with Descartes. At the age of seventy-one Burney was as excited by such praise from so eminent a man as he had ever been in his youth, for all his modesty: '*who's afraid*—this encouragem^t from *such* a Man, & such a supreme judge of my subject, if I was 50 years younger w^d turn my head—at present it remains in its usual place'.[1]

A correspondence now opened between the two men. Burney wrote in October 1797, describing the revisions which he had made as a result of his happy visit to Slough; and Herschel replied in the following month, answering various recondite queries and promising to answer others at the next dinner of the Royal Society. Although there is no evidence to indicate what Herschel really thought of Burney's poem, he undoubtedly respected his zeal and knowledge of the history of the science,

[1] CB to FB, 13 and 28 Sept. 1797, *DL*, v. 338-42, 344-7; to Mrs. Crewe, 15 and 30 Sept. 1797 (Osborn).

quite apart from the fact that he enjoyed his company. In November 1797 he looked forward to another visit from Burney and added, 'I cannot sufficiently express how happy that would make me and Mrs Herschel.'[1] Flattered by such encouragement and also by Fanny's news that the King and Queen had both recently expressed interest in his health and his poem,[2] Burney was as cheerful at the end of 1797 as he had been desperate a year earlier.

Realizing the precarious nature of her father's happiness, however, Fanny assiduously encouraged him with his poem, worrying whenever he failed to describe its progress in his letters: 'You do not tell me one word in the last 3 letters of Moons, Stars, & such little branches of the Heavens', she complained early in 1798. As he approached the discussion of contemporary astronomers at the end of his poem, she anxiously spurred him on with the thought that he now had not only plenty of material but also the pleasure 'of giving to living merit the meed so almost always reserved to lawrel its Manes'.[3] Burney was hard at work, however: by April 1798 he had completed his twelfth and final book and had transcribed the whole work neatly. He may well have been considering publication, for he now began trying it out on his friends, perhaps in the hope of being 'persuaded' to print it. He had not been alone in his excitement over the balloon experiments of the previous decade and astronomy had become a fashionable hobby for many of the ladies of his acquaintance. He was therefore assured of a suitably informed audience when Mrs. Crewe arranged a literary party in April 1798, at which he himself was to read part of his poem, William Windham what is described as his 'balloon journal', and George Canning 'a manuscript poem'.

Burney was invited to read first.

When I had finished the first book, '*Tocca lei*,' quo' I to Mr. Windham. 'No, no, not yet; another of your books first.' Well, when that was read, '*Tocca lei*,' said I to Mr. Canning. 'No, no,' they all cried out, 'let us go on,—another book.' Well, though hoarse, I read on; Mrs. Crewe relieved me, and then Miss Hayman, and then supper was announced; and so I was taken in: the rest, and the

---

[1] CB to Herschel, Oct. 1797, draft; Herschel to CB, 28 Nov. 1797 (Osborn 35. 18).   [2] FB to CB, 10 Dec. 1797 (Berg; *DL*, v. 363, 368).
[3] FB to CB, 19 Jan. 1798 (Berg).

'Balloon' and MS. poem, are to be read comfortably at Mrs. Crewe's villa at Hampstead, as soon as finished.[1]

Fanny was suitably amused by her father's account of this reading at which he had been 'the sole purveyor'; and like her we may wish that we could 'hear from Somebody else how the reading took'.[2] Windham and Canning have, however, left no comment for posterity and, in any case, whether or not their enthusiasm was sincere, Burney himself was triumphant.

His preoccupation with his poem sustained him once again during a period of great inconvenience in the summer of 1798, when reorganization within Chelsea College obliged him to move to a new apartment. In January he had feared that he would have to leave the College entirely and had begged Fanny to 'represent his difficulties, his books, health, time of life, and other circumstances' to the Queen, in the hope that some order in his favour might be procured. During a visit to Windsor Fanny mentioned her father's situation to the Queen, particularly the problem of moving his library, and she later believed that 'the accomodation then arranging, and since settled, as to his continuance in the College, has been deeply influenced by some Royal hint'. In the event, Burney had merely to move to a new apartment upstairs, in June 1798.[3] He was now living directly above Dr. Benjamin Moseley, the College Physician, who was to complain frequently about the noise made by Burney's servants and visitors. Burney himself, as he told Moseley, found his new quarters extremely noisy:

In his present apartments, immediately under the infirmary, Dr B. is not sure of one hour's stillness, out of the 24: as the changing the places of bedsteads, without wheels—rolling & rumbling of ponderous chairs, with & without casters—together with the poor mens wooden legs & crutches marking their painful steps—& the nocturnal occupations of the Nurses—render the bedroom & study of D^r B a very unfit residence for a hermit or Carthusian.[4]

An even worse problem was the disorder into which his recently re-catalogued library was thrown by the removal. As he told

[1] CB to FB, 24 Apr. 1798, *DL*, v. 407–8; cf. *Mem.* iii. 256–7.
[2] FB to CB, 25 Apr. 1798 (Berg).
[3] *DL*, v. 381, 383, 398–9; CB to FB, 4 June 1798 (Osborn).
[4] CB to Moseley, 26 Jan. 1799 (Shepard); Moseley to CB, 26 Jan. 1799, and n.d. (Osborn).

Mrs. Crewe, 'books that have been poked into holes & corners often cost me whole days to find, as I want them'.[1] The difficulty of finding the books he required obliged him to call a halt to the assistance he had been giving to a young composer, J. W. Callcott, who was working on a dictionary of music: 'even a secretary of state's search warrant, or a detachment from Bow Street w^d not be able to penetrate their lurking places, unless by accident, at present'.[2] A year later his 20,000 volumes seem to have been in no better order and, as he told Edmond Malone, 'the little leisure I have is spent in hunting, generally in vain, for what I am certain is in my possession, though *non est in veritas*'.[3]

Throughout this upheaval, however, Burney was cheered by the prospect of meeting Herschel once more in mid-September. During the summer he made his usual visits in the country, but when he arrived at West Humble to stay with the d'Arblays in their new cottage, Fanny noted with satisfaction that he was still deeply involved in his poem: 'he is grown now so extremely studious, that, when not engaged with company, or in discourse upon literary matters, it is evident he is impatient of lost time'.[4] The visit to Slough, however, had to be postponed because of the illness of Herschel's mother and Burney was instead plunged into 'gloom & agitation' by the elopement of his two children, James and Sarah Harriet.[5] Nevertheless, he stuck doggedly to his poem throughout the autumn, revising it and reading it to his female friends.[6] He was also helping Malone by providing additional notes to the third edition of Boswell's *Life of Johnson*, just as he was to help his friend with his edition and biography of Dryden in the following year.[7]

The postponed invitation to visit Slough arrived in November 1798. Although he was suffering from a persistent cough and was reluctant to travel, Burney was prepared to make this

---

[1] CB to Mrs. Crewe, 26 June [1798] (Osborn).

[2] CB to Callcott [June] and [July 1798] (Osborn).

[3] CB to [Malone], 30 June 1799 (PML).   [4] *DL*, v. 414; *Mem.* iii. 259.

[5] See *ante*, p. 387.   [6] *Frag. Mem.* (Berg).

[7] CB to Malone, 10 Oct. 1798 (B.M. Add. MS. 33965, f. 24) and 30 June 1799 (PML); Malone to CB, 6 Sept. 1798, 8 Jan. 1800, and to CB Jr., 15 Aug. 1799 (Folger); Prior, *Life of Malone*, p. 259 and n. 4. CB's new notes in the 3rd edn. of the *Life of Johnson* (1799) appear in vol. i. 18, 21, 46, 167, 177, 193, 219, 261, 378, 384, 397, 435, 438; vol. ii. 54, 171, 264, 334, 370; vol. iii. 458; vol. iv. 14, 19, 21, 464. See also *Correspondence of Percy and Malone*, ed. A. Tillotson, Louisiana State Univ., 1944, pp. 171–2.

important journey. Herschel seems eventually, however, to have offered to visit London instead and early in December he stayed at Chelsea College for two days, in the course of which he heard the first five books of the astronomy poem. To Burney's delight, Herschel could make few objections to the content of the work, doubtless because he knew very little of the early history of the science. As Burney proudly told Fanny, Herschel 'was so humble as to confess that I knew more of the history of astronomy than he did, and had surprised him with the mass of information I had got together'. The astronomer had, in fact, thanked Burney for the 'entertainment and instruction' which he had received during his visit. ('To *instruct* Herschel in astronomy!—'pon Honour!', dutifully exclaimed Fanny.) Herschel's praise of the poem was all the more gratifying because he had not yet heard Book XII, in which his own genius and discoveries were celebrated. For all his attempts at modesty, Burney could barely conceal his pride: 'Adad! I begin to be a little conceited.'[1]

III

1799 was probably the happiest year of Burney's life. It seemed to offer all the rewards for which he had laboured for so long and which he had always been too industrious or depressed to enjoy to the full. Although he was now in his seventy-fourth year, his health was better and his spirits higher than at any time during the decade and in the early months of the year he was as busy as ever with teaching, attendance at The Club and an endless round of social engagements. The opportunity for exuberant patriotism over Nelson's great naval victory at the mouth of the Nile in August 1798 was one factor which contributed to his cheerfulness. In the following October he had written to Latrobe, 'But huzzah! huzzah! Nelson for ever !. . . I do not remember in my long sojourning upon Earth, that any national event has given me so much pleasure.'[2] Such was his excitement on this occasion that, on the suggestion of Lady Spencer, he hastily wrote a song about the naval heroes and set it himself 'to an easy popular tune', in the belief that even 'the

---

[1] CB to FB, 10 Dec. 1798, *DL*, v. 429–30, cf. *Mem.* iii. 263–4; and 3 Jan. 1799 (Berg); FB to CB, 18 Dec. 1798 (Barrett).

[2] CB to Latrobe, 5 Oct. 1798 (Osborn).

most loyal subjects' were tiring of 'Rule, Britannia!' and 'God Save the King'. Copies of the song were duly presented to various friends and—most important of all—through Lady Harrington to the Queen. Princess Elizabeth soon wrote to tell Lady Harrington that the Queen admired the song so much that she wished it to be performed at Covent Garden and it was sung there, in the presence of Royalty, on 7 November 1798. It was not a success, however, as Burney himself admitted, although he blamed its failure on the ill-will of the performers, 'who had been singing songs of the same kind by other composers, & thought my poor ditty an interloper'.[1]

Burney's patriotism could not be easily discouraged, however, and in December 1798, having received a copy of Haydn's celebrated 'Hymn to the Austrian Emperor' (*'Gott, erhalte den Kaiser'*), he asked Latrobe to translate the German words into English and then himself versified them in a metre which would fit the tune. In January 1799 a copy of this English version was also loyally dispatched to the Queen, but Her Majesty's reaction to this latest display of zeal has not survived.[2] He had no doubt, however, that his efforts were appreciated, as he explained to Fanny in April 1799: 'I must tell you that your dear Royal Mistress never fails finding me out at the Concert of Anc^t Music—after the last time I was there—L^y Harington told me that she had seen me at the Concert, but that it was the Queen who shewed her where I sat.—is not this gracious & flattering?'[3]

Burney's wonderful summer therefore began in a glow of enthusiasm for his astronomy poem, of triumphant patriotism, and of renewed devotion to the Royal Family. In May he seemed already to detect something unusual in the air: 'the hurly burly of this Capital, was surely never so great before! & as well as a Ghost w^d make any thinking person cry out "Oh day & night! but this is wondrous strange!"'[4] On 4 June, the King's

[1] Princess Elizabeth to Lady Harrington [Nov. 1798], (Comyn); CB to FB, 2 Nov. 1798 (Osborn) and 3 Jan. 1799 (Berg); to CB Jr. [3 Nov. 1798] (Osborn); to Windham, 18 Nov. 1798 (Berg); FB to CB, 18 Dec. 1798 (Barrett); *Frag. Mem.* (Berg).

[2] CB to Latrobe, 18 Dec. 1798 (Osborn); to FB, 3 Jan. 1799 (Berg). See also O. E. Deutsch, 'Haydn's Hymn and Burney's Translation', *Music Review*, iv (1943), 157–62.

[3] CB to FB, 25 May 1799 (Barrett).   [4] CB to FB, 8 April 1799 (Barrett).

Birthday, his patriotic zeal had a new opportunity of expressing itself when the Chelsea Armed Association paraded at Chelsea College. Burney composed a march for the occasion, played the organ during the consecration of the Colours, and did most of the research into suitable precedents for the procession.[1]

Later in June Mrs. Crewe invited him to 'a delightful *Dejeuner*' at her Hampstead villa, 'made for the Princess of Wales & 50 illustrious persons'. Although he modestly believed that he had been invited merely as 'a makeweight', the Princess particularly asked to be introduced to him and at once said, 'How do you do, Dr B.? we are not strangers—I knew you before I came to England—*vous êtes un homme célèbre*.' Earlier in the year he had declined an invitation to give the Princess a weekly music lesson, partly because he disliked travelling at night, but also because he suspected that the Princess ('who is very poor') would be embarrassed by his fee, although he had added, 'I w^d rather attend her R.H. for $\frac{1}{2}$ a G^u in town, than for 5 at Night on black Heath.'

Now, however, he was captivated by his royal admirer, who talked to him about music for half an hour and, even thereafter, 'in little debates wch she had with individuals in the company, when she asserted an opinion, when I was by, she constantly, addressing herself to me, said—"is it not, Dr B.?" ' Burney was predictably gratified: 'Now don't you think, in the true spirit of Chivalry, that I w^d encounter, not only Knights, but Giants who sh^d dispute the beauty or basely traduce this Princess?' The Princess evidently thought equally well of Burney and invited him to a private concert in the following week, where she treated him 'like an old acquaintance'. Since an enjoyable dinner at Burlington House with the Duke of Portland, the Home Secretary, took place almost simultaneously, Burney could not contain his excitement, which sprang from precisely the same social sensitivity as had at once produced, and been the subject of, Fanny's *Evelina*, twenty years earlier, which he now significantly quoted (not quite accurately): 'Why Lord help your head! my dear Fanny—Why you thought you had *done* it, I'll warrant you, when you made young Brangton cry out:—"Sister! Sister! Miss has danced with a Lord!" But Hetty might, with greater wonderment, exclaim to you—Sister, sister!

[1] CB to FB, 21 June 1799 (Barrett); *Mem.* iii. 266–8.

Father last week not only *dined wth a Duke* on Thursday, but *drank Tea with a Princess,* on friday.'[1]

On 20 July Burney travelled from the scene of these social triumphs to Slough to stay with Herschel. The three days of his visit passed happily, 'in regions far *superior* to the little dirty planet on wch we crawl', and Books X, XI, and XII of his poem 'were heard with all the attention I wished, & approved beyond my most author-like expectations'. Other events of the weekend, however, almost overshadowed the successful reading of his poem. On the Sunday Burney accompanied Herschel to the Royal Terrace at Windsor, where he was deeply moved by the gay and loyal scene. As the royal party approached, the Queen said, 'There's Dr. Burney' and, as he liked to think, 'to the great mortification, probably, of many of my neighbours', for he was standing in a crowd 'of the first people in the kingdom for rank and office', both the King and Queen talked to him for some minutes. The King thought that he looked 'fat and young' and they were both 'so smiling and gracious that I longed to throw myself at their feet'.

In the evening Herschel—could he have been avoiding more of the poem?—persuaded Burney to accompany him to the royal concert in Windsor Castle. Once more they encountered the King:

the first question His Majesty asked me was,—'How does Astronomy go on?' I, pretending to suppose he knew nothing of my poem, said, 'Dr. Herschel will better inform your Majesty than I can.' 'Ay, ay,' says the King, 'but you are going to tell us something with your pen'; and moved his hand in a writing manner. 'What—what—progress have you made?' 'Sir, it is all finished, and all but the last of twelve books have been read to my friend Dr. Herschel.' The King, then looking at Herschel, as who would say, 'How is it?' 'It is a very capital work, Sir,' says H. 'I wonder how you find time?' said the King. 'I make time, Sir.' 'How, how?' 'I take it out of my sleep, Sir.' When the considerate good King, 'But you'll hurt your health. How long,' he adds, 'have you been at it?' 'Two or three years, at odd and stolen moments, Sir.' 'Well,' said the King. . . . 'Whatever you write, I am sure will be entertaining.' I bowed most humbly, as ashamed of

---

[1] CB to FB, 8 April, 2 July (Barrett) and 18 July 1799, (Berg); to Twining, 1 Oct. 1799 (Osborn). Cf. *Evelina* (1st edn., 1778), ii. 215. Hetty was CB's eldest daughter, Esther.

not deserving so flattering a speech. 'I don't say it to flatter you,' says the King; 'if I did not think it, I would not say it.'

The following morning Burney at last read Book XII of his poem to Herschel. Apparently overwhelmed by his interview with the King, however, he forgot to include any account of the astronomer's reaction to the versification of his own discoveries in his letters to Fanny, who had been awaiting that moment with baited breath for months.[1]

Late in August 1799 Burney travelled to Dover to stay with Mrs. Crewe. He had announced his impending arrival humbly, saying that he would come only if her house was 'not so full of better guests as to make me *de trop*'; but, through his hostess, he was soon happily meeting *'all the gentils* at this time in Dover & its vicinity'. The Duke of Portland and his daughter, Lady Mary Bentinck, were staying with the Crewes and Burney also met there such distinguished men as William Pitt, Henry Dundas, and George Canning. Whenever visits were returned by the Crewes, Burney, to his intense pleasure, was 'always of the Party'. He had never, perhaps, enjoyed himself quite so much. Throughout the summer he had been carrying about with him his version of Haydn's 'Hymn to the Emperor', which he now had the gratification of hearing 'very well sung in duo, I joining in the Chorus, by L^y Susan Ryder and Miss Crewe', as well as on another occasion when Pitt and Dundas obligingly beat time.

The only moment of stress occurred during a visit to Walmer Castle, when Canning told Burney that Pitt had acquired an elaborate telescope, designed by Herschel, which they were unable to put together, in spite of a large pamphlet of instructions. Having endured an evening of Burney's poem, Canning may have been teasing the historian of astronomy when he asked him to show them how to assemble the telescope, about which Burney knew even less than did Herschel about ancient Greek astronomers. Fortunately company entered the room before he was exposed and he quietly replaced the book of instructions in a drawer. Nevertheless, he promptly wrote to Herschel for advice and, when Pitt dined with the Crewes, was able to pro-

---

[1] CB to FB, 22–23 July 1799, *DL*, v. 437–42; FB to CB, 25 July 1799 (Osborn; cf. *DL*, v. 442–4); CB to Rosette Burney, 16 Aug. 1799 and to Twining, 1 Oct. 1799 (Osborn); *Frag. Mem.* (Berg).

duce the reply, which included flattering references to his poem. Since he could not conceal these compliments from the eyes of his female friends, he was obliged to satisfy popular demand by reading aloud sections of his poem.

Part of Burney's naïve but intense enjoyment of the high society in which he had been plunged—after, in his own significant words, 'becoming a gent^n & *leaving off practice*' (as a professional music-teacher) in June—arose from the conviction that he was being treated as an exception to all social rules and in a way that would make others acutely jealous. On 7 September, for example, he witnessed the embarkation of the British forces for Holland under the Duke of York:

Now mind!—if you read in the News-papers that the Duke of P[ortland] w⟨ent⟩ to Deal to see the last Embarkation, & had Lord *Cavan* in the Chaise with him—say ''tis a lie!—upon my soul, a lie!'—& for Ld Cavan read Dr B. the *Organer*—I was glad of the mistake, however—had my name appeared at such a time & wth such people—how sh^d I have been hated & Ministers abused—even by those who talk of *equality* as a good thing.

The same letter to Twining describes with similar relish a dinner at the Crewes when Pitt and his party were the guests and when Mr. Crewe could not be present:

Now pray be decent & keep your countenance, if you can—When the ladies retired from table, I was called up, and put in *the Chair* wch Mrs C. had left—stop bottle as I am—to put the bottle ab^t—I had heard that Mr Pitt drank a good deal of Wine—& Tocktor Purney dook gare not to *stop the Pottle*—for I watched the great Man's glass, & the Moment it was empty, tipt him the stuff—Well, but *only think*! take out your pencil & make a drawing for a print to please the lovers of Equality—Burney, on a level, between the first L^d of the Treasury & a Secretary of State—putting the bottle about![1]

It is impossible to begrudge the seventy-three-year-old Burney his youthfully exuberant pride, for his vulnerable happiness was already being threatened. For some months his family had been trying to conceal from him their anxiety about his favourite daughter, Susan Phillips, who was ill and desperately unhappy in Ireland.[2] During the autumn he learned of her ill-health and

[1] CB to [Mrs. Crewe], 16 Aug. 1799 and to FB, 9 Sept. 1799 (Osborn; *Mem.* iii. 272–7) and 15 Sept. 1799 (ibid., 278–80); to Twining, 1 Oct. 1799 (Osborn); *Frag. Mem.* (Berg).   [2] Hemlow, pp. 285–6.

the cruelty of her husband and realized that her return to England was imperative, but he had now reached a state of self-knowledge in which, as Fanny put it, he 'recoiled from the approach of excessive affliction with a horror of its power over his mind'.[1] Although he told Fanny, 'I am so sore by past disappointments, that my mind cannot be instantly healed', he did his best to ignore impending disaster and to believe that Susan would return safely. He could still enjoy a family party wholeheartedly:

we were as merry, & laughed as loud as the Burneys always do, when they get together and open their hearts; tell their old stories; & have no fear of being *Quizzed* by interlopers. It was so in my poor dear old father's time, & my boyish days—when my brother Thomas from London—or James from Shrewsbury came on a visit to Chester, we used, old & young, Male & female, to sit up all night—not to drink, but to laugh *à gorge deployée*. Who knows, when our dear Susey arrives, if something like this may not happen at *your* old father's?[2]

There was always, in any case, the astronomy poem to defend him against anxiety. Herschel wrote to him during the autumn, warmly inviting him to visit Slough once more. One compliment in his letter particularly gratified Burney: 'He who set off by saying "he did not love poetry"—now talks of my "valuable poetical communication".' Herschel's praise put him 'in such good humour wth my rhymes' that he began revising and expanding his poem.[3] He may well have been thinking seriously of publication at this time, for he was collecting suitable illustrations for the poem and had asked his nephew, Edward Burney the artist, to provide some drawings.[4]

Gloomy thoughts were thus kept at bay during the autumn of 1799, although Burney was waiting anxiously for Susan's arrival in England. In December Charles Burney set off to Chester to meet her and his father wrote constantly to him with advice. Burney must, however, have been optimistic, for he went to stay with Herschel for three days early in January 1800; but, although Susan reached England alive and was able to write to

---

[1] *Mem.* iii. 287.
[2] CB to FB, 29 Oct. 1799 (Osborn).
[3] Ibid., 19 Nov. 1799; Herschel to CB, 3 Oct. and 22 Dec. 1799 (Osborn).
[4] CB to FB, 29 Oct. and 1 Dec. 1799; J. C. Walker to CB, 4 Nov. 1799 (Osborn).

him, she died on 6 January.[1] Burney, like the rest of his family, was shattered and could find no consolation except by insisting that Susan's daughter, Fanny Phillips, come to live with him at Chelsea College.[2] For the first three months of the new century he refused all invitations and seems to have been roused by none of his usual interests until the performance of Haydn's new oratorio *The Creation* under Salomon in April 1800. On this occasion Burney was angered by some of the foolish criticism of Haydn's deliberately dissonant depiction of Chaos and he sent Latrobe a long letter describing his own unqualified admiration for the work.[3] Part of Burney's interest in this event was due to the fact that Haydn had written to him when he had first settled on the subject of his great oratorio; and in the previous summer had written again to inform him of the forthcoming publication of the score. Burney had enthusiastically collected the names of eighty-seven subscribers. As he proudly recorded in 1810, 'I procured him more subscribers to that sublime effort of genius —the Creation, than all his other friends, whether at home or abroad, put together.' After Susan's death, however, Burney could all too easily be hurt and, when the subscribers' copies reached England in July 1800, he was clearly distressed that the 'bale of books' contained 'no letter, or particular book for my own use . . . directed to me by Dr. Haydn'. It was not, in fact, until May 1804 that Haydn received the money which had been so devotedly collected for him and sent the grateful and affectionate letter that Burney had expected.[4]

As he slowly recovered from the shock of Susan's death, Burney resumed attendance at The Club and he paid his usual visits during the summer of 1800, but the rather scanty materials which survive suggest that he was doing nothing to any particular

[1] CB to CB Jr., 8 letters, 14 Dec. 1799–9 Jan. 1800 (Berg and Osborn); CB Jr. to CB, 5 letters, 27 Dec. 1799–10 Jan. 1800 (Barrett); Susan Phillips to CB, 30 Dec. 1799 (Barrett); Hemlow, pp. 286–90.

[2] FB to CB Jr. [Jan. 1800] (Osborn); *Mem.* iii. 294–5.

[3] CB to Latrobe [Apr. 1800] (Osborn). He also made a separate transcription of his defence of *The Creation*; and in 1811 sent another copy to L'Institut de France (Osborn).

[4] *Frag. Mem.* (Berg and Osborn); *Mem.* iii. 393; CB to Haydn, 19 Aug. 1799, *Harmonicon*, v (1827), 63; to Twining, 1 Oct. 1799 (Osborn); to FB, 19 Nov. 1799 (Osborn); to ——, 25 July 1800 (in grangerized Watt's *Byron*, B.M. C. 44 e-g, vol. xv; see *GDB*, ii. 118 n.); Haydn to CB, 19 May 1804 (Osborn); *Collected Correspondence and London Notebooks of Joseph Haydn*, ed. H. C. Robbins Landon, 1959, pp. 145, 165–6, 177, 230.

purpose or with any great enthusiasm. Apart from a letter in which Fanny refers to a 'head of Galileo' which William Locke had found for her father,[1] there is no mention of the astronomy poem. His health deteriorated during the autumn and his letters returned increasingly to the bitter subject of politics.[2] At last, in July 1801, with somewhat desperate energy, Burney threw himself into a new project, the compilation of the articles on music and musicians for Abraham Rees's *Cyclopaedia of Arts and Sciences*, an enormous work which was eventually to occupy forty-five volumes and was not to be completed until 1820.[3] The astronomy poem had in the end proved unavailing as a protection against depression and he had been forced to find a new preoccupation.

IV

It is necessary to bring the story of 'Astronomy, an historical & didactic Poem' to its sad conclusion. Burney's labours for Rees were soon swallowing all his time and energy, and, after mentioning Ursa Minor in a letter to Mrs. Crewe in September 1801, he added, 'All my astronomy will now go to the *dogs* not *bears*—definitions & dissertations now swallow my time & thoughts.'[4] He still saw Herschel occasionally,[5] but he did not attempt to conceal his reluctance to be involved in an astronomical dispute between two enthusiastic amateurs of the science, Mrs. H. Greville and Lady Templetown, who asked him to act as umpire, in 1802.[6]

Once his work for the *Cyclopaedia* was at an end, however, he seems to have returned to his poem, for he quoted twenty-two lines from it in a letter to his son Charles in 1805.[7] Not until 1807, nevertheless, are there any signs of a return of his original enthusiasm. In the summer of that year the prospect of meeting Lady Templetown, an old friend and an 'adept' in astronomy,

---

[1] FB to Fanny Phillips, 9 May 1800 (Hyde).
[2] CB to Mrs. Crewe, 5 letters, 8 Sept.–26 Nov. 1800 (Berg).
[3] See *post*, p. 408.
[4] CB to Mrs. Crewe, 26 Sept. 1801 (Osborn).
[5] CB to CB Jr., 10 May [1802] and to Mrs. Crewe [7 Dec. 1802] (Osborn). Through CB, CB Jr. provided Herschel with the name 'asteroid' for some new stars. Herschel first used the term in a paper read to the Royal Society on 6 May 1802, *Scientific Papers of Sir William Herschel*, 1912, ii, 196.
[6] CB to [Mrs. Greville], n.d., draft (Osborn); to Mrs. Crewe, 27 Sept. 1802 (Berg). [7] CB to CB Jr., 14 [Jan.] 1805 (Coke).

at the Duke of Portland's country house at Bulstrode, inspired the eighty-one-year-old Burney with the hope of enjoying 'astronomical speculations, with a little Music & back Gammon between the walks in the Paradisaical Gardens'.[1] One reason for the disappearance of his poem from his life was the fact that his friend Lord Macartney, who had died in 1806, 'had in a measure passed sentence upon my Versification, wch he had so highly praised in my Hist^y of Music & Commemoration of Handel'. Although he therefore had 'no great stomach' to re-read it, in anticipation of his meeting with Lady Templetown at Bulstrode Burney took his dusty manuscript down from the shelf and was surprised to find how interesting and amusing it was: 'In short, my coat was "caught in the wheel", and I did not stop till I read all my XII books through and most of the Notes, reading the Poem critically as I w^d revise the work of another.' In spite of Macartney's condemnation, all his former enthusiasm for his poem returned and, in the hope that, like Herschel, the scientific peeress might also benefit from an account of 'the inventions & discoveries of her predecessors', he 'packed up all my astronomical books and papers & promised myself great pleasure in reading my rhymes to so good a judge of the Subject'. Unfortunately, on reaching Bulstrode, Burney learned that Lady Templetown would not after all be coming.[2]

In reply to an account of this disappointment, Lady Crewe wrote Burney a letter in which she evidently made some disparaging remarks about his political views and, for good measure, after flattering and encouraging him for so many years, supported the judgement passed on his astronomy poem by her late kinsman, Lord Macartney. Burney could defend his politics, but he was clearly dazed by her remarks on his poem: 'Surely you under-rate yourself as well as me in speaking of my *crabbed chapters* ab^t *paralaxes* &c wch you seemed to like to read & talk ab^t—and as for me I did [? not] invent the crabbed words—I had them to explain, wch in my rhymes & my notes I was thought to have done by the very few in my confidence. . . .'[3] Lady Crewe's remarks must have hurt

---

[1] CB to Lady Templetown [Aug. 1807], draft (Berg); to Lord Ailesbury, 31 Aug. 1807, draft, and to Lady Crewe, 7 Sept. 1807 (Osborn).
[2] CB to [Lady Crewe], 2 Oct. 1807 (Osborn).
[3] Ibid. [Oct. 1807] (Osborn).

him deeply. The realization that for years he had been boring his friends in the belief that he was entertaining them must have been humiliating to one whose ambition in life was always to please. It is perhaps sufficient to explain the fate of his poem.

Burney himself never mentioned it again. When Fanny, after an absence of ten years in France, visited her eighty-six-year-old father in 1812, she found only that the poem, 'the last efforts of his genius, and last, and perhaps most cherished of his literary exercises . . . had been renounced, nay, committed to the flames!' She never learned the reason for this 'total relinquishment': 'the solemn look with which he announced that *it was over*, had an expression that she had not courage to explore'.[1]

As for the poem itself, Dr. Scholes produced what he believed to be the only surviving fragment of it, four lines concerning Newton in one of Burney's notebooks.[2] Three passages from the poem, however, have recently come to light. In a letter to his son in January 1805, Burney quoted twenty-two lines.[3] The second fragment contains some 400 lines of Book I, which is entitled 'Origin and progress of the art, previous to the time of Hypparchus'.[4] Although it is pleasing, more than 160 years after its composition, to be able to quote the opening of this work of Burney for the first time, it is simultaneously gratifying to discover, as one had suspected, that the world was not deprived of a masterpiece when the author decided to destroy it. The opening lines show Burney attempting an appropriate dignity and elevation:

> The various Orbs, by pow'r & wisdom plann'd,
> Which float in Aether by divine command;
> The Laws immutable by wch they run
> In never-ending circles round the sun;
> Their distance, magnitude, & motion's laws,
> Derived from Nature's Lord, the great First cause;
> The Sages who with toil essay'd to find
> The emanations of the Mighty Mind;
> The means they've us'd in science to excell,
> The Astronomic Muse essays to tell.

---

[1] *Mem.* iii. 415–16.   [2] *GDB*, ii. 157.
[3] See *ante*, p. 402 and n. 7.   [4] Osborn.

A third fragment, containing about 100 lines of a later book in much less finished state,[1] describes two eighteenth-century French expeditions to conduct experiments on the surface of the earth. Some idea of Burney's narrative style in his poem can be gathered from part of his account of the celebrated expedition by the French scientists, headed by Maupertuis, to Lapland in 1736:

> Another expedition, near the Pole,
> Was thought expedient to complete the whole,
> The measures to compair of diff'rent climes
> And from debate & doubt save future times.
> When sage Le Monnier, Clairaut, Camus join
> With ardent Maupertuis in this design,
> All geometricians of superior class,
> All eager expectation to surpass.
> Paris they quit, to icy regions steer,
> More late than southern brethren just one year.[2]
> But as their mission sooner was perform'd
> Though day & night by Arctic demons stormed
> Their enterprize shall here be first detail'd
> And hardships told o'er w[ch] their zeal prevail'd.
> From France, all blooming, in the Month of May
> To regions desert, barren, wild, they stray
> Where Nature poor & savage scarce can feed
> The insects w[ch] its transient summers breed;
> Where man's bereav'd of ev'ry social aid
> And implements of ev'ry useful trade
> To self reduc'd, bereav'd of all resource
> But mental vigour, & corporeal force.

Although we may not regret the loss of Burney's poem, it is perhaps proper to conclude with the thought that consoled Fanny: that, in spite of the unhappy end to the story, this curious undertaking had for several years served its function of distracting him from violent depression and had provided him with a purpose and with entertainment at a time when he believed that his life had been deprived of the possibility of either. Her closing words on the subject, moreover, remind us that 'Astronomy, an historical & didactic Poem', 'drawn up at

[1] Osborn.
[2] CB refers to the French expedition to Peru in 1735.

so advanced a period of a life—verging upon eighty—that had been spent in another and an absorbent study, must needs remain a monument of wonder for the general herd of mankind; and a stimulus to courage and enterprise for the gifted few, with whom longevity is united with genius'.[1]

[1] *Mem.* iii. 416–17.

X

BURNEY AND REES'S *CYCLOPAEDIA*

1801–1805

I

ONE of Burney's earliest ambitions had been to write a 'Dictionary of Music'. There is no reason to doubt Fanny's statement that, before embarking on his *History*, he had thought of translating Rousseau's *Dictionnaire de musique* (1767) and, although he was anticipated in this plan by William Waring in 1770, he had always planned eventually to compile a dictionary of his own. In 1777, when he had published only the first volume of the *History*, it had been on these grounds that he had dissuaded Thomas Twining from undertaking such a work. He may still have planned to take Rousseau as his basis, for William Bewley's review (about which he consulted Burney)[1] of the second edition of Waring's translation of the *Dictionnaire* (1779) seems clearly to have been influenced by his friend's jealousy of all rivals. Bewley described it as the most 'abominable' translation ever published in England and consigned it

to the oven of the pastry cook,
. . . 'from whose bourn
No traveller returns.'
It is not the smallest inconvenience resulting from such publications as the present, that they tend to prevent those who are qualified for the task from enriching our language with translations of works of merit.

In 1780 Burney was once more extremely irritated to learn that Samuel Arnold was planning to write a dictionary of music, but this threat did not materialize. Finally, if we may trust Fanny once more, he had been thinking of compiling a dictionary in 1796, when the death of his wife shattered all his plans.[2]

---

[1] Bewley to CB, 29 Mar. 1779 (Osborn); *Monthly Review*, lx (1779), 422–6.

[2] *Mem.* iii. 222–3; see *ante*, pp. 76, 238–9, 253.

By 1801 Burney had lost most of his enthusiasm for his poem on the history of astronomy and was ready for a new and absorbing task. Although he was now seventy-five, it is not surprising that he eagerly accepted an invitation to contribute the articles on music to a new *Cyclopaedia* to be edited by Dr. Abraham Rees and published by Longman and Rees (no relation of the editor). His old ambition was at last to be fulfilled, for this undertaking amounted, as Dr. Scholes has stated, to 'nothing less than the writing, single-handed, of a whole big *Encyclopaedia of Music*'.[1] When it is remembered that Burney's financial worries obliged him to continue teaching until he was seventy-eight, the additional attraction of the £1,000 which he was offered for the articles can easily be understood.

Burney can have had few illusions about the size of the task he had accepted and he was anxious to free himself from other literary obligations. In August 1801, a month after he started work for the *Cyclopaedia*, he decided to break his long connexion with the *Monthly Review*, to which he had been contributing since 1785. The abrupt manner in which he did so apparently hurt its editor, his octogenarian friend Ralph Griffiths, who replied,

I have been much affected by the contents of your last letter; especially that part of it in which you speak of your connection with the R—— as yielding *neither pleasure nor profit*. After this information, it would very ill accord with my real, unceasing, & affectionate regard for you, were I to press your continuance of a correspondence which you consider as of so cheerless a nature. You will, I hope, find yourself a gainer by the riddance of so undesirable a task: but certainly I shall very sensibly feel my own loss, on this *unthought-of* occasion. I trust, however, that you will still regard me as among the number of your true & disinterested friends; & that every kind of social intercourse between us will be closed only by that hand which dissolves all human ties & connections.

As soon as we have published the whole remainder of your valuable contributions, your account shall be made out. . . .[2]

Quite apart from his desire to concentrate his energies on the *Cyclopaedia*, it is clear that Burney had not been enjoying his reviewing in recent years. Once he had completed his *History of Music*, he had become a regular contributor to the *Monthly*

[1] *GDB*, ii. 184.   [2] Griffiths to CB, 31 Aug. 1801 (Osborn).

Review, dealing not only with books on music but also with travel books, biographies, poetry, and a varied assortment of foreign and domestic literary works. It had provided a steady addition to his income but Burney had also found in his anonymous reviewing a useful way of giving his own books some harmless publicity. Moreover, in spite of Griffiths's desire to preserve the impartiality of his journal, there was little he could do to prevent Burney from mercilessly exposing every sign of plagiarism of his own books by the younger generation of writers on music, or from occasionally attacking with unexpected harshness books by supposed friends, such as William Mason and J. C. Walker, with whom he otherwise conducted superficially polite correspondences. Burney was equally concerned, however, to defend and praise his real friends, living or dead, in his reviews; and Samuel Johnson, in particular, could have wished for no more vigilant and sturdy champion to protect his reputation against the many misrepresentations and falsehoods about his life and work which appeared after his death.

During the 1790's, however, as Ralph Griffiths approached his eightieth year and gradually lost his sight,[1] his son George played an increasingly important part in the direction of the periodical. Whereas the elder Griffiths had always been anxious to provide Burney with interesting books to review—'I would pick for you the best fruit in my garden', he had told him in 1791[2]—his son, a much less sympathetic editor who offended several of his father's reviewers,[3] may well have taken Burney less seriously. Whatever the reason, the books which he was sent to review after 1798 became noticeably less important and he himself referred derisively in February 1799 to the 'small-trash articles' and 'short Dabs' he was being asked to write for the 'Monthly Catalogue' of insignificant publications (dubbed the '*Cat's meat*' by the elder Griffiths).[4] It was in June 1799, however, that Burney wrote what is probably his most important review, a long article on the anonymous *Lyrical Ballads* which, in spite of some basically political objections, he praised with

[1] Ibid., 9 May 1801 (Osborn).
[2] Ibid., 31 Dec. [1791] (Osborn).
[3] B. C. Nangle, *The Monthly Review*, 2nd Series, Oxford, 1955, pp. vii–xii.
[4] CB to CB Jr., 8 Feb. 1799 (Coke).

unusual open-mindedness. It is possible that Wordsworth took account of some of Burney's observations in the famous Preface which he added to the second edition in 1800.[1]

After some three years of reviewing what usually amounted to little more than ephemeral rubbish, Burney resigned from the staff of the *Monthly Review*. Until June 1802 the articles which he had already written continued to appear and in that month Griffiths sent him £136 as a final payment for his contributions. In his reply Burney apologized for the manner of his resignation, indulging in an almost Johnsonian gloom at the conclusion of this episode in his life and expressing his anxiety to retain the affection of his old friend: 'There is something formal & solemn in this kind of *finale*, wch I do not like: it too much resembles Johnson's *horror of the last*. Yes—I remember well, that I felt compunction in the kind of farewell, wch I perhaps too pettishly made. . . .' Burney went on to mention his new labour for the *Cyclopaedia*, on which he had been working for almost a year: 'I have now such employment for my pen as will wear it to the stump, in all probability, long ere the curtain drops at the close of the vital drama. But these are melancholy reflexions, wch when I make, my kind friends, like Mrs Quickley to the dying Falstaff, "to comfort me, say, I sh^d no' think of those things." and so, heartily shaking hands, I beg you to regard this only as a temporary adieu. . . .'[2]

The pessimism with which Burney viewed his undertaking for Dr. Rees had been present from the very beginning, for he had soon realized the magnitude of his task and was haunted by the conviction that he would not live to complete it. He was already reflecting despondently on the impossibility of his task in a letter to J. W. Callcott (who was himself compiling a 'Musical Dictionary'), written on the day before he actually began work for Rees:

Time, like the Sibyl's leaves, becomes more precious in proportion to the little that remains. She put the same price on one third of her books as she had demanded for the whole 9. and I, who have expended more than 9 10^ths of my vitality, set as high a price on what is left, as the Cumaean prophetess did on her inspirations. During

---

[1] See R. Lonsdale, 'Dr. Burney and the *Monthly Review*', *RES*, xiv (1963), 346–58 and xv (1964), 27–37.

[2] CB to Griffiths, 9 June 1802 (Bodleian, MS. Add. C. 89. f. 3). CB slightly misquotes *Henry V*, II. iii. 20–21.

my whole existence I have been in the habit of cutting out more work than I c^d do—& now I have 10 years' work on my hands, & perhaps not 10 months to do it in.[1]

The earliest information about Burney's work for the *Cyclopaedia* is to be found in the title of one of the notebooks which he used: 'Memoranda for Musical Articles to be furnished to a new edition of the Cyclopaedia of Chambers commenced July 17th 1801.'[2] Rees was engaged, however, on a more ambitious project than merely a revision of the expanded edition of Ephraim Chambers's *Cyclopaedia*, which he had published between 1781 and 1786. Experts in many fields were to write entirely new articles, the original plan being to publish two volumes a year (each in two parts) over a period of ten years. For his contribution Burney was to receive £1,000, which was to be paid in instalments of £50 every six months, so that, if he kept pace with the proposed rate of publication, payment would be complete with the appearance of the final volume. He received the first payment of £50 in January 1802.[3]

Burney approved no more of his colleagues on the *Cyclopaedia* than he had of his fellow contributors to the *Monthly Review*, as he hastened to assure the King in May 1805, when asked about his current literary labours: ' "I am writing for the new Cyclopaedia, Sir." "I am glad the Subject of Music is in such good hands—but it's a sad set I believe"—"I fear, says I, that I am the only one of the set that is truly loyal—but all the men of letters, and artists seem now to be Jacobins"—"ay says the K. I believe to a Man—Not only professors of the beaux Arts but actors, singers, dancers, & fidlers".'[4] Burney was, nevertheless, quite independent of his colleagues and he respected the learned Dr. Rees. Indeed, if Burney deserves our admiration for accepting so enormous a task at such an advanced age, equal courage should perhaps be attributed to Rees himself, who can hardly have had more faith than Burney that death would not interrupt the supply of musical articles for his *Cyclopaedia*. While he could have obtained no more distinguished contributor on music than Burney, Rees may have

---

[1] CB to Callcott [16 July 1801] (Osborn).   [2] Osborn.
[3] CB to Longman, Rees & Co. [1805], draft (Berg).
[4] *Frag. Mem.* (Osborn). For FB's strangely distorted version of this conversation see *Mem.* iii. 361–2.

first approached younger men or, alternatively, have originally intended little revision of the musical articles in his earlier edition of Chambers. In any case, it certainly seems that Burney was called in at the last moment, for he later recorded in his notebook that '12 sheets were worked off ere my Copy was sent in', which suggests that he had been given little time to prepare his first articles.

What Burney later described as 'the musical department of the new Cyclopaedia on a large scale' included 'definitions in all the languages of Europe where Music has been much cultivated, with its history, biography, Criticism and discussions'. It was necessary to 'ferret out all my old books and papers which I had been collecting, ransacking, and commenting, for more than 50 years'. Dusty volumes and manuscripts reappeared from 'lumber rooms' and 'holes and corners out of the way', where he had stowed them, 'supposing I should never want them again'.[1] Even if Burney enjoyed returning to serious musicology for the first time since 1789, his research was not helped by the fact that, since his change of apartments in June 1798, he had not had the time or patience to reorganize or recatalogue his vast library. His books and papers were still 'truly in a chaotic state' several months later.[2]

Burney did not, of course, have to supply entirely new articles for the *Cyclopaedia*. His definitions of musical terms were often based on those (by Alexander Malcolm) in the 1781–6 edition of Chambers's *Cyclopaedia*, although he usually expanded them. For the biographies which he had to provide he turned first to his own earlier publications, from which many of his articles were transplanted without alteration, others consisting of a gathering of scattered references in his *Tours* or *History*, with an additional commentary merely to give coherence. Many of the articles, however, cannot be traced in these works or else were considerably expanded. In some cases Burney himself provided this additional material from first-hand knowledge or as a result of fresh thought upon the subject, but he was often heavily indebted to French and German musicologists, especially to works published since the completion of his *History*, and occasionally he even borrowed from his old rival Sir John

---

[1] CB to W. Crotch, 17 Feb. 1805 (Coke; Mercer, ii. 1032–6).
[2] CB to J. Huttner, 13 Mar. 1802 (transcript in Scholes Papers, Osborn).

Hawkins. Burney also eventually quoted so many articles from Rousseau's *Dictionnaire de musique* that his contribution to the *Cyclopaedia* incidentally fulfilled his old ambition of translating this work.

Burney's main task, therefore, consisted of transcribing (in many cases translating as well) and fusing the information and theories contained in a great number of different works. When he began work in mid-July 1801, his first aim was to catch up with the press and he quickly sent his first article (on 'Accompaniment') to Rees, covering '5 or 6 sides of copy paper'. From the beginning he did more than merely revise the articles in Rees's previous edition of Chambers. On 1 August he dispatched a '2ᵈ delivery consisting of Articles reformed, augmented, and entirely new, from the beginning of the letter A to *Ad libitum*. 25 Articles'. A further 45 articles were soon delivered, taking Burney to 'A plomb'.[1] As the first volume of the *Cyclopaedia*, published in January 1802, only reached 'AMA', Burney had quickly caught up with the press and he proceeded steadily to build up a pile of manuscript articles, which were ready when called for. During August 1801 he felt that he could allow himself his usual series of summer visits but, after visiting his ailing friend Richard Cox at Quarley, he decided to cut short his tour and return to Chelsea. As he had seemed much less relaxed than usual, Cox's companion, Miss Dowdeswell, wrote to find out if anything had offended him. Burney apologized for having been 'less cordial than usual', explaining that 'I was as happy at dear old Quarley as I cᵈ be with a head full of crotchets, pen-work & engagements.' Already the strain of his new employment was taking its toll and he had returned home with a cough and 'feeling myself as rheumatic as a dried toast'.[2]

As usual, once he was fully engaged with a new undertaking, Burney could think of nothing else. He was obliged to tell Mrs. Crewe that he had no time for astronomy: 'definitions & dissertations now swallow all my time & thoughts'.[3] During the autumn of 1801 he did, however, permit one series of engagements

---

[1] See *ante*, p. 411, n. 2.
[2] CB to Miss Dowdeswell, Oct. 1801, draft (Berg). Cf. *Henry IV, Pt. II*, ii. iv. 47–48: 'You are both, i' good truth, as rheumatic as two dry toasts.'
[3] CB to Mrs. Crewe, 26 Sept. 1801 (Osborn).

to distract him, for, at the request of his son Charles, he
sat for a bust to the famous sculptor Nollekens. Remembering
that Johnson had grumbled at the splendid doctoral robes
which he had worn in his portrait by Reynolds—'we want to
see *Burney* & he never comes to me in that dress'—he now
wavered between 'academic' and 'Roman' costume. Eventually,
however, he settled on a more modest academic dress than in his
portrait and borrowed Dr. Samuel Arnold's gown and hood for
the occasion. After one sitting had been wasted simply because
both he and Nollekens 'were such noodles we c^d not put them
on', the bust was executed, and casts were delivered early in
1803.[1]

Otherwise, with the coming of winter Burney felt overworked
and harrassed. An attempt at relaxation for a few days, such as a
visit with Mrs. Crewe to stay with Mrs. Burke at Beaconsfield
in November, resulted only in annoyance at the break in the
continuity of his work and at the difficulty of resuming it. Apart
from 'pen-work at home', he had still to attend to 'professional
work, and engagements in Town' and he found little time for
hospitality or correspondence: 'I eat people's dinners, but
never give them any in return—and often receive letters, wch I
never answer.'[2] In January 1802 he was gratified by an offer
of assistance from J. W. Callcott, whom he had helped with his
own 'Musical Dictionary',[3] but he took the opportunity to
indulge once more the gloomy reflections which his labours
inspired in him:

I am every day more & more frightened at the magnitude of my
undertaking at so late a time of life; at the large scale on wch I have
hitherto been working, and at the number of years it will require to
complete it! I find that it will absorb all my thoughts & occupy every
moment of that leisure wch I used to devote to friends & other pursuits. I have been doing little else, since last July, than hunt for books
& papers, wch I thought I sh^d never look into again; making indexes,
extracts, & memoranda.

After six months of hard work, he sadly reported, he had not
yet reached the end of letter 'B' and was convinced that he

---

[1] CB to CB Jr. [12 Oct.], [14 Oct.], [31 Oct.] (Osborn), and 9 Nov. 1801 (Berg);
see *post*, p. 418.   [2] CB to Rosette Burney, Nov. [1801] (Osborn).
[3] The unpublished and incomplete manuscript of this work, which is dedicated
to CB, is in the British Museum, Add. MSS. 27649–50.

would do well to finish his articles within the ten years in which the *Cyclopaedia* was to be published. It is difficult to establish the extent to which Callcott really assisted him. Later in 1802, they corresponded frequently for a few weeks on various musical topics, but no other letters between them concerning the *Cyclopaedia* have survived.[1]

Afflicted with the cough that was rarely to leave him for the rest of his life, to which a fever was added in February 1802,[2] Burney nevertheless did not spare himself in his anxiety to rid himself of his new burden. It is hard to suppress a suspicion, that, in a strange way, Burney derived a grim pleasure from telling his worried friends that he was 'deeply engaged in a work that can admit of no delay; and which occupies every instant I can steal from business, friends, or sleep'. Fanny, indeed, may well have rejoiced at his new and engrossing labour, for in April 1802 she left England to join her husband in Paris. Burney could not, of course, know that she would remain abroad for ten years, but if he had not been so anxiously preoccupied with the *Cyclopaedia*, Fanny's proposed absence of a year would have depressed him extremely. As it was, he seemed rather more worried in April 1802 by the fact that, after '*nine months*' *hard labour*', he had still not reached the end of the second letter of the alphabet.[3]

At Easter 1802 Burney permitted himself a few days with a large and distinguished group of visitors invited to Bulstrode by the Duke of Portland. For once, the old delight of moving in such society compensated for the distraction from his 'enormous *Cyclopaedia* jobb', as he proudly wrote to tell Fanny: 'We never sat down to table in a smaller N° than 30 each day—and *we* danced & *we* sung—& *we* walked, & *we* rode—& *we* prayed together at Chapel on Sunday, & were so sociable—"you have no notion".' Yet on his return to Chelsea Burney had to face the fact that he had completed only two letters of the alphabet by the middle of May.[4] By the end of July he was more eloquently depressed than ever about his work, complaining that a few hours of teaching had 'shivered the Lord knows how many

---

[1] CB to Callcott, 5 letters, 29 Jan. 1802–14 Jan. 1803 (Osborn); Callcott to CB, 8 letters, 27 Jan. 1802–13 Jan. 1803 (B.M. Add. MS. 27667, ff. 69–59).

[2] CB to Malone, 23 [Feb.] 1802 (Bodleian, MS. Malone 38, ff. 129–30).

[3] CB to — [April 1802], *Mem.* iii. 302–3.

[4] CB to FB, 20 May 1802 (Osborn; *Mem.* iii. 330, 353).

links of the chain of my Cyclopaedic work, & filled the next day with efforts to collect & put them together'. He had now been at work on his articles for a year: 'I had a mind to see what I c^d do in 12 months, by hunting after materials, and driving the quill at every possible moment I c^d steal from other occupations day & night, in bed & up, and I have found it impossible to finish 3 letters of the alphabet!' The aristocratic friends whom he had recently made at Bulstrode sent him invitations in vain: 'I'm now a slave, a Lexicographic slave, for life—I shall never be at leisure again—nor can I do anything from home for want of such books as I can find nowhere else.'[1]

During 1802, as if it were not enough that he was haunted by the conviction that he would never live to complete his articles, Burney was involved in some disagreement with Dr. Rees and his publishers, presumably connected with the financial arrange-ment between them and apparently negotiated by his solicitor, Edward Foss. In February 1802 Burney asked his son Charles, 'Where does our business hitch wth Dr Rees & Longman?—I hear not a Word from Mr Foss since I returned the draught of the Deed & Dr Rees from whom I have had a letter on another business does not even hint at it—'.[2] Burney may well have been endeavouring to obtain an agreement that, if he completed his articles before the whole *Cyclopaedia* had been published, he should receive the balance of the £1,000 due to him. Eventually Rees and Longman accepted these terms, although in June 1802 Foss had still not terminated the negotiations. 'It is going on very uncomfortably', Burney told Charles, 'in a business that weighs me down, & requires all the civility at least wch the Editors can bestow, to keep me in spirits.'[3]

Early in August 1802 Burney allowed himself his usual visit to Quarley, but he was not cheered to observe that Richard Cox was declining rapidly. In September he spent another two weeks with the Duke of Portland at Bulstrode, directing Call-cott's researches on his behalf in London by letter and sternly refusing to become involved in an astronomical dispute be-tween two ladies: 'My head & my hours are at present so fully occupied with other more serious matters, that I am equally

---

[1] CB to FB, 28 July 1802 (Osborn; misdated, *Mem.*, iii. 330–1).
[2] CB to CB Jr. [17 Feb. 1802] (Comyn).
[3] Ibid., 5 [June 1802] (Berg); misdated 5 May by CB.

unable to throw more light on the matter, or to seek it in books.'
If his labours provided him with any consolation at this period
it was only that he could now identify himself more closely than
ever with his greatest hero, whose *Dictionary* had been an
inspiration to Burney throughout his life; but it was with, at
best, a gloomy satisfaction that he quoted an observation from
the Preface to that work to Mrs. Crewe: 'Every other author
may aspire to praise; the lexicographer can only hope to escape
reproach, and even this negative recompence has been yet
granted to very few.'[1] Johnson's example certainly helped to
sustain Burney, who would recall what he had stated in a
footnote to Malone's edition of Boswell's *Life* in 1799: 'He owns
in his preface [to the *Dictionary*] the deficiency of the technical
part of his work; and he said, he should be much obliged to me
for definitions of musical terms for his next edition, which he
did not live to superintend.'[2] In a sense, therefore, Burney could
feel that he was at least providing a supplement to Johnson's
monumental work.

The cough, which he had lost in August, returned in September, but he worked indefatigably, resisting an offer by
Ralph Griffiths to let him 'peep at' a new and interesting book:
'alas! in the shackles with wch I have manacled myself, I have
no time for amusement.'[3] Few of his friends, indeed, at this
period escaped his gloomy reports on the impossibility of his
ever completing his undertaking and the phraseology of these
bitter complaints is often repeated from letter to letter. Christmas 1802 brought him only toothache to supplement his cough.[4]
His friends, who followed his slow progress with uneasy interest, did their best to cheer him, but Burney himself would
allow no one to take an optimistic view of his task. When J. W.
Callcott heard indirectly in January 1803 that Burney had
advanced as far as the article on Giardini, he wrote to congratulate him on this sudden progress through the alphabet.
Burney hastily accounted for this misleading information, for
his articles fell into different categories, which he sometimes
pursued separately through the alphabet: 'you must not

[1] CB to Mrs. Crewe, 27 Sept. 1802 (Berg); see *ante*, p. 402 and n. 6, p. 415 and
n. 1.   [2] 3rd edn. i. 261 n.
[3] CB to Griffiths, 12 Oct. 1802 (Bodleian, MS. Add. C. 89, f. 4).
[4] CB to Mrs. Anne Hunter [Dec. 1802], draft (Osborn); to Mrs. Crewe, 23 Dec.
1802 (Berg).

imagine that I have regularly worked my way through the Alphabet to *Giardini*—I jump from dry definitions and theory to Biography, and from Biography to Hist[y] just as they come across me—but I have not yet completed the letter C. . . .'[1]

During the early months of 1803 Burney could not avoid the usual distractions of teaching and of social engagements, but he was cheered a little in March by the arrival of his 'most magnificent representative', the bust by Nollekens, and he was able to mock his own delighted vanity: 'I shall become a very Narcissus & pine myself into a daffodil.'[2] When the fashionable season subsided in June, however, he returned grimly to uninterrupted work for the *Cyclopaedia*. In July he managed to arrange a meeting at Isleworth with Thomas Twining, whom he had seen rarely in recent years, but he could not know that this was the last occasion on which they would meet. Burney was more concerned at the time about another event of the same month, the marriage of his housekeeper, who had been in his service for thirteen years and whom, since the death of his wife, he had carefully trained to be his 'librarian' and to read his correspondence to him when he was busy. Of more immediate significance was the fact that 'She c[d] read my everyday writing of my foul copy of Articles for the press better than myself; & at last, transcribed for me fair as an Amanuensis, several entire letters of the Cyclopaedia for the press more legibly & correctly than any one copyist I employed.'[3]

Deprived of his amanuensis, Burney also lost one of his oldest friends later in the summer with the death of Richard Cox on 26 August 1803 at the age of eighty-five.[4] Having been in the habit of visiting him at Quarley in Hampshire for many years, Burney was now forced to take his summer holiday elsewhere. Late in August, after arranging that proofs of his articles for the *Cyclopaedia* should be sent to his son Charles, Burney went to stay with Mrs. Crewe at Cheltenham, in an attempt to get rid of his persistent cough.[5] His health did not noticeably improve but he met several old friends with whom he spent most of his time. Burney was not, however, taking a vacation from his lexico-

---

[1] CB to Callcott, 14 Jan. 1803 (Osborn).
[2] CB to CB Jr., [25 Mar. 1803] (Osborn).
[3] *Frag. Mem.* (Berg).
[4] *Gent. Mag.* lxxiii (1803), 887.   [5] CB to CB Jr., 22 Aug. [1803] (Osborn).

graphic labours and, although he was now making steady progress, he still would not permit his friends to cajole him into optimism. He was convinced that he would never live to see all his articles printed, for the whole of the letter 'B' was not yet completely published; and, as he told J. C. Walker, 'Though I advance more rapidly in my single department, I am every day more and more dismayed by the idea of not living to finish my MS.'[1]

Although he had no books with him at Cheltenham, he revised and corrected the fair copy of articles already written, usually working from five to eight or nine in the morning, and at night from eleven to one. He now felt acutely the loss of his trusted housekeeper, for he found that his granddaughter Fanny Phillips, who had taken over the duties of amanuensis, had transcribed some articles 'so ill, that the correction takes more time, & a great deal more patience to make it fit for the Compositor than if I had been my own amanuensis'.[2] Nevertheless, from such materials as he had taken with him to Cheltenham, he managed to complete a draft of another letter of the alphabet and he supervised the transcription of two others into a fair copy.[3]

During his stay at Cheltenham Mrs. Crewe's daughter had patiently helped him with his articles and, after his return to Chelsea late in September, Burney wrote to thank his friends for their hospitality and assistance. It was, however, one of the saddest letters he ever wrote: 'Going home to *vacuity* is a melancholy thing—I found my apartments neat, clean, & every thing in perfect order—But one must be in high health, spirits, & activity, to enjoy *loneliness*, or exercise one's faculties with energy when excited by no external stimulus. We are flints without a steel, or steels without flints, when alone, if mind & body concur not in fermenting ideas.'[4] Nevertheless, as Fanny was later to put it, there was a 'virtuously philosophical' purpose to his work for the *Cyclopaedia*, which partly served 'to while away enervating sadness upon those changes and chances that hang upon the very nature of mortal existence'.[5] Although in

---

[1] CB to Walker, Sept. 1803 (Shepard).
[2] CB to CB Jr., 4 Sept. [1803] (Osborn).
[3] CB to Malone, 6 Oct. 1803 (Bodleian, MS. Malone 38, ff. 131-2).
[4] CB to Mrs. Crewe, 26 Sept. [1803] (Osborn).
[5] *Mem.* iii. 302.

November 1803 he admitted to his son that he had 'not been in riotous spirits of late' and asked him to 'come; & bring hilarity with you',[1] he had been working hard on his articles. His housekeeper had been replaced by a new servant who predictably found his demands rather beyond her immediate capabilities. After a few weeks she was able to find books for him, but could emulate her predecessor in little else. Burney attempted to hasten the day when she too could enter the service of the *Cyclopaedia* by sending her to nightly lessons from a writing-master.[2] These efforts were in vain, for although in 1808 Burney referred to this woman as 'at once my Cook, my Nurse, & my Librarian', her claims to the third of these titles were limited: 'that is, she can find the books I want, but is unable to write or read writing'. Burney was thus obliged to do much of the drudgery of copying out his articles himself.[3]

Burney's work for the *Cyclopaedia* protected him to some extent from despondency at political events, although his letters were once more full of his usual distressed commentary on the subject. His patriotism had not diminished since he had written his songs on the naval heroes of 1798;[4] and when, in September 1803, the politician and poet John Courtenay asked him to provide 'some *hullabulloo* tunes' for some 'patriotic songs' he had written with Malone's help, Burney was pleased to oblige. Courtenay had sent a copy of his verses with a couplet at the head, which Burney could hardly resist:

> If Burney's Music w[d] the song inspire
> E'en strains like these might stir up British *fire*.

Burney modestly informed Courtenay that he was no longer 'a *Noted* man, & had no thoughts of ever composing Music again', but the simple tunes he provided—probably his last musical compositions—apparently satisfied the poet and he was soon distributing copies to his friends.[5]

Burney did not, however, allow himself to be distracted for long and during the winter he made rapid progress. By April

---

[1] CB to CB Jr., 3 Nov. [1803] (Comyn).
[2] *Frag. Mem.* (Berg); CB to Mrs. Crewe [19 Oct. 1803] (Osborn).
[3] CB to FB, 9 Oct. 1806 (Berg); to Huttner [6 July 1808] (Osborn).
[4] See *ante*, pp. 394-5.
[5] Courtenay to CB, 21 Sept. [1803] (Comyn); CB to Mrs. Crewe [19 Oct. 1803] (Osborn) and 9 [Jan.] 1804 (Berg).

1804 he was approximately half-way through the alphabet with his own articles, although only three volumes of the *Cyclopaedia* had as yet been published and had advanced no further than 'BAT'.[1] Burney was still reluctant, however, to view his undertaking any more cheerfully than in the past, almost as if his life would have been meaningless without this vast grievance: 'now in my 78th year, with incidental infirmities to a late time of life, I feel myself quite oppressed by the business w[ch] I have on my hands—I have been working night & day for near 3 years at these Articles, & have not yet gotten half through the Alphabet —but when the whole work will be issued from the press God knows who will live to see! For the letter B is not yet finished.'[2]

Although the tone of endless complaint and the condemnation of his own folly in ever having accepted the task had not changed, Burney must by now have realized that he would complete his articles in a much shorter time than he had at first expected. It had taken him several months to organize himself into a routine and to learn which books published since his own *History* were most useful for his purpose. There was, however, another factor which explains why, after the first two years, Burney began to move much more rapidly through the alphabet. His early despondency had arisen from the fallacious assumption that each letter would demand the same quantity of space and, therefore, of his time. If this had been the case, his horror at the fact that it had taken him two years to complete the first three letters would have been justified, but, after completing letter 'C', he had moved forward rapidly. The first three letters constituted, in fact, a quarter of the whole work, and not an eighth as he feared, as can be seen from the *Cyclopaedia* itself, the first three letters occupying ten of the thirty-nine volumes which were eventually published.

Burney, of course, showed no signs of relaxing as the end of his great labour became, if not exactly imminent, at least for the first time conceivable. So anxious was he, in fact, to rid himself of his burden that he at last decided to bring to an end his career as a teacher of music, which in London and Norfolk had continued for more than fifty-five years, with only occasional interruptions during illness and foreign travel. His failing sight

[1] CB to Twining, 10 Mar. 1804, copy (Osborn).
[2] CB to Mrs. C. M. Henslow, 30 Apr. 1804, draft (Osborn).

and hearing also prompted him to this decision and accordingly in April 1804 he decided 'to relinquish teaching and . . . musical patients' at the end of the season. He had no intention of abandoning his social life, however, and, on the contrary, he noted, 'I never, seemingly, have been more *in fashion* at any period of my life than this spring; never invited to more conversaziones, assemblées, dinners, and concerts.'[1] It was not perhaps coincidental that in May 1804, the month in which he gave up teaching, the Directors of the Concerts of Ancient Music presented Burney with a 'General Ticket' of perpetual admission, in recognition of 'his merits in the cause of music'. It was a gesture which gratified Burney extremely.[2]

Nevertheless, he could not bear his friends to think that he had any intention of leading an easier life. He assured Lord Lonsdale, for example,

It is not to be idle that I quit business. Nothing w^d make me more wretched than listless inactivity of mind however debilitated & in ruin may be its mansion. My literary pursuits in early life were undertaken to fill up the vacuum of summer vacations—mere amusement was never in the list of my pursuits. Your Lordship may probably remember Ant^y Chamier undersecretary of State to Ld Weymouth. He knew me so well, that when I was complaining of my laborious life to him. . . . after patiently hearing me detail my hardships he says—I pity you very much—but now do tell me Burney what you intend to set ab^t next? . . . Indeed without quitting the world entirely I never c^d afford to be totally idle if I had wished it. and the Society into wch I have long been honoured with admission, is too precious to be relinquished without infinite regret.[3]

Lord Lonsdale assured him in reply: 'I hope I may be able to quote you for years to come & to produce you as an Inducement to others, who would wish to arrive at the same Period of Life, retaining the same Strength Vigor & Chearfulness as you possess. . . .'[4]

Burney was now waiting only for the summer, when he would make a last assault on the remaining articles. Even before the end of the season, however, although he was teaching or en-

---

[1] *Mem.* iii. 335.
[2] Lord Dartmouth to CB, 27 May [1804]; CB to Lord Dartmouth, 27 May 1804, *Mem.* iii. 338–9.   [3] CB to Lonsdale, July 1804, draft (Osborn).
[4] Lonsdale to CB, 15 July 1804 (Osborn).

gaged on other business during the day and had 'afterwards night engagem^ts seldom less than two', he worked from five or six in the morning until his servants were up, and in the evening, he resumed his labours in bed, from whatever hour he returned home until one or two in the morning.[1] Eventually he shut himself up in Chelsea College for weeks at a time, admitting only his closest friends and relations.[2] Perhaps the only event which penetrated this complete absorption was the death of Thomas Twining on 6 August 1804.[3] Early in 1803 Twining, 'of whom Dr Burney speaks very highly, as not only a very learned, but an accomplished and agreable man', would almost certainly have been elected to The Club but he himself declined this honour. As Malone told Bishop Percy, 'He pleads being 69 and his scarcely ever visiting London'.[4] Although he and Burney had rarely met and had corresponded less regularly in recent years, Twining was still his oldest intimate friend, one 'who had been at my heart's Core more than 39 years!' He told Richard Twining, his friend's half-brother, that 'few incidents can happen in the last act of my vital drama more tragic than this!'[5] According to Fanny, 'It was a subject from which he shrunk ever after, both in conversation and by letter: it was a grief too concentrated for complaint.'[6]

Early in September 1804 Burney arranged that Charles should receive any proofs of his articles and went to stay at Bulstrode with the Duke of Portland. Just how hard he had worked since April can be seen from the fact that, while he was at Bulstrode, he almost completed his work for the *Cyclopaedia*. He had reached the end of the alphabet in foul copy and, for lack of a trustworthy amanuensis, had himself transcribed most of the articles for the press. What he had so often described as his 'rashly undertaken task' was almost at an end. 'And now for last revisal of Copy & insertion of omissions', he told Charles on 21 September, the day after his return to Chelsea.[7]

[1] CB to Rosette Burney, 28 May 1804 (Osborn).

[2] CB to Latrobe, 20 July 1804 (Osborn).

[3] *Gent. Mag.* lxxiv (1804), 790.

[4] *Correspondence of Percy and Malone*, ed. Arthur Tillotson, Lousiana State University, 1944, pp. 92, 121, 136, 144.

[5] CB to R. Twining, 13 Aug. 1804, draft (Osborn).

[6] *Mem.* iii. 339.

[7] CB to CB Jr., 1 Sept. and 21 Sept. 1804 and to Mrs. Blore, 12 Sept. 1804 (Osborn); *Frag. Mem.* (Berg).

II

As usual, Burney was granted little respite from anxiety. A few days later Charles brought news of a rumour, passed on confidentially by 'T.P.' (presumably the younger Tom Payne, the bookseller), that Burney's publishers, the Robinsons, were on the verge of bankruptcy. Burney was panicstricken by this information for, in the Robinsons' warehouse, lay all the unsold copies of the four volumes of his *History of Music*. They were still Burney's property and had been left with the Robinsons merely for convenience of storage and for sale to other booksellers and to the public. For some years this arrangement had been bringing Burney a steady income of some £50 or £60 a year, the Robinsons taking a 7s. 6d. profit on each volume they sold. Burney's first thought was to retrieve these remaining volumes immediately, for he feared that if the Robinsons did go bankrupt, all the property on their premises would be seized by their creditors. Unable to obtain any legal advice on the situation or, at first, to obtain any response from the harrassed booksellers themselves, Burney was plunged into the deepest despair at what he confidently foresaw as the loss of books worth at least £2,000. In various ways, he calculated early in October 1804, his *History* had cost him £5,000 to publish and, even if his anxiety, during this crisis, approached the hysterical, it is understandable that he should have been reluctant to lose any remaining profits from his monumental and expensive publication.[1]

Burney resolved that, if his urgent demand that the Robinsons instantly surrender his *History* was still unanswered by 8 October, he would himself seize them and have them transported in a cart to Chelsea College, where he had hired a 'dry room' for their storage. Since no mention could be made of the impending bankruptcy during his negotiations with the booksellers for the return of his property, he was unable to explain the necessity of the haste he required. Eventually the Robinsons made no objection to the removal of the books, which they promised to execute when they had time to pack them. Throughout October 1804 Burney's anguish increased steadily, as is suggested by the rise in his gloomy estimates of the expense

[1] CB to CB Jr., 28 Sept., 2 Oct. 1804 (Osborn); to Mrs. Crewe, 2 Oct. 1804 (Berg).

involved in the original publication of the *History*: £5,000 on 2 October, £6,000 on 5 November, and 'near £7,000' by 21 November. After a month of quite unnecessary mental agony, the *History of Music* returned to the protection of its author early in November 1804, in a 'caravan' borrowed for the purpose from Broadwood's music-shop. One hundred and twenty-five sets of the four volumes were left with five booksellers—Longman, White, Nicol, Payne and, as a gesture, the Robinsons—and the remainder were stacked, still in sheets, in Chelsea College. Having retrieved his *History*, Burney at once, on 5 November 1804, sent the booksellers a note for £50 which they owed him, and which he had been reluctant to demand while the fate of his property was in doubt, but payment had been stopped on the previous day.[1]

Worse was to follow immediately, for Burney discovered that, although he now possessed the sheets of his four volumes, the plates of musical examples and illustrations were missing, and the Robinsons had stored the parcels in 'so slovenly & dirty a manner that out of 312 complete sets, as I thought ready for sale, and 6 or 7 hundred copies of my 1ˢᵗ 3ᵈ & 4ᵗʰ Volˢ not one is furnished with plates or index fit for use'. He was obliged to hire two bookbinders to open and sort the 'immense bundles' of sheets, which were so 'torn and almost all dirtied so much, that I shall be ashamed to dispose of many of them'.[2] Before long the mislaid plates were found, but there were no impressions from them which could be used to complete the sets of sheets. For the benefit of one of his female friends Burney poured out the various items of his woe:

though with infinite difficulty I have recovered my books, they have been so neglected & ill-treated by their warehousemen, that many are spoiled by dirt & damage—plates mislaid & no impressions left either of the ornamental plates and frontispieces, plates of ancᵗ musical instrumᵗˢ, or music plates, wᶜʰ to the last 3 volˢ amount to 221. These I have to reprint, wᶜʰ will involve me in an enormous expense and all the trouble and anxiety of 1ˢᵗ publication. But till this cup is swallowed, I have not a single complete set of my Hist. Mus. the labour of 30 years, & near £7000 in printing fit for use or sale.[3]

[1] CB to CB Jr., 5 Oct. (Osborn), [12 Oct.], 31 Oct. 1804 (Berg); CB to G. and J. Robinson, 2 Nov. 1804 (Shepard); *Frag. Mem.* (Berg).

[2] CB to Latrobe, 5 Nov. [1804] (Osborn).

[3] CB to CB Jr. [? 12 Nov. 1804] (Berg); to Mrs. Blore, 21 Nov. 1804 (Osborn).

The 'trouble & vexation' arising from this situation kept Burney 'on the fret' for at least six months. In May 1805 he apparently tried to complete some sets of the *History* 'by reprinting the Plates at a most enormous expense',[1] but not until 1808 was any effective action taken towards the disposal of the bundles of sheets piled in Burney's storeroom in Chelsea College.[2]

When the news of the Robinsons' impending bankruptcy had, in Burney's words, 'first assailed my ear & occupied my mind', he had been working alphabetically through his articles for the *Cyclopaedia*, 'filling up gaps of omissions & dates'; but, as he told Charles with unusual understatement in November 1804, 'I have had my thoughts *turned away*, of late, sadly'. During October he had made almost no progress with his articles, apart from arriving at the depressing conclusion that 'What I am doing now will not be wanted these 20 y^{rs} I am sure'. Accordingly he took the sensible precaution of asking his son to send some particularly black and permanent ink, in case his manuscript should be illegible within a few years. Depressed and weak with nervous exhaustion, he now resumed what he hoped would be the last revision and expansion of the articles which had not yet been printed.[3] Working, perhaps for the very last time, with his old singleminded energy, he refused to admit any visitors: 'and if that negation was not resolutely practised at my door, the little time I have left, wch like the Sybil's leaves becomes more precious by diminution, w^d be squandered on gossiping visitors, from whom in return I sh^d neither receive amusement nor instruction'.[4] Consulting the great collection of newspapers assembled by his son, requesting help from friends, and preparing the illustrative plates for his articles, Burney worked resolutely into the early months of 1805.[5] In March he was unwell, but by May he was at last willing to admit to his friends that, in less than four years, he had completed a task which he had gloomily predicted he would not live to finish.[6]

---

[1] CB to Rosette Burney, 16 May [1805] (Osborn.   [2] See *post*, pp. 464–9.

[3] CB to CB Jr., 31 Oct. and [? 12 Nov.] 1804 (Berg).

[4] CB to Mrs. Blore, 21 Nov. 1804 (Osborn).

[5] CB to Malone [? Nov. 1804] (Osborn); to CB Jr. [13 Dec. 1804] (Osborn) and 14 [Jan.] 1805 (Coke); CB to [Latrobe] [1805], draft, and R. Wroughton to CB, 26 Dec. 1804 (Osborn).

[6] CB to Rosette Burney, 15 Mar. 1805 (Osborn); to Mrs. Waddington, 7 May 1805, 'George Paston' (E. M. Symonds), *Sidelights on the Georgian Period*, 1902, pp. 28–29.

Although his 'laborious and arduous undertaking' was thus effectually at an end, it brought in its wake numerous irritations and trials. For four years Burney had been sustained by the prospect of claiming the balance of the £1,000 he was to receive for his articles and during the summer he wrote to Longman and Rees, listing the half-yearly payments which he had already received (amounting to £300), and asking for the remaining £700. He was now prepared to hand over all the remaining articles if the publishers wished; or would alternatively retain the manuscript 'for any additions or corrections that may occur during his life'.[1] It is clear that he had some difficulty in persuading Longman and Rees to fulfil their obligations. In the following autumn Burney was having to economize because he could obtain nothing from 'Pater-Noster Row'; and he asked Charles to urge Tom Payne, the bookseller, 'to give the P.N. folks a *jog* for me. . . . I sh^d be glad to settle the business without a *rough attorney*.'[2] Legal action seems, however, to have been unnecessary and Burney apparently received his £700 in instalments before the end of 1806.[3]

It is difficult to tell from Burney's frequent complaints, which continued as long as he retained his unpublished articles, supplying them as they were called for, whether his publishers were really as unpleasant as they appeared to him. Certainly it would seem that they made little allowance for Burney's extreme sensitivity to suspected insult in his old age. The publishers were inclined, for example, to send him rather curt notes on various matters, which resulted in protests from Burney against their 'seeming ill breeding & total want of feeling or common humanity' and complaints that 'Nothing can be more rude & unfeeling than the whole gang'. In August 1807 he wrote, 'I have not been s⟨atis⟩fied of late with my employers in Pater Noster Row & Dr Rees. I have many ⟨com⟩plaints against them, though I relinquished every other employment & Ideas wch I had formed of other productions, & worked for them night & day during 5 years. . . .'[4] The incivilities from the publishers, calculated or not, continued; but that Burney was

[1] CB to Longman, Rees and Co. [1805], draft (Berg).
[2] CB to CB Jr., 31 Oct. 1805 (Osborn).
[3] Ibid., 4 Feb. 1807 (Osborn); cf. his will, 12 Jan. 1807, *GDB*, ii. 271.
[4] CB to CB Jr., 4 Feb. and 4 Mar. 1807; CB to Huttner, 15 Aug. 1807 (Osborn).

demanding no more than the attentive politeness which he felt
he deserved is clear from the ease with which he could be
consoled. In May 1808, for example, he was somewhat molli-
fied:

D[r] Rees has lately written me two friendly and feeling notes in
asking for the Copy of my MS. articles in letter D, which is now going
to press—and from the manner in which he speaks of my health and
seclusion from society, it inclines me and others to imagine that the
plagues and incivilities I received from Pater Noster Row, came from
the new partners, & their shopmen, who knew nothing of me or my
work—I believe during so long a life, few have gone through the
world in a more peacable manner than myself—and I now more
than ever wish to quit the world in peace and Christian charity with
all men.[1]

Yet even when Burney was not complaining about his
publishers, the manuscript articles which he retained did not
allow him to live his last years in the 'peace' to which he
aspired. As he had feared, those which had been written more
than five years earlier were sometimes illegibly faded by the
time they were called to press.[2] Years after they had been
written, the proofs of articles would suddenly arrive, with the
request that they be returned hastily, when he was too ill to read
them or to make the additions which he planned.[3] Similarly,
the engraver of the musical plates would arrive in the evening 'with the most tedious & tiresome Work of questions and
explanations of 2 Hours—till I was quite exhausted, and had a
most miserable Night—not a wink of sleep or ease'.[4]

Worst of all was the frequency with which he, or the publishers, lost, or thought they had lost, parts of the manuscript.
When the articles for a given letter of the alphabet were about
to be called for, Burney usually read them through and made
any necessary additions or alterations. In August 1806 he set
off for the country, only to discover during the journey that his
writing box was missing, 'w[ch] put me into an agony, as it was
not only a new one of red morocco, but the receptacle of 2
pocket books with notes, and Cyclopaedia papers that I have

---

[1] CB to Huttner, 20 May 1808 (Osborn).
[2] CB to Lady Crewe [Mar. 1808] (Osborn).
[3] CB to Belfour, 12 Nov. 1806, draft (Osborn); to Huttner, 6 Mar. 1807 (Berg;
draft, misdated 6 Feb. 1807, Osborn).
[4] CB to CB Jr. [12 May 1807] (Osborn).

been at work upon for 2 or 3 months—and a thousand dainties and curious papers, music, poetry, &c. to show the ladies at Bulstrode'. Burney rushed back to Chelsea to find that his servant had forgotten to put the box in his coach. His anxiety released itself in a fit of bad temper at the woman. Such small incidents were, at this period of his life, quite sufficient to put him 'in the greatest fright I ever experienced' and 'the utmost despair'.[1] There was similar panic in 1806 when Charles, who was reading proofs while his father was in the country, contrived to lose two pages of the manuscript.[2]

Late in the same year, Burney revised and delivered to the press 'all the remaining articles in letter C'. In January 1807, when he was trying to recover his health at Bath, he received an urgent request for the same set of articles. The incomprehensible disappearance of the manuscript which he had already delivered was 'a thunderbolt to me, & has made me sick at heart ever since', he wrote in February: 'if I were to live 20 years longer, I c^d never think of re-writing these articles, amounting to 50 or 60, some of them of considerable length'. When the missing articles were eventually found at the press, he was infuriated to receive only a 'laconic' note informing him of the fact.[3] In November 1807 the printers once more tortured him in the same way: he admitted to finding life as a whole increasingly harrassing, but 'The chief & direfully enraging of my plagues has been a 2^d loss of 3 leaves, containing more than 20 MSS. articles of the fair copy of the new Cyclopaedia, of wch I thought I had washed my hands 5 years ago—but the compositor, printer, or his *diavolo* delle mani nere have ingeniously contrived to keep my coat in the wheel of misfortune still longer'.[4]

There is no indication as to just how long Burney continued to expose himself to 'the wheel of misfortune'. His articles for the *Cyclopaedia* are not mentioned in his extant correspondence after May 1808 and it is more than likely, considering the anxiety they caused him in so many ways, that he eventually handed them over completely to Abraham Rees, as he had

---

[1] Ibid. [19 Aug.] (Berg) and [22 Aug.] 1806 (Osborn).
[2] Ibid., 31 Oct. and 7 Nov. 1806 (Osborn).
[3] Ibid., 4 Feb. and 4 Mar. 1807 (Osborn).
[4] CB to Lady Mary Lowther, 9 Nov. 1807, draft (Osborn).

offered in 1805. By 1808, in any case, it had become obvious that the manuscript articles would have to be handed over to Rees at some stage, for Burney could no longer hope to live to see the publication of the whole work, which was clearly going to be almost twice as large as had been anticipated. The twenty-eighth volume, taking the *Cyclopaedia* only to 'PUN', was not published until May 1814, the month after Burney's death;[1] and, until the work was completed in thirty-nine volumes in 1819, with six additional volumes of plates in 1820, the articles which had caused their author so much anguish, continued to be published posthumously.

Although for various reasons Burney's articles themselves are not easy to discuss and evaluate, the fact remains that they contain a considerable quantity of new material, written especially for Rees between 1801 and 1805, which deserves rather more attention than it has hitherto received. This material has been neglected, of course, because it is unusually difficult to isolate, scattered as it is through the hundreds of anonymous articles which he contributed to the *Cyclopaedia* and almost inextricably entangled with extracts from his own earlier works and those of other writers. In so far as it is possible and reasonable to consider this new material—Burney's last published literary undertaking—as a work in its own right, various characteristics can be observed which distinguish it from his other writings. One of the most surprising features of the completely new articles, considering the harrassed state of mind in which he wrote them, is their relaxed and good-humoured tone. Burney may have felt that old age permitted a kind of genial irresponsibility and, particularly in the early years of his work for Rees, he indulged his characteristic humour (and occasionally his various prejudices) more freely than in his earlier publications.

The most obvious feature of the new material, however, is the intrusion of memories of his youth, especially of his early years in London, for many of his articles are affectionate recollections of minor musicians and musical events unmentioned in the *History*. Although these reminiscences often resulted in some not unattractive irrelevance, Burney's style in his old age was

---

[1] B. D. Jackson, 'The Dates of Rees's Cyclopaedia', *Journal of Botany*, xxxiv (1896), 307–11.

XI

BURNEY'S 'MEMOIRS'

I

IN the spring of 1805, with the removal of the great burden which had caused him such anxiety for almost four years, Burney's spirits revived. More inclined to temperamental extremes in his old age than ever, after the despair which had so often afflicted him during his work for Rees's *Cyclopaedia*, the seventy-nine-year-old Burney returned enthusiastically to his old social life. On the whole, his health in the first years of the new century had been better than in the previous decade, although as he approached the age of eighty his sight, hearing and memory were beginning to fail. In one of his notebooks, after some remarks on Ménage's memory in his old age, 'the respectable Veteran of Chelsea College'[1] reported on his own senses in January 1805:

I was sensible of no decay of Memory till I was 77, the failure began by proper names, and extended to words in general. at 78 I seldom c^d recollect in writing or conversation the word I wanted immediately. . . . Add to this infirmity a decay in the auricular sense, not in distinguishing musical sounds the most delicate & minute; but in conversation, if not very near the person who addresses me, I lose the articulation, & am obliged to make them repeat what they have said!!—My Eyes too want a convex glass for pale ink & small letters!!![2]

Nevertheless, as his friends often observed, he still looked much younger than his age; and when the King met him at Chelsea College in May 1805 his first words were, 'Ten years younger than when I saw you last!'[3] His old charm and ease of manner had not diminished and for eighteen months after the completion of his articles for Rees, Burney led as full and various a social life as ever. After his death it was said of him, 'His manners were peculiarly easy, spirited, and gentlemanly, and

---

[1] Richard Porson to CB Jr., 18 Aug. 1802 (Osborn).
[2] Osborn.   [3] See *post*, p. 450.

XI

BURNEY'S 'MEMOIRS'

I

IN the spring of 1805, with the removal of the great burden which had caused him such anxiety for almost four years, Burney's spirits revived. More inclined to temperamental extremes in his old age than ever, after the despair which had so often afflicted him during his work for Rees's *Cyclopaedia*, the seventy-nine-year-old Burney returned enthusiastically to his old social life. On the whole, his health in the first years of the new century had been better than in the previous decade, although as he approached the age of eighty his sight, hearing and memory were beginning to fail. In one of his notebooks, after some remarks on Ménage's memory in his old age, 'the respectable Veteran of Chelsea College'[1] reported on his own senses in January 1805:

I was sensible of no decay of Memory till I was 77, the failure began by proper names, and extended to words in general. at 78 I seldom c^d recollect in writing or conversation the word I wanted immediately.... Add to this infirmity a decay in the auricular sense, not in distinguishing musical sounds the most delicate & minute; but in conversation, if not very near the person who addresses me, I lose the articulation, & am obliged to make them repeat what they have said!!—My Eyes too want a convex glass for pale ink & small letters!!![2]

Nevertheless, as his friends often observed, he still looked much younger than his age; and when the King met him at Chelsea College in May 1805 his first words were, 'Ten years younger than when I saw you last!'[3] His old charm and ease of manner had not diminished and for eighteen months after the completion of his articles for Rees, Burney led as full and various a social life as ever. After his death it was said of him, 'His manners were peculiarly easy, spirited, and gentlemanly, and

---

[1] Richard Porson to CB Jr., 18 Aug. 1802 (Osborn).
[2] Osborn.   [3] See *post*, p. 450.

he had all the graces of the Chesterfield school, without any of its studied formality.'[1] Maria Edgeworth recorded in June 1805 that her father, who met Burney at Mrs. Crewe's villa in Hampstead, had received precisely that impression: 'He was charmed with old Dr. Burney, who at eighty-two was the most lively, well-bred, agreeable man in the room. Lord Stanhope begged to be presented to him, and he thought him the most wonderful man he ever met.'[2] Similarly, a few years later, a friend of Fanny reported to her, 'He is *so French in his manners*! so attentive, so polite, so pleasing!—it's so rarely one sees an Englishman, however good and excellent, so charmingly well bred and engaging.'[3]

In spite of his return to a full social life, Burney was still not prepared to bring his literary activities to an end. For some years he was, of course, to be spasmodically occupied with the revision and proof-reading of his articles for Rees's *Cyclopaedia*; and in 1805 and 1807 he turned once more to his poem on the history of astronomy.[4] By the end of 1805, however, he was at work on a new project. He had started writing his 'Memoirs' in 1782, shortly after the publication of the second volume of his *History of Music*. Undertaken primarily as a diversion after years of heavy scholarship, the 'Memoirs' had inevitably been laid aside when work on the *History* was resumed. Nevertheless— and, in the light of Fanny d'Arblay's statements about her father's autobiography, it is highly important to establish as accurately as possible the various stages of its composition— Burney seems to have completed in 1782 a narrative of at least the first thirty-five or forty years of his life.

A note on a transcript of the opening pages of the original 'Memoirs', which Burney made in December 1805, reveals that they had originally been written in August 1782.[5] In April 1806 Burney told his son Charles that he had 'written down in 1782 all I c[d] then remember of dramatic transactions during these times, from 1744 to 1751, when I went to Lynn'.[6] As his letter was concerned only with 'dramatic transactions', he did not mention how much later than 1751 his narrative extended. It

---

[1] *Gent. Mag.* lxxxiv (1814), 421.
[2] *Life and Letters of Maria Edgeworth*, ed. A. J. C. Hare, 1894, i. 144. CB was in fact only seventy-nine.   [3] FB to CB, 29 May 1812, *DL*, vi. 58–59.
[4] See *ante*, pp. 402–3.   [5] Osborn. See *ante*, p. 272.
[6] CB to CB Jr., 19 Apr. 1806 (Comyn).

can be assumed, however, that it at least described his life from childhood until that year without interruption. A scrap of paper, entitled 'List of books and Papers in wch memoranda are made of my progress through life, from the cradle to decrepitude'[1] mentions three notebooks which may well constitute the 'Memoirs' of 1782. The first covered the years 1726 to 1743; the second continued the narrative to 1766; and the third contained 'Johnsoniana & Bons Mots', some pages of which have survived.[2] The new draft of the 'Memoirs' which Burney made in 1805 was written in larger notebooks, for a single volume contained the whole of the narrative to 1766.[3] The three notebooks listed by Burney must therefore represent an earlier draft, presumably that of 1782.

Burney did not return to his 'Memoirs' for twenty-three years. In December 1805, however, he set about revising and continuing the narrative he had written in 1782 and which, as has been suggested, covered his life at least until 1751 and probably to 1766. His memory of his youth was even sharper than it had been earlier and as well as transcribing the first draft he made considerable additions to it. Some of the new material had probably occurred to him whilst he was compiling the more reminiscential of his articles for the *Cyclopaedia* and he also reinforced his memory of his first years in London by consulting the great collection of early newspapers assembled by his son Charles.

Apart from the fact that he transcribed the 1782 draft of the 'Memoirs' in December 1805, however, little definite information about Burney's work on his autobiography has survived. In March 1806 he was working on his account of the performance at Drury Lane of *A Midsummer Night's Dream*, for which he had written music in 1763, for after a transcription of the 1782 draft of the unhappy story of this production, Burney added a note, dated 21 March 1806, concerning some new information about the adaptation which he had just acquired.[4] In the following month, April 1806, he sent Charles numerous queries about dates and details of events in the London theatre during the 1740's. Since Charles had himself made a special

---

[1] B.M. MS. Eg. 3009, f. 14.   [2] See *ante*, p.288.
[3] This is clear from fragments of the index, B.M. Add. MS. 48345, ff. 18–19.
[4] See *ante*, pp. 58–60.

collection of cuttings and notes about Garrick's career, Burney stressed that his own purpose was quite different. Thanking Charles for the information which he had already sent, he explained his own intention of writing a definitive, personal account of Garrick, which he felt was sorely needed:

Much obliged for your Garrickiana—but I shall not pillage the Memoranda wch you have been busy making of his Public character, & characters—His private life & character is all I shall meddle with —& that I will venture to say no one knows better, if so well as myself—nor has any one that I know of, among his biographers attempted to do him justice in that particular—Davies was never allowed to sit down in his house—Murphy never at his table—& Cumberland was his aversion—and he must have hated Garrick cordially—though for fear posterity sh^d know that such Men as Garrick and Sheridan were his Enemies, he praises them highly.[1]

Only fragments of this definitive account of Garrick have survived. Burney's low opinion of the actor's biographers recalls his similar scorn of those who had stepped forward to write the life of Johnson in 1784 and it is certain that this second great friend also received considerable space in the 'Memoirs'. Almost nothing, however, remains of Burney's account of his happy years as a member of the Streatham circle.

It is impossible to talk with any confidence of Burney's work on his 'Memoirs' after April 1806. He probably revised and expanded the 1782 draft of the work as he transcribed it but a number of surviving fragments were obviously written later than the first transcription. Thus his account of his courtship of his second wife in 1767 was to be inserted in 'Vol. II p. 16';[2] and that of his introduction to the Thrales in 1776 at page 19 of volume vii, 'Previous to the description of my sitting with Dr Johnson at Streatham'.[3] The fact that five volumes were required to cover the years 1766 to 1776 is explained by Burney's decision to include in his 'Memoirs' the unpublished portions of the journal of his travels in France and Italy in 1770. The three notebooks in the Osborn Collection which contain a transcription of this material seem to have been Volumes III,

---

[1] CB to CB Jr., 23 Apr. 1806 (Comyn); 7 Nov. 1806 (Osborn) contains further queries about Garrick.
[2] Berg and Osborn.   [3] Berg.

IV, and V of the 'Memoirs', for Burney's introduction to the first of these volumes explicitly links it with the main narrative of his life.[1]

Burney had no difficulty in continuing the narrative which he had written in 1782, for, as he told his son, since 1760 he had kept 'records in my pocket-books . . . to the present time, and c^d tell where & how I spent every hour of my life'.[2] Fragments of the later volumes of his 'Memoirs' show that he relied heavily on his diaries, for he usually described his social activities and other notable events in strict chronological order. No extant fragment of the continuous narrative deals with a later period than the summer of 1806 and Burney may well have completed it at about that time. Thereafter he seems to have contented himself with making occasional notes on important events and additions to the account of his early life.

Little more can be said, from Burney's point of view at least, about his 'Memoirs'. Although revision of the autobiography and examination of his letters and papers seem to have occupied him spasmodically until his death, these activities are hardly ever mentioned in his surviving correspondence. For reasons which will be discussed shortly, it must be assumed that Fanny d'Arblay deliberately attempted to suppress all references to her father's autobiography. Indications that at least until 1812 Burney continued reading through the hoards of his accumulated correspondence and other papers escaped her censorship more frequently. In November 1806 he mentioned in a letter that, having completed his articles for the *Cyclopaedia*, he was engaged on another work, begun many years earlier, which he did not expect to live to finish.[3] This should not be taken as evidence that, by this date, Burney had made little progress with his autobiography: the remark was made at a time when he believed that imminent death was hanging over him.

A more cheerful letter to Fanny in the previous month, October 1806, describes his pleasure in rediscovering the letter in which Rousseau had thanked him for a copy of *The Cunning Man*.[4] Such delighted recollection of the celebrated men whom he had known and of the honours which he had received in the course of his long life corresponds precisely to the predominant

---

[1] *Tours*, i. xxix–xxxi.   [2] See *ante*, p. 433, n. 6.
[3] CB to Belfour, 12 Nov. 1806, draft (Osborn).   [4] See *ante*, p. 101.

tone and content of his 'Memoirs', which were written to commemorate the same aspects of his life and indulged the same harmless vanity:

But is it not extraordinary, my d^r Fanny, that the most flattering letters I ever rec^d sh^d be from Dr Johnson and Rousseau, so little addicted to flattery? I can acc^t for it no other way than from my treating them wth that regard & reverence wch their great literary powers inspired. Much as I loved & respected the good & great Dr Johnson, I saw his prejudices, and severity of character—nor was I blind to Rousseau's eccentricities, principles, and Paradoxes, in all things but Music. . . . but as I had no power to correct the prejudices of the one, or the principles of the other of these extraordinary persons, was I to shun and detest the *Whole Man* because of his *peccant* Parts?[1]

Four years later, in 1810, Burney was still 'rummaging over heaps of old Correspondence',[2] and in 1811 and 1812 he was examining and preparing Twining's 'letters and confidential Papers' for his son Charles, probably with the intention that they should ultimately be returned to the Twining family.[3] One of these letters bears an inscription in Burney's hand: 'Pray Chas read the following letters & laugh when I'm no more— Decr 1811.'[4]

The rest of our information about Burney's 'Memoirs' and other papers comes from Fanny d'Arblay, who described their history and fate in a long letter to her sister Esther in 1820. Fanny claimed that, since she had undertaken the preliminary inspection of his correspondence with him in 1796, he had originally intended her to be the editor of his 'Memoirs' and papers. During her residence in France, between 1802 and 1812, Burney had turned instead to Charles, whom, next to Fanny herself, he considered to be 'most acquainted with his literary habits, intentions, & wishes'. On Fanny's return to England in August 1812, however, Charles (who was confident of the financial value of the 'Memoirs') had resigned the task to her, and until Burney's death in 1814, she helped him to sort and read his papers whenever opportunity presented itself.

[1] CB to FB, 12 Oct. 1806 (Osborn; *Mem.* iii. 371–3).
[2] Lord Lonsdale to CB, 6 Sept. 1810 (Osborn).
[3] CB to CB Jr., 7 Jan. 1812 (Comyn).
[4] Twining to CB, 8 Jan. 1776 (Add. MS. 39929, ff. 65–68`.

As Burney's will appointed no literary executor, Fanny was chosen by the family to edit his 'Memoirs' and correspondence and, after the manuscripts had accompanied her to France and then back to Bath, she devoted long periods of the next fifteen years of her life to examining the huge collection.[1]

Miss Hemlow has already described in detail the thoroughness of Fanny's editorial labours, her many misgivings and doubts concerning the right course of action, and her eventual decisions.[2] Fanny's first intention was to publish her father's 'Memoirs' in '3 Volumes in octavo' and to follow them with three volumes of his literary correspondence. After reading the twelve notebooks which contained the autobiography, however, she decided that the work was in no state to be published. His account of his early life in Condover, Shrewsbury, and Chester was, in her opinion, 'filled with *literal* nurses' tales . . . trivial to poverty, & dull to sleepiness'. It is clear, however, that she was really more disturbed by the discovery that Burney had described quite frankly the 'dissipated facility & negligence of his Witty & accomplished, but careless Father', and the 'niggardly unfeelingness of his nearly unnatural Mother'. This opening section of the 'Memoirs' was not only 'long, tedious, unnecessary' but, more significantly we may suspect, opened 'to the publick view a species of Family degradation to which the name of Burney now gives no similitude'.

The account of his early years in London was, according to Fanny at least, disappointingly concerned with musical and theatrical reminiscences and contained little about her own mother: '3 or 4 lines include all the history of his admiration & its effects'. This last statement is simply untrue, for at least two pages were devoted to Burney's courtship of Esther Sleepe and later passages described her popularity at Lynn and her death in 1762. Fanny herself admitted in 1832 that the account she gave of her mother in her *Memoirs* was written 'neither from fancy, nor remembrance, but from M:S:S: both in prose & verse of my dear Father'.[3] By 1820, however, Fanny was concerned less with facts than with reasons which might seem to justify her destruction of her father's autobiography. The

[1] FB to Esther Burney, 20 Nov. 1820 (Barrett). This letter is quoted also in the next two paragraphs.   [2] Hemlow, pp. 446–66.
[3] FB to Rebecca Sandford, Oct. 1832, draft (Berg).

section dealing with her father's life at Lynn she considered 'detached, vague, & unknit into any consistence'. Of the later volumes of the 'Memoirs' she had high expectations, but stated that Burney had done little more than copy out lists of his engagements from his pocket-books.

By 1820 Fanny had 'committed to the Flames' most of the autobiography, preserving only the torn fragments used in the present study. Her aim was to destroy anything 'that might have bred fevers, caused infectious ill-will, or have excited morbid criticism or ridicule'. By 1828, Fanny now aged seventy-six, had been joined by her seventy-nine-year-old sister, Esther, in the relentless destruction of whatever was useless or 'painful' in the 'enormous load of Letters, Memoirs, documents, mss: collections, copies of his own Letters, scraps of authorship, old pocket Books filled with personal & business memorandums, & fragments relative to the History of Musick. . . .' Although she had by now decided to publish neither his 'Memoirs' nor his correspondence, the threat that a biography of her father would appear from another quarter eventually compelled her to publish her own *Memoirs* of her father's life, ostensibly based on his autobiography, in 1832.[1]

There were two reasons why Fanny felt it imperative to suppress her father's 'Memoirs' and correspondence so extensively, although the nature of the first obliged her to emphasize only the second in public. Burney himself considered that his humble origins and the various problems of his childhood only emphasized by contrast the success of his later career and he had discussed with embarrassing frankness not only his relations, but most of the great men of his time with whom he had been acquainted. Fanny knew, however, that the family had no desire to be reminded of its origins and that her father's frankness about many celebrated personalities would be dangerous. Burney himself had realized that his 'Memoirs' would have to be published posthumously, for he wrote on the first page, 'They will be drawn up with too much sincerity and integrity to appear during the author's life'.[2] Although he can hardly have imagined that his autobiography would be destroyed, he acknowledged here one of the reasons which brought about that destruction. It was not one to which Fanny could

<hr>

[1] Hemlow, pp. 447–56.   [2] Osborn.

admit in public, however, and when she printed the opening pages of the 'Memoirs' in 1832, she omitted this sentence and deleted it heavily in the manuscript.

For the benefit of the public, Fanny had to provide a different explanation of her conduct. In her *Memoirs of Dr. Burney* in 1832 she justified the suppression of the autobiography entirely on the grounds that it had been written when her father was senile and in ill-health. At the very beginning of her biography she quoted the opening pages of Burney's 'Memoirs', stating explicitly that in 1782 he had been able to write no more than this brief account of his grandfather and father. She then asserted that the work had not been resumed until 1807, in spite of the fact that the manuscript which she had just transcribed was dated 1805 by Burney himself.

Fanny had good reason for making what may appear a trivial mistake of two years. In the autumn of 1806 Burney suffered a minor paralytic stroke in his left hand and, for some six months, he was depressed by the expectation that a worse affliction would follow. In 1832 Fanny repeatedly insisted that all but a few opening pages of her father's 'Memoirs' had been written *after* this stroke and while it still affected his spirits and literary powers. At the beginning of her biography, for example, she stated that he had not resumed work on the 'Memoirs' until 1807, 'when the Doctor had reached the age of eighty-one, and was under the dejecting apprehension of a paralytic seizure'.[1] Similarly, in her third volume, she mentioned his return to the writing of his 'Memoirs' only after she had devoted several pages to the stroke, which had affected him not only physically, but had dealt 'his spirits a suspensive shock, that caused a marked diminution of his resources for composition'. The stroke, according to Fanny, explained the 'nerveless laxity of expression' and the 'monotonous prolixity of detail' in the 'Memoirs', which justified her destruction of 'so immense a mass of morbid leisure, and minute personality'.[2]

That Fanny was consciously dishonest can not be doubted. Burney had written a narrative of almost half his life in 1782, when he was only fifty-six. Three more volumes contained a transcription of the unpublished journal which he had kept

---

[1] *Mem.* i. xvi.
[2] *Mem.* iii. 382–3. FB misdated CB's stroke 1807, instead of 1806.

during his travels in 1770. It is also clear that most of the additions and the later narrative were written in 1805 and 1806, *before* the stroke in his hand which, according to Fanny, crippled him mentally as well as physically. Even if it had been true that part of the 'Memoirs' had been written after the stroke in 1806, it is clear that Fanny greatly exaggerated its effect on her father. She herself provided some of the evidence which undermines her story. One of the annotations which she made when first reading her father's correspondence, with a view to publishing it separately, refers to a letter which he wrote in November 1806, less than six weeks after the stroke which she later described as having had so drastic an effect on his mental capacity. Her note explained that she had kept the letter because it illustrated 'the astonishing powers preserved of Mind, in old age & infirmities, as well as liberality & kindness of Heart, to the last of the Earthly career of Dr. Burney—with his unabated passion for his art'.[1]

Even when she was writing her *Memoirs*, Fanny was in constant danger of forgetting the senility which she had decided to attribute to him after 1806. Thus having quoted a letter which he wrote in 1810, she realized that it showed no signs of the mental decline which she had described. Her solution to this problem was to assert that, not only had Burney not resumed the writing of his 'Memoirs' until 1807, but that he had finished the work before an eventual recovery of his usual health and spirits: 'How merely an amanuensis had been the Editor of these Memoirs, had all the personal manuscripts of Dr. Burney been written at this healthy, though so much later period of his existence; instead of having fallen under his melancholy pen, to while away nerveless languor when paralysis, through the vision of his imagination, appeared to be unremittingly suspended over his head!'[2] Ultimately, therefore, Fanny was reduced to the demonstrably absurd assertion that Burney wrote the whole of his 'Memoirs' in a few months after his stroke in September 1806.

Miss Hemlow, who accepts Fanny's dating of her father's autobiography without question, also accepts what seemed to the guilty Fanny an important piece of evidence which retrospectively justified her suppression of the 'Memoirs'. In 1824

[1] CB to Belfour [Nov. 1806] (Osborn).   [2] *Mem.* iii. 387–8.

she discovered among Burney's papers what she took to be an admission on his part that his 'Memoirs' were tedious and use-less. Overjoyed by her discovery, Fanny wrote a long note on the other side of the piece of paper which bore this abject con-fession, excitedly claiming that it confirmed that it had been her duty to destroy the 'Memoirs' and that her father would have approved her action. This 'Wise, Candid, deeply judged pas-sage', as she described it, justified her in 'the Right Path I had already taken from conscientious tenderness to the true Fame of my reverend & gifted Father'.[1]

Not surprisingly, Fanny quoted her father's 'confession' in her *Memoirs* in 1832 as proof that 'Dr. Burney would have approved the destruction, or suppression of the voluminous records begun under his sickly paralytic depression', placing it just before her account of his death as if it represented a last wish on his part, although there is no indication when it was written. As she printed it, the paragraph read: 'These records of the numerous invitations with which I have been honoured, entered, at the time, into my pocket-books, which served as ledgers, must be very dry and uninteresting, without relating the conversations, *bons mots*, or characteristic stories, told by individuals, who struck fire out of each other, producing mirth and good-humour: but when these *entries* were made I had not leisure for details—and now—memory cannot recall them!'[2]

Unfortunately for Fanny, a comparison of Burney's original note with the version of it which she printed in 1832, reveals that it can take none of the weight she placed upon it, quite apart from the fact that it could not refer to the earlier narrative written in 1782 or to the travel journal of 1770. In Burney's manuscript the note begins: 'These short records of the numer-ous invitations wth wch I was honoured at this time entered in my Baldwin Pocket book, wch served as a ledger must be very dry & uninteresting. . . .' Burney expressed himself rather clumsily but quite unambiguously. The passage refers to invitations received 'at this time': in other words, at a specific period of his life, probably of no more than a few weeks. Al-though his diary reminded him of the bare facts, he could not recall anything in detail about these particular social activities. He was, therefore, apologizing for the dryness of only a small

[1] Berg.   [2] *Mem*. iii. 420.

section of his 'Memoirs', which is a completely different matter from admitting to the futility of his autobiography as a whole. Fanny herself must have realized, after her first rapture, that her father's note could not refer to the whole of his 'Memoirs'; but, reluctant to be deprived of what had seemed to be a justification of her conduct, she made some small but significant alterations to the first sentence when she printed it in 1832. It is hard not to admire the subtlety of the small grammatical and verbal changes she made. By omitting the word 'short' she contrived to make 'These records' appear to refer to the 'Memoirs' as a whole; and Burney's 'at this time', which makes it clear that he was talking about a limited period, is emended to 'at the time' and cunningly made dependent on 'entered' instead of 'honoured'. Burney's apology for his inability to recall a short period of his social life in vivid detail is transformed by these small alterations to an admission of failure which apparently refers to the entire work.

There was, moreover, a conclusion to the passage which Fanny wisely omitted in 1832. Having made his apology to the future readers of his 'Memoirs', Burney had cheerfully proceeded to justify the inclusion of these 'short records' of his social life by describing the pleasure it gave him to mention the fashionable 'company' which had so flatteringly honoured him in this way. At the worst, he knew that these *vain boasts* would be forgiven as *'human frailties,* or *amiable weaknesses'*. If there were no other evidence, these omitted sentences would make it clear that Fanny's all-important piece of exculpatory evidence was not after all a final condemnation by Burney of his 'Memoirs' but, on the contrary, an unimportant page of nonchalant humility from the autobiography itself.

Even if the manner in which Fanny justified her suppression and extensive destruction of her father's 'Memoirs' is demonstrably dishonest and the loss of the work regrettable, her motives —the wish to conceal his revelations about his family and his acquaintance, and the conviction that his literary reputation could only have been damaged by its publication—are perfectly understandable. The *Memoirs of Doctor Burney* which she published instead in 1832 raise different questions. Miss Hemlow admitted that the omission of 'painful episodes of the family history' limited the value of the biography but was aware of no other defect: 'While such omissions necessarily result in distortion, the evidence is that she did not fabricate or invent. While she did not always tell the full truth about some of the family difficulties, sins, and errors, she did not tell un-truths.' Trust in Fanny's veracity is important, as Miss Hemlow states, since that quality is 'one of the indispensable require-ments in a journalist or diarist whose writings are to be taken seriously as social or biographical records'. Her conviction that Fanny can be trusted led Miss Hemlow to the conclusion that 'As a biography, therefore, the *Memoirs* is limited by the point of view and the selection of material, but within its limits it is authoritative, and more authoritative than anything else written on Dr. Burney, or likely to be written'.[1]

Miss Hemlow's claims for Fanny's biography were made primarily with reference to John Wilson Croker's famous attack on the *Memoirs* in the *Quarterly Review* in 1833[2] which, with a later attack on Fanny's *Diary and Letters* in the same journal in 1842, has succeeded in scandalizing admirers of Fanny and her family ever since. It is impossible, however, to dismiss Croker merely as an irresponsibly malicious enemy of Fanny. Whatever his motives, his indictment of her *Memoirs* is extremely intelligent and, unless it is considered exclusively from Fanny's point of view, rather than that of her father, it is largely irrefutable. Croker's first objection was that Burney had clearly left his 'Memoirs' in the belief that, although they would be edited, they would be published substantially in the form in which he wrote them. Fanny, however, had appeared in her *Memoirs* as 'the *writer* of a work essentially her own, and not the *editor* of her father's recollections of his life'. Secondly, since Fanny had justified her destruction of most of Burney's 'Memoirs' on the grounds of the senility of the style, Croker protested that 'we do very much doubt whether what she has suppressed could have been more feeble, anile, incoherent, or "*sentant plus l'apoplexie*", than that which she has substituted for it'. He expanded this point by a derisive analysis of the 'pompous verbosity' of Fanny's convoluted, circumlocutory and inflated style, arguing that 'a judicious selection from the autograph manuscript would probably give a fuller and certainly a more intelligible account of this amiable man, than can be gathered

[1] Hemlow, p. 462.

[2] xlix. 97–125.

from the over-anxious piety and too elaborate care of his affectionate, but injudicious, biographer'.

Thirdly, Croker anticipated with peculiar perception Miss Hemlow's revelation of the hostility of the Burney children to their stepmother, detecting the insincerity in Fanny's account of her father's second marriage, which he felt that she had defended 'rather too eloquently'. Thereafter, he noted, Mrs. Burney was hardly mentioned again: 'in short, she is a cypher in Madame d'Arblay's history of the family—the doctor's own memoirs would probably have been more communicative.' Croker was, of course, correct, for surviving fragments of the 'Memoirs' describe the courtship of the second Mrs. Burney and her death at length. Fourthly, Croker insisted that a satisfactory biography of Burney had still to be written, for Fanny's *Memoirs* contained so much about her own career, that they would have been more accurately entitled 'Scattered Recollections of Miss Fanny Burney and her Acquaintance': 'Madame d'Arblay, with consummate art—or a confusion of ideas which has had the same effect as consummate art,— conceals from her readers, and perhaps from herself, that it is her *own Memoirs*, and *not* those of her father that she has been writing; and we confess that we have a strong suspicion, that it was *because* her father's auto-biography did not fulfil *this* object, that *it* has been suppressed. . . .'

The failure of her father's autobiography to deal at length with her own activities may well have been the ultimate reason for her suppression of it. Certainly, by 1832 the self-consciousness which had made Fanny so brilliant a diarist had hardened to ruthless egotism and from the point at which she describes the publication of *Evelina* in 1778 until her departure to France in 1802, her own career is given as much space in her *Memoirs* as the subject of her biography himself. Her private justification was that her own '*incipient* career of Notage took place just as *his* was at its meridian: for the second volume of his History of Music, & my own second work, Cecilia, came out in the same year. We basked, therefore, in public sunshine at the same time, & were tied together in innumerable little incidents.'[1] Twice, in fact, Burney and his daughter had published books in the same year. In her *Memoirs*, however, Fanny devotes more

[1] Hemlow, p. 465.

space to the appearance of her own novels than to that of her father's works; and, in both cases, gives the impression that the books were published with a much larger interval between them than was the case, in order that her own celebrity should not be in any way entangled with that of her father. In 1782, the interval between the publication of the second volume of Burney's *History* and Fanny's *Cecilia* was a matter of days. Fanny contrives, however, to give the impression that, only after his own book had been published, did her father urge her to set about writing her novel.[1] Burney's *Memoirs of Metastasio* and Fanny's *Camilla* were both published in 1796. In the *Memoirs* Fanny dates her father's biography 1795[2] and it is hard to think of any reason for such an error except that she was once more unwilling to share the limelight with her father.

Croker's fifth accusation was that Fanny deliberately withheld dates in the earlier part of her biography, especially that of her own birth, which, he observed, 'has been most *curiously* obliterated'. Her intention, he suspected, was to conceal her true age when *Evelina* was published in 1778. Part of the fame of the novel in the early nineteenth century depended on a popular belief that Fanny had written it at the age of seventeen, this confusion presumably resulting from the fact that the heroine of the story was seventeen when she entered fashionable society. In any case, many contemporary accounts of Fanny's life contained this important error.[3] At this point Croker made the apparent mistake which has enabled Fanny's admirers to dismiss the rest of his review with derision. He triumphantly produced the information that he had checked the registers at King's Lynn and had discovered that Fanny had been born in 1752 and was in fact aged twenty-five when *Evelina* was published. As her admirers have pointed out, Fanny herself had never stated that she was seventeen in 1778. On the other hand, she had never made any attempt to correct the mistake. Croker, moreover, did not accuse her of lying, but merely of having permitted a flattering error to circulate and of a studied attempt in her *Memoirs* of her father to perpetuate the myth by concealment of dates and by the implication that the authoress of *Evelina* was in her teens: 'we are . . . not much surprised that Madame d'Arblay, though she may have had no share in

[1] *Mem.* ii. 213–16, 240.   [2] Ibid., iii. 212–14.   [3] Hemlow, p. 458.

propagating the original error, should have shown so little anxiety to correct it'. Once again, Croker's accusation is plausible for, if the early part of the *Memoirs* is read with this problem in mind, Fanny's obfuscation of dates can have no other explanation. Miss Hemlow's defence of Fanny's failure to correct so widely circulated an error—that 'it was her consistent policy to avoid literary quarrels'[1]—curiously fails to meet the charge, since 'literary quarrels' were in no way involved.

Croker's conclusion was that the worst features of her *Memoirs*—the abominable style, the ludicrously heroic descriptions of many incidents in Burney's life, and the generally vague and over-idealized portrait of her father—could be explained only by Fanny's career as a novelist. Nor was he alone in making such an accusation. Mrs. Agnew, who had been housekeeper to Mrs. Delany when Fanny was at Court, objected to various details of Fanny's account of her former mistress. Whatever the facts about Mrs. Delany may be, Mrs. Agnew's general comments on Fanny's *Memoirs* are not unjust: 'she must fancy she was *writing a novel*, and therefore could embellish her story in any way she liked. Every character she has brought forward tends to raising herself and her family a step and a step higher, from the great connexions (of those persons), who had obtained a name in the world from their great abilities or rank in life.' So accustomed was Fanny to '*composing fictions*', Mrs. Agnew believed, 'that she was not to be depended upon where she desired to work up an effect, or *herself* to produce an impression'.[2]

The *Memoirs of Dr. Burney* can indeed be taken as Fanny's last novel. Yet if it had not been claimed for this work that it was 'authoritative in a way none other can ever be',[3] there would be little need to treat it more seriously than any biography of a father written by an affectionate daughter in the early nineteenth century. Quite apart from the understandable omission of painful episodes in the family history, however, it is possible to go even further than Croker's complaints about the disproportionate obtrusion of the biographer's personality and

[1] Ibid.
[2] *Correspondence of Mrs. Delany*, ed. Llanover, 2nd series, iii. 318, 320.
[3] Hemlow, p. 466.

career, the ludicrous idealization of Burney as the faultless hero
of the work and the deliberate vagueness with which certain
information is offered. Fanny's affectionate loyalty to the posthumous reputation of her father is not in question. The general
veracity of her biography and its claims to be authoritative are
another matter.

II

The general defects of Fanny's *Memoirs* can be illustrated
precisely in miniature by a comparison of passages from
Burney's manuscript autobiography, upon which she claimed to
have based her own work, with the actual use she made of them
in 1832. As the longest continuous fragment of Burney's
'Memoirs' to have survived is largely concerned with his life in
1805 and 1806, a comparison based on this material also permits
a return to the narrative of his life after the completion of his
articles for Rees's *Cyclopaedia*. The surviving pages of the fragment are numbered from 107 to 173, but many have been torn
out and others deleted, with the result that no more than thirty-
two have survived intact.[1] Since this material covered a period
when Fanny was in France and almost entirely out of touch with
her father, she quoted much of it without interruption though
not without alteration and rearrangement, in her *Memoirs*.
Sections of the fragment, however, were used at later points in
her narrative.[2]

1805 was a busy and enjoyable year for Burney, crowded
with engagements and remarkable for the literary honours and
flattering attention from Royalty which it brought him. During
the summer he received particular notice from the King and the
Prince of Wales. His own narrative describes in chronological
order a meeting with the Prince at a concert on 9 June 1805;[3]
the visit of the King and Queen to Chelsea College on 20 June;
other concerts early in July; and a dinner with the Prince on
9 July. Fanny's version disentangles the two strands of royal
attention, quoting the account of the King's visit to Chelsea
only after dealing with the meetings with the Prince of Wales,
to which she had added for good measure an undated descrip-

---

[1] Osborn.   [2] *Mem.* iii. 354–63, 374–6, 392–3.
[3] FB dates this meeting in May, *Mem.* iii. 354. The date given above is from CB
to CB Jr., 10 June 1805 (Osborn).

tion of another meeting, which did not in fact occur until March 1806. Although her dating of all these events is typically vague, she was clearly attempting to impart a coherent pattern to Burney's strictly chronological account.

The first feature of her treatment of Burney's narrative could be equally well illustrated by examination of any 'quotation' from his 'Memoirs' in the course of her work. It consists of a systematic 'improvement' of his prose, in which the idiosyncrasies and colloquial vigour of his style are replaced by her own tendency to verbosity and circumlocution. Such elevation of his style is never more apparent than when she reproduces his accounts of conversations with Royalty for, although no one could have been more appreciative of royal condescension than Burney himself, Fanny often seems to have felt that he had not been sufficiently respectful or grateful, either in the conversation which he was recalling or in his narrative as a whole. Thus, when Lady Melbourne, a former pupil of Burney, first broached the idea of a dinner to which the Prince of Wales would also be invited, Burney replied, according to his own account, 'I of course s^d I sh^d be most happy in such an honour. ay says the P[rince] & bring your son with you.—"it is singular (his Highness adds to Lady M.) that the Father sh^d be the best and almost the only good judge of Music in the Kingdom & his Son the best scholar".' Fanny did not, of course, tamper with the generous compliment to her father and her brother Charles, but the preceding sentence was expanded to 'Of course I expressed, as well as I could, my sense of so high and unexpected an honour; and the Prince, with a smile of unequalled courtesy, said, "Aye, do come, Dr. Burney, and bring your son with you".'[1]

Such alterations occur throughout the *Memoirs*. Although the result is that Fanny's quotations from her father's autobiography and from his letters cannot be trusted and although, in such cases as that just quoted, Burney's usual fascinated subservience and pride in such honours are ludicrously exaggerated, little harm perhaps is done. Sometimes, however, the effect of Fanny's interference is to destroy the true nature of Burney's personality. During the dinner given by Lord Melbourne on 9 July 1805, the Prince of Wales paid particular attention to Burney, persuading him to overcome 'the stubborn virtue of a long life'

[1] *Mem.* iii. 354.

by 'hobbing and nobbing' with him 'in a glass of *cherry brandy*!',
and by engaging him in a long conversation on music. Burney,
flattered by such condescension, recorded that 'We were
generally in perfect tune in our opinion, though once or 2^{ce} I
ventured to dissent from the Pr. but he condescended to come
over to my opinion; nothing however was *disputed* on either side.
I felt as much at my ease, as if comparing opinions with any
other well-bred man.' Fanny evidently decided that her father's
conversation had been rather too bold and the alterations she
made to the passage, small in themselves, completely change the
relations between Burney and the Prince: 'We were, generally,
in perfect tune in our opinions: though once or twice I ventured to dissent from his Royal Highness; and once he condescended to come over to my argument: and he had the skill,
as well as the nobleness, to put me as perfectly at my ease in
expressing my notions, as I should have been with any other
perfectly well-bred man.'[1] This small example will serve to
illustrate the way in which Fanny contrived to drain her father's
personality of any colour. Further conversation after dinner
received a similar infusion of servility.

The two versions of the visit by the King and Queen to
Chelsea College on 20 June 1805[2] reveal more sinister aspects of
Fanny's 'editing'. As an officer of the establishment Burney was
presented to the Royal Family and later accompanied them on
their inspection of the buildings, in the course of which the King
addressed several remarks to him. To some extent Fanny
improved the narrative by tidying up the conversation and
fusing remarks on similar topics which were separated in
Burney's version. Burney, however, described his presentation
to the King and Queen as follows: 'The first thing the K. said,
holding up both his hands: "Ten years younger than when I
saw you last!" The Queen most condescendingly said in a low
voice: "I am extremely obliged to you for the Hymn you sent
me"—'. (Burney was evidently still in the habit of sending the
Queen music which he thought she would appreciate).[3] In
Fanny's revised version the King's observation is substantially
the same but the Queen's first words differ strikingly: 'The first
words of the Queen were, "How does Madame d'Arblay do?"'

---

[1] *Mem*. iii. 356.   [2] Cf. *Gent. Mag.* lxxv (1805), 576.
[3] See *ante*, pp. 394-5.

And after my answer, and humble thanks, she added in a low voice, "I am extremely obliged to you, Dr. Burney, for the hymn you sent me".'[1]

No more precise illustration in miniature of Fanny's massive obtrusion on her account of her father's career could be offered. Her narrative of the Royal visit contains, however, further examples not only of such insertion of her own name, but also of a related feature of her *Memoirs*, the almost complete exclusion of mention of other members of the family by comparison with the prominent role which she gives herself. Burney's account mentions that the King and Queen did eventually inquire after Fanny, although she was merely linked with his granddaughter, Fanny Phillips, who was living at Chelsea with him at this time: 'Their Majesties condescended to ask many questions concerning my family, particularly of Mad^e d'Arblay, & Miss Phillips.' Fanny's emendation of this sentence is astonishing in its egotism: 'Their Majesties then both condescended to make some inquiries after my family, though by name only after my daughter d'Arblay.'[2]

Burney then described at some length the royal attentions to Fanny Phillips, whom he had summoned for presentation to their Majesties as soon as the Queen inquired after her. Although Fanny could hardly suppress this passage completely, she reduced it as much as possible and made up for lost ground at the very end of the account of the royal visit. Burney had concluded by mentioning that 'The K. did not forget to mention the fright I was in when my daughter Fanny (now d'Arblay) was s^d to have written a book, "*Evelina*, was not it?" says his Majesty. . . .' The rest of the sentence describes a final inquiry by the Queen about Fanny Phillips. Fanny d'Arblay's version omitted any mention of her niece and ludicrously exaggerated the King's interest in her first novel: 'The King then resumed again his old favourite topic of amusement, my daughter d'Arblay's concealed composition of Evelina; inquiring again and again into the various particulars of its contrivance and its discovery.'[3]

Such instances of the falsification of a text offered as direct quotation from her father's 'Memoirs' and of Fanny's senile egotism may be taken as characteristic of her biography as a whole. Further comparison of the long fragment of Burney's

[1] *Mem*. iii. 360. [2] Ibid. 361. [3] Ibid. 362.

autobiography with Fanny's use of it would only reinforce the
points which have already been made.[1] Two examples of
curiously unnecessary dishonesty on Fanny's part can be
found, however, in her use of the later pages of the fragment,
which contain only copies of letters and scattered reflections on
various subjects. The first case could, in fact, be illustrated
equally well from earlier examples in the *Memoirs*, for after
quoting Burney's autobiography briefly for 1803 and again for
1804, she stated that no other material for these years had
survived. With reference to 1804, she asserted, 'Here stop all
journals, all notes, all memorandums of Dr. Burney for the rest
of this year. Not another word remains bearing its date.'[2] If
Fanny was prepared to make such assertions, she would have
been wise to have destroyed completely fragments of Burney's
'Memoirs' of these years which she preserved and which flatly
contradict her statements.[3]

For the year 1811 she made a similar report: 'Of the year
1811, no species of event, nor detail of circumstance, has reached
this Memorialist, except the following letter, which is copied
from Doctor Burney's own handwriting near the conclusion of
his Journal. . . .'[4] Fanny then printed a letter from Burney to
A. F. C. Kollman, dated 24 March 1811, which appears on
pages 169–70 of the fragment of his 'Memoirs'. In spite of her
insistence that no other material survived from this year, page
171 of the same fragment contains a copy by Burney of another
letter to Kollman, dated 8 April 1811, which Fanny cannot have
overlooked since it bears her annotations. Some ten pages after
the pagination ceases appears another letter, from Burney to
William Shield, dated 9 May 1811, which is similarly annotated
by Fanny, one of her comments being 'This is the Last Letter
copied by the Doctor's own hand'. Although it is not clear whom
Fanny was trying to deceive by this annotation, unless it was intended for her edition of Burney's correspondence, the following
page bears yet another letter which, though heavily deleted, is
obviously in Burney's hand. Fanny's dishonesty, apparently
so often unnecessary, is tolerable only if one takes pity on the
octogenarian, who was presumably anxious to avoid spending
much time in discussion of her father's later years.

[1] See *ante*, p. 411, n. 4.   [2] *Mem.* iii. 334, 339.
[3] *Frag. Mem.* (Berg).   [4] *Mem.* iii. 393.

A final example of Fanny's technique of transforming her father's 'Memoirs' can be found in the same fragment and it supports the view that she was writing a novel rather than a biography. Before concluding her *Memoirs* with an account of Burney's death, she brought her narrative of his literary career to an impressive conclusion by drawing a parallel with Sir Joshua Reynolds:

> What next—and last—follows, is copied from the final page of Dr. Burney's manuscript journal: and closes all there is to offer of his written composition.
> Sir Joshua Reynolds desired that the last name he should pronounce in public should be that of Michael Angelo:[1] and Dr. Burney seems to purpose that the last name he should transmit—if so allowed—through his annals, to posterity, should be that of Haydn.

Fanny then quoted a note by Burney on the controversial depiction of Chaos in Haydn's *Creation*:

> Finding a blank leaf at the end of my Journal, it may be used in the way of postscriptum, in speaking of the prelude, or opening of Haydn's Creation, to observe, that though the generality of the subscribers were unable to disentangle the studied confusion in delineating chaos, yet, when dissonance was tuned, when order was established, and God said,
> > 'Let there be light!—and there was light!'
> > '*Que la lumière soit!—et la lumière fut!*'
> the composer's meaning was felt by the whole audience, who instantly broke in upon the performers with rapturous applause before the musical period was closed.[2]

It would, of course, have been pleasing if Burney's last written words had been such a tribute to his favourite composer. Fanny's transcription of this note, which appears on page 173 of the fragment in his 'Memoirs', is relatively accurate, the only significant alteration being to the first sentence. Burney had actually written, 'Finding a blank leaf at the end of my reflections on the prelude or opening of the Creation . . .'. (These reflections, heavily deleted by Fanny, appeared on the preceding page.) Fanny's emendation to 'at the end of my Journal' and her statement that the passage appeared on 'the final page'

---

[1] In his final *Discourse* to the Royal Academy in 1790.
[2] *Mem.* iii. 420–1.

of the journal give the impression that Burney was here making a conscious farewell to his literary career. In fact, he was merely transcribing an account of the first performance of *The Creation* which he had written in 1801 and which he sent to L'Institut de France in 1811.[1] In any case, the note does not appear on the 'final page' of his journal nor does it close 'all there is to offer of his written composition', for Burney went on to make further remarks about Haydn; and later pages of his notebook contain the letter to Shield already mentioned and deleted copies of two other letters.

Fortunately, most of the facts in Fanny's biography of her father and her quotations from his letters and 'Memoirs' can now be checked against other material. Although it is difficult to decide whether her crimes were always conscious, the fact that, just before her death, she was haunted by Croker's accusations—'I can use no softer term than Defamation for the least attack upon my veracity'—may indicate pangs of conscience.[2] The importance of what she destroyed can hardly be estimated, for it included almost all of Burney's 'Memoirs' of the most interesting period of his life, when he was the intimate friend of Johnson and Mrs. Thrale. It is characteristic that, apart from a few scraps, the only fragment which she preserved relating to this period should be his proud account of his discovery of the authorship of *Evelina*.[3]

It can be stated with confidence that hardly a single quotation from Burney's papers in her *Memoirs* escaped her interference; that, either through carelessness or design, simple factual information, especially dates, is often inaccurate; and that many episodes of Burney's life are blatantly misrepresented in her biography, as a result of her idealistic simplification. Nor can it be claimed that, allowing for omissions, errors of fact, and oversimplification, her *Memoirs* nevertheless contain a uniquely personal portrait of Burney. For this, at least, one might have hoped, but so concerned was Fanny to emphasize his virtues and unfailing literary and social success and to elevate his character above that of ordinary mortals, in the same way that her prose escapes the normal modes of human communication, that her biography fails conspicuously to focus on Burney's personality.

---

[1] See *ante*, p. 401, n. 3; and *post*, p. 471 and n. 3.
[2] Hemlow, p. 459.   [3] *Frag. Mem.* (Berg).

When there are no means of verifying information offered by Fanny in her *Memoirs*, her testimony must be considered better than nothing, for truth and distortion are subtly mingled. If complete reliance can never be placed on her statements, neither can they be completely dismissed. This, needless to say, does not amount to a confirmation of the view that her biography of Burney 'is authentic in a way none other can ever be'. Not a page of her *Memoirs* should be trusted implicitly. As Croker observed, 'As a literary work we have not a word to say in its favour; and . . . we wish we could have evaded the subject altogether.'[1]

---

[1] *Quarterly Review*, xlix (1833), 97.

XII

LAST YEARS

1805–1814

I

IN July 1806, three months after his eightieth birthday, Burney wrote to Fanny in Paris to describe his life in the preceding twelve months. Never, it seemed, had so many engagements and honours crowded upon him:

But Lord! Fanny, if I were to tell you half the honours I have lately rec^d from first-rate people for birth, worth, & talents in my *Octogenaire* state, it w^d make your hair stand on end. Dinners, concerts, conversazioni—more than ever—Though my Eyes, Ears, & memory, are very much impaired—& as to pedestrian abilities, I may say, when asked how I do, as Alderman Carey of Lynn did to me at 84—'I am pretty well; but od rabbit it! I don't know how it is, I can't walk so well as I used to do.'[1]

Although he had recently 'more than doubled, in number, the friends I have lost', the deaths of such friends as Richard Cox, Thomas Twining, Dorothy Young, Lord Macartney, Lady Mary Duncan, and Fulke Greville left gaps which he knew would never be filled. Yet the events of the previous year left him in high spirits and reasonable health. The polite attentions of the King and the Prince of Wales in the summer of 1805 had been only the beginning of a year which he recalled with the greatest pride. During July 1805 he had paid what was by now a customary visit to the Duke of Portland at Bulstrode, where he stayed for part of every summer from 1802 to 1809. The comforts of the great house, the beauty of the gardens, the society of the aristocratic and celebrated friends whom he met there, and the political importance of the Duke himself, who became Prime Minister in 1807, all contributed to Burney's intense enjoyment of these visits. Later in the summer of 1805

---

[1] CB to FB, 30 July 1806 (Osborn).

he stayed with Mrs. Crewe at Cheltenham and also visited Malvern, Birmingham, and Oxford.[1]

During the winter Burney suffered from the effects of a fall at Malvern, but his health generally remained satisfactory as he worked on his 'Memoirs'. In March 1806 an old ailment returned, but his description of it suggests that his spirits were not unduly affected: 'This morning at getting up, the Rheumatism seized my left leg like a mastiff . . . rendering me such a cripple that if I were to run a 100 yards with Sr Jos. Banks I sh^d be distanced.'[2] April, however, brought not only the warmer weather which could restore him, but at last, after years of disappointment, royal acknowledgement of his deserts in an official and concrete form. For several years Burney's friends, particularly Mrs. Crewe, had been trying to obtain some kind of pension for him. In September 1799 Burney had referred to such an attempt in a letter to Mrs. Crewe: 'I am always flattered by the zeal of my friends—& their good wishes, & merely *thinking* of me—&, as you observe, I have been too long in the habit of disappointm^t to be much disturbed by one aërial Castle, one "baseless fabric of a vision", more, being dissolved. I always loved Mr Canning before I knew myself in possession of his good wishes—& now here's gratitude added to natural inclination.'[3] Dr. Scholes quotes a draft of a letter from William Windham to some person in authority which describes at length Burney's uncertain health and precarious financial situation, mentioning that he was still obliged to teach and was writing for Rees's *Cyclopaedia*, and estimating his age at seventy-six.[4] This attempt to obtain a pension for Burney can therefore be dated in 1802, although once more it was unsuccessful.

In 1805, however, Mrs. Crewe and Windham made a last determined effort on Burney's behalf. Arthur Murphy, an old friend of Burney, died in June 1805 and the royal pension of £200 a year which he had been receiving since 1803 was available for another man of letters. According to Burney, the Princess of Wales had remarked, during the changes in the administration which were taking place at this time, that 'if the

---

[1] *Frag. Mem.*; CB to CB Jr., 31 Oct. 1805, and to Latrobe, 31 Oct. 1805 (Osborn).

[2] *Frag. Mem.* (Berg); for Banks's gout, cf. H. C. Cameron, *Sir Joseph Banks*, 1952, p. 270.   [3] CB to Mrs. Crewe, 25 Sept. 1799 (Osborn).

[4] *GDB*, ii. 255.

new Ministry did not do something for [him], she sh^d have no
opinion of them'. In the autumn Windham and Mrs. Crewe,
who were confident of success, began to engineer the bestowal
of the pension on their aged friend. On learning, however, that
this would depend on the approval of Lord Grenville, Burney,
having 'no interest or acquaintance' with the minister, 'fell
again into "the slough of despond"; blaming myself for having
been again the dupe of vain hopes'. The winter passed, as he
expected, without bringing any news of the pension and he
steeled himself against the inevitable disappointment, even to
the point of avoiding any communication with Lady Crewe (as
she had become in January 1806), who, he felt, was responsible
for the cruel rise and fall of his expectations.[1]

On 18 April 1806, however, appropriately enough Burney's
eightieth birthday, the news arrived that Grenville had approved a pension of £200 a year. The incredulous recipient of
this honour at once wrote a letter to Lady Crewe which has
often been quoted in the course of this study, in which he gave
what he described elsewhere as 'a short sketch of my hopes &
disappointments during the last 40 years of my life, to acc^t for
my scepticism in the smiles of Fortune, of wch I thought I sh^d
never again be the dupe'. The draft of this letter ends with the
sentence, 'This is the birth day and regeneration of the hopes of
a man born Apr. 7th O.S. 1726.'[2] Nine days later, at Grenville's request, the King approved the pension,[3] the first in-
stallment of which Burney received in the following November.[4]
Both Lady Crewe and his son Charles considered that the
annual pension should have been £300, as, apparently, did
Fanny, who adjusted the actual figure to that amount in her
Memoirs.[5] Burney himself, however, was content: while the
pension was financially a great comfort in his old age, he valued
the honour quite as much as the money. He was, as might be
expected, especially 'proud in being Johnson's successor in his
Majesty's bounty' and he was not displeased to learn that the

[1] *Frag. Mem.* (Osborn).

[2] *Frag. Mem.* (Osborn); CB to Lady Crewe, 18 Apr. 1806 (B.M. Add. MS.
37916, f. 16; draft, Osborn).

[3] Lord Grenville to George III, 25 Apr. 1806; George III to Grenville, 27 Apr.
1806, *Historical Manuscripts Commission Report on Fortescue MSS.*, vol. viii (1912),
pp. 120, 122.   [4] CB to Lady Crewe, 17 Nov. 1806 (Berg).

[5] *Mem.* iii. 368.

newspapers were reporting inaccurately that he had received 'the same pension as Dr Johnson had'.[1]

Two weeks after learning about his pension, Burney was flattered once more, by an invitation to attend the 'Annual Entertainment' and preview of the exhibition given by the Royal Academy to those who were considered 'judges & Patrons of the Art'. Burney particularly enjoyed this occasion as he had not been invited to it since the death of Reynolds in 1792, and he left a long account of it in his 'Memoirs'. In spite of his poor sight and hearing, he had a most agreeable time, for he met many friends who looked after him carefully, in particular Sir George Beaumont, the friend of Wordsworth, who was himself exhibiting several landscapes. Since, according to one report, Beaumont's 'the Thorn, from Lyrical Ballads' was particularly praised, we may wonder if Burney remembered his review of that famous volume in 1799.[2]

In July 1806 Burney was surprised to learn that his eccentric friend Lady Mary Duncan had left him in her will 'Six hundred p^ds and all my Papers of Music, and Music books'. Although he had little room to spare for these books, most of which merely duplicated his own collection, he was deeply touched by her remembrance of him.[3] In the same month there were rumours of further honours, for Burney heard from Fanny that the Institut de France was proposing to make him an honorary Correspondant of its 'Classe des Beaux Arts', in recognition of his contributions to musical history. Fanny apparently feared that her father, who had always detested French music and, more recently, French politics, would be offended rather than gratified by the proposed honour and she mentioned it to him only briefly and vaguely. That the Institut should honour him in this way in time of war, however, only increased his pleasure: 'are you afraid of turning my head with saying a word more of the honour wch the liberal members of the Institut have done me? or was it a false report? I own myself as much astonished as flattered even by the report, if that sh^d be all the notice bestowed on a man who has been all his life abusing the music in France, of the Anc^t _régime_, particularly the _Vocal_, as violently as Jean

[1] CB to CB Jr., 19 Apr. and 23 Apr. 1806 (Comyn).
[2] _Frag. Mem._ (Osborn); _Mem._, iii. 374–5; _Gent. Mag._ lxxvi (1806), 472.
[3] CB to FB, 9 Oct. 1806 (Berg); to CB Jr., 31 Oct. 1806 (Osborn).

Jacques—'.[1] Partly because of the difficulty of corresponding with France, however, Burney heard no more about his election until 1810.[2]

As a result of so many flattering honours, Burney was in high spirits during the summer of 1806. By comparison with his previous literary undertakings, the writing of his 'Memoirs' was a light and pleasant task and he was able to enjoy a busy social life without any of his former remorse. In July he was 'absolutely bewildered with affairs, engagements, & commissions for other people', although he was suffering from rheumatism and a cough.[3] In August he visited Bulstrode as usual, before proceeding to Bognor and Bristol in search of a cure for his ailments. He was not, however, seriously concerned about his health and was merely amused to find himself surrounded at Bristol by 'poor consumptive young ladies riding upon Donkeys, & cadaverous gentlemen in the last act of their vital drama'. Late in September he returned to Chelsea in better health and good spirits.[4]

Two days later, a slight paralytic seizure in his left hand brought this happy period of his life to an abrupt end. The whole character of his life changed, for, although medical treatment at once reduced the numbness, Burney expected that a more serious paralysis would soon follow. Accordingly, he refused to see any visitors except members of his family and permitted himself only 'an old Lady's airing in Hyde Park' each day. Yet although he feared for some six months that a worse affliction was imminent and, indeed, treated himself as an invalid from this period until his death, there can be no doubt that Fanny exaggerated his mental decline after this minor stroke, in order to justify her suppression of his 'Memoirs'. That he retained much of his characteristically self-derisive humour, is apparent from a letter to Malone in November 1806, in which he described his afflictions:

My hand is better, & the Torpor is now chiefly confined to the Thumb. Yet in gloomy moments, I cannot help imagining that Damocles' sword is is [*sic*] suspended over my head; wch is not a very

---

[1] CB to FB, 30 July 1806 (Osborn); *Mem.* iii. 389–90.   [2] See *post*, pp. 470–1.
[3] CB to Rosette Burney, 19 July 1806 (Osborn).
[4] CB to CB Jr., 30 Aug. 1806 (Berg); to Mrs. Fermor and Miss Willis [Sept 1806], draft (Osborn).

exhilerating idea. But to quicken *sensation* a little, I have the rheumatism frequently in my left shoulder, wch is nothing less than torpid. But Baretti used to say that 'two mistresses were better than one: as they divide the Attention.'[1]

What Burney himself described as 'the *foul fiend*, Hypochondria; with whom, till now, I was ever an utter stranger', however, became a frequent visitor and on 20 December 1806 he followed his doctors' advice and set out for Bath, by no means confident that he would ever return to Chelsea.[2] Shortly after his arrival he began making his will.[3] That he was suffering psychologically rather than physically, however, is clear from a letter which he wrote from Bath, in which he admitted that 'a *partial death* has more terrors in it wth me than entire dissolution, though, wth a rapid decay of sight, hearing, & memory, I am not tired of life'.[4] Mrs. Piozzi, who was also in Bath, evidently thought that his ailment was largely imaginary and irritated him by not taking his anxiety seriously enough.[5]

By March 1807, however, Burney had recovered his health and spirits sufficiently to return to Chelsea, where his life assumed a very simple pattern. He accepted no invitations, admitted visitors only in the afternoons, rarely ventured out-of-doors in cold weather, and never left London except 'to brace & fortify if possible my shattered frame before the departure of la belle saison' at Bulstrode during the summer. His health improved gradually and in the autumn of 1807 he could report that, during his walks in Kensington Gardens, he had 'mended my pace [so] that I overtake all invalide pedestrians in my path'.[6] Nevertheless, he dreaded the coming of winter, when his rheumatism and cough inevitably returned. He was not wasting his time at home, however, except in the sense that Fanny was to destroy the 'Memoirs' which he was now completing; nor was he crippled mentally to the extent which she chose to suggest. His daughter Sarah, who came to live with

---

[1] CB to Malone, 9 Nov. 1806 (Bodleian, MS. Malone 38, ff. 133-4).
[2] Ibid., 27 Nov. and 18 Dec. 1806 (Bodleian, MS. Malone 38, ff. 135-6, 159-60); to Flaxman, 15 Dec. 1806 (Osborn).   [3] *GDB*, ii. 261-73.
[4] CB to Lady Bruce [1807], draft (Osborn).
[5] CB to Mrs. Piozzi, 2 letters, 21 Jan. 1807 (JRL; Hyde; draft, Osborn); Mrs. Piozzi to CB, 21 Jan. 1807 (Osborn).
[6] CB to Miss Iremonger [June 1807], draft; to Mrs. Fermor and Miss Willis [1807], draft (Osborn).

him after the marriage of Fanny Phillips in June 1807, sometimes found him bad-tempered and unreasonable; but his old tendency to go to temperamental extremes, if it could plunge him into unnecessary periods of depression, was balanced at other times by a return of his old lively spirits and enthusiasm for life. Thus, his granddaughter Marianne Francis found him, in 1808, 'as young and gay as ever, reading & writing without spectacles, (which he has never used *yet*,) and cheerful and entertaining, and sprightly, and kind, as if he had been 23 instead of *eighty three*'.[1]

Burney was by no means cut off from the literary world, in spite of his enforced retirement from society. He corresponded frequently with Edmond Malone, answering his friend's queries and discussing literary and musical problems in amusing and lively letters. There were also requests for literary assistance from such writers as Henry Harington, who asked him to read over a manuscript;[2] John Belfour, who generously acknowledged Burney's somewhat reluctant assistance and advice in his translation of a Spanish poem on music;[3] and Uvedale Price.[4] The problems of another author kept Burney busy at this time, and, as much as any other factor, may have helped to rescue him from the morbidity which had followed his stroke. While Burney was at Bath early in 1807 he had received a letter from Johann Huttner (1765?–1847), a German writer who had settled in England, and who had accompanied Lord Macartney on his embassy to China in 1792.[5] Burney's article on 'Chinese Music', in which he acknowledged some assistance from Huttner, had recently appeared in the seventh volume of Rees's *Cyclopaedia* and Huttner wrote to thank Burney for his compliments, mentioning at the same time his financial difficulties, caused by the fact that the war with France had made it almost impossible for him to continue to earn his living as a translator of foreign books.

---

[1] Marianne Francis to Mrs. Piozzi, 13 Aug. 1808 (JRL, Eng. MS. 582); CB was eighty-two.

[2] Harington to CB, 4 June 1806 (Osborn). CB's remarks on his manuscript are in the Berg Collection.

[3] Belfour to CB, 11 Nov. 1806; CB to Belfour, 12 Nov. 1806 and n.d., drafts (Osborn). Cf. *Music, A Didactic Poem in Five Cantos. Translated from the Spanish of Don Tomas De Yriarte*, 1807, p. xi.   [4] Price to CB, 9 Mar. 1808 (Osborn).

[5] See *ante*, p. 362.

While he was still at Bath Burney had told Huttner's sad story to Lord Lonsdale, the husband of one of his former pupils and the friend of Wordsworth, who had promptly agreed to try to obtain a post for the German in the Foreign Office. Remembering Johnson's dying words to him—'Do all the good you can'—Burney obtained money from Lord Lonsdale for Huttner, lent him money himself, tried to assist the publication of a learned book the German had written, canvassed friends in the government and, with Lonsdale's help, eventually obtained a post for Huttner in the Pay Office. He clearly enjoyed acting as an intermediary between Lord Lonsdale and the impoverished author, to whom he felt free to write long moralistic and reminiscential letters on his own career as a man of letters.

In the end, however, he tired of the task of patronizing the depressed and helpless Huttner. When a post was at last obtained for him in July 1808, Huttner, who had always expressed his gratitude to Lord Lonsdale through Burney, now asked him to reply on his behalf to Canning's offer of employment. Burney was worn out, however, by the endless correspondence and negotiations in which Huttner's affairs had involved him; and the draft of a letter which he now sent to the unfortunate writer, inscribed 'Finale (It is hoped) to Huttner', unexpectedly and sternly rebukes the man whom he had been assisting so indefatigably for eighteen months: 'I see plainly from your temper that there will be no end of my servitude in acting as your secretary & solicitor to the end of at least one of our lives.' His dearest wish was to be allowed 'to glide quietly down to his grave after a long active laborious & not dishonourable life'. This was merely one of Burney's temperamental outbursts, however, for the two men were reconciled and Huttner took up his post in October 1808. Many years later he expressed to Fanny d'Arblay his deep gratitude for Burney's assistance in the unhappiest period of his life.[1]

Burney's almost constant confinement to Chelsea College and his intense desire to leave all his affairs in order had meanwhile brought once more to his attention a problem which had been

[1] CB to Huttner, 27 letters, 6 Mar. 1807–[Aug. 1808], (Berg; Osborn); Huttner to CB, 3 letters, 26 May–4 July 1808 (Osborn); CB to Lonsdale, 3 letters, drafts, Mar. 1807–Aug. 1807 (Hyde; Osborn; inset in Hawkins's *History*, B.M., C. 45, f. 4); Lonsdale to CB, 5 letters, 13 Oct. 1807–14 Aug. 1808 (Osborn); Huttner to FB, 18 Jan. 1833 (Osborn).

worrying him for some years. The sheets of his *History of Music* which he had rescued from the Robinsons' warehouse in 1804 were still piled, in hundreds of parcels, in the room in Chelsea College which he had hired for the purpose.[1] The problem of their disposal had inevitably occurred to him whenever friends asked for a set of the work, for he had no impressions of most of the plates and could offer them only a set in which the second, third and fourth volumes lacked the musical illustrations.[2] It was probably not until he made his will in January 1807, however, that Burney became seriously concerned about the fate of his *History*, although he did not yet fully realize the problems that were in store for him. In his will he stated that there were 'many impressions' of the 'frontispieces and ornamental plates' at Chelsea College and he added that

I think if the Pewter Plates of Music, which have been so injured by the Robinson's Warehouse Men and miserably reprinted by an ignorant person unused to the work, were to be restamped the expence would soon be made good by the Sale of the Work at six Guineas a Set, at least as far as the remaining Copies of the 2^d vol. go, and in time would enable the Proprietor of the work to reprint the 2^d Vol. intire which has long wanted a 2^d Edit.

The task of supervising the preparation of the *History* for sale was allotted to his son Charles.[3]

The problem was now, however, on Burney's mind and it was not long before he was urging his son to take immediate steps towards the disposal of the parcels of sheets. He was also irritated to find that the 125 sets of the *History*, which in 1804 he had divided between five booksellers,[4] were never advertised and he complained to Charles that his 'poor books sleep on the peacable shelves in the back shop—& I am perpetually asked where my Hist^y may be had': accordingly he urged his son to instruct Payne, one of the booksellers, to give the work more publicity.[5] The hundreds of sets at Chelsea College, however, soon became an even greater cause for anxiety and, although he had formally handed the problem over to Charles in his will, he himself began to worry endlessly about it.

[1] See *ante*, pp. 424–6.
[2] CB to Flaxman, 15 Dec. 1806 and to Mrs. Iremonger, [1807], draft (Osborn).
[3] *GDB*, ii. 267–8.   [4] See *ante*, p. 425.
[5] CB to CB Jr., 4 Mar. 1807 (Osborn).

The only feasible solution was to offer the copies of the *History* to the booksellers at a trade sale. It was now discovered, however, that the pewter plates of the numerous musical illustrations were so encrusted with dry ink that no new impressions could be obtained from them. Until they had been cleaned, so that examples of the impressions might be shown to interested booksellers, the *History* could not be offered for sale. At last, in May 1808, a serious attempt was made to have them cleaned and Burney's spirits rose at the prospect of getting rid of the stacks of sheets. Confident of success, he sent 'specimens of my pewter Music plates in their worst condition' to be cleaned by a method which had been recommended to him and 'to have 50 impressions of each worked off, and printed on good paper—as a stimulus to the Trade purchasing all the remaining copies of the letter-press work in a body or company subscribing for shares. . . .' He also asked Charles to help with the removal of the piles of sheets, pleading with him to 'save from annihilation a work which had cost me so much money, time, and labour, & which has been generally approved'.[1] By 20 May 1808 all Burney's hopes had been crushed. The recommended method of cleaning the plates had failed completely: 'the Ink in the heads of black notes, double bars, etc is become so impenetrable, so adamantine, that no tool can touch them'. He was plunged into despair: '*Je suis tombé de mon haut!*—I tremble for the *Trade-Sale*, for the complete riddance of the whole mountain of remaining Letter-press of my Hist. Mus. and emancipation of the poor benighted lumber-room'. 'Revive my drooping hopes', he begged Charles, '& send a dram of comfort, if you can to your feeble aged parent.'[2] Crushed by the failure of the experiment, he vented some of his irritation in a bad-tempered letter to his passive protégé, Johann Huttner.[3]

A week later his spirits were soaring once more, for his nephew Edward had successfully tried a different method (using 'soap lyxivium'), with the result that the very worst of the plates had been cleaned so effectively 'that they look like new plates, & the impressions from them are as black, clean, & sharp as the best of my first impressions! This is a most important

[1] Ibid., 13 May 1808 (Osborn).
[2] Ibid., 20 May [1808] (Osborn).
[3] CB to Huttner, 22 May 1808 (Osborn).

point gained, & w^d I sh^d think stimulate the book & Music sellers to bid high at a Trade Sale.'[1] Johann Huttner, who was doubtless rather dazed by his patron's rapid changes in mood, benefited from the success of the experiment to the extent of £40, which Burney promptly offered to lend him, ingenuously attributing his 'swaggering' spirits to the sunshine: 'I am indeed so revived by this warm weather that such a spirit of enterprize seems awakened, as makes me feel as if I were not only equal to the undertaking *new editions* of *old* works, but competent to entirely new *Enterprizes.* . . .'[2]

The next stage was to urge Payne to send Messenger, his foreman, to inspect the impressions which had been obtained from the cleaned plates and then to examine the sheets of the *History.* Messenger and some porters duly arrived on 6 June 1808 and moved the sheets into the passage of Burney's apartment. Three days later they examined and counted the volumes, which were packed in 'bundles of 5 sets each'. It was unfortunately necessary to 'throw aside damaged copies, many half devoured by rats & mice, stained, tattered & torn'; but, to the astonishment of Burney who, 'mobbled up' against the cold, 'with fear & trembling peeped at them now & then', the task was completed in a single day. Messenger was able to report that there were 164 complete sets of all four volumes, 480 additional copies of volume i (the 1789 edition) and 265 additional copies of both the third and fourth volumes.[3]

Burney was now obsessed with a desire to have the volumes moved out of Chelsea College as quickly as possible, not only to hasten the trade sale, but also to remove the packages 'out of the pilfering pensioners reach, who from the brown paper covers of my bales w^d proceed to the inside sheets themselves for their pipes & posteriours'. Although it would have been impossible for Payne to act quickly enough for Burney's taste, a fortnight after Messenger's visitation the bookseller sent word that he would take the volumes 'into his own territories . . . till an arrangement can be made for the Trade Sale'. The books were apparently removed a few days later, at the end of June 1808.[4] Burney could not rest, however, until they had ceased to

[1] CB to CB Jr. [26 May 1808] (Osborn).
[2] CB to Huttner, 28 May 1808 (Osborn).
[3] CB to CB Jr., 17 June [1808] (Berg).   [4] Ibid., 24 [June 1808] (Comyn).

be his property. By 4 July he was already urging Charles to remind Payne about the sale and in August he repeated the request, adding the threat that 'if something is not done for me in disposing of my Hist^y before the cold weather comes on, I shall be in despair and shut myself up in despair—perhaps for the rest of my life'.[1]

More than a year passed, however, before Burney heard, in October 1809, that the trade sale was at last being organized. The details of this long-awaited event were, nevertheless, humiliating and, in Burney's opinion, outrageous:

> What . . . do you think each complete set is to go for to the trade who purchase?—Why *2 guineas* a set!! Is not that humiliating, when it is remembered to have been a 30 years work in the collecting materials in all our own public & curiou [*sic*] private Lb^ys in travelling afterwards all over Europe & visiting all the great public libraries, having extracts made of original MSS. . . . hearing the great performers, conversing with the most learned Men, purchasing the best & most scarce printed books, & MS. Music—travelling at my own expence—advertising—paper—printing—ornamental plates . . . for a work wch has passed the Ordeal all over Europe!!! think of this my dear Chas & talk the matter over with Mr Payne, whom I have always regarded as my friend—whether another Guinea, at least, might not be added to the set. . . .[2]

Charles's protests seem to have had little effect for, three days later, on 23 October 1809 Burney wrote,

> Can Mr Payne's eloquence reconcile you or me to letting my 4 huge 4to Vol^s be sold for 2 Guineas! If sold by the pound, to a hugster, or Cheese-monger, as waste paper, they w^d fetch as much. . . . I *do* think if these cormorants cannot be skewed up to 3 Guineas, I w^d leave these books . . . to my executors—it is a Library book and will be always wanted for authorities concerning many facts & discoveries I made in all the great Libraries at Home and abroad throughout Europe; wch nobody else has done—

If Payne was merely anxious to get the books out of his warehouse, Burney would even consider hiring a room in which to keep them until more satisfactory negotiations could take place.[3] Although Burney next tried to raise the sale price to £3 a set

---

[1] Ibid., 4 July [1808] (Comyn) and 16 Aug. 1808 (Osborn).
[2] Ibid., 20 Oct. 1809 (Osborn).
[3] Ibid., 23 Oct. 1809 (Osborn).

and although Payne promised to 'do the best he could', anxiety to bring the business to an end seems eventually to have overcome his pride. 'Life is short, and bills are long', he sadly told Charles.[1] It was not until November 1810, however, that he was able to report that the *History* had at last been sold, apparently at two guineas a set: 'It was joyful news to me—Plates & Copy right included—£740 "Auction duty & some trifling expences to be deducted, the ballance to be p^d by Promissory notes at 3. 6. 9. 12. 15. 18. & 21 Months".'[2]

Burney was also delighted to hear that a new edition of the second volume of the *History* was being planned (presumably by Baynes, who had acquired the odd copies of the other three volumes), 'as it will make all the sets complete, & keep the work much longer alive than its Author'. Partly, no doubt, because this edition was no concern of Burney's, little information about it has survived. As only 250 copies of the second volume were required to complete the sets of the other three, it seems likely that no more were reprinted. This 'second edition', which was probably published in 1811 or 1812, was not described as such and, in fact, retained the original date of 1782 of the volume on the title-page. In 1935 Frank Mercer noted in his edition of the *History of Music* that there was a carelessly printed variant of volume ii, in which modern 's' was used throughout, which had no *Corrigenda* and in which all the musical examples were engraved (in the earlier edition, some of the smaller musical illustrations were printed from type).[3] Mercer did not, however, question the date of 1782, and it was left to Dr. Hazen to point out that the paper used in this variant edition could be dated 1809.[4]

The answer to Dr. Scholes's question—'why was it misdated

---

[1] CB to CB Jr., 6 Nov. 1809 (Osborn).

[2] Ibid., [Nov. 1810] (Osborn). On [3 Dec. 1810] CB wrote to tell CB Jr. that 18 booksellers had each bought 6 sets and one had bought 12 (a total of 120). Payne. Burney noted, 'retains 80'. A bookseller named Baynes bought 420 copies of vol. i and 250 copies each of vols. iii and iv, 'With the Copper & Pewter plates'. From these figures it appears that some of the sets left with various booksellers in 1804 must have been included in the sale (see *ante*, p. 425 and cf. p. 464). It is not easy to work out the price at which the books were finally sold. If Payne did not actually buy the 80 sets which he 'retained', however, the sale of the other sets at 2 guineas (the price originally proposed), and of additional volumes at half a guinea each, would bring in £735, a figure which is perhaps convincingly close to the £740 mentioned by Burney.   [3] Mercer, ii. 1050–1.

[4] *Johnson's Prefaces and Dedications*, p. 29.

and why was it carelessly printed?'[1]—can now be provided. The second volume was hastily reprinted in 1811 or 1812 to complete the 250 sets of the other three volumes. It was misdated because it was no more than a reproduction of the 1782 edition. If he ever knew of it, Burney was probably untroubled by this dishonesty. When the volumes of his *History of Music*, which had been lying for so many years in his storeroom and in booksellers' warehouses, were once more available for the edification of posterity, the last great anxiety of his literary career had been removed.

II

The paralysis in his left hand, which had afflicted him in September 1806, marked the first stage in Burney's withdrawal from society. The second stage was reached exactly three years later. Every summer since 1802 Burney had spent several weeks at Bulstrode at the invitation of the Duke of Portland and, after 1806, these excursions had been almost the only occasions on which he left Chelsea College for more than a few hours. The Duke's repeated invitations were one of the most flattering and happiest features of Burney's later years. In the summer of 1807 he made two separate visits to Bulstrode; and although he did not often see the Duke himself after he became Prime Minister in that year, he was warmly welcomed and made to stay for a long conversation when he called on him at Burlington House in July 1808. Such unnecessary attention gratified Burney enormously and he sent his friends long accounts of this interview, which had ended with the usual cordial invitation to Bulstrode.[2]

In July 1809 the invitation was repeated, when the Duke went so far as to press Burney to live permanently at Bulstrode.[3] Burney's visit ended in mid-September, but a fortnight later the Duke, who was in poor health, wrote to urge Burney to pay a second visit.[4] Almost immediately, however, the Duke was taken seriously ill, was forced to resign from the government and died on 30 October 1809. Burney felt this loss deeply, for

[1] *GDB*, ii. 334.
[2] CB to CB Jr., 4 July [1808] (Comyn); to Huttner [6 July 1808] (Osborn); to Lord Lonsdale [July 1808], draft (B.M., C. 45, f. 4).
[3] CB to Lady Manvers, 18 July 1809 (Osborn).
[4] Portland to CB, 28 Sept. 1809 (Osborn).

the Duke had always been particularly attentive to him and generously patient, when his memory failed and he was 'hammering for a word or a proper Name'. He hardly attempted to conceal the fact, however, that the death of the Duke signified more than the loss of a valued friend:

An irreparable loss to my heart—& to my circumstances the losses are incalculable—a beautiful Park & Gardens for riding out and walking; one of the best rooms in the Mansion on the Ground floor— due South—a Table & dinner of my own chusing at 5 o'Clock, and a pair of horses for my own warm Vehicle, with a careful driver for rides in the Park on fine days, when the Sun shines, all free from rent, Taxes, or expences of any kind—so that all I c^d possibly want in this abode was entirely my own.[1]

This letter suggests that Burney had considered accepting the Duke's invitation to live permanently at Bulstrode. Deprived of the hospitality and comforts of the great house, however, he now retired completely to Chelsea College. On 8 April 1811 he stated that he had not ventured out for a year and that he would probably never leave his apartment again.[2] Nevertheless, Marianne Francis had found him in good spirits in the summer of 1810, as 'industrious & occupied as ever'; and in 1811 he was still 'as full of business as the Sea of Sands, Books, papers, & anecdotes—plagued with a cough but otherwise well'.[3] In the afternoons he still received visitors, who ranged from former pupils, now elderly ladies, to Samuel Wesley, who zealously converted him from his former opinion that the music of J. S. Bach was mere pedantry to intense admiration for the composer. At the very end of his life Burney was able to atone for a glaring gap in his *History*, by advising and encouraging Wesley's campaign to introduce Bach's music to England.[4]

In 1810 Burney at last received an honour which had been delayed for some four years, for it was apparently not until this year that his willingness to become a Correspondent of the Institut de France was communicated to Joachim Le Breton, secretary of the 'Classe des Beaux Arts'. A diploma, dated

---

[1] CB to Lady Crewe [Nov. 1809], draft (Osborn).
[2] CB to Kollmann, 8 Apr. 1811, copy (Osborn).
[3] Hemlow, pp. 320–1.
[4] *GDB*, ii. 210–23; also, CB to Wesley, 6 letters, Mar. 1808–20 Dec. 1808 (Berg; Osborn); Wesley to CB, 8 letters, 22 Mar. 1808–17 July 1810 (Osborn).

28 April 1810, and an inscribed silver medal were brought to
England later in the year by Mrs. Solvyns, a friend of Fanny,
and Burney noted that he received the diploma on 23 November.[1]
Highly flattered, he nevertheless felt it necessary to be cautious
about mentioning such an honour in time of war: 'I shall be
quite silent as to the honour done me at the Institut—if I were
to blazon it in the Papers there w^d be no end of the remarks of
all kinds wch at this Crisis of our affairs the news may produce.
Therefore I shall remain *Mum* ab^t myself, as I have always
done.'[2] In January 1811, he received some of the Institut's
publications, including Le Breton's *Notice historique sur la Vie et
les Ouvrages de Joseph Haydn* (1810), and he transcribed his
account of the first performance of *The Creation* in England for
the benefit of his new colleagues.[3]

Most of Burney's time was now spent in examining his papers
and in reading in his library. Nothing gratified him more, however, than attentions from his aristocratic acquaintance, who
still sent him gifts of venison and game: 'To be remembered at
such a distance after totally renouncing the world, & convinced that I am not forgotten by some of the best & most
gracious part of it, gives a temporary glow to the cinder of
existence. . . .'[4] He still corresponded with his friends, although
he found this increasingly tiring. The most lively exchange
seems to have been with Molly Carter, whom he had known
since 1745.[5] Although they lived only a mile apart, they never
met, but exchanged instead cheerfully self-derisive accounts of
their ailments. As Burney told Lord Cardigan in 1810, 'She
dictates to her maid most ingenious and lively letters; while I,
as yet, can talk a little with my *fingers*, not, indeed, on the keys
of an Instrum^t, but on paper—and in this manner we keep alive
our remembrance & esteem for each other.'[6] For some years the
two octogenarians maintained their surprisingly spirited exchange of gloomy news. In December 1810, one of Molly
Carter's 'ingenious and lively letters' declared, 'Alas! I am a

---

[1] *Frag. Mem.* (Osborn). The diploma is in the Osborn Collection and the medal
belongs to Mr. J. R. G. Comyn.

[2] CB to CB Jr., 7 May 1810 (Berg).

[3] CB to —, Apr. 1811 (Osborn). See *ante*, pp. 401, 453.

[4] CB to Lady Manvers, n.d., draft (Osborn).

[5] *Frag. Mem.* (B.M. Add. MS. 48345, f. 9).

[6] CB to Lord Cardigan, 22 Nov. 1810, draft (Osborn).

Poor old worn out Post chaise without Wheels—a trim Equipage once that has measured many a Mile, I am Punished for my long health & Vagabond Life, by the loss of my active Powers. . . .' Her conversation with Lord Cardigan, she added, 'is reduced to what, when, who, how, where, for all which I am to find memory, neither of us have your Pointed recollection, I am affraid of being as twaddling as *Madame du Dufand* if I allow myself to praise you as much as you deserve'.[1] A year later Burney informed her that it had been so cold that he 'wished to be buried alive rather than suffer so torturing an existence', but he feared that, if he survived until a 'general thaw', 'I shall be p^d off . . . by tumbling to pieces, like an old rotten ruin'.[2]

Eventually Burney found that he was surviving not only his contemporaries but also his friends in a younger generation. In June 1808 he had written what must have been his last published work (apart from his articles in the *Cyclopaedia*), his 'Memoirs and Character of the late Mrs. Ord', one of the original 'Blue-Stockings' who had recently died at the age of eighty-two. On the advice of Malone, Burney sent his article to the *Gentleman's Magazine* and his affectionate recollections of his old friend appeared in July.[3] William Windham died in June 1810 and Burney provided Malone with information about the politician's father, whom he had known in Norfolk, in case it should be needed for a second edition of the short *Memoir* of his friend, which Malone had published during the summer.[4] In April 1812 Malone himself died, a great loss to Burney, for their correspondence had helped to brighten his later years of confinement.

The death of another of his correspondents, Molly Carter, in the following month[5] might have been a greater blow if it had not been followed so quickly by the return to England, after an

---

[1] Molly Carter to CB, 31 Dec. 1810 (transcript in Scholes Papers, Osborn).

[2] CB to [Molly Carter], 29 Dec. 1811, draft (Osborn).

[3] *Gent. Mag.* lxxviii (1808), 581–3; CB to Malone, 10 June and 23 June [1808], (Bodleian, MS. Malone 38, ff. 143–5, 161); Malone to CB, 8 June 1808 (Folger); CB to CB Jr., 24 June 1808 (Comyn).

[4] The first sketch of Malone's *Biographical Memoir of . . . William Windham* had appeared in June 1810, *Gent. Mag.* lxxx, Pt. I, 588–93; CB to Malone, Aug. 1810 (Bodleian, MS. Eng. Letters C. 15, f. 144); Malone to CB, 4 letters, 27 July–20 Aug. 1810 (Folger); CB to Lady Bruce, 17 Aug. 1810, draft (Osborn). CB also prepared 'Memoranda' on Windham for Courtenay in July 1810 (Osborn).

[5] *Gent. Mag.* lxxxii (1812), Pt. I, 499.

absence of ten years, of his daughter Fanny d'Arblay, who arrived at Chelsea College on 20 August 1812. She was deeply shocked by the drastic change in her father's appearance:

I found him . . . in his library, by himself—but oh! . . . very much altered indeed—weak, weak and changed—his head almost always hanging down, and his hearing most cruelly impaired. . . . In discourse, however, he reanimated, and was, at times, all himself. But he now admits scarcely a creature but of his family, and will only see for a short time even his children. He likes quietly reading, and lies almost constantly upon the sofa, and will never eat but alone! What a change![1]

For some time Burney had been intent on as complete a withdrawal from the life around him as possible and this gloomy and rarely penetrable mood was a constant source of worry to his family in his last years. Sarah Harriet Burney had been convinced in 1811 that 'the close seclusion he has doomed himself to' had only helped to lower her father's spirits: 'He wastes, and enfeebles, I think, almost visibly; but he will not hear the slightest representation from anybody on the subject—and to fret him would be worse than to see how thin he grows'.[2]

Fanny, now over sixty herself, tactfully did her best to the end to urge him to take some interest in his family. In 1813, after describing for him a happy gathering of Burneys, she added,

How I wish my beloved Father would permit himself to be more freely so surrounded by those whose first pride is to look up to him as their Chief! I often think he would be better, & feel his spirits lighter, if he could persuade himself to let them come in & go out, without taking the effort & forcing the violence upon his feelings of receiving & entertaining them as visitors. I would have them all permitted to offer what they can find to say, & accept their relations or prattling, & be content, in return, with sometimes a nod, & sometimes a wry face, just as approbation or dissent might dictate; & nothing more.[3]

Such well-intended advice seems to have had little effect. His main occupation was now 'Solitary reading, and lonely contemplation',[4] although a late letter (which Fanny, in fact, ascribed to 1814) to Mrs. Iremonger shows that, to the end of his life, he could still be cheered by the remembrance of his

---

[1] *DL*, vi. 83.   [2] Quoted by Hemlow, p. 321.
[3] FB to CB, 30 Jan. 1813 (Barrett).   [4] *Mem.* iii. 413.

friends: 'Such letters as yours are sufficient to make the most
desponding and dolorous son of Earth wish to extend his
existence to the length of the Patriarch Methuselah. I have no
desire to part with the remnant of life wch nature may allow me
though a Gulliverian Strulbruggh, as long as I can amuse &
divert thoughts from *self* when pain is not intolerable by the
most silly books, long forgotten, in my miscellaneous Lib^y'.[1]

Burney survived for twenty months after Fanny's return to
England. She dutifully wrote him cheerful letters to lighten his
depression, but a revival of his old spirits could now be shattered
all too easily by an unreasonable request from his son James to
use his influence on his behalf;[2] or from Charles, who asked
to borrow a book in March 1813. Burney complained that 'to
pick my lib^y to pieces as long as I have eyes to see it in its
present state w^d break my heart—It cannot be long ere I quit
sublunary concerns.'[3] Some of the short notes which he wrote to
members of his family during 1813 are lively and humorous,
but the approach of winter depressed him more than ever.
Sarah wrote in desperation to Charles in December 1813, 'We
are ... at our wits end to know what we can do to raise my poor
father's spirits.' She asked him to come and cheer up his father:
'He *says* he hates to be spoken to—but that is a fib: he only
hates it when the speaker has nothing amusing to talk about'.[4]

In March 1814 Burney was 'weak & suffering', but early in
April he was on his feet again and must have believed that he
had survived yet another painful winter.[5] Then, on 10 April,
Fanny, who was now living nearby in Lower Sloane Street,
heard that he had passed an 'alarming night' and hurried to
Chelsea College. She found him sitting on his sofa, 'his revered
head, as usual, hung upon his breast', in a state of such abstraction that he seemed not to hear her words. Eventually, however,
he moved:

He was now standing, and unusually upright; and, apparently,
with unusual muscular firmness. I was advancing to embrace him,
but his air spoke a rooted concentration of solemn ideas that repelled
intrusion.

[1] CB to Mrs. Iremonger, draft, n.d. (Osborn).
[2] FB to CB Jr. [27 Jan. 1813] (Comyn).
[3] CB to CB Jr., 9 Mar. 1813 (Osborn).
[4] Sarah Burney to CB Jr., 8 Dec. 1813 (Comyn).
[5] FB to CB Jr. [28 Mar. 1814] and 6 Apr. 1814 (Osborn).

Whether or not he recognized, or distinguished me, I know not! I had no command of voice to attempt any inquiry, and would not risk betraying my emotion at this great change since my last and happier admittance to his presence.

His eyes were intently bent on a window that faced the College burial-ground, where reposed the ashes of my mother-in-law, and where, he had more than once said, would repose his own.

He bestowed at least five or six minutes on this absorbed and melancholy contemplation of the upper regions of that sacred spot, that so soon were to enclose for ever his mortal clay.

No one presumed to interrupt his reverie.

He next opened his arms wide, extending them with a waving motion, that seemed indicative of an internally pronounced farewell! to all he looked at; and shortly afterwards, he uttered to himself, distinctly, though in a low, but deeply-impressive voice, 'All this will soon pass away as a dream!'

Burney's strength was ebbing fast. The striking irony underlying Fanny's account of his last hours was that, as he lay dying, the sky was brilliantly illuminated with the rockets and fireworks with which London was celebrating the defeat and capture of Napoleon, whose career had caused Burney such torment. Now, he was barely able to comprehend the news which Fanny repeated to him and which he had awaited so eagerly for so long.[1]

He died peacefully on 12 April 1814, a few days before his eighty-ninth birthday, and was buried a week later at Chelsea College: 'the funeral was numerously attended, by the governor, and chief officers of the College, and by the family and friends of this accomplished and excellent man'. There were none, however, of the friends of his prime present on this occasion. The pallbearers included Dr. Moseley, the Physician of Chelsea College, and Salomon, the musician and impresario, but most of them were members of a much younger generation, such as the Hon. Frederick North (the son of Lord North), and Samuel Rogers and Sir George Beaumont, both significantly friends of Wordsworth and Coleridge.[2] Apart from Fanny, only Mrs. Piozzi survived of the great Johnsonian circle; and even at the age of seventy-three and on the occasion of the death of one who had once been so great a friend, she was not disposed to forget or forgive the betrayal of which she imagined Burney to have

---

[1] *Mem.* iii. 423–33.   [2] See *post*, p. 476, n. 2.

been guilty: 'Burney—dead at last I am told at 89 Years old; and in the full possession of his Faculties:—They were extremely fine ones. He *thought* himself my Friend once I believe, whilst he *thought* the World was so'.[1]

Although a long obituary notice appeared in the *Gentleman's Magazine* in April and July 1814,[2] Burney had been so withdrawn from society for the last seven years of his life that his death did not leave a conspicuous vacancy at The Club, at concerts, or at literary parties. Even to his family his death could hardly come as an unexpected blow. Quite apart from the elation which affected the whole nation at the defeat of Napoleon, Fanny was preoccupied with the extremely profitable publication of her last novel, *The Wanderer*, which, ironically enough, contained an introductory letter, addressed to her father. At least one enthusiastic friend commented on the fact that Burney's death had occurred 'at a time, when the whole literary world, were engag'd in drawing amusement from a source so dear to him'.[3] By mid-June 1814 Fanny was frantically trying to move her father's possessions out of his apartment in Chelsea College, which had already been allocated to another official.[4] His 'Miscellaneous Library' had been auctioned on 9 June and the eight following week-days and had realized £1,414. 18s. 6d. In August his great collection of music was sold for £686. 0s. 6d., and, as Burney himself had hoped, his library of books on music was sold, without being separated, to the British Museum for £283.[5]

In 1816, when Fanny returned from a year in France, the family arranged for the erection of a monument to Burney in the North Choir Aisle of Westminster Abbey, which was completed in the summer of the following year. Miss Hemlow has already described the prolonged discussion to which Fanny's eloquent tribute was subjected: whether, for example, it was appropriate to mention Burney's conversational powers on such a monument.[6] There were other parts of her proposed inscription, however, which she was eventually persuaded to

[1] J. L. Clifford, *Hester Lynch Piozzi*, p. 414.

[2] lxxxiv, Pt. I, 420–1; Pt. II, 93–94.

[3] Harriet Rose to Rosette Burney, 23 Apr. 1814 (Comyn).

[4] FB to CB Jr., 16 June 1814 (Osborn).

[5] *GDB*, ii. 273–4; and A. Hyatt King, *Some British Collectors of Music*, Cambridge, 1963, pp. 30–32.   [6] Hemlow, pp. 391–2; *GDB*, ii. 274–5.

abandon and the letters in which she tried to defend her word-
ing reveal as much of her real attitude to her father and his
achievement as all the exaggerated filial reverence of the three
volumes of her *Memoirs*.

In April 1817 she wrote to her brother Charles:

High is still the only word that paints my Father's Principles; for
whether he had been

> 'Poet, Painter, or Musician,
> Churchman, Soldier, or Physician,'

his *Principles* would always have been the same, for they were innate,
& like those of Dr. Johnson, adhered to him in every part of his life,
& every use of his Reason.

As to *Chief*, it only can mean in his own *Country*, and in his own
Day: And who shall dispute it with him? All England, I am sure,
would name him First.

... But how can my dear Charles hesitate to allow *self*-acquired to
the attainments of our dear Father? Brought up at a Grammar
school, he was certainly *taught* his hic haec hoc;—&, apprentice to
Dr. Arne, he certainly did not *find out* the rules of Musick: But those
attainments through which he obtained Distinction from the Publick
were All the effects & efforts of his own studies, mental labour, &
indefatigable *self-directed* industry. This word here, my dear Carlos,
will be fully discussed & explained in the Memoirs.[1]

Although the inscription on the monument in Westminster
Abbey omitted the crucial word 'self-acquired', Fanny had
been right to insist on its importance. Burney's own proudest
and happiest memories arose from, and even depended on, the
contemplation of the distance he had travelled, through his
own efforts and in the face of so many difficulties, from the tiny
village of Condover to London's most fashionable literary
society, and to friendship with some of the most distinguished
men of his time. While his family was already forgetting its
origins[2] and could see little point in emphasizing the nature of
his struggle for fame, Fanny fully understood the importance to
her father of that upward climb as an end in itself, and she
claimed it as the justification of her biography:

Where the life has been as private as that of Dr. Burney, its history
must necessarily be simple, and can have little further call upon the

---

[1] FB to CB Jr. [25 Apr. 1817] (Osborn).   [2] Hemlow, p. 464.

attention of the world, than that which may belong to a wish of
tracing the progress of a nearly abandoned Child, from a small
village of Shropshire, to a Man allowed throughout Europe to have
risen to the head of his profession; and thence, setting his profession
aside, to have been elevated to an intellectual rank in society, as a
Man of Letters—

> 'Though not First, in the very first line'

with most of the eminent men of his day. . . .[1]

Fanny was also right to distinguish emphatically in this
passage between her father's professional activities as a musician
and his career as a 'man of letters'. While it is hardly fair to
describe him as 'The Great Dr. Burney', he has perhaps been
underestimated at times precisely because it has been difficult to
unify the different spheres of his activities and the different
images of him which have come down to posterity. In estimating
his achievement as a professional musician, however, we can at
once dispose of his claims on our attention as a composer in his
own right. In a poem which he wrote in October 1804, Burney
himself dismissed his own music as negligible, although it
should be remembered that he did this the more complacently
because of his conviction of the ephemeral nature of *all* music.
He described his early compositions as

> Dramatic Music long since old,
> Concertos, Trios, many fold;
> Lessons, Sonatas; Organ-pieces,
> Fugues on dry & barren theses. . . .

He had long since lost all ambition as a composer:

> For who can hope with utmost pains
> To equal such enchanting strains,
> As Haydn & Mozart have found
> Which lift each hearer off the ground,
> Where taste & genius ever flame,
> Whence all their inspirations came?
>   And still the road to fame is stopt
> And ev'ry verdant laurel cropt,
> By that gigantic youth, Beethoven,
> Whose feet, beyond a dout [*sic*], are cloven. . . .

---

[1] *Mem.* i. vii–ix; FB adapts Goldsmith's *Retaliation*, l. 96.

His true achievement, he considered, had been merely the un-
selfish commemoration of other musicians:

> My days in labour, study, toil
> Have long been spent, & nightly oil,
> Not to acquire for *self* a name,
> But loud to sound the trump of fame,
> And with an honest zeal to sing
> Each brother of the pipe & string.[1]

In spite of his modesty, it has been as a highly important
pioneer of musical history, whose writings were to exert an
enormous, if not always salutary, influence during the nineteenth century, that Burney has been most celebrated. Until
more recent and specialized scholarship exposed his shortcomings, later writers were often content to borrow information
and judgements from his *History of Music* without considering
that independent research and reflection were either necessary
or desirable. The lack of initiative of his successors cannot, of
course, be blamed on Burney and, although it is no longer
authoritative, his *History of Music* still provides a unique index
to eighteenth-century musical taste and, together with his
Musical Tours, remains a source of certain kinds of information
about the music of his own time which can hardly be super-
seded.

While Burney's achievement as a historian does not need to
be emphasized, his other contribution to music has received
comparatively little attention. It lies precisely in that escape
from the limitations of his own profession which has been stressed
throughout this study of his career. Nothing struck his contemporaries more than the manner in which, by proving himself an accomplished writer and a polished and elegant member
of 'polite society', Burney not only transcended his profession
but simultaneously elevated it, in the same way as Garrick and
Reynolds had won respect for the exponents of their arts by
their own achievements and social demeanour.[2] It should
perhaps be noted, however, that Burney himself tended to view
his own profession with very much the same reactions as the

---

[1] Berg.

[2] Johnson said that Garrick 'made his profession respectable', Hill–Powell, iii. 371,
n. 1.

society into which he had been admitted as an exception. He might well have said of musicians what he wrote of the members of another profession in 1801: 'Many actors and actresses . . . are ignorant, vulgar, without knowledge of the world, good morals, good breeding, wit, or any of the necessary talents for conversation; and would be at best but a dead weight on society, if admitted into what is *truly* called good company.' He probably had his own career in mind when he added that 'single instances only are to be found in any profession of superior worth and talents which enjoy or deserve unusual notice'.[1]

Reynolds described Burney as 'both a Philosopher & a Musician';[2] Sir William Jones observed that Burney 'gives dignity to the character of a modern musician by uniting it with that of a scholar and philosopher';[3] and Hazlitt wrote of him as 'an historian and a musician, but more of a courtier and man of the world than either'.[4] Thomas Twining went so far as to describe his friend's success in bridging the intellectual and social gap between the worlds of music and literature as 'contrary to the uniform course of nature'.[5] Nature would seem to have reasserted herself, however, for, as far as Burney is concerned, the gap has gradually widened again since his death. While his place in musical history is secure, Burney is now remembered by the literary historian only as a by no means dominating member of the Johnsonian and Streatham circles, who occasionally crosses the pages of Boswell's *Life of Johnson* and of *Thraliana*. By the side of such complex or powerful personalities as Johnson, Mrs. Thrale, Boswell, Walpole, and Burke, Burney inevitably remains a minor figure.

There is a third role, however, which Burney still performs for posterity, as the head of a family extraordinary for the diversity of its talents. Until recently, Burney has been confined in this capacity to the affectionate but emasculated image— invariably good-humoured, kind, charming, almost saintly— projected in his daughter's diary and letters. Although much can now be added to our picture of his family and in spite of the

---

[1] *Monthly Review*, xxxiv (1801), 385–6.
[2] F. W. Hilles, *Literary Career of Reynolds*, 1936, p. 246.
[3] *Works*, 1799, i. 419.
[4] *Works*, ed. P. P. Howe, 1934, viii. 209.   [5] See *ante*, p. 133.

various tensions in the household which Fanny understandably ignored, Burney must take at least some of the credit for the remarkable range of the achievements of his children. Mrs. Thrale certainly noticed the way in which the rest of the family were infected by Burney's own ambition and energy: 'their Esteem & fondness for the D^r seems to inspire them all with a Desire not to disgrace him; & so every individual of it must write and read & be literary. . . .'[1]

Such were Burney's ambitions for his children and his pride in their achievements that at times they were inevitably unable to answer the demands he made upon them. Occasionally they 'disgraced' him, and there were disagreements about politics with his sons and misgivings about the way his daughters chose to find happiness. These tensions occurred, however, only within an essential family unity which, perhaps as a result of his own peculiar childhood, Burney did much to foster. Nothing would have gratified him more than William Hazlitt's recognition of the achievement of the family as a whole, in his essay 'On the Aristocracy of Letters':

There are whole families who are born classical, and are entered in the heralds' college of reputation by the right of consanguinity. Literature, like nobility, runs in the blood. There is the B——family. There is no end of it or its pretensions. It produces wits, scholars, novelists, musicians, artists in 'numbers numberless'. The name is alone a passport to the Temple of Fame. Those who bear it are free of Parnassus by birth-right.[2]

The three surviving images of Burney as an eminent pioneer of musical history, as an intimate friend of the great literary figures of his time and as the proud father of distinguished novelists, scholars, musicians, and travellers, can be unified only by an understanding of his own aspirations and career. Burney was not a great man, for he was limited by his pursuit of social and literary success. Yet his intelligence, charm, and energy, the almost unremitting vitality of his response to life and to the demands he made upon himself, the diversity of his interests and the impressive range of his friendships, make him a unique, if not a profound, personality in his own right. The sheer length of his life involved him with many of the outstanding musical

---

[1] See *ante*, p. 263. [2] *Works*, ed. P. P. Howe, viii. 208-9.

and literary figures of the eighteenth century. Thomas Arne's apprentice, who played and taught for Handel, who met Europe's leading performers and composers, lived to be the friend of Haydn and to recognize Beethoven as the great composer of the nineteenth century. The young man who disturbed James Thomson's indolence, who became the intimate friend of Christopher Smart, Samuel Johnson, and Mrs. Thrale, lived to extend a public welcome to the *Lyrical Ballads.*

Burney himself was aware that, in the course of his long life, he had met an extraordinary diversity of men and, indeed, he believed that this would be one of the chief claims of the story of his life on the interest of posterity. At the very beginning of his ill-fated 'Memoirs' he wrote:

Perhaps few have been better enabled to describe truthfully & exactly from an actual survey, the manners & customs of the age in wch he lived, than myself: ascending from those of the most humble cottagers, & lowest mechanics, to the first Nobility, and most elevated personages in the kingdom with whom circumstances, situation, & accident, at different periods of my life, have rendered me familiar. Oppressed and laborious husbandmen, insolent & illiberal Yeomanry, overgrown Norfolk Farmers, generous, friendly & hospitable Merchants, Men of business & Men of pleasure, Men of Letters, Artists, Men of Science, sportsmen & country 'Squires, dissipated and extravagant Voluptuaries, Gamesters, Ambassadors, Statesmen, & even sovereign princes I have had opportunities of examining, in almost every point of view. All these & more it is my intention to display in their respective situations, to delineate their Virtues, Vices, and apparent degrees of happiness & misery, as well as the person and manner of Men of rank, learning, talents & abilities, wth whom I have lived, corresponded or been in some way connected.[1]

What little has survived of Burney's survey of human society has been embodied in the present study. Of his delineation of the 'apparent degrees of happiness & misery' of the men whose lives he described nothing seems to remain. The problem of happiness, however, is one which constantly comes to mind in contemplating Burney's own career. Confronted with an account of any intensely ambitious man, we are curious to know not only whether his aspirations were fulfilled, but also whether their attainment brought the envisaged happiness. At

---

[1] *Frag. Mem.* (Osborn).

times it may appear that Burney was always too frantically busy to enjoy the success for which he strove for so many years. The first half of his life passed in disappointment and frustration and, even when he embarked on the strenuous literary career which brought him the fame he sought, the rewards usually melted away just when he was ready to accept them. The brilliant circle at Streatham disintegrated precisely when he decided to give his enjoyment of it priority over his historical labours. The French Revolution, Fanny's resignation from Court, and his own illness destroyed his satisfaction and relief at having completed his huge *History of Music* in 1789. The few periods in which we can see him nearest to unqualified happiness—in 1796, 1799, and 1805, for example—were quickly shattered by the deaths of those whom he most loved or by his own ill-health.

For all his celebrated charm and poise, the restless energy which drove Burney to success also deprived him of the capacity to enjoy it with anything approaching serenity. Unremitting industry became so much a habit that, almost until the end of his life, he was uneasy without some large undertaking on his hands, and yet was depressed by the task as long as it remained unfinished. Since temperamental extremes of depression and exultation were, indeed, characteristic of Burney's state of mind, it is perhaps misguided to assume that serenity was the reward he sought. His happiness lay rather in the contemplation of all that he had achieved by his own efforts and in the face of many difficulties; the literary honours and social success which he and his children had won; and the memory of the great men like Samuel Johnson whose respect and friendship he had enjoyed. Just as in the first half of his life he had always looked expectantly to the future, at the end his happiness lay in looking to the past, in measuring the distance he had travelled from the Shropshire village in which he had spent his childhood.

All that remains of Burney's own discussion of happiness is Fanny d'Arblay's version of a passage from his 'Memoirs', in which he had recorded the views of his friend Sir Joshua Reynolds on the subject. The reason why he remembered these words is clear, for, as Reynolds himself acknowledged, he was defining the nature of Burney's happiness as well as his own:

Dr. Burney has left amongst his papers a note of an harangue which he had heard from Sir Joshua Reynolds, at the house of Dudley Long, when the Duke of Devonshire, and various other peers, were present, and when happiness was the topic of discussion. Sir Joshua for some time had listened in silence to their several opinions; and then impressively said: 'You none of you, my lords, if you will forgive my telling you so, can speak upon this subject with as much knowledge of it as I can. Dr. Burney perhaps might; but it is not the man who looks around him from the top of a high mountain at a beautiful prospect on the first moment of opening his eyes, who has the true enjoyment of that noble sight: it is he who ascends the mountain from a miry meadow, or a ploughed field, or a barren waste; and who works his way up to it step by step; scratched and harassed by thorns and briars; with here a hollow, that catches his foot; and there a clump that forces him all the way back to find out a new path;—it is he who attains to it through all that toil and danger; and with the strong contrast on his mind of the miry meadow, or ploughed field, or barren waste, for which it was exchanged,—it is he, my lords, who enjoys the beauties that suddenly blaze upon him. They cause an expansion of ideas in harmony with the expansion of the view. He glories in its glory; and his mind opens to conscious exaltation; such as the man who was born and bred upon that commanding height, with all the loveliness of prospect, and fragrance, and variety, and plenty, and luxury of every sort, around, above, beneath, can never know. . . .'[1]

[1] *Mem.* ii. 280–1.

BURNEY'S SETTING OF THORNTON'S BURLESQUE *ODE ON ST. CECILIA'S DAY*

ACCORDING to Boswell, Samuel Johnson admitted in July 1763 to having been greatly diverted by a burlesque *Ode on St. Cecilia's Day* by Bonnell Thornton,[1] which had first been published in 1749 and which was reprinted in June 1763, shortly before a performance to a musical setting at Ranelagh in the same month. Burney supplied Malone with the following footnote to Boswell's account for the third edition of the *Life of Johnson* (1799):

> In 1769 I set for Smart and Newbery Thornton's burlesque Ode on St. Cecilia's Day. It was performed at Ranelagh in masks, to a very crowded audience, as I was told; for I then resided in Norfolk. Beard sung the salt-box song, which was admirably accompanied on that instrument by Brent, the Fencing-master, and father of Miss Brent, the celebrated singer; Skeggs on the broomstick, as bassoon; and a remarkable performer on the Jew's-harp.— 'Buzzing twangs the iron lyre.' Cleavers were cast in bell-metal for this entertainment. All the performers of the old woman's Oratory, employed by Foote, were, I believe, employed at Ranelagh on this occasion.[2]

The trouble that this amusing footnote has caused may well seem to have been out of proportion to its importance. The problem it poses, however, is perplexing and, even if the following discussion of it is less conclusive than its predecessors, it will at least try to attend for the first time to all the relevant considerations.

In his edition of the *Life of Johnson*, Dr. G. B. Hill pointed out that, since Burney 'resided in Norfolk' only until 1760, the date he gave to his setting of the *Ode* 'cannot be correct'. Various solutions of the problem have been proposed. W. Barclay Squire, in his article on Burney in the *Dictionary of National Biography*, silently emended the date of the setting to 1759, as did W. H. Husk in his article on Charlotte Brent in Grove's *Dictionary of Music*. Dr. Scholes later agreed that Burney's date 'is clearly a misprint for 1759'.[3] In 1949, however, A. D. McKillop discussed the problem in an article which contained some useful information about burlesque music in the eighteenth century and made the first serious attempt to face the implications of the various statements in Burney's note. He found the usual emendation of Burney's date unacceptable and argued that 'until some

---

[1] Hill–Powell, i. 420 n.   [2] 3rd edn., i. 378 n.   [3] *GDB*, i. 95 n.

evidence for a performance in 1759 is forthcoming, it would seem
natural to connect Burney's account with the well-authenticated
performance of June 1763'.[1]

In 1957 Dr. Charles Ryskamp produced evidence which apparently
necessitated the rejection of both 1759 and 1763 as possible emendations of Burney's '1769'. An account of the performance of the *Ode* at
Ranelagh on 10 June 1763 in *The St. James's Chronicle* for 9–11 June
attributed the music composed for that occasion to Thomas Arne.
The same newspaper for 31 May–2 June had printed a letter (clearly,
however, no more than a 'puff') which expressed surprise that
Thornton's *Ode* had never been set to music before. From this evidence Ryskamp concluded not only that the 1763 setting was by
Arne but that it was the first setting of the *Ode*. Burney's setting must
therefore be dated later than 1763 and, since he was on holiday in
Norfolk in the summer of 1769 and had himself apparently dated his
setting in that year, Ryskamp argued that the original date should be
once more accepted without emendation.[2]

The wheel has thus come full circle. There are various aspects of
the problem, however, which have previously been ignored by those
who have solved it to their apparent satisfaction. For example,
Ryskamp's argument that Burney's setting can once more be dated
1769 may be dismissed immediately, if Burney's statement that he
wrote it for Smart and Newbery is accepted. John Newbery, the
bookseller and publisher who encouraged many of Smart's literary
and theatrical enterprises, died in December 1767. It may be added
that John Beard, who sang 'the salt-box song' in Burney's setting,
retired from the stage in May 1767, and is unlikely to have performed in the *Ode* in 1769.

A re-examination of the various statements in Burney's note makes
it clear, in fact, that a definite solution to the problem is not possible.
All that can be attempted is a full assessment of the available evidence
and a weighing of probabilities. It should, of course, be remembered
that Burney was seventy-two when he wrote the note for Malone and
that, in recollecting an event which had taken place some thirty or
forty years earlier, his memory may have been in fault in one or more
of the details. The following remarks by Burney must, nevertheless,
be taken into account:

(*a*) Burney stated that he set the *Ode* for Smart and Newbery. The
fact that Smart was confined in a lunatic asylum between 1757 and
1763 appears to limit the possible emendations of Burney's date, but

[1] 'Bonnell Thornton's Burlesque Ode', *Notes and Queries*, cxciv (1949), 321–4.
[2] 'Dr. Arne's Music for Thornton's Burlesque Ode', *Notes and Queries*, ccii (1957),
71–73.

neither of the previously proposed alternatives, 1759 and 1763, is necessarily affected. Smart was released from the madhouse between January and about August 1759 and a number of his friends including Garrick and Newbery, tried to assist him in various ways at this period. On the other hand, he was finally released in January 1763, so that he could have been involved in the performance of the *Ode* in the following June. Smart's biographers suggest, however, that by June 1763 Smart and Newbery were quarrelling and the poet undoubtedly broke his literary connexion with the publisher after his release from the asylum.[1] If previous emendations of Burney's date are disregarded, the period at which Smart is most likely to have co-operated with Newbery is before his first confinement: i.e. between 1750 and 1757, a period which can be limited further by the considerations in (*b*) and (*c*) below.

(*b*) Burney stated that he 'resided in Norfolk' when his setting was performed. If by 'resided' he meant that he was living permanently there, the setting must be ascribed to his years at Lynn, 1751–60. Burney could conceivably have meant that he was merely visiting Lynn at the time, or have confused a holiday there with his period of permanent residence in Norfolk. It can be shown that he often made summer visits to Lynn during the 1760's.

(*c*) The final sentence of Burney's note states that 'All the performers of the old woman's Oratory, employed by Foote, were, I believe, employed at Ranelagh on this occasion.' 'The Old Woman's Oratory', alternatively entitled 'Henley in Petticoats', was the name of a theatrical parody of the famous 'Orator' John Henley, which Smart and Newbery initiated in December 1751 and which included speeches, dancing, performing animals, songs, and ludicrous music, presented under the auspices of 'Mrs. Mary Midnight', Smart's pseudonym in his magazine *The Midwife*. Featured in these entertainments were performances on the salt-box, Jews' harp, broomstick, and other burlesque instruments, which are mentioned in Thornton's *Ode* and were employed in both Burney's setting and the performance in 1763. Thornton had first published his *Ode* in 1749, a year before he and Smart became leading contributors to *The Student* and *The Midwife*, both published by Newbery. In his own magazine *The Connoisseur*, Thornton frequently referred to the burlesque music at Mother Midnight's 'Oratory'.[2] Smart's biographers suggest that his own part in these entertainments had ended by May 1753 and in any case they had lapsed by 1754.[3]

[1] E. G. Ainsworth and C. E. Noyes, *Christopher Smart*, pp. 92–97, 104, 127.
[2] McKillop, op. cit., p. 323.
[3] Ainsworth and Noyes, op. cit., p. 62.

Between 1757 and 1760, however, the 'Old Woman's Oratory' and similar entertainments were occasionally revived, although it must seem unlikely that Smart had anything to do with them at this period. Theophilus Cibber appears to have been responsible for a series of 'Medley Concerts', some of which involved 'Miss Midnight', in the autumn of 1757, but the 'Oratory' itself was back at the Haymarket in May and June 1758.[1] 'Mrs. Midnight's Concert and Oratory, as it was originally performed in the year 1754' was again at the Haymarket in February, March, and April 1760 and another concert there in September featured 'Original Orations . . . by Mrs. Midnight'.[2] It is worth noting that 1759–60 is the only season in which Skeggs, a performer in Burney's setting, is known to have appeared at the Haymarket. He seems to have been involved in the 'Oratory' on 30 April 1760 when, as in the performance described by Burney, the band was 'all mask'd in the Venetian Taste'. Burney, of course, referred to 'the performers of the old woman's Oratory, employed by Foote'. Samuel Foote seems never to have been associated with Smart's version of the 'Oratory' but it is quite possible that in 1760, when Smart was in the madhouse, it was Foote who revived it at the Haymarket, a theatre with which he was often connected at this period and which he definitely hired in the summer of 1760.[3] It may also be significant that there is no record of any performances of the 'Old Woman's Oratory' after 1760.

(d) A minor consideration, which nevertheless bears on possible emendations and cannot be neglected, is that, if Burney's date of '1769' is incorrect, the error is much more likely to have affected only one of the final digits than both.

The almost absurdly complex and inconclusive nature of the evidence contained in Burney's note will now be readily apparent. All that remains is to consider three possible emendations of Burney's '1769' in the light of the information assembled above. If general likelihood alone were in question, there would undoubtedly be a strong case for ascribing Burney's setting of the burlesque Ode to the years 1751–3. Smart and Newbery were more closely connected in various enterprises at this period than they were ever to be again and Bonnell Thornton himself was often involved in them; the 'Old Woman's Oratory' was thriving and specializing in performances of burlesque music; and Burney, who had recently set to music a number of Smart's songs and had been an intimate friend of both the

[1] The London Stage 1660–1800, Part 4, ed. G. W. Stone, 1962, ii. 672.
[2] Ibid., 774, 791, 806; Ainsworth and Noyes, op. cit., p. 62 n.
[3] M. M. Belden, The Dramatic Work of Samuel Foote, New Haven, 1929, pp. 20–22, 85.

poet and Newbery, was definitely 'residing' in Norfolk. The obvious objections are that no performance of the *Ode* is known to have taken place at this period, that Foote had no connexion with the 'Oratory' while Smart was directing it, and that drastic emendation of both the final digits of the date would be involved.

The emendation to 1759 has always been favoured because Burney undoubtedly 'then resided in Norfolk' and because the alteration of only one digit is involved. But the same reasons could support an emendation to 1760, not hitherto suggested. Burney may well have stayed in Norfolk until the autumn of that year, although he had definitely been in London in April; and it is certain that the 'Oratory' was playing at the Haymarket during 1760. It is hard to see how Smart could have been involved in a performance of Burney's setting in 1760, however, although he had been at liberty between January and August 1759, when Foote might already have revived the 'Oratory' at the Haymarket. The main objection to an emendation to either 1759 or 1760 must be that once more no performance of the *Ode* is known to have taken place in either year and that, if it had been performed at Ranelagh and as successfully as Burney's note claims, it must seem unlikely that three or four years later the organizers of the 1763 performance would have felt able to claim with so much publicity that their setting was the first ever.

An emendation of Burney's date to 1763 has, of course, the unique support of the fact that a performance of the *Ode* is known to have taken place in that year and that contemporary accounts of it in no way contradict Burney's note. The main objection is that, on one occasion, the 1763 setting was attributed to Arne, although it is not impossible that this was ironic, considering Arne's reputation: in every other instance the setting was ascribed merely to 'an eminent master'. Burney was not, of course, living in Norfolk in 1763 but a fragment of his 'Memoirs' reveals that he left London on 9 June, the day before the performance, to stay with Mrs. Cibber in the country and that he visited King's Lynn later in the summer.[1] It could be argued that, thirty-five years later, he was confused about his actual whereabouts when the *Ode* was performed. Smart had conveniently been released from the asylum in the previous January, although it can be objected that his relations with Newbery were strained thereafter. Samuel Foote had the Haymarket under his control at this period, although there is no evidence that the 'Old Woman's Oratory' was ever performed after 1760. After his wife's death in 1762 Burney's interest returned markedly to the theatre, and in the autumn of 1763 he was engaged as musical director for A *Midsummer*

[1] Berg.

Night's Dream at Drury Lane. It is also worth noting that the 1763 performance of the *Ode* was for the benefit of Miss Brent and that Burney lists her father as one of the performers of his own setting, a fact that may not be unconnected.

Apart from the fact that a performance of Thornton's *Ode* actually took place in 1763, there is little to choose between the three emendations which have been discussed and which have their own advantages and disadvantages. If there is any consolation to be found in this perplexing situation, it can only be that there is now some evidence by which to identify the cause of all the trouble. Burney sent Malone his additional notes to the *Life of Johnson* in the late summer of 1798. On 6 September Malone replied:

> In your remarks on Boswell, there is a word that I cannot make out. It is in the Account of the Mock Cantata of B. Thornton, as performed at Ranelagh— '——were cast in bell-mettle on this occasion.' The word appears to my eyes *Chaus*; but unluckily there is no such word. I have been forced to send the Copy today to the press, leaving a blank. Pray tell me how to fill it up.[1]

It is clear that it was Malone who transcribed Burney's note for the press and that he had had some difficulty in reading his friend's handwriting. We can only regret that, since he had to admit his inability to read the word 'cleavers', Malone did not bother to make quite sure that he had correctly transcribed the date which Burney gave to his setting.

[1] Folger.

CANCELLATIONS IN THE *HISTORY OF MUSIC*, VOLUME I

THE letter, dated 24 December 1775, in which Burney informed Twining that any further 'Criticisms & corrections' must wait until a second edition, contains bibliographical information which must be added to the description of the first volume of the *History* provided by Dr. Hazen.[1] Regretting that he could afford to make no more changes, Burney wrote: 'at present more I could not do without ruin & destruction of the whole impression. 20 cancelled pages. 11 of addit. notes. 26 double & 2 of errata, will considerably inflame the reckoning with the printer & stationer, & make my book, as I feared some time ago *600* instead of 500 pages.'[2] Burney's remarks raise a number of problems. There are, as he states, eleven pages of 'Additional Notes' at the end of the volume, mainly the work of Twining (pp. 497–507); but only one, instead of two, of 'Errata' (p. 523). Burney was perhaps merely being pessimistic. There are two sequences of pages with duplicated numbering, marked with asterisks (pp. *81–*86 and *217–*232), amounting to only twenty-two in all. His statement that there were '26 double' pages was, however, no casual slip, for he repeated in his 'Directions to the Book-Binder' that 'There are . . . twenty-six *double pages*, marked with asterisms' (p. 523). For some reason Burney counted four too many.

More attention should perhaps be paid to his reference to '20 cancelled pages', for Dr. Hazen detected only eight. Signatures E4 and F1 (pp. 31–34) are both cancels and, according to Hazen, 'they were perhaps printed in the same half-sheet, but were cut and then pasted separately'. These four pages concern the Diatonic, Chromatic, and Enharmonic Genera in Greek music and the cancellation was undoubtedly caused by Burney's desire to take account of Twining's 'hypothesis' on this subject. The second cancellation described by Hazen is more complex, affecting signature L, which has seven leaves and includes six 'double pages'. In Hazen's opinion L3 and L4 were cancelled; a new sheet was inserted, signed L3 and L4 on the first two leaves and with the third and fourth unsigned; and a single leaf, signed *L, 'was pasted to the stub (of the original L3 or L4) in some manner so that L1 & L2 were both held firmly'.

---

[1] A. T. Hazen, *Johnson's Prefaces and Dedications*, p. 27.
[2] CB to Twining, 24 Dec. 1775, copy (Osborn).

The section in which these cancellations and insertions occur deals
with rhythm in ancient music and, particularly in the affected area,
with classical metre, a subject about which Twining clearly knew
much more than Burney. Twining sent his corrections to what
Burney had already written and his own views on the subject in
November 1774.[1] The cancellation was made a few months later. As
a cryptic note by Twining reveals, he sent Burney 'Addend to the
Rhythmic §' in May 1775.[2] In the following month Burney replied:
'I have . . . accepted almost every correction for the cancelled ½ sheet
excepting the rejection of Note (y) which contains an Idea that I am
loath to part with.'[3] The note to which Burney referred appears on
L3ᵛ (p. 78).

Dr. Hazen thus noted eight of the twenty cancelled pages mentioned by Burney. Four more can be identified as follows. Signature
G2 (pp. 43–44) is a cancel, the content of these pages being once
more Twining's theory of the Enharmonic Genus. Signature Ooo3
(pp. 469–70) is also a cancel. These pages contain three examples of
Burney's verse translations and the cancellation was once more
caused by Twining. In October 1775 he suggested alterations to
'Aristotle's Hymn to Hermias'[4] and in December 1775 was particularly derisive of the first poem on page 469.[5] His repeated criticism
evidently drove Burney to make the cancellation and revise his
translations.

Eight cancelled pages remain unaccounted for and, since they
cannot otherwise be detected, it is reasonable to assume that they
constituted a full sheet. Since some cancellation must have taken
place in Burney's chapter on Egyptian Music, to permit the insertion
of James Bruce's letter,[6] it may also be assumed that a full sheet was
replaced at this point. In his note for the bookbinder (p. 523),
Burney explained that the 'double pages' were 'occasioned by the
late arrival of Mr. Bruce's communications, and by other additions
to the text, occurring after the Press was broken up; and this method
of inserting them was preferred to that of giving the reader the
trouble of turning to a *Supplement*'. It is clear that Burney did not
decide, or did not receive permission, to include Bruce's letter in its
expanded form until his chapter on Egyptian Music (originally pp.
198–216) had been printed. Burney could have added the letter on

[1] Twining to CB, 14 and 30 Nov. 1774, copies (Add. MS. 39933, ff. 118–31),
and notes (Add. MS. 39936, ff. 55–56).
[2] Ibid., 12 May 1775, notes (Add. MS. 39936, f. 57).
[3] CB to Twining, June 1775, copy (Osborn).
[4] Twining to CB, 16 Oct. 1775, notes (Add. MS. 39936, f. 59).
[5] Ibid., 3 Dec. 1775, copy (Add. MS. 39933, ff. 170–3).
[6] See *ante*, pp. 160–1.

double pages at the end of the chapter but, to give it the prominence which he felt it deserved, he inserted it in the middle. As a result he was obliged to cancel the last sheet of the chapter and to transfer most of this material to the double pages (pp. *217–*232). In this way the remaining eight cancelled pages mentioned by Burney in his letter to Twining can be accounted for.

Brief mention may be made here of the three ornamental plates which grace the first volume of the *History*. In his 'List and Description of the Plates' Burney explained that these engravings by Bartolozzi from designs by Cipriani had originally served as tickets for fashionable concerts. He felt that it was 'a hardship upon the admirable artists who designed and engraved them, as well as upon the public, that such productions should be buried in oblivion' and, inspired by 'a wish to publish and preserve them in a work to which they seemed naturally to belong', he had decided to use them as additional illustrations. He was doubtless hoping once more to appeal to his more general readers who would appreciate a handsomely produced book and who might find the other plates of ancient musical instruments less enticing.

Burney purchased six engravings in all, at 'great expence' as he himself admitted,[1] intending to use three in each of his two volumes. This transaction with Bartolozzi probably took place early in 1774, for in the following May Bewley warned him, 'If they are merely emblematical, I shall abuse you for your extravagant donation to the publick.'[2] The plates were indeed 'merely emblematical' and some of Burney's more scholarly readers agreed that such embellishment was unnecessary. Richard Gough, who evidently knew something of Burney's dealing with the engraver, expressed his opinion, after the publication of the *History*, that he 'might have saved the hundred guineas which he gave Bartolozzi for three Bach's Concert-tickets'.[3] (Gough was evidently referring to Johann Christian, the son of J. S. Bach.) It seems more likely, however, that Burney received all six, rather than only three, of the engravings for his hundred guineas. Of the three which were not used in 1776, one would appear in the second volume in 1782.

Dr. Scholes described 'two slightly varying forms' of the 1776 edition of the first volume of the *History*.[4] These variations, however, affected only the placing of the plates and may be attributed to the vagaries of different bookbinders. In some copies of the 1776 edition Bartolozzi's engraving (1784) of Reynolds's portrait of Burney

[1] CB to [C. Davy], 3 Nov. 1774 (Osborn).
[2] Bewley to CB, 30 May 1774 (Osborn).
[3] Gough to M. Tyson, 6 Mar. 1776, J. Nichols, *Literary Anecdotes*, viii. 619.
[4] *GDB*, ii. 333–4.

appears as the frontispiece and the list of subscribers is omitted. Since Burney himself stated that there were no copies of the first edition left in 1789, such copies, with the portrait and without the subscription list, were put together after 1784 and before 1789.

A number of the engravings in the later volumes are from drawings by Burney's nephew, Edward Francesco, which are now in the Print Room of the British Museum. Some of these drawings, not all of which were used, bear notes by Burney.

BIBLIOGRAPHY

I. MANUSCRIPT SOURCES

Collection of Mr. James M. Osborn of Yale University:
(Now (1986) in the Beinecke Rare Book Library at Yale where it has been recatalogued.)

(*a*) 496 letters, and copies and drafts of letters, by Burney.
387 letters to Burney.

(*b*) 'Dizionario portativo Italiano ed Inglese, compilato da Carlo Burney per l'uso proprio di se stesso. MDCCLVI.'

(*c*) Journal of his travels in France and Italy in 1770, 3 vols.

(*d*) 5 notebooks containing materials for the *History of Music*.

(*e*) 'Sketch of a Plan for a Public Music School', 1774, 2 copies.

(*f*) 'The Trial of Midas the II^d', 1777.

(*g*) 1 leaf of the material supplied to Boswell for the *Life of Johnson* in 1787.

(*h*) Translation of chapter xii of Metastasio's *Estratto* on Aristotle's *Poetics*.

(*i*) Fragments of 'Astronomy, an Historical and Didactic Poem'.

(*j*) Notebook of poems and other miscellaneous poems.

(*k*) Notebook containing 'Memoranda for Musical Articles' for Rees's *Cyclopaedia*, 1801.

(*l*) 25 fragments of his 'Memoirs' and pocket-books, and the skeleton of a volume of the 'Memoirs'.

(*m*) 'Memoranda of the Burney Family 1603–1845' (anonymous typescript).

(*n*) Dr. P. A. Scholes's notes for, and correspondence concerning, *The Great Doctor Burney*, 1948. This material contains a few transcripts of untraced letters by Burney.

Berg Collection of the New York Public Library:

(*a*) 143 letters, and copies and drafts of letters, by Burney.
65 letters to Burney.

(*b*) *c.* 104 fragments of his pocket-books, verses, and 'Memoirs', in 11 folders.

Barrett Collection of the British Museum (Egerton MSS. 3690–708):

(*a*) 27 letters by Burney.
63 letters to Burney.
(Eg. MS. 3690, ff. 1–111, containing correspondence with Fanny; and Eg. MS. 3700A, ff. 1–40.)

(b) Fanny's account of the quarrel between Burney and Greville, omitted from *Memoirs of Dr. Burney* (Eg. MS. 3696, ff. 127–30.)

(c) Skeleton of a notebook, including 'Johnsoniana'. (Eg. MS. 3700B, ff. 1–9.)

British Museum, excluding the Barrett Collection:

(a) 31 letters by Burney (Add. MSS. 11730, ff. 33, 35; 33965, ff. 22, 24, 26; 35027, f. 12; 35126, ff. 157–8, 349–50, 488–9; 35127, ff. 74–75, 84–88, 125–6, 161–2, 257–8; 35130, ff. 17–18; 35532, ff. 364–5; 37909, f. 160; 37914, ff. 56–57; 37915, ff. 186–7; 37916, ff. 16–17; 39929, ff. 54–56, 59–64, 324–6; 39932, ff. 165–6; 48345, ff. 21, 41–45; Egerton 3009, f. 13; inset in Hawkins's *History of Music*, 1776, vol. i, C. 45, f. 4 and in Watt's *Byron*, C. 44. e-g, vol. xv).

(b) 122 letters, and copies of and notes on letters, from Twining to Burney. (Add. MSS. 39929, 39933, 39934, 39936; for full details of the extant Burney–Twining Correspondence see *ante*, p. 134, n. 1). 8 letters from J. W. Callcott to Burney, copies. (Add. MS. 27667, ff. 69–59, reversed foliation).

(c) Journal of his travels in France and Italy in 1770 (Add. MS. 35122).

(d) Fragments of his 'Memoirs' (Add. MS. 48345, ff. 1–20, 22). Fragment of a notebook, 1755–60 (Add. MS. 48345, ff. 23–36). Miscellaneous notes on music (Add. MS. 48345, ff. 37–40). Madame d'Arblay's notes on Christopher Smart (Add. MS. 48345, ff. 46–47).

Bodleian Library, Oxford:

(a) 24 letters, or copies of letters, by Burney (MS. Malone 38, ff. 129–47, 150–61; MS. Add. C. 89, ff. 1–4; MS. Eng. misc. c. 75, f. 98; MS. Eng. letters d. 74, f. 150; MS. Don. c. 56, ff. 87–88, 128; MS. Montagu d. 6, f. 312; MS. Eng. letters c. 15, ff. 144–5).

(b) Burney's Mus.D. Exercise, 1769 (MS. Mus. Sch. Ex. c. 15).

Collection of John R. G. Comyn, Esquire, of Turnastone, Herefordshire:

29 letters by Burney.
49 letters to Burney.

Collection of Mr. and Mrs. Donald F. Hyde of Somerville, New Jersey:

(a) 16 letters by Burney.

(b) 1 leaf of the material supplied to Boswell for his *Life of Johnson* in 1787.

John Rylands Library, Manchester:

(a) 16 letters by Burney. (Eng. MSS. 545, 913.)

(b) 'The Trial of Midas the II^d', 1777. (Eng. MS. 648.)

(c) Proof-sheets (4 pp.) of the *History of Music*, corrected by Burney (Eng. MS. 655.)

Smaller Public Collections:

Folger Library, Washington: 18 letters from Malone to Burney.
Pierpont Morgan Library, New York: 3 letters by Burney.
         9 letters to Burney.
Biblioteca Communale annessa al Conservatorio Musicale, Bologna:
        6 letters by Burney.
Yale University Library: 3 letters by Burney.
        An anecdote supplied to Boswell for his *Life of Johnson*.
Cambridge University Library: 1 letter by Burney.
King's Lynn Museum: 1 letter by Burney.
St. Michael's College, Tenbury: 1 letter by Burney.
Ashmolean Museum, Oxford: fragment of 1 letter by Burney.
Houghton Library, Harvard: 2 letters from Smart to Burney.
        Charlotte Burney's Commonplace Book, containing 11 poems by Burney. (MS. Eng. 926.)

Smaller Private Collections:

Mr. Gerald Coke, of Bentley, Hampshire: 7 letters by Burney.
        6 letters to Burney.
Professor F. W. Hilles, Yale University: 6 letters by Burney.
        1 letter to Burney.
Mr. Brooks Shepard, Yale University: 7 letters by Burney.
The Warden of All Souls College, Oxford: 1 letter to Burney.

II. BURNEY'S PUBLISHED WORKS

1766

The Cunning-Man, a Musical Entertainment, in Two Acts. As it is Performed at the Theatre Royal in Drury-Lane. Originally written and composed by M. J. J. Rousseau. London: Printed for T. Becket and P. A. de Hondt. 1766. 8⁰.

Second edition, 1766, with the addition to the title-page of 'Imitated, and adapted to his original music, by Charles Burney'; and a quotation from *Hudibras*. The 'Advertisement', now dated 29 Nov. 1766, announces that the music is available from Bremner. (For editions and arrangements of the music, see *GDB*, ii. 345–6.)

Reprinted at Dublin, 1767, 12⁰. Also in vol. ii of the *Supplement* to *Bell's British Theatre*, 1784; and in *A Collection of the Most Esteemed British Farces*, Edinburgh, 1786, ii. 196–207 (second edition, 1792).

1769

An Essay towards a History of the Principal Comets that have appeared since the Year 1742. Including a particular Detail of the Return of the famous Comet of 1682 in 1759, according to the Calculation and Prediction of Dr. Halley. Compiled from the

Observations of the most eminent Astronomers of this Century. With Remarks and Reflections upon the Present Comet. To which is prefixed, by way of Introduction, A Letter upon Comets. Addressed to a Lady, by the late M. de Maupertuis. Written in the Year 1742. London: Printed for T. Becket and P. A. de Hondt. 1769. 8°.

The translation of Maupertuis's *Letter* to Madame du Châtelet was by Esther Burney, Burney's first wife. The 'Postscript' is dated 25 October 1769.

Reprinted at Glasgow, for Robert Urie, 1770, 12°. This edition omits the Dedication to the Countess of Pembroke.

1771

The Present State of Music in France and Italy: or, The Journal of a Tour through those Countries, undertaken to collect Materials for a General History of Music. By Charles Burney, Mus.D. London: Printed for T. Becket and Co. 1771. 8°.

Second edition, corrected, printed for T. Becket, J. Robson and G. Robinson, 1773.

Dr. Burney's Continental Travels, 1770–1772, ed. C. H. Glover, 1927. Contains selections from the *Italian Tour* and previously unpublished material from Burney's travel journal. (British Museum, Add. MS. 35122.)

Dr. Burney's Musical Tours in Europe, ed. P. A. Scholes, 2 vols., 1959. Vol. i: *An Eighteenth-Century Musical Tour in France and Italy.* A conflation of the text of the second edition with the unpublished travel journal. (Two copies, British Museum, Add. MS. 35122 and Osborn 73. 1.)

TRANSLATIONS:

Carl Burney's der Musik Doctors Tagebuch einer Musikalischen Reise durch Frankreich und Italien welche er unternommen hat um zu einer allgemeinen Geschichte der Musik Materialen zu sammlen. Aus dem Englischen übersetzt von C. D. Ebeling, Aufsehern der Handlungsakademie zu Hamburg. Hamburg: J. J. C. Bode. 1772. 8°. Facsimile, ed. Richard Schaal, *Documenta musicologica,* xix, Basel, 1959.

Rijk gestoffeerd verhaal van de eigenlijke Gesteldheid der hedendaagsche Toonkunst of sir Karel Burneys Dagboek van Zyne onlangs gedaane Reizen door Frankryk, Italien en Deutschland. Groningen. 1786. 8°. Translated by J. W. Lustig. Another edition, Utrecht, 1790.

De l'état présent de la Musique en France et en Italie, dans les Pays-Bas, en Hollande et en Allemagne, ou Journal des Voyages faits dans ces différents Pays avec l'intention d'y recueillir des matériaux pour servir à une Histoire générale de la Musique, par Ch. Burney, Professeur de Musique, Traduit de l'Anglais par Ch. Brack, de la Société Royale de Gottingue. Gênes: J. Giossi. Volume i, 1809; volumes ii and iii, 1810.

Viaggio musicale in Italia, 1770. Traduzione di Virginio Attanasio. [Milan.] 1921. 8°. Translated into Italian from Brack's French translation.

Lettera del defonto Signor Giuseppe Tartini alla Signora Maddalena Lombardini inserviente ad una importante Lezione per i Suonatori di Violino. With English title: *A Letter from the late Signor Tartini to Signora Maddalena Lombardini (now Signora Sirmen) Published as an Important Lesson to Performers on the Violin. Translated by Dr. Burney.* London: R. Bremner. 1771. 4°. The Italian and English texts are on facing pages.

Second edition, 1779. Reprinted as *An Important Lesson to Performers on the Violin*, London, W. Reeves, 1879 and 1913.

1773

The Present State of Music in Germany, the Netherlands, and the United Provinces. Or, The Journal of a Tour through those Countries, undertaken to collect Materials for a General History of Music. By Charles Burney, *Mus.D.*, *F.R.S.* London: T. Becket, J. Robson and G. Robinson. 1773. 2 vols., 8°.
Second edition, corrected, 1775.
Dr. Burney's Continental Travels, 1770–1772, ed. C. H. Glover, 1927. Contains extracts.
Dr. Burney's Musical Tours in Europe, ed. P. A. Scholes, 2 vols., 1959. Vol. ii: *An Eighteenth-Century Musical Tour in Central Europe and the Netherlands*. A reprint of the second edition.

TRANSLATIONS:

Carl Burney's der Musik Doctors Tagebuch seiner Musikalischen Reisen. Zweyter Band. Durch Flandern, die Niederlande und am Rhein bis Wien. Aus dem Englischen übersetzt; and *Dritter Band. Durch Böhmen, Sachsen, Brandenburg, Hamburg und Holland. Aus dem Englischen übersetzt. Mit einigen Zusätzen und Anmerkungen zum zweyten und dritten Bande.* Hamburg: J. J. C. Bode. 1773. 8°. Translated by C. D. Ebeling and J. J. C. Bode. The two volumes were considered to be the second and third of the series which had begun with the *Italian Tour*. Facsimile, ed. Richard Schaal, *Documenta musicologica*, xix, Basel, 1959.
For the Dutch translation by J. W. Lustig, Groningen, 1786, and the French translation by Charles Brack, Gênes, 1810, see under '1771'.
Dr. Ch. Burney. La Musique dans les cours allemandes en 1772. Extrait du 'Voyage musical en Allemagne', traduit et annoté par Émile le Roy. Paris; J. Baur. 1881. 8°.

1776

A General History of Music, from the Earliest Ages to the Present Period. To which is prefixed, a Dissertation on the Music of the Ancients. By Charles Burney. *Mus.D. F.R.S. Volume the First.* London: Printed for the Author; and sold by T. Becket, J. Robson, and G. Robinson. 1776. 4°.
Second edition, corrected and revised, 1789.
A General History of Music . . . by Charles Burney, with critical and historical notes by Frank Mercer, 2 vols., London, 1935. Reprinted, New York, 1957. The text of volume i is taken from the second edition.

TRANSLATION:

Dr. Karl Burney's Abhandlung über die Musik der Alten . . . übersetzt, und mit einigen Anmerkungen begleitet von J. J. Eschenburg. Leipzig. 1781. 4°. A translation of the opening *Dissertation*.

1779

Account of an Infant Musician [*William Crotch*]. By Charles Burney, Doctor of Music, *F.R.S. Read at the Royal Society, Feb. 18, 1779.* London: J. Nichols. 1779. 4°.

Reprinted in *Philosophical Transactions of the Royal Society for 1779*, lxix (Pt. I), 183–206.

1782

'Advice to the *Herald*': a poem in *The Morning Herald*, 12 March 1782.

A General History of Music. From the Earliest Ages to the Present Period . . . Volume the Second. London: Printed for the Author; and sold by J. Robson and G. Robinson. 1782. 4°.

Reprinted, with the original date, but with modern 's' throughout, by [? W. Baynes], in 1811 or 1812.

Edited by Frank Mercer, London, 1935. Reprinted, New York, 1957.

A review, with Twining's assistance, of Francis Maxwell's *An Essay upon Tune*, in *Critical Review*, liv (Aug. 1782), 117–25.

1785

An Account of Mademoiselle Theresa Paradis, of Vienna, the Celebrated Blind Performer on the Piano Forte, including a *Cantata in German Written for Mademoiselle Paradis, by her blind friend M. Pfeffel, of Colmar, and set to music by her musicmaster, M. Leopold Kozeluch, of Vienna, 11th November 1784. Imitated by Dr. Burney.*

This narrative and translation appeared in many periodicals and newspapers (see p. 309). A few copies were printed separately and are rare. There is a copy in the Osborn Collection.

An Account of the Musical Performances in Westminster-Abbey, and the Pantheon, May 26th, 27th, 29th; and June the 3d, and 5th, 1784. In Commemoration of Handel. London: Printed for the Benefit of the Musical Fund, and sold by T. Payne and Son and G. Robinson. 1785. 4°.

An edition, without the plates, was published at Dublin, 1785, 8°.

Extracts were printed in G. F. Graham's *Account of the First Edinburgh Musical Festival held between the 30th October and 5th November 1815*, Edinburgh, 1815; and in a prospectus for a Musical Festival in Westminster Abbey, with the original title, *To which is added, A Notice of the Forthcoming Royal Musical Festival of 1834*, 1834. 8°.

TRANSLATION:

Dr. Karl Burney's Nachricht von Georg Friedrich Händel's Lebensumständen und der ihm zu London im Mai und Jun. 1784 angestellten Gedächtnissfeyer. Aus dem Englischen übersetzt von Johann Joachim Eschenburg. Berlin: F. Nicolai. 1785. 4°.

1785–1802

Book reviews, and contributions to the 'Correspondence' section, in the *Monthly Review*. For a full list of Burney's articles, see B. C. Nangle, *The Monthly Review, First Series, 1749–1789, Indexes of Contributors and Articles*, Oxford, 1934; and *Second Series, 1790–1815*, Oxford, 1955.

1789

*A General History of Music, from the Earliest Ages to the Present Period. . . .
Volume the Third* and *Volume the Fourth.* London: Printed for the Author; and
sold by Payne and Son, Robson and Clark, and G. G. J. and J. Robinson,
1789. 4°.
Edited by Frank Mercer, London, 1935. Reprinted, New York, 1957.

TRANSLATION:

The introduction to volume iii was translated by J. J. E. Eschenburg in
Berliner Musik-Wochenblatt, 1792, pp. 73–75 and 81–88.

1791

Verses on the Arrival in England of the Great Musician Haydn. T. Payne. 1791.
4°.

1796

*Memoirs of the Life and Writings of the Abate Metastasio. In which are incorpor-
ated, Translations of his Principal Letters. By Charles Burney, Mus.D. F.R.S.*
London: Printed for G. G. and J. Robinson. 1796. 3 vols. 8°.
*Didon abandonée; traduit de l'Italien . . . par Madlle. M. Grignon. Together with
an extract from Memoirs of the Life and Writings of the Abate Metastasio: by Charles
Burney,* London [?1810]. 12°.

1799

Hymn for the Emperor. Translated by Dr. Burney. Composed by Doctor Haydn.
London: Broderip and Wilkinson.

1802–1819

Articles on music and musicians contributed to *The Cyclopaedia; or, Universal Dictionary of Arts, Sciences, and Literature,* ed. Abraham Rees. London:
Printed for Longman, Hurst, Rees, Orme and Brown. 1802–19. 39 vols. 4°.
6 volumes of plates completed the work in 1820.

1803

A hymn, 'Again the day returns of holy rest', *Gentleman's Magazine,* lxiii
(Dec. 1803), 1140.

1808

'Memoirs and Character of the late Mrs. Ord', *Gentleman's Magazine,*
lxxviii (July, 1808), 581–3.

NOTE

The *Ode: To the People of Great Britain on the Threatened Invasion,* 1804, tenta-
tively attributed to Burney by Dr. Scholes, *GDB,* ii. 338–9, was written by
his son Charles, as is clear from a letter from Burney to Charles, 4 September
1803 (Osborn.)

III. OTHER WORKS QUOTED OR CITED

(Unless otherwise stated, the place of publication is London.)

AINSWORTH, EDWARD G., and NOYES, CHARLES E. *Christopher Smart: A Biographical and Critical Study* (University of Missouri Studies, xviii. 4), Columbia, 1943.

BARRY, JAMES. *Account of a Series of Pictures, in the Great Room of the Society of Arts, Manufactures, and Commerce, at the Adelphi*, 1783.

BELDEN, MARY MEGIE. *Dramatic Work of Samuel Foote*, New Haven, 1929.

BELFOUR, JOHN. *Music, A Didactic Poem in Five Cantos. Translated from the Spanish of Don Tomas de Yriarte*, 1807.

BENKOVITZ, MIRIAM. 'Dr. Burney's Memoirs', *RES*, x (1959), 257–68.

BICKNELL, JOHN. *Musical Travels through England. By Joel Collier, Organist*, 1774. 2nd edn., expanded, 1775; 3rd edn., with appendix, 1775; 4th edn., 1776; 5th edn., 1785; 6th edn. [? by George Veal], 1818.

Biographia Dramatica, or, A Companion to the Playhouse, by David Erskine Baker, 2 vols., 1764; new edns. by Isaac Reed, 2 vols., 1782 and by Stephen Jones, 4 vols., 1812.

BOSWELL, JAMES. *Life of Samuel Johnson*, 3rd edn., ed. Edmond Malone, 4 vols., 1799; ed. G. B. Hill, revised L. F. Powell, 6 vols., Oxford, 1934–50. *See also* CROKER, J. W.

—— *Boswell's London Journal 1762–1763*, ed. Frederick A. Pottle, London, 1950.

—— *Boswell for the Defence*, ed. William K. Wimsatt, Jr. and Frederick A. Pottle, London, 1960.

BOTTING, ROLAND B. 'Johnson, Smart and the *Universal Visiter*', *Modern Philology*, xxxvi (1938–9), 293–300.

BURNEY, FRANCES. *Evelina, or, a Young Lady's Entrance into the World*, 3 vols., 1778.

—— *Memoirs of Doctor Burney, arranged from his own Manuscripts, from Family Papers, and from Personal Recollections. By his daughter, Madame d'Arblay*, 3 vols., 1832.

—— *Diary and Letters of Madame d'Arblay*, ed. Austin Dobson, 6 vols., 1904–5.

—— *Early Diary of Frances Burney, 1768–1778*, ed. Annie Raine Ellis, revised edn., 2 vols., 1907.

BUSBY, THOMAS. *Concert Room and Orchestra Anecdotes of Music and Musicians*, 3 vols., 1825.

CAMERON, H. C. *Sir Joseph Banks, K.B., P.R.S., the Autocrat of the Philosophers*, 1952.

CHESTERFIELD, EARL OF. *Letters to his Son*, ed. C. Stokes Carey, 2 vols., 1912.

CLIFFORD, JAMES L. *Hester Lynch Piozzi (Mrs. Thrale)*, Oxford, 1941.

COLLISON-MORLEY, LACY. *Giuseppe Baretti and his Friends*, 1909.

COPELAND, THOMAS W. *Our Eminent Friend Edmund Burke*, New Haven, 1949.

COURTENAY, JOHN. *Four Patriotic Songs, addressed to the British Sailors, Soldiers and Volunteers*, 1803.

CRADOCK, JOSEPH. *Literary and Miscellaneous Memoirs*, 4 vols., 1828.

CRAMMER-BYNG, J. L. *An Embassy to China*, 1962.

CROKER, JOHN WILSON. 'Madame d'Arblay's Memoirs of Dr. Burney', *Quarterly Review*, xlix (1833), 97–125.
—— *Life of Samuel Johnson . . . by James Boswell*, 2nd edn. [by John Wright], 10 vols., 1835.
CUMMINGS, WILLIAM HAYMAN. *Dr. Arne and Rule, Britannia*, 1912.
CUNNINGHAM, GEORGE GODFREY. *Lives of Eminent and Illustrious Englishmen*, 8 vols., 1836.
DAVIES, THOMAS. *Memoirs of the Life of David Garrick*, 2 vols., 1780.
DELANY, MARY. *Autobiography and Correspondence of Mary Granville, Mrs. Delany*, ed. Lady Llanover, 1st series, 3 vols., 1861; 2nd series, 3 vols., 1862.
DEUTSCH, OTTO ERICH. 'Haydn's Hymn and Burney's Translation', *Music Review*, iv (1943), 157–62.
DEVLIN, CHRISTOPHER. *Poor Kit Smart*, 1961.
DRAPER, JOHN W. *William Mason. A Study in Eighteenth-Century Culture*, New York, 1924.
EDGEWORTH, MARIA. *Life and Letters*, ed. Augustus J. C. Hare, 2 vols., 1894.
EDWARDS, F. G. 'Dr. Charles Burney (1726–1814). A Biographical Sketch', *Musical Times*, xlv (1904), 435–9, 513–15, 575–80.
FÉTIS, FRANÇOIS JOSEPH. *Biographie universelle des musiciens*, 2nd edn., 8 vols., Paris, 1860–5.
FOSTER, JOSEPH. *Alumni Oxonienses, 1715–1886*, 4 vols., Oxford, 1887–8.
GARRICK, DAVID. *Private Correspondence . . . with the Most Celebrated Persons of his Times* [ed. James Boaden], 2 vols., 1831–2.
—— *Letters*, ed. David M. Little and George M. Kahrl, 3 vols., 1963. *See also* DAVIES, T., MURPHY, A., OMAN, C., *and* STONE, G. W.
GENEST, JOHN. *Some Account of the English Stage, from the Restoration in 1660 to 1830*, 10 vols., Bath, 1832.
GOTWALS, VERNON. *Joseph Haydn*, Madison, 1963.
GRAY, THOMAS. *Correspondence*, ed. Paget Toynbee and Leonard Whibley, 3 vols., Oxford, 1935.
Grove's Dictionary of Music and Musicians, 5th edn., ed. Eric Blom, 9 vols., 1954.
Harmonicon, The, 11 vols., 1823–33:
'Dr. Burney's Letter to Haydn', v (1827), 63.
'Memoir of Sir John Hawkins', ix (1831), 79–81.
'Memoir of Charles Burney, Mus.Doc., F.R.S.', x (1832), 215–17.
HAWKINS, SIR JOHN. *The Complete Angler*, 1760.
—— *General History of the Science and Practice of Music*, 5 vols., 1776; new edns., 2 vols., 1853, 3 vols., 1875, and 2 vols., 1963.
See also SCHOLES, PERCY A.
HAWKINS, LAETITIA-MATILDA. *Anecdotes, Biographical Sketches and Memoirs*, vol. i, 1822. No more published under this title.
HAYDN, JOSEPH. *Collected Correspondence and London Notebooks*, ed. H. C. Robbins, 1959.
HAZEN, ALLEN T. *Samuel Johnson's Prefaces and Dedications*, New Haven, 1937.
HAZLITT, WILLIAM. *Complete Works*, ed. P. P. Howe, 21 vols., 1930–4.

HEDGCOCK, F. A. *A Cosmopolitan Actor. David Garrick and his French Friends*, [1912].

HEMLOW, JOYCE. *History of Fanny Burney*, Oxford, 1958.

HERSCHEL, SIR WILLIAM. *Scientific Papers . . . Collected and edited under the direction of a joint committee of the Royal Society and the Royal Astronomical Society*, 2 vols., 1912.

HILL, CONSTANCE. *Fanny Burney at the Court of Queen Charlotte*, 1912.

HILLES, FREDERICK WHILEY. *Literary Career of Sir Joshua Reynolds*, Cambridge, 1936.

Historical Manuscripts Commission, Report on the Fortescue MSS., vol. viii, 1912.

HOOLE, JOHN. *Dramas and Other Poems; of the Abbe Pietro Metastasio*, 3 vols., 1800.

HUGHES, ROSEMARY S. M. 'Dr. Burney's Championship of Haydn', *Musical Quarterly*, xxvii (1941), 90–96.

HUME, DAVID. 'Calendar of Hume MSS. in the possession of the Royal Society of Edinburgh', by J. Y. T. Greig and Harold Beynon, *Proceedings of the Royal Society of Edinburgh*. lii (1931–2).

—— *Letters*, ed. J. Y. T. Greig, 2 vols., Oxford, 1932.

See also MOSSNER, E. C.

HUTTON, WILLIAM HOLDEN. *Burford Papers, being Letters of Samuel Crisp to his Sister at Burford; and other Studies of a Century (1745–1845)*, 1905.

JACKSON, B. DAYDON. 'The Dates of Rees's Cyclopaedia', *Journal of Botany*, xxxiv (1896), 307–11.

JEFFERSON, THOMAS. *Papers*, ed. J. P. Boyd (in progress), vols. 1– , Princeton, 1950– .

JOHNSON, R. BRIMLEY. *Fanny Burney and the Burneys*, 1926.

JOHNSON, SAMUEL. *Letters*, ed. R. W. Chapman, 3 vols., Oxford, 1952.

JONES, SIR WILLIAM. *Works*, 6 vols., 1799.

KETTON-CREMER, R. W. *A Norfolk Gallery*, 1948.

KIDSON, FRANK. 'James Oswald, Dr. Burney, and "The Temple of Apollo"', *Musical Antiquary*, ii (1910–11), 34–41.

KING, A. HYATT. *Some British Collectors of Music*, Cambridge, 1963.

KNAPP, LEWIS MANSFIELD. *Tobias Smollett, Doctor of Men and Manners*, Princeton, 1949.

LANGLEY, HUBERT. *Doctor Arne*, Cambridge, 1938.

LANSDOWNE, MARQUIS OF. *Queeney Letters, being Letters addressed to Hester Maria Thrale by Doctor Johnson, Fanny Burney and Mrs. Thrale-Piozzi*, 1934.

'LEE, VERNON' (Violet Paget). *Studies of the Eighteenth Century in Italy*, 1880.

LEIGH, R. A. 'Les Amitiés françaises du Dr. Burney', *Revue de littérature comparée*, xxv (1951), 161–94.

LOEWENBERG, ALFRED. 'Midsummer Night's Dream Music in 1763', *Theatre Notebook*, i (1945–7), 23–26.

LONSDALE, ROGER. 'Dr. Burney and the Integrity of Boswell's Quotations', *Papers of the Bibliographical Society of America*, liii (1959), 327–31.

—— 'Dr. Burney, John Weaver and the Spectator', in *Famed for Dance: Essays on the Theory and Practice of Theatrical Dancing in England, 1660–1740*, New York, 1960.

LONSDALE, ROGER. 'Christopher Smart's First Publication in English', RES, xii (1961), 402-4.

—— 'William Bewley and the *Monthly Review*: a Problem of Attribution', *Papers of the Bibliographical Society of America*, lv (1961), 309-18.

—— 'Dr. Burney and the *Monthly Review*,' RES, xiv (1963), 346-58 and xv (1964), 27-37.

LYNCH, JAMES J. *Box, Pit and Gallery: Stage and Society in Johnson's London*, Berkeley and Los Angeles, 1953.

MACMILLAN, DOUGALD. *Drury Lane Calendar, 1747-1776*, Oxford, 1938.

MACAULAY, LORD. 'Diary and Letters of Madame d'Arblay', *Edinburgh Review*, lxxvi (1842-3), 523-70.

MALLET, DAVID. *Alfred, a Masque. Acted at the Theatre-Royal in Drury-Lane*, 1751.

McKILLOP, ALAN DOUGALD. 'Bonnell Thornton's Burlesque Ode', *Notes and Queries*, cxciv (1949), 321-4.

METZDORF, ROBERT A. *Catalogue of the Tinker Library*, New Haven, 1959.

MOSSNER, ERNEST CAMPBELL, *Life of David Hume*, Edinburgh, 1954.

MURPHY, ARTHUR. *Life of David Garrick*, 2 vols., 1801.

NANGLE, BENJAMIN CHRISTIE. *The Monthly Review, First Series, 1749-1789: Indexes of Contributors and Articles*, Oxford, 1934; and *Second Series, 1790-1815*, Oxford, 1955.

—— 'Charles Burney, Critic', in *The Age of Johnson: Essays Presented to Chauncey Brewster Tinker*, New Haven, 1949.

NICHOLS, JOHN. *Literary Anecdotes of the Eighteenth Century*, 9 vols., 1812-15.

—— *Illustrations of the Literary History of the Eighteenth Century*, 8 vols., 1817-58.

NICHOLS, R. H., and WRAY, F. A. *History of the Foundling Hospital*, 1935.

NISARD, CHARLES. *Mémoires et correspondances historiques et littéraires inédits*, Paris, 1858.

OLDHAM, J. BASIL. *History of Shrewsbury School, 1552-1952*, Oxford, 1952.

OLIVER, J. W. *Life of William Beckford*, 1932.

OMAN, CAROLA. *David Garrick*, 1958.

OWEN, H., and BLAKEWAY, J. B. *History of Shrewsbury*, 2 vols., 1825.

'PASTON, GEORGE' (Emily Morse Symonds). *Sidelights on the Georgian Period*, 1902.

PERCY, THOMAS. *Reliques of Ancient English Poetry*, 3rd edn., 3 vols., 1775.

—— *Correspondence of Thomas Percy and Edmond Malone*, ed. Arthur Tillotson, Louisiana State University, 1944.

PINKERTON, JOHN. *Literary Correspondence*, ed. Dawson Turner, 2 vols., 1830.

PIOZZI, HESTER LYNCH (Thrale). *Thraliana: the Diary of Mrs. Hester Lynch Thrale (later Mrs. Piozzi) 1776-1809*, ed. Katharine C. Balderston, 2nd edn. corrected, 2 vols., Oxford, 1951. *See also* CLIFFORD, J. L.

PRICE, CECIL. 'Six Letters by Christopher Smart', *RES* viii (1957), 145-8.

PRIESTLEY, JOSEPH. *Memoirs of Dr. Joseph Priestley, to the year 1795, written by himself; with a continuation by his son, Joseph Priestley*, London, 1807.

PRIOR, SIR JAMES. *Life of Edmond Malone*, 1860.

ROBBERDS, J. W. *Memoir of the Life and Writings of the late William Taylor of Norwich*, 2 vols., 1843.

ROBERTS, W. WRIGHT. 'Charles and Fanny Burney in the light of the new

Thrale Correspondence in the John Rylands Library', *Bulletin of the John Rylands Library*, xvi (1932), 115–36.

ROBERTS, W. WRIGHT. 'The Trial of Midas the Second', *Bulletin of the John Rylands Library*, xvii (1933), 322–32; reprinted in *Music and Letters*, xiv (1933), 303–12.

ROBINSON, HENRY CRABB. *Diary, Reminiscences, and Correspondence*, ed. T. Sadler, 3 vols., 1869.

ROGERS, SAMUEL. *Recollections of the Table-Talk of Samuel Rogers. To which is added Porsoniana* [ed. A. Dyce], 1856.

ROUSSEAU, JEAN-JACQUES. *Lettre à M. le Docteur Burney, auteur de l'Histoire générale de la Musique*, in *Traités sur la musique*, Geneva, 1781, pp. 375–427.

—— *Correspondance générale*, ed. Théophile Dufour, 20 vols., Paris, 1924–34.

RYSKAMP, CHARLES. 'Dr. Arne's Music for Thornton's Burlesque Ode', *Notes and Queries*, ccii (1957), 71–73.

SCHOLES, PERCY A. *The Great Doctor Burney*, 2 vols., 1948.

—— *Life of Sir John Hawkins*, 1953.

SEWARD, WILLIAM. *Anecdotes of Some Distinguished Persons*, 4th edn. enlarged, 4 vols., 1798.

—— *Biographiana*, 2 vols., 1799.

SMART, CHRISTOPHER. *Poems on Several Occasions*, 1752.

—— *The Midwife: or, The Old Woman's Magazine*, 3 vols., 1751–3.

—— *Poems*, ed. Christopher Hunter, 2 vols., Reading, 1791.

—— *Collected Poems*, ed. Norman Callan, 2 vols., 1949.

—— *Selected Poems*, ed. Robert Brittain, Princeton, 1950.

See also AINSWORTH, E. G., BOTTING, R. B., DEVLIN, C., LONSDALE, R., *and* PRICE, C.

SMITH, D. NICHOL. *Oxford Book of Eighteenth Century Verse*, Oxford, 1926.

SMITH, JOHN THOMAS. *Nollekens and his Times*, 2 vols., 1828.

SQUIRE, WILLIAM BARCLAY. *Catalogue of the King's Music Library, Part I: the Handel Manuscripts*, 1927.

STEVENSON, R. 'The Rivals—Hawkins, Burney, and Boswell', *Musical Quarterly*, xxxvi (1950), 67–88.

STOCKDALE, PERCIVAL. *Memoirs*, 2 vols., 1809.

STONE, GEORGE WINCHESTER, Jr. '*A Midsummer Night's Dream* in the hands of Garrick and Colman', *Publications of the Modern Language Association of America*, liv (1939), 467–82.

—— *The London Stage 1660–1800: Part 4*, 3 vols., Carbondale, 1962.

THOMSON, JAMES. *The Castle of Indolence and Other Poems*, ed. Alan D. McKillop, Lawrence, Kansas, 1961.

TREND, J. B. 'R. J. S. Stevens and his Contemporaries', *Music and Letters*, xiv (1933), 128–37.

TWINING, THOMAS. *Recreations and Studies of a Country Clergyman of the Eighteenth Century*, ed. Richard Twining, 1882.

ULLRICH, HERMANN. 'Maria Theresia Paradis in London', *Music and Letters*, xliii (1962), 16–24.

WALKER, RALPH S. 'Charles Burney's Theft of Books at Cambridge', with an additional note by J. C. T. Oates, *Transactions of the Cambridge Bibliographical Society*, iii (1962), 313–26.

WALPOLE, HORACE. *Last Journals*, ed. A. Francis Steuart, 2 vols., 1910.
—— *Letters*, ed. Mrs. Paget Toynbee, 16 vols., Oxford, 1903–5; and *Supplement*, ed. Paget Toynbee, 3 vols., Oxford, 1918–25.
—— *Correspondence*, ed. Wilmarth S. Lewis (in progress), vols. i– , 1937–
WARDLE, RALPH M. *Mary Wollstonecraft*, Lawrence, Kansas, 1951.
WELCH, CHRISTOPHER. *Six Lectures on the Recorder*, 1911.
WILLIAMS, C. F. ABDY. *Short Historical Account of the Degrees in Music at Oxford and Cambridge*, 1894.
WOLCOT, JOHN ('Peter Pindar'). *Ode upon Ode; or, A Peep at St. James's*, 7th edn., 1787.
WOOLF, VIRGINIA. 'An Evening at Dr. Burney's', *The Second Common Reader*, 1932, pp. 108–25.
WORDSWORTH, WILLIAM. *Early Letters*, ed. E. de Selincourt, Oxford, 1935.
YOUNG, ARTHUR. *Autobiography . . . with Selections from his Correspondence*, ed. M. Betham-Edwards, 1898.

Additions to Bibliography (1986)

BROFSKY, H. 'Dr. Burney and Padre Martini: Writing a General History of Music', *Music Quarterly*, LXV (1979), 313–46.
BURNEY, CHARLES. *Music, Men, and Manners in France and Italy 1770*, ed. H. Edmund Poole, 1969. (The text of Burney's MS. journal of his travels from British Library, Add. MS. 35122.)
GRANT, KERRY S. *Dr. Burney as Critic and Historian of Music*, Ann Arbor, 1983.
HEMLOW, JOYCE (and others). *A Catalogue of the Burney Family Correspondence 1749–1878*, New York, 1971.
LIPKING, LAWRENCE. *The Ordering of the Arts in Eighteenth-Century England*, Princeton, 1970, ch. x.
LONSDALE, ROGER. 'Johnson and Dr. Burney', in *Johnson, Boswell and Their Circle: Essays Presented to Lawrence Fitzroy Powell*, ed. Mary Lascelles (and others), Oxford, 1965, pp. 21–40.
—— 'Dr. Burney's "Dictionary of Music"', *Musicology* v (1977), 159–71.
—— 'Dr. Burney, "Joel Collier" and Sabrina', in *Evidence in Literary Scholarship: Essays in Memory of James Marshall Osborn*, ed. René Wellek and Alvaro Ribeiro, Oxford, 1979, pp. 281–308.

INDEX